T0325616

Intelligent Soft Computation and Evolving Data Mining:
Integrating Advanced Technologies

Leon Shyue-Liang Wang
National University of Kaohsiung, Taiwan

Tzung-Pei Hong
National University of Kaohsiung, Taiwan

INFORMATION SCIENCE REFERENCE

Hershey · New York

Director of Editorial Content:	Kristin Klinger
Director of Book Publications:	Julia Mosemann
Acquisitions Editor:	Lindsay Johnston
Development Editor:	Joel Gamon
Publishing Assistant:	Deanna Zombro
Typesetter:	Deanna Zombro
Quality control:	Jamie Snavely
Cover Design:	Lisa Tosheff
Printed at:	Yurchak Printing Inc.

Published in the United States of America by
Information Science Reference (an imprint of IGI Global)
701 E. Chocolate Avenue
Hershey PA 17033
Tel: 717-533-8845
Fax: 717-533-8661
E-mail: cust@igi-global.com
Web site: http://www.igi-global.com/reference

Library of Congress Cataloging-in-Publication Data

Intelligent soft computation and evolving data mining : integrating advanced technologies / Leon Shyue-Liang Wang and Tzung-Pei Hong, editor.   p. cm.
  Summary: "This book provides a reference to researchers, practitioners, and students in both soft computing and data mining communities for generating creative ideas of securing and managing data mining"--Provided by publisher. Includes bibliographical references and index. ISBN 978-1-61520-757-2 (hardcover) -- ISBN 978-1-61520-758-9 (ebook) 1. Data mining. 2. Soft computing. 3. Computational intelligence. I. Wang, Leon Shyue-Liang, 1955- II. Hong, Tzung-Pei, 1963-
  QA76.9.D343I578 2010
  006.3--dc22
                        2009035762

British Cataloguing in Publication Data
A Cataloguing in Publication record for this book is available from the British Library.

All work contributed to this book is new, previously-unpublished material. The views expressed in this book are those of the authors, but not necessarily of the publisher.

To my wife Molly, and my two children, David and Angela.
- S.L.

To my parents, my wife, my two sons and daughter.
- T.P.

Table of Contents

Section 1
Integrating Soft Computation and Data Mining

J. Alcalá-Fdez, University of Granada, Spain
I. Robles, University of Granada, Spain
F. Herrera, University of Granada, Spain
S. García, University of Jaén, Spain
M.J. del Jesus, University of Jaén, Spain
L. Sánchez, University of Oviedo, Spain
E. Bernadó-Mansilla, University Ramon Llull, Spain
A. Peregrín, University of Huelva, Spain
S. Ventura, University of Córdoba, Spain

Pei-Wei Tsai, National Kaohsiung University of Applied Sciences, Taiwan
Jeng-Shyang Pan, National Kaohsiung University of Applied Sciences, Taiwan
Bin-Yih Liao, National Kaohsiung University of Applied Sciences, Taiwan
Shu-Chuan Chu, Cheng Shiu University, Taiwan
Mei-Chiao Lai, Diwan University, Taiwan

Shyue-Liang Wang, National University of Kaohsiung, Taiwan
Ju-Wen Shen, Chunghwa Telecom Co., Ltd., Taiwan
Tuzng-Pei Hong, National University of Kaohsiung, Taiwan

Section 2
Soft Computation

Section 3
Data Mining

Detailed Table of Contents

Section 1
Integrating Soft Computation and Data Mining

J. Alcalá-Fdez, University of Granada, Spain

I. Robles, University of Granada, Spain

F. Herrera, University of Granada, Spain

S. García, University of Jaén, Spain

M.J. del Jesus, University of Jaén, Spain

L. Sánchez, University of Oviedo, Spain

E. Bernadó-Mansilla, University Ramon Llull, Spain

A. Peregrín, University of Huelva, Spain

S. Ventura, University of Córdoba, Spain

KEEL is a Data Mining software tool to assess the behaviour of evolutionary learning algorithms in particular and soft computing algorithms in general for different kinds of Data Mining problems including as regression, classification, clustering, pattern mining and so on. It allows us to perform a complete analysis of some learning model in comparison to existing ones, including a statistical test module for comparison. In this chapter the authors will provide a complete description of KEEL, the kind of problems and algorithms implemented, and they will present a case of study for showing the experimental design and statistical analysis that we they can do with KEEL.

Pei-Wei Tsai, National Kaohsiung University of Applied Sciences, Taiwan

Jeng-Shyang Pan, National Kaohsiung University of Applied Sciences, Taiwan

Bin-Yih Liao, National Kaohsiung University of Applied Sciences, Taiwan

Shu-Chuan Chu, Cheng Shiu University, Taiwan

Mei-Chiao Lai, Diwan University, Taiwan

This chapter reviews the basic idea and processes in data mining and some algorithms within the field of evolutionary computing. The authors focus on introducing the algorithms of computational intelligence since they are useful tools for solving problems of optimization, data mining, and many kinds of industrial issues. A feasible model of combining computational intelligence with data mining is presented at the end of the chapter with the conclusions.

Chapter 3

Shyue-Liang Wang, National University of Kaohsiung, Taiwan

Ju-Wen Shen, Chunghwa Telecom Co., Ltd., Taiwan

Tuzng-Pei Hong, National University of Kaohsiung, Taiwan

Discovery of functional dependencies (FDs) from relational databases has been identified as an important database analysis technique. Various mining techniques have been proposed in recent years to deal with crisp and static data. However, few have emphasized on fuzzy data and also considered the dynamic nature that data may change all the time. In this work, the authors propose a partition-based incremental data mining algorithm to discover fuzzy functional dependencies from similarity-based fuzzy relational databases when new sets of tuples are added. Based on the concept of tuple partitions and the monotonicity of fuzzy functional dependencies, we avoid re-scanning of the database and thereby reduce computation time. An example demonstrating the proposed algorithm is given. Computational complexity of the proposed algorithm is analyzed. Comparison with pair-wise comparison-based incremental mining algorithm (Wang, Shen & Hong, 2000) is presented. It is shown that with certain space requirement, partition-based approach is more time efficient than pair-wise approach in the discovery of fuzzy functional dependencies dynamically.

Chapter 4

Peitsang Wu, I-Shou University, Taiwan, R.O.C.

Yung-Yao Hung, I-Shou University, Taiwan, R.O.C.

In this chapter, a meta-heuristic algorithm (Electromagnetism-like Mechanism, EM) for global optimization is introduced. The Electromagnetism-like mechanism simulates the electromagnetism theory of physics by considering each sample point to be an electrical charge. The EM algorithm utilizes an attraction-repulsion mechanism to move the sample points towards the optimum. The electromagnetism-like mechanism (EM) can be used as a stand-alone approach or as an accompanying algorithm for other methods. Besides, the electromagnetism-like mechanism is not easily trapped into local optimum. Therefore, the purpose of this chapter is using the electromagnetism-like mechanism (EM) to develop an electromagnetism-like mechanism based fuzzy neural network (EMFNN), and employ the EMFNN to train fuzzy if-then rules.

Section 2
Soft Computation

Chapter 5

Yuanyuan Chai, Beijing Jiaotong University, China

This chapter is a survey of CI and indicates the Simulation Mechanism-Based (SMB) classification method for Computational Intelligence through reviewing on the definitions of CI and existed classification methods. The classification method divides all CI branches into three categories: organic mechanism simulation class, inorganic mechanism simulation class and artificial mechanism simulation class. Furthermore, branches in organic mechanism simulation class are introduced in detail, by which the chapter concludes the nonlinear mapping model for each class. The work presented in this chapter will provide an efficient approach to understand essence of CI.

Chapter 6

Shangce Gao, University of Toyama, Japan
Zheng Tang, University of Toyama, Japan
Hiroki Tamura, University of Miyazaki, Japan

Artificial Immune System as a new branch in computational intelligence is the distributed computational technique inspired by immunological principles. In particular, the Clonal Selection Algorithm (CS), which tries to imitate the mechanisms in the clonal selection principle proposed by Burent to better understand its natural processes and simulate its dynamical behavior in the presence of antigens, has received a rapid increasing interest. However, the description about the mechanisms in the algorithm is rarely seen in the literature and the related operators in the algorithm are still inefficient. In addition, the comparison with other algorithms (especially the genetic algorithms) lacks of analysis. In this chapter, several new clonal selection principles and operators are introduced, aiming not only at a better understanding of the immune system, but also at solving engineering problems more efficiently. The efficiency of the proposed algorithm is verified by applying it to the famous traveling salesman problems (TSP).

Chapter 7

Takashi Hasuike, Osaka University, Japan

This chapter considers various types of risk-management models based on the portfolio theory under some social uncertainty that received historical data includes ambiguity, and that they are assumed not to be constant. These models with uncertainty are represented many social problems such as assets allocation, logistics, scheduling, urban project problems, etc.. However, since these problems with uncertainty are formulated as stochastic and fuzzy programming problems, it is difficult to solve them analytically in the sense of deterministic mathematical programming. Therefore, introducing possibility and necessity measures based on the fuzzy programming approach and considering the concept of risk-management based on the portfolio theory, main problems are transformed into the deterministic programming problems. Then, in order to solve the deterministic problems efficiently, the solution method is constructed.

Neuro-fuzzy modeling is a computing paradigm of soft computing and very efficient for system modeling problems. It integrates two well-known modeling approaches of neural networks and fuzzy systems, and therefore possesses advantages of them, i.e., learning capability, robustness, human-like reasoning, and high understandability. Up to now, many approaches have been proposed for neuro-fuzzy modeling. However, it still exists many problems need to be solved. In this chapter, the authors firstly give an introduction to neuro-fuzzy system modeling. Secondly, some basic concepts of neural networks, fuzzy systems, and neuro-fuzzy systems are introduced. Also, they review and discuss some important literatures about neuro-fuzzy modeling. Thirdly, the issue for solving two most important problems of neuro-fuzzy modeling is considered, i.e., structure identification and parameter identification. Therefore, the authors present two approaches to solve these two problems, respectively. Fourthly, the future and emerging trends of neuro-fuzzy modeling is discussed. Besides, the possible research issues about neuro-fuzzy modeling are suggested. Finally, the authors give a conclusion.

Forecasting data from a time series is to make predictions for the future from available data. Thus, such a problem can be viewed as a traditional data mining problem because it is to extract rules for prediction from available data. There are two kinds of forecasting approaches. Most traditional forecasting approaches are based on all available data including the nearest data and far away data with respect to the time. These approaches are referred to as the global prediction scheme in the authors' study. On the other hand, there also exist some prediction approaches that only construct their prediction model based on the most recent data. Such approaches are referred to as the local prediction schemes. Those local prediction approaches seem to have good prediction ability in some cases but due to their local characteristics, they usually fail in general for long term prediction. In this chapter, the authors shall detail those ideas and use several commonly used models, especially those model free estimators, such as neural networks, fuzzy systems, grey systems, etc., to explain their effects. Another issues discussed in the chapter is about multi-step predictions. From the author's study, it can be found that those often-used global prediction schemes can have fair performance in both one-step-ahead predictions and multi-step predictions. On the other hand, good local prediction schemes can have better performance in the one-step-ahead prediction when compared to those global prediction schemes, but usually have awful performance for multi-step predictions. In this chapter, the authors shall introduce several approaches of combining local and global prediction results to improve the prediction performance.

Yunong Zhang, Sun Yat-Sen University, China
Ning Tan, Sun Yat-Sen University, China

Artificial neural networks (ANN), especially with error back-propagation (BP) training algorithms, have been widely investigated and applied in various science and engineering fields. However, the BP algorithms are essentially gradient-based iterative methods, which adjust the neural-network weights to bring the network input/output behavior into a desired mapping by taking a gradient-based descent direction. This kind of iterative neural-network (NN) methods has shown some inherent weaknesses, such as, 1) the possibility of being trapped into local minima, 2) the difficulty in choosing appropriate learning rates, and 3) the inability to design the optimal or smallest NN-structure.

To resolve such weaknesses of BP neural networks, we have asked ourselves a special question: Could neural-network weights be determined directly without iterative BP-training? The answer appears to be YES, which is demonstrated in this chapter with three positive but different examples. In other words, a new type of artificial neural networks with linearly-independent or orthogonal activation functions, is being presented, analyzed, simulated and verified by us, of which the neural-network weights and structure could be decided directly and more deterministically as well (in comparison with usual conventional BP neural networks).

Cha-Hwa Lin, National Sun-Yat Sen University, Taiwan
Jin-Fu Wang, National Sun-Yat Sen University, Taiwan

Mobile agent planning (MAP) is one of the most important techniques in the mobile computing paradigm to complete a given task in the most efficient manner. To tackle this challenging NP-hard problem, Hopfield-Tank neural network is modified to provide a dynamic approach which not only optimizes the cost of mobile agents in a spatio-temporal computing environment, but also satisfies the location-based constraints such as the starting and ending nodes of the routing sequence which must be the home site of the traveling mobile agent. Meanwhile, the energy function is reformulated into a Lyapunov function to guarantee the convergence to a stable state and the existence of valid solutions. Moreover, the objective function is designed to estimate the completion time of a valid solution and to predict the optimal routing path. This method can produce solutions rapidly that are very close to the minimum cost of the location-based and time-constrained distributed MAP problem.

Cheng-Jian Lin, National Chin-Yi University of Technology, Taiwan, R.O.C.
Cheng-Hung Chen, National Chin-Yi University of Technology, Taiwan, R.O.C.

This chapter presents an evolutionary neural fuzzy network, designed using the functional-link-based neural fuzzy network (FLNFN) and a new evolutionary learning algorithm. This new evolutionary learning algorithm is based on a hybrid of cooperative particle swarm optimization and cultural algorithm. It is thus called cultural cooperative particle swarm optimization (CCPSO). The proposed CCPSO method, which uses cooperative behavior among multiple swarms, can increase the global search capacity using the belief space. Cooperative behavior involves a collection of multiple swarms that interact by exchanging information to solve a problem. The belief space is the information repository in which the individuals can store their experiences such that other individuals can learn from them indirectly. The proposed FLNFN model uses functional link neural networks as the consequent part of the fuzzy rules. This chapter uses orthogonal polynomials and linearly independent functions in a functional expansion of the functional link neural networks. The FLNFN model can generate the consequent part of a nonlinear combination of input variables. Finally, the proposed functional-link-based neural fuzzy network with cultural cooperative particle swarm optimization (FLNFN-CCPSO) is adopted in several predictive applications. Experimental results have demonstrated that the proposed CCPSO method performs well in predicting the time series problems.

Chapter 13

The load frequency control (LFC) is to maintain the power balance in the electrical power system such that the system's frequency deviates from its nominal value to within specified limits and according to practically acceptable dynamic performance of the system. The control strategy evolved may also result in overall high efficiency (fuel saving) and minimum additional equipment to avoid cost, maintenance etc. The supplementary controller i.e. of a diesel or steam turbine generating unit, called the load frequency controller, may satisfy these requirements. The function of the controller is to generate, raise or lower command signals to the speed-gear changer of the prime mover (i.e. diesel engine) in response to the frequency error signal by performing mathematical manipulations of amplification and integration of this signal. The speed-gear changer must not act too fast, as it will cause wear and tear of the engine and, also, should not act too slow, as it will deteriorate system's performance. Therefore, an optimum load frequency controller is required for satisfactory operation of the system. In this Chapter, intelligent controllers for the LFC problem are analyzed and discussed. The use of any single technique or even a combination of genetic algorithms, fuzzy logic and neural networks is explored instead of conventional methods.

Chapter 14

Multimedia products today broadcast over networks and are typically compressed and transmitted from host to client. Adding watermarks to the compressed domain ensures content integrity, protects copyright, and can be detected without quality degradation. Hence, watermarking video data in the compressed domain is important. This work develops a novel video watermarking system with the aid of computational intelligence, in which motion vectors define watermark locations. The number of watermark bits varies dynamically among frames. The current study employs several intelligent computing methods including

K-means clustering, Fuzzy C-means clustering, Swarm intelligent clustering and Swarm intelligence based Fuzzy C-means (SI-FCM) clustering to determine the motion vectors and watermark positions. This study also discusses and compares the advantages and disadvantages among various approaches. The proposed scheme has three merits. First, the proposed watermarking strategy does not involve manually setting watermark bit locations. Second, the number of embedded motion vector clusters differs according to the motion characteristics of each frame. Third, the proposed special exclusive-OR operation closely relates the watermark bit to the video context, preventing attackers from discovering the real watermark length of each frame. Therefore, the proposed approach is highly secure. The proposed watermark-extracting scheme immediately detects forgery through changes in motion vectors. Experimental results reveal that the watermarked video retains satisfactory quality with very low degradation.

Section 3
Data Mining

Chapter 15

Data mining (DM) is the key process in knowledge discovery. Many theoretical and practical DM applications can be found in science and engineering. However there are still such areas where data mining techniques are still at early state of growth and application. In particular, an unsatisfactory progress is observed in DM applications in the analysis of Internet and Web performance issues. This chapter gives the background of network performance measurement and presents our approaches, namely Internet Performance Mining and Web Performance Mining as the ways of DM application to Internet and Web performance issues. The authors present real-life examples of the analysis where explored data sets were collected with the aid of two network measurement systems WING and MWING developed at our laboratory.

Chapter 16

As vast numbers of web services have been developed over a broad range of functionalities, it becomes a challenging task to find relevant or similar web services using web services registry such as UDDI. Current UDDI search uses keywords from web service and company information in its registry to retrieve web services. This method cannot fully capture user's needs and may miss out on potential matches. Underlying functionality and semantics of web services need to be considered. This chapter introduces a methodology for predicting similarity of web services by integrating hierarchical clustering, nearest neighbor classification, and algorithms for natural language processing using WordNet. It can be used to facilitate the development of intelligent applications for retrieving web services with imprecise or vague requests. The authors explore semantics of web services using WSDL operation names and parameter names along with WordNet. They compute semantic interface similarity of web services and use this data to generate clusters. Then, they represent each cluster by a set of characteristic operations to predict similarity of new web services using nearest neighbor approach. The empirical result is promising.

Chapter 17

This chapter discusses two different types of text data mining focusing on the biomedical literature. One deals with explicit information or facts written in articles, and the other targets implicit information or hypotheses inferred from explicit information. A major difference between the two is that the former is bound to the contents within the literature, whereas the latter goes beyond existing knowledge and generates potential scientific hypotheses. As concrete examples applied to real-world problems, this chapter looks at two applications of text data mining: gene functional annotation and genetic association discovery, both considered to have significant practical importance.

Chapter 18

This chapter presents an automatic meteorological data mining system based on analyzing and mining heterogeneous remote sensed image datasets, with which it is possible to forecast potential rainstorms in advance. A two-phase data mining method employing machine learning techniques, including the C4.5 decision tree algorithm and dependency network analysis, is proposed, by which a group of derivation rules and a conceptual model for metrological environment factors are generated to assist the automatic weather forecasting task. Experimental results have shown that the system reduces the heavy workload of manual weather forecasting and provides meaningful interpretations to the forecasted results.

Chapter 19

This chapter describes a machine learning approach for classification problems in safety-related domains. The proposed method is based on ensembles of low-dimensional submodels. The usage of low-dimensional submodels enables the domain experts to understand the mechanisms of the learned solution. Due to the limited dimensionality of the submodels each individual model can be visualized and can thus be interpreted and validated according to the domain knowledge. The ensemble of all submodels overcomes the limited predictive performance of each single submodel while the overall solution remains interpretable and verifiable. By different examples from real-world applications the authors will show that their classification approach is applicable to a wide range of classification problems in the field of safety-related applications - ranging from decision support systems over plant monitoring and diagnosis systems to control tasks with very high safety requirements.

Foreword

It is my great honor to be the first reader of this excellent book edited by two world class specialists in the filed of Artificial Intelligence, Prof. Leon S.L. Wang and Prof. Tzung-Pei Hong.

This edited book treats a very important topic of Artificial Intelligence, which is related to Integrating Advanced Technology for Intelligent Soft Computation and Data Mining. The book presents an international forum for the synergy of new developments from these two significant, but different research disciplines. It is very good idea of the Editors for making the fusion of diverse techniques and applications, owing to which new and innovative ideas will be stimulated and integrated.

This book contains nineteen original and high quality chapters authored by leading researchers of soft computing and data mining communities as well as practitioners from medical science, space and geo-information science, transportation engineering, and innovative life science. The book is organized into three sections. The first section includes four innovative chapters that give a flavor of how soft computation and data mining can be integrated for various applications. In the second section nine new soft computation techniques for different real world applications are presented. The last section includes five real life problems for which the authors proposed new data mining techniques.

The research results presented in the chapters of this book are original and very interesting. I would like to congratulate Professor Leon S.L. Wang and Professor Tzung-Pei Hong for the excellent work and all the authors for their wonderful contributions.

In my opinion, the techniques for integrating advanced technologies for intelligent soft computation and data mining included in this book are very valuable and many readers such as postgraduate and Ph.D. students in Computer Science, scientists who are working on intelligent computing, knowledge management, data mining, will find it interesting and helpful.

Ngoc Thanh Nguyen
Wroclaw University of Technology, Poland

Ngoc Thanh Nguyen *works at Wroclaw University of Technology, Poland, and is the head of Knowledge Management Systems Department in the Faculty of Computer Science. His scientific interests consist of knowledge integration methods, collective intelligence, intelligent technologies for conflict resolution, inconsistent knowledge processing, multi-agent systems, and E-learning methods. He has edited 20 special issues in international journals, 10 books and 8 conference proceedings. He is the author of 4 monographs and about 190 other publications. Prof. Nguyen serves as Editor-in-Chief of International Journal of Intelligent Information and Database Systems; Editor-in-Chief of two book series: Advances in Applied Intelligence Technologies and Computational Intelligence and its Applications for IGI Global Publishers (USA); Associate Editor of Neurocomputing, International Journal of Innovative Computing & Information Control, Journal of Information Knowledge System Management and KES Journal; and a Member of Editorial Review Boards of several other prestigious international journals. He has been General Chair or Program Chair of more than 10 international conferences. Prof. Nguyen has been selected as the Vice-President of International Society of Applied Intelligence (ISAI); In 2008 for his activities the President of Poland has rewarded Prof. Nguyen the Bronze Medal for Education. In 2009 he received the Title of Professor granted by the President of Poland.*

Preface

Since its inception, data mining has been described as "the nontrivial extraction of implicit, previously unknown, and potentially useful information from data". It was usually used by business intelligence organizations and analysts to extract useful information from databases. But increasing applications of data mining have been found in other areas to extract information from the enormous data sets generated by modern experimental and observational methods. However, due to the intractable computational complexity of many existing data mining techniques for real world problems, techniques that are tolerable to imprecision, uncertainty, and approximation are very desirable.

In contrast to conventional hard computing, the basic ideas underlying soft computing is to exploit the tolerance for imprecision, uncertainty, partial truth, and approximation to achieve tractability, robustness and low solution cost. At this juncture, the principal constituents of soft computing are Fuzzy Logic (FL), Neural Computing (NC), Evolutionary Computation (EC), Genetic Algorithms (GA), Swam Intelligence (SI), Machine Learning (ML) and Probabilistic Reasoning (PR), with the latter subsuming belief networks, chaos theory and parts of learning theory. It has been demonstrated in many areas that the soft computing methodologies are complementary to many existing theories and technologies.

As such, the objective of this book is to present an international forum for the synergy of new developments from two different research disciplines. It is hoped that through the fusion of diverse techniques and applications, new and innovative ideas will be stimulated and shared.

This book contains nineteen chapters written by leading experts from researchers of soft computing and data mining communities as well as practitioners from medical science, space and geo-information science, innovative life science, and traffic and transportation engineering. The book is organized into three sections. The first section shows four innovative works that give a flavor of how soft computation and data mining can be integrated for various applications. The second section compiles nine new soft computation techniques for different real world applications, with a leading chapter of survey to classify current computational intelligence technologies. The third section is devoted to five real life problems that can be addressed by the proposed new data mining techniques. Since the chapters are written by many researchers with different backgrounds around the world, the topics and content covered in this book provides insights which are not easily accessible otherwise.

While integrating advanced technologies clearly falls in the emerging category because of recency, it is now beginning to reach popularity and more books on this topic becomes desirable. It is hoped that this book will provide a reference to researchers, practitioners, students in both soft computing and data mining communities and others, for the benefit of more creative ideas.

We are grateful to all authors for their contributions and the referees for their vision and efforts. We would like to express our thanks to IGI Global and National University of Kaohsiung for realizing this book project.

June 2009
Leon S.L. Wang
Tzung-Pei Hong

Section 1
Integrating Soft Computation and Data Mining

Chapter 1
Introduction to the Experimental Design in the Data Mining Tool KEEL

J. Alcalá-Fdez
University of Granada, Spain

I. Robles
University of Granada, Spain

F. Herrera
University of Granada, Spain

S. García
University of Jaén, Spain

M.J. del Jesus
University of Jaén, Spain

L. Sánchez
University of Oviedo, Spain

E. Bernadó-Mansilla
University Ramon Llull, Spain

A. Peregrín
University of Huelva, Spain

S. Ventura
University of Córdoba, Spain

ABSTRACT

KEEL is a Data Mining software tool to assess the behaviour of evolutionary learning algorithms in particular and soft computing algorithms in general for different kinds of Data Mining problems including as regression, classification, clustering, pattern mining and so on. It allows us to perform a complete analysis of some learning model in comparison to existing ones, including a statistical test module for comparison. In this chapter the authors will provide a complete description of KEEL, the kind of problems and algorithms implemented, and they will present a case of study for showing the experimental design and statistical analysis that they can do with KEEL.

DOI: 10.4018/978-1-61520-757-2.ch001

INTRODUCTION

Data Mining (DM) is the process for automatic discovery of high level knowledge by obtaining information from real world, large and complex data sets (Ham & Kamber, 2006). This idea of automatically discovering knowledge from databases is a very attractive and challenging task, both for academia and industry. Hence, there has been a growing interest in DM in several Artificial Intelligence (AI)-related areas, including Evolutionary Algorithms (EAs) (Eiben & Smith, 2003).

EAs are optimization algorithms based on natural evolution and genetic processes. Nowadays in AI, they are considered as one of the most successful search techniques for complex problems and they have proved to be an important technique for learning and Knowledge Extraction. This makes them also a promising tool in DM (Cordón, Herrera, Hoffmann, & Magdalena, 2001; Freitas, 2002; Jain & Ghosh, 2005; Grefenstette, 1994; Pal & Wang, 1996; Wong & Leung, 2000). The main motivation for applying EAs to Knowledge Extraction tasks is that they are robust and adaptive search methods that perform a global search in place of candidate solutions (for instance, rules or other forms of knowledge representation).

The use of EAs in problem solving is a widespread practice (Stejic, Takama, & Hirota, 2007; Mucientes, Moreno, Bugarín, & Barro, 2006; Romero, Ventura, & Bra, 2004), however, their use requires a certain programming expertise along with considerable time and effort to write a computer program for implementing the often sophisticated algorithm according to user needs. This work can be tedious and needs to be done before users can start focusing their attention on the issues that they should be really working on. In the last few years, many software tools have been developed to reduce this task. Although a lot of them are commercially distributed (some of the leading commercial software are mining suites such as SPSS Clementine [1], Oracle Data Mining [2] and KnowledgeSTUDIO [3]), a few are available as open source software (we recommend visiting the KDnuggets software directory [4] and The-Data-Mine site [5]). Open source tools can play an important role as is pointed out in (Sonnenburg et al., 2007).

In this chapter, we provide a complete description of a non-commercial Java software tool named KEEL (Knowledge Extraction based on Evolutionary Learning) [6]. This tool empowers the user to assess the behaviour of evolutionary learning for different kinds of DM problems: regression, classification, clustering, pattern mining, etc. This tool can offer several advantages:

- It reduces programming work. It includes a library with evolutionary learning algorithms based on different paradigms (Pittsburgh, Michigan and IRL) and simplifies the integration of evolutionary learning algorithms with different preprocessing techniques. It can alleviate researchers from the mere "technical work" of programming and enable them to focus more on the analysis of their new learning models in comparison with the existing ones.

- It extends the range of possible users applying evolutionary learning algorithms. An extensive library of EAs together with easy-to-use software considerably reduce the level of knowledge and experience required by researchers in evolutionary computation. As a result researchers with less knowledge, when using this framework, would be able to apply successfully these algorithms to their problems.

- Due to the use of a strict object-oriented approach for the library and software tool, these can be used on any machine with Java. As a result, any researcher can use KEEL on his machine, independently of the operating system.

In order to describe KEEL, this chapter is arranged as follows. The next section introduces a brief background to demonstrate our position on the book's topic. Section KEEL DESCRIPTION describes KEEL and its main features and modules. Section EVOLUTIONARY ALGORITHMS IN KEEL introduces a brief description of the algorithms implemented in KEEL. In Section CASE STUDIES, one case study is given to illustrate how KEEL should be used. Finally, some conclusions and future work are pointed out.

BACKGROUND

A search on the Internet for DM software reveals the existence of many commercial and non-commercial DM tools and libraries, developed throughout the scientific community. We can distinguish between libraries whose purpose is to develop new EAs for specific applications and DM suites that incorporate learning algorithms (some of them including evolutionary learning methods)

and which in addition provide mechanisms to establish scientific comparisons among them. Over the Internet and in specialized literature we can find a large number of libraries dedicated to evolutionary computation. For instance, table 1 and 2 show some libraries designed for a specific type of EA and some generic tools by which it is possible to develop different EAs for many problems, respectively.

Nowadays, many researchers base their work on DM tools (Rodríguez, Kuncheva, & Alonso, 2006), or they employ tools specifically designed for an area of DM, such as (Wang, Nauck, Spott, & Kruse, 2007). We centre our interest on free distributions of software dedicated to the whole range of the DM field. Moreover, we are interested in tools where developers, since the source code is available, have the choice of extending their functionality. Probably the most well-known open source DM package is Weka (Witten & Frank, 2005), a collection of Java implementations of Machine Learning (ML) algorithms. However, there are others open source software packages available

Table 1. Libraries designed for a specific type of EA

Type	Reference
Genetic Algorithms	Chuang, 2000
Genetic Programming	Punch & Zongker, 1998
Memetic Algorithms	Krasnogor & Smith, 2000
Learning Classifier Systems	Meyer & Hufschlag, 2006
Evolutionary Multiobjective Optimization	Tan, Lee, Khoo, & Khor, 2001
Distributed EAs	Tan, Tay, & Cai, 2003

Table 2. Generic tools for developing EAs

Name	Reference
ECJ	Luke et al., 2007
EO	Keijzer, Guervós, Romero, & Schoenauer, 2002
Evolvica	Rummler, 2007
JCLEC	Ventura, Romero, Zafra, Delgado, & Hervás, 2007
Open Beagle	Gagné & Parizeau, 2006

in internet, for example: ADaM (Rushing et al., 2005), D2K (with E2K) (Llorà, 2006), KNIME (Berthold et al., 2006), MiningMart (Morik & Scholz, 2004), Orange (Demšar, Zupan, Leban, & Curk, 2004), Tanagra (Rakotomalala, 2005) or RapidMiner (formerly YALE) (Mierswa, Wurst, Klinkenberg, Scholz, & Euler, 2006).

All these software tools provide several functionalities, but each one supports them in a different way. We have established a set of basic and advanced characteristics that these tools may possess or not. The objective is to detect the major differences in the software tools and then to categorize KEEL as an alternative to these tools when other research requirements are needed. All of them have been selected by evaluating all the software tools, tutorials and guidelines for the usage of such tools, the only characteristic that we have added for a different reason is EAs integration given that this is the main motivation for KEEL. Selected characteristics are briefly explained as follows:

- *Language* is the programming language used in the development of the software. C++ language is less portable with respect to Java.
- *Graphical Interface* includes functionality criteria which tool can be managed through a handy interface by the user, and how
  ○ *Graph representation* indicates that the experiment or knowledge flows are represented by graphs with node-edge connections. This alternative is more interpretable and user-friendly than using a chain of processes or a tree representation of modules.
  ○ *Data visualization* includes tools for representing the data sets through charts, tables or similar mechanisms.
  ○ *Data management* comprises of a set of toolkits that allow us to perform basic manual operations with the data, such as removing or modifying rows, columns, etc.

- *Input/Output* functionality criteria pointing out the different data formats supported, such as *ARFF* (the Weka standard), *others* (including C4.5 input.names standard (Quinlan, 1993),.xls,.csv, XML) and *database connection*. The tool supports this functionality if it can load or save data in these formats or can transform them into a standard one that it uses.
- *Pre-processing Variety.* This comprises of *discretization* (Liu, Hussain, Tan, & Dash, 2002), *feature selection* (Lee, 2004), *instance selection* (D. R. Wilson & Martinez, 2000) and *missing values imputation* (Batista & Monard, 2003). The trend of most of the suites is to offer a good feature selection and discretization set of methods, but they overlook specialized methods of missing values imputation and instance selection. Usually, the contributions included are basic modules of replacing or generating null values and methods for sampling the data sets by random (stratified or not) or by value-dependence.
- *Learning Variety* is support over main areas of DM, such as predictive tasks (*classification, regression, anomaly/deviation detection*), and descriptive tasks (*clustering, association rule discovery, sequential pattern discovery*) (P.-N. Tan, Steinbach, & Kumar, 2005). Intermediate level is awarded if the tool includes the classical models, and advance level is awarded it the tool contains advanced DM models from these areas.
- *Off/On-line run* of the experiment set up. An On-line run implies that the tool interface and algorithm modules need to be in the same machine and the experiments are completely dependent on the software tool. An off-line run entails the independence of the experiments created with respect to the suite interface, allowing the experiment to be executed in other machines.

- *Advanced Features* includes some of the less common criteria incorporated for extending the functionality of the software tool.
- *Post-processing*, usually for tuning the model learned by an algorithm.
- *Meta-learning*, which includes more advanced learning schemes, such as bagging or boosting, or meta learning of the algorithm parameters.
- *Statistical tests* for establishing comparisons of results. An advanced support of this property requires a complete set of parametric and nonparametric statistical tests; a basic support implies the existence of well-known standard statistical tests (such as t-test).
- *EA* support indicates the integration of EAs into the DM areas that the software tool offers. A basic support of this feature implies the use of genetic algorithms in some techniques (usually, genetic feature selection). To upgrade the level it is necessary to incorporate EAs in learning or meta-learning models.

Table 3 shows a summary of the studied characteristics. We distinguish four levels of support in these characteristics: none (N), basic support (B), intermediate support (I) and advanced support (A). If features do not have intermediate levels of support, the notation used is Yes (Y) for supporting and No (N) for no-supporting.

If we analyze the characteristics presented in these DM package we will be able to highlight that most of software tools have a none/basic support for two type of pre-processing (instance selection and missing values imputation), statistical tests and EAs. Moreover, these software tools usually integrate a representative set of algorithms for each type of learning and pre-processing task. However, the experiments are meant to be run in the same environment, which is not practical if the algorithms require high computation times (as with the EAs).

KEEL solves these disadvantages since the users can analyze the behaviour of evolutionary and non-evolutionary algorithms in each type of learning and preprocessing task, as well as run their experiments in both modes (off-line and on-line). In the next section, we will describe KEEL in detail.

Table 3. Summary of the characteristics of each DM software tool

Software	Language	Representation	Visualization	Management	ARFF Format	Other Formats	Data Base	Discretization	Feature S.	Instance S.	Missing Values	Classification	Regression	Clustering	Association R.	On-Line	Off-Line	Postprocessing	Meta Learning	Statistical Test	EAs
		Graphical Interface			Input / Output			Pre-processing Variety				Learning Variety				Run Type		Advanced Features			
ADaM	C++	N	N	I	Y	N	N	N	A	B	N	I	N	A	B	Y	N	N	N	N	B
D2K	Java	Y	A	I	Y	Y	Y	I	A	B	B	A	A	A	A	Y	N	N	N	N	I
KNIME	Java	Y	A	A	Y	Y	Y	I	A	B	B	A	A	A	A	Y	N	N	N	I	B
MiningMart	Java	Y	B	A	N	N	Y	I	A	B	I	B	B	N	N	Y	N	N	N	N	B
Orange	C++	Y	A	A	N	Y	N	A	I	B	B	I	N	I	I	N	Y	N	N	N	N
Tanagra++	C++	A	A	Y	Y	N	B	A	B	N	A	I	A	A	Y	N	N	I	A	N	N
Weka	Java	Y	A	A	Y	Y	Y	I	A	B	B	A	A	A	A	Y	N	N	I	N	B
RapidMiner	Java	N	A	A	Y	N	Y	I	A	B	B	A	A	A	A	Y	N	N	A	B	I

Figure 1. Screenshot of the main window of KEEL software tool

KEEL

KEEL is a software tool that facilitates the analysis of the behaviour of evolutionary learning in the different areas of learning and pre-processing tasks, making the management of these techniques easy for the user. The presently available version of KEEL consists of the following function blocks[7] (see Figure 1):

- *Data Management*: This part is made up of a set of tools that can be used to build new data, to export and import data in other formats to or from KEEL format, data edition and visualization, to apply transformations and partitioning to data, etc.
- *Design of Experiments (off-line module)*: The aim of this part is the design of the desired experimentation over the selected data sets and providing for many options in different areas: type of validation, type of learning (classification, regression, unsupervised learning), etc.
- *Educational Experiments (on-line module)*: With a similar structure to the previous part, this allows for the design of

experiment that can be run step-by-step in order to display the learning process of a certain model by using the software tool for educational purposes.

This structure makes KEEL software useful for different types of user, who expect to find different functionalities in a DM software. In the following subsections we explain its main features and the different integrated function blocks.

Main Features

KEEL is a software tool developed to ensemble and use different DM models. Notice that this is the first software toolkit of this type containing a library of evolutionary learning algorithms with open source code in Java. The main features of KEEL are:

- EAs are presented in predicting models, pre-processing (evolutionary feature and instance selection) and postprocessing (evolutionary tuning of fuzzy rules).
- It includes data pre-processing algorithms proposed in specialized literature

are included: data transformation, discretization, instance selection and feature selection.

- It has a statistical library to analyze algorithms' results. It comprises a set of statistical tests for analyzing the suitability of the results and performing parametric and non-parametric comparisons among the algorithms.
- Some algorithms have been developed using the Java Class Library for Evolutionary Computation (JCLEC)[8] (Ventura et al., 2007).
- It provides a user-friendly interface, oriented to the analysis of algorithms.
- The software is aimed to create experimentations containing multiple data sets and algorithms connected among themselves to obtain an expected results. Experiments are independently script-generated from the user interface for an off-line run in the same or other machines.
- KEEL also allows creating experiments in on-line mode, aiming an educational support in order to learn the operation of the algorithms included.
- It contains a Knowledge Extraction Algorithms Library[9] with the incorporation of multiple evolutionary learning algorithms, together with classical learning approaches. The principal families of techniques included are:
- Evolutionary rule learning models. Including different paradigms of evolutionary learning.
- Fuzzy systems. Fuzzy rule learning models with a good trade-off between accuracy and interpretability.
- Evolutionary neural networks. Evolution and pruning in neural networks, product unit neural networks, and radial base models.
- Genetic programming. Evolutionary algorithms that use tree representations for knowledge extraction.

- Subgroup discovery. Algorithms for extracting descriptive rules based on patterns subgroup discovery.
- Data reduction (instance and feature selection and discretization). EAs for data reduction.

Data Management

The Data Management module integrated in KEEL allows us to perform the data preparation stage independently of the remaining of the DM process itself. This module is focused on the group of users denoted as domain experts. They are familiar with their data, they know the processes that produce the data and they are interested in reviewing those to improve upon or analyze them. On the other hand, domain users are those whose interest lies in applying processes to their own data and they usually are not experts in DM.

Figure 2 shows an example window of the Data Management module in the section of Data Visualization. The module has seven sections, each of which is accessible through the buttons on the left side of the window. In the following, we will briefly describe them:

- **Creation of a new data set:** This option allows us to generate a new data set compatible with the other KEEL modules.
- Import data to KEEL format: Since KEEL works with a specific data format (alike the ARFF format) in all its modules, this section allows us to convert various data formats to KEEL format, such as CSV, XML, ARFF, extracting data from data bases, etc.
- **Export data from KEEL format:** This is the opposite option to the previous one. It converts the data handled by KEEL procedures in other external formats to establish compatibility with other software tools.
- **Visualization of data:** This option is used to represent and visualize the data. With it, we can see a graphical distribution of each

Figure 2. Data management

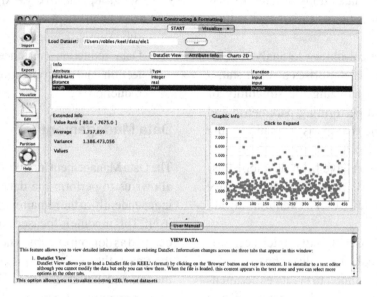

attribute and comparisons between two attributes.

- **Edition of data:** This area is dedicated to managing the data manually. The data set, once loaded, can be edited by terms of modifying values, adding or removing rows and columns, etc.
- **Data Partition:** This zone allows us to make the partitions of data needed by the experiment modules to validate results. It supports k-fold cross validation, 5x2 cross validation and hold-out validation with stratified partition.
- **Data Preparation:** This section allows us to perform automatic data preparation for DM, including cleaning, transformation and reduction of data. All techniques integrated in this section are also available in the experiments-related modules.

Design of Experiments: Off-Line Module

This module is a Graphical User Interface (GUI) that allows the design of experiments for solving various problems of regression, classification and unsupervised learning. Having designed the experiments (see Figure 3, step 1), it generates the directory structure and files required (see Figure 3, step 2) for running them in any local machine with Java (see Figure 3, step 3).

The experiments are graphically modeled, based on data flow and represented by graphs with node-edge connections. To design an experiment, we have first to indicate the type of validation (k-fold cross validation (Kohavi, 1995) or 5x2 cross validation (Dietterich, 1998)) and the type of learning (regression, classification or unsupervised) to be used. Then, we have to select the data sources, drag the selected methods into the workspace and connect methods and datasets, combining the evolutionary learning algorithms with different pre-processing and post-processing techniques, if needed. Finally, we can add statistical tests to achieve a complete analysis of the methods being studied, and a report box to obtain a summary of the results. Notice that each component of the experiment is configured in separate dialogues that can be opened by doubleclicking the respective node. Figure 4 shows an example of an experiment following the MOGUL methodology (Cordón, Jesus, Herrera, & Lozano, 1999) and using a re-

Figure 3. Steps of the design of experiments off-line

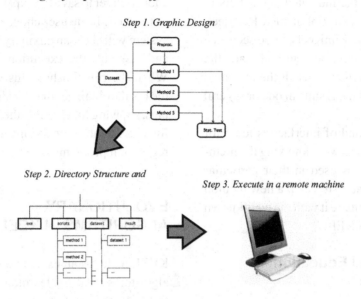

Figure 4. Example of an experiment and the configuration window of a method

port box to obtain a summary of the results. The configuration window of the MOGUL method is also shown in this figure.

When the experiment has been designed, the user can choose either to save the design in a XML file or to obtain a zip file. If the user chooses a zip file, then the system will generate the file with the directory structure and required files for running the designed experiment in any local machine with Java. This directory structure contains the data sources, the jar files of the algorithms, the configuration files in XML format, a script file with all the indicated algorithms in XML format, and a Java tool, named RunKeel, to run the experiment. RunKeel can be seen as a simple EA scripting environment that reads the script file in XML format, runs all the indicated algorithms and saves the results in one or several report files.

Obviously, this kind of interface is ideal for experts of specific areas who, knowing the methodologies and methods used in their particular area of interest, intend to develop a new method and would like to compare it with the well-known methods available in KEEL.

Computer-Based Education: On-Line Module

This module is a GUI that allows the user to design an experiment (with one or more algorithms), run it and visualize the results on-line. The idea is to use this part of KEEL as a guideline to demonstrate the learning process of a certain model. This module has a similar structure as the previous one but includes only those algorithms and options that are suitable for academic purposes.

When an experiment is designed the user can choose either to save the experiment in a XML file or to run it. If the user chooses to run it, then the system will show an auxiliary window to manage and visualize the execution of each algorithm. When the run finishes, this window will show the results obtained for each algorithm in separate tags, showing for example the confusion matrices for classification or the mean square errors for regression problems (see Figure 5).

EVOLUTIONARY ALGORITHMS IN KEEL

KEEL includes an extensive set of evolutionary algorithms used for learning and preprocessing tasks. In this section, we will present an enumeration of the evolutionary methods which can be used in KEEL for experimental purposes. In order to do this, three tables will contain a list of methods depending on the task they are used for: data preparation, classification and regression. The name used in KEEL for each method together with the reference is given.

Table 4 shows the data preparation evolutionary algorithms included in KEEL. Table 5 and Table 6

Figure 5. Auxiliary window of an experiment with two algorithms

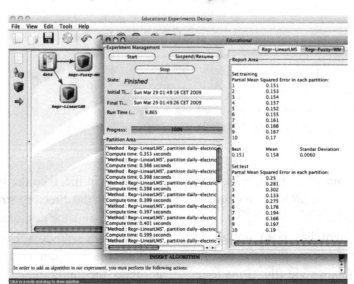

enumerate the evolutionary algorithms contained in KEEL for classification and regression tasks respectively.

EXPERIMENTAL EXAMPLES OF KEEL

This section is dedicated to present some case studies as examples of the functionality and process of creating an experiment in the KEEL software tool. We will show, in each one of the following subsections, an example of classification, regression and unsupervised experimentation.

Classification Example

This study is focused on the development of a comparison of two evolutionary interval rule based learning algorithms and a subsequent analysis of the results over 12 problems for classification. These problems are summarized in Table 7.

The methods considered for the experiment are XCS (Wilson, 1995) and SIA (Venturini, 1993). XCS is rule based inductive learning algorithms based on the Michigan approach and SIA is an interval rule learning algorithm based on IRL.

To develop the experiment we consider a *10-fold cross validation* model. For each one of the 10 partitions, both algorithms have been run 3 times

since these methods are probabilistic (a total of 30 runs). Moreover, a pairwise Wilcoxon test was applied in order to ascertain if differences in the performance of the methods are significant.

The values considered for the input parameters of each method are:

XCS parameters:

- Number of Explores = 100000.
- Population Size = 6400.
- $\alpha = 0.1$, $\beta = 0.2$, $\delta = 0.1$, $\nu = 10.0$, $\theta_{mna} = 2$, $\theta_{del} = 50.0$, $\theta_{sub} = 50.0$, $\varepsilon_0 = 0$.
- Do action set subsumption = false.
- Fit reduction = 0.1.
- Initial prediction = 10.0, initial fitness = 0.01, initial prediction error = 0.0.
- Prediction error reduction = 0.25.
- Probability of crossover = 0.8.
- Probability of mutation = 0.04.
- $\theta_{ga} = 50.0$.
- Do genetic algorithm subsumption = true.
- Type of selection = Roulette wheel selection.
- Type of mutation = free.
- Type of crossover = 2 points.
- Probability of "Don't care" = 0.33.
- $R_0 = 1.0$, $m_0 = 0.1$, $l_0 = 0.1$.
- Do specify operator = false.

SIA parameters:

Table 4. Evolutionary algorithms included in KEEL for data preparation tasks

Type	Name	Reference
Feature selection	FS-SSGA-Integer-knn	Casillas, Cordón, Jesus, & Herrera, 2001
	FS-GGA-Binary-Inconsistency	Lanzi, 1997
Instance selection	IS-CHC	Cano, Herrera, & Lozano, 2003
	IS-GGA	Cano et al., 2003
	IS-SGA	Cano et al., 2003
	IS-PBIL	Cano et al., 2003
	IS-IGA	Ho, Liu, & Liu, 2002
	IS-GA_MSE_CC_FSM	Gil-Pita & Yao, 2007
	IS-SSMA	García, Cano, & Herrera, 2008

Table 5. Evolutionary algorithms included in KEEL for classification tasks

Type	Name	Reference
Neural networks	Clas-NNEP	F. Martínez, Hervás, Gutiérrez, & Martínez, 2008
	Clas-GANN	Miller, Todd, & Hedge, 1989
		Yao, 1999
Fuzzy rules	Clas-Fuzzy-SAP	Sánchez, Couso, & Corrales, 2001
	Clas-Fuzzy-GP	Sánchez et al., 2001
	Clas-Fuzzy-AdaBoost	Jesus, Hoffmann, Navascués, & Sánchez, 2004
	Clas-Fuzzy-LogitBoost	Otero & Sánchez, 2006
	Clas-Fuzzy-GAP	Sánchez et al., 2001
	Clas-Fuzzy-MaxLogitBoost	Sánchez & Otero, 2007
	Clas-Fuzzy-Ishib-Selec	Ishibuchi, Nozaki, Yamamoto, & Tanaka, 1995
	Clas-Fuzzy-SLAVE	González & Pérez, 2001
	Class-Fuzzy-MOGUL	Cordón, Jesus, & Herrera, 1998
		Cordón, Jesus, Herrera, & Lozano, 1999
	Clas-Fuzzy-Ishibuchi99	Ishibuchi, Nakashima, & Murata, 1999
	Clas-Fuzzy-Ishib-Hybrid	Ishibuchi, Yamamoto, & Nakashima, 2005
	Clas-Fuzzy-Shi-Eberhart-Chen	Shi, Eberhart, & Chen, 1999
Interval rules	Clas-GAssist-ADI	Bacardit & Garrell, 2003, 2004
	Clas-PGIRLA	Corcoran & Sen, 1994
	Clas-SIA	Venturini, 1993
	Clas-XCS	Wilson, 1995
	Clas-Hider	Aguilar-Ruiz, Riquelme, & Toro, 2003
		Aguilar-Ruiz, Giraldez, & Riquelme, 2007
	Clas-GAssist-Intervalar	Bacardit & Garrell, 2007
	Clas-LogenPro	Wong & Leung, 2000
	Clas-UCS	Bernadó-Mansilla & Garrell, 2003
	Clas-PSO_ACO	Sousa, Silva, & Neves, 2004
	Clas-Ant_Miner	Parpinelli, Lopes, & Freitas, 2002b
	Clas-Advanced_Ant_Miner	Parpinelli et al., 2002b
		Parpinelli, Lopes, & Freitas, 2002[a]
	Clas-Ant_Miner_Plus	Parpinelli et al., 2002b
	Clas-Advanced_Ant_Miner_Plus	Parpinelli et al., 2002b
		Parpinelli, Lopes, & Freitas, 2002[a]

- Number of Iterations = 200.
- $\alpha = 150$, $\beta = 0$.
- Threshold Strength = 0.

To do this experiment in KEEL, first of all we click the Experiment option in the main menu of the KEEL software tool, define the experiment as a Classification problem and use a 10-fold cross validation procedure to analyze the results. Next, the first step of the experiment graph setup is to choose the data sets of the Table 7 to be used. The partitions in KEEL are static, allowing that

Table 6. Evolutionary algorithms included in KEEL for regression tasks

Type	Name	Reference
Neural networks	Regr-GANN	Miller, Todd, & Hegde, 1989 Yao, 1999
	Regr-NNEP	A. Martínez, Martínez, Hervás, & García, 2006
Fuzzy rules	Regr-Fuzzy-TSK-IRL	Cordón & Herrera, 1999
	Regr-Fuzzy-MOGUL-IRLSC	Cordón & Herrera, 1997
	Regr-Fuzzy-GP	Sánchez et al., 2001
	Regr-Fuzzy-MOGUL-IRLHC	Cordón & Herrera, 2001
	Regr-Fuzzy-MOGUL-TSK	Alcalá, Alcalá-Fdez, Casillas, Cordón, & Herrera, 2007
	Regr-Fuzzy-SAP	Sánchez et al., 2001
	Regr-COR_GA	Casillas, Cordón, & Herrera, 2002
		Casillas, Cordón, Herrera, & Villar, 2004
	Regr-Thrift	Thrift, 1991
	Regr-GFS-RB-MF	Homaifar & McCormick, 1995
		Cordón & Herrera, 1997
	Regr-Fuzzy-MOGUL-IRL	Cordón & Herrera, 1997
	Regr-Fuzzy-SEFC	Juang, Lin, & Lin, 2000
	Regr-Fuzzy-P_FCS1	Carse, Fogarty, & Munro, 1996
Fuzzy rules post-processing	Post-G-G-Tuning-FRBSs	Cordón & Herrera, 1997
	Post-A-G-Tuning-FRBSs	Herrera, Lozano, & Verdegay, 1995
	Post-Rules-Selection	Cordón & Herrera, 1997
		Ishibuchi et al., 1995
	Post-G-T-FRBSs-Weights	Alcalá, Cordón, & Herrera, 2003
	Post-G-S-Weight-FRBS	Alcalá et al., 2003
	Post-GB-NFRM	Park, Kandel, & Langholz, 1994
Symbolic	Regr-Fuzzy-GAP-RegSym	Sánchez & Couso, 2000
	Regr-SAP	Sánchez & Couso, 2000
		Sánchez et al., 2001;
	Regr-Interval-GAP-RegSym	Sanchez & Couso, 2007
	Regr-Interval-GAP-RegSym	Cordón & Herrera, 1997
	Regr-Interval-SAP-RegSym	Sanchez & Couso, 2007
		Sánchez et al., 2001
	Regr-GAP	Sánchez & Couso, 2000

further experiments carried out will give up being dependent on particular data partitions. Optionally, a user could create new partitions with the function block *Data Management*.

The graph in Figure 6 represents the flow of data and results from the algorithms and statistical techniques. A node can represent an initial data flow (group of data sets), a pre-process/post-process algorithm, a learning method, test or a visualization of results module. They can be easily distinguished according the color of the node. All their parameters can be adjusted by clicking twice

Table 7. Data sets summary descriptions

Data set	#Examples	#Atts.	#Classes
Bupa	345	6	2
Cleveland	297	13	5
Ecoli	336	7	8
Glass	214	9	7
Haberman	306	3	2
Iris	150	4	3
Monk-2	432	6	2
New-thyroid	215	5	3
Pima	768	8	2
Vehicle	846	18	4
Wine	178	13	3
Wisconsin	683	9	2

on the node. Notice that KEEL incorporates the option of configure the number of runs for each probabilistic algorithm, including this option in the configuration dialog of each node (3 in this case study). Logically, directed edges connecting two nodes represent a relationship between them (data or results interchange). When the data is interchanged, the flow includes pairs of train-test data sets. Thus, the graph in this specific example describes a flow of data from the 12 data sets to the nodes of the two learning methods (*Clas-XCS* and *Clas-SIA*).

After the models are trained, the instances of the data set are classified. These results are the inputs for the visualization and test modules. The module *Vis-Clas-Tabular* receives these results as input and generates output files with several performance metrics computed from them, such as confusion matrixes for each method, accuracy and error percentages for each method, fold and class, and a final summary of results. Figure 6 also shows another type of results flow, the node *Stat-Clas-Wilcoxon* which represents the statistical comparison, results are collected and a statistical analysis over multiple data sets is performed by following the indications given in Demsar,

2006. The test used in this example is a pairwise Wilcoxon test.

Once the graph is defined, we can set up the associated experiment and save it as zip file for an off-line run. Following the structure of directories shown in Figure 3, the experiment is set up as a set of XML scripts and a JAR program for running it. Within the *results* directory, there will be directories used for housing the results of each method during the run. For example, the files allocated in the directory associated to an interval learning algorithm will contain the knowledge or rule base. In the case of a visualization procedure, its directory will house the results files. The results obtained by the analyzed methods are shown in Table 8, where Acc_{tra} and Acc_{tst} stand respectively for the averaged accuracy obtained over the training and test data.

In case of using a test procedure, the *Stat-Clas-Wilcoxon* directory will house the results files. Test modules in KEEL provide the output in text and Latex formats. They generate associated tables with information of the statistical procedure. In this case, Tables 9 and 10 are generated by the *Stat-Clas-Wilcoxon* module when the run is finished.

Figure 6. Experiment graph of the case study of classification

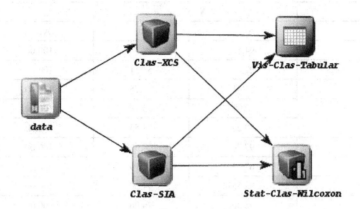

Analysing the results shown in Table 8, 9 and 10; we can highlight that, although XCS algorithm does not obtain the best training accuracy in all the data sets, the test accuracy is the best in 10 of the 12 data sets. Moreover, the statistical analysis (pairwise comparisons Wilcoxon's test) obtains that XCS algorithm clearly outperforms SIA assuming a high level of significance $p=0.005040$.

Regression Example

We show an example of regression experimentation which is focused on a comparison of two fuzzy rule based learning algorithms over a real-world electrical energy distribution problem (ele1).

The methods considered for the experiment are Thrift (Thrift, 1991) and WM (Wang & Mendel, 1992). Thrift learns the consequent of the fuzzy rules in the Rule Base by means of a decision table representation of the fuzzy rule base following a Pittsburgh approach, and WM is Wang and Mendel's well-known ad hoc data-driven rule generation method.

To develop the experiment we consider a *10-fold cross validation* model. The values considered for the input parameters of each method are:

Thrift parameters:

- Number of labels = 3
- Population Size = 61
- Number of Evaluations = 10000
- Crossover Probability = 0.6
- Mutation Probability = 0.1

Wang-Mendel parameters:

- Number of Labels = 3.

Following a similar procedure to the classification example, first of all we click the Experiment option in the main menu of the KEEL software tool, define the experiment as a Regression problem and use a 10-fold cross validation procedure to analyze the results. Next, we choose the ele1 data set.

The graph in Figure 7 represents the flow of data and results from the algorithms and visualization modules. After the set of rules are obtained, the objects of the data set are modeled. These results are the inputs for the visualization module. The module *Vis-Regr-Tabular* receives these results as input and generates output files with several performance metrics computed from them.

The results obtained by the analyzed methods are shown in Table 11, where MSE_{tra} and MSE_{tst} stand respectively for the mean square error ob-

Table 8. Results obtained in the 12 data sets

Data set	XCS		SIA	
	Acc_{tra}	Acc_{tst}	Acc_{tra}	Acc_{tst}
Bupa	94.68	69.10	100.00	56.55
Cleveland	92.81	54.51	100.00	53.78
Ecoli	89.35	82.75	100.00	80.70
Glass	92.41	75.17	100.00	70.31
Haberman	80.28	72.53	97.24	69.55
Iris	97.70	94.67	100.00	95.33
Monk-2	67.23	68.19	67.13	67.19
New-thyroid	98.55	94.50	100.00	93.46
Pima	92.36	76.06	100.00	70.07
Vehicle	91.15	74.12	100.00	61.94
Wine	100.00	96.67	100.00	95.52
Wisconsin	98.36	96.34	99.95	96.93
Average	91.24	**79.55**	**97.03**	75.95

Table 9. Ranks. Positive ranks correspond to XCS. Negative ranks correspond to SIA

		N	Mean Rank	Sum of Ranks
XCS vs. SIA	Positive Ranks	10	7.5	75.0
	Negative Ranks	2	1.5	3.0
	Ties	0		
	Total	12		

Table 10. Test statistics. Positive ranks (R⁺) correspond to XCS. Negative ranks (R⁻) correspond to SIA

Comparison	R^+	R^-	p-value
XCS vs. SIA	75.0	3.0	0.005040

tained over the training and test data in each fold of the 10fcv.

Unsupervised Learning Example

Finally, we illustrate an example of unsupervised experimentation concerning the employment of a well-known association rules algorithm to a small data set. The method considered for the experiment is Apriori (Agrawal, Mannila, Srikant, Toivonen & Verkamo, 1996). The parameters used are:

Apriori parameters:

- MinSupport = 5
- MinConfidence = 0.75
- AntecedentMaxSize = 1
- ConsecuentMaxSize = 1

Figure 7. Experiment graph of the case study of regression

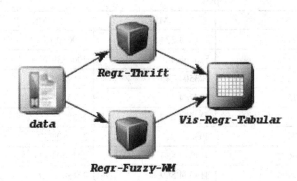

Following a similar procedure to the classification example, first of all we click the Experiment option in the main menu of the KEEL software tool, define the experiment as a Unsupervised problem and use no validation procedure to analyze the results. Next, we choose the "weather" data set.

The graph in Figure 8 represents the experiment graph. Once the experiment is run, the set of resulting rules can be located within the *results* directory. In this case, the rules, with their associated confidence and support, are the following ones:

1. if (humidity = "normal") then play = "yes" (0.857 / 6)
2. if (windy = "false") then play = "yes" (0.750 / 6)

FUTURE TRENDS

The KEEL software tool is being continuously updated and improved. At the moment, we are developing a new set of evolutionary learning algorithms and a test tool that will allow us to apply parametric and non-parametric tests on any set of data. We are also developing data visualization tools for the on-line and off-line modules. Finally, we are also working on the development of a data set repository that includes the data set

partitions and algorithm results on these data sets, the KEEL-dataset[10].

CONCLUSION

In this chapter, we have provided a complete description KEEL, a software tool to assess the behaviour of evolutionary learning algorithms in particular and soft computing algorithms in general for DM problems. It relieves researchers of much technical work and allows them to focus on the analysis of their new learning models in comparison with the existing ones. Moreover, the tool enables researchers with a basic knowledge of evolutionary computation to apply EAs to their work.

We have shown some case studies to illustrate functionalities and the experiment set up processes in KEEL. We have tackled a classification study, a regression problem and an example of unsupervised learning by means of the obtaining of association rules. In the classification case, in which various data sets have been employed, the results have been contrasted through statistical analysis (pairwise comparisons Wilcoxon's test), obtaining that XCS algorithm clearly outperforms SIA assuming a high level of significance $p = 0.005040$. As regression problem, we have used the ele1 data set and we have run the algorithms

Table 11. Results obtained in the ele1 data set

Data set	Thrift		Wang-Mendel	
	MSE_{tra}	MSE_{tst}	MSE_{tra}	MSE_{tst}
Fold0	533199.911	421974.224	600050.154	494157.506
Fold1	641411.264	515168.487	2066539.7	1919242.2
Fold2	480059.424	483504.735	556088.251	592182.225
Fold3	630683.155	427784.492	2083337.96	1766343.77
Fold4	554593.603	556084.297	2079715.15	1799318.74
Fold5	510154.74	403075.917	2057802.57	2294985.16
Fold6	544968.667	414878.833	2042403.52	2138930.7
Fold7	524193.999	414554.569	2013886.29	2390803.51
Fold8	507660.871	535250.587	1516655.06	1525392.13
Fold9	543274.626	404593.359	2086352.03	1745858.38
Average	**547020.026**	**457686.95**	1710283.07	1666721.43

Figure 8. Experiment graph of the case study of unsupervised learning

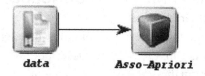

data   Asso-Apriori

Thrift and Wang-Mendel. Finally, we conduct an small experiment involving the well-known Apriori algorithm to a small data set, showing the resulting base of rules.

ACKNOWLEDGMENT

This paper has been supported by the Spanish Ministry of Education and Science under Project TIN2008-06681-C06-(01, 02, 03, 04, 05 and 06).

REFERENCES

Agrawal, R., Mannila, H., Srikant, R., Toivonen, H., & Verkamo, A. I. (1996). Fast Discovery of Association Rules. *Advances in Knowledge Discovery and Data Mining, 12,* 307–328.

Aguilar-Ruiz, J., Giraldez, R., & Riquelme, J. (2007). Natural encoding for evolutionary supervised learning. *IEEE Transactions on Evolutionary Computation, 11*(4), 466–479. doi:10.1109/TEVC.2006.883466

Aguilar-Ruiz, J., Riquelme, J., & Toro, M. (2003). Evolutionary learning of hierarchical decision rules. *IEEE Transactions on Systems, Man, and Cybernetics. Part B, 33*(2), 324–331.

Alcalá, R., Alcalá-Fdez, J., Casillas, J., Cordón, O., & Herrera, F. (2006). Hybrid learning models to get the interpretability-accuracy trade-off in fuzzy modeling. *Soft Computing, 10*(9), 717–734. doi:10.1007/s00500-005-0002-1

Alcalá, R., Alcalá-Fdez, J., Casillas, J., Cordón, O., & Herrera, F. (2007). Local identification of prototypes for genetic learning of accurate tsk fuzzy rule-based systems. *International Journal of Intelligent Systems, 22*(9), 909–941. doi:10.1002/int.20232

Alcalá, R., Cordón, O., & Herrera, F. (2003). Combining rule weight learning and rule selection to obtain simpler and more accurate linguistic fuzzy models. In J. Lawry, J. Shanahan, & A. Ralescu (Eds.), Modelling with words (Vol. 2873, pp. 44–63). Berlin: Springer.

Bacardit, J., & Garrell, J. (2003). Evolving multiple discretizations with adaptive intervals for a pittsburgh rule-based learning classifier system. In Genetic and evolutionary computation conference (gecco'03) (p. 1818-1831). Berlin: Springer-Verlag.

Bacardit, J., & Garrell, J. (2004). Analysis and improvements of the adaptive discretization intervals knowledge representation. In Genetic and evolutionary computation conference (gecco'04) (p. 726-738). Berlin: Springer-Verlag.

Bacardit, J., & Garrell, J. (2007). Bloat control and generalization pressure using the minimum description length principle for a pittsburgh approach learning classifier system. In Learning classifier systems (Vol. 4399, pp. 59–79). London: Springer Berlin-Heidelberg.

Batista, G. E., & Monard, M. C. (2003). An analysis of four missing data treatment methods for supervised learning. *Applied Artificial Intelligence, 17*(5-6), 519–533. doi:10.1080/713827181

Bernadó-Mansilla, E., & Garrell, J. (2003). Accuracy-based learning classifier systems: models, analysis and applications to classification tasks. *Evolutionary Computation, 1*(3), 209–238. doi:10.1162/106365603322365289

Bernadó-Mansilla, E., & Ho, T. K. (2005). Domain of competence of xcs classifier system in complexity measurement space. *IEEE Transactions on Evolutionary Computation, 9*(1), 82–104. doi:10.1109/TEVC.2004.840153

Berthold, M. R., Cebron, N., Dill, F., Fatta, G. D., Gabriel, T. R., Georg, F., et al. (2006). Knime: the konstanz information miner. In Proceedings international workshop on multi-agent systems and simulation (mas & s), 4th annual industrial simulation conference (isc 2006) (p. 58-61), Palermo, Italy.

Cano, J. R., Herrera, F., & Lozano, M. (2003). Using evolutionary algorithms as instance selection for data reduction in kdd: an experimental study. *IEEE Transactions on Evolutionary Computation, 7*(6), 561–575. doi:10.1109/TEVC.2003.819265

Carse, B., Fogarty, T., & Munro, A. (1996). Evolving fuzzy rule based controllers using genetic algorithms. *Fuzzy Sets and Systems, 80*(3), 273–293. doi:10.1016/0165-0114(95)00196-4

Casillas, J., Cordón, O., del Jesus, M. J., & Herrera, F. (2001). Genetic feature selection in a fuzzy rule-based classification system learning process for high-dimensional problems. *Information Sciences, 136*(1-4), 135–157. doi:10.1016/S0020-0255(01)00147-5

Casillas, J., Cordón, O., & Herrera, F. (2002). Cor: a methodology to improve ad hoc data-driven linguistic rule learning methods by inducing cooperation among rules. *IEEE Transactions on Systems, Man, and Cybernetics. Part B, 32*(4), 526–537.

Casillas, J., Cordón, O., Herrera, F., & Villar, P. (2004). A hybrid learning process for the knowledge base of a fuzzy rule-based system. In X international conference on information processing and management of uncertainty in knowledge-based systems (ipmu´04) (pp. 2189-2196), Perugia, Italy.

Chuang, A. (2000). An extendible genetic algorithm framework for problem solving in a common environment. *IEEE Transactions on Power Systems*, *15*(1), 269–275. doi:10.1109/59.852132

Corcoran, A., & Sen, S. (1994). Using real-valued genetic algorithms to evolve rule sets for classification. In *Proceedings of the first ieee conference on evolutionary computation,* (Vol. 1, p. 120-124), Orlando, FL.

Cordón, O., del Jesus, M. J., & Herrera, F. (1998). Genetic learning of fuzzy rule-based classification systems cooperating with fuzzy reasoning methods. *International Journal of Intelligent Systems*, *13*(10-11), 1025–1053. doi:10.1002/(SICI)1098-111X(199810/11)13:10/11<1025::AID-INT9>3.0.CO;2-N

Cordón, O., del Jesus, M. J., Herrera, F., & Lozano, M. (1999). Mogul: A methodology to obtain genetic fuzzy rule-based systems under the iterative rule learning approach. *International Journal of Intelligent Systems*, *14*(9), 1123–1153. doi:10.1002/(SICI)1098-111X(199911)14:11<1123::AID-INT4>3.0.CO;2-6

Cordón, O., & Herrera, F. (1997). A three-stage evolutionary process for learning descriptive and approximate fuzzy logic controller knowledge bases from examples. *International Journal of Approximate Reasoning*, *17*(4), 369–407. doi:10.1016/S0888-613X(96)00133-8

Cordón, O., & Herrera, F. (1999). A two-stage evolutionary process for designing tsk fuzzy rule-based systems. *IEEE Transactions on Systems, Man, and Cybernetics. Part B*, *29*(6), 703–715.

Cordón, O., & Herrera, F. (2001). Hybridizing genetic algorithms with sharing scheme and evolution strategies for designing approximate fuzzy rule-based systems. *Fuzzy Sets and Systems*, *118*(2), 235–255. doi:10.1016/S0165-0114(98)00349-2

Cordón, O., Herrera, F., Hoffmann, F., & Magdalena, L. (2001). Genetic fuzzy systems: Evolutionary tuning and learning of fuzzy knowledge bases. Singapore: World Scientific.

del Jesus, M. J., Hoffmann, F., Navascués, L. J., & Sánchez, L. (2004). Induction of fuzzy-rule-based classiffers with evolutionary boosting algorithms. *IEEE transactions on Fuzzy Systems*, *12*(3), 296–308. doi:10.1109/TFUZZ.2004.825972

Demsar, J. (2006). Statistical comparisons of classifiers over multiple data sets. *Journal of Machine Learning Research*, 7, 1–30.

Demsar, J., Zupan, B., Leban, G., & Curk, T. (2004). Orange: From experimental machine learning to interactive data mining. In Knowledge discovery in databases: Pkdd 2004 (p. 537-539). Berlin: Springer.

Dietterich, T. G. (1998). Approximate statistical tests for comparing supervised classification learning algorithms. *Neural Computation*, *10*(7), 1895–1923. doi:10.1162/089976698300017197

Eiben, A. E., & Smith, J. E. (2003). Introduction to Evolutionary Computing. Berlin: Springer Verlag.

Freitas, A. A. (2002). Data mining and knowledge discovery with evolutionary algorithms. Secaucus, NJ: Springer-Verlag New York, Inc.

Gagné, C., & Parizeau, M. (2006). Genericity in evolutionary computation software tools: Principles and case-study. *International Journal of Artificial Intelligence Tools*, *15*(2), 173–194. doi:10.1142/S021821300600262X

García, S., Cano, J., & Herrera, F. (2008). A memetic algorithm for evolutionary prototype selection: A scaling up approach. *Pattern Recognition, 41*(8), 2693–2709. doi:10.1016/j.patcog.2008.02.006

Gil-Pita, R., & Yao, X. (2007). Using a genetic algorithm for editing k-nearest neighbor classifiers. In *Proceedings of the 8th international conference on intelligent data engineering and automated learning (ideal)* (pp. 1141-1150), Birmingham, UK.

González, A., & Pérez, R. (1999). Slave: a genetic learning system based on an iterative approach. *IEEE transactions on Fuzzy Systems, 7*(2), 176–191. doi:10.1109/91.755399

González, A., & Pérez, R. (2001). Selection of relevant features in a fuzzy genetic learning algorithm. *IEEE Transactions on Systems, Man, and Cybernetics. Part B, 31*(3), 417–425.

Grefenstette, J. J. (1994). Genetic algorithms for machine learning. Norwell, MA: Kluwer Academic Publishers.

Han, J., & Kamber, M. (2006). Data mining: Concepts and Techniques (2nd ed.). San Francisco: Morgan Kaufmann Publishers Inc.

Herrera, F., Lozano, M., & Verdegay, J. (1995). Tuning fuzzy logic controllers by genetic algorithms. *International Journal of Approximate Reasoning, 12*(3-4), 299–315. doi:10.1016/0888-613X(94)00033-Y

Ho, S.-Y., Liu, C.-C., & Liu, S. (2002). Design of an optimal nearest neighbor classifier using an intelligent genetic algorithm. *Pattern Recognition Letters, 23*(13), 1495–1503. doi:10.1016/S0167-8655(02)00109-5

Homaifar, A., & McCormick, E. (1995). Simultaneous design of membership functions and rule sets for fuzzy controllers using genetic algorithms. *IEEE transactions on Fuzzy Systems, 3*(2), 129–139. doi:10.1109/91.388168

Ishibuchi, H., Nakashima, T., & Murata, T. (1999). Performance evaluation of fuzzy classifier systems for multidimensional pattern classification problems. *IEEE Transactions on Systems, Man, and Cybernetics. Part B, 29*(5), 601–618.

Ishibuchi, H., Nozaki, K., Yamamoto, N., & Tanaka, H. (1995). Selecting fuzzy if-then rules for classification problems using genetic algorithms. *IEEE transactions on Fuzzy Systems, 3*(3), 260–270. doi:10.1109/91.413232

Ishibuchi, H., Yamamoto, T., & Nakashima, T. (2005). Hybridization of fuzzy gbml approaches for pattern classification problems. *IEEE Transactions on Systems, Man, and Cybernetics. Part B, 35*(2), 359–365.

Juang, C., Lin, J., & Lin, C.-T. (2000). Genetic reinforcement learning through symbiotic evolution for fuzzy controller design. *IEEE Transactions on Systems, Man, and Cybernetics. Part B, Cybernetics, 30*(2), 290–302. doi:10.1109/3477.836377

Keijzer, M., Guervós, J. J. M., Romero, G., & Schoenauer, M. (2002). Evolving objects: A general purpose evolutionary computation library. In Selected papers from the 5th european conference on artificial evolution (pp. 231-244). London, UK: Springer-Verlag.

Kohavi, R. (1995). A study of cross-validation and bootstrap for accuracy estimation and model selection. In 14th international joint conference on artificial intelligence (pp. 1137-1145), Montreal, Quebec, Canada.

Krasnogor, N., & Smith, J. (2000, July 8-12). Mafra: A java memetic algorithms framework. In *Proceedings of the 2000 international genetic and evolutionary computation conference (GECCO 2000)* (pp. 125–131), Las Vegas, NV.

Lanzi, P. (1997). Fast feature selection with genetic algorithms: A filter approach. In *Conference on ieee international evolutionary computation,* (pp. 537-540), Indianapolis, IN.

Lee, J.-S. (2004). Hybrid genetic algorithms for feature selection. *IEEE Transactions on Pattern Analysis and Machine Intelligence, 26*(11), 1424–1437. doi:10.1109/TPAMI.2004.105

Liu, H., Hussain, F., Tan, C., & Dash, M. (2002). Discretization: An enabling technique. *Data Mining and Knowledge Discovery, 6*(4), 393–423. doi:10.1023/A:1016304305535

Llorà, X. (2006). E2k: evolution to knowledge. *SIGEVOlution, 1*(3), 10–17. doi:10.1145/1181964.1181966

Llorà, X., & Garrell, J. M. (2003). Prototype induction and attribute selection via evolutionary algorithms. *Intelligent Data Analysis, 7*(3), 193–208.

Luke, S., Panait, L., Balan, G., Paus, S., Skolicki, Z., Bassett, J., et al. (2007). *Ecj: A java based evolutionary computation research system*. Retrieved from http://cs.gmu.edu/ eclab/projects/ecj

Martínez, A., Martínez, F., Hervás, C., & García, N. (2006). Evolutionary product unit based neural networks for regression. *Neural Networks, 19*(4), 477–486. doi:10.1016/j.neunet.2005.11.001

Martínez, F., Hervás, C., Gutiérrez, P., & Martínez, A. (in press). Evolutionary product-unit neural networks classifiers. *Neurocomputing.*

Meyer, M., & Hufschlag, K. (2006). A generic approach to an object-oriented learning classifier system library. *Journal of Artificial Societies and Social Simulation, 9* (3). Available from http://jasss.soc.surrey.ac.uk/9/3/9.html

Mierswa, I., Wurst, M., Klinkenberg, R., Scholz, M., & Euler, T. (2006). Yale: rapid prototyping for complex data mining tasks. In *Kdd '06: Proceedings of the 12th acm sigkdd international conference on knowledge discovery and data mining,* (pp. 935–940). New York: ACM.

Miller, G., Todd, P., & Hedge, S. (1989). Designing neural networks using genetic algorithms. In *Proceedings of the 3rd international conference on genetic algorithm and their applications* (p. 379-384). Arlington, VA: George Mason University.

Miller, G., Todd, P., & Hegde, S. (1989). Designing neural networks using genetic algorithms. In *Proceedings of the 3rd international conference on genetic algorithms* (pp. 379–384). San Francisco, CA: Morgan Kaufmann Publishers Inc.

Morik, K., & Scholz, M. (2004). The miningmart approach to knowledge discovery in databases. In N. Zhong & J. Liu (Eds.), Intelligent technologies for information analysis (pp. 47-65). Berlin: Springer-Verlag.

Mucientes, M., Moreno, L., Bugarín, A., & Barro, S. (2006). Evolutionary learning of a fuzzy controller for wall-following behavior in mobile robotics. *Soft Computing, 10*(10), 881–889. doi:10.1007/s00500-005-0014-x

Otero, J., & Sánchez, L. (2006). Induction of descriptive fuzzy classifiers with the logitboost algorithm. *Soft Computing, 10*(9), 825–835. doi:10.1007/s00500-005-0011-0

Pal, S. K., & Wang, P. P. (1996). Genetic algorithms for pattern recognition. Boca Raton, FL: CRC Press, Inc.

Park, D., Kandel, A., & Langholz, G. (1994). Genetic-based new fuzzy reasoning models with application to fuzzy control. *IEEE Transactions on Systems, Man, and Cybernetics*, *24*(1), 39–47. doi:10.1109/21.259684

Parpinelli, R., Lopes, H., & Freitas, A. (2002a). An ant colony algorithm for classification rule discovery. In H. Abbass, R. Sarker, & C. Newton (Eds.), Data mining: a heuristic approach (pp. 191-208). Hershey, PA: Idea Group Publishing.

Parpinelli, R., Lopes, H., & Freitas, A. (2002b). Data mining with an ant colony optimization algorithm. *IEEE Transactions on Evolutionary Computation*, *6*(4), 321–332. doi:10.1109/TEVC.2002.802452

Punch, B., & Zongker, D. (1998). *Lib-gp 1.1 beta*. Retrieved from http://garage.cse.msu.edu/software/lil-gp

Quinlan, J. R. (1993). C4.5: programs for machine learning. San Francisco: Morgan Kaufmann Publishers Inc.

Rakotomalala, R. (2005). Tanagra: un logiciel gratuit pour l'enseignement et la recherche. In proceedings of the 5th journées d'extraction et gestion des connaissances (Vol. 2, p. 697-702), Paris, France.

Rivera, A. J., Rojas, I., Ortega, J., & del Jesús, M. J. (2007). A new hybrid methodology for cooperative-coevolutionary optimization of radial basis function networks. *Soft Computing*, *11*(7), 655–668. doi:10.1007/s00500-006-0128-9

Rodríguez, J. J., Kuncheva, L. I., & Alonso, C. J. (2006). Rotation forest: A new classifier ensemble method. *IEEE Transactions on Pattern Analysis and Machine Intelligence*, *28*(10), 1619–1630. doi:10.1109/TPAMI.2006.211

Romero, C., Ventura, S., & de Bra, P. (2004). Knowledge discovery with genetic programming for providing feedback to courseware author. user modeling and user-adapted interaction. *The Journal of Personalization Research*, *14*(5), 425–465.

Rummler, A. (2007). *Evolvica: a java framework for evolutionary algorithms*. Retrieved from http://www.evolvica.org.

Rushing, J., Ramachandran, R., Nair, U., Graves, S., Welch, R., & Lin, H. (2005). Adam: a data mining toolkit for scientists and engineers. *Computers & Geosciences*, *31*(5), 607–618. doi:10.1016/j.cageo.2004.11.009

Sánchez, L., & Couso, I. (2000). Fuzzy random variables-based modeling with ga-p algorithms. In B. Bouchon, R. Yager, & L. Zadeh (Eds.), Information, uncertainty and fusion (pp. 245-256). Norwell, MA: Kluwer Academic Publishers.

Sanchez, L., & Couso, I. (2007). Advocating the use of imprecisely observed data in genetic fuzzy systems. *IEEE transactions on Fuzzy Systems*, *15*(4), 551–562. doi:10.1109/TFUZZ.2007.895942

Sánchez, L., Couso, I., & Corrales, J. A. (2001). Combining gp operators with sa search to evolve fuzzy rule based classifiers. *Information Sciences*, *136*(1-4), 175–191. doi:10.1016/S0020-0255(01)00146-3

Sánchez, L., & Otero, J. (2007). Boosting fuzzy rules in classification problems under single-winner inference. *International Journal of Intelligent Systems*, *22*(9), 1021–1034. doi:10.1002/int.20236

Shi, Y., Eberhart, R., & Chen, Y. (1999). Implementation of evolutionary fuzzy systems. *IEEE transactions on Fuzzy Systems*, *7*(2), 109–119. doi:10.1109/91.755393

Sonnenburg, S., Braun, M. L., Ong, C. S., Bengio, S., Bottou, L., & Holmes, G. (2007). The need for open source software in machine learning. *Journal of Machine Learning Research, 8*, 2443–2466.

Sousa, T., Silva, A., & Neves, A. (2004). Particle swarm based data mining algorithms for classification tasks. *Parallel Computing, 30*(5-6), 767–783. doi:10.1016/j.parco.2003.12.015

Stejic, Z., Takama, Y., & Hirota, K. (2007). Variants of evolutionary learning for interactive image retrieval. *Soft Computing, 11*(7), 669–678. doi:10.1007/s00500-006-0129-8

Tan, K., Lee, T., Khoo, D., & Khor, E. (2001). A multiobjective evolutionary algorithm toolbox for computer-aided multiobjective optimization. *IEEE Transactions on Systems, Man, and Cybernetics. Part B, 31*(4), 537–556.

Tan, K., Tay, A., & Cai, J. (2003). Design and implementation of a distributed evolutionary computing software. *IEEE Transactions on Systems, Man, and Cybernetics. Part C, 33*(3), 325–338.

Tan, P.-N., Steinbach, M., & Kumar, V. (2005). Introduction to data mining, (first edition). Boston: Addison-Wesley Longman Publishing Co., Inc.

Thrift, P. (1991). Fuzzy logic synthesis with genetic algorithms. In *Proceedings of the fourth international conference on genetic algorithms (icga)* (pp. 509-513), San Diego, USA.

Ventura, S., Romero, C., Zafra, A., Delgado, J. A., & Hervás, C. (2007). JCLEC: a java framework for evolutionary computation. *Soft Computing, 12*(4), 381–392. doi:10.1007/s00500-007-0172-0

Venturini, G. (1993). Sia: A supervised inductive algorithm with genetic search for learning attributes based concepts. In Machine learning: Ecml-93 (Vol. 667, pp. 280–296). London: Springer Berlin-Heidelberg.

Wang, X., & Mendel, J. M. (1992). Generating fuzzy rules by learning from examples. *IEEE Transactions on Systems, Man, and Cybernetics, 22*(6), 1414–1427. doi:10.1109/21.199466

Wang, X., Nauck, D., Spott, M., & Kruse, R. (2006). Intelligent data analysis with fuzzy decision trees. *Soft Computing, 11*(5), 439–457. doi:10.1007/s00500-006-0108-0

Wilson, D. R., & Martinez, T. R. (2000). Reduction techniques for instance-based learning algorithms. *Machine Learning, 38*(3), 257–286. doi:10.1023/A:1007626913721

Wilson, S. W. (1995). Classifier fitness based on accuracy. *Evolutionary Computation, 3*(2), 149–175. doi:10.1162/evco.1995.3.2.149

Witten, I., & Frank, E. (2005). Data mining: Practical machine learning tools and techniques, (2nd ed.). San Francisco: Morgan Kaufmann Publishers.

Wong, M. L., & Leung, K. S. (2000). Data mining using grammar-based genetic programming and applications. Norwell, MA: Kluwer Academic Publishers.

Yao, X. (1999). Evolving artificial neural networks. *Proceedings of the IEEE, 87*(9), 1423–1447. doi:10.1109/5.784219

ENDNOTES

1. http://www.spss.com/clementine
2. http://www.oracle.com/technology/products/bi/odm
3. http://www.angoss.com/products/studio/index.php
4. http://www.kdnuggets.com/software
5. http://the-data-mine.com/bin/view/Software

6   http://www.keel.es

7   http://www.keel.es/software/prototypes/
      version1.1/ManualKeel.pdf

8   http://jclec.sourceforge.net/

9   http://www.keel.es/algorithms.php

10   http://www.keel.es/datasets.php

Chapter 2
Cat Swarm Optimization Supported Data Mining

Pei-Wei Tsai
National Kaohsiung University of Applied Sciences, Taiwan

Jeng-Shyang Pan
National Kaohsiung University of Applied Sciences, Taiwan

Bin-Yih Liao
National Kaohsiung University of Applied Sciences, Taiwan

Shu-Chuan Chu
Cheng Shiu University, Taiwan

Mei-Chiao Lai
Diwan University, Taiwan

ABSTRACT

This chapter reviews the basic idea and processes in data mining and some algorithms within the field of evolutionary computing. The authors focus on introducing the algorithms of computational intelligence since they are useful tools for solving problems of optimization, data mining, and many kinds of industrial issues. A feasible model of combining computational intelligence with data mining is presented at the end of the chapter with the conclusions.

INTRODUCTION

Data Mining (DM) is a series of processes, which analyses the data and sieves some useful information or interesting knowledge out from real-world large and complex data sets (Ghosh & Jain, 2005). Various statistics, analysis, and modeling methods are employed to find patterns and relationships in

DM. The process of *Knowledge Discovery from Data (KDD)* is the key, which makes the outcome of DM being meaningful. Nevertheless, the fast development of computer science, the database management system (DBMS) and Data Warehouse (DW) pushes the size of the datasets increases forward with an astounding speed. It results in that precisely extracting the knowledge or finding the relationships and patterns become more difficult. Hence, the need for powerful tools to assist DM is clear. To build such

DOI: 10.4018/978-1-61520-757-2.ch002

tools for assisting DM, one of the ways is to lead in the evolutionary computing.

In this chapter, the concept of DM is reviewed, and several algorithms in evolutionary computing are presented. In addition, a feasible solution, which combines the intelligent computing and DM, is proposed. Finally, the discussion that concludes the chapter is made.

CONCEPT OF DATA MINING

Data mining is an essential step in the process of KDD as depicted in Figure 1 (Han & Kamber, 2007). By using data mining as a tool, several models, which are used to simulate the situations in the real world, can be created to describe the relationships between social behaviors in the real world and the patterns observed in the data. These patterns and relationships are very useful for increasing enterprise profit. For instance, the patterns and their relations to the actual shopping behaviors in customers help the store owners understand how to place their goods to make the customers feel more convenient when shopping. Hence, discovering the knowledge, which is hidden in the data, via data mining is very important.

In data mining, we can create 6 kinds of model to assist us to discover knowledge from the data. The models are listed as follows:

1. Regression.
2. Classification.
3. Time-Series Forecasting.
4. Clustering.
5. Association Rule.
6. Sequence Discovery.

No matter which model is employed, the training data is required to construct the knowledge from mining. The training data may comes from the historical records in the database or simply separates the data into two parts. One part of the data is used as the training dataset, and the other part of the data is used as the test dataset.

Regression

It is a kind of data analysis method used to fit an equation to a dataset. The simplest form of linear regression consists of a linear formula of a straight line in equation (1). After determining the appropriate values of a and b, the predicted value of y can be found based upon a given value of x. In more complicated system, such as multi regression, the acceptable number of the input variable is increased, and the model can be constructed by a quadratic equation. (Chapple, n.d.)

$$y = a \cdot x + b \tag{1}$$

Figure 1. Data mining as a step in the process of knowledge discovery

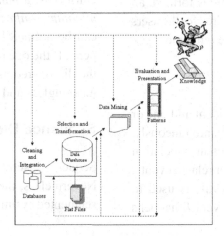

Classification

Classification in data mining classifies the outcomes into different classes according to the calculation result of the input variables. The classes of the outcomes are generally defined to be the discrete values in order to discriminate the classes from the others. For example, the classification can be employed in the case of sending advertisement to predict whether the customer will reply the mail. In this case, the outcome C of the classifier is set to two (C=reply∪not reply) or three (C=reply∪not reply∪unknow) classes.

Time-Series Forecasting

The outcome of time-series forecasting is a mathematical formula, which generates the patterns appear in the history data approximately. Usually, it is used to make long-term or short-term predictions of future values. (Han & Kamber, 2007) Time-series forecasting is similar to regression, but the input data for time-series forecasting is always related to time.

Clustering

The objects of clustering are to find out the similarity of the data in the same cluster and to figure out the differences between clusters. Since it separates the data into several clusters without the predetermined criteria and the users will not be able to know how the outcome is formed, an expert of clustering analyst is required for the users to understand the meaning of the outcome.

Association Rule

Assume a sign appears in an incident and one or more events or item must appear simultaneously, we may say that this sign represents an association between the incident and the other related events. In other words, the association rule is used to find out the probability $P(\cdot)$ of event B happens when event A occurs. The mathematical form of the definition of association rule is expressed as $P(B)|_A$. In data mining, the same case is formulated as follows:

$$Event(X, "A") \Rightarrow event(X, "B") \text{ [support=}S_X\%, \text{confidence=}c_X\%] \tag{2}$$

The *event* is a function that represents the relation between the input variables, X indicates the item, which drives the event, and S_X and C_X are constant. The definition of the term, "support", represents that about S_X percentages of the whole transactions under analysis conform to this association rule, and the term "confidence", indicates the change of when X is associated to A conditional on the *event*, and then X will be associated to B conditional on the *event*. If the *event* is the same for both A and B, the association rule can be reformed in equation (3).

$$A \Rightarrow B \text{ } [S_X\%, C_X\%] \tag{3}$$

For example, if a customer buys the fried chicken, then the probability for the same customer to buy the cola together is *82%*, and there are *3%* records of those under considered matches this association rule. Then this case can be presented as *buys*(*X*,"fried chicken")⇒*buys*(*X*,"cola") [3%,82%].

Typically, association rule in data mining is only concerned subject to it satisfies two constrains: a *minimum support threshold* and a *minimum confidence threshold*. These thresholds can be defined by the users or the domain experts. If the one of the thresholds is not satisfied, the discovered association rule is established as meaningless and is discarded.

Sequence Discovery

Sequence discovery is similar to association rule. Nevertheless, the item in sequence discovery is segmented by time series. Sequence discovery can be used to find the frequently occurring ordered events. In general, sequence discovery is used to deal with the data mining process for the time-series database, which consists of sequences of values or events obtained over repeated measurements of time (Han & Kamber, 2007).

An example of sequential pattern is "If a man overeats today, he may be overweight within two days." Sequence discovery can be a powerful tool helps the salesclerks to place the merchandise on the shelves since it discovers the relations between items related to time. Once the customer grabs an item into the shopping bag, the items with larger chance for him to buy right away can be located near by according to the knowledge got from sequence discovery.

Definition of Interesting Rules and Patterns

It is very easy for a data mining system to generate more than thousands of rules or patterns, but not all the generated rules or patterns is useful and interesting. Han et al. has defined *4* criteria for determine whether the rules or patterns are interesting. (Han & Kamber, 2007) The criteria are listed as follows:

1. Easily understood by humans.
2. Valid on new or test data with some degree of certainty.
3. Potentially useful.
4. Novel.

A rule or a pattern presents knowledge in case it satisfies the criteria listed above.

COMPUTATIONAL INTELLIGENCE AND EVOLUTIONARY COMPUTING

Computational intelligence is a broad field containing Fuzzy Logic, Artificial Neural Network, and *Evolutionary Computing*. Each of them

includes various practical theories, algorithms, and applications. For example, fuzzy logic is applied to the control system of the high speed rail with a big success; artificial neural network is applied to real-time control system (Xia, Tian, Sun & Dong, 2008), and evolutionary computing is applied to design and control the power systems (Kassabaldis, El-Sharkawi, Marks, Moulin, Alves & da Silva, 2002).

Swarm intelligence is one of the branches in evolutionary computing. The algorithms in swarm intelligence are often applied to solve problems of optimization. These algorithms are proofed that they can solve the problems effectively. Swarm intelligence includes *Cat Swarm Optimization (CSO)* (Chu & Tsai, 2007),(Chu, Tsai & Pan, 2006), Ant Colony Optimization (ACO) (Chu, Roddick & Pan, 2004),(Chu, Roddick, Su, & Pan, 2004),(Dorigo & Gambardella, 1997), Bacterial Foraging (BF) (Passino, 2002), Particle Swarm Optimization (PSO) (Chang, Chu, Roddick & Pan, 2005), (Shi & Eberhart, 1999) etc. GA, PSO and ACO are well-known and are applied to solve engineering, and economic problems for several years, and there exists various applications of them for data mining (Atkinson-Abutridy, Mellish, & Aitken, 2004), (Hong, Chen, Lee, & Wu, 2008), (Li, Chen & Li, 2007), (Zhao, Zeng, Gao & Yang, 2006) . The introduction of these algorithms is easily to be found. Therefore, in this section, we are going to introduce CSO and its parallel version, which is called *Parallel Cat Swarm Optimization (PCSO)* (Tsai, Pan, Chen, Liao & Hao, 2008).

Cat Swarm Optimization (CSO)

CSO is proposed by Chu et al. in *2006* (Chu, Tsai & Pan, 2006) by employing the particular behaviors of animals, and the performance analysis is given in *2007* (Chu & Tsai, 2007). Two sub-modes, namely the seeking mode and the tracing mode, are proposed in CSO to simulate the motions of cats. There are about *32* different species of creatures in cat, e.g. lion, tiger, leopard etc. according to the classification of biology. Though they live in different environments, most of their behaviors are still similar. The instinct of hunting ensures the survival of outdoor cats, which live in the wild. Nevertheless, this instinct of the indoor cats behaves on the strongly curious about any moving things. Contrary to the instinct of hunting, the cats are usually inactive when they are awake. The alertness of cats is very high. They always stay alert even if they are resting. Thus, you can simply see that the cats usually look lazy, but stare their eyes hugely looking around to observe the environment. Chu et al. utilize the conduct of cats to construct CSO and find that the outcomes of employing CSO to solve problems of optimization present high performance.

In different algorithms of evolutionary computing, the solutions are presented in different forms. The solutions are presented by chromosomes in Genetic Algorithm (GA) (Goldberg, 1989), (Pan, McInnes & Jack, 1996); the solutions are presented by particles in PSO; and CSO forms the solutions with the coordinates of the cats. Each cat in CSO carries *4* kinds of different information, namely, the coordinate of the current position, the velocities in each dimension, the fitness value, and a flag that presents the motion of it-self. Suppose the population size is chosen to be N, and the problem to be solved is an M-dimensional problem. Figure 2 presents the structure of CSO. The operation of CSO can be described in *5* steps and is listed as follows:

1. Create N cats and randomly sprinkle the cats into the M-dimensional solution space within the constrain ranges of the initial value and the velocities for each dimension are also generated. Set the motion flag of the cats to make them move into the tracing mode or the seeking mode according to the ratio *MR*.

2. Evaluate the fitness value of the cats by taking the coordinates into the fitness function,

which represents the benchmark and the characteristics of the problem you want to solve. After calculating the fitness values one by one, record the coordinate (x_{best}) and the fitness value of the cat, which owns the best fitness value we find so far.

3. Move the cats by taking the operations in seeking mode or tracing mode according to the information form the motion flag.

4. Reset the motion flag of all cats and separate them into statuses that indicating seeking or tracing according to *MR*.

5. Check if the process satisfies the termination condition. If the process is terminated, output the coordinate, which presents the best solution we find, otherwise go back to step *2* and repeat the process.

The Seeking Mode Process

In seeking mode, the cat moves slowly and conservatively. It observes the environment before it moves. Four essential factors are defined in seeking mode:

*   *Seeking Memory Pool (SMP)*
*   *Seeking Range of the selected Dimension (SRD)*
*   *Counts of Dimension to Change (CDC)*
*   *Self-Position Considering (SPC).*

SMP is used to define the size of seeking memory for each cat to indicate the points sought by the cat. The cat would pick a point from the memory pool according to the rules described later. *SRD* declares the mutative ratio for the selected dimensions. *CDC* discloses how many dimensions will be varied. In seeking mode, if a dimension is selected to mutate, the difference between the new value and the old one cannot be out of the range of which is defined by *SRD*. *SPC* is a Boolean variable, which decides whether the point, where the cat is already standing, will be one of the candidates to move to. No matter the value of

Figure 2. The flowchart of Cat Swarm Optimization

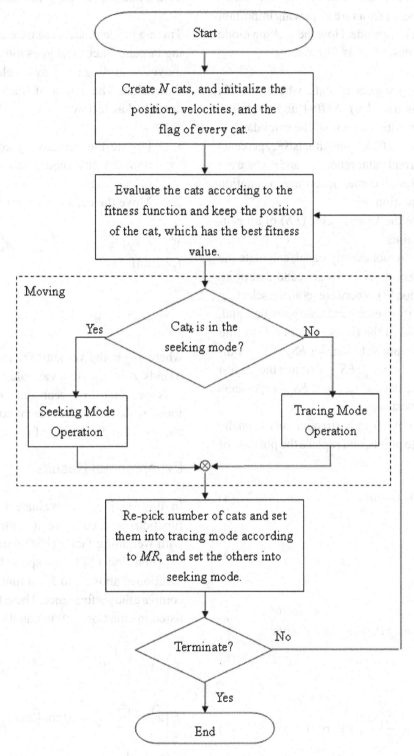

SPC is true of false; the value of *SMP* will not be influenced. These factors are all playing important roles in the seeking mode. How the seeking mode works can be described as follows:

1. Generate *j* copies of cat$_k$, where *j=SMP*. If *SPC* is true, let *j=SMP*-1 and retain the present position as one of the candidates.
2. According to *CDC*, plus/minus *SRD* percents of the current value randomly and replace the old one for all copies according to equation (4) to equation (6).
3. Calculate the fitness value (*FS*) of all candidate points.
4. If all *FS* are not exactly equal, calculate the selecting probability of each candidate point by equation (7), otherwise set all the selecting probability of each candidate point be equal. If the goal of the fitness function is to find the minimum solution, let $FS_b=FS_{max}$, otherwise $FS_b=FS_{min}$. FS_{max} denotes the largest *FS* in the candidates, and FS_{min} represents the smallest one.
5. Pick the point to move to randomly from the candidate points, and replace the position of cat$_k$.

$$M = Modify \cup (1 - Modify) \qquad (4)$$

$$|Modify| = CDC \times M \qquad (5)$$

$$x_{jd} = \begin{cases} x_{jd} & ,d \notin Modify \\ (1 + rand \times SRD) \times x_{jd} & ,d \in Modify \end{cases} \bigg|_{d=1,2,...,M} \forall j \qquad (6)$$

$$P_i = \frac{|FS_i - FS_b|}{FS_{max} - FS_{min}} \text{ , where } 0 < i < j \qquad (7)$$

The Tracing Mode Process

Tracing mode models the case of the cat in tracing targets. Once a cat goes into tracing mode, it moves according to its own velocities for every dimension. The action of tracing mode can be described as follows:

1. Update the velocity by equation (8). The new velocity should satisfy the constraint of the range.
2. Move the cat according to equation (9).

$$v_{k,d}^{t+1} = v_{k,d}^{t} + r_1 \times c_1 \times \left(x_{best} - x_{k,d}^{t} \right), \text{ where } d = 1,2,...,M \qquad (8)$$

$$x_{k,d}^{t+1} = x_{k,d}^{t} + v_{k,d}^{t+1} \qquad (9)$$

where $v_{k,d}$ is the velocity for cat$_k$, *t* denotes the rounds, r_1 is a random variable satisfies $r_1 \in [0,1]$, c_1 is a constant, x_{best} represents the best solution found so far, $x_{k,d}$ is the current position of the cat, and *M* is the dimension of the solution.

Experimental Results

In this section, we evaluate CSO by six test functions and compare it with PSO and PSO with weighting factor (PSO with WF), which is the modified PSO. We applied the algorithms mentioned above into 5 test functions in order to compare the performance. These test functions are listed in equation (10) to equation (14).

$$f_1\left(\vec{x} \right) = \sum_{d=1}^{M-1} 100 \left(x_{d+1} - x_d^2 \right)^2 + \left(x_d - 1 \right)^2 \qquad (10)$$

$$f_2\left(\vec{x} \right) = \sum_{d=1}^{M} \left(x_d^2 - 10\cos\left(2\pi x_d\right) + 10 \right) \qquad (11)$$

$$f_3\left(\vec{x} \right) = \frac{1}{4000} \left[\sum_{d=1}^{M} \left(x_d - 100 \right)^2 \right] - \left[\prod_{d=1}^{M} \cos\left(\frac{x_d - 100}{\sqrt{d}} \right) \right] + 1 \qquad (12)$$

Table 1. The Limitation ranges of dimensions for every test function

Function Name	Limitation Range
Test Function 1	$x_d \in [15, 30]$
Test Function 2	$x_d \in [2.56, 5.12]$
Test Function 3	$x_d \in [300, 600]$
Test Function 4	$x_d \in [-30, 30]$
Test Function 5	$x_d \in [-100, 100]$

$$f_4\left(\vec{x}\right) = 20 + e - 20 \cdot e^{-0.2\sqrt{\frac{\sum_{d=1}^{M} x_d^2}{M}}} - e^{\sum_{d=1}^{M} \frac{\cos(2\pi x_d)}{M}}$$

(13)

$$f_5\left(x\right) = \sum_{d=1}^{M} \left\lfloor x_d + 0.5 \right\rfloor^2$$

(14)

In the experiments, we aim at finding the minimum of the fitness values of all the test functions. In other words, the goal of our experiments is to find the minimum values of the fitness functions. For each test function, we limit the initial ranges for every dimension according to Table 1. The limits are only applied to constrain the cats in the process of initialization. When the process moves to the evaluation and movement stage, there is no limit on any dimension for every cat.

The parameter settings for CSO are listed in Table 2, and the settings for PSO and PSO with WF are listed in Table 3. The usage of the parameters for PSO and PSO with WF can be found in (Shi & Eberhart, 1999). The dimensions of all fitness functions are set to be *30*, the population sizes are set to *160*. For each algorithm, *2000* generations are applied per cycle and *50* cycles per test function. The final results are composed of the average of the *50* cycles. The *SPC* flag for CSO is set to be true. For PSO-type algorithms, the maximum velocities for each test function are listed in Table 4. The experimental results are listed in order in Figure 3 to Figure 7. The test function *1* to test function *3*, namely Rosenbrock, Rastrigrin, and Griewank function, are well-known in the research

field of swarm intelligence and used to examine the performance of the algorithms.

Discussion

The initial ranges of the first three functions do not include the global best solution. The global best solution is, however, included in the last two functions. According to the experimental results, CSO presents better performance of finding the global best solution, no matter whether the global best solution is included in the initial range or not. Discovering rules and relationships in data mining can also be treated as a high-dimensional problem of optimization. Since CSO presents good performance in the experiments, it should be able to perform effectively to find the rules or relationships in data mining as a useful tool.

Parallel Cat Swarm Optimization (PCSO)

The parallel version of CSO is proposed by Tasi et al. in *2008* (Tsai, Pan, Chen, Liao & Hao, 2008). According to the experience and the knowledge from our life, things will be done in the best way when the consideration is complete and is observed from different angles. Sometimes, an expert may get a new idea or a breakthrough by the opinions from a novice. Hence, the power of cooperation has the potential to be stronger than the power of solo.

The precedents of splitting the amount of the population into several sub-populations to

Table 2. Parameter settings for CSO

Parameter	Value or Range		Parameter	Value or Range
MP	5		MR	2%
SRD	20%		c_1	2.0
CDC	80%		r_1	[0, 1]

Table 3. Parameter settings for PSO and PSO with WF

Parameter	Value or Range
Initial Weight	0.9
Final Weight	0.4
c_1	2.0
c_2	2.0
r_1	[0, 1]
r_2	[0, 1]

Table 4. Maximum velocities for PSO and PSO with WF

Function Name	Maximum Velocity
Test Function 1	100.0
Test Function 2	10.0
Test Function 3	600.0
Test Function 4	100.0
Test Function 5	10.0

Figure 3. The experimental result of test function 1

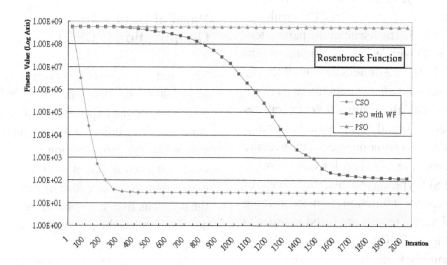

Figure 4. The experimental result of test function 2

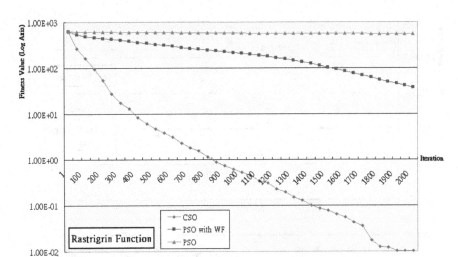

Figure 5. The experimental result of test function 3

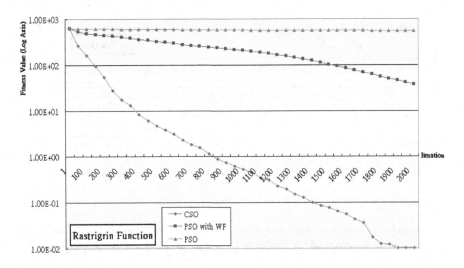

construct the parallel structure can be found in several algorithms, such as Island-model Genetic Algorithm, Parallel Genetic Algorithm (Abramson & Abela, 1991) and Parallel Particle Swarm Optimization Algorithm with Communication Strategies (Chang, Chu, Roddick & Pan, 2005). Each of the sub-populations evolves independently and shares the information they have occasionally. Although it results in the reducing of the population size for each sub-population, the benefit of cooperation is achieved.

By inspecting the structure of CSO, the individuals work independently when they stay in the seeking mode. Oppositely, they share the identical information, the global best solution, as they know according to their knowledge to the present in the tracing mode. In PCSO, it still follows the structure of this framework.

Underneath the structure of CSO, most of the individuals work as a stand along system. To parallelize these individuals in CSO, The procedure in the tracing mode is modified to make it

Figure 6. The experimental result of test function 4

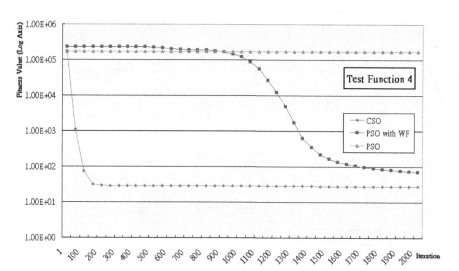

Figure 7. The experimental result of test function 5

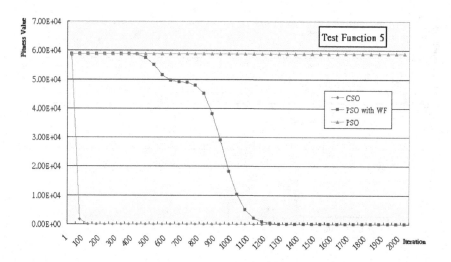

seems more cooperative. In PCSO, the individuals are separated into several sub-populations at the beginning. Hence, the individuals in tracing mode do not move forward to the global best solution directly, but they move forward to the local best solution of its own group in general. Only if the predetermined iteration is achieved, the sub-populations pop the local best solutions at present and randomly pick a sub-population

to replace the worst individual in the selected sub-population.

Basically, the main framework of PCSO is similar to CSO. Assume that we set G equals to 1; then the PCSO becomes the original CSO. At the beginning of the algorithm, N individuals are created and separate into G groups. The Parallel tracing mode process and the information exchanging process are described as follows:

Parallel Tracing Mode Process

The parallel tracing mode process can be described as follows:

1. Update the velocities for every dimension $v_{k,d}(t)$ for the cat_k at the current iteration according to equation (15), where $x_{l_{best},d}(t-1)$ is the position of the cat, who has the best fitness value, at the previous iteration in the group that cat_k belongs to.
2. Check if the velocities are in the range of maximum velocity. In case the new velocity is over-range, it is set equal to the limit.
3. Update the position of catk according to equation (16).

$$v_{k,d}(t) = v_{k,d}(t-1) + r_1 \cdot c_1 \cdot \left[x_{l_{best},d}(t-1) - x_{k,d}(t-1) \right]$$
$$\text{where } d = 1, 2, ..., M \qquad (15)$$

$$X_{k,d}(t) = x_{k,d}(t-1) + v_{k,d}(t) \qquad (16)$$

Information Exchanging

The procedure forces the sub-populations exchange their information, and achieve somehow the cooperation. We define a parameter ECH to control the exchanging of the information between sub-populations. The information exchanging is applied once per ECH iterations. The information exchanging consists of 4 steps:

1. Pick up a group of the sub-populations sequentially and sort the individuals in this group according to their fitness value.
2. Randomly select a local best solution from an unrepeatable group.

3. The individual, whose fitness value is worst in the group, is replaced by the selected local best solution.
4. Repeat step *1* to *3* until all the groups exchanged information to someone else.

Experimental Results

To evaluate the performance of PCSO, equations (7) to equation (9) are applied to be the test function, and the results are compared with CSO and PSO with weighting factor (PSO with WF). The initial range still follows the values listed in Table 1, and the rest of the parameter settings are exactly the same as those in the previous section. For PCSO, the group number G is set to *2* and *4* as two individual experiments, and the value of ECH is set to *20*. During the experiments, we focus on the case when the optimization has to be done with only a small size of the population and less iterations. Hence, the population sizes are all set to *16*. For each algorithm, we apply only *500* iterations per cycle and 50 cycles per test function, and the final results are composed of the average of the 50 cycles. The experimental results are represents in Figure 8 to Figure 10.

Discussion

According to the experimental results, we notice that PCSO converges faster than CSO and PSO with weighting factor. To further observe the convergence at the end of the generations, the outcomes at the last *20* generations of the experiments are plotted in Figure 11 to Figure 13. The results exhibit that the convergence and the searching ability of PCSO is higher in case the iteration is less and the population size is small. The information exchanging plays a key role to improve the searching ability of CSO, and it performs the cooperation between sub-populations.

Figure 8. PCSO experiment with test function 1

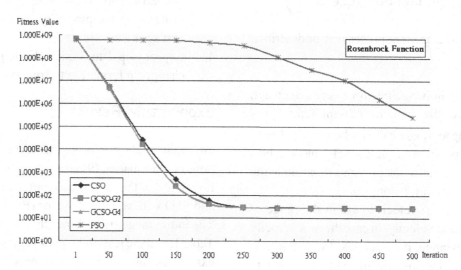

Figure 9. PCSO experiment with test function 2

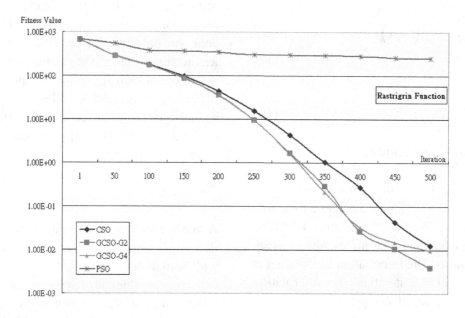

FEASIBLE SOLUTIONS OF COMPUTATIONAL INTELLIGENCE FOR DATA MINING

The first step of employing algorithms in computational intelligence, especially in evolutionary computing, to solve problems is to design the *fitness function*. The user defined fitness function should be able to describe the application domain completely and clearly in mathematical form. Normally, the goal of employing algorithms in evolutionary computing is designed to find the solutions that minimize the outcome of the fitness function. Suppose M elements are concerned and treated as the input, they are put into the solution set one by one in different dimensions. The fitness

Figure 10. PCSO experiment with test function 3

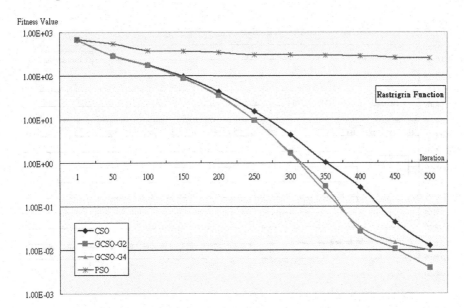

Figure 11. The stretched result of Rosenbrock function

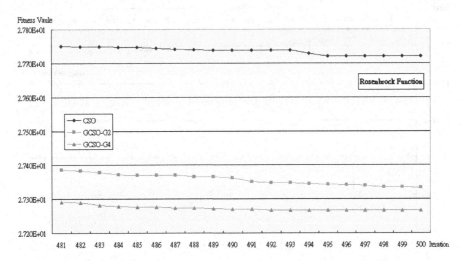

function should be somehow the combinations or operations between the elements, and the output, namely the fitness value, represents result of evaluation according to the fitness function.

To combine the evolutionary computing with data mining, the design of the fitness function that fits the goal is required. Fortunately, series of formula used to examine the properties in data mining have already been defined. Therefore,

we may combine these formulas to structure the fitness function.

Existing Criteria of Evaluation in Data Mining

There exist many criteria for evaluating the accuracy or the value of the discovered rules by data mining. Some of them are listed as follows:

Figure 13. The stretched result of Griewank function

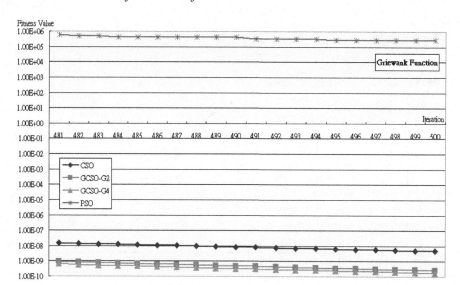

Figure 12. The stretched result of Rastrigrin function

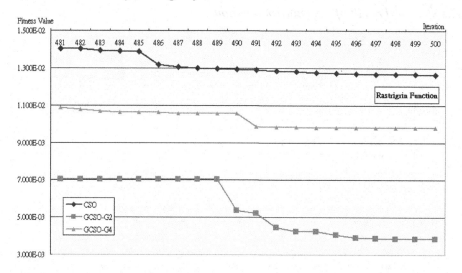

1. Central Tendency, Variance and Standard Deviation

Central tendency indicates the arithmetic mean value of a dataset. Finding out the center of a dataset is necessary for calculating the variance and the standard deviation of the dataset. They tell the distributed form of the dataset, and they are useful to eliminate the noise data and some outlanders in the pre-process, e.g. data cleaning.

The mean value, of the data set composed of $X=\{x_1,x_2,x_3,\ldots\ldots,x_M\}$ is described in equation (17), the variance and standard deviation are listed in equation (18) and equation (19).

$$\bar{x} = \frac{\displaystyle\sum_{d=1}^{M} x_d}{M} \qquad (17)$$

$$\sigma^2 = \frac{1}{M}\sum_{d=1}^{M}\left(x_d - \overline{x}\right)^2 = \frac{1}{M}\left[\sum_{d=1}^{M}x_d^2 - \frac{1}{M}\left(\sum_{d=1}^{M}x_d\right)^2\right]$$

(18)

$$\sigma = \sqrt{\sigma} = \sqrt{\frac{1}{M}\sum_{d=1}^{M}\left(x_d - \overline{x}\right)^2} = \sqrt{\frac{1}{M}\left[\sum_{d=1}^{M}x_d^2 - \frac{1}{M}\left(\sum_{d=1}^{M}x_d\right)^2\right]}$$

(19)

2.   Confidence

A confidence is the probability of event B occurs conditional on event A exists. It is formed in equation (20) as follows:

$$Confidence = P(B)|_A \qquad (20)$$

The confidence can be used as a threshold for eliminating the outcome to maintain the final result being pure, and it is also called the minimum confidence threshold.

3.   Support

A support is defined as the authentic ratio of the number of predicted outcome matches the real data. If the support is too low for an association rule in data mining, it means that this association rule should be abandoned.

4.   Split Info

The split info is defined to be the potential information generated by splitting the training dataset, D, into v partitions corresponding to the v outcomes of a test on attribute A (Han & Kamber, 2007). Actually the split information provides the same information called "entropy". It considers the information you will have in case you get a certain clue. The split info is represented as follows:

$$SplitInfo_A\left(D\right) = -\sum_{j=1}^{v}\frac{\left|D_j\right|}{\left|D\right|} \times \log_2\left(\frac{\left|D_j\right|}{\left|D\right|}\right) \qquad (21)$$

Feasible Solutions Combines Intelligence Soft Computing with Data Mining

As we mentioned above, employing the algorithms in computational intelligence to assist in data mining requires the fitness function for evaluating the generated outcomes. Several advanced methods are proposed one after another: Ghosh presents a fitness function for rule discovery with the designed rules, which are encoded in the form of chromosomes. (Ghosh, 2005), Yu et al. propose a fitness function, which considers the true positive, false positive, true negative and false negative in the outcome with a penalty factor (Yu, Tan & Lee, 2005).

In this section, we would like to concern some basic rules that we can easily get to construct the fitness function. Suppose we are employing CSO to discover the relations between the items from the dataset, C, the solution set may consist of several items, which are picked randomly or with a pre-selecting process, e.g. based on the frequency of occurrence, and combined in pairs. The dataset and the solution set are described in equation (22) and equation (23). The fitness function in this case can be a simple combination of the support and the confidence. Assume each encoded solution set contains M items, the fitness function can be formulated in equation (23). Under this consideration, the goal of employing CSO is to find the maximum value of *fitness*(X), and the solution set, whose fitness value equals to *2* should be the optimal in ideal.

$$U = \{y_1, y_2, y_3, \ldots\ldots, y_N\} \qquad (22)$$

$$X = \{x_1, x_2, x_3, \ldots\ldots, x_M\}, \text{ where } X \in U \text{ and } M < N \quad (23)$$

$$fitness\left(X\right) = \frac{2}{M} \sum_{d=1}^{(M/2)} \left(confidence_{2d} + support_{2d+1}\right)$$

(24)

Since the solution sets are combined in pairs, the repeated items and the reversed items should be avoid in each pair in the initialization and the movement of CSO. Moreover, if the size of the dataset is extremity large, to reduce the computational complexity and the computation time, we may apply the algorithms in clustering in the pre-process, or segment the training dataset into subsets for increasing the searching capacity for CSO.

CONCLUSION

In this chapter, a brief review of data mining is presented and two algorithms in swarm intelligence are introduced. The review of some criteria using for evaluating the result of data mining are given and a feasible solution for employing computational intelligence algorithms to support data mining is presented.

The experimental results indicate that CSO performs well and effectively on finding the near best solution. By designing a suitable fitness function, which approximately reflects the problem you want to solve, the algorithms in computational intelligence can provide a powerful assistance for data mining.

REFERENCES

Abramson, D., & Abela, J. (1991). *A parallel genetic algorithm for solving the school timetabling problem*. Technical Report, Division of Information Technology, CSIRO.

Atkinson-Abutridy, J., Mellish, C., & Aitken, S. (2004). Combining information extraction with genetic algorithms for text mining. *IEEE Intelligent Systems*, 22–30. doi:10.1109/MIS.2004.4

Chang, J. F., Chu, S. C., Roddick, J. F., & Pan, J. S. (2005). A Parallel Particle Swarm Optimization Algorithm with Communication Strategies. *Journal of Information Science and Engineering, 21*(4), 809–818.

Chapple, M. (n.d.). *Regression (data mining) definition*. About.com: Databases. Retrieved from http://databases.about.com/od/datamining/g/regression.htm

Chu, S. C., Roddick, J. F., & Pan, J. S. (2004). Ant Colony System with Communication Strategies. *Information Sciences, 167*, 63–76. doi:10.1016/j.ins.2003.10.013

Chu, S. C., Roddick, J. F., Su, C. J., & Pan, J. S. (2004). Constrained ant colony optimization for data clustering. In *8th Pacific Rim International Conference on Artificial Intelligence*, (LNAI Vol. 3157, pp. 534-543).

Chu, S. C., & Tsai, P. W. (2007). Computational Intelligence Based on the Behaviors of Cats. *International Journal on Innovative Computing . Information & Control, 3*(1), 163–173.

Chu, S. C., Tsai, P. W., & Pan, J. S. (2006). Cat swarm optimization. *9th Pacific Rim International Conference on Artificial Intelligence* (LNCS Vol. 4099, pp. 854-858). Berlin: Springer.

Dorigo, M., & Gambardella, L. M. (1997). Ant Colony System: A Cooperative Learning Approach to the Traveling Salesman Problem. *IEEE Transactions on Evolutionary Computation, 26*(1), 53–66. doi:10.1109/4235.585892

Ghosh, A. (2005). *Evolutionary algorithms for data mining and knowledge discovery. Evolutionary computation in data mining*. In A. Gohsh & L. C. Jain (Eds.), *Studies in Fuzziness and Soft Computing,* (Vol. 163, pp. 1-19).

Ghosh, A., & Jain, L. C. (2005). *Evolutionary computation in data mining*. In A. Gohsh & L. C. Jain, (Eds.), *Studies in Fuzziness and Soft Computing,* (Vol. 163).

Goldberg, D. E. (1989). *Genetic algorithm in search. Optimization and machine learning.* Reading. MA: Addison-Wesley Publishing Company.

Han, J., & Kamber, M. (2007). *Data mining: Concepts and techniques,* (2nd Ed.). San Francisco: Morgan Kaufmann.

Hong, T. P., Chen, C. H., Lee, Y. C., & Wu, Y. L. (2008). Genetic-Fuzzy Data Mining with Divide-and-Conquer Strategy. *IEEE Transactions on Evolutionary Computation, 12*(2), 252–265. doi:10.1109/TEVC.2007.900992

Kassabalidis, I.N., El-Sharkawi, M.A., Marks, R.J. II, Moulin, L.S., & Alves, A.P. da Silva. (2002). Dynamic Security Border Identification Using Enhanced Particle Swarm Optimization. *IEEE Transactions on Power Systems, 17*(3). doi:10.1109/TPWRS.2002.800942

Li, S. T., Chen, C. C., & Li, J. W. (2007). A multi-objective particle swarm optimization algorithm for rule discovery. *3rd International Conference on Intelligent Information Hiding and Multimedia Signal Processing,* (pp. 597-600).

Pan, J. S., McInnes, F. R., & Jack, M. A. (1996). Application of parallel genetic algorithm and property of multiple global optima to VQ codevector Index assignment. *Electronics Letters, 32*(4), 296–297. doi:10.1049/el:19960194

Passino, K. M. (2002). Biomimicry of Bacterial Foraging for Distributed Optimization and Control. *Control Systems Magazine, IEEE,* 52-67.

Shi, Y., & Eberhart, R. (1999). Empirical study of particle swarm optimization. *Congress on Evolutionary Computation,* 1945-1950.

Tsai, P. W., Pan, J. S., Chen, S. M., Liao, B. Y., & Hao, S. P. (2008). Parallel cat swarm optimization. *7th International Conference on Machine Learning and Cybernetics,* 3328-3333.

Xia, F., Tian, Y.C., Sun, Y., & Dong, J. (2008). Neural Feedback Scheduling of Real-time Control Tasks. *International Journal on Innovative Computing, Information & Control, 4*(11).

Yu, O., Tan, K. C., & Lee, T. H. (2005). Knowledge discovery in data mining via an evolutionary algorithm. In A. Gohsh & L. C. Jain, (Eds.), *Evolutionary computation in data mining: Studies in Fuzziness and Soft Computing,* (Vol. 163, pp. 101-121).

Zhao, X. Z., Zeng, J. F., Gao, Y. B., & Yang, Y. P. (2006). A particle swarm algorithm for classification rules generation. In *6th International Conference on Intelligent Systems Design and Applications,* (pp. 957-962).

Chapter 3
Dynamic Discovery of Fuzzy Functional Dependencies Using Partitions

Shyue-Liang Wang
National University of Kaohsiung, Taiwan

Ju-Wen Shen
Chunghwa Telecom Co., Ltd., Taiwan

Tuzng-Pei Hong
National University of Kaohsiung, Taiwan

ABSTRACT

Discovery of functional dependencies (FDs) from relational databases has been identified as an important database analysis technique. Various mining techniques have been proposed in recent years to deal with crisp and static data. However, few have emphasized on fuzzy data and also considered the dynamic nature that data may change all the time. In this work, the authors propose a partition-based incremental data mining algorithm to discover fuzzy functional dependencies from similarity-based fuzzy relational databases when new sets of tuples are added. Based on the concept of tuple partitions and the monotonicity of fuzzy functional dependencies, we avoid re-scanning of the database and thereby reduce computation time. An example demonstrating the proposed algorithm is given. Computational complexity of the proposed algorithm is analyzed. Comparison with pair-wise comparison-based incremental mining algorithm (Wang, Shen & Hong, 2000) is presented. It is shown that with certain space requirement, partition-based approach is more time efficient than pair-wise approach in the discovery of fuzzy functional dependencies dynamically.

INTRODUCTION

A functional dependency describes the relationship between attributes in a database relation. It states that the value of an attribute is uniquely determined by the values of some other attributes. It serves as a constraint between the attributes and is being used in the normalization process of relational database design. Therefore the discovery of functional dependencies from databases has been identified as an important technique for analyzing attribute

DOI: 10.4018/978-1-61520-757-2.ch003

semantics and redesign of relational schemas. It has received considerable research interest in recent years. For examples, from a database of chemical compounds, it is valuable to discover compounds that are functionally dependent on a certain structure attribute (Huhtala, Karkkainen, Porkka, & Toivonen, 1998). In addition, as a kind of data dependency, a large dataset can be losslessly decomposed into a set of smaller datasets using the discovered functional dependencies.

To find all functional dependencies from a given database relation *r*, we need to search for all possible dependencies and test their validity. There are essentially two approaches for searching for all possible functional dependencies: top-down searching and bottom-up searching. The top-down approach starts with the set of trivial functional dependencies and adds those functional dependencies that are satisfied by *r*. It can be further classified into depth-first search and level-wise (breadth-first) search. The dependencies discovery techniques proposed in Bell et al. (1995), Huhtala et al. (1998), Mannila et al. (1997), Yao et al. (2002) are top-down approach. The bottom-up approach starts with the set of all possible functional dependencies and removes those functional dependencies that are contradicted by *r*. The discovery techniques proposed in Flach, (1990), Flach & Savnik (1999), Mannila et al. (1997) are bottom-up approach. To test the validity of a given dependency, pair wise comparison method between any two tuples, decision-tree method and a tuple-partition method have been proposed. However, current data mining techniques of determining functional dependencies deal only with crisp databases. Although various forms of fuzzy functional dependencies have been proposed for fuzzy databases, they emphasized conceptual viewpoints, and few mining algorithms are given.

To extend functional dependency, there are many approximate dependencies proposed and defined on the crisp relational data model. For example, Haux and Eckert (1985) have extended

functional dependency to probabilistic dependency. Saharia and Barron (1995) have extended functional dependency to cluster dependency. To extend functional dependency to fuzzy databases, there are different forms of fuzzy functional dependency on various types of fuzzy relational data models. For example, Raju and Majumdar (1988), Bosc et al. (1997), Chen (Chen, 1998), have defined various forms of fuzzy functional dependencies on the possibility-based fuzzy relational data model. For the similarity-based fuzzy relational data model Buckles et al. (1982), Sachar (1985), and Yazici et al. (1999) have defined a fuzzy functional dependency based on conformance. Wang et al. (2001) proposed a form of fuzzy functional dependency based on equivalence classes induced by level values on given similarity relations. Belohlavek et al. (2006) proposed a fuzzy functional dependency using fuzzy predicate logic on ranked database relations over domains with similarities. For equivalence-class-based fuzzy relational data model, Shenoi et al. (1990) defined a fuzzy functional dependency based on redundancy. These fuzzy functional dependencies are basically intended to preserve the functionality of classical functional dependency on the new fuzzy relational data models so that semantics between fuzzy attributes can be captured.

Mining extended functional dependencies has been studied in recent years. Currently, most of the discovered dependencies are used for answering imprecise or fuzzy queries. For example, Bosc et al. (1997) proposed mining extended functional dependencies for linguistic summaries of data content and fuzzy-rule-based functional dependency as knowledge from databases. Rasmussen et al. (1999) proposed mining techniques of fuzzy functional dependency using SummarySQL for linguistic summaries of database. Nambiar et al. (2004) proposed mining approximate functional dependencies to answer imprecise queries. Carrasco et al. (2000) and Galindo (2006) proposed FSQL for obtaining fuzzy dependencies and data summarization. However, similar to the application of discovered classical functional dependencies, the mining results of fuzzy functional dependency could potentially be used for decomposition of a large dataset into joins of smaller datasets Galindo et al. (2002). In addition, it could play a role as semantic information extractor (e.g. extracting keys, foreign keys, functional dependencies...) in the first phase of database reverse engineering. Database reverse engineering usually consists of two major phases: semantic information extraction from legacy databases and mapping semantic information to extended entity relationship diagrams.

In Wang et al. (2001), we have proposed a form of fuzzy functional dependency on the similarity-based fuzzy data model that is based on equivalence classes induced by level values on given similarity relations. The fuzzy functional dependency proposed is more general than the fuzzy functional dependency defined by Sachar (1985) and Yazici et al. (1999). It is similar to the fuzzy functional dependency defined by Hale et al. (1996) and Shenoi et al. (1990), but on the similarity-based data model. A non-incremental searching algorithm based on a top-down approach to discover all functional dependencies was given. In (Wang, Shen & Hong, 2000), an incremental searching algorithm based on pair-wise comparison to discover all functional dependencies, when a new tuple is added to the database, was proposed. In this work, we further propose a partition-based incremental data mining algorithm to discover fuzzy functional dependencies from similarity-based fuzzy relational databases when new sets of tuples are added. Based on the concept of tuple partitions and the monotonicity of fuzzy functional dependencies, we avoid re-scanning of the database and thereby reduce computation time. Comparison with pair-wise comparison-based incremental mining algorithm (Wang, Shen & Hong, 2000) is presented. It is shown that with certain space requirement, partition-based approach is more time efficient than pair-wise approach in the discovery of fuzzy functional dependencies dynamically.

The rest of our paper is organized as follows. Section 2 reviews the similarity-based fuzzy relational data model. Section 3 presents the fuzzy functional dependencies based on equivalence classes and a technique to validate fuzzy functional dependencies base on tuple partitions. Section 4 presents the partition-based incremental searching algorithm. Section 5 shows the computational complexity of the proposed algorithm and comparison with pair-wise incremental mining algorithm. Section 6 presents some numerical results demonstrating the proposed algorithm. A conclusion is given at the end of the paper.

A SIMILARITY-BASED FUZZY RELATIONAL DATA MODEL

In this section, we first review the similarity relation and its relationship with respect to equivalence relations and domain partitions. Next, we review a fuzzy relational data model that is based on similarity relations, proposed by Buckles and Petry.

Similarity Relation and Domain Partition

The concept of a similarity relation is essentially a generalization of the concept of an equivalence relation (Zadeh, 1971). It is useful for describing how similar two elements from the same domain are, as the name implies. For a given domain D, a similarity relation s is a mapping of every pair of elements in the domain onto the unit interval $[0, 1]$. More specifically:

Definition 1: A similarity relation, s, in domain D is a binary relation in D, such that for any a, b, $c \in D$,

(1) $s(a, a) = 1$,
(2) $s(a, b) = s(b, a)$,
(3) $s(a, c) \geq \max [\min (s(a, b), s(b, c))]$ for all $b \in D$.

Example 1: An example of a similarity relation s on the domain D of attribute *EDUCATION* is $\{Ph.D., B.S., M.S., A.D., H.S.\}$, as shown in Table 1. The grade of membership $\mu_S(B.S., M.S.)=0.8$ can be interpreted as the similarity between domain elements $B.S.$ and $M.S.$ is a degree of 0.8.

The relationship between similarity relations and equivalence relations can be observed from the property below. If s is a similarity relation, then for each α-level value in s, it creates an equivalence relation that represents the presence of similarity between the elements at least to the degree α. Each of these equivalence relations forms a partition π_A^α on the domain D of attribute A. Clearly, two elements d_1 and d_2 belong to the same equivalence class of this partition iff $s(d_1, d_2) \geq \alpha$. Therefore, a similarity relation s defined on domain D of attribute A is associated with the set $DP(s)=\{\pi_A^\alpha \mid \alpha \in (0, 1]\}$ of domain partitions. These domain partitions are nested in the sense that $\pi_A^{\alpha_1}$ is a refinement of $\pi_A^{\alpha_2}$ iff $\alpha_1 \geq \alpha_2$.

Example 2: Consider the similarity relation in Table 1, a nested sequence of domain partitions $\pi_{EDU}^{1.0}=\{\{Ph.D.\}, \{B.S.\}, \{M.S.\}, \{A.D.\}, \{H.S.\}\}$, $\pi_{EDU}^{0.8}=\{\{Ph.D.\}, \{B.S., M.S.\}, \{A.D., H.S.\}\}$, $\pi_{EDU}^{0.6}=\{\{M.S., B.S., A.D., H.S.\}, \{Ph.D.\}\}$, $\pi_{EDU}^{0.5}=\{\{Ph.D., M.S., B.S., A.D., H.S.\}\}$, may be formed from the similarity relation.

A Similarity-Based Fuzzy Relational Data Model

Let $R(A_1, A_2, ..., A_m)$ be a relational database schema and r a relational instance of R. Let D_j be the domain for attribute A_j. A similarity-based fuzzy relational database (Buckles & Petry, 1982) is defined as a set of relations consisting of tuples with the following extensions. Let t_i represent the i-th tuple of a relation r, and have the form $(t_{i1}, t_{i2}, ..., t_{im})$ where t_{ij} is defined on the domain D_j, $1 \leq j \leq m$. Unlike the ordinary relational database, two simple but important extensions are defined. The first extension is that the tuple component t_{ij} selected from D_j is not constrained to be singleton, instead, $t_{ij} \subseteq D_j$ and $t_{ij} \neq \emptyset$. Allowing a tuple component t_{ij} to be a subset of the domain D_j means that fuzzy information can be represented. If t_{ij} consists of a single element, it represents the most precise information; whereas if t_{ij} is the domain D_j itself, it corresponds to the fuzziest information.

The second extension of the fuzzy relational database is that, for each domain D_j of a relation, a similarity relation s_j is defined over the set elements. The similarity relation introduces different degrees of similarity to the elements in each domain and this is another mechanism for the representation of "fuzziness" in this fuzzy relational data model. This leads to the following definition:

Table 1. A similarity relation on the domain of attribute EDUCATION

	H.S.	A.D.	M.S.	B.S.	Ph.D.
H.S.	1	0.8	0.6	0.6	0.5
A.D.	0.8	1	0.6	0.6	0.5
M.S.	0.6	0.6	1	0.8	0.5
B.S.	0.6	0.6	0.8	1	0.5
Ph.D.	0.5	0.5	0.5	0.5	1

Definition 2: A similarity-based fuzzy database relation r is a subset of the set cross product $\underline{2}^{D_1} \times \underline{2}^{D_2} \times ... \times \underline{2}^{D_m}$, where $\underline{2}^{D_j} = 2^{D_j} - \varphi$, 2^{D_j} represents the power set of D_j. For each domain D_j, a similarity relation s_j is defined over the domain elements.

Example 3: A simple illustration of a fuzzy database relation is shown in Table 2 below representing the *NAME, EDUCATION, AGE* and *CONSUMPTION* of six *CUSTOMERS*. The similarity relations for these attributes are shown in Figures 1 and 2. For simplicity, tuple components shown here do not include subsets of domain elements, although it is permitted in the data model.

FUZZY FUNCTIONAL DEPENDENCIES ON THE SIMILARITY-BASED DATA MODEL

In this section, we first give the definition of a fuzzy functional dependency based on equivalence classes on the similarity-based fuzzy relational database. A method based on tuple partitions for testing the validity of fuzzy functional dependencies is then proposed. The following is a list of notation used in this paper.

R: a relational schema.

r: a relational instance on *R*.

t_i, $1 \le i \le$ n: *i*-th tuple of relation *r*.

A_j, $1 \le j \le m$: relational attribute, e.g. *JOB*.

Table 2. A fuzzy database relation (CUSTOMERS)

Row ID	NAME	EDUCATION	AGE	CONSUMPTION
1	Jill	Ph.D.	50	High
2	Ann	B.S.	35	Average
3	May	M.S.	25	Low
4	Bob	B.S.	27	Low
5	Ruth	A.D.	30	Moderate Low
6	William	H.S.	27	Moderate High

Figure 1 The lattice-structured ordering between $\{EDU_{1.0}, AGE_{1.0}\} \rightarrow CON_{1.0}$ and $\{EDU_{0.8}, AGE_{0.9}\} \rightarrow COM_{0.8}$

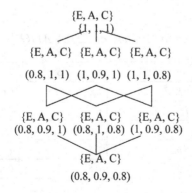

Table 3. Similarity relations for attributes NAME, AGE and CONSUMPTION

	Jill	Ann	May	Bob	Ruth	William			25	27	30	35	50
Jill	1	0	0	0	0	0		25	1	0.9	0.7	0.7	0.5
Ann	0	1	0	0	0	0		27	0.9	1	0.7	0.7	0.5
May	0	0	1	0	0	0		30	0.7	0.7	1	0.9	0.5
Bob	0	0	0	1	0	0		35	0.7	0.7	0.9	1	0.5
Ruth	0	0	0	0	1	0		50	0.5	0.5	0.5	0.5	1
William	0	0	0	0	0	1							

NAME={ Jill, Ann, May, Bob, Ruth, William } AGE= {25, 27, 30, 35, 50}

	Low	Moderate Low	Average	Moderate High	High
Low	1	0.8	0.6	0.3	0.3
Moderate Low	0.8	1	0.6	0.3	0.3
Average	0.6	0.6	1	0.3	0.3
Moderate High	0.3	0.3	0.3	1	0.8
High	0.3	0.3	0.3	0.8	1

CONSUMPTION={Low, Moderate Low, Average, Moderate High, High}

t.A: value of tuple t with respect to attribute A.

D_j, $1 \leq j \leq m$: domain of attribute A_j, e.g. {Sec, Sw Eng, Acct, Sys Eng, VP, Dn Eng}.

d_{jk}, $1 \leq j \leq m$: domain values of D_j, e.g. Sw Eng.

s_j, $1 \leq j \leq m$: similarity relation on domain D_j.

$\mu_{Sj}(d_{jk}, d_{jl})$: degree of similarity defined by s_j on D_j.

α: level value, $\alpha \in (0, 1]$.

$s_j^{\alpha j}$: equivalence relation induced by level value α_j on domain D_j of attribute A_j.

Λ_{A_j}: the set of all level value of s_j on attribute A_j.

$\left| \Lambda_{A_j} \right|$: number of level values in Λ_{A_j}.

$\left[d_{jk} \right]_{A_j}^{\alpha_j}$: domain equivalence class induced by $s_j^{\alpha j}$ on domain D_j of attribute A_j, i.e., {$d_{jl} | \mu_{Sj}(d_{jk}, d_{jl}) \geq \alpha_j$}.

$\pi_{Aj}^{\alpha j}$: domain partition of D_j with level value α_j, i.e., {$\left[d_{jk} \right]_{A_j}^{\alpha_j}$}

$[t_i A_j]_{A_j}^{\alpha j}$: domain equivalence class containing $t_i A_j$

$\left[t_i \right]_{A_j}^{\alpha_j}$: tuple equivalence class induced by domain equivalence classes, i.e., {$t_j | t_j A_j$ and $t_i A_j$ fall in the same domain equivalence class on domain D_j of attribute A_j with level value α_j}.

$\Pi_{A_j}^{\alpha_j}$: tuple partition with respect to attribute A_j and level value α_j, i.e., {$\left[t_i \right]_{A_j}^{\alpha_j}$}.

$X_{\alpha_X} \rightarrow A_{\alpha_A}$: a fuzzy functional dependency with level value α_X on attribute set X and level value α_A on attribute A, e.g., {$JOB_{0.8}$, $EXP_{0.9}$} $\rightarrow SALARY_{0.8}$.

$FD_\alpha r$): the set of all coarsest fuzzy functional dependencies with respect to α in relation r;

$COVER_\alpha r$): a cover of r, i.e., $FD\alpha_{(r)}$) is the deductive closure of this set of fuzzy functional dependencies.

Fuzzy Functional Dependencies

Functional dependencies are relationships between attributes of a relation: a functional dependency states that the value of an attribute is uniquely determined by the values of some other attributes.

Definition 3: Let R be a relation schema and r be a non-fuzzy relation over R. A functional dependency is expressed as $X \rightarrow A$, where $X \subseteq R$ and $A \in R$. The functional dependency $X \rightarrow A$ holds or is valid in r if, for all pairs of tuples t_1 and $t_2 \in r$,

$$t_1.X = t_2.X \text{ implies } t_1.A = t_2.A,$$

where $t_i.X$ denotes the attribute value of the tuple t_i with respect to the attribute set X.

In [21], we have defined a functional dependency on the similarity-based fuzzy relational databases based on equivalence classes. It states that if $t_1.X$ and $t_2.X$ fall in the same equivalence class in X then $t_1.A$ and $t_2.A$ also fall in the same equivalence class in A, with respect to level values α_X and α_A respectively. This notion motivates the following definitions regarding tuple partitions and their equivalence classes.

Definition 4: Let r be a similarity-based relational instance on schema $R(A_1, A_2, ..., A_m)$, D_j be the domain of attribute A_j, s_j be the similarity relation defined on domain D_j, $1 \leq j \leq m$, and $\pi_{A_j}^{\alpha j}$ be the domain partition with level value α_j. A tuple equivalence class of t_i on attribute A_j, denoted as $\left[t_i \right]_{A_j}^{\alpha_j}$, is a set of tuples in r such that their tuple components with respect to A_j belong to the same equivalence class as t_i in $\pi_{A_j}^{\alpha_j}$, where α_j is a level value in s_j.

Example 4: Consider the fuzzy database relation in Table 2 and the similarity relations in Figures 1 and 2. Attribute *EDUCATION* with level value 0.8 forms a domain partition $\pi_{EDU}^{0.8} = \{\{Ph.D.\}, \{B.S., M.S.\}, \{A.D., H.S.\}\}$. For the given database relation, tuple one induces a tuple equivalence class on attribute *EDUCATION*: $\left[1 \right]_{EDU}^{0.8} = \{1\}$. Tuple two induces a tuple equivalence class: $\left[2 \right]_{EDU}^{0.8} = \{2, 3, 4\}$ because tuples two, three, and four contain attribute values in the same domain equivalence class $\{B.S., M.S.\}$. Tuple five

induces a tuple equivalence class: $\left[5 \right]_{EDU}^{0.8} = \{5, 6\}$. Therefore, the fuzzy database relation is divided into three tuple equivalence classes corresponding to the domain partition $\pi_{EDU}^{0.8}$. In fact, a set of tuple equivalence classes $\{ \left[t_i \right]_{A_j}^{\alpha_j} \}$ forms a tuple partition of a relation r. For example, tuple partition $\Pi_{EDU}^{0.8} = \{ \left[1 \right]_{EDU}^{0.8}, \left[2 \right]_{EDU}^{0.8}, \left[5 \right]_{EDU}^{0.8} \} = \{\{1\}, \{2, 3, 4\}, \{5, 6\}\}$, where $\Pi_{A_j}^{\alpha_j}$ represents the tuple partition of a relation with respect to attribute A_j with level value α_j. In addition, this tuple partition induces a domain partition $\pi_{EDU}^{0.8}$ of the corresponding attribute *EDUCATION* with level value 0.8. This leads to the following property between tuple and domain partitions.

Lemma 1: Let $\left[t_i \right]_{A_j}^{\alpha_j}$ be the tuple equivalence class containing tuple t_i in relation r corresponding to domain partition $\pi_{A_j}^{\alpha_j}$, then $\Pi_{A_j}^{\alpha_j} = \{ \left[t_i \right]_{A_j}^{\alpha_j} \mid t_i \in r \}$ forms a tuple partition of the relation r with respect to attribute A_j and level value α_j.

Based on the concept of domain partition and tuple partition, a fuzzy functional dependency on a similarity-based fuzzy relation is defined as follows:

Definition 5: Let r be a similarity-based relational instance on schema $R(A_1, A_2, ..., A_m)$, D_j the domain of attribute A_j, $X \subseteq R$, and $A \in R$. The fuzzy relational instance r is said to satisfy the fuzzy functional dependency $X_{\alpha_X} \rightarrow A_{\alpha_A}$ if, for all pairs of tuples t_i and $t_k \in r$,

$$\left[t_i \right]_{A_j}^{\alpha_j} = \left[t_k \right]_{A_j}^{\alpha_j} \text{ for all } A_j \in X, \text{ implies } \left[t_i \right]_A^{\alpha_A} =$$

$$\left[t_i \right]_{A_j}^{\alpha_j} \left[t_k \right]_{A_j}^{\alpha_j} \left[t_i \right]_A^{\alpha_A} \left[t_k \right]_A^{\alpha_A} = \left[t_k \right]_{A_j}^{\alpha_j} \text{ for all } A_j \in X,$$

implies $\left[t_i \right]_A^{\alpha_A} = \left[t_k \right]_A^{\alpha_A}$,

where α_X is the set of level values consisting of α_j's on A_j, $A_j \in X$.

<u>Example 5</u>: Consider the fuzzy database relation in Table 2 and the similarity relations in Figures 1 and 2. Attribute *EDUCATION* with level value 0.8 forms a domain partition with $\pi_{EDU}^{0.8}$ ={{*Ph.D.*}, {*B.S., M.S.*}, {*A.D., H.S.*}}. Attribute *AGE* with level value 0.9 forms a domain partition with $\pi_{AGE}^{0.9}$ ={{*25, 27*}, {*30, 35*}, {*50*}}. Attribute *CONSUMPTION* with level value 0.8 forms a domain partition with $\pi_{CON}^{0.8}$ ={{*Low, Moderate Low*}, {*Average*}, {*Moderate High, High*}}. It can be checked easily that the fuzzy functional dependency {$EDU_{0.8}$, $AGE_{0.9}$} $\rightarrow CON_{0.8}$ holds, since only tuples 3 and 4 have attribute values that fall in the same equivalence classes {*B.S., M.S.*} and {*25, 27*} of $\pi_{EDU}^{0.8}$, $\pi_{AGE}^{0.9}$ respectively and they have attribute values fall in the same equivalence class {*Low, Moderate Low*} of $\pi_{CON}^{0.8}$.

For a set of attributes X and A, the number of possible functional dependencies $X_{\alpha_X} \rightarrow A_{\alpha_A}$ depends on the number of level values in the similarity relations of each attribute. Let Λ_X and Λ_A be the sets of level values of attributes X and A respectively. Let $|\Lambda_X|$ and $|\Lambda_A|$ be the ranks (i.e. the number of elements) of Λ_X and Λ_A. Then the number of possible functional dependencies for $X \rightarrow A$ is $|\Lambda_X| * |\Lambda_A|$. If X contains multiple attributes, e.g., X_1 and X_2, then $|\Lambda_X| = |\Lambda_{X1}| * |\Lambda_{X2}|$.

<u>Example 6</u>: Consider the fuzzy relation in Table 2 and the similarity relations for attributes *EDUCATION, AGE* and *CONSUMPTION* as shown in Figures 1 and 2. The level value sets for each attribute are Λ_{EDU} = {1.0, 0.8, 0.6, 0.5}, Λ_{AGE} = {1.0, 0.9, 0.7, 0.5}, and Λ_{CON} = {1.0, 0.8, 0.6, 0.5, 0.3}. The ranks for these attributes are $|\Lambda_{EDU}|$ = 4, $|\Lambda_{AGE}|$ = 4, and $|\Lambda_{CON}|$ = 5. If X = {*EDU, AGE*} and A = {*CON*}. Then the number of possible functional dependencies is 4×4×5 = 80.

In fact, a lattice-structured ordering exists among these fuzzy functional dependencies. It is defined as follows:

<u>Definition 6</u>: Let $X_{\alpha_X} \rightarrow A_{\alpha_A}$ and $X_{\alpha_X'} \rightarrow A_{\alpha_A'}$ be two fuzzy functional dependencies on attri-butes X and A. Then $X_{\alpha_X'} \rightarrow A_{\alpha_A'}$ is a *coarser* dependency than $X_{\alpha_X} \rightarrow A_{\alpha_A}$ (and $X_{\alpha_X} \rightarrow A_{\alpha_A}$ is *finer* than $X_{\alpha_X'} \rightarrow A_{\alpha_A'}$) if $\alpha_X' \leq \alpha_X$ and $\alpha_A' \leq \alpha_A$. Thus, *coarser than* defines a lattice-structured ordering on the fuzzy functional dependencies of $X \rightarrow A$.

<u>Example 7</u>: Continuing Example 6, the lattice-structured ordering between {$EDU_{1.0}$, $AGE_{1.0}$} $\rightarrow CON_{1.0}$ and {$EDU_{0.8}$, $AGE_{0.9}$} $\rightarrow CON_{0.8}$ is shown in Figure 1. It can be observed that the FD {$EDU_{0.8}$, $AGE_{0.9}$} $\rightarrow CON_{0.8}$ is coarser than the FD {$EDU_{1.0}$, $AGE_{0.9}$} $\rightarrow CON_{1.0}$, which in turn is coarser than the FD {$EDU_{1.0}$, $AGE_{1.0}$} $\rightarrow CON_{1.0}$.

It is possible to compute all possible fuzzy functional dependencies for a given set of attri-butes. However, it is also desirable to determine the coarsest fuzzy functional dependency that is greater than a specified universal level value on a given set of attributes. For example, for X = {*EDU, AGE*} and A = {*COM*}, the coarsest fuzzy functional dependency $X \rightarrow A$ that is greater than 0.8 is {$EDU_{0.8}$, $AGE_{0.9}$} $\rightarrow CON_{0.8}$, the coarsest fuzzy functional dependency that is greater than 0.9 is {$EDU_{1.0}$, $AGE_{0.9}$} $\rightarrow CON_1$, and the coarsest fuzzy functional dependency that is greater than 1 is {$EDU_{1.0}$, $AGE_{1.0}$} $\rightarrow CON_1$, as can be observed from Figure 1.

In the searching algorithm given in section 4.1, we will be searching for the coarsest fuzzy functional dependencies with respect to a given universal level value α, i.e., the least α_X and α_A that is greater than or equal to α.

Validation of Fuzzy Functional Dependencies

A partition Π is a refinement of another partition Π' if every equivalence class in Π is a subset of some equivalence class of Π'. A dependency, $X_{\alpha_X} \rightarrow A_{\alpha_A}$, is a valid fuzzy functional depen-dency if $\Pi_X^{\alpha_X}$ is a refinement of $\Pi_A^{\alpha_A}$ (Wang, Tsai & Hong, 2001). In this work, we further extend the above concept by checking the number of equivalence classes in the tuple partitions. This leads to the following lemma:

Lemma 2: A functional dependency $X_{\alpha_X} \to A_{\alpha_A}$ holds if $\left| \Pi_X^{\alpha_X} \right| = \left| \Pi_{X \cup \{A\}}^{(\alpha_X, \alpha_A)} \right|$.

Example 8: Continuing Example 4, the tuple partitions for the fuzzy database relation in Table 2 are $\Pi_{EDU}^{0.8} = \{\{1\}, \{2, 3, 4\}, \{5, 6\}\}$, $\Pi_{AGE}^{0.9} = \{\{1\}, \{2, 5\}, \{3, 4, 6\}\}$ and $\Pi_{CON}^{0.8} = \{\{1, 6\}, \{2\}, \{3, 4, 5\}\}$. The fuzzy functional dependency $\{EDU_{0.8}, AGE_{0.9}\} \to CON_{0.8}$ holds, since $\Pi_{\{EDU,AGE\}}^{(0.8,0.9)} = \{\{1\}, \{2\}, \{3, 4\}, \{5\}, \{6\}\}$, $\Pi_{\{EDU,AGE,CON\}}^{(0.8,0.9,0.8)} = \{\{1\}, \{2\}, \{3, 4\}, \{5\}, \{6\}\}$, and $\left| \Pi_{\{EDU,AGE\}}^{(0.8,0.9)} \right| = 5 = \left| \Pi_{\{EDU,AGE,CON\}}^{(0.8,0.9,0.8)} \right|$.

INCREMENTAL SEARCHING OF FUZZY FUNCTIONAL DEPENDENCIES

As described in section 3.1, we will be searching for the coarsest functional dependencies with respect to a given universal level value. Let $FD_\alpha(r)$ be the set of all coarsest fuzzy functional dependencies, $X_{\alpha_X} \to A_{\alpha_A}$, satisfied by a fuzzy relational instance r with respect to a given level value α. A set of fuzzy functional dependencies forms a *cover* for $FD_\alpha(r)$ if $FD_\alpha(r)$ is the deductive closure of this set, i.e., $FD_\alpha(r)$ can be logically implied by the functional dependencies in the *cover*. A *cover* is non-redundant, if for any two fuzzy functional dependencies $X \to A$ and $Y \to A$, it implies $X \not\subset Y$. It can be shown that each element of a non-redundant cover can be written in the form of $X \to A$, where A is a single attribute such that $A \notin X$. In this work, we will confine ourselves to incremental searching for a non-redundant *cover* of fuzzy functional dependencies with respect to a given level value, i.e., we restrict ourselves to fuzzy functional dependencies with a single attribute on the right hand side.

The monotonicity of functional dependencies on conventional crisp relational databases has been shown in (Carrazco, Vila, Galindo & Cubero,

2000). It shows that functional dependencies are monotonic in the following sense: $r_1 \subseteq r_2$ implies $FD(r_1) \supseteq FD(r_2)$, where $FD(r)$ represents the set of all functional dependencies on r. In (Rasmussen & Yager, 1999), we have shown that the monotonicity also holds for the equivalence-class-based fuzzy functional dependencies on the similarity-based fuzzy relational databases. Let r_1 and r_2 be fuzzy relational instances on R. If $r_1 \subseteq r_2$, then $FD_\alpha r_1 \supseteq FD\alpha_{(r_2)}$ for any given level value $\alpha \in (0, 1]$. An incremental algorithm based on pair-wise comparisons was then proposed to find the fuzzy functional dependencies based on this property. In this work, an improved incremental data mining algorithm based on tuple partitions is proposed. Given a fuzzy relation r1, a non-redundant co*ver* of $FD\alpha_{(r1)}$ and a new set of tuples r2, our algorithm finds a cover *of* new functional dependencies of $FD\alpha_{(r_1 \cup r2)}$ in a more time efficient manner.

The proposed algorithm first tries to validate existing fuzzy functional dependencies from both r1 and r2. It uses the validation technique proposed in lemma 2. To validate a given dependency X→A, it calculates the tuple partition of the left hand side X and tuple partition of both left hand side and right hand side X and A. If $|\Pi LHS| == |\Pi LR|$ then the dependency is valid. Otherwise, it tries to find more specialized (or less general) dependencies and add them to the queue to be validated later. When all dependencies are validated, it removes all the less general fuzzy functional dependencies and returns a cover *of* the coarsest fuzzy functional dependencies with respect to a given level value α.

The Incremental Searching Algorithm for Fuzzy Functional Dependencies

Input: a fuzzy relation r1 on $R(A1, A2, ..., Am)$;

similarity relations s_j on the domain of attribute A_j, $1 \le j \le$ m;

a non-redundant $COVER_\alpha(r_1)$ of r_1 w.r.t. a given level value α;

a set of new tuples r_2 on R, with optional $COVER_a(r_2)$.

Output: a non-redundant cover of the set of fuzzy functional dependencies satisfied by $r_1 \cup r_2$.

Procedure FD-INCR(r_1, r_2, $COVER_a(r_1)$, $COVER_a(r_2)$, R)

1. $QUEUE := COVER_a(r_1) \cap COVER_a(r_2)$; //assumes all FD's if $COVER_a(r_2)$ is unknown
2. $FD\_SET := \emptyset$;
3. For each attribute $A \in R$ and the least $\alpha_A \geq \alpha$
4. $\pi_A^{\alpha_A} := $ DOMAIN-PARTITION(A, s_A, α_A); // domain partitions
5. $\Pi_A^{\alpha_A} := $ TUPLE-PARTITION($r_1 \cup r_2, A, \alpha_A$); // tuple partitions
6. While $QUEUE \neq \emptyset$ Do
7. $FD := $ Dequeue from $QUEUE$; // $X_{\alpha_X} \to A_{\alpha_A}$
8. $LHS := $ Left-hand-side of FD; // X_{α_X}
9. $RHS := $ Right-hand-side of FD; // A_{α_A}
10. $A := $ Get and Remove first attribute of LHS; // lines 10-14 compute partition of X_{α_X}
11. $\Pi_{LHS} := \Pi_A$;
12. While $|LHS| \geq 1$ Do
13. $A' := $ Get and Remove first attribute of LHS;
14. $\Pi_{LHS} := $ REFINE-PARTITION($\Pi_{LHS}, \Pi_{A'}$);
15. $\Pi_{LR} = $ REFINE-PARTITION(Π_{LHS}, Π_{RHS}); // partition of $X_{\alpha_X} \cup \{A_{\alpha_A}\}$
16. If ($|\Pi_{LHS}| == |\Pi_{LR}|$) Then
17. $FD\_SET := FD\_SET \cup \{FD\}$
18. Else Enqueue FD_SPECIALIZE($FD, r_1 \cup r_2$) to $QUEUE$; //finds more specialized FD's
19. REMV_REDUNDANT(FD_SET); // removes less general FD's
20. Return(FD_SET);

The procedure DOMAIN-PARTITION(A, s_A, α_A) above computes the domain partition for each attribute. The procedure TUPLE-PARTITION($r_1 \cup r_2, A, \alpha_A$) computes the tuple partition of the

relation $r_1 \cup r_2$ with respect to attribute A_{α_A}. The procedure REFINE-PARTITION(Π', Π'') refines the partitions Π' and Π''. The procedure FD_SPECIALIZE($X_{\alpha_X} \to A_{\alpha_A}$, R) finds the set of least specialized fuzzy functional dependencies of a contradicted fuzzy functional dependency, $X_{\alpha_X} \to A_{\alpha_A}$. The procedure REMV_REDUNDANT(FD_SET) removes those fuzzy functional dependencies from FD_SET that are less general than others. These procedures are stated in detail as follows:

Procedure 1: Compute Domain Partition for Attribute A W.R.T. Level Value α_A

Input: Attribute A, similarity relation s_A of A, level value α_A

Output: $\pi_A^{\alpha_A}$, domain partition of A w.r.t. α_A

Procedure DOMAIN-PARTITION(A, s_A, α_A)

1. $\pi_A^{\alpha_A} := \emptyset$; //initial set of partition
2. For any $x, y \in$ domain(A)
3. If $s(x,y) \geq \alpha_A$ Then
4. $\pi_A^{\alpha_A} := $ Add $\{x, y\}$ to appropriate equivalence class in $\pi_A^{\alpha_A}$;
5. Else $\pi_A^{\alpha_A} := $ Add $\{x\}$, $\{y\}$ to appropriate equivalence classes in $\pi_A^{\alpha_A}$;
6. Return($\pi_A^{\alpha_A}$);

Procedure 2: Compute tuple Partition of R W.R.T. Attribute A and Level Value α_A

Input: A relation r, an attribute A in the relation, and the least $\alpha_A \geq \alpha$

Output: $\Pi_A^{\alpha_A}$, tuple partition of r w.r.t. A_{α_A}

Procedure TUPLE-PARTITION($r_1 \cup r_2, A, \alpha_A$)

1. $K := 1$;
2. $C_k := \{1\}$; // first equivalence class containing tuple one

3. $\Pi_A^{\alpha_A} := \left\{ C_k \right\}$; // initial partition contains first equivalence class

4. For $i=2$ to $|r|$ Do

5. If $t_i.A \in \left\{ \left[t_1.A \right]_A^{\alpha_A} ..., \left[t_{i-1}.A \right]_A^{\alpha_A} \right\}$ Then // equivalence class already exists

6. Add i to appropriate C_k;

7. Else $k:=k+1$;

8. $C_{k+1}:=\{i\}$; // create new equivalence class

9. $\Pi_A^{\alpha_A} :=$ Add $\{C_{k+1}\}$ to $\Pi_A^{\alpha_A}$;

10. Return($\Pi_A^{\alpha_A}$);

Procedure 3: Compute the Refinement of Two Tuple Partitions

Input: Partitions $\Pi' = \left\{ c_1', ..., c_{|\Pi'|}' \right\}$ and $\Pi'' = \left\{ c_1'', ..., c_{|\Pi''|}'' \right\}$

Output: Partition $\Pi=\Pi'\cdot\Pi''$

Procedure REFINE-PARTITION(Π',Π'')

1. $\Pi:=\varphi$;

2. For $i:=1$ to $|\Pi'|$ Do

3. For each $t \in c_i'$ Do $T[t]:=i$;

4. $S[i]:=\varphi$;

5. For $i:=1$ to $|\Pi''|$ Do

6. For each $t \in c_i''$ Do

7. $S\left[T\left[t \right] \right] := S\left[T\left[t \right] \right] \cup \{t\}$;

8. For each $t \in c_i''$ Do

9. If $S\left[T\left[t \right] \right] \neq \varphi$ Then $\Pi := \Pi \cup \left\{ S\left[T\left[t \right] \right] \right\}$;

10. $S\left[T\left[t \right] \right] := \varphi$;

11. For $i:=1$ to $|\Pi'|$ Do

12. For each $t \in c_i'$ Do $T[t]=NULL$;

13. Return(Π);

Procedure 4: Find Least Specialization of a Contradicted Functional Dependency

Input: Contradicted functional dependency $X_{\alpha_X} \rightarrow A_{\alpha_A}$ and R

Output: the set of least specialization of $X_{\alpha_X} \rightarrow A_{\alpha_A}$

Procedure FD_SPECIALIZE($X_{\alpha_X} \rightarrow A_{\alpha_A}$, R)

1. $FD\_SP: = \emptyset$;

2. $DIS: = R - (X \cup \{A\})$;

3. For each ($ATTR$ with the least $\alpha_{ATTR} \geq \alpha$) in DIS Do

4. Add $\left(X_{\alpha_X} \cup \left\{ ATTR_{\alpha_{ATTR}} \right\} \right) \rightarrow A_{\alpha_A}$ to FD_SP;

5. Return (FD_SP);

Procedure 5: Remove More Specialized Functional Dependencies

Input: A set of functional dependencies satisfied by $r_1 \cup r_2$

Output: A non-redundant set of functional dependencies

Procedure REMV_REDUNDANT(FD_SET)

1. For each pair $FD1$, $FD2$ from FD_SET Do

2. If (RHS of $FD1$) $==$ (RHS of $FD2$) Then // check right hand side of FD's

3. If (LHS of $FD1$) $\subseteq$ (LHS of $FD2$) Then // check left hand side of FD's

4. Remove $FD2$ from FD_SET

5. Else If (LHS of $FD2$) $\subseteq$ (LHS of $FD1$) Then

6. Remove $FD1$ from FD_SET

7. Return (FD_SET);

An example is given below to show how the proposed algorithm can be used to discover functional dependencies incrementally. For simplicity, we assume that one tuple is added to the database.

Example 9: Consider the database in Table 2. A new tuple {*George, MS, 30, Moderate Low*} is added to the relation. The following shows the steps of the proposed incremental searching algorithm in detail.

Input: a fuzzy relation r_1 on $R(NAME, EDU, AGE, CON)$;

a non-redundant $COVER_{0.8}(r_1) = \{NAME_1 \rightarrow EDU_{0.8}, \quad NAME_1 \rightarrow AGE_{0.9}, NAME_1 \rightarrow CON_{0.8}, \{AGE_{0.9}, CON_{0.8}\} \rightarrow EDU_{0.8}, \{EDU_{0.8}, CON_{0.8}\} \rightarrow AGE_{0.9}, \{EDU_{0.8}, AGE_{0.9}\} \rightarrow CON_{0.8}\}$ with $\alpha = 0.8$;

a new relation $r_2 = \{t\} = \{George, MS, 30, Moderate\ Low\}$;

Output: a non-redundant cover of the set of FD's satisfied by $r_1 \cup \{t\}$

Line 1: QUEUE: $= \{ NAME_1 \rightarrow EDU_{0.8}, NAME_1 \rightarrow AGE_{0.9}, NAME_1 \rightarrow CON_{0.8}, \{AGE_{0.9}, CON_{0.8}\} \rightarrow EDU_{0.8}, \{EDU_{0.8}, CON_{0.8}\} \rightarrow AGE_{0.9}, \{EDU_{0.8}, AGE_{0.9}\} \rightarrow CON_{0.9} \}$

Line 2: FD_SET:= $\emptyset$;

Line 6: (Loop1) QUEUE $\neq \emptyset$;

Line 7: FD:= $NAME_1 \rightarrow EDU_{0.8}$;

Line 16: $\left| \Pi_{NAME}^{1.0} \right| = \left| \Pi_{\{NAME, EDU\}}^{(1.0, 0.8)} \right|$;

Line 17: FD_SET:= $\{ NAME_1 \rightarrow EDU_{0.8} \}$;

Line 6: (Loop2) QUEUE $\neq \emptyset$;

Line 7: FD:= $NAME_1 \rightarrow AGE_{0.9}$;

Line 16: $\left| \Pi_{NAME}^{1.0} \right| = \left| \Pi_{\{NAME, AGE\}}^{(1.0, 0.9)} \right|$;

Line 17: FD_SET:= $\{ NAME_1 \rightarrow EDU_{0.8}, NAME_1 \rightarrow AGE_{0.9} \}$;

Line 6: (Loop3) QUEUE $\neq \emptyset$;

Line 7: FD:= $NAME_1 \rightarrow CON_{0.8}$;

Line 16: $\left| \Pi_{NAME}^{1.0} \right| = \left| \Pi_{\{NAME, CON\}}^{(1.0, 0.8)} \right|$;

Line 17: FD_SET:= $\{ NAME_1 \rightarrow EDU_{0.8}, NAME_1 \rightarrow AGE_{0.9}, NAME_1 \rightarrow CON_{0.8} \}$;

Line 6: (Loop4) QUEUE $\neq \emptyset$;

Line 7: FD:= $\{AGE_{0.9}, CON_{0.8}\} \rightarrow EDU_{0.8}$;

Line 16: $\left| \Pi_{\{AGE, CON\}}^{(0.9, 0.8)} \right| \neq \left| \Pi_{\{AGE, CON, EDU\}}^{(0.9, 0.8, 0.8)} \right|$;

Line 18: QUEUE:= $\{ \{EDU_{0.8}, CON_{0.8}\} \rightarrow AGE_{0.9}, \{EDU_{0.8}, AGE_{0.9}\} \rightarrow CON_{0.9}, \{NAME_1, AGE_{0.9}, CON_{0.8}\} \rightarrow EDU_{0.8} \}$;

//Noted that a new fuzzy functional dependency is added to the QUEUE

Line 6: (Loop5) QUEUE $\neq \emptyset$;

Line 7: FD:= $\{EDU_{0.8}, CON_{0.8}\} \rightarrow AGE_{0.9}$;

Line 16: $\left| \Pi_{\{EDU, CON\}}^{(0.8, 0.8)} \right| \neq \left| \Pi_{\{EDU, CON, AGE\}}^{(0.8, 0.8, 0.9)} \right|$;

Line 18: QUEUE:= $\{\{EDU_{0.8}, AGE_{0.9}\} \rightarrow CON_{0.8}, \{NAME_1, AGE_{0.9}, CON_{0.8}\} \rightarrow EDU_{0.8}, \{NAME_1, EDU_{0.8}, CON_{0.8}\} \rightarrow AGE_{0.9}\}$;

Line 6: (Loop6) QUEUE $\neq \emptyset$;

Line 7: FD:= $\{EDU_{0.8}, AGE_{0.9}\} \rightarrow CON_{0.8}$;

Line 16: $\left| \Pi_{\{EDU, AGE\}}^{(0.8, 0.9)} \right| \neq \left| \Pi_{\{EDU, AGE, CON\}}^{(0.8, 0.9, 08)} \right|$;

Line 18: QUEUE:= $\{ \{NAME_1, AGE_{0.9}, CON_{0.8}\} \rightarrow EDU_{0.8}, \{NAME_1, EDU_{0.8}, CON_{0.8}\} \rightarrow AGE_{0.9}, \{NAME_1, EDU_{0.8}, AGE_{0.9}\} \rightarrow CON_{0.9}\}$;

Line 6: (Loop7) QUEUE $\neq \emptyset$;

Line 7: FD:= $\{NAME_1, AGE_{0.9}, CON_{0.8}\} \rightarrow EDU_{0.8}$;

Line 16: $\left| \Pi_{\{NAME, AGE, CON\}}^{(1.0, 0.9, 0.8)} \right| = \left| \Pi_{\{NAME, AGE, CON, EDU\}}^{(1.0, 0.9, 0.8, 08)} \right|$;

Line 17: FD_SET:= $\{ NAME_1 \rightarrow EDU_{0.8}, NAME_1 \rightarrow AGE_{0.9}, NAME_1 \rightarrow CON_{0.8}, \{NAME_1, AGE_{0.9}, CON_{0.8}\} \rightarrow EDU_{0.8}\}$;

Line 6: (Loop8) QUEUE $\neq \emptyset$;

Line 7: FD:= $\{NAME_1, EDU_{0.8}, CON_{0.8}\} \rightarrow AGE_{0.9}$;

Line 16: $\left| \Pi_{\{NAME, EDU, CON\}}^{(1.0, 0.8, 0.8)} \right| = \left| \Pi_{\{NAME, EDU, CON, AGE\}}^{(1.0, 0.8, 0.8, 0.9)} \right|$;

Line 17: FD_SET:= $\{ NAME_1 \rightarrow EDU_{0.8}, NAME_1 \rightarrow AGE_{0.9}, NAME_1 \rightarrow CON_{0.8}, \{NAME_1, AGE_{0.9}, CON_{0.8}\} \rightarrow EDU_{0.8}, \{NAME_1, EDU_{0.8}, CON_{0.8}\} \rightarrow AGE_{0.9}\}$

Line 6: (Loop8) QUEUE $\neq \emptyset$;

Line 7: FD:= $\{NAME_1, EDU_{0.8}, AGE_{0.9}\} \rightarrow CON_{0.8}$;

Line 16: $\left| \Pi_{\{NAME, EDU, AGE\}}^{(1.0, 0.8, 0.9)} \right| = \left| \Pi_{\{NAME, EDU, AGE, CON\}}^{(1.0, 0.8, 0.9, 0.8)} \right|$;

Line 17: FD_SET:= $\{NAME_1 \rightarrow EDU_{0.8}, NAME_1 \rightarrow AGE_{0.9}, NAME_1 \rightarrow CON_{0.8}, \{NAME_1, AGE_{0.9}, CON_{0.8}\} \rightarrow EDU_{0.8}, \{NAME_1, EDU_{0.8}, CON_{0.8}\} \rightarrow AGE_{0.9}, \{NAME_1, EDU_{0.8}, AGE_{0.9}\} \rightarrow CON_{0.8}\}$

Line 19: FD_SET:= $\{ NAME_1 \rightarrow EDU_{0.8}, NAME_1 \rightarrow AGE_{0.9}, NAME_1 \rightarrow CON_{0.8} \}$;

The algorithm thus returns a non-redundant cover of the set of FD's $\{ NAME_1 \rightarrow EDU_{0.8},$

$NAME_1 \rightarrow AGE_{0.9}$, $NAME_1 \rightarrow CON_{0.8}$ } at line 20.

ANALYSIS

This section analyzes the time and space complexities of the proposed incremental searching algorithm. The comparisons with pair-wise comparison incremental algorithm in (Wang, Shen & Hong, 2000) are also presented.

Let $|R|$ be the number of attributes in schema R, $|r|$ be the number of tuples in r, $|COVER_\alpha r|$ be the number of fuzzy functional dependencies in $COVER\alpha_{(r)}$. Let $|D|$ be the number of elements in domain D. Table 4 shows the best-case and worst-case analyses of time and space complexities of the proposed algorithm and pair-wise comparison algorithm, for the case that one tuple is added to a relation r. For the proposed algorithm, the time complexities of TUPLE-PARTITION and REFINE-PARTITION are both $O(|r|)$. In procedure FD-*INCR*, lines 4 and 5 compute domain and tuple partitions of all attributes in R *and* require $O(|D|2\cdot|R|)$ and $O(|r|\cdot|R|)$ respectively. The best case occurs when the QUEUE in line 6 remains unchanged and $|LHS|=1$. In this case, line 15 requires $O(|r|\cdot|COVER(r)|)$ computation time. In total, the algorithm has time complexity $O(|D|2\cdot|R|+|r|\cdot(|R|+|COVER(r)|))$. However, the worst case occurs when QUEUE contains all possible fuzzy functional dependencies in the whole

searching space. In this case, the algorithm has time complexity $O(|D|2\cdot|R|+|r|\cdot2|R|)$. The space complexity is $O(|R|\cdot(|r|+|D|))$ for storing both tuple and domain partitions.

In the pair-wise comparison algorithm (Wang, Shen & Hong, 2000), for each fuzzy functional dependency in $COVER(r)$, the newly added tuple t must be compared with every tuple in r. For the best case that the $COVER(r)$ remains unchanged, $O(|D|^2\cdot|R|\cdot|COVER(r)|\cdot|r|\cdot|R|)$ computation time is required. The worst case occurs when all possible fuzzy functional dependencies in the whole searching space must be examined. In this case, the time complexity is $O(|D|^2\cdot|R|\cdot|r|\cdot2^{|R|})$. The space complexity is $O(|R|\cdot|D|)$ for storing domain partitions. It is observed that the proposed algorithm requires less computation time, especially when $|R|$ or $|COVER(r)|$ is large in the best case.

Table 5 shows the time and space complexities of the same two algorithms when k tuples are added to a relation. The pair-wise comparison approach requires that the incremental searching be executed k times. However, the proposed approach requires only one execution of the algorithm. It is observed form Table 5 that the proposed approach requires much less computation time than pair-wise-comparison approach. This is due to k repetitions must be executed by the pair-wise algorithm.

Table 4. Time and space complexities when one tuple is added

	Proposed Algorithm	Pair-wise Algorithm
Time Complexity (Best-Case)	$O\left(|D|^2 \cdot |R| + |r| \cdot \left(|R| + |COVER(r)|\right)\right)$	$O\left(|D|^2 \cdot |R| \cdot |COVER(r)| \cdot |r| \cdot |R|\right)$
Time Complexity (Worst-Case)	$O\left(|D|^2 \cdot |R| + |r| \cdot 2^{|R|}\right)$	$O\left(|D|^2 \cdot |R| \cdot |r| \cdot 2^{|R|}\right)$
Space Complexity	$O\left(|R| \cdot \left(|r| + |D|\right)\right)$	$O\left(|R| \cdot |D|\right)$

Table 5. Time and space complexities when k tuples are added

	Proposed Algorithm	Pair-wise Algorithm
Time Complexity (Best-Case)	$O\left(\|D\|^2 \cdot \|R\| + (\|r\| + k) \cdot (\|R\| + \|COVER(r)\|)\right)$	$O\left(\|D\|^2 \cdot \|R\| \cdot k \cdot \|COVER(r)\| \cdot \|r\| \cdot \|R\|\right)$
Time Complexity (Worst-Case)	$O\left(\|D\|^2 \cdot \|R\| + (\|r\| + k) \cdot 2^{\|R\|}\right)$	$O\left(\|D\|^2 \cdot \|R\| \cdot k \cdot \|r\| \cdot 2^{\|R\|}\right)$
Space Complexity	$O\left(\|R\| \cdot (\|r\| + k + \|D\|)\right)$	$O\left(\|R\| \cdot \|D\|\right)$

NUMERICAL EXAMPLES

In this section, we describe the numerical results concerning the relationship between the fuzzy functional dependencies discovered and the number of tuples $|r|$ in a fuzzy relation.

Tables 6, 7 and 8 show the fuzzy functional dependencies discovered from the fuzzy relational database shown in Table 2, for level values α=1.0, 0.9, 0.8 respectively. For cases that $|r|$ = 7, 8, 9, 10, we have inserted extra tuples accordingly. These results justify the property that $r_1 \subseteq r_2$ implies $FD_\alpha(r1) \supseteq FD\alpha_{(r}2)$

Table 9 summarizes the number of fuzzy functional dependencies discovered for different number of tuples and level values. It further justifies the monotonic characteristics that the number of fuzzy functional dependencies decreases when the number of tuples increases, for all level val-

ues. Notice that for fixed $|r|$, the number of fuzzy functional dependencies is not monotonic with respect to the level value. That is, the number of fuzzy functional dependencies does not decrease monotonically when the level value decreases. This is due to the effect of different similarity relations on different attribute domains.

CONCLUSION

In this work, we have presented a partition-based incremental data mining algorithm to discover fuzzy functional dependencies from dynamic similarity-based fuzzy relational databases. Based on the concept of tuple partition and partition refinement, a simple validation technique for fuzzy functional dependencies is proposed. The behavior of fuzzy functional dependencies with respect to

Table 6. The FD's discovered for α=1.0

$|r|$	# of FD's	FD's, α=1.0
6	9	$NAME_1 \rightarrow EDU_1$, $NAME_1 \rightarrow AGE_1$, $NAME_1 \rightarrow CON_1$, $\{EDU_{1.0}, AGE_{1.0}\} \rightarrow NAME_1$, $\{EDU_{1.0}, AGE_{1.0}\} \rightarrow CON_1$, $\{EDU_{1.0}, AGE_{1.0}\} \rightarrow NAME_1$, $\{EDU_{1.0}, AGE_{1.0}\} \rightarrow AGE_1$ $\{EDU_{1.0}, AGE_{1.0}\} \rightarrow NAME_1$, $\{EDU_{1.0}, AGE_{1.0}\} \rightarrow EDU_1$
7	7	$NAME_1 \rightarrow EDU_1$, $NAME_1 \rightarrow AGE_1$, $NAME_1 \rightarrow CON_1$, $\{EDU_{1.0}, AGE_{1.0}\} \rightarrow NAME_1$, $\{EDU_{1.0}, AGE_{1.0}\} \rightarrow CON_1$, $\{EDU_{1.0}, AGE_{1.0}\} \rightarrow NAME_1$, $\{EDU_{1.0}, AGE_{1.0}\} \rightarrow AGE_1$
8	5	$NAME_1 \rightarrow EDU_1$, $NAME_1 \rightarrow AGE_1$, $NAME_1 \rightarrow CON_1$, $\{EDU_{1.0}, AGE_{1.0}\} \rightarrow CON_1$, $\{EDU_{1.0}, AGE_{1.0}\} \rightarrow AGE_1$
9	4	$NAME_1 \rightarrow EDU_1$, $NAME_1 \rightarrow AGE_1$, $NAME_1 \rightarrow CON_1$, $\{EDU_{1.0}, AGE_{1.0}\} \rightarrow AGE_1$
10	4	$NAME_1 \rightarrow EDU_1$, $NAME_1 \rightarrow AGE_1$, $NAME_1 \rightarrow CON_1$, $\{EDU_{1.0}, AGE_{1.0}\} \rightarrow AGE_1$

Table 7. The FD's discovered for α=0.9

$|r|$	# of FD's	FD's, α=0.9
6	7	$NAME_1 \rightarrow EDU_1$, $NAME_1 \rightarrow AGE_{0.9}$, $NAME_1 \rightarrow CON_1$, $CON_1 \rightarrow AGE_{0.9}$, $\{EDU_{1.0}, AGE_{0.9}\} \rightarrow CON_1$, $\{EDU_{1.0}, AGE_{0.9}\} \rightarrow NAME_1$, $\{EDU, CON\}_{(1,1)} \rightarrow NAME_1$
7	7	$NAME_1 \rightarrow EDU_1$, $NAME_1 \rightarrow AGE_{0.9}$, $NAME_1 \rightarrow CON_1$, $CON_1 \rightarrow AGE_{0.9}$, $\{EDU_{1.0}, AGE_{0.9}\} \rightarrow CON_1$, $\{EDU_{1.0}, AGE_{0.9}\} \rightarrow NAME_1$, $\{EDU_{1.0}, AGE_{1.0}\} \rightarrow NAME_1$
8	5	$NAME_1 \rightarrow EDU_1$, $NAME_1 \rightarrow AGE_{0.9}$, $NAME_1 \rightarrow CON_1$, $CON_1 \rightarrow AGE_{0.9}$, $\{EDU_{1.0}, AGE_{0.9}\} \rightarrow CON_1$
9	4	$NAME_1 \rightarrow EDU_1$, $NAME_1 \rightarrow AGE_{0.9}$, $NAME_1 \rightarrow CON_1$, $CON_1 \rightarrow AGE_{0.9}$
10	4	$NAME_1 \rightarrow EDU_1$, $NAME_1 \rightarrow AGE_{0.9}$, $NAME_1 \rightarrow CON_1$, $CON_1 \rightarrow AGE_{0.9}$

Table 8. The FD's discovered for α=0.8

$|r|$	# of FD's	FD's, α=0.8
6	6	$NAME_1 \rightarrow EDU_{0.8}$, $NAME_1 \rightarrow AGE_{0.9}$, $NAME_1 \rightarrow CON_{0.8}$, $\{AGE_{0.9}, CON_{0.8}\} \rightarrow EDU_{0.8}$, $\{EDU_{0.8}, CON_{0.8}\} \rightarrow AGE_{0.9}$, $\{EDU_{0.8}, AGE_{0.9}\} \rightarrow CON_{0.8}$
7	3	$NAME_1 \rightarrow EDU_{0.8}$, $NAME_1 \rightarrow AGE_{0.9}$, $NAME_1 \rightarrow CON_{0.8}$
8	3	$NAME_1 \rightarrow EDU_{0.8}$, $NAME_1 \rightarrow AGE_{0.9}$, $NAME_1 \rightarrow CON_{0.8}$
9	3	$NAME_1 \rightarrow EDU_{0.8}$, $NAME_1 \rightarrow AGE_{0.9}$, $NAME_1 \rightarrow CON_{0.8}$
10	3	$NAME_1 \rightarrow EDU_{0.8}$, $NAME_1 \rightarrow AGE_{0.9}$, $NAME_1 \rightarrow CON_{0.8}$

Table 9. The number of FD's for different number of tuples and level values

	1.0	0.9	0.8	0.7	0.6	0.5	0.3
6	9	7	6	4	5	7	9
7	7	7	3	4	5	7	9
8	5	5	3	4	5	7	9
9	4	4	3	4	5	7	9
10	4	4	3	4	5	7	9

the number of tuples has also been shown numerically. It justifies the monotonic characteristics that the number of fuzzy functional dependencies decreases when the number of tuples increases, for all level values. Computational complexity of the proposed algorithm is analyzed. Comparison with pair-wise comparison-based incremental mining algorithm (Raju & Majumdar, 1988) is presented. For the case of adding one tuple to a fuzzy database relation, it is shown that with certain space requirement, partition-based approach is more time efficient than pair-wise approach in the discovery of fuzzy functional dependencies dynamically. When multiple tuples are added to a fuzzy database relation in the same time, partition-based approach requires even much less time than pair-wise comparison approach.

Although the proposed mining method works well on the similarity-based data model, it is just a beginning. There is still much work to be done in this field. Various forms of dependencies have been defined on the possibility-based and similarity-based fuzzy relational data models. Mining of different types of dependencies from different data models remains to be investigated. In fact, we have started to develop mining algorithms for discovering fuzzy functional dependencies from possibility-based fuzzy relations. We will also attempt to discover inclusion dependencies between fuzzy relations.

REFERENCES

Bell, S., & Brockhausen, P. (1995). *Discovery of data dependencies in relational databases.* Tech. Rep. LS-8. No. 14. Dortmund, Germany: University of Dortmund.

Belohlavek, R., & V. (2006). Relational Model of Data over Domains with Similarities: An Extension for Similarity Queries and Knowledge Extraction. In *Proceedings of IEEE IRI* (pp. 207-213).

Bosc, P., Lietard, L., & Pivert, O. (1997). Functional dependencies revisited under graduality and imprecision. In *Proceedings of NAFIPS* (pp. 57-62).

Buckles, B. P., & Petry, F. E. (1982). A fuzzy representation of data for relational databases. *Fuzzy Sets and Systems, 7,* 213–226. doi:10.1016/0165-0114(82)90052-5

Carrasco, R. A., Vila, M. A., Galindo, J., & Cubero, J. C. (2000). FSQL: a Tool for obtaining fuzzy dependencies. In *8th International Conference on Information Processing and Management of Uncertainty in Knowledge-Based Systems,* (pp. 1916-1919).

Chen, G. Q. (1998). *Fuzzy Logic in Data Modeling: Semantics, Constraints, and Database Design.* Amsterdam: Kluwer Academic Publishers.

Flach, P. A. (1990). *Inductive characterization of database relations.* ITK Research Report.

Flach, P. A., & Savnik, I. (1999). Database dependency discovery: a machine learning approach. *AI Communications, 12*(3), 139–160.

Galiano, F. B., Cubero, J. C., Cuenca, F., & Medina, J. M. (2002). Relational decomposition through partial functional dependencies. *Data & Knowledge Engineering, 43*(2), 207–234. doi:10.1016/S0169-023X(02)00056-3

Galindo, J., Urrutia, A., & Piattini, M. (2006). *Fuzzy databases: modeling, design and implementation.* Hershey, PA: Idea Group Publishing.

Hale, J., & Shenoi, S. (1996). Analyzing FD inference in relational databases. *Data and Knowledge Engineering Journal, 18,* 167–183. doi:10.1016/0169-023X(95)00033-O

Haux, R., & Eckert, U. (1985). Nondeterministic dependencies in relations: an extension of the concept of functional dependency. *Information Systems, 10*(2), 139–148. doi:10.1016/0306-4379(85)90032-8

Huhtala, Y., Karkkainen, J., Porkka, P., & Toivonen, H. (1998). Efficient discovery of functional and approximate dependencies using partitions. In *Proceedings of IEEE International Conference on Data Engineering* (pp. 392-410).

Mannila, H., & Toivonen, H. (1997). Levelwise search and borders of theories in knowledge discovery. *Data Mining and Knowledge Discovery, 1*(3), 241–258. doi:10.1023/A:1009796218281

Nambiar, U., & Kambhampati, S. (2004). Mining approximate functional dependencies and concept similarities to answer imprecise queries. In *Seventh International Workshop on the Web and Databases,* (pp. 73-78).

Raju, K. V. S. V. N., & Majumdar, A. K. (1988). Fuzzy functional dependencies and losses join decomposition of fuzzy relational database systems. *ACM Transactions on Database Systems, 13*(2), 129–166. doi:10.1145/42338.42344

Rasmussen, D., & Yager, R. R. (1999). Finding fuzzy and gradual functional dependencies with SummarySQL. *Fuzzy Sets and Systems, 106*, 131–142. doi:10.1016/S0165-0114(97)00268-6

Sachar, H. (1986). *Theoretical aspects of design of and retrieval from similarity-based relational database systems.* Ph.D. Dissertation, University of Texas at Arlington, TX.

Saharia, A. N., & Barron, T. M. (1995). Approximate dependencies in database systems. *Decision Support Systems, 13*, 335–347. doi:10.1016/0167-9236(93)E0049-J

Shenoi, S., Melton, A., & Fan, L. T. (1990). An equivalence class model of fuzzy relational databases. *Fuzzy Sets and Systems, 38*, 153–170. doi:10.1016/0165-0114(90)90147-X

Wang, S. L., Shen, J. W., & Hong, T. P. (2000). Discovering Functional Dependencies Incrementally from Fuzzy Relational Databases. In *Proceedings of the Eighth National Conference on Fuzzy Theory and Its Applications,* (17).

Wang, S. L., Tsai, J. S., & Hong, T. P. (2001). Discovering Functional Dependencies from Similarity-based Fuzzy Relational Databases. *Journal of Intelligent Data Analysis, 5*(1), 131–149.

Yao, H., Hamilton, H., & Butz, C. (2002). *FD_Mine: discovering functional dependencies in a database using equivalences.* Technical Report TR 2002-04. Regina, Canada: University of Regina.

Yazici, A., & George, R. (1999). *Fuzzy Database Modeling.* Heidelberg: Physica-Verlag.

Zadeh, L. A. (1971). Similarity relations and fuzzy orderings. *Information Sciences, 3*(1), 177–200. doi:10.1016/S0020-0255(71)80005-1

Chapter 4
An Intelligent Data Mining System Through Integration of Electromagnetism–Like Mechanism And Fuzzy Neural Network

Peitsang Wu
I-Shou University, Taiwan, R.O.C.

Yung-Yao Hung
I-Shou University, Taiwan, R.O.C.

ABSTRACT

In this chapter, a meta-heuristic algorithm (Electromagnetism-like Mechanism, EM) for global optimization is introduced. The Electromagnetism-like mechanism simulates the electromagnetism theory of physics by considering each sample point to be an electrical charge. The EM algorithm utilizes an attraction-repulsion mechanism to move the sample points towards the optimum. The electromagnetism-like mechanism (EM) can be used as a stand-alone approach or as an accompanying algorithm for other methods. Besides, the electromagnetism-like mechanism is not easily trapped into local optimum. Therefore, the purpose of this chapter is using the electromagnetism-like mechanism (EM) to develop an electromagnetism-like mechanism based fuzzy neural network (EMFNN), and employ the EMFNN to train fuzzy if-then rules.

INTRODUCTION

The six generation systems (SGS) are constituted by fuzzy logic, neural networks and genetic algorithms (Wang, 1999). During the last decades, there are a lot of researchers employed the above methods on their researches (Buckley and Hayashi, 1992,

1994; Ishibuchi et al., 1992, 1993, 1995; Lin and Lu, 1995). These studies were focus on not only the modification of architectures but also the improvement of performances. Many investigations for SGS werefocus on the optimization problems (Aliev et al., 2001; Goldberg, 1989). Moreover, the merging of fuzzy logic, neural networks and genetic algorithms was also an interesting field (Kuo et al., 1999, 2001, 2002; Shapiro, 2002).

DOI: 10.4018/978-1-61520-757-2.ch004

Fuzzy logic has been shown highly promising performance in the area of control (Fukuda and Shibata, 1992; Jang, 1991, 1992, 1993; Lin, 1991, 1995). Fuzzy neural networks (FNN), associates the fuzzy logic with neural networks, has been used to learn the fuzzy if-then rules. There are many literatures that have addressed the architectures of fuzzy neural networks (Gupta and Knopf, 1990; Ishibuchi et al., 1992, 1993, 1995; Takagi and Hayashi, 1991). And each of them has different capability for problem solving. Since the experts' knowledge is quite subjective, the fuzzy logic attempts to capture it. The fuzzy neural network is used to learn fuzzy IF-THEN rules which can represent the qualitative factors. Recently, the genetic algorithm combined with fuzzy neural network has been proposed (Buckley, 1996; Kuo et al., 2001), and the training results were better than those of the conventional fuzzy neural network.

The Electromagnetism-like Mechanism (EM) is a new meta-heuristic algorithm developed for global optimization (Birbil and Fang, 2003). The Electromagnetism-like Mechanism simulates the electromagnetism theory of physics by considering each sample point to be an electrical charge. The algorithm utilizes an attraction-repulsion mechanism to move the sample points towards the optimality. The EM-like algorithm has been tested and verified to prove it can be converged rapidly (in terms of the number of function evaluations) to the global optimum, and to produce highly efficient results for those problems with varying degree of difficulty (Birbil and Fang, 2003; Birbil et al, 2005).

The original EM was revised by Birbil et al. (2005) in order to make it convergent and after some modifications in the original EM, they proved that their new revised EM exhibits global convergence with probability one. Yang (2002) was the first to use the electromagnetism algorithm for training neural network with great saving on the computation memories and training time.

The results indicated that the electromagnetism algorithm performed much better than the genetic algorithm in finding optimal solution globally (Wu et al., 2004).

Wu et al. are the first to combine the EM algorithm with fuzzy neural network to obtain fuzzy if–then rules (Wu et al., 2005). For EM's merit of simple concept and economic computational cost, Wu and Chiang used the EM algorithm to solve the traveling salesman problem (TSP) (Wu and Chiang a,b,c, 2005). Debels et al. (2006) integrated a scatter search with EM for the solution of resource constraint project scheduling problems. Furthermore, Wu and Fang used the revised EM algorithm to solve large scaled TSP problem (Wu and Fang, 2006).

Since the Electromagnetism-like Mechanism is a new heuristic algorithm for global optimization and there are fewer investigations on it until now, we are motivated to utilize the EM algorithm for fuzzy neural network training. In this article, we introduce a new heuristic algorithm (Electromagnetism-like Mechanism, EM) and develop an electromagnetism-like mechanism based fuzzy neural network (EMFNN). There are several objectives that we want to accomplish. They are listed following:

- The fuzzy neural network and the electromagnetism-like mechanism will be introduced.
- The electromagnetism-like mechanism based fuzzy neural network (EMFNN) will be developed.
- Two systems of FNN and EMFNN will be established.
- The comparisons between FNN and EMFNN will be done by two examples and a sales forecasting case.
- The simulation results of conventional fuzzy neural network (FNN) and EMFNN will be presented.

FUZZY NEURAL NETWORKS

The Artificial neural networks (ANN), fuzzy logic, and genetic systems constitute the three independent research fields regarding sixth generation systems (SGS). ANN and the fuzzy model have been used in many application areas (Lee, 1990; Lippmann, 1987), each pairing its own advantages and disadvantages. Therefore, how to successfully combine these two approaches, ANNs and fuzzy modeling, is a relevant concern for further studies.

Takagi and Hayashi (1991) introduced a feed-forward ANN into fuzzy inference. Each rule is represented by an ANN while all the membership functions are represented by only one ANN. The algorithm is divided into three major parts: (1) the partition of inference rules; (2) the identification of IF parts; and (3) the identification of THEN parts. Since each rule and all the membership functions are represented by different ANNs, they are trained separately. In other words, the parameters cannot be updated concurrently. Jang (1991, 1992, 1993) proposed a method which transformed the fuzzy inference system into a functional equivalent adaptive network, and then employed the Error Back-Propagation (EBP)-type algorithm to update the premise parameters and least square method to identify the consequence parameters. Nakayama et al. (1992) proposed a so-called the FNN (fuzzy neural network) which had a special structure for realizing a fuzzy inference system. Each membership function consisted of one or two sigmoid functions for each inference rule. Due to the lack of a membership function setup procedure, the rule determination and membership function setup were decided by so-called experts where the decision was very subjective. Lin and Lee (1991) proposed the so-called neural-network-based fuzzy logic control system (NN-FLCS). They introduced the low-level learning power of neural networks in the fuzzy logic system and provided high-level human-understandable meaning to the normal connectionist architecture. Also,

Kuo and Cohen (1998) introduced a feed-forward ANN into fuzzy inference represented by Takagi's fuzzy modeling and applied it to multi-sensor integration.

Buckley and Hayashi (1994) surveyed recent findings on learning algorithms and applications for fuzzy neural networks with fuzzy inputs, weights and outputs (Buckley and Hayashi, 1992; Hayashi et al., 1993). Gupta and Knopf (1990) and Gupta and Qi (1991, 1992) presented some models with fuzzy neurons, but no learning algorithms were proposed in the paper. Ishibuchi et al. (1993) and Ishibuchi et al. (1995) proposed learning methods of neural networks to utilize not only numerical data but also expert knowledge represented by fuzzy IF-THEN rules. The authors summarized the direct fuzzification of conventional neural networks which was to extend connection weights, inputs and outputs. The types of neural network fuzzifications are list as follows.

- Type 1: fuzzy inputs, crisp weights, crisp outputs
- Type 2: fuzzy inputs, crisp weights, fuzzy outputs
- Type 3: crisp inputs, fuzzy weights, fuzzy outputs
- Type 4: fuzzy inputs, fuzzy weights, fuzzy outputs
- Type 5: crisp inputs, crisp weights, fuzzy outputs
- Type 6: crisp inputs, fuzzy weights, crisp outputs
- Type 7: fuzzy inputs, fuzzy weights, crisp outputs

The Fuzzy neural networks (FNN) in Type 1 were used in the classification problem of a fuzzy input vector to a crisp class. In order to implement the fuzzy IF-THEN rules by neural networks, a FNN with fuzzy inputs, fuzzy targets and crisp weights were used (i.e. Type 2). Ishibuchi et al. (1995) were focused on Type 3 and Type 4 which weights were fuzzified. Nevertheless, the last three cases are not realistic. Since both inputs and weights are real numbers, the outputs are always real numbers. Consequently, weights should be fuzzified for handling fuzzy targets in Type 5. The fuzzy weights are not necessary because targets are real numbers.

Kuo and Xue (1999) proposed a fuzzy neural network whose inputs, outputs, and weights were all fuzzified with asymmetric Gaussian functions. The learning algorithm was EBP-type learning procedure. Moreover, genetic algorithm was integrated with the proposed FNN in order to yield better results both in speed and accuracy (Kuo et al., 2001). Kuo (2001) integrated the ANN and GFNN (fuzzy neural network with initial weights generated by genetic algorithm) that provided more reliable forecasts, and GFNN can also learn the expert's knowledge which is fuzzy. Kuo et al. (2002) proposed a FNN with fuzzy weight elimination which can really improve FNN's performance.

For a neural network to be called a fuzzy neural network (FNN), the signals and/or the weights must be in a fuzzy set (Buckley and Hayashi, 1994). Ishibuchi et al. (1992) have proposed a classification method of fuzzy vectors using a multilayer feed-forward neural network. In the method, people can classify unknown fuzzy input vectors using the corresponding fuzzy outputs from the trained neural network. Besides, Ishibuchi et al. (1993) have delivered learning methods of neural network for utilizing expert knowledge represented by the fuzzy IF-THEN rules. In the learning of neural networks for constructing classification system, the fuzzy IF-THEN rules such as "IF x_{p1} is large and x_{p2} is small, THEN $x_p = (x_{p1}, x_{p2})$ belongs to class 1" are utilized as well as numerical data that are usually employed in conventional supervised learning methods. On the other hand, for constructing fuzzy control systems, the fuzzy IF-THEN rules such as "IF x_1 is large and x_2 is small, THEN y is small" are utilized in the learning of neural networks as well as numeri-

cal data. In the cause of dealing with linguistic values such as "large", "medium" and "small", architecture of neural networks that can handle fuzzy input vectors is first proposed by Ishibuchi et al. (1995). In this article, the architecture of the FNN with fuzzy inputs and crisp weights and fuzzy outputs is illustrated as following.

Operations of Fuzzy Numbers

First, before describing architecture of neural networks, operations on fuzzy numbers and intervals required for defining the architecture and deriving its learning algorithm are briefly described. The addition and multiplication of intervals are used here.

$$
X + Y = \left[x^{L}, x^{U}\right] + \left[y^{L} + y^{U}\right]
$$
$$
= \left[x^{L} + y^{L}, x^{U} + y^{U}\right] \tag{1}
$$

$$
k \cdot X = k \cdot \left[x^{L}, x^{U}\right]
$$
$$
= \begin{cases} \left[kx^{L}, kx^{U}\right] & \text{if } k \geq 0, \\ \left[kx^{U}, kx^{L}\right] & \text{if } k < 0, \end{cases} \tag{2}
$$

where $X = \left[x^{L}, x^{U}\right]$ and $Y = \left[y^{L}, y^{U}\right]$ are intervals and k is a real number. The superscripts L and U represent the lower bound and the upper bound of the intervals, respectively. Moreover, intervals are denoted by uppercase letters and real numbers are denoted by lowercase. The activation function of neural networks can also be extended to an interval input-output relation as

$$
f\left(\text{Net}\right) = f\left(\left[\text{net}^{L}, \text{net}^{U}\right]\right)
$$
$$
= \left[f\left(\text{net}^{L}\right), f\left(\text{net}^{U}\right)\right], \tag{3}
$$

where $\text{Net} = \left[\text{net}^{L}, \text{net}^{U}\right]$ is an interval input and $f(x) = (1 + \exp(-x))^{-1}$ is the logistic function used in many BP algorithms.

In the proposed algorithm, real numbers are denoted by lowercase letters (e.g. a; b; . . .) and fuzzy numbers are denoted by uppercase letters under a bar (e.g. $\tilde{A}$; $\tilde{B}$; . . .), respectively. Since fuzzy input vectors of multilayer feed-forward neural networks are in the proposed FNN, the addition, multiplication of the fuzzy numbers is necessary for defining the proposed FNN. Thus, they are defined as follows:

$$\tilde{Z}(z) = \tilde{X}(x) + \tilde{Y}(y) = \max\left\{\tilde{X}(x) \wedge \tilde{Y}(y) \big| z = x + y\right\}, \quad (4)$$

$$\tilde{Z}(z) = \tilde{X}(x) \cdot \tilde{Y}(y) = \max\left\{\tilde{X}(x) \wedge \tilde{Y}(y) \big| z = x \cdot y\right\}, \quad (5)$$

$$f\left(\widetilde{Net}\right)(z) = \max\left\{\widetilde{Net}(x) \big| z = f(x)\right\}. \quad (6)$$

Here $\widetilde{Net}$ and $f\left(\widetilde{Net}\right)$ are a fuzzy input and a fuzzy output, respectively. The fuzzy activation defined by equation (6) of each unit of a neural network are means the membership function of each fuzzy number, $\wedge$ is the minimum operator, and $f(x) = (1 + \exp(-x))^{-1}$ denotes the activation function of hidden units and output units of the proposed FNN.

The α-cut of fuzzy number is defined as

$$\tilde{X}[\alpha] = \left\{x \big| \tilde{X}(x) \geq \alpha, x \in \Re\right\},$$
$$\text{for } 0 < \alpha \leq 1, \quad (7)$$

where $\tilde{X}[\alpha] = \left[\tilde{X}[\alpha]^{L}, \tilde{X}[\alpha]^{U}\right]$, $\tilde{X}[\alpha]^{L}$ and $\tilde{X}[\alpha]^{U}$ are the lower boundary and the upper boundary of the α-cut set $\tilde{X}[\alpha]$.

FNN Learning Algorithm

The proposed FNN learning algorithm is similar to the EBP-type learning algorithm. Some as-

sumptions should be clarified before discussing the algorithm:

- Employing a three layer feed-forward neural network with n_I input units, n_H hidden units, and n_O output units where input vectors and output vectors are fuzzified.
- These fuzzy numbers are defined by triangular fuzzy numbers.

The input–output relation of the proposed FNN is defined by the extension principle and can be written as follows:

Input layer:

$$\tilde{O}_{pi}[\alpha] = \tilde{X}_{pi}[\alpha], \quad i = 1, 2, ..., n_I. \quad (8)$$

Hidden layer:

$$\tilde{O}_{ph}[\alpha] = f(\widetilde{Net}_{ph}[\alpha]), \quad h = 1, 2, ..., n_H. \quad (9)$$

$$\widetilde{Net}_{ph}[\alpha] = \sum_{i=1}^{n_I} W_{hi}[\alpha] \cdot \tilde{O}_{pi}[\alpha] + \Theta_h. \quad (10)$$

Output layer:

$$\tilde{O}_{pk}[\alpha] = f(\widetilde{Net}_{pk}[\alpha]), \quad k = 1, 2, ..., n_O. \quad (11)$$

$$\widetilde{Net}_{pk}[\alpha] = \sum_{h=1}^{n_H} \tilde{W}_h[\alpha] \cdot \tilde{O}_{ph}[\alpha] + \Theta_k. \quad (12)$$

From equations (8)–(12), Θ_h, Θ_k are fuzzy biases, and the α-cut sets of the fuzzy output $\tilde{O}_p$ are calculated from the α-cut sets of the fuzzy inputs. If the α-cut set of the fuzzy outputs $\tilde{O}_p$ is required, then the above relation can be rewritten as follows:

Input layer:

$$\tilde{O}_{pi}[\alpha] = \left[\tilde{O}_{pi}[\alpha]^{L}, \tilde{O}_{pi}[\alpha]^{U}\right]$$
$$= \left[\tilde{X}_{pi}[\alpha]^{L}, \tilde{X}_{pi}[\alpha]^{U}\right], \quad i = 1, 2, ..., n_I. \quad (13)$$

Hidden layer:

$$\tilde{O}_{ph}[\alpha] = \left[\tilde{O}_{ph}[\alpha]^{\mathrm{L}}, \tilde{O}_{ph}[\alpha]^{\mathrm{U}}\right]$$
$$= \left[f(\widetilde{Net}_{ph}[\alpha])^{\mathrm{L}}, f(\widetilde{Net}_{ph}[\alpha])^{\mathrm{U}}\right],$$
$$h = 1, 2, \ldots, n_{\mathrm{H}}. \tag{14}$$

$$\widetilde{Net}_{ph}[\alpha]^{\mathrm{L}} = \sum_{\substack{i=1 \\ W_{hi} \geq 0}}^{n_{\mathrm{I}}} W_{hi} \cdot \tilde{O}_{pi}[\alpha]^{\mathrm{L}}$$

$$+ \sum_{\substack{i=1 \\ W_{hi} < 0}}^{n_{\mathrm{I}}} W_{hi} \cdot \tilde{O}_{pi}[\alpha]^{\mathrm{U}} + \Theta_h. \tag{15}$$

$$\widetilde{Net}_{ph}[\alpha]^{\mathrm{U}} = \sum_{\substack{i=1 \\ W_{hi} \geq 0}}^{n_{\mathrm{I}}} W_{hi} \cdot \tilde{O}_{pi}[\alpha]^{\mathrm{U}}$$

$$+ \sum_{\substack{i=1 \\ W_{hi} < 0}}^{n_{\mathrm{I}}} W_{hi} \cdot \tilde{O}_{pi}[\alpha]^{\mathrm{L}} + \Theta_h. \tag{16}$$

Output layer:

$$\tilde{O}_{pk}[\alpha] = \left[\tilde{O}_{pk}[\alpha]^{\mathrm{L}}, \tilde{O}_{pk}[\alpha]^{\mathrm{U}}\right]$$
$$= \left[f(\widetilde{Net}_{pk}[\alpha])^{\mathrm{L}}, f(\widetilde{Net}_{pk}[\alpha])^{\mathrm{U}}\right],$$
$$k = 1, 2, \ldots, n_{\mathrm{O}}. \tag{17}$$

$$\widetilde{Net}_{pk}[\alpha]^{\mathrm{L}} = \sum_{\substack{h=1 \\ W_h \geq 0}}^{n_{\mathrm{H}}} W_h \cdot \tilde{O}_{ph}[\alpha]^{\mathrm{L}}$$

$$+ \sum_{\substack{h=1 \\ W_h < 0}}^{n_{\mathrm{H}}} W_h \cdot \tilde{O}_{ph}[\alpha]^{\mathrm{U}} + \Theta_k. \tag{18}$$

$$\widetilde{Net}_{pk}[\alpha]^{\mathrm{U}} = \sum_{\substack{h=1 \\ W_h \geq 0}}^{n_{\mathrm{H}}} W_h \cdot \tilde{O}_{ph}[\alpha]^{\mathrm{U}}$$

$$+ \sum_{\substack{h=1 \\ W_h < 0}}^{n_{\mathrm{H}}} W_h \cdot \tilde{O}_{ph}[\alpha]^{\mathrm{L}} + \Theta_k. \tag{19}$$

After above calculation, we define the n_{O}-dimensional fuzzy target vectors, $\tilde{T}_p = (\tilde{T}_{p1}, \tilde{T}_{p2}, \ldots, \tilde{T}_{pn_{\mathrm{O}}})$, corresponding to the fuzzy input vectors $\tilde{X}_p = \left(\tilde{X}_{p1}, \ldots, \tilde{X}_{pn_I}\right)$. The objective is to minimize the cost function defined as:

$$E_p = \sum_{\alpha} \sum_{k=1}^{n_{\mathrm{o}}} \alpha \cdot \left(E_{k(\alpha)}^{\mathrm{L}} + E_{k(\alpha)}^{\mathrm{U}}\right)$$
$$= \sum_{\alpha} E_{p(\alpha)}, \tag{20}$$

where

$$E_{p(\alpha)} = \sum_{k=1}^{n_{\mathrm{o}}} \alpha \cdot \left(E_{k(\alpha)}^{\mathrm{L}} + E_{k(\alpha)}^{\mathrm{U}}\right), \tag{21}$$

$$E_{k(\alpha)}^{\mathrm{L}} = \frac{(\tilde{T}_{pk}[\alpha]^{\mathrm{L}} - \tilde{O}_{pk}[\alpha]^{\mathrm{L}})^2}{2}$$

$$E_{k(\alpha)}^{\mathrm{U}} = \frac{(\tilde{T}_{pk}[\alpha]^{\mathrm{U}} - \tilde{O}_{pk}[\alpha]^{\mathrm{U}})^2}{2}. \tag{22}$$

The $E_{k(\alpha)}^{\mathrm{U}}$ and $E_{k(\alpha)}^{\mathrm{L}}$ can be viewed as the squared errors for the upper boundaries and lower boundaries of the α-cut set.

Therefore, each weight is updated in a similar way from the approach of Ishibuchi et al. (1993). The gradient search method is derived for each parameter. It is the amount of adjustment for each parameter using the cost function $E_{p(\alpha)}$ as follows:

$$\Delta W_h(t+1) = -\eta \frac{\partial E_{p(\alpha)}}{\partial W_h} + \beta \Delta W_h(t), \tag{23}$$

$$\Delta W_{hi}(t+1) = -\eta \frac{\partial E_{p(\alpha)}}{\partial W_{hi}} + \beta \Delta W_{hi}(t), \tag{24}$$

where t indexes the epoch number, and η and β are a learning rate and a momentum constant, respectively. We can train a neural network for several values of α by using the cost function. If the sum of cost functions over all the given fuzzy vectors becomes very small of learning, the α-cut sets of the given fuzzy vectors can be correctly classified using the trained neural network.

A META-HEURISTIC ALGORITHM FOR GLOBAL OPTIMIZATION – THE ELECTROMAGNETISM-LIKE MECHANISM (EM)

In the last decades, variously novel meta-heuristic algorithms for global optimization have been proposed. Such meta-heuristic algorithms are inspired by careful observations of natural phenomena and some of them are developed simply by implementing practical ideas. In this section, we study some famous and potential meta-heuristic algorithms for global search.

In the early 1970s, John Holland, one of the founders of evolutionary computation, introduced the concepts of the genetic algorithms (evolutionary algorithms) (Holland, 1975). The Genetic Algorithms (GAs) are derivation-free stochastic optimization methods based on the concepts of nature selection and evolutionary process. They work by repeatedly modifying a population of artificial structures through the application of genetic operators and need only fitness information instead of gradient information. The Genetic Algorithms have recently become popular global optimization techniques, specifically in combinatorial optimization (Goldberg, 1989). Besides, in optimization applications, they have been used in many fields such as function optimization, image processing, traveling salesman problem, system identification, and control system. In machine learning, genetic algorithms have been used to learn syntactically simple string the IF-THEN rules in an arbitrary environment. Excellent references on Gas and their implement and application are in (Davis, 1991; Goldberg, 1989; Michalewicz, 1994).

The genetic algorithms operate on the potential solutions (also called chromosome) to problems. The conception of fitness is used in GA to measure the "adaptation" of a candidate solution (chromosome). The genetic operators of selection, crossover, and mutation are repeatedly applied to the population to increase the fitness of chromosomes (Goldberg, 1989; Michalewicz, 1994).

The inquiry for robust search has made genetic algorithms become fundamentally different from classical algorithms. The differences are based on four principles (Goldberg, 1989).

- GAs use a coded representation of the parameters, not the parameters themselves.
- GAs search from a population of solution vectors, not a single solution vector.
- GAs exclusively use values of the function under study, and do not consider auxiliary information, such as the derivative.
- GAs use probabilistic transition rules, not deterministic rules.

From the above discussion, it can be seen that evolutionary algorithms such as GAs differ substantially from more traditional search and optimization methods. The most significant differences are:

- GAs search a population of points in parallel, not a single point.
- GAs do not require derivative information or other auxiliary knowledge; only the objective function and corresponding fitness levels influence the directions of search.
- GAs use probabilistic transition rules, not deterministic ones.
- GAs are generally more straightforward to apply.
- GAs can provide a number of potential solutions to a given problem. The final choice is left to the user.

The idea of network optimization using genetic algorithms during the training process is quite popular (Alpaydin et al., 2002; Devert et al., 2002; Mandischer, 2002). Methods using GA to modify the weight of neural network connections are usually considered as less efficient and more computing-intensive than those based on gradient back propagation algorithm. Furthermore, Aliev et al. (2001) have proposed a genetic algorithm-based learning mechanism for adjusting fuzzy weights expressed as LR-type fuzzy numbers of fuzzy neural networks with fuzzy inputs and outputs. This method differed from the existing approaches by the following. The proposed method does not require differentiability of error performance index of the FNN. The derived algorithm for learning FNN was not crisp. The proposed mechanism based on the GA was more likely to locate the global minimum of error performance of the FNN than the existing algorithms, mainly based on α-cuts which sometimes may fail.

The Simulated Annealing (SA) is a stochastic single-point search technique, which has been applied successfully in various optimization fields. The SA guides the search by specifying a cooling scheme that allows the acceptance of randomly generated neighbor solutions which are relatively unfavorable as compared with the current solution (Kirkpatrick et al., 1983; Laarhoven and Aarts, 1987). Using the latter feature, the SA aims to get away trapping at local optima. The temperature described by the cooling scheme is reduced as the search makes progress so that the search is intensified around the global optimum.

The first influential work on the Tabu Search (TS) was published in late 1980's by Glover (1986). The Tabu Search is an iterative scheme, which is based on moving from one point to a neighborhood point in single iteration. Throughout this search, main idea is to keep track of not only the local information but also some information related to the exploration process. This scheme requires a systematic handling of Tabu lists, which hold the history of moves and prevents them to be revisited. Though no rigorous convergence proof has been shown, many successful applications of the Tabu Search are reported (Glover and Laguna, 1997).

The Electromagnetism-like Mechanism (EM), a new meta-heuristic algorithm for global optimization, was developed by Birbil and Fang (2003). The EM algorithm utilizes the attraction-repulsion mechanism of the electrically charges toward the optimality. EM converges rapidly to optimum when the number of function evaluations is used as a performance measure without using the first or second order information. The EM can be used as a stand-alone approach or as an accompanying algorithm for other methods.

The EM algorithm has a mechanism that encourages the points to converge to the highly attractive valleys, and contrarily, discourages the points to move further away from steeper hills. This idea is similar to the attraction–repulsion mechanism of the electromagnetism theory. In the approach, the charge of each point relates to the objective function value, which we are trying to optimize. The principle of superposition states that the electromagnetic force on a charged particle caused by any number of other particles can be calculated by adding together vectorially the forces from each of the other particles calculated separately. The points observing better objective values would signal the other points to converge to the global or local minimums. In the algorithm, each sample point is treated like a charged particle. This charge basically determines the magnitude of attraction or repulsion of the point over the population. The attraction directs the points towards better regions, whereas repulsion allows particles to exploit the unvisited regions.

General Scheme

We apply the algorithm to the optimization problems with bounded variables of the form:

$$\min f(x) \; s.t. \; x \in S \tag{25}$$

where $S=\{x \in R^n | l_k \leq x_k \leq u_k; l_k, u_k \in R, k=1,2,\dots n\}$, and the parameters are defined as:

n: dimension of the problem,

u_k : upper bound in the kth dimension,

l_k : lower bound in the kth dimension,

$f(x)$: pointer to the function that is minimized, respectively.

In the general scheme of the EM (Table 1), x^i is used to specify the ith point of the population. There are two points in the population that are indexed separately. The free particle, namely the perturbed point is denoted by x^p and the point has the best objective function value in the current iteration (i.e., tile current best point) is indicated by x^{best}. The heuristic electromagnetism algorithm consists of four phases.

In this algorithm, there are four procedures: "Initialization", "Local search", "Total force calculation", and "Move along the total force". "Initialization" is used to sample m points from the feasible region. A typical way for initialization is sampling the points from the feasible region uniformly. The next procedure, "Local search", is used to search around the neighborhood information to get better solutions. The major procedures of the EM algorithm are the "Total force calculation" and "Move along the total force" procedures. The "Total force calculation" procedure is used for calculating the total force exerted on each point, whereas "Move along the total force" procedure is used for moving the sample points along the direction of the total force (Yang, 2002).

Initialization

"Initialize" is used to randomize m sample points from the feasible domain, which is a n dimensional hyper-cube. Each coordinate of a point is assumed to be uniformly distributed between the corresponding upper bound and lower bound. After a point is sampled from the space, the objective function value for the point is calculated using the function pointer $f(x)$. The procedure ends with m points identified, and the point that has the best function value is stored in x^{best}. The words *particle* and *point* are interchangeably used (Birbil and Fang, 2003).

Initialization ()

1: **for** $i = 1$ to m **do**

2:     **for** $k = 1$ to n **do**

3:         $\lambda \leftarrow U(0, 1)$

4: ($x_k^i \leftarrow l_k + \lambda\, u_k - l_k$)

5:     **end for**

6:     Calculate $f(x^i)$

7: **end for**

8: $x^{best} \leftarrow \mathrm{argmin}\{ f(x^i), \forall i\}$

Table 1. General scheme of the EM

ALGORITHM EM (m, *MAXITER*, *LSITER*, δ)
m: number of sample points
MAXITER: maximum number of iterations
LSITER: maximum number of local search iterations
δ: local search parameter, $\delta \in [0,1]$
1. Initialization ()
2. iteration $\leftarrow 1$
3. **while** (iteration< *MAXITER*) **do**
4. Local Search (*LSITER*, δ)
5. **F** $\leftarrow$ Calculation of Total Force Vector_CalcF()
6. Movement (**F**)
7. iteration $\leftarrow$ iteration +1
8. end **while**

Local Search

"Local search" is applied to gather the neighborhood information for each sample point. In this procedure, a new feasible point y is moved along the direction of a sample point x^i within the maximum feasible random step length $\delta \in [0,1]$. If the new point y observes a better point in fixed iterations, the sample point x^i is replaced by this new point y. And the neighborhood search ends. Hence the current best point is updated. This is a simple random line search algorithm that is applied to each coordinate. This procedure does not require any gradient information to perform the local search that is different from other local search methods (Birbil and Fang, 2003).

Local Search (*LSITER*, δ)

1: counter $\leftarrow 1$

2: Length $\leftarrow \delta(\max_k \{u_k - l_k\})$

3: **for** $i = 1$ to m **do**

4:    **for** $k = 1$ to n **do**

5:       $\lambda_1 \leftarrow U(0, 1)$

6:       **while** counter $<$ *LSITER* **do**

7:          $y \leftarrow x_i$

8:          $\lambda_2 \leftarrow U(0, 1)$

9:          **if** $\lambda_1 > 0.5$ **then**

10:            $y_k \leftarrow y_k + \lambda_2 (\text{Length})$

11:          **else**

12:            $y_k \leftarrow y_k - \lambda_2 (\text{Length})$

13:          **end if**

14:          **if** $f(y) < f(x^i)$ **then**

15:            $x^i \leftarrow y$

16:            counter $\leftarrow$ *LSITER* $- 1$

17:          **end if**

18:          counter $\leftarrow$ counter $+ 1$

19:       **end while**

20:    **end for**

21: **end for**

22: $x^{\text{best}} \leftarrow \text{argmin}\{ f(x^i), \forall\} i$

Calculation of Total Force Vector

The total force on each particle is calculated in spirit of the Coulomb's Law. The charge of each point, q^i, determines its power of attraction or repulsion. This charge is evaluated by using the objective function value of the point, x^i, relative to the objective function value of the current best point (Birbil and Fang, 2003).

$$q^i = \exp\left[-n \times \frac{f(x^i) - f(x^{best})}{\sum_{k=1}^{m}\left[f(x^k) - f(x^{best})\right]} \right],$$
$$i = 1, 2, \cdots m. \tag{26}$$

After determining the charge of each point on x^i, the total force F^i is calculated by the equation below:

$$F^i = \begin{cases} \sum_{j\neq i}^{m}(x^j - x^i)\cdot \dfrac{q^i q^j}{\| x^j - x^i\|^2}, & if \ f(x^j) < f(x^i) \\ \sum_{j\neq i}^{m}(x^i - x^j)\cdot \dfrac{q^i q^j}{\| x^j - x^i\|^2}, & if \ f(x^j) \le f(x^i) \end{cases}, \forall i. \tag{27}$$

Calculation of Total Force Vector _CalcF()

1: **for** i = 1 to m **do**

2:    $q^i \leftarrow \exp\left[-n\dfrac{f(x^i) - f(x^{\text{best}})}{\sum_{k=1}^{m}\left(f(x^k) - f(x^{\text{best}})\right)} \right]$

3:    $F^i \leftarrow 0$

4: **end for**

5: **for** i = 1 to m **do**

6:    **for** j = 1 to m **do**

7:       **if** $f(x^j) < f(x^i)$ **then**

8:          $F^i \leftarrow F^i + (x^j - x^i)\dfrac{q^i q^j}{\|x^j - x^i\|^2}$ {Attraction}

9:       **else**

10:          $F^i \leftarrow F^i - (x^j - x^i)\dfrac{q^i q^j}{\|x^j - x^i\|^2}$ {Repulsion}

11:       **end if**

12:    **end for**

13: **end for**

Movement According to Total Force Vector

After evaluating the total force F^i, the point is moved towards the direction of the force by a random step length as given in Eq. (28). We select the step length randomly because we want to incorporate a diversification effect to the algorithm. In the equation, λ is the random step length, which is uniformly distributed between 0 and 1. The *RNG* is a vector whose components denote the allowed feasible movement towards the current upper bound, u^k, or the lower bound, l^k, for the corresponding dimension (Birbil and Fang, 2003).

$$x^i = x^i + \lambda \frac{F^i}{\left\|F^i\right\|}(RNG), i = 1, 2, \cdots m. \quad (28)$$

Movement(F)

```
1: for i = 1 to m do
2:     if i ≠ best then
3:         λ ← U (0, 1)
4:         F^i ← F^i / ‖F^i‖
5:         for k = 1 to n do
6:             if F_k^i > 0 then
7:                 x_k^i ← x_k^i + λ F_k^i(u_k − x_k^i)
8:             else
9:                 x_k^i ← x_k^i + λ F_k^i(x_k^i − l_k)
10:            end if
11:        end for
12:    end if
13: end for
```

THEORETICAL STUDY OF THE EM

Bribil et al. (2005) had investigated the theoretical structure of EM. After reviewing the original method, the authors presented some necessary modifications for the convergence proof. They showed that in the limit, the modified method converged to the vicinity of global optimum with probability one. In their paper, a convergence property of the recently proposed electromagnetism-like method, (EM) had been studied. Their main task had been showed that when the number of iterations is large enough, one of the points in the current population moves into the ε-neighborhood of the global optimum. In order to achieve this result, they had given a detailed mathematical construction, which could be easily applied to some of the other population-based stochastic search algorithms. The derivations of the convergence proof for the EM algorithm can be found at Bribil et al. (2005).

ELECTROMAGNETISM-LIKE MECHANISM BASED FUZZY NEURAL NETWORK (EMFNN)

By incorporating the electromagnetism-like mechanism, we now have our fuzzy neural network learning algorithm that is so-called the electromagnetism-like based fuzzy neural network mechanism (EMFNN) as following:

- *Step 1*: Initialize the connected weights of fuzzy neural network randomly through the EM, there are n dimensional hypercube if the neural network with n connected weights.
- *Step 2*: Evaluating each point in the population in terms of fitness value using E_p.
- *Step 3*: If termination conditions are met, go to step 7.
- *Step 4*: The procedure of local search is used to find a better point in the neighborhood. If the new point y observes a better point in fixed iterations, the sample point x^i is replaced by this new point y. And the neighborhood search ends. Hence the current best point is updated.

- *Step 5*: This charge is evaluated by using the objective function value of the point, x^i, relative to the objective function value of the current best point. After determining the charge of each point on x^i, the total force F^i is calculated.

- *Step 6*: After evaluating the total force F^i, the point is moved towards the direction of the force by a random step length. Return to step 2.

- *Step 7*: Stop, return the best point and translate it into the weights of the FNN. This iterative process leads to the improved performance of candidate set of weights.

COMPUTATIONAL RESULTS

In this section, we demonstrate the learning algorithms of conventional fuzzy neural network (FNN) and electromagnetism-like mechanism based fuzzy neural network (EMFNN) by computer simulation on two examples that were studied by Ishibuchi et al. (1995). We evaluate the simulation results of the conventional FNN and EMFNN by two cases, and the parameter designs are also illustrated.

Example One

We first apply both the conventional FNN and EMFNN to the approximate realization of the nonlinear mapping of fuzzy numbers. The fuzzy numbers used in the thesis are triangular fuzzy numbers. The training patterns of example one is shown in Figure 1.

We use a three layers fuzzy neural network with single input node, five hidden nodes and single output node for the conventional FNN and EMFNN training. The training patterns with five α-cut levels are shown in Figure 1. After the simulation, Figure 2 illustrates fuzzy outputs from the trained FNN and EMFNN with three training patterns and two new fuzzy inputs, respectively. We can find that the EMFNN get better generalization for the new fuzzy inputs as well as good fitting to the fuzzy training data from the comparison with Figure 1 and Figure 2.

Example Two

In example two, we will try to learn the fuzzy IF-THEN rules with one precondition variables (X) and one consequence variable (Y) through the conventional FNN and EMFNN. Let us assumed that the following three fuzzy IF-THEN rules are given:

Figure 1. Training patterns of example one

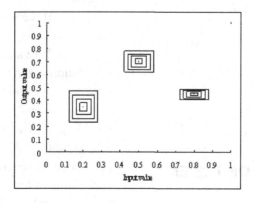

Figure 2. Fuzzy outputs from the trained FNN and EMFNN in example one

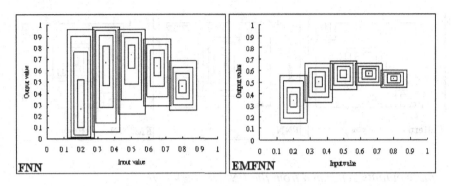

- If *X* is *small*, then *Y* is *small*.
- If *X* is *medium*, then *Y* is *medium*.
- If *X* is *large*, then *Y* is *large*.

The membership function of linguistic values such as "*small*", "*medium*", "*large*" are shown in Figure 3, where **S** represents "*small*", **MS** represents "*medium small*", **M** represents "*medium*", **ML** represents "*medium large*", and **L** represents "*large*", respectively.

We use the training patterns with five *α*-cut levels, then train the conventional FNN and EMFNN with single input node, five hidden nodes and single output node. Figure 4 represent the training patterns and fuzzy outputs from the trained FNN and EMFNN. According to Figure 4,

we can note the EMFNN has better fitting to the training data. Besides, we apply the conventional FNN and EMFNN for learning two new fuzzy inputs "medium small" and "medium large", we can also find the good generated new fuzzy inputs of the EMFNN (see Figure 5).

Figure 5 shows the two fuzzy inputs can be linguistically explained as "*medium small*" and "*medium large*", and the EMFNN have better generated new fuzzy inputs. Consequently, we can obtain two new fuzzy IF-THEN rules:

- If *X* is *medium small*, THEN *Y* is *medium small*.
- If *X* is *medium large*, THEN *Y* is *medium large*.

Figure 3. Membership functions of five linguistic values

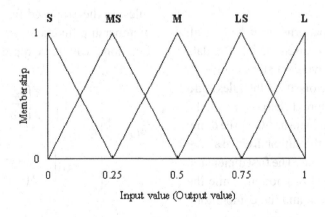

Figure 4. Fuzzy training patterns and trained fuzzy outputs of the FNN and EMFNN

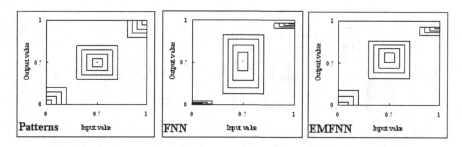

Figure 5. New fuzzy outputs generated from the FNN and EMFNN

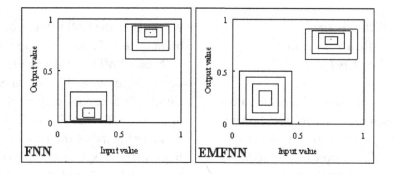

According to the above two examples, we can observe that the trained EMFNN have good capability for learning the fuzzy IF-THEN rules in our illustrated examples. Therefore, we will apply the conventional FNN and EMFNN for learning the fuzzy IF-THEN rules on a sales forecasting case.

Sales Forecasting Case

We quote the training patterns form Kuo et al. (2000) for testing our proposed model. The data are collected form a convenient store company. Because of numerous factors affect the sales and a different product has different characteristics, the discussion and analysis of data needed to be done. After the previous work, the author divided all the factors into three dimensions. The first dimension represents the methods of promotion, while the types of advertising media and the competitors'

actions are presented in the second and third dimension, respectively. Table 2 presents the fuzzy number of each event from Kuo et al. (2000). According to Table 2, we have 42 (3 × 7 × 2) fuzzy IF-THEN rules for training the conventional FNN and EMFNN as presented in Table 3. The network topology with three inputs (three dimensions) and one output that representing the promotion effect on sales is utilized for learning the fuzzy IF-THEN rules. In the proposed fuzzy IF-THEN rules, the membership functions are asymmetric Gaussian functions, which are represented as:

$$\tilde{A}(x) = \begin{cases} \exp\left(-\frac{1}{2}\left(\frac{x-\mu}{\sigma^L}\right)\right) & x < \mu, \\ 1, & x = \mu, \\ \exp\left(-\frac{1}{2}\left(\frac{x-\mu}{\sigma^U}\right)\right) & \text{otherwise.} \end{cases}$$

(29)

Thus, the asymmetric Gaussian fuzzy numbers are specified by their three parameters (i.e., center (μ), right width (σ^U) and left width(σ^L)). Figure 6 shows the asymmetric Gaussian functions.

We apply the two proposed methods to train the fuzzy IF-THEN rules. In order to analyze the effects of these parameters, we select several parameters of the conventional FNN and EMFNN for implementing the following experiments.

Experiment 1

In order to determine the best network topology, we implement two experiments for the conventional FNN and EMFNN. In experiment 1, the conventional FNN and EMFNN have been implemented 2000 and 100 epochs. The purpose of experiment 1 is desirable to know how many hidden nodes will construct the best network topology. And the simulation results (Mean Square Error, MSE) of experiment 1 for the conventional FNN and EMFNN are presented in Table 4.

According to Table 4, we calculate the average error of each hidden nodes level, and decide the number of hidden nodes of the conventional FNN and EMFNN. After that, we execute experiment 2 for the purpose of determine best parameter setup.

Experiment 2

In the example 2, the conventional FNN with three hidden nodes and the EMFNN with nine hidden nodes have been implemented, respectively. The designed parameters of experiment 2 and the simulation results are as shown in Table 5. According to Table 5, we can observe the network error decrease if training epochs reduce and the training results of the EMFNN is better than those of the conventional FNN after the comparison of network error. In this section, we discuss the factors of the EMFNN that impact the network error, and we would like to inquire the relationship among the number of sample points (m), local search iterations (LS) and step length parameter (δ). The levels of factors were selected with local search iterations (LS = 2, 4), sample points (m = 25, 50) and step length parameter (δ = 0.01, 0.1, 1). According to

Table 2. Fuzzy numbers of each event

Factors	Events	$\sigma^L = \dfrac{l-\mu}{3}$	Average(μ)	$\sigma^u = \dfrac{u-\mu}{3}$
Promotion methods	10 dollars discount	0.2000	8.6000	0.2333
	5 dollars discount	0.2333	4.9000	0.3000
	Buy 2 get 1 free	0.2000	6.8000	0.3000
Advertising media	At night on TV	0.2667	7.6000	0.3000
	At noon on TV	0.1667	2.5000	0.3333
	In the evening on TV	0.1333	3.1000	0.4667
	Radio	0.2667	4.5000	0.4000
	Newspaper	0.1667	3.8000	0.5000
	POP notice	0.1000	6.5000	0.4333
	Poster	0.2000	6.6000	0.3000
Competitor's action	Related products without promotion	0.2000	7.6000	0.4000
	Related products with promotion	0.1000	4.5000	0.3333

Table 3. The fuzzy IF-THEN rules of sales forecasting events

		IF			THEN	
		Fuzzy number			Fuzzy number	
	Promotion	Media	Competitor	Left σ ^{L}	μ	Right σ ^{U}
1	10 dollars discount	At night on TV	No	0.2000	7.8000	0.2667
2	10 dollars discount	At noon on TV	No	0.0333	2.1000	0.5667
3	10 dollars discount	In the evening on TV	No	0.1000	3.9000	0.4333
4	10 dollars discount	Radio	No	0.2000	4.6000	0.2667
5	10 dollars discount	Newspaper	No	0.2333	5.5000	0.3000
6	10 dollars discount	POP notice	No	0.2000	7.0000	0.3333
7	10 dollars discount	Poster	No	0.1000	6.5000	0.3000
8	5 dollars discount	At night on TV	No	0.2000	6.0000	0.4000
9	5 dollars discount	At noon on TV	No	0.0333	1.1000	0.3000
10	5 dollars discount	In the evening on TV	No	0.1000	3.3000	0.3667
11	5 dollars discount	Radio	No	0.1333	3.4000	0.3333
12	5 dollars discount	Newspaper	No	0.2000	4.2000	0.3333
13	5 dollars discount	POP notice	No	0.1333	5.0000	0.4000
14	5 dollars discount	Poster	No	0.1000	5.3000	0.3000
15	Buy 2 get 1 free	At night on TV	No	0.2333	7.3000	0.3000
16	Buy 2 get 1 free	At noon on TV	No	0.0000	3.2000	0.4667
17	Buy 2 get 1 free	In the evening on TV	No	0.0333	3.7000	0.4333
18	Buy 2 get 1 free	Radio	No	0.2000	5.2000	0.3333
19	Buy 2 get 1 free	Newspaper	No	0.2000	5.4000	0.3333
20	Buy 2 get 1 free	POP notice	No	0.2333	6.5000	0.3000
21	Buy 2 get 1 free	Poster	No	0.2000	6.6000	0.2667
22	10 dollars discount	At night on TV	Yes	0.2333	7.7000	0.3000
23	10 dollars discount	At noon on TV	Yes	0.1000	3.7000	0.3667
24	10 dollars discount	In the evening on TV	Yes	0.1000	4.1000	0.4333
25	10 dollars discount	Radio	Yes	0.2000	4.8000	0.2667
26	10 dollars discount	Newspaper	Yes	0.2333	5.7000	0.3000
27	10 dollars discount	POP notice	Yes	0.2333	6.1000	0.3667
28	10 dollars discount	Poster	Yes	0.2000	7.1000	0.2333
29	5 dollars discount	At night on TV	Yes	0.2000	5.8000	0.4000
30	5 dollars discount	At noon on TV	Yes	0.0000	2.4000	0.4000
31	5 dollars discount	In the evening on TV	Yes	0.0333	2.1000	0.4333
32	5 dollars discount	Radio	Yes	0.1333	3.4000	0.3333
33	5 dollars discount	Newspaper	Yes	0.1333	4.4000	0.4000
34	5 dollars discount	POP notice	Yes	0.1000	4.7000	0.3667
35	5 dollars discount	Poster	Yes	0.1667	6.0000	0.3333
36	Buy 2 get 1 free	At night on TV	Yes	0.2000	6.8000	0.2667
37	Buy 2 get 1 free	At noon on TV	Yes	0.1000	3.5000	0.3667

continued on next page

Table 3. continued

38	Buy 2 get 1 free	In the evening on TV	Yes	0.1000	3.5000	0.3667
39	Buy 2 get 1 free	Radio	Yes	0.1000	4.6000	0.4000
40	Buy 2 get 1 free	Newspaper	Yes	0.1000	4.5000	0.3667
41	Buy 2 get 1 free	POP notice	Yes	0.2000	6.2000	0.2667
42	Buy 2 get 1 free	Poster	Yes	0.2000	7.1000	0.2333

Figure 6. Asymmetric Gaussian functions

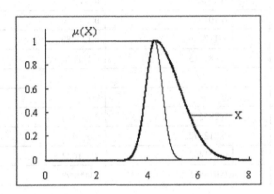

Table 4. Simulation results of FNN and EMFNN for experiment 1

FNN			Hidden nodes		
η	β		3	5	7
0.3	0.7		0.134276	0.138658	0.143546
0.7	0.3		0.100977	0.134618	0.141929
Avg. Error			0.091620	0.117626	0.136638
EMFNN			Hidden nodes		
m	LS		5	7	9
50	7		0.009063	0.008715	0.008914
100	3		0.011198	0.011459	0.010275
Avg. Error			0.021524	0.010131	0.010087

the simulation results, we implement an Analysis of Variance for the EMFNN (see Table 6).

From the analysis of variance that shown in Table 6, we can obviously find that the main effect of the sample points (m) is significant. Besides, there are no significant interactions among local search iterations (LS), sample points (m) and step length parameter (δ). Furthermore, the main ef-fect of local search iterations (LS) and step length parameter (δ) are not significant and we could also observe there is a significant effect on step length parameter between 0.01 and 0.1.

Table 5. Simulation results of the FNN and EMFNN for experiment 2

FNN			Epochs		
η	β		2000	4000	8000
	0.1		0.091137	0.113212	0.113749
0.1	0.5		0.121449	0.117693	0.120290
	0.9		0.102550	0.117908	0.126531
	0.1		0.114394	0.119166	0.122908
0.5	0.5		0.109345	0.119061	0.130512
	0.9		0.127069	0.143546	0.143546
	0.1		0.101322	0.129350	0.143036
0.9	0.5		0.117356	0.127089	0.145345
	0.9		0.081115	0.111160	0.109816
EMFNN			δ		
LS	m		0.01	0.1	1
2	25		0.285559	0.126384	0.014919
	50		0.012774	0.011418	0.013369
4	25		0.321435	0.011622	0.014663
	50		0.013475	0.009090	0.013409

Table 6. Analysis of variance for network error of the EMFNN

Source of Variation		Sum of Squares	D.F.	Mean square	F_0	F*
δ		0.0473829	2	0.0236914	15.96	19.000
LS		0.0005431	1	0.0005431	0.37	18.513
m		0.0409557	1	0.0409557	27.59 *	18.513
δ * LS		0.0032189	2	0.0016094	1.08	19.000
LS * m		0.0005012	1	0.0005012	0.34	18.513
δ * m		0.0468140	2	0.0234070	15.77	19.000
Error		0.0029685	2	0.0014842		
Total		0.1423842	11			

Summary

After the computer simulations of examples and cases, we can conclude that the training results and learning capability of our proposed EMFNN are better than those of the conventional fuzzy neural network (FNN) in the illustrated two examples and cases. And we also discovered that the step length parameter (δ) and sample points (m) are two important factors of the EMFNN for decreasing the network error. In other words, we can realize that when we run the EMFNN with suitable step length parameter (δ) or when we increase the number of points in the population, the chance of finding the best network topology increases.

CONCLUSION AND FUTURE RESEARCH DIRECTIONS

In this chapter, we have studied a novel meta-heuristic algorithm, the Electromagnetism-like Mechanism (EM) (Birbil and Fang, 2003), for global optimization. The method imitates the behavior of electrically charged particles where a set of points in the population corresponding to a set of charged particles. The strength of the method lies in the idea of directing sample points toward local optimizers, which point out attractive regions of the feasible space. Without using the higher order information, the EM algorithm has converged rapidly (in terms of the number of function evaluations) to the global optimum and produced highly efficient results for problems of varying degree of difficulty.

Since the EM algorithm is a new method for global optimization, the applications of the algorithm are not many. Although there were some studies proposed several learning algorithms for fuzzy neural network training (for example: delta learning rule, genetic algorithm etc.), the electromagnetism-like mechanism for fuzzy neural network training was first proposed by the authors of this article. In this article, we also studied the architecture and learning algorithm of conventional fuzzy neural network. In order to evaluate the training results of the electromagnetism-like mechanism for the fuzzy neural network training, we have established two systems for the conventional FNN and EMFNN in C++ codes, and the comparisons between two fuzzy neural network architectures have also been done by two simple examples and a sales forecasting case.

From the simulation results of the performance measures, we have collected the following conclusions:

- The number of training epochs of EMFNN is less than the conventional FNN.
- According to the examples, we could find the EMFNN have better learning capability than FNN, and it can also successfully generalize new fuzzy IF-THEN rules.
- For our case, the parameters of the number of sample points (m) and the step length (δ) are main factors of EMFNN for decreasing the network error.
- When we run the EMFNN with suitable step length parameter (δ) or when we increase the number of points in the population the chance of finding the best network topology increases.
- The main effect of the parameters of step length and sample points are much significant than that of local search iterations in our cases.
- For other difficult cases, the parameters of the step length and sample points should be increased.
- Besides, it should be noticed that if the parameters of the sample points, the number of local search iterations and the range of weights increase, the search time would also increase.

The potential future research directions are described as following:

- In future works, more real world problems could be applied for the EMFNN training, and the parameter design for performance measures could be carried out carefully.
- Applying the EM algorithm for other architectures of the fuzzy neural network training.
- The comparisons of the EMFNN and other meta-heuristic algorithms based fuzzy neural network could be implemented.
- Since the EM algorithm converges rapidly to optimum when the number of function evaluations is used as a performance measure without using the first or second order information, the further research will be pursued on using the first or second order

information of the functions instead of Local Search procedure.

REFERENCES

Aliev, R. A., Fazlollahi, B., & Vahidov, R. M. (2001). Genetic algorithm- based learning of fuzzy neural networks. Part 1: Feed-forward fFuzzy neural networks. *Fuzzy Sets and Systems, 118*, 351–358. doi:10.1016/S0165-0114(98)00461-8

Alpaydin, G., Dundar, G., & Balkir, S. (2002). Evolution-based design of fuzzy networks using self-adapting genetic parameters. *IEEE transactions on Fuzzy Systems, 10*(2), 211–221. doi:10.1109/91.995122

Baker, J. E. (1985). Adaptive selection methods for genetic algorithms. In *Proceedings of an International Conference on Genetic Algorithms and their Application (pp.* 101–111). Hillsdale, NJ: Lawrence Erlbaum Associates.

Birbil, S. I., Fang, S., & Sheu, R. (2005). On the convergence of a population-based global optimization algorithm. *Journal of Global Optimization, 30*, 301–318. doi:10.1007/s10898-004-8270-3

Birbil, S. I., & Fang, S. C. (2003). Electromagnetism- like mechanism for global optimization. *Journal of Global Optimization, 25*, 263–282. doi:10.1023/A:1022452626305

Buckley, J. J., & Hayashi, Y. (1992). Fuzzy neural nets and applications. *Fuzzy Systems and AI, 3*, 11–41.

Buckley, J. J., & Hayashi, Y. (1994). Fuzzy neural networks. In R. Yager, L. Zadeh (Eds.), Fuzzy Sets, Neural Networks, and Soft Computing. New York: Van Nostrand Reinhold.

Buckley, J. J., Reilly, K. D., & Penmetcha, K. V. (1996). "Backpropagation and genetic algorithms for training fuzzy neural nets", *IEEE International Conference on Fuzzy Systems, 1*, 2–6.

Davis, L. (1991). Handbook of Genetic Algorithms. New York: Van Nostrand Reinhold.

Debels, D., Reyck, B. D., Leus, R., & Vanhoucke, M. (2006). A hybrid scatter search/electromagnetism meta-heuristic for project scheduling. *European Journal of Operational Research, 169*, 638–653. doi:10.1016/j.ejor.2004.08.020

Devert, W., Mateen, M. R., & Louis, A. T. (2002). E-Net: Evolutionary neural network synthesis. *Neurocomputing, 42*, 171–196. doi:10.1016/S0925-2312(01)00599-9

Emmeche, C. (1994). Garden in the Machine: The Emerging Science of Artificial Life. Princeton, NJ: Princeton University Press.

Fogel, D. B. (1994). Applying evolutionary programming to selected control problems. *Computers & Mathematics with Applications (Oxford, England), 11*(27), 89–104. doi:10.1016/0898-1221(94)90100-7

Fukuda, T., & Shibata, T. (1992). Hierarchical intelligent control for robotic motion by using fuzzy. artificial intelligence. and neural network. In . *Proceedings of IJCNN, 92*, I-269–I-274.

Glover, F. (1986). Future paths for integer programming and links to artificial intelligence. *Computers & Operations Research, 13*, 533–549. doi:10.1016/0305-0548(86)90048-1

Glover, F., & Laguna, M. (1997). Tabu Search. Dordrecht, The Netherlands: Kluwer Academic Publishers.

Goldberg, D. E. (1989). Genetic Algorithms in Search, Optimization, and Machine Learning. Reading, MA: Addison-Wesley.

Gupta, M. M., & Knopf, G. K. (1990). Fuzzy neural network approach to control systems. In *Proceedings of the First International Symposium on Uncertainty Modeling and Analysis*, (pp. 483–488).

Gupta, M. M., & Qi, J. (1991). On fuzzy neuron models. In . *Proceedings of International Joint Conference on Neural Networks, II,* 4312–4436.

Hayashi, Y., Buckley, J. J., & Czogula, E. (1993). Fuzzy neural network. *International Journal of Intelligent Systems, 8,* 527–537. doi:10.1002/int.4550080405

Holland, J. H. (1975). Adaptation in Natural and Artificial System. Ann Arbor, MI: The University of Michigan Press.

Ishibuchi, H., Fujioka, R., & Tanaka, H. (1992). An architecture of neural networks for input vectors of fuzzy numbers. In *Proc. IEEE Int. Conf. Fuzzy Syst. (FUZZ-IEEE'92),* (pp. 1293–1300).

Ishibuchi, H., Kwon, K., & Tanaka, H. (1995). A learning algorithm of fuzzy neural networks with triangular fuzzy weights. *Fuzzy Sets and Systems, 71,* 277–293. doi:10.1016/0165-0114(94)00281-B

Ishibuchi, H., Okada, H., Fujioka, R., & Tanaka, H. (1993). Neural networks that learn from fuzzy If-Then rules. *IEEE transactions on Fuzzy Systems, FS-1*(2), 85–89. doi:10.1109/91.227388

Ishibuchi, H., & Tanaka, H. (1991). Regression analysis with interval model by neural networks. In Proc. Int. Joint Conf. Neural Networks (IJCNN'91-Singapore), (pp. 1594–1599).

Jang, J.-S. R. (1991). Fuzzy modeling using generalized neural networks and Kalman Filter algorithm. In *Proceedings of Ninth National Conference on Artificial Intelligence,* (pp. 762–767).

Jang, J.-S. R. (1992). Fuzzy controller design without domain expert. *IEEE International Conference on Fuzzy Systems,* (pp. 289–296).

Jang, J.-S. R., & Sun, C.-T. (1993). Functional equivalence between radial basic function networks and fuzzy inference systems. *IEEE Transactions on Neural Networks, 4*(1), 156–159. doi:10.1109/72.182710

Kirkpatrick, A., Gelatt, A. K. C. J., & Vechi, M. P. (1983). Optimization by simulated annealing. *Science, 220,* 671–680. doi:10.1126/science.220.4598.671

Kuo, R. J. (2001). A sales forecasting system based on fuzzy neural network with initial weights generated by genetic algorithm. *European Journal of Operational Research, 129,* 496–517. doi:10.1016/S0377-2217(99)00463-4

Kuo, R. J., Chen, C. H., & Hwang, Y. C. (2001). An intelligent stock trading decision support system through integration of genetic algorithm based fuzzy neural network and artificial neural network. *Fuzzy Sets and Systems, 118,* 21–45. doi:10.1016/S0165-0114(98)00399-6

Kuo, R. J., & Cohen, P. H. (1998). Manufacturing process control through integration of neural networks and fuzzy model. *Fuzzy Sets and Systems, 98*(1), 15–31. doi:10.1016/S0165-0114(96)00382-X

Kuo, R. J., Wu, P., & Wang, C. P. (2000). Fuzzy neural networks for learning fuzzy If-Then rules. *Applied Artificial Intelligence, 14,* 539–563. doi:10.1080/08839510050076963

Kuo, R. J., Wu, P., & Wang, C. P. (2002). An intelligent sales forecasting system through integration of artificial neural networks and fuzzy neural networks with fuzzy weight elimination. *Neural Networks, 15,* 909–925. doi:10.1016/S0893-6080(02)00064-3

Kuo, R. J., & Xue, K. C. (1999). Fuzzy neural networks with application to sales forecasting. *Fuzzy Sets and Systems, 108,* 123–143. doi:10.1016/S0165-0114(97)00326-6

Laarhoven, P. J. M. V., & Aarts, E. H. L. (1987). Simulated Annealing: Theory and Applications. Dordrecht, The Netherlands: Kluwer Academic Publishers.

Lee, C. C. (1990). Fuzzy logic in control systems: Fuzzy logic controller- Part I. *IEEE Transactions on Systems, Man, and Cybernetics, 20*(2), 404–418. doi:10.1109/21.52551

Lee, C. C. (1990). Fuzzy logic in control systems: Fuzzy logic controller- Part II. *IEEE Transactions on Systems, Man, and Cybernetics, 20*(2), 419–435. doi:10.1109/21.52552

Lin, C. T. (1995). A neural fuzzy control system with structure and parameter learning. *Fuzzy Sets and Systems, 70*, 183–212. doi:10.1016/0165-0114(94)00216-T

Lin, C. T., & Lee, C. S. G. (1991). Neural network-based fuzzy logic control and decision system. *IEEE Transactions on Computers, C-40*(12), 1320–1336. doi:10.1109/12.106218

Lin, C. T., & Lu, Y. C. (1995). A neural fuzzy system with linguistic teaching signals. *IEEE transactions on Fuzzy Systems, 3*(2), 169–189. doi:10.1109/91.388172

Lippmann, R. P. (1987). An introduction to computing with neural nets. *IEEE ASSP Magazine*, 4–22. doi:10.1109/MASSP.1987.1165576

Mandischer, M. (2002). A comparison of evolution strategies and backpropagation for neural network training. *Neurocomputing, 42*, 87–117. doi:10.1016/S0925-2312(01)00596-3

Michalewicz, Z. (1994). Genetic Algorithms +Data Structures=Evolution Programs, New York: Springer-Verlag.

Nakayama, S., Horikawa, S., Furuhashi, T., & Uchikawa, Y. (1992). Knowledge acquisition of strategy and tactics using fuzzy neural networks. In *Proc. IJCNN'92*, (pp. II-751–756).

Rooij, A. V., Lakhmi, J., & Ray, J. (1998). Neural Networks Training Using Genetic Algorithms. Singapore: World Scientific.

Shapiro, A. F. (2002). The merging of neural networks, fuzzy logic, and genetic algorithms. *Insurance, Mathematics & Economics, 31*, 115–131. doi:10.1016/S0167-6687(02)00124-5

Takagi, T., & Hayashi, I. (1991). NN-driven fuzzy reasoning. *International Journal of Approximate Reasoning, 5*, 191–212. doi:10.1016/0888-613X(91)90008-A

Wang, C. P. (1999). *A shipping forecasting model of distribution center through integration of genetic algorithm and fuzzy neural network.* Unpublished Master thesis, I-Shou University, Kaohsiung County, Taiwan.

Wu, P., & Chiang, H. C. (2005). *The application of electromagnetism-like mechanism for solving the TSP problems.* TMS & AMS Joint International Conference, Tunghai Univerity, Taichung, Taiwan, R.O.C.

Wu, P., & Chiang, H. C. (2005). The application of electromagnetism-like mechanism for solving the traveling salesman problems. In *Proceeding of the Chinese Institute of Industrial Engineering Annual Meeting*, HsinChu, Taiwan, R.O.C.

Wu, P., & Chiang, H. C. (2005). An EM+K-opt methods for the TSPs. In *Proceeding of the Operations Research Society of Taiwan Annual Meeting*, Taipei, Taiwan, R.O.C.

Wu, P., & Fang, H. C. (2006). A revised electromagnetism-like mechanism for the traveling salesman problem. In *Proceeding of the 36th International Conference on Computers & Industrial*, Taipei, Taiwan, R.O.C.

Wu, P., Yang, K. J., & Hung, Y. Y. (2005). *The study of electromagnetism-like mechanism based fuzzy neural network for learning fuzzy if–then rules.* (. LNCS, 3684, 382–388.

Wu, P., Yang, W. H., & Wei, N. C. (2004). An electromagnetism algorithm of neural network analysis -an application to textile retail operation . *Journal of the Chinese Institute of Industrial Engineers, 21*(1), 59–67.

Yager, R. R. (1980). On choosing between fuzzy subsets. *Kybernetes, 9*, 151–154. doi:10.1108/eb005552

Yang, W. H. (2002). *A study on the intelligent neural network training using the electromagnetism algorithm*. Unpublished Master Thesis, I-Shou University, Kaohsiung County, Taiwan.

KEY TERMS AND DEFINITIONS

Artificial Neural Network (ANN): An artificial neural network (ANN), often just called a "neural network" (NN), is a mathematical model or computational model based on biological neural networks. It consists of an interconnected group of artificial neurons and processes information using a connectionist approach to computation. In most cases an ANN is an adaptive system that changes its structure based on external or internal information that flows through the network during the learning phase.

Electromagnetism-Like Mechanism (EM): The EM algorithm simulates the electromagnetism theory of physics by considering each sample point to be an electrical charge. The EM algorithm utilizes an attraction-repulsion mechanism to move the sample points towards the optimum. EM can be used as a stand-alone approach or as an accompanying algorithm for other methods. Besides, the electromagnetism-like mechanism is not easily falling into local optimum.

Fuzzy Neural Network (FNN): A feedforward artificial neural networks (ANN) was introduced into fuzzy inference. Each rule is represented by an ANN while all the membership functions are represented by only one ANN. The algorithm is divided into three major parts: (1) the partition of inference rules; (2) the identification of IF parts; and (3) the identification of THEN parts.

Global Optimization Methods: In the field of global optimization, it is quite common to classify the methods into two main categories: deterministic methods and stochastic (or probabilistic) methods. As the names imply, the methods that do not involve random elements go into the former category, whereas the methods that utilize probabilistic schemes go into the latter category.

Meta-Heuristic: A meta-heuristic is a heuristic method for solving a very general class of computational problems by combining user-given black-box procedures -usually heuristics themselves - in the hope of obtaining a more efficient or more robust procedure.

Section 2
Soft Computation

Chapter 5
Computational Intelligence–Revisited

Yuanyuan Chai
Beijing Jiaotong University, China

ABSTRACT

This chapter is a survey of CI and indicates the Simulation Mechanism-Based (SMB) classification method for Computational Intelligence through reviewing on the definitions of CI and existed classification methods. The classification method divides all CI branches into three categories: organic mechanism simulation class, inorganic mechanism simulation class and artificial mechanism simulation class. Furthermore, branches in organic mechanism simulation class are introduced in detail, by which the chapter concludes the nonlinear mapping model for each class. The work presented in this chapter will provide an efficient approach to understand essence of CI.

INTRODUCTION

IEEE academic conferences on neural networks, fuzzy systems, evolutionary computation which held the first "World Congress on Computational Intelligence (WCCI'94)" in Orlando, Florida represented the birth of CI. From then on, CI emerging as a new field of study has gained widespread concern from a growing number of scholars.

Plenty of CI branches have made considerable progress and have become hot issues in various fields of research and applications in recent years. The CI branches, although different from each other, share

the property of being non-symbolic and operating in a bottom-up model, where structure emerges from an unordered begin.

We consider that CI mainly adopts the connectionism idea and actually uses the bionics ideas for reference; it is a computational method which origins from emulating intelligent phenomenon in nature and is described in abstract mathematical language. Computational intelligent systems depend on numerical data supplied by manufactured sensors and do not rely upon "knowledge", and it can establish the relationship through training and solve the complex problems.

From comprehensive discussion on definitions of CI and correct understanding the nature and com-

DOI: 10.4018/978-1-61520-757-2.ch005

putational mechanism of CI branches, this chapter introduces the Simulation-Mechanism-Based (SMB) method for CI according to the collection of all CI branches and all the different classification methods. This classification method divides all CI branches into three categories: organic mechanism simulation class (OMS), inorganic mechanism simulation class (IMS) and artificial mechanism simulation class (AMS). Among them, organic mechanism simulation class is the most important part of CI, many branches in this class such as fuzzy logic, neural network and GA are the major tools in many research fields.

Organic mechanism simulation class can be also divided into group mechanism simulation class and individual mechanism simulation class. Group mechanism simulation class can be divided into group evolution mechanism simulation class and group collaboration mechanism simulation class according to the different group intelligent behaviors which they attempt to simulate. Individual mechanism simulation class attempts to simulate life phenomenon in different level of the individual. DNA computing simulates the DNA molecule structure in molecule level. Artificial Neural Network simulates the brain structure in organ structure level. Artificial immune system simulates the biology immune systems in organism function level. Fuzzy logic simulates human thinking manner in cognitive level. SVM simulates the human ability of pattern identify in perception level. Artificial life simulates the whole life character in human being level.

This chapter also introduces the nonlinear mapping models for them through elaboration on the essence and computational mechanism of each branch.

DEFINITIONS OF CI

From birth of CI in 1992, there are plenty of definitions about Computational Intelligence. But there isn't a uniform definition. In the following section, we summarize various definitions about CI. Finally, a wide-covered definition is given.

Background

The first published definition is due to Bezdek (1992) who states that computational systems depend on numerical data supplied by manufactured sensors and do not rely upon "knowledge". Bezdek (1994) notes that there are many variations on the theme of intelligent systems, and characterizes them according to the ABC's: Artificial intelligence, Biological intelligence and Computational intelligence. Artificial loosely refers to systems with a symbolic knowledge component; biological refers to physical, chemical and organic systems, while computational systems include a knowledge component and interaction with sensory information that is described in numerical models.

Bezdek (1994) offers that CI is low-level computation in the style of the mind, whereas AI is mid-level computation in the style of the mind. The envisioned difference is that mid-level systems include knowledge, while low level systems do not.

His proposal is to call a system computationally intelligent when it deals only with numerical (low-level) data, has a pattern recognition component, and does not use knowledge in the AI sense; and additionally, when it (begins to) exhibit (i) computational adaptivity; (ii) computational fault tolerance; (iii) speed approaching human-like turnaround, and (iv) error rates that approximate human performance (Bezdek, 1994).

Mark's (1993) definition is listing neural networks as one of the building blocks of CI, the others being genetic algorithm, fuzzy systems, evolutionary programming, and artificial life.

Eberhart et al. (1996) elaborate further on the very notion of CI and relate their vision to that of Bezdek. Their view is summarized as that CI is defined as a methodology involving computing that exhibits an ability to learn and/or deal with new situations such that the system is perceived to possess one or more attributions of reason, such as generalization, discovery, association, and abstraction. The output of a computationally intelligent system includes predictions and/or decisions. Put another way, CI comprises practical adaptation concepts, paradigms, and implementations that enable or facilitate appropriate actions (intelligent behavior) in complex and changing environments (Eberhart, Simpson, & Dobbins, 1996).

One of the main differences between this view and that of Bezdek is the emphasis on adaptation, rather than pattern recognition. Eberhart (1995) considers that adaptation is arguably the most appropriate term for what computationally intelligent systems do. In fact, it is not too much of a stretch to say that computational intelligence and adaptation are synonymous.

Fogel (1995) states that technologies of neural, fuzzy and evolutionary systems were brought together under the rubric Computational Intelligence, a relatively new field to generally describe methods of computation that can be used to adapt solutions to new problems and do not rely on explicit human knowledge.

Actually, Fogel's view is an amplification of that of Eberhart et al. in the sense that he sees intelligence and adaptation as synonyms. Fogel (1995) presents that any system which generates adaptive behaviors to meet goals in a range of environments can be said to be intelligent. In contrast, any system that cannot generate adaptive behaviors and can only perform in a single limited environment demonstrates no intelligence.

A particular interpretation of computational (and artificial) intelligence is after Poole, where the author states that CI is the study of the design of intelligence agents. An intelligence agent is a system that acts intelligently: What it does is appropriate for its circumstances and its goal, it is flexible to changing environments and changing goals, it learns from experience, and it makes appropriate choice given perceptual limitations and finite computation (Poole, Goebel, & Mackworth, 1998).

Now many researchers identify "computational intelligence" as "soft computing".

Soft computing differs from conventional (hard) computing in that, unlike hard computing, it is tolerant of imprecision, uncertainty and partial truth. In effect, the role model for soft computing is the human mind. The guiding principle of soft computing is: Exploit the tolerance for imprecision, uncertainty and partial truth to achieve tractability, robustness and low solution cost (Zadeh, 1994). The principal constituents of soft computing (SC) are fuzzy logic (FL), neural network theory (NN) and probabilistic reasoning (PR), with the latter subsuming belief networks, genetic algorithms, chaos theory and parts of learning theory. What is important to note is that SC is not a melange of FL, NN and PR. It is a partnership in which each of the partners contributes a distinct methodology for addressing problems in its domain. In this perspective, the principal contributions of FL, NN and PR are complementary rather than competitive (Zadeh, 1994).

There are also a lot of definitions about CI.

Some researchers consider that CI is the study of the design of intelligent agents. The central scientific goal of computational intelligence is to understand the principles that make intelligent behavior possible, in natural or artificial systems.

Others consider that CI is certainly more than just the study of the design of intelligent agents; it also includes study of all non-algorithmizable processes that humans (and sometimes animals) can solve with various degree of intelligence (Duch, 2007).

In CI these interest generally focus on problems that only humans and animals can solve, problems requiring intelligence. Specific interests also focus on methods and tools that are applicable to this type of problems (Duch, 2007).

CI studies problems for which there are no effective algorithms, either because it is not possible to formulate them or because they are NP-hard and thus not effective in real life applications. This is quite broad definition: computational intelligence is a branch of computer science studying problems for which there are no effective computational algorithms (Duch, 2007).

Definition and Description

All the above definitions are obtained from the following critical aspects: 1)simulation the action of intelligent agents; 2)adaptability; 3)problems that CI can solve; 4)all CI branches. So we generalize:

Computational intelligence actually uses the bionics ideas for reference, it origins from emulating intelligent phenomenon in nature. CI attempts to simulate and reappearance the characters of intelligence, such as learning and adaptation, so that it can be a new research field for reconstructing the nature and engineering. In other words, CI simulates the biological mechanism of intelligent systems in nature, such as brain structure, evolution and immunity, so it can deal with difficult work efficiently and achieve robustness and low solution cost. We can also say that CI is based on the natural mechanisms like fuzzy inference, neural network and evolution, it is a new methodology described in mathematics language. CI is a new stage of intelligence development.

CI has some superiority to traditional artificial intelligence. The most important advantage is that CI doesn't need to construct the precise model for the problem, and it is very fit for solving the difficult and inextricable problems which can't be modeled by traditional technology.

All CI branches that we have collected are: fuzzy logic (FL), artificial neural network (ANN), evolutionary computing (EC), swarm intelligence (SI), particle swarm optimization(PSO), ant colony optimization (ACO), Intelligent Agent(IA), Multi-Agent System(MAS), support vector machines(SVM), artificial immune system (AIS), DNA computing, artificial life(AL), simulated annealing(SA), natural computation(NC), quantum computation(QC), rough sets(RS), taboo search(TS), Granular Computing (GrC), Chaos

Optimization algorithm(COA), local search, fractal science(FC).

CLASSIFICATION METHODS

At present, emphases in the research of CI are mostly concentrated on the study of hybrid algorithms. Many new hybrid algorithms gain plenty of success in specific application areas. The SMB method for CI provides a theoretical basis and reference for further study on the instinct of CI and invention of new hybrid algorithms.

Because CI has many branches, so does its classification methods. Firstly, this section presents some different classification methods briefly. SMB method will be introduced in the end.

Different Classification Method

The following methods divide CI branches from different perspective. Here, we only use EC, FC, NC, DNAC and QC for examples to show various classification methods.

Computational-Medium-Based Classification Method

One perspective is that of the applied computational medium. This separates the fields of EC, FC, and NC on the one hand and DNAC and QC on the other hand. Namely, the first group of techniques belongs to the traditional silicon medium. This approach has its limitations originating from the underlying physics. DNA computing and QC represent an alternative by relying on a different medium. Quantum computing is an approach to overcome some of the limitations by going down to the level of quantum mechanics. The distinguishing feature of DNA computing is the fact that the medium in which computations are realized consists of biomolecules and enzymes. This medium is often called bioware, as opposed to hardware.

Parallelism Based Classification Method

Another perspective is offered by considering parallelism. Since the traditional computer hardware is essentially built for sequential computing, most of the algorithms are sequential as well. Nature is intrinsically parallel. One single brain consists of billions of neurons working simultaneously and any given animal population is performing the main adaptation task by trying out many solutions parallelly. NN and EC can be viewed as mimicking these natural phenomena, and hence being fundamentally parallel. DNAC and QC go further in this respect by their different computational medium they are truly parallel. Thus, DNAC, EC, NN and QC can be seen as building on parallelism to various extents. Fuzzy computing is the outlier from this perspective.

Natural-Biology-Based Classification Method

Inspiration from nature forms the third aspect. The so-called natural computation consists of research fields in computer science that is inspired by natural processes. In this context, natural is often interpreted as biological, bio-chemical. Among the five areas in this chapter three are clearly members of the natural computation family. In particular, evolutionary computation is based on ideas from Darwinian evolution, neural computation builds on abstract models of brains, and DNA computing is effectively carried out in a biological medium. FC and QC do not belong to natural computation (Furuhashi, 2001).

Problem-Space-Based Classification Method

The fourth method is proposed by Roger Jang, who is a student of Zadeh and is the inventor of ANFIS. He divided SC into two categories. One is model space including neural networks, adaptive neural network, and fuzzy inference system. Another is approach space including derivative-free optimization and derivative-based optimization (Jang, Sun, & Mizutani, 1997).

Computational-Intelligent-Based Classification Method

The last division we make here is based on emphasizing the computational, respectively the intelligent aspect within CI. The computational aspect forms the focus of DNAC and QC. Both disciplines are concerned with redefining the very basics of computation and the computers that carry out computational tasks. This aspect is closely related to the issue of the used medium as discussed above. EC, FC, and NC follow a complementary approach in that they emphasize the "intelligence" within CI. EC and NC form a further sub-group by their shared vision of how to interpret intelligence. Evolutionary computation and neural computation are also often named together under the umbrella of adaptive systems (Craenen & Eiben, 2003).

SMB Classification Method

All these classification methods divided the branches of CI into different subfields from distinct perspective. The classification method introduced in this paper is different from all the above methods.

At first, Let us look at the definition of CI introduced above: CI actually uses the bionics ideas for reference, it origins from emulating intelligent phenomenon in nature. CI attempts to simulate and reappearance the characters of intelligence, such as learning and adaptation (Zadeh, 1993), so that it can be a new research field of reconstructing the nature and engineering. We simply consider that CI is a sort of simulation science and it attempts to simulate natural intelligent behaviors,

Figure 1. SMB classification method

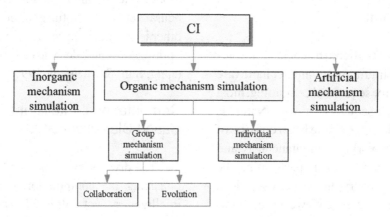

such as self-organize, leaning, and adaptation. CI can offer us a new kind of approaches for solving problems.

The essence of CI is a universal approximator, and it has the great function of non-linear mapping and optimization (Yager, 1993). Then, from the perspective of "emulation", we can make classification through the different objects which CI attempts to simulate and we define such classification method as Simulation-Mechanism-Based (SMB) classification method. Here we note that nature refers to nature in broad sense, which not only includes biology or organic nature, but also includes inorganic nature and artificial nature. According to this definition, we divide CI into three categories: CI branches which simulate the intelligent behaviors in organic nature can be defined as organic mechanism simulation class; CI branches which simulate the intelligent behaviors in inorganic nature can be defined as inorganic mechanism simulation class; CI branches which simulate the intelligent behaviors in artificial nature can be defined as artificial mechanism simulation class.

So in general, we have three classes: organic mechanism simulation class, inorganic mechanism simulation class and artificial mechanism simulation class. Organic mechanism simulation class can be divided into group mechanism simulation class and individual mechanism simulation class. Group

mechanism simulation class can be also divided into group collaboration mechanism simulation class and group evolution mechanism simulation class. The details are as follows Figure 1.

ORGANIC MECHANISM SIMULATION CLASS

CI branches based on organic mechanism simulation are enlightened by the biology kingdom in nature. This kind of methods attempt to simulate various intelligent behaviors in the natural biology. According to different simulation objects, organic mechanism simulation class (OMS) can be also divided into group mechanism simulation class and individual mechanism simulation class.

Group mechanism simulation class refers to CI branches which attempt to simulate the intelligent behaviors of biology group. This class includes EC, Swarm intelligence, ACO, PSO, IA and MAS. According to the different intelligent behaviors, group mechanism simulation class can be also divided into group collaboration mechanism simulation class and group evolution mechanism simulation class. Individual mechanism simulation class refers to CI branches which attempt to simulate the intelligent behaviors of biology individual. It includes Fuzzy logic (FL), Neural network (NN), Support vector machine (SVM), artificial immune system (AIS), DNA computing and artificial life (AL) (Zadeh, 1988; Zadeh, 1965; Rumelhart, 1994).

In this section, branches of each class will be introduced in detail. The nonlinear model for each class will be discussed after that.

Group Mechanism Simulation Class

Group mechanism simulation class includes such branches: EC, Swarm intelligence, ACO, PSO, IA and MAS. Evolutionary computing (EC): simulating principle of Darwin's evolution theory; Swarm intelligence (SI): simulating the group intelligent behaviors; Particle swarm optimization (PSO): simulating the bird group; Ant colony optimization (ACO): simulating the ant group; intelligent agent (IA): simulating the behavior of intelligent agents; Multi agent system (MAS): simulating the collaboration behavior of multi agents.

All these algorithms have the following common characters: they simulate the nature biology colony evolution or collaboration process for solving complex problems. They are all under the umbrella of group mechanism simulation class and bring us a new computational method for the problems difficult to handle. We consider EC simulates the biology group evolution mechanism; while the others such as swarm intelligence, PSO, ACO, MAS simulate the biology group collaboration mechanism.

Group Evolution Mechanism Simulation Class

The most representative method among them is evolutionary computing (EC). The survival of any biology group is following the Darwin's evolution theory which indicates only the fittest survive in the end. Whether the individual in a group can be selected or be eliminated by the nature is according to its adaptation ability to the environment. From the 1960's, how to simulate biology and construct effective algorithm which can be applied to complex optimization problems is becoming a hot issue (Bonarini, 2001). EC is born from such background. EC includes: genetic algorithms (GA), evolution strategies (ES), evolutionary programming (EP).

GA simulates the biology genetics and natural selection mechanism. It is a sort of optimization search algorithm. GA is very different from traditional mathematics model in that it can find an effective solution for the problems which can't be modeled by traditional approaches. In 1975, Holland first proposed GA in his book named "Adaptation in Natural and Artificial Systems", and also brought forward the term "Schema Theorem". Holland established the theory foundation of GA. GA is based on the evolutionary principle of survival of the fittest. It uses the genetics operations on the group which consist of likely solutions time after time, and make the group evolve constantly; eventually it can search the excellent individual (solution) which satisfies the requires well in the group by the global parallel search technique. ES simulates the natural evolution theory; it is a kind of parameter optimization algorithm. In 1964, ES is proposed by Rechenberg, Schwefel, and Peter Bienert in German. EP is proposed by Fogel in 1962, it is a methodology simulating human intelligence. The process of EP is searching the computer program individual with the highest fitness from the all likely computer programs. The algorithms with high fitness can be saved as the father generation to form new filial generation. This process recycles constantly until EP finds the most reliable program.

About EC, we summarize as: EC adopts the simple coding technique for expressing the complex structures, and instruct orientation of learning and searching through simple genetic operations and natural selection until it finds the best solution which satisfies the conditions well. EC fully shows the process of group evolution, it also simulates the characters of biology group such as self-organize, adaptation and self-study. EC provides an efficient, easy-handled, and cur-

Figure 2. Biology group evolution process

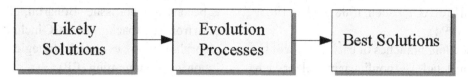

rent computational methodology for optimization problems in complex system. In fact, it is a bionics algorithm simulating biology group evolution. So we define the general process about EC in Figure 2.

Group Collaboration Mechanism Simulation Class

Swarm intelligence tries to simulate the complex behaviors produced by biology group collaboration, and so SI can bring us some new approaches and algorithms for solving the complex behaviors in complex systems.

Swarm intelligence can solve such problems: function optimization, the shortest path, attempter, analysis of image and data. Swarm intelligence means that "simple intelligent agent can represent complex intelligent behaviors through collaboration." This kind of intelligent model requires plenty of simple agents for achieving best solution of one problem. As for the simple agent, it travels in the solution space without discipline until it gets the total information feedback from the whole intelligent swarm. Swarm intelligence is a distributing algorithm enlightened by the collective behaviors of biology group. Its main branches are PSO and ACO.

Particle Swarm Optimization (PSO) was proposed by Kennedy and Eberhart in 1995. It attempts to simulate the migration and infest of bird kingdom. PSO is an optimization tool based on group and iteration. A set of random solutions follow the best particle in the solution space though iteration and eventually find the best solution. In PSO, we adopt information share mechanism; it has the profound background of intelligence.

Ant colony algorithm (ACO) also simulates the biology behavior. Some italic researchers propose the ACO through the study on ant behavior in 1990s. The core of this theory is Pheromone, which can be felt by ants and affect their behaviors. So the ant colony can search the new route according to the changing environment and produce the best choice. Now ACO has displayed its advantage in solving complex optimization problems, especially in discrete optimization problems.

Through the above, we can conclude: swarm intelligence computing is a kind of algorithm simulating group collaboration. The algorithm achieves the solution through the collaboration of numbers of intelligent agents. The simple intelligent agent represents the complex intelligent behaviors by colony collaboration. The whole group can finish specific mission by colony collaboration and show the character of self-organize. So we can define the general process about swarm intelligence as Figure3.

Nonlinear Mapping Model for Group Mechanism Simulation class

The paper considers that EC, Swarm intelligence, ACO, PSO, IA and MAS are all under the umbrella of group mechanism simulation class. We can regard this kind of algorithms as nonlinear mapping process and the intermediate process can be seen as a non-linear mapping machine in Figure 4.

1. **IN(swarm)**: Biology group/colony (the initial group consists of all the likely solutions; any intelligent colony).

Figure 3. Biology group collaboration process

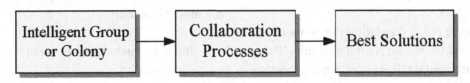

2. **Non-linear mapping machine**: biology evolution or collaboration process
3. **OUT(swarm)**: The best solution

We can define "Non-linear mapping machine" as:

Non-linear mapping machine= (**Input, Output, F(xi), O(F(xi)), E(xi)**), Process pseudo-code can be expressed as follows:

```
Procedure SwarmNonMapMach (In
(swarm))
BEGIN
For each agent
    Initialize a group
END For
WHILE maximum iterations or
minimum error criteria is not
attained do
    For each agent do
        Calculate fitness
value F(xi)O(F(xi))
    End For
END While
RETURN Out(swarm)
END
```

where,

Input: The initial group consists of all the likely solutions or any intelligent colony;\\

Output: The best solution;

F(xi): Fitness function. Fitness function is the index which can estimate the individual in the group according to their performance. It is also the basis of evolution or collaboration. In EC, the individual with high fitness will be selected, whereas the individual with low fitness will be eliminated; in the collaboration process, we judge whether one particle is the best one according to its fitness.

O(F(xi)): Evolution operation or collaboration operation. Operation is according the fitness of individual. In EC, the selected individuals can produce new individual through various genetic operations; in the collaboration process, we update the speed and displacement of individuals according to their fitness function, make the individuals approach to the best solution.

E(xi): Estimation index. We use the estimation index to judge whether the performance of individual reach our predict standard or not. If performance of individual reaches our standard, we can stop the algorithm.

Individual Mechanism Simulation Class

Individual mechanism simulation class includes such branches: Fuzzy logic (FL), Neural network (NN), Support vector machine (SVM), artificial

Figure 4. Nonlinear mapping model for group mechanism simulation class

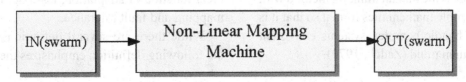

immune system (AIS), DNA computing and artificial life (AL).

Fuzzy logic (FL): simulating the human uncertainty about the world; Neural network (NN): simulating the neural cell in brain; Support vector machine (SVM): simulating the human ability of pattern identify; Artificial immune system (AIS): simulating the biology immune system; DNA computing: simulating the DNA structure; Artificial life (AL): simulating life of nature.

All these algorithms have the following common characters: they simulate the intelligent phenomenon in different level of the individual organism in nature. Artificial life simulates the whole life character. DNA computing simulates the DNA molecule structure. Artificial immune system simulates the biology immune systems. SVM simulates the human ability of pattern identify. Fuzzy logic simulates human thinking manner in cognitive level. NN simulates the brain structure.

This paper focuses on fuzzy logic and artificial neural networks.

Fuzzy Logic

Since introduced by Zadeh in 1965, Fuzzy sets theory has gained an increasing level of acceptance in science and engineering. Fuzzy sets theory broke through the limitation of classical set theory founded by German mathematician George Cantor in the end of 19th century and created a new branch of mathematics, which is fuzzy mathematics, and laid the foundation of fuzzy theory (Zadeh, 1965). Gupta defines fuzzy sets theory as "a body of concept and techniques aimed at providing a systematic framework for dealing with the vagueness and imprecision inherent to human thought process" (Zadeh, 1988). The introduction of fuzzy sets can express the human thinking method with relatively simple mathematics format so that it is possible to handle complex systems consistent with the human mind (Zadeh, 1973).

The general process of fuzzy inference system is a model that maps:

- Input characteristics to input membership functions,
- Input membership function to rules,
- Rules to a set of output characteristics,
- Output characteristics to output membership functions, and
- Output membership function to a single-valued output.

A fuzzy inference system implements a nonlinear mapping from its input space to output space. The Stone-Weierstrass theorem indicates that a fuzzy inference system can approximate arbitrary nonlinear function (Zadeh, 1994). We can also define the process as Figure5.

Recent interest has developed in the use of fuzzy set theory for the modeling of complex systems. We call such a representation a fuzzy model of a system (FMS). Fuzzy modeling based on fuzzy inference is used to describe the model of the object using fuzzy if-then rules. The construction of these systems involves modeling a, usually nonlinear, relationship between system input and output. Conceptually a fuzzy logic controller or more generally any FMS (fuzzy model of a system) can be seen as a function f mapping input to output (Yager, 1993).

Neural Networks

Neural network is built by a large number of artificial neurons (processing units, PE) according to certain topology structure. It is a network system with parallel computing capacity (Rumelhart, 1994). Neural network originated from study on information processing of human brain, it has the great function of adaptation, learning, nonlinear mapping and fault tolerance.

While there are several definitions for NN, the following definition emphasizes the key fea-

Figure 5. Reasoning process of FIS

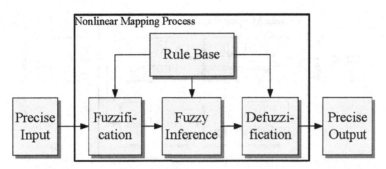

tures of such models. An NN can be defined as a distributed, adaptive, generally nonlinear learning machine built from interconnecting different processing elements (PE).

NN has the ability to perform nonlinear pattern classification and function approximation. Its mapping capability is believed to approximate any arbitrary mathematical function.

The inherent parallel architecture and the fault tolerance nature of NN are appealing to address problems in variety of application areas. NN find their application in function approximation, pattern recognition, system identification and prediction.

So we conclude that there are three basic elements in NN:

1. A set of connection presented by weights, Wij.
2. A sum unit.
3. A activation function f.

The process of one neuron is shown in Figure 6.

Mathematically, the information processing ability of a neuron can be represented as a nonlinear mapping operation, *Ne*, from the input vector $X(t) \in R^n$ to the scalar output $y(t) \in R^1$; that is (Gupta, 1996),

$$Ne:X(t)\in R^n \rightarrow y(t)\in R^1$$

Neural networks have been applied very successfully in the identification and control of dynamic systems. The universal approximation capabilities of the Multi-Layer Perceptron (MLP) have made it a popular choice for modeling nonlinear systems and for implementing general-purpose non-linear controllers (Jang, Sun, & Mizutani, 1997).

Nonlinear Mapping Model for Individual Mechanism Simulation class

Neural networks and fuzzy inference methods can approximate any continuous nonlinear functions and can be implemented by a non-linear mapping process from inputs to outputs. So we can depict the basic structure of NN and FL as Figure 7.

1. **IN(indiv)**: a set of inputs. In fuzzy logic, input means precise inputs; in NN, input means a set of weighted neurons.
2. **Non-linear mapping machine**: reasoning and learning process
3. **OUT(indiv)**: In fuzzy logic, output means precise output, such as decision; in NN, output means the output value of one neuron.

We can define "Non-linear mapping machine" as:

Non-linear mapping machine= (**II (Xi), RB, LR (II (Xi)), IO (LR (II (Xi))))**, Process pseudocode can be expressed as follows:

Figure 6. Training process of NN

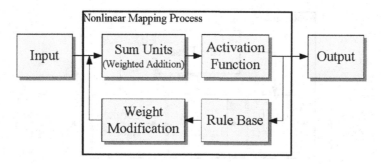

Procedure IndivNonMapMach (IN (indiv))

```
Procedure IndivNonMapMach (IN
(indiv))
BEGIN
For the whole system do
    Initialize RB and weights;
END For
WHILE minimum error criteria is
not attained do
    For each input unit do
            Calculate
II(Xi);
            LR (II(Xi));
            Calculate
IO(LR(II(Xi)));
    End For
END While
RETURN OUT(indiv)
END
```

II(Xi): Integrated Input (Xi), which can change the inputs to our required inputs. In fuzzy logic, it means "fuzzification" through the membership function, so we can change the precise inputs to the fuzzy input sets; in NN, it means the weighted addition of every input neuron.

RB: rules base, which contains prepared rules by the experience of experts. In fuzzy logic, it means the fuzzy rules base; in NN, it means the study rules. The systems make learning and reasoning according to RB.

LR(II(Xi)): Learning and reasoning (Integrated Input (Xi)), which is the process of learning and reasoning of integrated inputs according to the RB. In fuzzy logic, it means fuzzy inference on fuzzy input sets, and we can achieve the aggregated fuzzy output sets. In NN, the neuron can learn based on study rules, and modify the connection weights, so we can get the changed weighted addition of every input neuron.

IO (LR (II (Xi))): Integrated Output (learning and reasoning (Integrated Input (Xi))), which means change the outcomes of learning and reasoning. In fuzzy logic, it means "defuzzification" to the aggregated fuzzy output sets, so we can get the precise output; in NN, we make activation function on the weighted addition of every input neuron, so we can get the output value of one neuron.

Figure 7. Nonlinear mapping model for individual mechanism simulation class

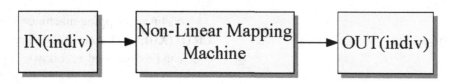

Table 1. Inorganic mechanism simulation class

Branches	Descriptions
Simulated annealing	Simulating the annealing process of solid substances in physics
Natural computation	Simulating the nature and is the mapping of simulation computation
Quantum computation	Simulating the "tunnel effect" and other quantum mechanical effects

INORGANIC MECHANISM SIMULATION CLASS

CI branches simulating inorganic mechanism derive from the various laws of nature, such as anneal, sun photon and quantum. We can use the intelligence of such nature laws to develop many computational methods, and solve many complicated problems according to these methods. See in table 1.

Inorganic mechanism simulation class (IMS) attempts to simulate various nature phenomenon to produce new algorithms. It uses the nature inorganic disciplines or laws to solve practical problems. With our deep understanding of nature, we can develop more computational methods based on inorganic mechanism simulation.

ARTIFICIAL MECHANISM SIMULATION CLASS

Artificial mechanism simulation class (AMS) attempts to simulate the discipline of nature man-made product to solve practical problems. Artificial mechanism simulation class includes such branches: Rough sets (RS), Taboo search (TS), Ordinal optimization (OO), Granular Computing (GrC), Chaos Optimization algorithm (COA), Local search (LS), Fractal science (FC).

With the invention of more and more man-made products, we will have a growing number of artificial mechanism simulation algorithms.

FUTURE TRENDS

It is becoming less common to read about an application that uses just neural networks, or just evolutionary computation, or just fuzzy logic (Eberhart, 1998). There are many possibilities for combining the above mentioned CI branches.

In large measure, fuzzy logic, neuro computing, and probabilistic reasoning are complementary, not competitive. It is becoming increasingly clear that in many cases it is advantageous to combine them. A case in point is growing number of "neurofuzzy" consumer products and systems that use a combination of fuzzy logic and neural-network techniques (Zadeh, 1994).

System Modeling based on conventional mathematical tools (e.g., differential equations) is not well suited for dealing with ill-defined and uncertain systems. By contrast, a fuzzy inference system employing fuzzy if-then rules can model the qualitative aspects of human knowledge and reasoning processes without employing precise quantitative analyses. Hybrid tools developed using combinations of neural networks; evolutionary computation and fuzzy logic solve difficult problems, require relatively short development times, and are robust.

It should be noted that more research endeavors are necessary to develop hybrid methods for CI so that these models are made applicable in system modeling and control of complex systems. SMB classification method presented in this chapter give a guide for invention of hybrid methods in theory; while nonlinear mapping models discussed above will help us in understanding common computation mechanism of CI branches. It is believed that these theories will have effective influence on new CI hybrid methods.

CONCLUSION

In recent years, CI has been the hot issue in various research fields and a lot of computational intelligence branches have achieved tremendous success in many applications. In essence, any CI branch can be understood as a nonlinear mapping machine and can solve many complex problems such as optimization, classification and decision-making (Eberhart, 1998).

The biggest difference between traditional methods and CI is that the latter solve the problems by simulating the intelligent behaviors in nature, not by precise calculation method. Recently research in CI concentrates on the classification method and nonlinear mapping model of each branch (Denai, Palis & Zeghbib, 2007). From fully understanding the nature of CI, this chapter gives the general definition of CI; this paper also puts forward the simulation-mechanism-based(SMB) classification method based on simulating feature of CI. This method divides CI into three categories: organic mechanism simulation class, inorganic mechanism simulation class and artificial mechanism simulation class.

Organic mechanism simulation class is the most important part of CI including many main branches such as fuzzy logic, neural networks and evolutionary computing. According to the different simulation objects, organic mechanism simulation class can be also divided into group mechanism simulation class and individual mechanism simulation class. Group mechanism simulation class includes such methods: EC, Swarm intelligence, ACO, PSO, IA and MAS. Individual mechanism simulation class includes such methods: Fuzzy logic (FL), Neural network (NN), Support vector machine (SVM), artificial immune system (AIS), DNA computing and artificial life (AL). From fully understanding and analyzing the computing mechanism of each branch, this paper brought forward the nonlinear mapping model for group mechanism simulation class and individual mechanism simulation class which laid a theoretical foundation for next work.

SMB classification method and the nonlinear mapping model for group mechanism simulation class and individual mechanism simulation class which discussed in this paper will provide a theoretical basis and reference for further study on the nature of CI and invention of new hybrid algorithms.

REFERENCES

Bezdek, J. C. (1992). On the Relationship between Neural Networks, Pattern Recognition and Intelligence. *International Journal of Approximate Reasoning*, 6, 85–107. doi:10.1016/0888-613X(92)90013-P

Bezdek, J. C. (1994). What is Computational Intelligence? Computational Intelligence: Imitating Life, (pp. 1-11). Piscataway, NJ: IEEE Press.

Bonarini, A. (2001). Evolutionary Learning, Reinforcement Learning, and Fuzzy Rules for Knowledge Acquisition in Agent-Based Systems. *Proceedings of the IEEE*, 89(9), 1334–1346. doi:10.1109/5.949488

Craenen, B. C., & Eiben, A. E. (2003). Computational Intelligence. Encyclopedia of Life Support Sciences. Oxford, UK: EOLSS Publishers Co. Ltd.

Denai, M. A., Palis, F., & Zeghbib, A. (2007). Modeling and Control of Non-Linear Systems Using Soft Computing Techniques. *Applied Soft Computing*, 7(3), 728–738. doi:10.1016/j.asoc.2005.12.005

Duch, W. (2007). What is Computational Intelligence and What Could It Become? Tech. Rep., Department of Informatics, Nicolaus Copernicus University and School of Computer Engineering, Nanyang Technological University.

Eberhart, R., Simpson, P., & Dobbins, R. (1996). Computational Intelligence PC Tools. Boston: Academic Press.

Eberhart, R. C. (1995). Computational Intelligence: A Snapshot. Computational Intelligence - A Dynamic System Perspective Piscataway (pp. 9-15). Piscataway, NJ: IEEE Press.

Eberhart, R. C. (1998). Overview of Computational Intelligence. *Proceedings of the 20th Annual International Conference of the IEEE Engineering in Medicine and Biology Society, 3*, 1125-1129.

Fogel, D. B. (1995). Review of Computational Intelligence: Imitating Life. *IEEE Transactions on Neural Networks, 6*(6), 1562–1565.

Furuhashi, T. (2001). Fusion of Fuzzy/ Neuro/ Evolutionary Computing for Knowledge Acquisition. *Proceedings of the IEEE, 89*(9), 1266–1274. doi:10.1109/5.949484

Gupta, M. M. (1996). Fuzzy Logic and Fuzzy Systems: Recent Developments and Future Directions. In *The Biennial Conference of the North American Fuzzy Information Processing Society*, (pp. 155-159).

Jang, J. S., Sun, C. T., & Mizutani, E. (1997). Neuro-Fuzzy and Soft Computing: A Computational Approach to Learning and Machine Intelligence, (1st. Ed.). Upper Saddle River, NJ: Prentice Hall.

Marks, R. (1993). Computational versus Artificial. *IEEE Transactions on Neural Networks, 4*(5), 737–739.

Poole, D. I., Goebel, R. G., & Mackworth, A. (1998). Computational Intelligence: A Logical Approach. Computational Intelligence and Knowledge, (pp. 1-22). New York: Oxford University Press.

Rumelhart, D. E. (1994). The Basic Ideas in Neural Networks. *Communications of the ACM, 37*(3), 87–92. doi:10.1145/175247.175256

Yager, R. R. (1993). On a Hierarchical Structure for Fuzzy Modeling and Control. *IEEE Transactions on Systems, Man, and Cybernetics, 23*(4), 1189–1197. doi:10.1109/21.247901

Zadeh, L. A. (1965). Fuzzy Set. *Information and Control, 8*, 338–353. doi:10.1016/S0019-9958(65)90241-X

Zadeh, L. A. (1973). Outline of a New Approach to the Analysis of Complex Systems and Decision Processes. *IEEE Transactions on Systems, Man, and Cybernetics, 3*(1), 28–44.

Zadeh, L. A. (1988). Fuzzy Logic. *IEEE Computer, 21*(4), 83–93.

Zadeh, L. A. (1993). *Fuzzy Logic, Neural Networks and Soft Computing*. Tech. Rep. University of California at Berkeley, November.

Zadeh, L. A. (1994). Soft Computing and Fuzzy Logic. *IEEE Software, 11*(6), 48–56. doi:10.1109/52.329401

Chapter 6
Artificial Clonal Selection Model and Its Application

Shangce Gao
University of Toyama, Japan

Zheng Tang
University of Toyama, Japan

Hiroki Tamura
University of Miyazaki, Japan

ABSTRACT

Artificial Immune System as a new branch in computational intelligence is the distributed computational technique inspired by immunological principles. In particular, the Clonal Selection Algorithm (CS), which tries to imitate the mechanisms in the clonal selection principle proposed by Burent to better understand its natural processes and simulate its dynamical behavior in the presence of antigens, has received a rapid increasing interest. However, the description about the mechanisms in the algorithm is rarely seen in the literature and the related operators in the algorithm are still inefficient. In addition, the comparison with other algorithms (especially the genetic algorithms) lacks of analysis. In this chapter, several new clonal selection principles and operators are introduced, aiming not only at a better understanding of the immune system, but also at solving engineering problems more efficiently. The efficiency of the proposed algorithm is verified by applying it to the famous traveling salesman problems (TSP).

INTRODUCTION

Most living organisms exhibit extremely sophisticated learning and processing abilities that allow them to survive and proliferate generation after generation in their dynamic and competitive environments. For this reason, nature has always served as inspiration for several scientific and technological developments.

This area of research is often referred to as Biologically Inspired Computing. The motivation of this field is primarily to extract useful metaphors from natural biological systems, in order to create effective computational solutions to complex problems in a wide range of domain areas. The more notable developments have been the neural networks inspired by the working of the brain, and the evolutionary algorithms inspired by neo-Darwinian theory of evolution.

DOI: 10.4018/978-1-61520-757-2.ch006

More recently however, there has been a growing interest in the use of the biological immune system as a source of inspiration to the development of these computational systems. The immune system contains many useful information-processing abilities, including pattern recognition, learning, memory and inherent distributed parallel processing. For these and other reasons, the immune system has received a significant amount of interest to use as a metaphor within computing. This emerging field of research is known as Artificial Immune Systems (AIS).

Essentially, AIS are the use of immune system components and process as inspiration to construct computational systems. The system is an emerging area of biologically inspired computation and has received a significant amount of interest from researchers and industrial sponsors in recent years. Applications of AIS include such areas as learning (Hunt & Cooke, 1996; Ichimura et.al, 2005; Nanni, 2006), fault diagnosis and fault tolerant (Canham, 2003; Branco, Dente, & Mendes, 2003), computer security and intrusion detection (Aickelin et.al., 2003; Dasgupta, 1999), and optimization (Engin & Doyen, 2004; Khilwani et.al, 2008). The field of AIS is showing great promise of being a powerful computing paradigm.

In this chapter, we further study the constructs and immune mechanism of natural immune system and present artificial immune systems based on the clonal selection principle. The mechanisms used in the algorithm are interpreted and several improvements of the algorithm are also introduced.

First and foremost, we study the receptor editing which is one of the most important mechanisms in the immune cell tolerance. Both hypermutation (HM) and receptor editing (RE) operators are used to maintain the diversity of the repertoire of B cells. And hypermutation is good for exploring local optimum, whereas receptor editing may help immune system to escape from local optima. Therefore the hypermutation and receptor editing might play complementary roles in affinity maturation process. Besides, by using

the characteristics of ergodicity and dynamic of chaos variables, the chaotic initialization mechanism is introduced into the clonal selection model to improve its global search capabilities. In order to overcome the inefficient local search ability of the algorithm, a distance-based hypermutation (DHM) operator which makes use of the information during gene positions is proposed. In this improved operator, the gene which is nearer to the preselected gene has higher probability to be selected. As a result, the improved hypermutation operator has a remarkable ability to generate higher affinity antibodies. Moreover, for the purpose of realizing the cooperation and communication among different antibodies, we also introduce a greedy crossover operator to the polyclonal selection algorithm and combined it to the traditional simulated annealing (SA) strategy. By using SA the probability of local minimum can be reduced because of the introduction of jump probability which can be adjusted by controlling the temperature. Furthermore, in order to solve the inherent disadvantages such as the information exchange during different antibodies, a literal interactive receptor editing (LIRE) is also presented. Inspired by the Idiotypic Network Theory, LIRE enables the system to realize the communication during different antibodies and therefore the performance is improved. Last but not least, we also proposed a pheromone-linker to combine the clonal selection algorithm with another nature phenomena inspired algorithm (Ant Colony Optimization) to construct a hybridization model. The pheromone-linker is utilized not only to realize the cooperation and communication between different elite pools in the clonal selection algorithm, but also to give the ant colony optimization some initial pheromones to accelerate its convergence speed. Simulations based on several traveling salesman problems demonstrated the efficiency and robustness of the proposed clonal selection models mentioned above.

Finally, some suggestions for future research are proposed, and the general remarks of this chapter are given to conclude this chapter.

Background

Over the past few decades there has been a growing interest in the use of biology as a source of inspiration for solving computational problems. Natural organisms exhibit powerful learning and processing abilities that allow them to survive and proliferate generation after generation in ever changing and challenging environments.

Significant attention has been given to the extraction of metaphors and ideas from the nervous system for the construction of Artificial Neural Networks (ANNs) and of neo-Darwinian evolution for the creation of evolutionary algorithms (EA). More recently however, attention has been drawn to the use of the immune system as another powerful metaphor. The immune system is incredibly robust; it is adaptive, inherently distributed, posses powerful pattern recognition, learning and memory capabilities. It is for these reasons (and more) the immune system is attracting such attention.

Natural Immune System

Natural immune system, one of the most intricate biological systems, is a complex of cells, molecules and organs that possesses an identification mechanism capable of distinguishing between self cells and non-self cells. In this section, we first present an overview of the natural immune system. Followed by this, we introduce the immune cells - the basic items of immune system, and systemic behavior of immune response respectively.

Overview of the Immune System

Although *Immunology* is a relatively new science, its origin can be retrospected to approximately 200 years ago. In 1796, E. Jenner discovered that the *vaccinia*, or *cowpox*, induced protection against human *smallpox*, a frequently lethal disease (Janeway Jr. & Travers, 1997).

Functionally, an immune response process can be divided into two related activities. One is immune recognition, and the other is immune response. The immune system can not only distinguish on foreign pathogen from another, but also can discriminate between foreign molecules and self cells and proteins. Once a foreign invader has been recognized, the immune system recruits a variety of immune cells and molecules to mount an appropriate response.

As an amazingly complex biological system, the immune system includes two inter-related systems: the *innate (natural) immune system* and the *adaptive (acquired) immune system*. Innate immunity, which is also known as nonspecific immunity, refers to the defense mechanism against foreign invaders that individuals are born with. Innate immunity is mainly composed of the following mechanisms: physiologic barriers, phagocytic barriers, and inflammatory response. Adaptive immunity, also called acquired or specific immunity, represents the part of the immune system that is able to specifically recognize and selectively eliminate foreign microorganism and molecules. The main characteristics of the adaptive immunity are the following: antigenic specificity, diversity, immunologic memory, and self/non-self discrimination

It is important to note that the acquired immunity does not act independently of the innate immunity; on the contrary, they work together to eliminate foreign invaders. For instance, the phagocytic cells (innate immunity) are involved in the activation of the adaptive immune response. Also, some soluble factors, produced during a specific immune response, have been found to augment the activity of these phagocytic cells. An important part of the adaptive immune system is managed by white blood cells, called lymphocytes. These cells are produced in the bone marrow, circulate in the blood and lymph system, and reside in various lymphoid organs to perform immunological functions.

Immune Organs and Cells

The immune system consists of many different immune organs and tissues that are found throughout the body. These organs are known as lymphoid organs and can be divided functionally into two main types: *primarily lymphoid organs*, responsible for the production of new lymphocytes, and *second lymphoid organs* where the lymphocyte repertoires meet the antigenic universe. *Tonsils, adenoids, lymphatic vessels, bone marrow, lymph nodes, the thymus, the spleen and the appendix* are all immune organs.

Lymphocytes are small *leukocytes* that possess a major responsibility in the immune system. They are responsible for adaptive immune response and the immunologic attributes such as diversity, specificity, memory and self/non-self discrimination. There are two main types of lymphocytes: B lymphocyte and T lymphocyte. We also call them B cell and T cell. These two types of immune cells are rather similar, but differ with relation to how they recognize antigens and by their functional roles.

B cell: The B cell derived its letter designation from its site of maturation, in the *Bursa* of *Fabricius* in birds. The main task of B cells includes generation and secretion of antibodies (Ab) as a response to invaders. Each B cell is programmed to produce a specific antibody. For example, one B cell will make an antibody that blocks a virus that causes the common cold, while another produces an antibody that attacks a bacterium that causes pneumonia. When a B cell encounters its triggering antigen, it gives rise to many large cells known as plasma cells. Every plasma cell is essentially a factory for producing an antibody. Each of the plasma cells descended from a given B cell manufactures millions of identical antibody molecules and pours them into the bloodstream.

T cell: T cells derive their name from their site of maturation in the *Thymus*. Their functions include the regulation of other cells' actions and directly attack the host infected cells. Unlike the membrane-bound antibody on B cells, the T cell receptor (TCR) does not recognize free antigen directly. Instead the TCR recognizes only antigen that is bound to particular classes of self-molecules, most T cells recognize antigen only when it is bound to a self-molecules encoded by major histocompatibility complex (MHC). MHC molecules are proteins recognized by T cells when distinguishing between self and non-self. A self MHC molecule provides a recognizable scaffolding to present a foreign antigen to the T cell.

Immune Response

Different immune cells play unique role in antigen recognition, and ensure that the immune system can recognize and respond to different types of antigens. In this section, we simply illustrate the basic immune response process as shown in Figure 1.

Immune system constitutes the defense mechanism of the body by means of physical barriers, physiologic barriers, innate immune response, and adaptive immune responses. Among these, adaptive immune response is more important for human being because it contains metaphors like recognition, memory acquisition, and etc. The main component of adaptive immune response is lymphocytes, which divide into two classes as T and B lymphocytes (cells), each having its own function. B cells have a great functionality because of their secreted antibodies (Ab) that take very critical roles in adaptive immune response. Figure 1 presents a simplified architecture of the basic immune mechanisms of defense. The first layer in the immune system is a diverse army of antigens. An antigen, which can cause diseases, is a foreign substance from the environment such as chemicals, viruses, pollen and so on. The ultimate target of all immune response is to prevent or eliminate the antigens. The second layer is composed of three kinds of components involving the physical barriers such as the skin and mucous membranes, the physiologic barriers such as saliva, sweat and tears, and the innate immune response. Through the second layer, a certain portion of antigens are

Figure 1. Multi-layered immune response

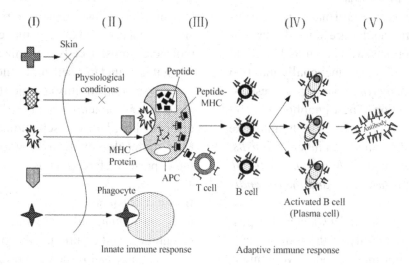

recognized and destroyed. The remaining antigens are subjected to the specialized antigen presenting cells (APC) where those encountered antigens are ingested and fragmented into antigenic peptides. The pieces of these peptides are displayed on the cell surface by major histocompatibility complex (MHC) molecules existing in the digesting APC. The presented MHC-peptide combination on the cell surface is recognized by the T cells causing them to be activated. Activated T cells secrete some chemicals as alert signals to B cells in response to this recognition. Those stimulated B cells proliferate (divide) and eventually mature into terminal (non-dividing) antibody secreting cells, called plasma cells. This process is known as the adaptive immune response. Finally, antibodies which are secreted on the surfaces of plasma cells bind the existing antigens and neutralize them signaling other components of immune system to destruct the antigen-antibody complex.

Artificial Immune Systems (AIS)

AIS are the use of immune system components and processes as inspiration to construct computational systems. As a result, theoretical immunology plays an important role in the development of AIS. In

the following, we will introduce some basic immune theories and their applications in artificial immune system.

Negative Selection Based Algorithm

During the generation of T cells, receptors are made through a pseudo-random genetic rearrangement process. Then, they undergo a censoring process in the thymus, called the negative selection. During this process, T cells that react against self antigens are destroyed; only those that do not bind to self antigens are allowed to leave the thymus. Accordingly, all T cells that leave the thymus are said to be tolerant to self, that is to say, they do not respond to self.

Forrest et al. (1994) developed a negative selection algorithm based on the principles of self/non-self discrimination in the natural immune system. The general ideas of the negative selection algorithm can be described as follows. In generation stage, the detectors are generated by some random process and censored by trying to match self samples. Those candidates that match are eliminated and the rest are kept as detectors. In the detection stage, the collection of detectors (or detector set) is used to check whether an incoming data instance is self or non-self. If it matches any detector, then it is claimed as non-self or anomaly. Furthermore, the feature space is restricted to binary string of fixed length and the matching between detectors and elements is defined by a process called *r*-contiguous matching. It is necessary to point out that the number of random detectors that is required to be generated is exponential on the size of self.

Immune Network Theory Based Algorithm

The immune network theory (Jerne, 1974), originally proposed by Jerne in 1974, suggests that the immune system is composed of a regulated network of molecules and cells that recognize on another even in the absence of antigens.

As mentioned in the previous section, the immune system is activated when it encounters a foreign antigen. However, it is reasonable that we want to keep minimum number of active immune system members, even if no antigenic attacks.

The immune network theory suggests that the immune system is formally defined as an enormous and complex network of *paratopes* that recognize sets of *idiotopes*, and *idiotopes* that are recognized by sets of *paratopes*, thus it can recognize as well as be recognized. Furthermore, the immune cells can respond either positively or negatively to the recognition signal. A positive response would lead to cell proliferation, cell activation and antibody secretion, whereas a negative response would result into tolerance and suppression.

Immune network theory based artificial immune models have also received amount attention. Hunt and Cooke (1996) started the works on immune network theory since 1995. Timmis (2001) and other researchers continued this work and made some improvements.

In artificial immune network (AIN) models, a B-cell population is made of two sub-populations: the initial population and the cloned population. The initial set is generated from a subset of raw training data to create the B-cell network. The remainders are used as antigen training items. Antigens are then selected randomly from the

training set and presented to the areas of the B-cell network. If the binding is successful, then the B-cell is cloned and mutate. The mutation yields a diverse set of antibodies that can be used in the classification procedure. Once a new B cell is created, an attempt is made to integrate it into the network at the closest B Cells. If the new B cell can not be integrated, it is removed from the population. If no bind is successful, then a B-cell is generated using the antigen as a template and is then incorporated into the network.

An updated version, called AINE (Timmis, 2001) uses artificial recognition ball (ARB) to represent a number of similar B-cells (not a single B cell). This resembles the idea of recognition ball in immunology, which refers to the region in the shape space of antigen that an antibody can recognize. It represents a single *n*-dimensional data item that could be matched by Euclidean distance to an antigen or another ARB. A link between two B-cells is created if the affinity (distance) between two ARBs is below a network affinity threshold (NAT). The results show that the combination of normalizing the stimulation levels of ARBs in the network and the resource allocation mechanism leads to the biasing of AINE towards the strongest pattern in the data set to emerge.

Clonal Selection Based Algorithm

Clonal selection principle is a form of natural selection. It establishes the idea that only those cells that recognize the antigens proliferate, thus being selected against those which do not.

Figure 2 depicts the clonal selection theory. When an animal is exposed to an antigen, some subpopulation of its bone marrow derived cells (B lymphocytes) can recognize the antigen with a certain affinity (degree of match), the B lymphocytes will be stimulated to proliferate (divide) and eventually mature into terminal (non-dividing) antibody secreting cells, called plasma cells. Proliferation of the B lymphocytes is a mitotic process whereby the cells divide themselves, creating a set of clones identical to the parent cell. The proliferation rate is directly proportional to the affinity level, i.e. the higher affinity levels of B lymphocytes, the more of them will be readily selected for cloning and cloned in larger numbers.

More specifically, during asexual reproduction, the repertoire of antigen-activated B cells is diversified basically by two mechanisms: somatic hypermutation and receptor editing. A rapid accumulation of hypermutation is necessary for a fast maturation of the immune response. More often than not, a large proportion of the cloned population becomes dysfunctional or develops into harmful anti-self cells after the mutation. However, occasionally an effective change enables the offspring cell to bind better with the antigen, hence affinity is improved. In the event that a mutated cloned cell with higher affinity is found, it in turn will be activated to undergo proliferation. It should be noted that the mutation on the cloned cells occurs at a rate which is inversely proportional to the antigen affinity. Clones of higher affinity cells are subjected to less mutation compared to those from cells which exhibit lower affinity. This process of constant selection and mutation of

only the B-cells with antibodies which can better recognize specific antigens is known as affinity maturation. Though the repertoire of antibodies in the immune system is limited; through affinity maturation, it is capable of evolving antibodies to successfully recognize and bind with known and unknown antigens, leading to their eventual elimination. On the other hand, those cells with low affinity receptors may be further mutated and are programmed for cell death by the immune system through a process called apoptosis if they do not improve their clone size of antigenic affinity.

In addition to somatic hypermutation and receptor editing, about 5-8% of the least stimulated lymphocytes is replaced per cell generation by newcomer cells from the bone marrow and join the pool of available antigen recognizing cells to maintain the diversity of the population.

Besides, the immune system also possesses memory properties as a portion of B-cells will differentiate into memory cells, which do not produce antibodies but instead remembers the antigenic pattern in anticipation of further re-infections. These memory cells circulate through the blood, lymph and tissues. When exposed to

Figure 2. The clonal selection principle

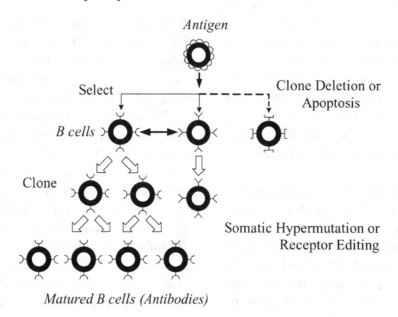

Matured B cells (Antibodies)

a second antigenic stimulus, they commence to differentiate into plasma cells capable of producing high-affinity antibodies, preselected for the specific antigen that had stimulated the primary response.

The early work of artificial immune system inspired by the clonal selection theory is carried out using genetic algorithm (GA) and evolutionary algorithm (EA). Forrest et al (1993) argue that a reasonable clonal selection model is a genetic algorithm (GA) without crossover. However, the standard genetic algorithm does not account for important properties such as affinity proportional reproduction and mutation. To fulfill the basic processes involved in clonal selection, other authors (de Castro & Von Zuben, 2002) proposed a clonal selection algorithm, named *CLONALG*.

In clonal selection algorithms, antigen usually means the problem and its constraints, while antibody represents the candidate solution of the problem. Mathematically, we use the Shape-space (Perelson, 1993) to quantitatively describe the interaction among them. The shape-space idea is that the degree of binding between a receptor and a molecule that it binds and it is presented a theoretical argument showing that a complete repertoire is attainable within the known parameters of immune recognition. Due to the fact that the antibody can be represented by a set of coordinates in a $_N$-dimensional shape-space, we express the antibody's receptor gene sequence as $R = (r_1, r_2, \ldots, r_N)$. Then the processes of the clonal selection algorithm can be generally described as follows.

- Step 1. Create an initial pool of $_m$ antibodies (candidate solutions $(Ab_1, Ab_2, \ldots, Ab_m)$).
- Step 2. Compute the affinity of all antibodies $(D(Ab_1), D(Ab_2), \ldots, D(Ab_m))$, where $D(.)$ is the function to compute the affinity.
- Step 3. Select $n(n < m)$ best (fittest) individuals based on their affinities from the $_m$ original antibodies. These antibodies will be referred to as the elites.

- Step 4. Place each of the $_n$ selected elites in $_n$ separate and distinct pools in an ascending order $(Ab_1, Ab_2, \ldots, Ab_n)$. They will be referred to as the elite pools. (Note: There is no crossover of antibodies between pools).
- Step 5. Clone the elites in each elite pool with a rate proportional to its fitness, i.e., the fitter the antibody, the more clones it will have. The amount of clone generated for these antibodies is given by:
$p_i = \text{round}(\frac{n-i}{n} \times Q)$ where $_i$ is the ordinal number of the elite pools, Q is a multiplying factor which determining the scope of the clone and round(.) is the operator that rounds its argument towards the closest integer. After this step, we can obtain $\sum P_i$ antibodies just as $(Ab_{11}, Ab_{12}, \ldots, Ab_{1p_1}; \ldots; Ab_{n1}, Ab_{n2}, \ldots, Ab_{np_n})$
- Step 6. Subject the clones in each pool through hypermutation process.
- Step 7. Determine the fittest individual B_i $D(B_i) = \max(D(Ab_{i1}), \ldots, D(Ab_{ip_i})), i = 1, 2, \ldots, n$ in each elite pool from amongst its mutated clones.
- Step 8. Update the parent antibodies in each elite pool with the fittest individual of the clones. If the clone is fitter than its parent, then it replaces its parent and vice-versa.
- Step 9. Replace the worst $_c$ ($\beta = c/n$) elite pools with new random antibodies once every $_k$ generations to introduce diversity and prevent the search from being trapped in local optima.
- Step 10. Determine if the maximum number of generation G_{max} to evolve is reached. If it has, terminate and return the best antibody; if it has not, return to Step 4.

Advanced Clonal Selection Model

In order to solve the inherent disadvantages in the previous clonal selection models, several improvements are proposed with respect to the operators, the initialization method, the antibody updating strategy, and so on.

Receptor Editing Operator

Receptor editing as a mechanism of immune cell tolerance is reported in several laboratories. Unlike the clonal deletion in classical clonal selection theory, occasionally immune cells are found undergo change of receptor specificity by secondary gene fragment rearrangements. As a result, the autoreactive immune cells can be salvaged before deletion by altering their receptors to express novel non-autoreactive immune cell receptors. This phenomenon is initially identified as a process that eliminates autoreactive receptors in newly generated immune cells and is termed receptor editing.

The basic mechanisms of the receptor editing can be illustrated in Figure 3. It has played a major role in shaping the lymphocyte repertoire. Both B and T lymphocytes that carry antigen receptors are able to change specificity through subsequent receptor gene rearrangement. This phenomenon is achieved by the unique structure of the antibody molecule, which is composed of two chains, each resulting from the somatic rearrangement of various genetic segments. In the case of B lymphocytes, which express at their surface a receptor (Ig for immunoglobulin, composed of heavy and light chains) allowing them to specifically recognize antigens, such as pathogenic microbes. The rearrangement takes place at the stage of the pro-B cells. In the primal rearrangement, the heavy chain locus is rearranged to produce a VDJ segment, which locus encodes numerous variable (V), diversity (D) and junction (J) segments. Within each individual pro-B cell, rearrangement starts when one D segment and one J segment join together. A V segment is then joined to the assembled DJ, forming a unique VDJ combination. Secondary rearrangement

also plays an important function in the process governing B lymphocyte tolerance. It occurs in the light chain, whose locus lack D regions, only V and J segments be assembled. Following an initial VJ rearrangement, upstream V segments can be further rearranged to downstream J segment, deleting or displacing the previously rearrange VJ segment. Furthermore, numerous V regions are in reverse orientation on the chromosome, these V are rearranged by inversion rather than by deletion of the intervening sequences, and hence preserve the V segments encoded in it. This retains a high number of V for more rearrangement. Moreover, Pelanda and Torres (2006) interpret that clonal deletion, previously regarded as the major mechanism of central B cell tolerance, has been shown to operate secondarily and only when receptor editing is unable to provide a non-autoreactive specificity.

In the receptor editing clonal selection algorithm, a new operator is added into the step 6 (as in the original clonal selection algorithm) and the clones are subjected to either hypermutation or receptor editing operators. The new receptor editing operator based on Figure 3 can be introduced in the following. The editing on heavy chains occurs mostly by deletion of the intervening gene sequence while in the case of light chain receptor gene editing can occur either by deletion or by inversion of the intervening gene fragment. When applying the model to the Traveling Salesman Problem (TSP), we just use the inversion operator since the deletion operator can produce an illegal tour for TSP. If receptor gene position $_i$ and $_j$ are selected, then the novel gene sequences based on inversion can be illustrated as:

$$r_1 \cdots \to r_{i-1} \to \mathbf{r_i} \to r_{i+1} \cdots r_{j-1} \to \mathbf{r_j} \to r_{j+1} \cdots \to r_N$$
$$\Downarrow$$
$$\text{inversion}(\mathbf{r_i} \to r_{i+1} \cdots r_{j-1} \Rightarrow r_{j-1} \cdots r_{i+1} \cdots \mathbf{r_i})$$
$$\Downarrow$$
$$r_1 \cdots \to r_{i-1} \to r_{j-1} \cdots r_{i+1} \to \mathbf{r_i} \to \mathbf{r_j} \to r_{j+1} \cdots \to r_N$$

Figure 3. Gene fragment rearrangement on heave chain (a) and on light chain (b).

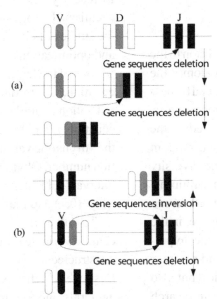

Some of the clones in each elite pool undergo the hypermutation process and the remainder of the clones passes the receptor editing process. The mutation number (P_{hm} and P_{re} for hypermutation and receptor editing, respectively) are defined as follows: $P_{hm}=\lambda \cdot p_i$; $P_{re}=(1-\lambda)\cdot p_i$, where λ is a user-defined parameter which determines the complementary intensity between the hypermutation and receptor editing and we also find that an equivalent level of $P_{hm}:P_{re}$, that is $\lambda=0.5$ will lead the algorithm to a better performance.

As to the efforts of the receptor editing taking on the hypermutation, we declare that the receptor editing can prevent the search process from becoming "premature" and increase the global search ability. If a particular immune cell is selected during the primary immune response, then the immune system explores the local area around the selected cell, by hypermutation, with small alterations in the shape of the antigen-binding site. The higher affinity mutated immune cell will be selected. As a result of this, after a series of small steps, the selected immune cell reaches a maximum. According to the clonal selection theory, low affinity cells are deleted. Hence, facing the enormous number of different antigens, an immune cell undergoing hypermutation might become stuck at a local optimal and cannot improve affinity further. As mentioned above, receptor editing allows the immune system to rescue immune cells before deletion. This also provides a chance to immune system to escape from local optimum. Nevertheless, some studies found that receptor editing might promote not only tolerance but also autoreactive. In other words, most cases of editing will land the immune cells in a locale where the affinity is lower than current affinity. Occasionally, the editing will produce a higher affinity immune cell. The higher affinity cell can then improve its affinity to better state by hypermutation.

In general, hypermutation is good for exploring local optimum, whereas receptor editing may help immune system to escape from local optima. Thus the conclusion that the hypermutation and receptor editing might play complementary roles in the affinity maturation process is presented.

Chaotic Initialization and Distance-Based Hypermutation

In the clonal selection algorithm, in addition to the initial antibody repertoire generated randomly, the low affinity antibodies have to be replaced by new random antibodies during the mutation process. No doubt, these random antibodies will reduce the complexity of the algorithm. However, random antibodies have a bad influence on the diversity of repertoire. As a result, the search within affinity landscape will become premature and can not produce better solutions. Furthermore, in the process of greedy search, both somatic hypermutation of clonal selection theory and receptor editing generate not only high affinities, but also low affinity antibodies usually. Hence, the search efficiency is reduced. To solve this mechanism, a distance-based hypermutation operator for all selected antibodies is constructed. According to this mechanism, a gene which is nearer to the preselected gene has higher probability to be selected.

The basic ideas of the two methods can be illustrated as follows. First, the solution space of the optimization problem is mapped to the ergodic space of chaotic variables; and thus optimization variables are represented by chaotic variables which are coded into an antibody. Then, taking full advantages of the ergodic and stochastic properties of chaotic variables, both distance-based somatic hypermutation and receptor editing are performed in the neighborhoods of high affinity antibodies to exploit the local solution space, and the motion of chaotic variables in their ergodic space is used to explore the whole solution space.

Chaotic Initialization

As a kind of characteristic of nonlinear systems, chaos is a bounded unstable dynamic behavior that exhibits sensitive dependence on initial conditions and infinite unstable periodic motions. Although it appears to be stochastic, it occurs in a deterministic nonlinear system under deterministic conditions.

In recent years, growing interest from physics, chemistry, biology, and engineering has stimulated the studies of chaos for control, synchronization and optimization.

One of the famous chaos systems, the Logistic equation, is introduced in the process of the initialization of antibodies defined by the following equation: $z_i(k+1)=4z_i(k)(1-z_i(k))$, where z_i denotes the i-th chaotic variable and k represents the iteration number. Obviously, $z_i(k)$ is distributed in the interval $(0,1)$ under the conditions that the initial $z_i(k) \in (0,1)$ and that $z_i(0) \notin \{0.25,0.5,0.75\}$.

To solve traveling salesman problems, each chaotic variable corresponding to a valid tour is constructed according to the permutation theory. First, we will discuss the transform rule with the numerals one to three as an example. There are $3!=6$ total permutations of these numerals illustrated in Table 1.

Here, the construction is in lexicographic order. D is the serial number and $V=(v_1,v_2)$ indicates the vector of the permutations, where v_1, v_2 means the ordering of firstly and secondly selected elements respectively. The relationship between D and V can be constructed as follows:

$$
\begin{cases}
D_0 = D \\
v_i = \dfrac{D_{i-1}}{(n-i)!} & i = 1,2,\ldots,n-1 \\
D_i = D_{i-1} - (v_i - 1)(n-i)!
\end{cases}
$$

where the function x rounds the elements of x to the nearest integers greater than or equal to x. Then C is constructed according to the pointer of V. For example, $V=v_1v_2=21$ (where D=3), we can obtain $C=C_1C_2C_3=213$ shown as follows:

In order to generate chaotic permutations, we set $D_0=n!z_i$ and $d_i=nz_i$ where the chaotic variable z_i can be obtained according to the Logistic equation. Thus the transform rule is modified as follows:

Table 1. The DVC table of R=(1,2,3)

D	V	C
1	11	123
2	12	132
3	21	213
4	22	231
5	31	312
6	32	321

$$\begin{cases} v_1 = d_1 \\ d_i = (n-i+1)(d_{i-1} - v_{i-1} + 1) \\ \quad v_i = d_i \qquad\qquad i = 1,2,\ldots,n-1 \end{cases}$$

So we have established a one-to-one correspondence between the permutation C (i.e. the antibody's receptor gene sequence) and the chaotic variable z_i.

Distance-Based Hypermutation Operator

In order to account for the enormous number of antigens, immune cells possess the unique ability to acquire large numbers of somatic hypermutation in the immune cell's gene sequence. In the former clonal selection model, the somatic hypermutation was simply performed by swapping pairs of gene positions in the antibodies and can be illustrated as follows:

$$r_1 \rightarrow r_2 \ldots \rightarrow r_i \rightarrow r_{i+1} \ldots \rightarrow r_j \rightarrow r_{j+1} \ldots \rightarrow r_N$$
$$\Downarrow$$
$$r_1 \rightarrow r_2 \ldots \rightarrow r_j \rightarrow r_{i+1} \ldots \rightarrow r_i \rightarrow r_{j+1} \ldots \rightarrow r_N$$

However, the original hypermutation operator usually generates low affinity antibodies rather than high ones and thus has inefficient local search ability. Therefore we can overcome this problem by utilizing information from genes. Suppose $d(i,j)$ indicates the distance between the gene position i and j, and the current randomly selected position is i. Then the probability to select the following position j can be calculated according to the equation shown as follows:

$$p_j = \frac{d_{max} - d(i,j)}{\sum_{k=1}^{n}(d_{max} - d(i,k))}$$

where $d_{max} = \max\{d(i,j)\}$, ($j=1,2,\ldots,N$ and $j \neq i$). According to this equation, the gene position which is nearer to the preselected gene position has a higher probability to be selected. So in this condition the distance-based hypermutation operator can be illustrated as follows:

Table 2.

$v_1=2$	123	$C_1=2$
$v_2=1$	13	$C_2=1$
		$C_3=3$
$C=C_1C_2C_3=213$		

$$r_1 \rightarrow r_2 \cdots \rightarrow \mathbf{r_i} \rightarrow r_{i+1} \cdots \rightarrow \mathbf{r_j} \rightarrow r_{j+1} \cdots \rightarrow r_N$$
$$\Downarrow$$
$$r_1 \rightarrow r_2 \cdots \rightarrow \mathbf{r_i} \rightarrow \mathbf{r_j} \rightarrow r_{i+1} \cdots \rightarrow r_{j+1} \cdots \rightarrow r_N$$

Generally speaking, by using the characteristics of ergodicity and dynamic of chaos variables, the chaotic initialization mechanism is introduced into the clonal selection algorithm to improve its global search capabilities. On the other hand, to overcome the inefficient local search ability of the algorithm, the proposed algorithm uses a distance-based hyper-mutation operator utilizing the information during gene positions and thus the gene which is nearer to the preselected gene has higher probability to be selected. As a result, the improved hypermutation operator has a remarkable ability to generate higher affinity antibodies.

Polyclonal Selection Algorithm with Simulated Annealing (PCASA)

As a class of meta-heuristic optimization algorithm, simulated annealing (SA) is based on the analogy between simulation of the annealing solids and the problem of solving large combinatorial optimization problems. The effectiveness of SA is attributed to the nature that it can explore the design space by means of neighborhood structure and escape from local minima by probabilistically allowing uphill moves controlled by the temperature parameter.

By using the polyclonal selection algorithm, which is also derived from the clonal selection theory, the solution space can be exploited and explored parallelly and effectively. In addition, the advantage of using SA which, in general, is able to obtain improvement even into the late phase of the process, is that the probability to be trapped in local minimum can be reduced by employing a jump, and as such this jump can by adjusted by controlling the temperature.

The polyclonal selection algorithm is realized by utilizing a greedy crossover operator which carries out the cooperation and communication among different antibodies and the conceptual graph is shown in Figure 4.

Greedy Crossover Operator

In order to fulfill the purpose of realizing the cooperation and communication among the different antibodies which would enable us to obtain the diversity and high convergence speed, we have added a greedy crossover operator into the algorithm. Greedy crossover selects the first city of one parent, compares the distance between the first city and the city next to it in both of the parents. From this comparison, the city with the shorter distance is chosen. The newly chosen city will then be used for the same comparison with the next city in both the parents as mentioned earlier. If one city has already appeared in the tour, the other alternate city will then be selected. However, in the case where by both the cities have already

Figure 4. The conceptual graph of the multiple clonal operator (polyclonal)

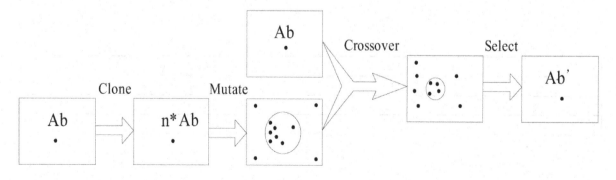

appeared, the non-selected city which is the closest to the current city will then be chosen.

Simulated Annealing Strategy

Simulated annealing is based on thermodynamics and can be considered as an algorithm that generates a sequence of Markov chains controlled by gradually decreasing temperature of the system. The algorithm employs a random search which not only accepts changes that decrease objective function, but also some changes that increases it with a probability. Its major advantage over other methods is the ability to obtain improvements even into the late phase of the process and thus avoids being trapped at local minima.

The simulated annealing strategy is incorporated into the antibody updating process (step 8). At each temperature T, if the affinity of the best offspring B_i is larger than the affinity of the parents, the offspring is accepted into the elite pools or else it can also be accepted with probability P. The probability $P(Ab_i \rightarrow B_i)$ is according to the role followed by:

$$P = \begin{cases} 1 & D\left(Ab_i\right) < D(B_i) \\ 0 & D\left(Ab_i\right) \geq D(B_i) \\ \exp(\dfrac{D\left(B_i\right) - D(Ab_i)}{T}) & \text{otherwise} \end{cases}$$

and the cooling scheme is defined as $T(t+1)=T(t)*(1-\delta)$. According to this updating rule, if the fittest individual of the clones B_i in each elite pool has higher affinity than its parent antibody Ab_i, update with probability "1". As a result, the elite in the offspring have been preserved and enter into the following generation. On the contrary, if B_i is not better than its parent, then update according to an exponential function to maintain the diversity of the population, where the temperature is related to the diversity. Generally, the better the diversity is, the bigger

T is. Otherwise, T is smaller. It is obvious that by controlling T, the population diversity can be easily manipulated. In the earlier searching phase the diversity is well maintained to enhance the global search, while in the latter searching phase the algorithm concentrates on finding a local-optimal solution. Furthermore, in order to save the information of the original population such that the best antibody during the parents could not be replaced, the exponential function is not used for AB_i.

Lateral Interactive Receptor Editing (LIRE)

In order to solve the inherent disadvantages of the clonal selection algorithm, such as the information exchange during different antibodies, we propose a lateral interactive receptor editing. Similar to the crossover operator in the genetic algorithms (GA), the information exchange or communication during different antibodies (chromosomes) has been demonstrated to be a powerful strategy to improve the search performance of the algorithms. However, according to the clonal selection principle, there is no crossover of genetic material between members of the repertoire in the immune response process. Aiming at the realization of the communication during different antibodies, we construct a literal interactive receptor editing (LIRE) which is inspired by the Idiotypic Network Theory. Different from the crossover in GA which is a binary operator, the LIRE just manipulates a single antibody. It is realized based on the idiotopes of an antibody. The idiotopes are a set of particular substances of an antibody; they can recognize other antibodies to some extent. Thus, even though there is no genetic material exchange during antibodies, the information communication can also be accomplished.

In the affinity maturation process, not only the hypermutation and receptor editing react on paratopes, but also the literal reaction during different antibodies takes place. Figure 5 illustrates the idiotypic network. Once an antigen is presented to the immune system, its epitope is recognized by a set of different paratopes on antibodies (taking B1 as an example) with various degrees of precision (affinity). These paratopes occur on antibody and receptor molecules together with certain idiotopes. As a result, the set of paratopes is associated with a set of idiotypes. Within the immune network, the idiotopes on B1 can recognize other paratopes on B2 and B3. That is to say, each paratope on an antibody can not only recognize a foreign antigen, but also can be recognized by external idiotopes. In Figure 5, the recognition of an antigen denotes the antibody receives stimulation from the antigen; and the restraint actions represent the recognitions during idiotopes and paratopes.

Due to fact that the antibody can be represented by a set of coordinates in a N-dimensional shape-space, we express the paratopes of an antibody to be a gene sequence as $P=(p_1, p_2, \ldots, p_N)$, and the idiotopes to be a set of gene segments as $I=(i, \ldots, i_n)$ (here, the variable n ($n<N$) means the number of the idiotopes of an antibody, and the value of n denotes the degree of the literal interaction from other antibodies). Thus, an antibody can be described as Ab=(P,I). The affinity is the degree of match between the paratopes of an antibody and the epitope of the antigen. In this section, we use

$$E(Ab) = E(P) = \sum_{i=1}^{N-1} E(p_i, p_{i+1}) + E(p_1, p_N)$$

to quantitatively describe it, where E(.) denotes the affinity function and is determined according the problem. The object of the algorithm is to find a maximum value of E(P) based on the problem. Figure 6 shows an example of the literal interaction during different antibodies, where the paratope size is supposed to be eight and there are three different antibodies B1, B2 and B3. The paratopes of these antibodies are P_1=(abcdefgh), P_2=(fgdbecha), and P_3=(bcfghaed). Initially, the idiotopes of the antibodies are empty. Once B1 receives stimuli from B2 and B3 and the reaction gene on B1 is c, some genes will be memorized on the idiotopes of B1. The genes on the paratopes of B2 and B3 that are the same as c will be recognized and those genes that are the successors of c will be memorized on the idiotopes of B1. In our example, h and f are the literal interaction results from B2 and B3, respectively.

In the idiotypic network, an antibody will receive stimuli from all of the other antibodies. That is to say, after the literal interaction, n (n=m-1) idiotopes of an antibody will be filled in. In the model, the clone $Ab_{ij} \rightarrow P=(p_1, p_2, \ldots, p_N)$

Figure 5. Idiotypic network representation

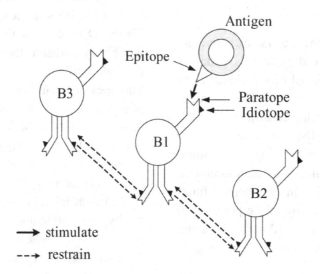

of antibody Ab_1 undergone this step will become $Ab_{ij} \rightarrow (P,I) = (p_1, p_2, \ldots, p_N, i_1, \ldots, i_{m-1})$, where the idiotopes $i_1, \ldots, i_{m-1}$ are the literal interaction results from antibodies Ab_j ($j=1,2,\ldots,m$ and $j \neq i$), respectively.

Then, the literal interactive receptor editing operator is utilized to manipulate these clones. Figure 7 illustrates an example of this process. Based on the idiotopes of the antibody B1, i.e. f and h, the original receptor editing is carried out. One of the inversion positions is the successor of reaction gene c, i.e. d in our example. We use the idiotopes of B1 as the other inversion position one by one. After inversion, we will get (abcfedgh) and (abchgfed) based on f and h, respectively. Then, an update rule takes place. Among these m-1 clones that have undergone LIRE, the one with the fittest affinity will be selected to replace the parent antibody.

Fast Algorithm for the Implementation of LIRE

First, we define two functions pos(.) and gene(.) on the paratopes $P_i = (p_1, \ldots, p_N)$ of an antibody Ab_i as follows: gene(r)=s and pos(s)=r when gene r is located on the s-th element of P_i. Taking B1 in Figure 6 as an example, we have gene(2)=b and pos(b)=2.

Then, in order to fill in the idiotopes of Ab_i (suppose the reaction gene is c), we need to find the same gene as c on the other antibodies Ab_j ($j=1,2,\ldots,m$ and $j \neq i$). The functions defined on Ab_i and Ab_j are $pos_i(.), gene_i(.)$, and $pos_j(.), gene_j(.)$, respectively. As a result, the idiotopes of Ab_i can be enumerated as follows: $gene_j(pos_i(c)+1)$, for $j=1,2,\ldots,m$ and $j \neq i$. The fast algorithm for the implementation of LIRE on antibody Ab_i is represented in the following:

01: **Begin**
02: randomly choose a reaction gene h_1 among P on Ab_i
03: $h_2 := gene_i(pos_i(c)+1)$
04: **for** j:=1 **to** m and $j \neq i$ **do**
05: $h_3 := gene_j(pos_j(h_1)+1)$
06: $h_4 := gene_i(pos_i(h_3)+1$
07: gain$:= E(h_1,h_3)+E(h_2,h_4)-E(h_1,h_2)-E(h_3,h_4)$
08: **if** (gain≥ 0) **then**
09: inverse the genes between h_2 and h_3
10: **end-for**
11: **End**

There are several characteristics of the implementation of LIRE. First and foremost, the operator LIRE is unary. It spends much less computation time in comparison with binary operators. Besides,

Figure 6. An example of the literal interaction during different antibodies

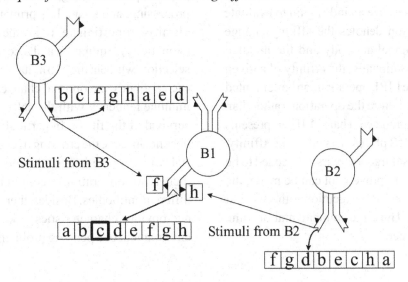

Figure 7. An example of the literal interaction receptor editing operator

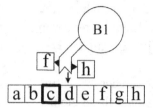

B1: Paratope: a b c d e f g h
     Reaction Gene : c
     Idiotope: f h

LIRE(B1): a b c f e d g h

a b c h g f e d

there are some knowledge exchanges between antibodies, at least one gene segment (h_1,h_3). Thus, the elitist part of the genes (as the common genes during different antibodies are regarded as elites, similar to the crossover in GA) can be memorized. Furthermore, LIRE has the ability of generating a new gene segment, such as (h_2,h_4), without which the algorithm would perform the search only among gene segments present in the initial population. Therefore, the diversity of the population can be maintained to some extent. Last but not least, we utilize an index gain to evaluate the inversion. gain denotes the affinity change between the original antibody and the mutated one. And computationally, the affinity of a given antibody after the LIRE operation can be computed from the affinity before the operation, rather than needing to be recomputed. That is, LIRE represents cutting the tour at 2 places. To update the affinity, only 4 addition-subtraction pairs are needed to be carried out. If an improvement can be made, the inversion is carried into execution; otherwise, it takes no effect. Thus, the implementation time can also be reduced.

CSA Combined with Ant Colony Optimization (CSACO)

Among those nature phenomena inspired algorithms, the clonal selection algorithm (CSA) and ant colony optimization (ACO) are two main branches. CSA is designed based on the basic features of adaptive immune response to antigenic stimulus and has been verified as having a great number of useful mechanisms from the viewpoint of programming, controlling, information processing, and so on. It is primarily based upon affinity-proportionate reproduction, mutation (somatic hypermutation and receptor editing) and selection, wherein the two mutation operators give each antibody the optimal chance and ensure the immune tendency with the select mechanism of survival of the fittest. In particular, the mutation does not involve the crossing over of genetic material between members of the repertoire and thus there is no cooperation or communication among different antibodies. Besides, there are many basic and obvious characteristics or knowledge in the environment of a pending problem. Utilization of the feedback information from the environment may be a good alternative method for improving the search performance of an algorithm. However, in CSA, the mutation and selection mechanisms lack the capability to capture the hits provided by the environment, so may be torpid when solving complex problems. On the other hand, ACO is a class of constructive multi-agent metaheuristic algorithms that are analogous with the behavior of real ants. It has been widely used as search algorithms in various applications and has demonstrated satisfactory performance. It tries to imitate the basic mechanisms that allow ants to find the shortest path from their colony to a food source. Compared with CSA, ACO has some attractive characteristics. Ants can communicate with the environment through secreting pheromone (aromatic substances) in their traveling paths. They can sense the density of the pheromone and have the tendency to choose a specific path is positively correlated to the density of a found trail. Moreover, ACO has constructive cooperation between ants; that is, ants in the colony share information among themselves through pheromone. If many ants choose a certain path and lay down pheromones, the density of the trail increases and thus this trail attracts more and more ants. General speaking, in ACO, the ability of utilizing environment feedback information is preeminent, but its inherent shortcoming that slows convergence speed is also visible. Based on this consideration, we propose a pheromone-linker to combine CSA and ACO. The basic idea of the proposed model can be interpreted as follows. First, the solution space of the optimization problem was explored by CSA parallelly and effectively. Then, based on the pheromone-linker, that is, the pheromones that secreted by the best antibody of each elite pool in CSA, ACO was utilized not only to exploit the local solution space but also to realize the cooperation and communication during different elite pools.

An Overview of Ant Colony Optimization

The ant colony optimization is a metaheuristic approach first proposed by M. Dorigo (2004). The inspiring source of ACO is the foraging behavior of ants. This behavior enables ants to find the shortest route between a food source and their nest. The key to such effectiveness is pheromone--a chemical substance deposited by ants as they travel. Pheromone provides ants with ability to communicate with each other. Ants essentially move randomly, but when they encounter a pheromone trail, they decide whether or not to follow it. If they do so, they deposit their own pheromone on the trail, which reinforces the path. The probability that an ant chooses one path over another is governed by the amount of pheromone on the potential path of interest. Because of the pheromone, trails that are more frequently traveled by ants become more attractive alternative for other ants. Subsequently, less traveled paths become less likely paths for other ants. With time, the amount of pheromone on a path evaporates. Prior to the establishment of the most desirable pheromone trails, individual ants will use all potential paths in equal numbers, depositing pheromone as they travel. But the ants taking the shorter path will return to the nest first with food. The shorter pathway will have the most pheromone because the path has fresh pheromone and has not yet evaporated, and will be more attractive to those ants that return to the food source. There is, however, always a probability that an ant will not follow a well-marked pheromone trail. This probability (although small) allows for exploration of other trails, which is beneficial because it allows discovery of shorter or alternate pathways, or new sources of food. Given that the pheromone trail evaporates over time, the trail will become less detectable on longer trails, since these trails take more time to traverse. The longer trails will hence be less attractive, which benefit to the colony as a whole.

Till now, there are several versions of ant colony optimization. The first one presented in the literature is called ant system (AS). Later many developments have taken place in ACO methodologies, such as elitist strategy for ant system (EAS), rank based ant system, ant colony system (ACS) and MAX-MIN ant system (MMAS). These variants of ACO differ from each other in that their idiographic realizations are different. Thus, for the purpose of making our hybrid algorithm be general and fundamental, all those well-known improvements were not introduced in our model, although they might be able to improve the performance of the hybrid algorithm. In other words, we adopted the ant system algorithm to be combined with CSA.

Pheromone-Linker to Combine CSA with ACO

For the sake of combining CSA with ACO more elaborately and smoothly, the pheromone-linker has been proposed in this chapter. There are two main functions of this pheromone-linker. One is to realize the cooperation and communication during different elite pools in CSA. The other is to give ACO some initial pheromones and accelerate its convergence speed. In our proposed model, the pheromone-linker is constructed as follows:

First, determine the fittest antibodies in each elite pool from amongst its updated clones. Then the selected antibodies deposit pheromones on the whole repertoire (corresponding to the map in TSP) according to the following rule:

$$\tau_{ij}(k) = \begin{cases} D(k) & \text{if gene segment } (r_i, r_j) \text{ is contained by antibody } k. \\ \varepsilon & \text{otherwise.} \end{cases}$$

where k denotes the selected antibody. τ_{ij} is the quantum of pheromone on gene segment (r_i, r_j). $D(k)$ is the affinity of antibody k, while ε is a small constant in order to avoid producing invalid solutions in the following ACO search step by giving all the gene segments not contained by the antibodies a small survival chance. By this pheromone-secreting rule, the higher affinity of the selected antibody, the more pheromone is

received by the gene segment belonging to this antibody. Then each antibody B_i deposits pheromone in the repertoire.

Based on the initialized pheromones, the repertoire is judged through an ACO search procedure. Initially, n' (usually set to be equal to the value of elite pool n) ants are placed on randomly chosen gene positions. Then, in each construction step, each ant moves, according to a probabilistic decision, to a gene position it has not yet visited. Ant k currently located at position i chooses to go to position j with a probability:

$$P_{ij}(k) = \frac{[\tau_{ij}]^{\alpha}[\eta_{ij}]^{\beta}}{\sum_{l \in N_k}[\tau_{il}]^{\alpha}[\eta_{il}]^{\beta}} \quad \text{if} \quad j \in N_k$$

where the locally available heuristic information η_{ij} is usually set to be $1/d(I,j)$. Parameters α and β determine the relative importance of the pheromone trail and the heuristic information, and N_k denotes the feasible neighborhood of ant k. After all ants have completed the tour construction, the pheromone trails are updated according to:

$$\tau_{ij} \rightarrow \rho\tau_{ij} + \sum_{k=1}^{n'}\Delta\tau_{ij}(k)$$

$$\Delta\tau_{ij}(k) = \begin{cases} 1/L(k) & \text{if gene segment } (r_i, r_j) \text{ is traveled by ant } k \\ 0 & \text{otherwise} \end{cases}$$

where the parameter ρ is the trail persistence and $L(k)$ is the tour length of the k-th ant. Through this procedure, n' new antibodies (solutions) has been produced by the n' ants.

The primary characteristics of the proposed hybridization can be summarized as follows: Based on the initial pheromones on the repertoire (i.e. the map in TSP) secreted by the fittest antibodies in each elite pool, ACO is utilized to act as a local search operator. As a result, the local search ability of CSA can be enhanced. Moreover, due to all of the elite pools take effects synchronously and interact with each other that is realized by the pheromones, all of the elitist gene segments in each pool have been memorized by the repertoire and thus the repertoire can give some hits to lead the immune system to construct fitter antibodies based on these segments in the next generation. On the other hand, the speed at which the traditional ACO gives the solution is slow if there is little information pheromone on the path early. To solve this problem, in our proposed algorithm, ACO adopts CSA to give information pheromone to distribute and thus the convergence speed of ACO can be accelerated.

Application to the Traveling Salesman Problem (TSP)

The Traveling Salesman Problem (TSP) is a classic combinatorial optimization problem, which is simple to state but very difficult to solve. The problem is to find the shortest possible tour through a set of cities so that each city is visited exactly once. This problem is known to be NP-hard, and cannot be solved exactly in polynomial time.

In the traveling salesman problem, we are given a set $\{c_1, c_2, \ldots, c_N\}$ of cities and for each pair $\{c_i, c_j\}$ of distinct cities a distance $d(c_i, c_j)$. Here, the subscript N denotes the number of cities in a tour. The objective of the TSP is to find an ordering π (Hamiltonian cycle) of the cities that minimize the following equation (where $D(\pi)$ denotes the total tour length of the ordering π):

$$D\left(\pi\right) = \sum_{i=1}^{N-1} d(c_{\pi(i)}, c_{\pi(i+1)}) + d(c_{\pi(N)}, c_{\pi(1)})$$

In this chapter, we concentrate our attention upon the symmetric TSP, in which the distance satisfies $d(c_i, c_j) = d(c_j, c_i)$ for $1 \leq i, j \leq N$. The number of the Hamiltonian cycles, i.e. the size of feasible solutions in the TSP, is actually $(N-1)!/2$.

The choice of data structure for tour representation plays a critical role in the efficiency of exploitation and exploration for the traveling salesman problem. There are several traditional types of the representation, such as the Permutation representation, the Matrix representation which is usually adopted in the Artificial Neural Networks (ANNs) and the Tree representation (involving Splay Tree, Two-Level Tree and Segment Tree) whose implementation is efficient but programming is more complex.

Due to the simplicity of programming and the analogy with the gene representation in the immune system, the Permutation $V = (v_1, v_2, \ldots, v_i, \ldots, v_N)$ is utilized in this study, where $v_i = k$ denotes that the city k is in the position i in the tour. Thus this permutation represents a feasible solution for TSP that the first city to be visited is the value of v_1 and the i-th city to be visited is the value of v_i. The last city to be visited before going back to the city v_1 is the city v_N. It should be noticed that with this representation the direction is not arbitrary. For instance, although the state (A,B,C,D)) is different from the state (B,C,D,A)), they represent the same tour.

In order to verify the effectiveness of the proposed clonal selection model, fifteen instances of TSP are tested. These problem instances of TSP are taken from TSPLIB. There are two types of the selected instances involving EUC_2D and ATT. The meanings of them are distance and pseudo-Euclidean distance respectively. A detailed description can be found in TSPLIB. Then five variants of the clonal selection are constructed involving RECS making use of the receptor editing operator, CDCS which utilizes the chaotic initialization and distance-based hypermutation, PCSSA which incorporates the simulated annealing into the polyclonal selection algorithm, LICS which uses distance-based hypermutation and literal interactive receptor editing operators, and CSACO which combines the clonal selection algorithm with the ant system. In addition, the conventional genetic algorithm (GA) is used to make a comparison. In GA, we utilizes the roulette wheel selection and elite preservation strategy. The traditional mutate operator 2-opt and greedy crossover operator with mutate probability 0.03 and 0.85 respectively are adopted.

Figure 8 illustrates the simulation results based on the fifteen TSP instances. The horizontal axis indicates the name of the instance, while the vertical axis denotes the quality of the solution produced by each algorithm. In this study, it is evaluated as the deviation from the known best result of the solution. From Figure 8, we can find that each algorithm incorporated with a new proposed mechanism (or operator) can produce better solutions and construct a much smoother curve than the previous one. As a result, the efficiency and the robustness of the proposed clonal selection model have been demonstrated.

FUTURE TRENDS

Objectively, the interrelated algorithms of the artificial immune system (especially the clonal selection algorithm) are mostly put forward after the year 1997. As these algorithms are almost exclusive to specific problems, there are very few profound and universal achievements of the computational complexity and convergence which have been gained. Thus, likewise most researchers, this chapter conveys to the public that the current period of research should focus on resolving the basis of its existence, which includes:

1. Go a step further on various kinds of algorithm mechanisms of immune system. That is because only with deeper understanding of immune mechanism, it could be possible to keep digging in the study of the construction (or architecture) of new algorithm. Furthermore, the discovery of new mechanism would undoubtedly promote the emergence of new methods of algorithm.

2. Improve the already existed matrix of artificial immune system. Like mentioned above, the now existed matrix of artificial immune system is over-simple, still cannot lay solid foundations for the application of artificial intelligence. More specifically,

Figure 8. Comparison of the average quality of the solutions during six algorithms for all tested instances.

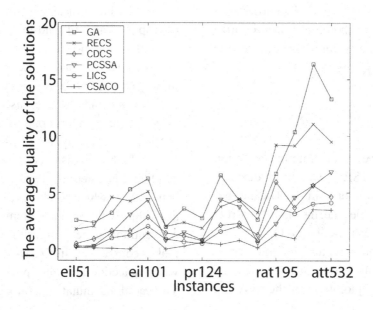

make it possible to thoroughly master the implementation of the algorithm, analyze the convergence and computational complexity of the algorithm, hence make room for further criticism and improvement.

3. Open up brand new implement fields for the artificial immune system. Like other artificial intelligence methods, the utility of method research is the standard of evaluating whether or not this algorithm is feasible, when has been put into application. While the artificial immune system research including the clonal selection model has been widely and rapidly applied within ten years, it has been hardly evaluated as highly as other intelligent algorithms in engineering application.

4. Based on the research of hybridization of the artificial immune system with other nature-inspired methods, the immune mechanism could be used to improve many current existed algorithms. Numerous algorithms like immune-evolution, immune-neural network and so forth have been brought up for discussion, meanwhile successfully applied. The newly emerged thoughts and methods during hybridization expand the ability of dealing more complicate issues. The artificial immune mechanism research could be a major contribution towards science of artificial intelligence in a totally new perspective.

5. Among these existent frame theories, the study of neural network has advanced onto an upper stage; meanwhile the immune mechanism is in the process of emerging. Although the research about the mechanism and algorithm of the incretion system has not been reported yet, it is for sure another newly emerged field coming along with the research of immune mechanism.

CONCLUSION

In this chapter, we discussed the clonal selection model. Several new clonal selection principles and related operators were incorporated into the clonal selection algorithm.

In the antibody's initialization stage, the chaotic initialization method was introduced to improve the global search capabilities of the algorithm by using the characteristics of ergodicity and dynamic of chaos variables. As for the mutate operators in the algorithm, based on the newly found receptor editing mechanism in the immune response process, the receptor editing operator was proposed to carry out the global search ability of the algorithm. The relationship between the hypermutation and receptor editing operators that they played complementary roles in the affinity maturation process was revealed. Furthermore, the enhanced operators of the hypermutation and receptor editing were introduced, respectively. The distance-based hypermutation could utilize the information during gene positions and therefore have a remarkable ability to generate higher affinity antibodies, while the literal interactive receptor editing enabled the system to realize the information exchanges during different antibodies and meanwhile to maintain the diversity of the population. In addition, two hybrid clonal selection algorithms which combined with the traditional simulated annealing strategy together with the greedy crossover operator and the ant colony optimization respectively were introduced. They exposed that the hybridization can be recognized to be an essential aspect of high performing algorithms.

The application of the clonal selection model to the traveling salesman problem demonstrated the effectiveness and robustness of the algorithm. To conclude the chapter, several general remarks about the future trends were also presented.

REFERENCES

Aickelin, U., Bentley, P., Cayzer, S., Kim, J., & Mcleod, J. (2003) Danger theory: The link between AIS and IDS. In *Proceedings ICARIS-2003, 2nd International Conference on Artificial Immune Systems*, (pp.147-155).

Branco, P. J. C., Dente, J. A., & Mendes, R. V. (2003). Using immunology principles for fault detection. *IEEE Transactions on Industrial Electronics*, *50*(2), 362–374. doi:10.1109/TIE.2003.809418

Canham, R. O., & Tyrrell, A. M. (2003). A hardware artificial immune system and embryonic array for fault tolerant systems. *Genetic Programming and Evolvable Machines*, *4*, 359–382. doi:10.1023/A:1026143128448

Dasgupta, D. (1999). *Artificial Immune System and Their Applications*. Berlin: Springer-Verlag.

de Castro, L. N., & Von Zuben, F. J. (2002). Learning and optimization using clonal selection principle. *IEEE Transactions on Evolutionary Computation*, *6*(3), 239–251. doi:10.1109/TEVC.2002.1011539

Dorigo, M., & Stutzle, T. (2004). *Ant Colony Optimization*. Cambridge, MA: MIT Press.

Engin, O., & Doyen, A. (2004). A new approach to solve hybrid flow shop scheduling problems by artificial immune system. *Future Generation Computer Systems*, *20*, 1083–1095. doi:10.1016/j.future.2004.03.014

Forrest, S., Javornik, B., Smith, R. E., & Perelson, A. S. (1993). Using genetic algorithm to explore pattern recognition in the immune system. *Evolutionary Computation*, *1*(3), 191–211. doi:10.1162/evco.1993.1.3.191

Forrest, S., Perelson, A., Allen, L., & Cherukuri, R. (1994). Self-nonself discrimination in a computer. In *IEEE Symposium on Research in Security and Privacy*, (pp. 202-212).

Hunt, J. E., & Cooke, D. E. (1996). Learning using an artificial immune system. *Journal of Network and Computer Applications*, *19*, 189–212. doi:10.1006/jnca.1996.0014

Ichimura, T., Oeda, S., Suka, M., & Yoshida, K. (2005). A learning method of immune multi-agent neural networks. *Neural Computing & Applications*, *14*, 132–148. doi:10.1007/s00521-004-0448-6

Janeway, C. A., Jr., & Travers, P. (1997). *Immunobiology: The Immune System in Health and Disease*. São Paulo, Brazil: Artes Medicas.

Jerne, N. K. (1974). Towards a network theory of the immune system. *Annals of Immunology*, *125C*, 373–389.

Khilwani, N., Prakash, A., Shankar, R., & Tiwari, M. (2008). Fast clonal algorithm. *Engineering Applications of Artificial Intelligence*, *21*, 106–128. doi:10.1016/j.engappai.2007.01.004

Nanni, L. (2006). Mechine learning algorithms for T-cell epitopes prediction. *Neurocomputing*, *69*, 866–868. doi:10.1016/j.neucom.2005.08.005

Pelanda, R., & Torres, R. M. (2006). Receptor editing for better or for worse. *Current Opinion in Immunology*, *18*, 184–190. doi:10.1016/j.coi.2006.01.005

Perelson, A. S. (1993). Immune network theory. *Immunological Reviews*, *110*, 5–36. doi:10.1111/j.1600-065X.1989.tb00025.x

Timmis, J., & Neal, M. (2001). A resource limited artificial immune system. *Knowledge-Based Systems*, *14*(3), 121–130. doi:10.1016/S0950-7051(01)00088-0

Chapter 7
Risk–Management Models Based on the Portfolio Theory Using Historical Data under Uncertainty

Takashi Hasuike
Osaka University, Japan

ABSTRACT

This chapter considers various types of risk-management models based on the portfolio theory under some social uncertainty that received historical data includes ambiguity, and that they are assumed not to be constant. These models with uncertainty are represented many social problems such as assets allocation, logistics, scheduling, urban project problems, etc.. However, since these problems with uncertainty are formulated as stochastic and fuzzy programming problems, it is difficult to solve them analytically in the sense of deterministic mathematical programming. Therefore, introducing possibility and necessity measures based on the fuzzy programming approach and considering the concept of risk-management based on the portfolio theory, main problems are transformed into the deterministic programming problems. Then, in order to solve the deterministic problems efficiently, the solution method is constructed.

INTRODUCTION

A mission in this chapter is to extend previous mathematical programming problems using historical data to stochastic and fuzzy programming problems under uncertainty, particularly considering the risk-management. In the practice decision making, it is necessary to take various constraints and assumptions into consideration as well as un-

certainty, such as the probability derived from the statistical analysis of historical data and the ambiguity derived from lack of reliable information and decision maker's subjectivity. Since it is difficult that decision makers know precise information due to such uncertainty, they need to make appropriate decisions under uncertainty.

Until now, in order to deal with uncertainty in the sense of mathematical programming, many studies with respect to stochastic and fuzzy programming have been performed. Stochastic programming is

DOI: 10.4018/978-1-61520-757-2.ch007

a field of mathematical methods to deal with the optimization problems under uncertainty characterized by stochastic fluctuation. The application areas of stochastic programming include many fields (inventory, finance and marketing, etc.). Particularly, the portfolio selection problem, which is combined probability and optimization theory with the investment behavior, is one of the most important problems in stochastic programming problems. Since portfolio theories have focused on risk management under random and ambiguous conditions, they have greatly advanced since the initial important study proposed by Markowitz. Then, some measures for the risk management have been developed such as Semi-variance model, Absolute deviation model, Safety first model, Value-at-Risk, etc.. Thus, in the research field of portfolio selection problem, researchers have studied models with uncertainty and proposed efficient and versatile models of appropriate risk management. Furthermore, some researchers have also considered applying the portfolio theory to general mathematical programming problems such as the asset allocation in production processes and logistics. Therefore, the stochastic programming based on the portfolio theory has become an important field to the mathematical programming from the view point of theory as well as practice.

On the other hand, with respect to the ambiguity such as lack of reliable information and decision maker's subjectivity, they are assumed to be rather fuzziness than randomness. The centre of social behavior in economy, investment and production fields is the human behavior, and so it is obvious that psychological aspects of decision makers have a major impact on social behaviors. Then, it is also clear that some factors in historical data include the ambiguity. Therefore, in order to represent such ambiguity and subjectivity, a fuzzy number was introduced in some previous researches. The fuzzy number is roughly a number to represent the degrees of attribution and preference to objectives directly. Thus, the concept of fuzzy number is dif-

ferent from that of random variable. Many previous researches have been dealt with random variables or fuzzy numbers in mathematical programming problems, separately. However, practical social systems obviously weave such randomness with fuzziness. Therefore, in the case that decision makers consider the present social problems as mathematical programming problems, they need to consider not only randomness but also fuzziness, simultaneously.

Therefore, by extending risk management models using historical data based on the portfolio theory, standard stochastic and fuzzy programming models under uncertainty to general decision making problems, we propose several types of general risk-management problems under uncertainty. The proposed models include many previous stochastic and fuzzy programming problems by considering the parameters setting, and so they become very versatile problems to apply various social situations. However, in the sense of the deterministic mathematical programming, these mathematical models are not well-defined problems due to random and fuzzy variables, and so we need to set a criterion for each objective or constraint involving random and fuzzy variables in order to solve them analytically using the mathematical programming. In this chapter, using the standard stochastic and fuzzy programming approaches, we perform the deterministic equivalent transformations to main problems. Furthermore, deterministic equivalent problems derived from such stochastic and fuzzy programming problems are generally complicate problems, and so it is often difficult to apply standard programming approaches to these problems. Therefore, we develop the efficient and analytical solution method to each proposed model considering the analytical strictness and simple usage in practical social situations.

This chapter is organized as follows. In Background section, we provide the brief literature review of stochastic, fuzzy programming and portfolio selection problems under uncertainty. Then, we introduce some risk-management models based on the portfolio theories and perform the equivalent transformations using multi-scenario to the future returns. In Fuzzy Extension of Risk-Management Models section, we propose the fuzzy extension of risk-management models based on the portfolio theories and construct the efficient solution method. Then, in order to represent properties of our proposed models, the simple numerical example is provided. Finally, we provide Future Trends and Conclusion on this study.

BACKGROUND

Literature Review

In classical mathematical programming problems, coefficients of objective functions or constraints are assumed to be completely known. However, in practical social systems, these parameters are often not known exactly since they are variable, unreliable or imprecise in some way, and so they are rather uncertain than constant. In order to deal with such uncertainty, stochastic programming (Danzig, 1955; Vajda, 1982) and fuzzy programming have been considered. They are useful tools for the decision making under stochastic and fuzzy environments, respectively. Particularly, the fuzzy mathematical programming has been developed for treating uncertainty in the setting of optimization problems. Until now, there are many studies from the theoretical as well as from the computational point of view (for example, Dubois & Prade, 1980; Hasuike & Ishii, 2008; Inuiguchi et al., 1990;, Liu, 2002, 2004; Luhandjura, 1987; Maeda, 2001; Sakawa, 1993; Zimmermann, 1978). In fuzzy programming problems, the objective function is fuzzy-valued and there is no universal concept of optimal solutions to be accepted widely, it is important to define some concepts for the fuzzy objective functions and constraints and to investigate their properties. From this viewpoint, there are many ideas such as parametric linear programming problems in order to obtain a

reasonable optimal solution (Tanaka et al, 1984), possibility and necessity programming problems (Inuiguchi & Ramik, 2000; Katagiri et al., 2004), interactive programming problems (Katagiri et al., 2008; Sakawa, 1993), etc..

On the other hand, as one of the most important risk-management problems in the real world, Markowitz (1952) initially introduced portfolio selection problems, combined probability and optimization theory with investment behavior, and formulated the portfolio selection problem mathematically as follows: (1) minimizing variance for a given expected value, and (2) maximizing expected value for a given variance. It has been the centre of research activity in the real financial field and numerous researchers have contributed to the development of modern portfolio theory (cf. Luenberger, 1997; Campbell.et al., 1997; Elton & Gruber, 1995; Jorion, 1992). In particular, portfolio theories have focused on the risk management under random and ambiguous conditions and advanced greatly since Markowitz's study. Until now, many researchers have proposed models of portfolio selection problems which extended Markowitz model; Capital Asset Pricing Model (CAPM) (Sharpe, 1964; Lintner, 1965; Mossin, 1966), mean-absolute-deviation model (Konno, 1990; Konno et al., 1993), semi-variance model (Bawa & Lindenberg, 1977), safety-first model (Elton & Gruber, 1995), Value at Risk and conditional Value at Risk model (Rockafellar & Uryasev, 2000), etc.. Recently, some researches have recently considered portfolio selection problems under both randomness and fuzziness. Guo & Tanaka (1998), Tanaka et al. (2000) and Watada (1997) considered the portfolio selection based on fuzzy probabilities and possibility distributions. Inuiguchi & Ramik (2000) considered a fuzzy portfolio selection problem and compared it with a stochastic programming problem. Vercher et al. (2007) considered the fuzzy portfolio optimization under downside risk measures. Katagiri et al. (2005) and Huang (2007) considered portfolio selection problems under both random and ambiguous situations, and proposed solution methods. Hasuike and Ishii (2007) also investigated the portfolio selection problem, in particular, the case that involves some probabilistic and multi-scenario situations. Thus, in the field of portfolio selection problems, researchers have studied models that include uncertainty, and have proposed efficient and versatile models of appropriate risk management.

Therefore, by extending approaches of the risk-management used in the portfolio theory to general mathematical programming problems, we propose new and versatile risk-management models. In particular, we propose the following flexible models under randomness, fuzziness, and flexibility: (a) mean-variance and mean-absolute deviation models, (b) a probability fractile optimization model of total future profits, and (c) a probability maximization model of total future profits. These mathematical programming problems with randomness and fuzziness are called stochastic and fuzzy programming problems (for example, Liu, 2002, 2004), and are usually transformed into nonlinear programming problems by setting the target values and using chance constraints. Since it is almost impossible to obtain their global optimal solutions directly, we construct the efficient solution method to obtain them by performing the equivalent transformations for several nonlinear programming problems.

Notations of Parameters and Assumptions

In this paper, the following parameters are used.

$\bar{r}$: Mean value of n-dimensional Gaussian random variable row vectors

V: Gaussian random variance

r_G: Minimum value of the goal for expected total return

a_{ij}: Cost coefficient of jth decision variable to ith constraint

b_i: Maximum value to ith constraint

x: n-dimensional decision variable column vector

n: Total number of decision variables

In this chapter, we assume that the main object in the following problems is minimizing the total risk, which generates in the case that a decision maker earns the total profit of assets or products more than the target value. Then, in simplify of the following discussion, we also assume that the coefficients of parameter r_j are only fuzzy numbers. In the case that cost coefficients of constraints are assumed to be fuzzy or random variables, we discuss to the problems including such fuzzy or random variables in the same manner.

Mathematical Definitions of Fuzzy Set, Number and Variable

For centuries, probability theory and error calculus have been the only models to treat uncertainty. However, a lot of new models recently have been introduced for handling incomplete numerical and linguistic information, decision maker's subjectivity, etc.. For example, "tall", "reputable", "similar", "satisfactory", "large number", "approximately equal to 10". They are neither tractable by the classical set theory nor probability theory. In order to deal with such uncertainty, Zadeh (1965) first defined the fuzzy set theory, and it has been well developed and applied in a wide variety of real problems. The notion of the fuzzy set is non-statistical in nature and the concept provides a natural way of dealing with problems in which the source of imprecision is the absence of sharply defined criteria of class membership function rather than the presence of random variables. The concept of fuzzy set is as follows:

Definition 1

A fuzzy set A in a universe X is a mapping from X to [0,1]. For any $x \in X$ the value $A(x)$ is called the degree of membership of x in A. X is called the carrier of the fuzzy set A. The degree of membership can also be represented by x instead of $A(x)$. The class of all fuzzy sets in X is denoted by $F(x)$.

Then, the definition of fuzzy number is provided as the following form based on the fuzzy set:

Definition 2

A fuzzy number a is a fuzzy set on the real line R satisfying the following conditions:

(a)   linearity: $E_\lambda = \{x | \mu_a(x) \geq \lambda\}$ is a close space.
(b)   normality: $^\exists x$ satisfying $\mu_a(x) = 1$.
(c)   convexity:
$$\mu_a \left(\lambda x_1 + (1 - \lambda) x_2 \right) \geq \mu_a (x_1) \wedge \mu_a (x_2),$$
$$^\forall \lambda \in [0, 1]$$

Furthermore, the notion of fuzzy variable is first introduced by Kaufmann (1975) and then it appeared in Zadeh (1975, 1978) and Nahmias (1978).

Definition 3

A fuzzy variable is defined as a function from the possibility space $(\Theta, P(\Theta), Pos)$ to the real line R. Subsequently, let Θ be a nonempty set, and $P(\Theta)$ be the power set of Θ. For each $A \in P(\Theta)$, there is a nonnegative number $Pos\{A\}$, called its possibility, such as

(i) $Pos\{\varphi\} = 0, Pos\{\Theta\} = 1$, and
(ii) $Pos\{\cup_k A_k\} = \sup_k Pos\{A_k\}$ for any arbitrary collection $\{A_k\}$ in $P(\Theta)$.

Definition 4

Let ξ be a fuzzy variable on the possibility space $(\Theta, P(\Theta), Pos)$. Then, its membership function is derived from the possibility measure Pos by

$$M(x) = Pos\{\theta \in \Theta | \xi(\theta) = x\}$$

Furthermore, let $\tilde{a}_i, (i = 1, 2, ..., n)$ be fuzzy variables defined on the possibility space $(\Theta, P(\Theta), Pos)$, respectively. Their membership function are also derived from the possibility measures as follows:

$$\mu_{\tilde{a}_i}(x) = Pos_i \left\{ \theta \in \Theta_i \middle| \tilde{a}_i(\theta) = x \right\},$$
$$i = 1, 2, ..., n$$

From these definitions, the following theorem holds.

Theorem 1

Then, the membership function $\mu_{\tilde{a}}(x)$ of $\tilde{a} = f(\tilde{a}_1, \tilde{a}_2, ..., \tilde{a}_n)$ is derived from the membership functions $\mu_{\tilde{a}_i}(x), i = 1, 2, ..., n$ as follows:

$$\mu_{\tilde{a}}(x) = \sup_{x_1, x_2, ..., x_n \in R} \left\{ \min_{\leq i \leq n} \mu_{\tilde{a}_i}(x_i) \middle| x = f(x_1, x_2, ..., x_n) \right\}$$

Definition 4 coincides with the extension principle of Zadeh. Now let us illustrate the operation on fuzzy variables.

Example 1

We introduce a trapezoidal fuzzy variable represented by (r_1, r_2, r_3, r_4) of crisp numbers with $r_1 < r_2 < r_3 < r_4$, whose membership function can be denoted by

$$\mu\left(x\right) = \begin{cases} \dfrac{x - r_1}{r_2 - r_1} & \left(r_1 \leq x \leq r_2\right) \\ 1 & \left(r_2 \leq x \leq r_3\right) \\ \dfrac{r_4 - x}{r_4 - r_3} & \left(r_3 \leq x \leq r_4\right) \\ 0 & \text{otherwise.} \end{cases}$$

Thus, the fuzzy variable is useful tools for the decision making under uncertain environment. Then, the fuzzy mathematical programming has been developed for treating uncertainty in the setting of optimization problems. Until now, there are many studies from the theoretical as well as from the computational point of view. Some fuzzy programming problems consider that the objective function is fuzzy-valued and there is no universal concept of optimal solutions to be accepted widely. Therefore, it is important to define some concepts for the fuzzy objective functions and constraints and to investigate their properties. With respect to this viewpoint, there are many ideas such as parametric linear programming problems in order to obtain a reasonable optimal solution (Tanaka et al, 1999, 2000), possibility and necessity programming problems (Inuiguchi & Ramik, 2000; Katagiri et al., 2005, 2008), etc..

Possibility and Necessity Measure

In deterministic problems of the fuzzy programming, possibility and necessity measures are introduced. Possibility theory was first proposed by Zadeh (1978), and developed by many researchers such as Dubois and Prade (1988). Now, let a and b be fuzzy variables on the possibility spaces $(\Theta_1, P(\Theta_1), \text{Pos}_1)$ and $(\Theta_2, P(\Theta_2), \text{Pos}_2)$, respectively. Then, $\tilde{a} \leq \tilde{b}$ is a fuzzy event defined on the product possibility space $(\Theta, P(\Theta), \text{Pos})$, whose possibility is

$$\text{Pos}\left\{\tilde{a} \leq \tilde{b}\right\} = \sup_{x,y \in R}\left\{\mu_{\tilde{a}}\left(x\right) \wedge \mu_{\tilde{b}}\left(y\right) \middle| x \leq y\right\}$$

where the abbreviation Pos represents possibility. This means that the possibility of $\tilde{a} \leq \tilde{b}$ is the largest possibility that there exists at least on pair of values $x, y \in R$ such that $x \leq y$, and the values of $\tilde{a}$ and $\tilde{b}$ are x and y, respectively.

More generally, the possibility of fuzzy event is provided as follows:

Definition 5

Let $\tilde{a}_i$, $\left(i = 1, 2, \ldots, n\right)$ be fuzzy variables, and $f_j : R^n \rightarrow R, (j = 1, 2, \ldots, m)$ be continuous functions.

Figure 1. Membership function of trapezoidal fuzzy variable

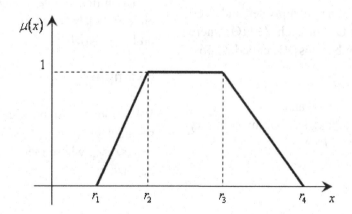

Then, the possibility of the fuzzy event characterized by $f_j\left(\tilde{a}_1, \tilde{a}_2, ..., \tilde{a}_n\right) \leq 0$, $(j=1,2,...,m)$ is as follows:

$$\text{Pos}\left\{f_j\left(\tilde{a}_1, \tilde{a}_2, ..., \tilde{a}_n\right) \leq 0, \ j = 1,2,...,m\right\}$$
$$= \sup_{x_1, x_2, ..., x_n \in R} \left\{\min_{1 \leq i \leq n} \mu_{\tilde{a}_i}\left(x_i\right) \middle| f_j\left(x_1, x_2, ..., x_n\right) \leq 0, \ \left(j = 1,2,...,m\right)\right\}$$

In a similar way to the possibility measure, the necessity measure of a set A is defined as the impossibility of the opposite set A^c.

Definition 6

Let $(\Theta, P(\Theta), \text{Pos})$ be a possibility space, and A be a set in $P(\Theta)$. Then, the necessity measure of A is defined by $\text{Nec}\{A\} = 1 - \text{Pos}\{A^c\}$.

Thus, the necessity measure is the dual of possibility measure, i.e. $\text{Pos}\{A\} + \text{Nec}\{A^c\} = 1$ for any $A \in P(\Theta)$.

Example 2

Let us consider a trapezoidal fuzzy variable $\xi = (r_1, r_2, r_3, r_4)$ and the target fixed value λ. From the definitions of possibility and necessity, we obtain the following results:

$$\text{Pos}\{\xi \leq \lambda\} = \begin{cases} 1 & (r_2 \leq \lambda) \\ \dfrac{\lambda - r_1}{r_2 - r_1} & (r_1 \leq \lambda < r_2), \\ 0 & \text{otherwise} \end{cases} \quad \text{Nec}\{\xi \leq \lambda\} = \begin{cases} 1 & (r_4 \leq \lambda) \\ \dfrac{r_3 - \lambda}{r_3 - r_4} & (r_3 \leq \lambda < r_4) \\ 0 & \text{otherwise} \end{cases}$$

Fuzzy Chance Constrained Programming

In a way similar to the stochastic chance constraint, we introduce the fuzzy chance constraint. Assume that x is a decision vector, ξ is a fuzzy vector, $f(x,\xi)$ is a return function, and $g_j(x,\xi), (j=1,2,...,m)$ are continuous functions. Since the fuzzy constraints $g_j(x,\xi) \leq 0$ do not define a deterministic feasible set, a natural idea is to provide a possibility α where it is desired that the fuzzy constraints hold. Thus, we introduce the chance constraint as follows:

$$\text{Pos}\{g_j(x,\xi) \leq 0\} \geq \alpha, \ (j=1,2,...,m)$$

Using these fuzzy stochastic constraints and the similar manner of the stochastic programming, we first introduce the possibility fractile optimization model as follows:

Maximize $\overline{f}$

subject to $\text{Pos}\left\{f\left(x, \boldsymbol{\xi}\right) \geq \overline{f}\right\} \geq \beta$

$\text{Pos}\left\{g_j\left(x, \boldsymbol{\xi}\right) \leq 0\right\} \geq \alpha, \quad \left(j = 1,2,...,m\right)$

Figure 2. Possibility measure for the trapezoidal fuzzy variable

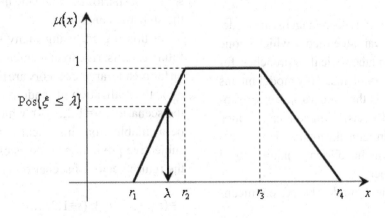

Figure 3. Necessity measure for the trapezoidal fuzzy variable

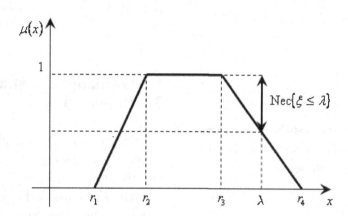

where α and β are the predetermined confidence levels. Then, in a similar way to this approach, we also introduce the following possibility maximization model.

$$\text{Maximize} \quad \text{Pos}\left\{f(x,\xi) \geq \bar{f}\right\}$$
$$\text{subject to} \quad \text{Pos}\left\{g_j(x,\xi) \leq 0\right\} \geq \alpha, \quad (j=1,2,...,m)$$

where $\bar{f}$ is the predetermined confidence level to the object. In order to solve these problems, there are various types of solution approaches using not only deterministic programming approaches but also genetic algorithm (GA), neural network (NN), and the other heuristics.

Risk Management Model Based On Mean-Variance Theory

First, we introduce a risk-management model based on the mean-variance theory which is one of the traditional mathematical approaches for portfolio selection problems. This model means that the risk factor is the total variance for random variables and decision maker can reduce uncertainty by minimizing the total variance. This model is formulated as the following mathematical programming problem:

(Risk-management model based on mean-variance theory)

$$\text{Minimize} \quad V(x) = x^t \mathbf{V} x$$
$$\text{subject to} \quad E(x) = \bar{r}^t x \geq r_G$$
$$\sum_{j=1}^{n} a_{ij} x_j \leq b_i, \; x \geq \mathbf{0}, \; (i=1,2,...,m)$$

$$(1)$$

The mean-variance model has long served as the basis of financial theory. In the sense of mathematical programming, this problem is a quadratic programming problem, and so we find the optimal solution using standard convex or nonlinear programming approaches. However, it is not efficient to solve the large scale quadratic programming problem directly. Furthermore, in the case that a decision maker predicts the future return of each product, she or he doesn't consider only one scenario of the future return, but often several scenarios based on the historical data and the statistical analysis.

In this regard, using many scenarios of the future returns, risk-management model (1) based on the mean-variance theory are reformulated. Let r_{sj} be the realization of random variable R_s about the scenario s, $s=1,2,...,S$), which we assume to be available from historical data and from the subjective prediction of decision makers. Then, the return vector of scenario i is as follows;

$$r_s = (r_{s1}, r_{s2}, ..., r_{sn}), \; (s=1,2,...S) \tag{2}$$

where each probability by scenarios is as follows:

$$p_s = \Pr\{r = r_s\}, \ (s = 1, 2, \ldots S) \tag{3}$$

We also assume that the expected value of the random variable can be approximated by the average derived from these data. Particularly, we let

$$\bar{r}_j \equiv E\left[R_j\right] = \sum_{s=1}^{S} p_s r_{sj} \tag{4}$$

Then, the mean value $E(x)$ and variance $V(x)$ derived from the data are as follows:

$$E\left(\boldsymbol{x}\right) = \sum_{j=1}^{n} \bar{r}_j x_j = \sum_{j=1}^{n} \left(\sum_{s=1}^{S} p_s r_{sj}\right) x_j \tag{5}$$

$$V\left(\boldsymbol{x}\right) = \sum_{s=1}^{S} p_s \left(\sum_{j=1}^{n} r_{sj} x_j - E\left(\boldsymbol{x}\right)\right)^2$$

$$= \sum_{s=1}^{S} p_s \left(\sum_{j=1}^{n} r_{sj} x_j - \sum_{j=1}^{n} \left(\sum_{s=1}^{S} p_s r_{sj}\right) x_j\right)^2$$

$$= \sum_{j=1}^{n} \sum_{k=1}^{n} \sigma_{jk} x_j x_k \tag{6}$$

For simplify of the following discussion, we assume each probability p_s to become same value $\frac{1}{S}$. From above parameters, we transformed risk-management model (1) into the following problem:

$$\text{Minimize} \quad \frac{1}{S} \sum_{s=1}^{S} \left(\sum_{j=1}^{n} \left(r_{sj} - \bar{r}_j\right) x_j\right)^2$$

$$\text{subject to} \quad \bar{r}_j = \frac{1}{S} \sum_{s=1}^{S} r_{sj}$$

$$\sum_{j=1}^{n} \bar{r}_j x_j \geq r_G, \ \sum_{j=1}^{n} a_{ij} x_j \leq b_i, \ \boldsymbol{x} \geq \boldsymbol{0}, \ \left(i = 1, 2, \ldots, m\right) \tag{7}$$

Furthermore, introducing parameters $z_s = \sum_{j=1}^{n} \left(r_{sj} - \bar{r}_j\right) x_j, \left(s = 1, 2, \ldots, S\right)$, we equivalently transformed problem (7) into the following problem:

$$\text{Minimize} \quad \frac{1}{S} \sum_{s=1}^{S} z_s^2$$

$$\text{subject to} \quad z_s - \sum_{j=1}^{n} \left(r_{sj} - \bar{r}_j\right) x_j = 0, \ \left(s = 1, 2, \ldots, S\right)$$

$$\bar{r}_j = \frac{1}{S} \sum_{s=1}^{S} r_{sj},$$

$$\sum_{j=1}^{n} \bar{r}_j x_j \geq r_G, \ \sum_{j=1}^{n} a_{ij} x_j \leq b_i, \ \boldsymbol{x} \geq \boldsymbol{0}, \ \left(i = 1, 2, \ldots, m\right) \tag{8}$$

Since this problem is a quadratic programming problem not to include the variances, we can set each parameter more easily than initial model (1) and solve it analytically. However, this problem is not a linear programming problem which is efficiently solved using linear programming approaches.

Risk Management Model Based on Mean-Absolute Deviation Theory

In order to construct the risk-management model to solve efficiently, the risk measure needs to be represented by not variance but the other simple measure. Therefore, we consider the other risk-management model based on the mean-absolute deviation theory proposed by Konno (1990). This problem is formulated as a linear programming problem and it is essentially equivalent to the model based on the mean-variance theory if the rate of the return of assets is multivariate normally distributed. Now, let the absolute deviation (AD)

$$AD \equiv \frac{1}{S} \sum_{s=1}^{S} \left|\sum_{j=1}^{n} \left(r_{sj} - \bar{r}_j\right) x_j\right| \equiv \frac{1}{S} \sum_{s=1}^{S} \left|r_s - \bar{r}_P\right| \tag{9}$$

With respect to this absolute deviation, in the case that random variables occur according to normal distributions, the absolute deviation is equivalently transformed into the variance (Konno, 1990). Therefore, we also equivalently transformed the mean-absolute deviation model with the mean-variance model. By introducing this definition of absolute deviation, he proposed the following portfolio selection problem:

Minimize $\dfrac{1}{S}\sum_{s=1}^{S}\left|\sum_{j=1}^{n}\left(r_{sj}-\bar{r}_{j}\right)x_{j}\right|$

subject to $\bar{r}_{j}=\dfrac{1}{S}\sum_{i=1}^{m}r_{sj}$

$\qquad \sum_{j=1}^{n}\bar{r}_{j}x_{j}\geq r_{G},\ \sum_{j=1}^{n}a_{ij}x_{j}\leq b_{i},\ \boldsymbol{x}\geq\boldsymbol{0},\ \left(i=1,2,...,m\right)$

$$(10)$$

Then, introducing parameters $z_{s}=\sum_{j=1}^{n}\left(r_{sj}-\bar{r}_{j}\right)x_{j}$, problem (10) is equivalently transformed into the following problem based on the result of the previous study of Konno (1990):

Minimize $\dfrac{2}{S}\sum_{s=1}^{S}z_{s}$

subject to $z_{s}+\sum_{j=1}^{n}r_{sj}x_{j}\geq\sum_{j=1}^{n}\bar{r}_{j}x_{j},\ \left(s=1,2,...,S\right)$

$\qquad \bar{r}_{j}=\dfrac{1}{S}\sum_{s=1}^{S}r_{sj},$

$\qquad \sum_{j=1}^{n}\bar{r}_{j}x_{j}\geq r_{G},\ \sum_{j=1}^{n}a_{ij}x_{j}\leq b_{i},\ \boldsymbol{x}\geq\boldsymbol{0},\ \left(i=1,2,...,m\right)$

$$(11)$$

Consequently, by using the risk-management model based on the mean-absolute deviation theory, we easily solve a large scale problem.

Risk Management Model Based on Mean-Variance Theory

With respect to the risk-management models based on mean-variance and mean-absolute deviation theories, the main concept is that the risk-management is equal to minimizing the total variance and absolute deviation, i.e., the reduction of variation risk. However, the nonfulfillment probability, which means that the total return is less than the target value, is also considered as one of the most important factor of risk-management. Therefore, we extend one of traditional safety first models with respect to portfolio selection problems, Roy model to the risk-management model.

This model has been formulated as the following mathematical programming problem.

(risk-management models based on Roy model)

Minimize $\Pr\left\{R\left(\boldsymbol{x}\right)\leq r_{f}\right\}$

subject to $\bar{\boldsymbol{r}}^{t}\boldsymbol{x}\geq r_{G}$

$\qquad \sum_{j=1}^{n}a_{ij}x_{j}\leq b_{i},\ \boldsymbol{x}\geq\boldsymbol{0}$ $\qquad(12)$

where each notation means as follows:

$R(x)$: Total profit
r_f: Goal of the total profit

Subsequently, probability chance constraint $\Pr\{R(x){\leq}r_{f}\}$ means the probability satisfying the total return $R(x)$ is less than target goal r_f. Furthermore, the other risk-management models based on other safety first models, Kataoka model and Telser model are as follows:

(risk-management models based on Kataoka model)

Maximize r_{f}

subject to $\Pr\left\{R\left(\boldsymbol{x}\right)\leq r_{f}\right\}\leq\alpha,$

$\qquad \bar{\boldsymbol{r}}^{t}\boldsymbol{x}\geq r_{G},\ \sum_{j=1}^{n}a_{ij}x_{j}\leq b_{i},\ \boldsymbol{x}\geq\boldsymbol{0}$

$$(13)$$

where α is a goal of nonfulfillment probability.

(risk-management models based on Telser model)

Maximize $\bar{\boldsymbol{r}}^{t}\boldsymbol{x}$

subject to $\Pr\left\{R\left(\boldsymbol{x}\right)\leq r_{f}\right\}\leq\alpha,$

$\qquad \sum_{j=1}^{n}a_{ij}x_{j}\leq b_{i},\ \boldsymbol{x}\geq\boldsymbol{0}$ $\qquad(14)$

Kataoka model means that decision maker considers maximizing the target level of total return under the target nonfulfillment probability. Then, Telser model means that she or he considers maximizing the expected total return under the stochastic constraint. Consequently, these safety first models are focused on the minimization of negative profit and also have long served as the basis of financial theory as well as mean-variance and mean-absolute deviation models. In mathematical programming, these problems are stochastic programming problems, and so we obtain the optimal solution using stochastic programming approaches. In some previous researches, each future return is assumed to be a random variable including the fixed expected return and variance. However, it is hard to observe variances of each asset in real market accurately and determine them as fixed values. Furthermore, in the case that decision makers expect the future return of each product, they don't consider the only one scenario of the future return, but often several scenarios.

Therefore, in a way similar to mean-variance an mean-absolute deviation models, we introduce the scenario of return vector (2) and the occurrence probability (3). Then, we assume each probability to be $p_s = \dfrac{1}{S}$. Using these parameters, we transform the risk-management models based on the basic safety first models into the following problems introducing the parameters $z_s \in \{0,1\}$, $(s=1,2,...,S)$, respectively:

(risk-management models based on Roy model)

Minimize $\dfrac{1}{S}\sum_{s=1}^{S} z_s$

subject to $\sum_{j=1}^{n} r_{sj} x_j + M \cdot z_s \geq r_f, \ \left(s=1,2,...,S\right)$

$\bar{r}^t x \geq r_G, \ \sum_{j=1}^{n} a_{ij} x_j \leq b_i, \ x \geq 0, \ \left(i=1,2,...,m\right)$

$$(15)$$

(risk-management models based on Kataoka model)

Maximize r_f

subject to $\dfrac{1}{S}\sum_{s=1}^{S} z_s \leq \alpha,$

$\sum_{j=1}^{n} r_{sj} x_j + M \cdot z_s \geq r_f, \ \left(s=1,2,...,S\right)$

$\bar{r}^t x \geq r_G, \ \sum_{j=1}^{n} a_{ij} x_j \leq b_i, \ x \geq 0, \ \left(i=1,2,...,m\right)$

$$(16)$$

(risk-management models based on Telser model)

Maximize $\bar{r}^t x$

subject to $\dfrac{1}{S}\sum_{s=1}^{S} z_s \leq \alpha,$

$\sum_{j=1}^{n} r_{sj} x_j + M \cdot z_s \geq r_f, \ \left(s=1,2,...,S\right)$

$\sum_{j=1}^{n} a_{ij} x_j \leq b_i, \ x \geq 0, \ \left(i=1,2,...,m\right)$

$$(17)$$

where M is a sufficiently large number satisfying

$$M \geq r_G - \min\left\{\sum_{j=1}^{n} r_{sj} x_j\right\}.$$ These models are 0-1 mixed linear programming problems. Therefore, we obtain these optimal portfolios using integer programming approaches such as Branch-bound method.

FUZZY EXTENSION OF RISK-MANAGEMENT MODELS

Fuzzy Extension of Risk-Management Model with the Mean-Variance

In previous mathematical programming models, each return in scenarios is considered as a fixed value derived from a random variable. However, considering psychological aspects and subjectivity of decision makers, it is difficult to predict the future return as the fixed value. Furthermore, even if decision makers hold a lot of effective linguistic information, the linguistic information must be transformed into a number in order to determine the optimal decision using the mathematical methods, and so some ambiguity occurs by this numerical conversion. Therefore, we need to consider that the future return is ambiguous. Then we propose the risk-management models based on the portfolio theory using scenarios where the return is ambiguous. In this paper, the return including the ambiguity is assumed to the following triangular fuzzy number:

$$\tilde{r}_{sj} = \left\langle \bar{r}_{sj}, \alpha_j, \alpha_j \right\rangle = \left\langle \bar{r}_{sj}, \alpha_j \right\rangle \qquad (18)$$

In this paper, for simplify of the following discussion, we assume $\bar{r}_{sj} - \alpha_j \geq 0$. In basic risk-management problem (7) based on the mean-variance theory, since $\tilde{r}_{sj}$ is a fuzzy variable, the objective function and the parameters including the fuzzy variable $\tilde{r}_{sj}$ are also assumed to be fuzzy variables. Therefore, we can't optimize this problem without transforming the objective function into another form.

In previous researches, some criteria with respect to fuzzy portfolio problems have been proposed. For example, Liu (2002, 2007), and Huang (2006) considered a portfolio selection problems using fuzzy or hybrid (fuzzy and random) expected value and its variance. Katagiri (2005) proposed a portfolio selection problem using possibility measure and probability measure. Carlsson (2002) proposed a portfolio selection problem using the possibility mean value. In, this paper, we assume the following cases:

(a) Since the main object is minimizing the total variance and the decision maker considers minimize it as small as possible even if the aspiration level becomes smaller.

(b) On the other hand, it is clear that the decision maker also considers that she or he never

Figure 4. Shape of the membership function $\mu_{\tilde{r}_{sj}}\left(\omega\right)$

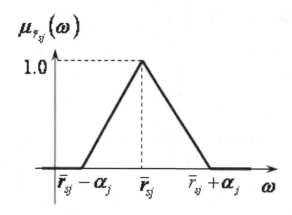

fails to earn the total return more than the goal in the variance constraint.

Therefore, we consider fuzzy risk-management models based on the portfolio theory for probabilistic expected value and variance. Then, we introduce a possibility measure for total variance based on assumption (a) and a necessity measure for the expected total return based on assumption (b). Then, we convert basic mean-variance problem (7) into the following problem including the chance-constraint:

$$
\begin{aligned}
\text{Minimize} \quad & \sigma_G \\
\text{subject to} \quad & \text{Pos}\left\{\tilde{V}(\boldsymbol{x}) \le \sigma_G\right\} \ge h, \\
& \text{Nec}\left\{\tilde{E}(\boldsymbol{x}) \ge r_G\right\} \ge h, \\
& \sum_{j=1}^{n} a_{ij} x_j \le b_i, \ \boldsymbol{x} \ge \boldsymbol{0}, \ (i = 1, 2, \dots, m)
\end{aligned}
\tag{19}
$$

where $\text{Pos}\left\{\tilde{V}(\boldsymbol{x}) \le \sigma_G\right\}$ is a possibility measure and this means $\text{Pos}\left\{\tilde{V}(\boldsymbol{x}) \le \sigma_G\right\} = \sup_{\sigma \le \sigma_G} \mu_{\tilde{V}(\boldsymbol{x})}(\sigma)$, then $\text{Nec}\left\{\tilde{E}(\boldsymbol{x}) \ge r_G\right\}$ is a necessity measure and this means $\text{Nec}\left\{\tilde{E}(\boldsymbol{x}) \ge r_G\right\} = 1 - \sup_{r \ge r_G} \mu_{\tilde{E}(\boldsymbol{x})}(r)$. In this problem, membership functions $\mu_{\tilde{E}(\boldsymbol{x})}(r)$ and $\mu_{\tilde{V}(\boldsymbol{x})}(\sigma)$ are assumed to be the following forms using fuzzy extension principle. First, fuzzy number $\tilde{E}(\boldsymbol{x})$ is given as the following triangular fuzzy numbers:

$$
\tilde{E}(\boldsymbol{x}) = \left\langle \frac{1}{S} \sum_{j=1}^{n} \left(\sum_{s=1}^{S} \overline{r}_{sj} \right) x_j, \sum_{j=1}^{n} \alpha_j x_j \right\rangle
\tag{20}
$$

Therefore, we obtain membership function $\mu_{\tilde{E}(\boldsymbol{x})}(r)$ as follows:

$$
\mu_{\tilde{E}(\boldsymbol{x})}(\omega) =
\begin{cases}
\dfrac{\frac{1}{S} \sum_{j=1}^{n} \left(\sum_{s=1}^{S} \overline{r}_{sj} \right) x_j - \omega}{\sum_{j=1}^{n} \alpha_j x_j} & (q^- \le \omega \le q) \\[4ex]
\dfrac{\omega - \frac{1}{S} \sum_{j=1}^{n} \left(\sum_{s=1}^{S} \overline{r}_{sj} \right) x_j}{\sum_{j=1}^{n} \alpha_j x_j} & (q \le \omega \le q^+) \\[4ex]
0 & (\omega < q^-, \ q^+ < \omega)
\end{cases}
$$

$$
q^- = \frac{1}{S} \sum_{j=1}^{n} \left(\sum_{s=1}^{S} \overline{r}_{sj} \right) x_j - \sum_{j=1}^{n} \alpha_j x_j, \quad q^+ = \frac{1}{S} \sum_{j=1}^{n} \left(\sum_{s=1}^{S} \overline{r}_{sj} \right) x_j + \sum_{j=1}^{n} \alpha_j x_j, \quad q = \frac{1}{S} \sum_{j=1}^{n} \left(\sum_{s=1}^{S} \overline{r}_{sj} \right) x_j
\tag{21}
$$

Next, we consider another membership function $\mu_{\tilde{V}(\boldsymbol{x})}(\sigma)$. In a way similar to $\mu_{\tilde{E}(\boldsymbol{x})}(r)$, we obtain the fuzzy number for $\tilde{z}_s = \sum_{j=1}^{n} \left(\tilde{r}_{sj} - \tilde{r}_j \right) x_j = \sum_{j=1}^{n} \tilde{r}_{sj} x_j - \tilde{E}(\boldsymbol{x})$ as the following triangular fuzzy number:

$$
\tilde{z}_s = \left\langle \sum_{j=1}^{n} \overline{r}_{sj} x_j - \frac{1}{S} \sum_{j=1}^{n} \left(\sum_{s=1}^{S} \overline{r}_{sj} \right) x_j, 2 \sum_{j=1}^{n} \alpha_j x_j \right\rangle
$$

$$
= \left\langle z_s, 2 \sum_{j=1}^{n} \alpha_j x_j \right\rangle
\tag{22}
$$

Therefore, we obtain membership function $\mu_{\tilde{z}_s}(\omega)$ as follows:

$$
\mu_{\tilde{z}_s}(\omega) =
\begin{cases}
\dfrac{z_s - \omega}{2 \sum_{j=1}^{n} \alpha_j x_j} & \left(z_s - 2 \sum_{j=1}^{n} \alpha_j x_j \le \omega \le z_s \right) \\[4ex]
\dfrac{\omega - z_s}{2 \sum_{j=1}^{n} \alpha_j x_j} & \left(z_s \le \omega \le z_s + 2 \sum_{j=1}^{n} \alpha_j x_j \right) \\[4ex]
0 & \left(\omega < z_s - 2 \sum_{j=1}^{n} \alpha_j x_j, \ z_s + 2 \sum_{j=1}^{n} \alpha_j x_j < \omega \right)
\end{cases}
\tag{23}
$$

Furthermore, we consider the membership function for $\tilde{S}_s = \left(\sum_{j=1}^{n} \left(r_{sj} - \overline{r}_j \right) x_j \right)^2$. In general cases using fuzzy numbers, membership functions often become much complicate functions. Therefore, with respect to $\mu_{\tilde{z}_s}(\omega)$, we introduce the h-cut of this membership function in order to represent briefly:

$$\tilde{z}_s = \left[\mu_{Z_s}^{(L)}(h), \mu_{Z_s}^{(R)}(h)\right] =$$
$$\left[\mu_{r^t x}^{(L)}(h) - \mu_{E(x)}^{(R)}(h), \mu_{r^t x}^{(R)}(h) - \mu_{E(x)}^{(L)}(h)\right] \quad (24)$$

where

$$\tilde{r}^t x = \left[\mu_{r^t x}^{(L)}(h), \mu_{r^t x}^{(R)}(h)\right]$$
$$= \left[\sum_{j=1}^{n}\overline{r}_{sj}x_j - (1-h)\sum_{j=1}^{n}\alpha_j x_j, \sum_{j=1}^{n}\overline{r}_{sj}x_j + (1-h)\sum_{j=1}^{n}\alpha_j x_j\right]$$

$$\tilde{E}(x) = \left[\mu_{E(x)}^{(L)}(h), \mu_{E(x)}^{(R)}(h)\right]$$
$$= \left[\frac{1}{S}\sum_{j=1}^{n}\left(\sum_{s=1}^{S}\overline{r}_{sj}\right)x_j - (1-h)\sum_{j=1}^{n}\alpha_j x_j, \frac{1}{S}\sum_{j=1}^{n}\left(\sum_{s=1}^{S}\overline{r}_{sj}\right)x_j + (1-h)\sum_{j=1}^{n}\alpha_j x_j\right]$$

From the h-cut of membership function $\mu_{\tilde{z}_s}(\omega)$, that of membership function $\mu_{\tilde{S}_s}(\omega)$ is the following form:

$$\tilde{S}_s = \left[\mu_{S_s}^{(L)}(h), \mu_{S_s}^{(R)}(h)\right]$$
$$\left[\mu_{S_s}^{(L)}(h) = \min\left\{0, \left(\mu_{Z_s}^{(L)}(h)\right)^2, \left(\mu_{Z_s}^{(R)}(h)\right)^2\right\}\right.$$
$$\left.\mu_{S_s}^{(R)}(h) = \max\left\{\left(\mu_{Z_s}^{(L)}(h)\right)^2, \left(\mu_{Z_s}^{(R)}(h)\right)^2\right\} \quad (25)$$

Therefore, the membership function $\mu_{\tilde{V}(x)}(\sigma)$ is obtained as follows.

$$\tilde{V}(x) = \left[\frac{1}{S}\sum_{s=1}^{S}\mu_{S_s}^{(L)}(h), \frac{1}{S}\sum_{s=1}^{S}\mu_{S_s}^{(R)}(h)\right] \quad (26)$$

By using these membership functions, we transform the problem (19) into the following problem:

Minimize σ_G

subject to $\dfrac{1}{S}\sum_{s=1}^{S}\mu_{S_s}^{(L)}(h) \leq \sigma_G,$

$$\frac{1}{S}\sum_{j=1}^{n}\left(\sum_{s=1}^{S}\overline{r}_{sj}\right)x_j - h\sum_{j=1}^{n}\alpha_j x_j \geq r_G,$$

$$\sum_{j=1}^{n}a_{ij}x_j \leq b_i, \; x \geq 0, \; (i=1,2,...,m) \quad (27)$$

where the left part of membership function $\mu_{S_s}^{(L)}(h)$ is as follows:

$$\mu_{S_s}^{(L)}(h) = \left(\sum_{j=1}^{n}\overline{r}_{sj}x_j \pm (1-h)\sum_{j=1}^{n}\alpha_j x_j\right)^2 + \left(\frac{1}{S}\sum_{j=1}^{n}\left(\sum_{s=1}^{S}\overline{r}_{sj}\right)x_j \mp (1-h)\sum_{j=1}^{n}\alpha_j x_j\right)^2$$
$$-2\left(\sum_{j=1}^{n}\overline{r}_{sj}x_j \pm (1-h)\sum_{j=1}^{n}\alpha_j x_j\right)\left(\frac{1}{S}\sum_{j=1}^{n}\left(\sum_{s=1}^{S}\overline{r}_{sj}\right)x_j \mp (1-h)\sum_{j=1}^{n}\alpha_j x_j\right)$$
$$= \left(\sum_{j=1}^{n}\overline{r}_{sj}x_j - \frac{1}{S}\sum_{j=1}^{n}\left(\sum_{s=1}^{S}\overline{r}_{sj}\right)x_j\right)^2 - 4(1-h)\left(\sum_{j=1}^{n}\alpha_j x_j\right)\left(\sum_{j=1}^{n}\overline{r}_{sj}x_j\right)$$
$$\quad (28)$$

Then, introducing parameters $z_s^{(h)}$, problem (27) is equivalently transformed into the following problem:

Minimize $\dfrac{1}{S}\left[z_i^2 - 4(1-h)\left(\sum_{j=1}^{n}\alpha_j x_j\right)\left(\sum_{j=1}^{n}\overline{r}_{sj}x_j\right)\right]$

subject to $z_s - \sum_{j=1}^{n}\overline{r}_{sj}x_j + \dfrac{1}{S}\sum_{j=1}^{n}\left(\sum_{s=1}^{S}\overline{r}_{sj}\right)x_j = 0, \; (s=1,2,...,S)$

$$\frac{1}{S}\sum_{j=1}^{n}\left(\sum_{s=1}^{S}\overline{r}_{sj}\right)x_j - h\sum_{j=1}^{n}\alpha_j x_j \geq r_G,$$

$$\sum_{j=1}^{n}a_{ij}x_j \leq b_i, \; x \geq 0, \; (i=1,2,...,m)$$
$$\quad (29)$$

In problem (29), the objective function is a convex quadratic function, and so problem (29) is equivalent to a convex quadratic programming problem. Therefore, we obtain a global optimal solution by using standard convex programming approaches. Furthermore, in the case that each return does not include fuzziness, i.e., each $\alpha_j=0, (j+1,2,...,n)$, problem (29) is degenerated to the following problem:

Minimize $\dfrac{1}{S}\sum_{s=1}^{S}z_s^2$

subject to $z_s - \sum_{j=1}^{n}\overline{r}_{sj}x_j + \dfrac{1}{S}\sum_{j=1}^{n}\left(\sum_{s=1}^{S}\overline{r}_{sj}\right)x_j = 0, \; (s=1,2,...,S)$

$$\frac{1}{S}\sum_{j=1}^{n}\left(\sum_{s=1}^{S}\overline{r}_{sj}\right)x_j \geq r_G,$$

$$\sum_{j=1}^{n}a_{ij}x_j \leq b_i, \; x \geq 0, \; (i=1,2,...,m)$$
$$\quad (30)$$

This problem is equivalent to basic mean-variance portfolio selection problem (8). Consequently, we find that problem (30) is certainly a fuzzy extended model for the basic mean-variance model.

Fuzzy Extension of Risk-Management Model with the Mean-Absolute Deviation

In a way similar to the model based on the mean-variance theory, we consider the fuzzy extension of the risk-management model based on the mean-absolute deviation theory. First, we rewrite the risk-management model based on the mean-absolute deviation theory:

$$
\begin{aligned}
\text{Minimize} \quad & \frac{1}{S}\sum_{s=1}^{S}\left|\sum_{j=1}^{n}\left(r_{sj}-\bar{r}_j\right)x_j\right| \\
\text{subject to} \quad & \bar{r}_j = \frac{1}{S}\sum_{i=1}^{m}r_{sj} \\
& \sum_{j=1}^{n}\bar{r}_j x_j \geq r_G, \ \sum_{j=1}^{n}a_{ij}x_j \leq b_i, \ \boldsymbol{x}\geq \boldsymbol{0}, \ \left(i=1,2,...,m\right)
\end{aligned}
\tag{31}
$$

In this problem, the objective function and parameters including fuzzy variables $\tilde{r}_{sj}$ are also assumed to be fuzzy variables. Therefore, we convert problem (31) into the following problem by using chance constraints:

$$
\begin{aligned}
\text{Minimize} \quad & \sigma_G \\
\text{subject to} \quad & \text{Pos}\left\{\tilde{D}(\boldsymbol{x})\leq \sigma_G\right\}\geq h, \\
& \text{Nec}\left\{\tilde{E}\left(\boldsymbol{x}\right)\geq r_G\right\}\geq h, \\
& \sum_{j=1}^{n}a_{ij}x_j \leq b_i, \ \boldsymbol{x}\geq \boldsymbol{0}, \ \left(i=1,2,...,m\right)
\end{aligned}
\tag{32}
$$

The same kind of membership functions is given in Section 3, so we consider membership function $\mu_{\tilde{D}(\boldsymbol{x})}\left(\omega\right)$. The h-cut of membership function becomes the following form in a way similar to the mean-variance model:

$$
\begin{aligned}
\tilde{D}\left(\boldsymbol{x}\right) &= \left[\mu_D^{(L)}\left(h\right),\mu_D^{(R)}\left(h\right)\right] \\
&= \left[\frac{1}{S}\sum_{s=1}^{S}\mu_{Z_s'}^{(L)}\left(h\right)\frac{1}{S}\sum_{s=1}^{S}\mu_{Z_s'}^{(R)}\left(h\right)\right]
\end{aligned}
\tag{33}
$$

where

$$
\mu_{Z_s'}^{(L)}\left(h\right) = \begin{cases} \mu_{Z_s}^{(L)}\left(h\right) & \left(\mu_{Z_s}^{(L)}\left(h\right)\geq 0\right) \\ 0 & \left(\mu_{Z_s}^{(L)}\left(h\right)<0\leq \mu_{Z_s}^{(R)}\left(h\right)\right) \\ -\mu_{Z_s}^{(R)}\left(h\right) & \left(\mu_{Z_s}^{(R)}\left(h\right)<0\right) \end{cases}
$$

$$
\mu_{Z_s'}^{(R)}\left(h\right) = \begin{cases} \mu_{Z_s}^{(R)}\left(h\right) & \left(\mu_{Z_s}^{(L)}\left(h\right)\geq 0\right) \\ \max\left\{0,-\mu_{Z_s}^{(L)}\left(h\right),\mu_{Z_s}^{(R)}\left(h\right)\right\} & \left(\mu_{Z_s}^{(L)}\left(h\right)<0\leq \mu_{Z_s}^{(R)}\left(h\right)\right) \\ -\mu_{Z_s}^{(L)}\left(h\right) & \left(\mu_{Z_s}^{(L)}\left(h\right)<0\right) \end{cases}
$$

and

$$
\begin{aligned}
\tilde{z}_s &= \left[\mu_{Z_s}^{(L)}\left(h\right),\mu_{Z_s}^{(R)}\left(h\right)\right] \\
&= \left[\mu_{\boldsymbol{r}^t\boldsymbol{x}}^{(L)}\left(h\right)-\mu_{E(\boldsymbol{x})}^{(R)}\left(h\right),\mu_{\boldsymbol{r}^t\boldsymbol{x}}^{(R)}\left(h\right)-\mu_{E(\boldsymbol{x})}^{(L)}\left(h\right)\right] \\
&= \left[z_s - 2\left(1-h\right)\sum_{j=1}^{n}\alpha_j x_j, z_s + 2\left(1-h\right)\sum_{j=1}^{n}\alpha_j x_j\right]
\end{aligned}
$$

$$
z_s = \sum_{j=1}^{n}\bar{r}_{sj}x_j - \frac{1}{S}\sum_{j=1}^{n}\left(\sum_{s=1}^{S}\bar{r}_{sj}\right)x_j, \ \left(s=1,2,...,S\right)
$$

Using this membership function, problem (32) is transformed into the following problem:

$$
\begin{aligned}
\text{Minimize} \quad & \sigma_G \\
\text{subject to} \quad & \frac{1}{S}\sum_{s=1}^{S}\mu_{Z_s'}^{(L)}\left(h\right)\leq \sigma_G \\
& \frac{1}{S}\sum_{j=1}^{n}\left(\sum_{s=1}^{S}\bar{r}_{sj}\right)x_j - h\sum_{j=1}^{n}\alpha_j x_j \geq r_G, \\
& \sum_{j=1}^{n}a_{ij}x_j \leq b_i, \ \boldsymbol{x}\geq \boldsymbol{0}, \ \left(i=1,2,...,m\right)
\end{aligned}
\tag{34}
$$

In order to solve problem (34) analytically, we introduce the following parameters:

$$z_s = v_s - v_s^- + v_s^+,$$

$$-\bar{\alpha}(h) \le v_s \le \bar{\alpha}(h),$$

$$v_s^- = \bar{\alpha}(h) - z_s, \quad \left(v_s^+ = 0, z_s \ge \alpha(h)\right),$$

$$v_s^+ = z_s - \left(-\bar{\alpha}(h)\right), \quad \left(v_s^- = 0, z_s \le -\alpha(h)\right),$$

$$\bar{\alpha}(h) = 2(1-h)\left(\sum_{j=1}^{n} \alpha_j x_j\right)$$

By using these parameters, problem (34) is equivalently transformed into the following problem based on the previous study of King (1993):

Minimize $\dfrac{1}{S}\displaystyle\sum_{s=1}^{S}\left(2z_s - 2\bar{\alpha}(h)\right)$

subject to $z_s = v_s - v_s^- + v_s^+, \quad -\bar{\alpha}(h) \le v_s \le \bar{\alpha}(h),$

$$z_s - \alpha(h) \ge 0, \; z_s + \alpha(h) \ge 0,$$

$$\frac{1}{S}\sum_{j=1}^{n}\left(\sum_{s=1}^{S}\bar{r}_{sj}\right)x_j - h\sum_{j=1}^{n}\alpha_j x_j \ge r_G,$$

$$\sum_{j=1}^{n}a_{ij}x_j \le b_i, \; \boldsymbol{x} \ge \boldsymbol{0}, \; \left(i = 1,2,...,m\right)$$

(35)

Since this problem is a linear programming problem, we obtain the global optimal solution by using linear programming approaches such as Simplex method and Interior point method. Furthermore, in a way similar to the proposed fuzzy mean-variance model in Section 3, in the case that each return does not include fuzziness, i.e., each $\alpha_j=0,(j+1,2,...,n)$, problem (35) is degenerated to the following problem:

Minimize $\dfrac{2}{S}\displaystyle\sum_{s=1}^{S}\left(2z_s - 2\bar{\alpha}(h)\right)$

subject to $z_s - \left(\displaystyle\sum_{j=1}^{n}\bar{r}_{sj}x_j - \frac{1}{S}\sum_{j=1}^{n}\left(\sum_{s=1}^{S}\bar{r}_{sj}\right)x_j\right) \ge 0,$

$$\left(\sum_{j=1}^{n}\bar{r}_{sj}x_j - \frac{1}{S}\sum_{j=1}^{n}\left(\sum_{s=1}^{S}\bar{r}_{sj}\right)x_j\right) - z_s \ge 0,$$

$$\frac{1}{S}\sum_{j=1}^{n}\left(\sum_{s=1}^{S}\bar{r}_{sj}\right)x_j \ge r_G,$$

$$\sum_{j=1}^{n}a_{ij}x_j \le b_i, \; \boldsymbol{x} \ge \boldsymbol{0}, \; \left(i = 1,2,...,m\right)$$

(36)

This problem is equivalent to basic mean-absolute deviation model (11). Consequently, we find that problem (36) is certainly a fuzzy extended model for the basic mean-absolute deviation model.

Fuzzy Extension of Risk-Management Models with the Safety-First Theory

In a way similar to risk-management models using mean-variance and mean-absolute deviation, we consider the case based on the safety-first theory. These problems (15), (16) and (17) include fuzzy numbers in objective functions and constraints; for example, each membership function of the objective function

$$\tilde{f}_s = \sum_{j=1}^{n}\tilde{r}_{sj}x_j + M \cdot z_s, \quad \left(s = 1,2,...,S\right) \text{ is given}$$

as follows:

$$\tilde{f}_s = \left\langle \sum_{j=1}^{n}\bar{r}_{sj}x_j + M \cdot z_s, \sum_{j=1}^{n}\alpha_j x_j \right\rangle \tag{37}$$

In the case that we introduce these membership functions in problems (15), (16) and (17), directly, these problems are not well-defined problems due to fuzzy numbers, and we need to transform these problems into deterministic equivalent problems in the sense of mathematical programming. In the case that a decision maker deals with each safety first model, it is obvious that she or he focuses on its objective function more greatly than the other constraint. With respect to its objective function, she or he considers that the object is realized as well as possible even if the possibility decreases a little. Then, with respect to constraint $\bar{r}^t\boldsymbol{x} \ge r_G$, we introduce the possibility mean function based on the result of previous research [3].

$\bar{r}'x \geq r_G$

$$\Leftrightarrow \int_0^1 \gamma \left(\sum_{j=1}^n \left[\frac{1}{S} \sum_{s=1}^S \bar{r}_{sj} - (1-\gamma)\alpha_j \right] x_j \right) d\gamma + \int_0^1 \gamma \left(\sum_{j=1}^n \left[\frac{1}{S} \sum_{s=1}^S \bar{r}_{sj} + (1+\gamma)\beta_j \right] x_j \right) d\gamma \geq r_G$$

$$\Leftrightarrow \sum_{j=1}^n \left(\frac{1}{S} \sum_{s=1}^S \bar{r}_{sj} x_j \right) - \left(\int_0^1 \gamma (1-\gamma) d\gamma \right) \sum_{j=1}^n \alpha_j x_j + \left(\int_0^1 \gamma (1-\gamma) d\gamma \right) \sum_{j=1}^n \beta_j x_j \geq r_G$$

$$\Leftrightarrow \sum_{j=1}^n \left(\frac{1}{S} \sum_{s=1}^S \bar{r}_{sj} x_j \right) - \frac{1}{6} \sum_{j=1}^n \alpha_j x_j + \frac{1}{6} \sum_{j=1}^n \beta_j x_j \geq r_G$$

$$(38)$$

Furthermore, if target value r_G is sufficiently small, the maximum value of aspiration level for each object is sufficiently large. However, a decision maker often has a goal to each object such as "Total future return $\tilde{f}_s$ is approximately larger than the goal f_1." and "The goal of nonfulfillment probability is less than about p_1.". Furthermore, in a similar way to each return involving the decision maker's subjectivity and ambiguity, taking account of the vagueness of human judgment and flexibility for the execution of a plan, the decision maker has some subjectivity and ambiguity with respect to each goal. In this paper, we introduce such subjective goals for the total return r_G, nonfulfillment probability $p = \frac{1}{S} \sum_{s=1}^S z_s$ and expected total return r_G as fuzzy goals. First, the fuzzy goal of r_G is assumed to be the following membership function:

$$\mu_G \left(r_G \right) = \begin{cases} 1 & \left(r_G \leq r_{G1} \right) \\ \dfrac{r_{G0} - r_G}{r_{G0} - r_{G1}} & \left(r_{G1} < r_G \leq r_{G0} \right) \\ 0 & \left(r_{G0} < r_G \right) \end{cases} \quad (39)$$

In a similar way to r_G, fuzzy goals of p and r are assumed to be the following forms:

$$\mu_G \left(p \right) = \begin{cases} 1 & \left(p \leq p_1 \right) \\ \dfrac{p_0 - p}{p_0 - p_1} & \left(p_1 < p \leq p_0 \right) \\ 0 & \left(p_0 < p \right) \end{cases} \quad (40)$$

$$\mu_G \left(r \right) = \begin{cases} 1 & \left(r_1 \leq r \right) \\ \dfrac{r - r_0}{r_1 - r_0} & \left(r_0 \leq r < r_1 \right) \\ 0 & \left(r < r_0 \right) \end{cases} \quad (41)$$

Then, we introduce the following possibility measure $\Pi_{\tilde{f}_s} \left(\tilde{G} \right)$ and necessity measure $N_{\tilde{f}_s} \left(\tilde{G} \right)$

$$\Pi_{\tilde{f}_s} \left(\tilde{G} \right) = \sup_\omega \min \left\{ \mu_{\tilde{f}_s} \left(\omega \right), \mu_G \left(\omega \right) \right\}$$

$$N_{\tilde{f}_s} \left(\tilde{G} \right) = \inf_\omega \max \left\{ 1 - \mu_{\tilde{f}_s} \left(\omega \right), \mu_G \left(\omega \right) \right\} \quad (42)$$

We assumed the following cases:

(a) In the case that the object is maximizing the total return, we deal with possibility measure $\Pi_{\tilde{f}_s} \left(\tilde{G} \right)$ since a decision maker strongly considers that she or he manages to earn the total return as much as possible.

(b) In the case that the object is not maximizing the total return but other objects such as minimizing the nonfilfullment probability, we deal with necessity measure $N_{\tilde{f}_s} \left(\tilde{G} \right)$ since a decision maker consider that the total return is sure to be hold more than the goal satisfying the other object.

From these assumptions, in this paper, we possibility maximization models with respect to each objective function of basic safety first model satisfying this aspiration level becomes more than the other aspiration level. Therefore, safety first models (15), (16) and (17) are transformed into the following problems introducing parameter h:

(risk-management model based on Roy model)

Maximize h

subject to $\mu_G(p) \geq N_{\tilde{I}_s}(\tilde{G}) \geq h, \quad (s=1,2,...,S)$

$\mu_G(p) \geq \mu_G(r) \geq h,$

$\sum_{j=1}^{n} a_{ij}x_j \leq b_i, \ \boldsymbol{x} \geq \boldsymbol{0}, \ (i=1,2,...,m), \ z_s \in \{0,1\}$

(43)

(risk-management model based on Kataoka model)

Maximize h

subject to $\Pi_{\tilde{I}_s}(\tilde{G}) \geq \mu_G(p) \geq h, \quad (s=1,2,...,S)$

$\Pi_{\tilde{I}_s}(\tilde{G}) \geq \mu_G(r) \geq h, \quad (s=1,2,...,S)$

$\sum_{j=1}^{n} a_{ij}x_j \leq b_i, \ \boldsymbol{x} \geq \boldsymbol{0}, \ (i=1,2,...,m), \ z_s \in \{0,1\}$

(44)

(risk-management model based on Telser model)

Maximize h

subject to $\mu_G(r) \geq \mu_G(r_G) \geq h,$

$\mu_G(r) \geq N_{\tilde{I}_s}(\tilde{G}) \geq h, \quad (s=1,2,...,S)$

$\sum_{j=1}^{n} a_{ij}x_j \leq b_i, \ \boldsymbol{x} \geq \boldsymbol{0}, \ (i=1,2,...,m), \ z_s \in \{0,1\}$

(45)

In these problems, each constraint is transformed into the following inequality:

$\mu_G(p) \geq h \ \Leftrightarrow \ p \leq (1-h)p_0 + hp_1$

$\mu_G(r) \geq h \ \Leftrightarrow \ r \geq (1-h)r_0 + hr_1$

$\Pi_{\tilde{I}_s}(\tilde{G}) \geq h \ \Leftrightarrow \ \sup_{\omega} \min\{\mu_{\tilde{I}_s}(\omega), \mu_G(\omega)\} \geq h$

$\Leftrightarrow \ \mu_{\tilde{I}_s}(\omega) \geq h, \ \mu_G(\omega) \geq h$

$\Leftrightarrow \ \sum_{j=1}^{n} \bar{r}_{sj}x_j + R^*(h)\sum_{j=1}^{n} \alpha_j x_j + M \cdot z_s \geq g_{\tilde{I}_s}^{-1}(h)$

$N_{\tilde{I}_s}(\tilde{G}) \geq h \ \Leftrightarrow \ \inf_{\omega} \min\{1-\mu_{\tilde{I}_s}(\omega), \mu_{r_G}(\omega)\} \geq h$

$\Leftrightarrow \ ^\exists h, \ 1-\mu_{\tilde{I}_s}(\omega) \leq h \Rightarrow \mu_{r_G}(\omega) \geq h$

$\Leftrightarrow \ \sum_{j=1}^{n} \bar{r}_{sj}x_j - L^*(1-h)\sum_{j=1}^{n} \alpha_j x_j + M \cdot z_s \geq g_{\tilde{I}_s}^{-1}(h)$

(46)

Furthermore, introducing a parameter $\bar{h}$ into problems (43), (44) and (45), we also obtain the similar inequalities with respect to $\bar{h}$ using the same manner to (46). From these inequalities, we transform these safety first models into the following problems:

(risk-management model based on Roy model)

Maximize h

subject to $\frac{1}{S}\sum_{s=1}^{S} z_s \leq (1-\bar{h})p_0 + \bar{h}p_1,$

$\sum_{j=1}^{n} \bar{r}_{sj}x_j - L^*(1-h)\sum_{j=1}^{n} \alpha_j x_j + M \cdot z_s \geq g_{\tilde{I}_s}^{-1}(h), \quad (s=1,2,...,S)$

$\sum_{j=1}^{n} \bar{r}_{sj}x_j - L^*(1-\bar{h})\sum_{j=1}^{n} \alpha_j x_j + M \cdot z_s \leq g_{\tilde{I}_s}^{-1}(\bar{h}), \quad (s=1,2,...,S)$

$(1-h)r_0 + hr_1 \leq \sum_{j=1}^{n}\left(\frac{1}{S}\sum_{s=1}^{S}\bar{r}_{sj}x_j\right) - \frac{1}{6}\sum_{j=1}^{n}\alpha_j x_j + \frac{1}{6}\sum_{j=1}^{n}\beta_j x_j \leq (1-\bar{h})r_0 + \bar{h}r_1,$

$\sum_{j=1}^{n} a_{ij}x_j \leq b_i, \ \boldsymbol{x} \geq \boldsymbol{0}, \ (i=1,2,...,m), \ z_s \in \{0,1\}$

(47)

(risk-management model based on Kataoka model)

Maximize h

subject to $(1-\bar{h})p_0 + \bar{h}p_1 \leq \frac{1}{S}\sum_{s=1}^{S} z_s \leq (1-h)p_0 + hp_1,$

$\sum_{j=1}^{n} \bar{r}_{sj}x_j + R^*(\bar{h})\sum_{j=1}^{n} \alpha_j x_j + M \cdot z_s \geq g_{\tilde{I}_s}^{-1}(\bar{h}), \quad (s=1,2,...,S)$

$(1-h)r_0 + hr_1 \leq \sum_{j=1}^{n}\left(\frac{1}{S}\sum_{s=1}^{S}\bar{r}_{sj}x_j\right) - \frac{1}{6}\sum_{j=1}^{n}\alpha_j x_j + \frac{1}{6}\sum_{j=1}^{n}\beta_j x_j \leq (1-\bar{h})r_0 + \bar{h}r_1,$

$\sum_{j=1}^{n} a_{ij}x_j \leq b_i, \ \boldsymbol{x} \geq \boldsymbol{0}, \ (i=1,2,...,m), \ z_s \in \{0,1\}$

(48)

(risk-management model based on Telser model)

Maximize h

subject to $(1-\bar{h})p_0 + \bar{h}p_1 \leq \frac{1}{S}\sum_{s=1}^{S} z_s \leq (1-h)p_0 + hp_1,$

$\sum_{j=1}^{n} \bar{r}_{sj}x_j - L^*(1-h)\sum_{j=1}^{n} \alpha_j x_j + M \cdot z_s \geq g_{\tilde{I}_s}^{-1}(h), \quad (s=1,2,...,S)$

$\sum_{j=1}^{n} \bar{r}_{sj}x_j - L^*(1-\bar{h})\sum_{j=1}^{n} \alpha_j x_j + M \cdot z_s \leq g_{\tilde{I}_s}^{-1}(\bar{h}), \quad (s=1,2,...,S)$

$(1-h)r_0 + hr_1 \leq \sum_{j=1}^{n}\left(\frac{1}{S}\sum_{s=1}^{S}\bar{r}_{sj}x_j\right) - \frac{1}{6}\sum_{j=1}^{n}\alpha_j x_j + \frac{1}{6}\sum_{j=1}^{n}\beta_j x_j,$

$\sum_{j=1}^{n} a_{ij}x_j \leq b_i, \ \boldsymbol{x} \geq \boldsymbol{0}, \ (i=1,2,...,m), \ z_s \in \{0,1\}$

(49)

These problems are 0-1 mixed nonlinear programming problems, and so it is almost impossible to solve them directly and efficiently. However, in the case that parameters h and $\bar{h}$ is fixed such as $h=h_f$ and $\bar{h} = \bar{h}_f$, by considering the following problems;

(risk-management model based on Roy model)

Maximize $\frac{1}{S}\sum_{s=1}^{S}z_s$

subject to
$$\sum_{j=1}^{n}\overline{r}_{sj}x_j - L'\left(1-h_f\right)\sum_{j=1}^{n}\alpha_j x_j + M\cdot z_s \geq g_{L_s}^{-1}\left(h_f\right),\ \left(s=1,2,...,S\right)$$
$$\sum_{j=1}^{n}\overline{r}_{sj}x_j - L'\left(1-\overline{h}_f\right)\sum_{j=1}^{n}\alpha_j x_j + M\cdot z_s \leq g_{L_s}^{-1}\left(\overline{h}_f\right),\ \left(s=1,2,...,S\right)$$
$$\left(1-h_f\right)r_0 + h_f r_1 \leq \sum_{j=1}^{n}\left[\frac{1}{S}\sum_{s=1}^{S}\overline{r}_{sj}x_j\right] - \frac{1}{6}\sum_{j=1}^{n}\alpha_j x_j + \frac{1}{6}\sum_{j=1}^{n}\beta_j x_j \leq \left(1-\overline{h}_f\right)r_0 + \overline{h}_f r_1,$$
$$\sum_{j=1}^{n}a_{ij}x_j \leq b_i,\ \mathbf{x}\geq \mathbf{0},\ \left(i=1,2,...,m\right),\ z_s\in\{0,1\}$$

$$(50)$$

(risk-management model based on Kataoka model)

Maximize $\overline{r}_G$

subject to
$$\left(1-\overline{h}_f\right)p_0 + \overline{h}_f p_1 \leq \frac{1}{S}\sum_{s=1}^{S}z_s \leq \left(1-h_f\right)p_0 + h_f p_1,$$
$$\sum_{j=1}^{n}\overline{r}_{sj}x_j + R'\left(\overline{h}_f\right)\sum_{j=1}^{n}\alpha_j x_j + M\cdot z_s \geq \overline{r}_G,\ \left(s=1,2,...,S\right)$$
$$\left(1-h_f\right)r_0 + h_f r_1 \leq \sum_{j=1}^{n}\left[\frac{1}{S}\sum_{s=1}^{S}\overline{r}_{sj}x_j\right] - \frac{1}{6}\sum_{j=1}^{n}\alpha_j x_j + \frac{1}{6}\sum_{j=1}^{n}\beta_j x_j \leq \left(1-\overline{h}_f\right)r_0 + \overline{h}_f r_1,$$
$$\sum_{j=1}^{n}a_{ij}x_j \leq b_i,\ \mathbf{x}\geq \mathbf{0},\ \left(i=1,2,...,m\right),\ z_s\in\{0,1\}$$

$$(51)$$

(risk-management model based on Telser model)

Maximize $\sum_{j=1}^{n}\left[\frac{1}{S}\sum_{s=1}^{S}\overline{r}_{sj}x_j\right] - \frac{1}{6}\sum_{j=1}^{n}\alpha_j x_j + \frac{1}{6}\sum_{j=1}^{n}\beta_j x_j$

subject to
$$\left(1-\overline{h}_f\right)p_0 + \overline{h}_f p_1 \leq \frac{1}{S}\sum_{s=1}^{S}z_s \leq \left(1-h_f\right)p_0 + h_f p_1,$$
$$\sum_{j=1}^{n}\overline{r}_{sj}x_j - L'\left(1-h_f\right)\sum_{j=1}^{n}\alpha_j x_j + M\cdot z_s \geq g_{L_s}^{-1}\left(h_f\right),\ \left(s=1,2,...,S\right)$$
$$\sum_{j=1}^{n}\overline{r}_{sj}x_j - L'\left(1-\overline{h}_f\right)\sum_{j=1}^{n}\alpha_j x_j + M\cdot z_s \leq g_{L_s}^{-1}\left(\overline{h}_f\right),\ \left(s=1,2,...,S\right)$$
$$\sum_{j=1}^{n}a_{ij}x_j \leq b_i,\ \mathbf{x}\geq \mathbf{0},\ \left(i=1,2,...,m\right),\ z_s\in\{0,1\}$$

$$(52)$$

and evaluating whether each objective function is equal to $g_p^{-1}\left(\overline{h}_f\right)$, $g_{f_s}^{-1}\left(\overline{h}_f\right)$ and $g_r^{-1}\left(\overline{h}_f\right)$ using the bisection algorithm for parameter h, respectively, we obtain each optimal solution each global optimal solution. Consequently, the following solution method is constructed with respect to the risk-management model based on Roy model (47).

Solution Method

- STEP 1: Elicit the membership function of a fuzzy goal with respect to total profit, nonfulfillment probability and expected total return.

- STEP 2: Set $h\leftarrow 1$ and solve problem (47). If the optimal objective value $Z(h)$ of the problem satisfies $Z\left(h\right)\leq g_p^{-1}\left(h\right)$ and its feasible solution including constraints exists, then terminate. In this case, the obtained current solution is an optimal solution of main problem. Otherwise, go to STEP 3.

- STEP 3: Set $h\leftarrow 0$ and solve problem (47). If the optimal objective value $Z(h)$ of the problem satisfies $Z\left(h\right)\leq g_p^{-1}\left(h\right)$ or the feasible solution including constrains does not exist, then terminate. In this case, there is no feasible solution and it is necessary to reset a fuzzy goal for each objective function. Otherwise, go to STEP 4.

- STEP 4: Set $U_h\leftarrow 1$ and $L_h\leftarrow 0$.

- STEP 5: Set $h\leftarrow\dfrac{U_h+L_h}{2}$

- STEP 6: Solve problem (47) and calculate the optimal objective value $Z(h)$ of the problem. If $Z\left(h\right)\leq g_p^{-1}\left(h\right)$, then set $U_h\leftarrow h$ and return to STEP 5. If $Z\left(h\right)< g_p^{-1}\left(h\right)$, then set $L_h\leftarrow h$ and return to STEP 5. If $Z\left(h\right)= g_p^{-1}\left(h\right)$, then terminate the algorithm. In this case, $x^*(h)$ is equal to a global optimal solution of main problem.

In a similar way to this solution method for the risk-management model based on Roy model, the solution methods for the risk-management model based on Kataoka model and Telser model are constructed. Furthermore, in problems (50), (51) and (52), a decision maker considers that all the fuzzy numbers and fuzzy goals is not included in each problem, each problem is degenerated to basic safety first model (15), (16) or (17), respectively. Therefore, we find that our proposed models (50), (51) and (52) include many previous risk-management models based on safety first theory.

Table 1. Numerical example in the case of nine decision variables and ten return scenarios

	R1	R2	R3	R4	R5	R6	R7	R8	R9
Scenario1	0.082	0.061	0.162	0.179	0.191	0.053	0.129	0.136	0.122
Scenario2	0.072	0.062	0.141	0.163	0.210	0.062	0.142	0.121	0.119
Scenario3	0.075	0.055	0.153	0.177	0.204	0.060	0.119	0.111	0.125
Scenario4	0.070	0.051	0.149	0.182	0.205	0.054	0.128	0.127	0.113
Scenario5	0.084	0.070	0.143	0.162	0.189	0.067	0.135	0.120	0.115
Scenario6	0.066	0.064	0.152	0.159	0.195	0.049	0.144	0.118	0.107
Scenario7	0.076	0.071	0.146	0.163	0.191	0.053	0.135	0.125	0.126
Scenario8	0.072	0.058	0.140	0.167	0.202	0.046	0.118	0.107	0.119
Scenario9	0.065	0.053	0.155	0.181	0.190	0.069	0.138	0.123	0.115
Scenario10	0.078	0.072	0.164	0.169	0.188	0.064	0.133	0.111	0.124
Spread α	0.01	0.02	0.02	0.05	0.1	0.02	0.04	0.06	0.08

Table 2. Numerical example in the case of three constrains and their upper value

	R1	R2	R3	R4	R5	R6	R7	R8	R9	Upper
Scenario1	2	3	5	6	8	2	4	5	6	500
Scenario2	1	2	6	4	7	3	4	3	5	600
Scenario3	4	2	4	7	8	2	6	7	4	650

Numerical Example

In order to compare our proposal models with one of the most important portfolio model, mean-variance model, let us consider an example shown in Tables 1 and 2. We assume that there are nine decision variables whose returns are assumed to be symmetric triangle fuzzy numbers involving spread α. Then, we assumed that 10 scenarios for returns are generated randomly from data based on Markowitz (1959) and spread α for each return is equal among all scenarios. Table 2 shows that the number of constraints in all problems is 3.

This example may be considered as the practical problem in production processes with constraints of human and feedstock resources under the decision maker's prediction to returns of productions. In this case, we solve the following three problems; (P1) Basic mean-variance model, (P2) Fuzzy mean-variance model, (P3) Fuzz mean-

Table 3. Optimal solutions with respect to each problem

Problem	R1	R2	R3	R4	R5	R6	R7	R8	R9
P1	3.243	1.010	14.990	1.190	13.159	0.154	5.068	7.556	14.940
P2	0	0	0	0	25	0	75	0	0
P3	18.579	0	0	0	4.250	18.620	37.314	0	40.389
P4	8.419	0	25.350	9.761	2.934	0	17.616	3.707	0
P5	1.283	10.644	0.120	4.967	20.594	0.048	23.921	0.097	0.096
P6	0.538	2.403	4.471	8.721	20.216	4.699	15.339	6.680	1.733

absolute deviation model, (P4) Fuzzy Roy model, (P5) Fuzzy Kataoka model and (P6) Fuzzy Telser model. Then, membership functions of fuzzy goals $\mu_G(r_G)$, $\mu_G(p)$ and $\mu_G(r)$ proposed in the previous section are assumed to be the following linear functions set by the decision maker.

$$\mu_G(r_G) = \begin{cases} 1 \\ r_G - 8, \\ 0 \end{cases} \quad \mu_G(p) = \begin{cases} 1 \\ \dfrac{0.2 - p}{0.1}, \\ 0 \end{cases} \quad \mu_G(r) = \begin{cases} 1 \\ r - 8 \\ 0 \end{cases}$$

Consequently, we solve these problems using standard approaches or the proposed solution method, and obtain each optimal portfolio shown in Table 3:

Form these optimal solutions, while we find that the all decision variables in the basic mean-variance model P1 does not become 0, we also find that some decision variables in fuzzy mean-variance and mean- absolute deviation risk-management models become 0 even if these models consider the well-decentralized concept. This result means that the concept to fuzzy extension of risk-management models using the variance is that unnecessary decision variables are not selected under the well-decentralization. Furthermore, with respect to results of fuzzy safety-first based risk-management models, they are similar to the result of basic mean-variance model in the sense of well-decentralized.

FUTURE TRENDS

Most recently, the role of risk-management is more and more important due to the uncertain and complex social systems such as financial crisis and fluctuation in demands. Particularly, in the sense of economics and management science, the concept of risk-management is requisite in many production companies which sustain the economic infrastructure all over the world. Therefore, our

proposed risk-management models are expected to be more standard and versatile under various uncertainty in the economic and management fields. Then, the proposed models may play a part of risk-management fields under various uncertain social conditions.

As the future studies in the sense of the mathematical programming, we need to consider risk-management models in the case that decision variables are restricted to be integer. For instance, in production processes, individual products such as home electric appliances and commodities cannot be divided. Therefore, we should consider integer programming problems for the risk-management. However, it is much difficult to solve them analytically and efficiently due to NP-hard of integer programming problems. Consequently, we need to propose not only the more versatile models but also the efficient solution method.

CONCLUSION

In this chapter, we have proposed some fuzzy extended risk-management models using multi-scenario based on portfolio theories such mean-variance, mean-absolute deviation and safety first theories, and considered models minimizing the total variance, maximizing the aspiration level for nonfulfillment probability, total profit or expected total return, respectively. Furthermore, to solve it more efficiently, we have transformed main problem into the deterministic equivalent 0-1 mixed linear programming problem. We may be able to apply this solution method to the case including not only fuzziness but also both randomness and fuzziness, which is called to fuzzy random variable or random fuzzy variable. Then, we will also apply our proposed method to the other portfolio selection problems and be able to extend all the portfolio selection problems to the models considering various uncertainty situations.

REFERENCES

Bawa, V. S., & Lindenberg, E. B. (1977). Capital market equilibrium in a mean-lower partial moment framework. *Journal of Financial Economics*, *5*, 189–200. doi:10.1016/0304-405X(77)90017-4

Bilbao-Terol, A., Perez-Gladish, B., Arenas-Parra, M., & Rodriguez-Uria, M. V. (2006). Fuzzy compromise programming for portfolio selection. *Applied Mathematics and Computation*, *173*, 251–264. doi:10.1016/j.amc.2005.04.003

Campbell, J. Y., Lo, A. W., & MacKinlay, A. C. (1997). *The Econometrics of Finance Markets*. Princeton, NJ: Princeton University Press.

Carlsson, C., Fullér, R., & Majlender, P. (2002). A possibilistic approach to selecting portfolios with highest utility score. *Fuzzy Sets and Systems*, *131*, 13–21. doi:10.1016/S0165-0114(01)00251-2

Danzig, D. B. (1955). Linear programming under uncertainty. *Management Science*, *1*, 197–206. doi:10.1287/mnsc.1.3-4.197

Dubois, D., & Prade, H. (1980). Systems of linear fuzzy constraints. *Fuzzy Sets and Systems*, *3*, 37–48. doi:10.1016/0165-0114(80)90004-4

Dubois, D., & Prade, H. (1988). *Possibility Theory: An Approach to Computerized Processing of Uncertainty*. New York: Plenum.

Elton, E. J., & Gruber, M. J. (1995). *Modern Portfolio Theory and Investment Analysis*. New York: Wiley.

Guo, P., & Tanaka, H. (1998). Possibility data analysis and its application to portfolio selection problems. *Fuzzy Economic Rev.*, *3*, 3–23.

Hasuike, T., & Ishii, H. (2005). Portfolio selection problem with two possibilities of the expected return. In *Proceedings of Nonlinear Analysis and Convex Analysis Okinawa,* (pp.115-25). Yokohama: Yokohama Publishers.

Hasuike, T., & Ishii, H. (2008). Portfolio selection problems considering fuzzy returns of future scenarios. *International Journal of Innovative Computing . Information and Control*, *4*(10), 2493–2506.

Huang, X. (2007). Two new models for portfolio selection with stochastic returns taking fuzzy information. *European Journal of Operational Research*, *180*, 396–405. doi:10.1016/j.ejor.2006.04.010

Inuiguchi, M., Ichihasi, H., & Tanaka, H. (1990). Fuzzy programming: A survey of recent development. In R. Slowinski & J. Teghem (Ed.), *Stochastic versus Fuzzy Approaches to Multiobjective Mathematical Programming under Uncertainty*, (pp. 45-68).

Inuiguchi, M., & Ramik, J. (2000). Possibilisitc linear programming: A brief review of fuzzy mathematical programming and a comparison with stochastic programming in portfolio selection problem. *Fuzzy Sets and Systems*, *111*, 3–28. doi:10.1016/S0165-0114(98)00449-7

Inuiguchi, M., & Tanino, T. (2000). Portfolio selection under independent possibilistic information. *Fuzzy Sets and Systems*, *115*, 83–92. doi:10.1016/S0165-0114(99)00026-3

Jorion, P. (1992). Portfolio optimization in practice, *Financial Analysis Journal*, (Jan.-Feb.), 68-74.

Katagiri, H., Ishii, H., & Sakawa, M. (2004). On fuzzy random linear knapsack problems. *Central European Journal of Operations Research*, *12*(1), 59–70.

Katagiri, H., Sakawa, H., Kato, K., & Nishizaki, H. (2008). Interactive multiobjective fuzzy random linear programming: Maximization of possibility and probability. *European Journal of Operational Research*, *188*, 530–539. doi:10.1016/j.ejor.2007.02.050

Katagiri, H., Sakawa, M., & Ishii, H. (2005). A study on fuzzy random portfolio selection problems using possibility and necessity measures. *Scientiae Mathematicae Japonocae, 65*(2), 361–369.

Katagiri, H., Sakawa, M., Kato, K., & Nishizaki, I. (2004). A fuzzy random multiobjective 0-1 programming based on the expectation optimization model using possibility and necessity measure. *Mathematical and Computer Modelling, 40*, 411–421. doi:10.1016/j.mcm.2003.08.007

Kaufmann, A. (1975). *Introduction to the Theory of Fuzzy Subsets*, (Vol.I). New York: Academic Press.

King, A. J. (1993). Asymmetric risk measure and trcking models for portfolio optimization under uncertainty. *Annals of Operations Research, 45*, 205–220. doi:10.1007/BF02282047

Konno, H. (1990). Piecewise linear risk functions and portfolio optimization. *Journal of the Operations Research Society of Japan, 33*, 139–159.

Konno, H., Shirakawa, H., & Yamazaki, H. (1993). A mean-absolute deviation-skewness portfolio optimization model. *Annals of Operations Research, 45*, 205–220. doi:10.1007/BF02282050

Lintner, B. J. (1965). Valuation of risky assets and the selection of risky investments in stock portfolios and capital budgets. *The Review of Economics and Statistics, 47*, 13–37. doi:10.2307/1924119

Liu, B. (2002). *Theory and Practice of Uncertain Programming*. Heidelberg, Germany: Physica Verlag.

Liu, B. (2004). *Uncertainty Theory*. Heidelberg, Germany: Physica Verlag.

Luenberger, D. G. (1997). *Investment Science*. Oxford, UK: Oxford Univ. Press.

Luhandjura, M. K. (1987). Linear programming with a possibilistic objective function. *European Journal of Operational Research, 13*, 137–145.

Maeda, T. (2001). Fuzzy linear programming problems as bi-criteria optimization problems. *Applied Mathematics and Computation, 120*, 109–121. doi:10.1016/S0096-3003(99)00237-4

Markowitz, H. (1959). *Portfolio Selection*. New York: Wiley.

Mossin, J. (1966). Equilibrium in capital asset markets. *Econometrica, 34*(4), 768–783. doi:10.2307/1910098

Nahmias, S. (1978). Fuzzy variables. *Fuzzy Sets and Systems, 1*, 97–110. doi:10.1016/0165-0114(78)90011-8

Rockafellar, R. T., & Uryasev, S. (2000). Optimization of conditional value-at-risk. *Journal of Risk, 2*(3), 1–21.

Sakawa, M. (1993). *Fuzzy sets and Interactive Multiobjective Optimization*. New York: Plenum.

Sharpe, W. F. (1964). Capital asset prices: A theory of market equivalent under conditions of risk. *The Journal of Finance, 19*(3), 425–442. doi:10.2307/2977928

Tanaka, H., & Guo, P. (1999). Portfolio selection based on upper and lower exponential possibility distributions. *European Journal of Operational Research, 114*, 115–126. doi:10.1016/S0377-2217(98)00033-2

Tanaka, H., Guo, P., & Turksen, I. B. (2000). Portfolio selection based on fuzzy probabilities and possibility distributions. *Fuzzy Sets and Systems, 111*, 387–397. doi:10.1016/S0165-0114(98)00041-4

Tanaka, H., Ichihashi, H., & Asai, K. (1984). A formulation of fuzzy linear programming problem based on comparison of fuzzy numbers. *Control Cybernet, 13*(3), 185–194.

Vajda, S. (1982). *Probabilistic Programming.* New York: Academic Press.

Vercher, E., Bermúdez, J. D., & Segura, J. V. (2007). Fuzzy portfolio optimization under downside risk measures. *Fuzzy Sets and Systems, 158,* 769–782. doi:10.1016/j.fss.2006.10.026

Watada, J. (1997). Fuzzy portfolio selection and its applications to decision making. *Tatra Mountains Math. Pub., 13,* 219–248.

Zadeh, L. A. (1965). Fuzzy sets. *Information and Control, 8,* 338–353. doi:10.1016/S0019-9958(65)90241-X

Zadeh, L. A. (1975). The concept of a linguistic variable and its application to approximate reasoning. *Information Sciences, 8,* 199–251. doi:10.1016/0020-0255(75)90036-5

Zadeh, L. A. (1978). Fuzzy sets as a basis for a theory of possibility. *Fuzzy Sets and Systems, 1,* 3–28. doi:10.1016/0165-0114(78)90029-5

Zimmermann, H. J. (1978). Fuzzy programming and linear programming with several objective functions. *Fuzzy Sets and Systems, 1,* 45–55. doi:10.1016/0165-0114(78)90031-3

Chapter 8
Neuro–Fuzzy System Modeling

Chen-Sen Ouyang
I-Shou University, Taiwan, R.O.C.

ABSTRACT

Neuro-fuzzy modeling is a computing paradigm of soft computing and very efficient for system modeling problems. It integrates two well-known modeling approaches of neural networks and fuzzy systems, and therefore possesses advantages of them, i.e., learning capability, robustness, human-like reasoning, and high understandability. Up to now, many approaches have been proposed for neuro-fuzzy modeling. However, it still exists many problems need to be solved. In this chapter, the authors firstly give an introduction to neuro-fuzzy system modeling. Secondly, some basic concepts of neural networks, fuzzy systems, and neuro-fuzzy systems are introduced. Also, they review and discuss some important literatures about neuro-fuzzy modeling. Thirdly, the issue for solving two most important problems of neuro-fuzzy modeling is considered, i.e., structure identification and parameter identification. Therefore, the authors present two approaches to solve these two problems, respectively. Fourthly, the future and emerging trends of neuro-fuzzy modeling is discussed. Besides, the possible research issues about neuro-fuzzy modeling are suggested. Finally, the authors give a conclusion.

INTRODUCTION

System modeling concerns modeling the operation of an unknown system from a set of measured input-output data and/or some prior knowledge (e.g., experience, expertise, or heuristics) about the system. It plays a very important role and has

a wide range of applications in various areas such as control, power systems, communications, networks, machine intelligence, etc. To understand the underlying properties of the unknown system and handle it properly, we can measure the system outputs by feeding a set of inputs and then construct a simulated system model from the obtained input-output dataset. Besides, some prior knowledge about the unknown system will also be helpful

DOI: 10.4018/978-1-61520-757-2.ch008

to construct the model. Usually, the problem of system modeling becomes very difficult when the unknown system is highly nonlinear and complex. Therefore, efficient approaches for solving this problem are necessary.

So far, there are many approaches proposed for system modeling. Quantitative approaches (hard computing) based on conventional mathematics (e.g., statistics, regression, differential equations, or numerical analysis) theoretically tend to be more accurate. However, they have disadvantages of the difficulty in deriving the corresponding mathematical forms, and the lack of adaptability and robustness. Especially, they are not suitable when the underlying system is complex, ill-defined, or uncertain. Therefore, many researchers have paid attention to intelligent problem-solving approaches, like conventional artificial intelligence and soft computing. Conventional artificial intelligence focuses on an attempt to mimic human intelligent behavior by expressing it in language forms or symbolic rules, and manipulating on the symbolic knowledge. One of the most popular and successful conventional artificial intelligence approaches is expert systems. However, it suffers from the difficulties in knowledge acquisition and representation. Soft computing differs from conventional (hard) computing in that, unlike hard computing, it is tolerant of imprecision, uncertainty, partial truth, and approximation. It is still not a closed and clearly defined discipline at present. Generally speaking, soft computing mainly consists of several computing paradigms (Jang et al., 1997), including neural networks, fuzzy systems, evolutionary computation, machine learning, probabilistic reasoning, etc. Moreover, the integration of several of these paradigms is also included in soft computing. Among these paradigms, neural networks and fuzzy systems are the most popular two to be chosen. Neural networks possess the advantages of parallel processing, capabilities of learning and adaptation, and fault tolerance. However, this approach usually encounters the problems

of slow convergence, local minima, difficulty in constructing the network architecture, and low understandability of the associated numerical weights. Fuzzy systems can deal with uncertain information and represent it with fuzzy rules which are easy to be comprehended. Besides, the human-like inference process used in this approach is quite understandable. However, this approach lacks a definite method to determine the number of fuzzy rules required and the membership functions associated with each rule. Moreover, it lacks an effective learning algorithm to refine the fuzzy rules to minimize output errors. Because of the complementary characteristics of neural networks and fuzzy systems, the integration of these two paradigms results in a very effective approach called neuro-fuzzy systems. It has attracted a lot of attention in recent years since it possesses the advantages of fuzzy systems and neural networks. Up to now, many approaches have been proposed for neuro-fuzzy modeling. However, it is still an open problem how to model an unknown system with neuro-fuzzy techniques.

BACKGROUND

In this section, the preliminary knowledge of neural networks and fuzzy systems, which is related to neuro-fuzzy modeling, is briefly introduced. Then, the focus of this chapter, i.e., neuro-fuzzy modeling, is introduced in detail. Also, some important literatures about neuro-fuzzy modeling are reviewed and discussed.

Neural Networks

Artificial neural networks, commonly referred to as neural networks or connectionist models, are models inspired by the structure and behavior of the human brain. The brain is a highly complex, nonlinear, and parallel information-processing system since it consists of a large number (approximately 10^{11}) of highly connected elements (approximately 10^4 connections per element) called neurons (Hagan et al., 1996). Through the massively parallel structure and simple functions of neurons, the brain is able to perform many complex tasks (e.g., pattern recognition, motor control, perception, etc.) much faster than the fastest digital computer in existence today. Besides, one important capability of the brain is acquiring knowledge for solving problems through learning. Therefore, artificial neural networks are designed to model the way in which the brain performs a particular task or function of interest. By mimicking the human brain, neural networks possess the advantages of parallel processing, capabilities of learning and adaptation, and fault tolerance. Moreover, some neural networks have been proved to be universal approximators of function approximation. Therefore, the research in neural networks has been an active research field for decades and has been successfully applied to many practical fields such as aerospace, automotive, banking, electronics, financial, medical, robotics, securities, speech, and telecommunication (Hagan et al., 1996).

The research in neural networks mainly considers the development of architectures and learning algorithms, and examines the applicability of these models to information-processing tasks (Nauch, 1997). In the following, we describe the categorization of neural networks according to the network architectures and learning algorithms.

Network Architectures

A network architecture means the manner in which the neurons and weighted connections of a neural network are structured. It mainly decides the functionality of the network and is intimately linked with the learning algorithm used to train the network. In general, architectures of neural networks are categorized into two classes, i.e., feedforward neural networks and recurrent neural networks. We describe these two classes as follows.

A generic feedforward neural network usually consists of several layers (one input layer, one or more hidden layers, and one output layer). Each layer contains several nodes acting as neurons. A node in each layer, except the input layer, has weighted connections from nodes in the previous layer. In other words, each node accepts the weighted output signals from nodes in the previous layer and sends its own output signal to nodes in the next layer. Figure 1 shows an L-layer feedforward neural network. The functionality of each node is usually simple. Suppose the number of nodes in layer l, $1 \leq l \leq L$, is represented by $s^{(l)}$. The output $o_i^{(l)}$ of node i, $1 \leq i \leq s^l$, in layer l, except the input layer, is computed by the following equations:

$$o_i^{(l)} = f_i^{(l)}(n_i^{(l)}), \ n_i^{(l)} = g_i^{(l)}(\vec{o}^{(l-1)}, \vec{\omega}_i^{(l)}) \qquad (1)$$

where $\vec{o}^{(l-1)} = [o_1^{(l-1)} \ o_2^{(l-1)} \ \cdots \ o_{s^{(l-1)}}^{(l-1)}]$, $\vec{\omega}_i^{(l)} = [\omega_{i1}^{(l)}, \omega_{i2}^{(l)}, ..., \omega_{is^{(l-1)}}^{(l)}]$ are weights connected to node i in layer l, $n_i^{(l)}$ is the net input computed by a net-input function $g_i^{(l)}$, and $o_i^{(l)}$ is the node output computed by an activation function $f_i^{(l)}$. Note that $s^{(0)}$ and $\vec{o}^{(0)}$ are the number of nodes contained in the input layer and the output vector of the input layer, respectively. Indeed, $\vec{o}^{(0)} = \vec{x} = [x_1 \ x_2 \ \cdots \ x_{s^{(0)}}]$ is the input vector. The net-input function g and the activation function f usually take the following forms:

$$f(n_i^{(l)}) = \frac{1}{1 + e^{-n_i^{(l)}}}, \ g(\vec{o}^{(l-1)}, \vec{\omega}_i^{(l)})$$
$$= \vec{o}^{(l-1)} \times (\vec{\omega}_i^{(l)})^T + b_i^{(l)} \qquad (2)$$

where $(v)^T$ is the transpose of a vector v and $b_i^{(l)}$ is the bias term. Other types of the activation functions can be found in (Hagan et al., 1996). To obtain the network output $\vec{y}$ for the input pattern $\vec{x}$, we firstly calculate the output $\vec{o}^{(1)}$ for the first hidden layer and send it to the next layer for

Figure 1. L-layer feedforward neural network

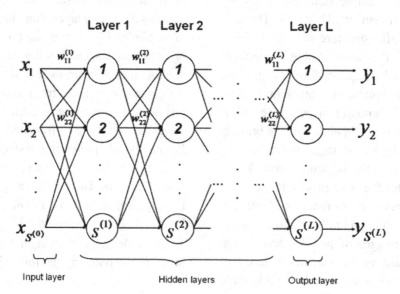

calculating the next layer output. This process goes on until the output of the final layer, $\vec{o}^{(L)}$, is obtained. Finally, we have the network output $\vec{y} = \vec{o}^{(L)}$ for the input pattern $\vec{x}$.

A recurrent neural network (Hagan et al., 1996) is quite different from a feedforward neural network because it has at least one feedback loop. For example, the outputs of a discrete-time recurrent network with one recurrent layer depend on not only the present inputs but also the past outputs. The feedback loops involve the use of particular branches composed of unit-delay elements (denoted by z^{-1}), which result in a nonlinear dynamical behavior of the network. The functionality of each recurrent node is similar to that of the node in feedforward networks except the addition of feedbacks as inputs. Generally speaking, compared with feedforward neural networks, recurrent neural networks are more powerful in performance. However, they require much more computation power.

LEARNING ALGORITHM

Learning algorithms of neural networks support rules for refining the adaptive parameters of the networks to have a better performance. There have been many different learning algorithms proposed for different network architectures. They can be generally categorized into two classes, i.e., learning with a teacher and leaning without a teacher (Haykin, 1999). We describe these two classes as follows.

Learning with a teacher is a kind of learning paradigm. A teacher possesses the knowledge represented by a set of input-output examples about the environment and is able to provide the neural network with the desired response for an input training example. The network parameters are adjusted iteratively by a learning algorithm to minimize the error between the desired responses and the actual responses. Therefore, this kind of learning paradigm is also referred to as supervised learning since a teacher exists to oversee the learning process. Backpropagation algorithm (Rumehart & McClelland, 1986), also known as generalized delta rule or error back-propagation algorithm, is a well-known and typical supervised learning algorithm for multi-layer feedforward neural networks. The detailed derivation of back-propagation can be found in (Haykin, 1999), which is mainly based on the gradient descent method (GDM) (Hagan et al., 1996) and the chain rule of calculus.

In the paradigm of learning without a teacher, there is no teacher to oversee the learning process. Therefore, this kind of learning paradigm is also referred to as unsupervised learning. A task independent measure is used for the quality of representation that the network is required to learn, and the adaptive parameters of the network are optimized with respect to that measure. Some well-known neural networks with unsupervised learning, like self-organizing maps (SOM), adaptive resonance theory (ART), and Hopfield network have been widely researched and applied to many applications (Hagan et al., 1996).

Fuzzy Systems

Since Zadeh, the founder of fuzzy logic, proposed the fuzzy set theory (Zadeh, 1965) in 1965 to characterize and deal with nonprobabilistic uncertainties, many researchers have actively pursued the research on fuzzy systems also known as fuzzy-rule-based systems, fuzzy expert systems, fuzzy models, fuzzy associative memories, or fuzzy logic controllers (Jang et al., 1997). Unlike classical models which usually try to avoid vague, imprecise, or uncertain information, fuzzy systems make use of fuzzy sets to characterize such kind of information and represent the domain knowledge of the considered problem in a set of fuzzy IF-THEN rules. Moreover, a fuzzy reasoning process is performed on the set of fuzzy rules to make decisions. Because of mimicking the interpretation and reasoning styles of human,

fuzzy systems usually lead to simpler and more suitable models, which are easier to be handled and are more familiar to human thinking. Besides, fuzzy systems, like neural networks, have also been proved to be universal approximators of function approximation. Therefore, fuzzy systems have been successfully applied to many areas such as automatic control, signal processing, information retrieval, pattern recognition, database management, and decision-making.

System Architecture

A fuzzy system is usually composed of several components, i.e., fuzzification module, fuzzy rule base, fuzzy inference engine, and defuzzification module, as shown in Figure 2. We briefly describe the functionality of each component and the operation of the whole system as follows:

1. Fuzzification. For each crisp input value, the fuzzification module transfers it into a fuzzy set to express the associated measurement uncertainty.

2. Fuzzy reasoning. Fuzzy reasoning is performed by the fuzzy inference engine based on the fuzzy sets obtained in step 1 and the fuzzy rule base composed of a set of fuzzy IF-THEN rules. One example of fuzzy IF-THEN rules is defined as the following (Jang et al., 1997):

$$\textbf{IF } x_1 \textbf{ IS } A_1 \textbf{ AND } x_2 \textbf{ IS } A_2 \textbf{ AND} \dots \textbf{AND } x_n \textbf{ IS } A_n \textbf{ THEN } y \textbf{ IS } B \qquad (3)$$

where $x_1, x_2 \dots, x_n$, and y are linguistic variables (e.g., temperature, age, height, etc.), and $A_1, A_2, \dots, A_n$, and B are linguistic values (e.g., high, young, tall, etc.) defined by fuzzy sets on universes of discourse $x_1, x_2 \dots, x_n$, and y, respectively. Besides, the most popular fuzzy reasoning method is the compositional rule of inference (Klir & Yuan, 1995). After reasoning, we have a conclusion represented by a fuzzy set for each output variable.

Figure 2. Block diagram of a fuzzy system

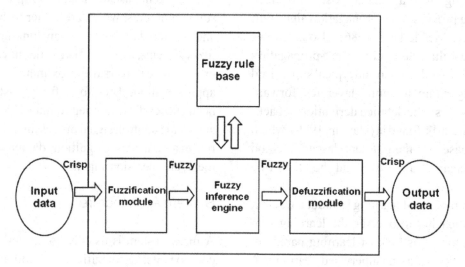

3. Defuzzification. To obtain a crisp output value for each output variable, a defuzzification method is used in the defuzzification module to convert the related fuzzy conclusion obtained in step 2 to a single real number. A lot of defuzzification methods have been proposed in literatures (Klir & Yuan, 1995). The center of area (COA) method, sometimes called the center of gravity method or centroid method, is a popular one and defined as the following continuous version:

$$d(B') = \frac{\int_y \mu_{B'}(y)y\,dy}{\int_y \mu_{B'}(y)\,dy} \qquad (4)$$

or the following discrete version:

$$d(B') = \frac{\sum_y \mu_{B'}(y)y}{\sum_y \mu_{B'}(y)} \qquad (5)$$

where $d(B')$ is the defuzzification value of fuzzy set B' and $\mu_B(y)$ is the membership degree of output value y belonging to B'.

Some Types of Fuzzy Systems

In the following, we introduce three well-known types of fuzzy systems, i.e., Mamdani-type, Tsukamoto-type, and TSK-type. The difference between them is mainly based on the type of the conclusion parts of fuzzy rules.

A Mamdani-type fuzzy system (Mamdani & Assilian, 1975) takes the following form for each rule j:

IF x_1 IS A_{1j} AND x_2 IS A_{2j} AND … AND x_n IS A_{nj} THEN y IS B_j $\qquad (6)$

An example for illustrating the reasoning process of the Mamdani-type fuzzy system is given in Figure 3(a), where $n=2$, the number of rules is two, and each membership function is in the triangular form. Besides, we adopt 'min' and 'max' operators for the t-norm and t-conorm (Klir & Yuan, 1995), respectively. A Tsukamoto-type fuzzy system (Gupta et al., 1979) takes the following form for each rule j:

IF x_1 IS A_{1j} AND x_2 IS A_{2j} AND … AND x_n IS A_{nj} THEN y IS C_j $\qquad (7)$

Figure 3. Three well-known types of fuzzy systems. (a) Mamdani-type. (b) Tsukamoto-type. (c) TSK-type

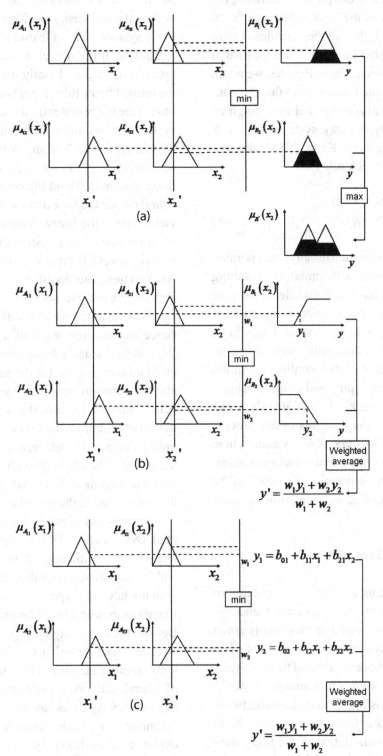

where C_j is a monotonic membership function. Figure 3(b) shows an example for illustrating the reasoning process of the Tsukamoto-type fuzzy system, where $n=2$, the number of rules is two, and each membership function in the premise of a rule is in the triangular form. Besides, we adopt 'min' operator for the t-norm. Note that the conclusion is a crisp value calculated by a weighted average. A TSK-type fuzzy system (Takagi & Sugeno, 1985; Sugeno & Kang, 1988) takes the following form for each rule j:

$$\text{IF } x_1 \text{ IS } A_{1j} \text{ AND } x_2 \text{ IS } A_{2j} \text{ AND } \dots$$
$$\text{AND } x_n \text{ IS } A_{nj} \text{ THEN } y = f(x_1, x_2, \dots, x_n) \qquad (8)$$

where f is a crisp function usually a polynomial. When f is a first-order polynomial, the resulting fuzzy system is called a first-order TSK-type fuzzy system. When f is a constant, it is called a zero-order TSK-type fuzzy system. Essentially, a TSK-type fuzzy system with linear rule consequents describes a global nonlinear relation between the system inputs and outputs using a set of local linear models. Figure 3(c) shows an example for illustrating the reasoning process of the first-order TSK-type fuzzy system, where $n=2$, the number of rules is two, and each membership function in the premise of a rule is in the triangular form. Besides, we adopt 'min' operator for the t-norm.

Neuro-Fuzzy Systems

Neuro-fuzzy systems are integrated systems of neural networks and fuzzy systems. Generally speaking, there are two basic viewpoints about the neuro-fuzzy systems. One viewpoint is to discover or refine the parameters of fuzzy systems using learning algorithms of neural networks. A fuzzy system is transformed into a neural network architecture called a fuzzy neural network. In other words, the initialization of the fuzzy neural network, including the number of layers, the number of nodes in each layer, the functionality

of each node, the connections between nodes, and the initial values of all adaptive parameters, is directly and easily decided according to the fuzzy system. Then, a learning algorithm is used to train the fuzzy neural network until a desired precision is reached. Finally, we can extract a set of the refined fuzzy rules to replace the original rule base of the fuzzy system and use this refined fuzzy system for symbolic inference. Alternatively, we can apply the learning algorithms of neural networks directly to refine partial parameters of fuzzy systems without the construction of fuzzy neural networks. Note that the leading role in this view point is the fuzzy system. The other viewpoint is using a fuzzy system to initialize a fuzzy neural network for a system modeling problem. As we know, the decision of a neural network architecture and its associated weights is not easy. Besides, the initial weights influence the convergence rate and the result of a training process. We can firstly use a fuzzy clustering method to build a fuzzy system for the set of training data and then convert the fuzzy system into a fuzzy neural network. Usually, the obtained parameters of the network from the fuzzy system are close to optimal values. Therefore, a refined fuzzy neural network can be obtained with a fast training for numeric inference. Note that the leading role in this view point is the neural network.

For the types of neuro-fuzzy systems, Nauck et al. (Nauch et al., 1997) proposed a taxonomy based on the combination style of neural networks and fuzzy systems. They distinguish neuro-fuzzy systems into two types, i.e., cooperative neuro-fuzzy systems and hybrid neuro-fuzzy systems. Besides the taxonomy based on the combination style between neural networks and fuzzy systems, another taxonomy is based on the classes of neural network architectures. Two kinds of neuro-fuzzy systems are distinguished in this taxonomy, i.e., static neuro-fuzzy systems and dynamic neuro-fuzzy systems. The difference between these two types is mainly the adopted architecture of neural networks and rule forms.

The neural network module used in the former is a multi-layer feedforward neural network, while the neural network module used in the latter is a multi-layer recurrent neural network.

Literature Survey

A lot of approaches have been proposed for neuro-fuzzy modeling in literatures. We survey some important ones of them in the following.

For the static neuro-fuzzy modeling, we consider two types of static neuro-fuzzy modeling in the following, i.e., cooperative type and hybrid type, as mentioned earlier. Most of static neuro-fuzzy system modeling approaches belong to the second type. For approaches in the cooperative type, most of them are mixtures of the three basic forms described in (Nauch et al., 1997). Nomura et al. (1992) employed a supervised learning to determine the corresponding fuzzy sets of a TSK-type fuzzy system from a set of existing fuzzy rules and a set of training data. A problem associated with this approach is the difficulty in interpreting the obtained fuzzy sets. Kosko (1992) proposed fuzzy associative memories each of which represents a fuzzy rule. Fuzzy sets are supposed to be known in advance, and fuzzy associative memories (fuzzy rules) and the corresponding rule weights are learned from a set of training data by a learning procedure of adaptive vector quantization. The disadvantage of this approach is the difficulties of knowing the fuzzy sets about the problem in advance and obtaining the suitable values of rule weights. Pedrycz and Card (1992) used a learning procedure of self-organizing feature map to determine the fuzzy rules composed by a set of specified linguistic terms. However, this approach also encounters the problem of specifying linguistic terms. Besides, it consumes much computation power of examining all possible combinations of linguistic terms.

For hybrid neuro-fuzzy system modeling, there are two important problems which should be dealt with, i.e., structure identification and parameter identification. For structure identification, many clustering methods have been proposed to extract fuzzy rules from a given set of training data. According to the way the data are presented, the methods can be categorized into nonincremental and incremental ones. For non-incremental methods, the whole data set is considered all at once. Bezdek (1981) proposed the fuzzy c-means algorithm which generalizes the hard c-means algorithm to produce a fuzzy partition for a given dataset. Yager and Filev (1994) proposed a mountain method based on the calculation of mountain functions. The computation power and time increase substantially when the number of grid nodes is large. Lin et al. (1997) obtained fuzzy partitions by iteratively cutting each dimension of the input space into two parts. However, it is difficult to decide the locations of best cuts. Yen et al. (1998) developed several approaches that attempt to reduce the number of fuzzy rules by assessing their degree of importance using singular-value decomposition (SVD). They start with an over-sized rule base and then remove redundant or less important fuzzy rules. However, data patterns may not be properly described due to the removal of such fuzzy rules. Wong and Chen (1999) proposed another idea for clustering. Reference vectors attract one another and form different clusters according to a similarity measure. However, convergence is very slow especially when the amount of given data is huge. Gonzalez et al. (2002) proposed a clustering technique which increases the density of prototypes in the input areas where the target function presents a more variable response. However, the number of clusters can not be determined automatically and needs to be set by the user. Azeem et al. (2003) used one of the three suggested clustering methods to identify the structure of generalized adaptive neuro-fuzzy inference systems. It takes much time and computation power to decide the suitable number of generalized radial basis function (GRBF) units, since a set of possible values for the number of GRBF units has to be evaluated by several cluster validity measures. All these non-incremental algorithms have one advantage that they are independent of the input order of training instances. However, they often take a long time and need a large amount of memory. The whole set of rules have to be generated from the scratch when new training data are considered. Besides, they cannot be applied to an environment where data are acquired on-line. Panella and Gallo (2005) proposed a new adaptive neuro-fuzzy inference systems (ANFIS) synthesis procedure where clustering is applied in the joint input–output data space. Sun et al. (2007) applied a relatively novel neural network technique, i.e., extreme learning machine (ELM), to realize a TSK-type neuro-fuzzy system. The proposed method is an improved version of the regular TSK-type neuro-fuzzy system.

Incremental clustering methods, on the other hand, consider training data one at a time. Clusters are built up, with none at the beginning, incrementally. The method proposed by Juang (2002) extracts fuzzy rules from a given dataset via an aligned clustering-based algorithm and a projection-based correlation measure. Wang and Lee (2002) developed a clustering algorithm by which rule nodes and term-set nodes are created adaptively and dynamically via simultaneous self-organizing learning and parameter learning procedures. Less significant rules are pruned and similar input term sets are combined. Kasabov and Song (2002) proposed an evolving, distance-based connectionist clustering method to partition the input space for the purpose of creating fuzzy inference rules. In any cluster, the maximum distance between an example point and the cluster center is less than a predefined threshold value. Kukolj and Levi (2004) proposed a heuristic self-organizing network (HSON) for partitioning of the input-output space. However, HSON is sensitive to the initial number of cluster nodes and the associated initial weights. Incremental algorithms can run efficiently, but they suffer from the data presentation ordering problem, i.e., the performance of

an incremental method may be greatly affected by the input order of training instances. One important problem which should be considered in rule generation is rule redundancy. The rule redundancy occurs when some of fuzzy rules are similar enough in a fuzzy system. Most of rule generation methods by clustering training data sets do not possess mechanisms to detect and reduce redundant rules. Therefore, some rule reduction approaches have been proposed for solving this problem. Roubos and Setnes (2001) and Jin (2000) proposed similarity-based approaches by merging a pair of similar fuzzy sets and fuzzy rules, respectively, at a time. However, it is time-consuming if only two fuzzy sets or fuzzy rules are merged at a time. Besides, they only consider the information about the input subspace of training data for the calculation of similarity, and the information about the output subspace is ignored. Wang and Lee (2002) proposed a mapping-constrained agglomerative clustering algorithm in which a procedure is used for combining compatible clusters. However, it is time-consuming especially when the initial number of seed clusters is large. Sudkamp et al. (2003) proposed a greedy merging based method by gradually partitioning the input data subspace into grids and then merging neighbor regions in several directions of input domains. However, the number of rules and the number of the considered directions for merging increase exponentially with the number of input dimensions. Besides, the merging results are sensitive to the order of directions.

For parameter identification, most systems use backpropagation to refine parameters of the system. However, backpropagation suffers from the problems of local minima and slow convergence rate. To alleviate these difficulties, different methods of least squares estimation (LSE) have been proposed. Many researchers (Wu et al., 2001) applied pseudo-inverse techniques to obtain optimal solutions for LSE. However, in most cases, pseudo-inverse is hard to find. Even though it can be found, it is usually memory/time demanding when the amount of training data is large. Jang and Sun (1995) proposed sequential formulas and Gomm and Yu (2000) proposed orthogonal least squares training for LSE. However, these methods suffer from either the necessity of initializing a certain parameter by the user or the restriction of usage to full rank problems. A lot of attention has been paid to solving LSE based on singular value decomposition (SVD) of the underlying matrix (Golub & Van Loan, 1996). The Golub-Kahan-Reinsch method (Golub & Reinsch, 1970) and Jacobi-like methods (Berry & Sameh, 1989) applied orthogonal transformations for the decomposition of small and dense matrices. After SVD, the optimal solution to LSE can be obtained. The Lanczos methods, LSQR and LSCG (Golub & Van Loan, 1996), used the Lanczos bidiagonalization process of Golub et al. (1996), for solving LSE problems. However, the amount of memory these methods consume depends on the number of training patterns. A lot of memory is required when the set of training patterns is large. Furthermore, the convergence rate of these methods is sensitive to the proper initialization of a certain parameter set by the user.

NEURO-FUZZY SYSTEM MODELING

In this chapter, we focus on hybrid neuro-fuzzy system modeling. Therefore, there are two important problems which should be dealt with, i.e., structure identification and parameter identification. Structure identification focuses on initializing the structures of neuro-fuzzy systems, including the rule form, the number of fuzzy rules, the linguistic terms and associated parameters of each fuzzy rule, the fuzzification and defuzzification methods, and the mechanism of fuzzy reasoning. As mentioned earlier, most of neuro-fuzzy systems employ fuzzy clustering methods to generate fuzzy rules from a set of input-output data. The purpose of the parameter identification in neuro-fuzzy modeling is refining the parameters

of initial fuzzy rules, obtained in the structure identification phase, for better precision. The refinement is usually through neural networks with learning algorithms. A corresponding fuzzy neural network is constructed from the obtained initial fuzzy rules and trained with neural learning methods, like backpropagation. Sometimes, the neural leaning methods are applied to the fuzzy rules directly without the construction of fuzzy neural networks. Several approaches have been proposed for this issue and possess advantages and disadvantages, as mentioned earlier. However, how to refine the initial fuzzy rules efficiently is still an open problem at present.

STRUCTURE IDENTIFICATION

We present in the following a similarity-and-merge-based rule generation (SMRG) method (Ouyang et al., 2005) for structure identification. It contains two steps, i.e., fuzzy cluster generation and fuzzy rule extraction. In SMRG, initial fuzzy clusters are generated incrementally and quickly form the training data set based on input-similarity and output-variance tests. Membership functions associated with each fuzzy cluster are also defined according to statistical means and deviations of the data points included in the cluster. Then, similar clusters are merged dynamically together through input-similarity, output-similarity, and output-variance tests. To obtain a fuzzy rule-base, we extract a fuzzy rule from each cluster directly. Apparently, SMRG supports a mechanism for cluster merging to alleviate the problems of data-input-order bias and redundant clusters.

Similarity-and-Merge-Based Rule Generation

The task of SMRG is to partition the given input-output data set into fuzzy clusters, with the degree of association being strong for data within a cluster and weak for data in different clusters.

Then, the corresponding fuzzy rule of each cluster is extracted. SMRG is an incremental one and consists of two steps, i.e., fuzzy cluster generation and fuzzy rule extraction. For the fuzzy cluster generation, there are two stages, i.e., data partitioning and cluster merge. In the data partitioning stage, the data are considered one by one and are partitioned into a set of clusters for which membership functions are derived. Like other incremental clustering algorithms, the clusters obtained from the data partitioning stage are sensitive to the input order of the training patterns, and maybe some of them are redundant. The influence of these two problems is reduced by the second stage, i.e., the cluster merge stage, in which similar clusters are merged together. Therefore, more clusters are located in the local areas with a highly variant output surface and fewer clusters are located in the areas with less variant output values. We then extract a fuzzy IF-THEN rule from each cluster in the step of fuzzy rule generation.

Let $\vec{x}$ be the input vector, i.e., $\vec{x} [x_1 \, x_2 \dots x_n]$. A fuzzy cluster C_j is defined as a pair $(I_j(\vec{x}), O_j(y))$ where $I_j(\vec{x})$ describes the input distribution and $O_j(y)$ describes the output distribution of the training patterns included in cluster C_j. Both $I_j(\vec{x})$ and $O_j(y)$ are Gaussian functions defined as:

$$I_j(\vec{x}) = \prod_{i=1}^{n} g(x_i; m_{ij}, \sigma_{ij}) = \prod_{i=1}^{n} \exp\left[-\left(\frac{x_i - m_{ij}}{\sigma_{ij}}\right)^2\right], \quad (9)$$

$$O_j(y) = g(y; m_{0j}, \sigma_{0j}) = \exp\left[-\left(\frac{y - m_{0j}}{\sigma_{0j}}\right)^2\right] \quad (10)$$

w h e r e $\vec{m}_j = [m_{1j} \, m_{2j} \dots m_{nj}]$ and $\vec{\sigma}_j = [\sigma_{1j} \, \sigma_{2j} \dots \sigma_{nj}]$ denote the mean vector and the deviation vector, respectively, for $I_j(\vec{x})$, and m_{0j} and σ_{0j} denote the mean and deviation, respectively, for $O_j(y)$.

Data Partitioning Stage

Assume that we have a set of N training patterns and each pattern t_v, $1 \leq v \leq N$, is represented by $(\vec{p}_v, q_v)$ where $\vec{p}_v = [p_{1v} \, p_{2v} \dots p_{nv}]$ denotes input values and q_v denotes the desired output value for $\vec{p}_v$. The size, S_j, of cluster C_j is defined to be the number of patterns that belong to C_j. Before we proceed, we define several operators to help the description later. The operator '*comb*' combines a cluster C_j and a pattern t_v to result in a new cluster C'_j, i.e.,

$$C'_j = comb(C_j, t_v) \quad (11)$$

where $C'_j = (I'_j(\vec{x}), O'_j(y))$ and

$$I'_j(\vec{x}) = comb\_x(I_j(\vec{x}), \vec{p}_v),$$
$$O'_j(y) = comb\_y(O_j(y), q_v). \quad (12)$$

The mean and deviation vectors, $\vec{m}'_{ij}$ and $\vec{\sigma}'_{ij}$, associated with $I'_j(\vec{x})$ are computed by:

$$m'_{ij} = \frac{S_j m_{ij} + p_{iv}}{S_j + 1}, \quad (13)$$

$$\sigma'_{ij} = \sqrt{\frac{(S_j - 1)(\sigma_{ij} - \sigma_0^I)^2 + S_j(m_{ij})^2 + (p_{iv})^2}{S_j} - \frac{(S_j + 1)}{S_j}\left(\frac{S_j m_{ij} + p_{iv}}{S_j + 1}\right)^2} + \sigma_0^I \quad (14)$$

for $1 \leq i \leq n$ while the mean and deviation, m'_{0j} and σ'_{0j} associated with $O'(y)$ are computed by:

$$m'_{0j} = \frac{S_j m_{0j} + q_v}{S_j + 1}, \quad (15)$$

$$\sigma'_{0j} = \sqrt{\frac{(S_j - 1)(\sigma_{0j} - \sigma_0^O)^2 + S_j(m_{0j})^2 + (q_v)^2}{S_j} - \frac{S_j + 1}{S_j}\left(\frac{S_j m_{0j} + q_v}{S_j + 1}\right)^2} + \sigma_0^O \quad (16)$$

with σ_0^I and σ_0^O being user-defined constants and denoting initial deviations for input dimensions and output dimension, respectively, of new generated clusters.

Let J be the number of existing fuzzy clusters. Initially, J is 0 since no cluster exists at the beginning. For training instance t_v, we calculate $I_j(\vec{p}_v)$ which measures the degree that t_v is close to C_j regarding to input dimensions. We say that instance t_v passes the input-similarity test on cluster C_j if

$$I_j(\vec{p}_v) \geq \rho \tag{17}$$

where ρ $0 \leq \rho \leq 1$ is a user-defined threshold. Then we check the output variance induced by the addition of t_v as follows. For each cluster C_j on which t_v has passed the input similarity test, we calculate

$$O'_j(y) = comb\_y(O_j(y), q_v) \tag{18}$$

We say that instance t_v passes the output-variance test on cluster C_j if

$$\sigma'_{0j} \leq \tau \tag{19}$$

where τ is a user-defined threshold.

Two cases may occur. First, there are no existing fuzzy clusters on which instance t_v has passed both the input-similarity test and the output-variance test. For this case, we assume that instance t_v is not close enough to any existing cluster and a new fuzzy cluster C_k, $k=J+1$, is created with

$$\vec{m}_k = \vec{p}_v, \quad \vec{\sigma}_k = \left[\sigma_0^I\ \sigma_0^I, ..., \sigma_0^I\right],$$
$$m_{0k} = q_v, \quad \sigma_{0k} = \sigma_0^O \tag{20}$$

Note that the new cluster C_k contains only one member, instance t_v. The reason that $\vec{\sigma}_k$ and $\vec{\sigma}_{0k}$ are initialized to non-zero values is to avoid the null width of a singleton cluster. Of course, the

number of clusters is increased by 1 and the size of cluster C_k should be initialized, i.e.,

$$J=J+1, S_k=1 \tag{21}$$

On the other hand, if there are existing fuzzy clusters on which instance t_v has passed both the input-similarity test and the output-variance test, let clusters $C_{m1}, C_{m2}, ..., C_{mf}$ be such clusters and let the cluster with the largest input-similarity measure be cluster C_a, i.e.,

$$I_a(\vec{p}_v) = \max(I_{m1}(\vec{p}_v),$$
$$I_{m2}(\vec{p}_v), ..., I_{mf}(\vec{p}_v)). \tag{22}$$

If two or more clusters are found, we consider the one with minimum output-variance. If, again, two or more clusters are found, we choose one to be C_a randomly from them. We assume that instance t_v is closest to cluster C_a and cluster C_a should be modified to include instance t_v as follows:

$$C_a = comb(C_a, t_v), S_a = S_a + 1 \tag{23}$$

Note that J is not changed in this case. The above process is iterated until all the training instances have been processed. At the end, we have J fuzzy clusters.

Cluster Merge Stage

The basic idea is to merge together the clusters in the areas where training patterns present less variant output response. Before we continue, we define some operators for merging clusters together. The operator $comb\_g$ combines k clusters, $C_1, C_2, ..., C_k$, $k \geq 2$, into a new cluster C'_j, i.e.,

$$C'_j = comb\_g(C_1, C_2, ..., C_k) \tag{24}$$

where $C'_j = (I'_j(\vec{x}), O'_j(y))$ and

$$I'_j(\vec{x}) = comb\_g\_x(I_1(\vec{x}), I_2(\vec{x}), \ldots, I_k(\vec{x})),$$
$$O'_j(y) = comb\_g\_y(O_1(y), O_2(y), \ldots, O_k(y)). \tag{25}$$

The mean and deviation vectors, $\vec{m}'_j$ and $\vec{\sigma}'_j$, associated with $I'_j(\vec{x})$ are computed by:

$$m'_{ij} = \frac{\sum_{d=1}^{k} S_d m_{id}}{\sum_{d=1}^{k} S_d}, \tag{26}$$

$$\sigma'_{ij} = \sqrt{\frac{\sum_{d=1}^{k}[(S_d-1)(\sigma_{id}-\sigma_0^I)^2 + S_d(m_{id})^2] - (m'_{ij})^2 \sum_{d=1}^{k} S_d}{\sum_{d=1}^{k} S_d - 1}} + \sigma_0^I \tag{27}$$

for $1 \le i \le n$, while the mean and deviation, m'_{0j} and σ'_{0j}, associated with $O'_j(y)$ are computed by:

$$m'_{0j} = \frac{\sum_{d=1}^{k} S_d m_{0d}}{\sum_{d=1}^{k} S_d}, \tag{28}$$

$$\sigma'_{0j} = \sqrt{\frac{\sum_{d=1}^{k}[(S_d-1)(\sigma_{0d}-\sigma_0^O)^2 + S_d(m_{0d})^2] - (m'_{0j})^2 \sum_{d=1}^{k} S_d}{\sum_{d=1}^{k} S_d - 1}} + \sigma_0^O. \tag{29}$$

Let A contains the J clusters obtained from the data partitioning stage, and let B be an empty set. Firstly, we group the clusters in A into candidate classes for merging. For any two different clusters C_i and C_j in A, we calculate

$$r_{ij}^I = \frac{I_i(\vec{m}_j) + I_j(\vec{m}_i)}{2},$$
$$r_{ij}^O = \frac{O_i(m_{oj}) + O_j(m_{0i})}{2} \tag{30}$$

where r_{ij}^I and r_{ij}^O are the input-similarity measure and the output-similarity measure, respectively, between C_i and C_j. C_i and C_j are grouped into the same candidate class if

$$r_{ij}^I \ge \rho, \quad r_{ij}^O \ge \varepsilon \tag{31}$$

where ε, $0 \le \varepsilon \le 1$, is a user-defined threshold. In this way, the clusters in A are grouped into a set of candidate classes. If every candidate class contains only one cluster, we stop and the clusters in A are desired ones. Otherwise, we check whether the constituent clusters of each candidate class can be merged together to form a new fuzzy cluster. Let $C_1, C_2, \ldots, C_k$ be the constituent clusters of a candidate class X. If $k=1$, the class has only one cluster and nothing can be merged, and so we remove the cluster in X from A to B. Otherwise, we calculate

$$O'_j = comb\_g\_y(O_1(y), O_2(y), \ldots, O_k(y)) \tag{32}$$

If the output-variance test is successful, i.e.,

$$\sigma'_{0j} \le \tau \tag{33}$$

then we remove $C_1, C_2, \ldots, C_k$ from A, merge them into a new cluster C'_j by

$$C'_j = comb\_g(C_1, C_2, \ldots, C_k),$$
$$S'_j = \sum_{d=1}^{k} S_d \tag{34}$$

and put C'_j into B. If the output-variance test fails, we do not merge. Instead, we remove $C_1, C_2, \ldots, C_k$ of X from A to B. This process iterates until A is empty. Then we remove all the clusters from B to A, increase ρ and ε to become $(1+\theta)\rho$ and $(1+\theta)\varepsilon$, respectively, with θ being a predefined constant rate, and do the whole process again, until every candidate class has only one cluster. The purpose of increasing threshold values, ρ and ε, is to refine the partitioning of A into candidate classes for merging. Finally, we have a set of J', $J' \le J$, fuzzy clusters, $\varsigma = \{C_1, C_2, \ldots, C_{J'}\}$.

Fuzzy Rule Extraction

After the J' fuzzy clusters are obtained, we extract a fuzzy IF-THEN rule from each cluster. Note that each cluster C_j is described as $(G_j(\vec{x}), c_j)$ where $G_j(\vec{x})$ contains mean vector $\vec{m}_j = [m_{1j} \ m_{2j} \ ... \ m_{nj}]$ and deviation vector $\vec{\sigma}_j = [\sigma_{1j} \ \sigma_{2j} \ ... \ \sigma_{nj}]$. Alternatively, we can represent cluster C_j by a fuzzy rule having the following form of a zero-order TSK-type fuzzy IF-THEN rule (Takagi & Sugeno, 1985; Sugeno & Kang, 1988):

$$\textbf{IF} x_1 \textbf{IS } \mu_{1j}(x_1) \textbf{ AND} x_2 \textbf{IS } \mu_{2j}(x_2) \textbf{ AND} ...$$
$$\textbf{AND} x_n \textbf{IS } \mu_{nj}(x_n) \textbf{ THEN} y \textbf{ IS} C_j \qquad (35)$$

where $\mu_{ij}(x_i)$ are membership functions each of which is a Gaussian function, i.e.,

$$\mu_{ij}(x_i) = g(x_i; m_{ij}, \sigma_{ij})$$
$$= \exp\left[-\left(\frac{x_i - m_{ij}}{\sigma_{ij}}\right)^2\right] \qquad (36)$$

with mean m_{ij} and deviation σ_{ij}. Note that m_{ij}, σ_{ij}, and c_j can be refined in the parameter identification phase. Gaussian functions are adopted for representing clusters because of their superiority over other functions in performance. Now we end up with a set of J' initial fuzzy rules, $R = \{R_1, R_2, ..., R_{J'}\}$, for the given input-output data set. Note that with this approach, the data contained in a cluster have a high degree of similarity. Besides, when new training data are considered, the existing clusters can be adjusted or new clusters can be created, without the necessity of generating the whole set of rules from the scratch.

We can alternatively represent cluster C_j by the following first-order TSK type form (Takagi & Sugeno, 1985; Sugeno & Kang, 1988):

$$\text{IF } x_1 \text{ IS } \mu_{1j}(x_1) \text{ AND } x_2 \text{ IS } \mu_{2j}(x_2)$$
$$\text{AND } ... \text{ AND } x_n \text{ IS } \mu_{nj}(x_n)$$
$$\text{THEN } y \text{ IS } f_j(\vec{x}) = b_{0j} + b_{1j}x_1 + ... + b_{nj}x_n \quad (37)$$

where $\mu_{ij}(x_i)$ is the same as that in Eq.(36), and $b_{0j}, b_{1j}, ..., b_{nj}$ are called consequent parameters and are set as $b_{0j} = c_j$ and $b_{1j} = b_{2j} = ... = b_{nj} = 0$ initially. Note that m_{ij}, σi_j, and $b0_j, b1_j, ..., bn_j$ can be refined in the parameter identification phase.

PARAMETER IDENTIFICATION

We present a hybrid leaning algorithm (HLA) (Lee & Ouyang, 2003; Ouyang et al., 2005) in the following for the parameter identification in neuro-fuzzy modeling. This hybrid learning algorithm is mainly composed of a recursive SVD-based least squares estimator and the gradient descent method (GDM). The former is developed based on the well-known matrix decomposition technique, i.e., singular value decomposition (SVD), while the latter is derived based on gradient descent method. Such a learning algorithm is suitable for refining a zero-order or first-order TSK-type fuzzy system. Firstly, a zero order or first-order TSK-type fuzzy neural network is constructed according to the set of initial fuzzy rules obtained in the structure identification phase. Then, the hybrid leaning algorithm is used to train the network. In each iteration in which all training patterns are presented, the recursive SVD-based least squares estimator and the gradient descent method are applied to refine antecedent parameters and consequent parameters of rules, respectively. This process is iterated until the desired approximation precision is achieved. Finally, the trained fuzzy neural network can be used as they are for numeric inference, or final fuzzy rules can be extracted from the network for symbolic reasoning. This hybrid learning algorithm has the advantage of alleviating the local minimal problem. Besides, it learns faster, consumes less memory, and produces lower approximation errors than other methods.

Zero-Order TSK-Type Fuzzy Neural Networks

A four-layer fuzzy neural network, with input variables $\vec{x} = [x_1 \ x_2 \ ... \ x_n]$ and output variable y, is constructed based on the set of zero-order TSK-type fuzzy rules obtained in the structure identification phase. Such a network with J fuzzy rules is called zero-order TSK-type fuzzy neural network and shown in Figure 4(a). The four layers are called the fuzzification layer (layer 1), the conjunction layer (layer 2), the normalization layer (layer 3), and the output layer (layer 4), respectively. Note that links between the inputs and layer 1 are weighted by ($\mu i_j, \sigma i j$, $1 \leq i \leq n$, $1 \leq j \leq J$, links between layer 3 and layer 4 are weighted by cj, $1 \leq j \leq J$, and the other links are weighted by 1.

The operation of the fuzzy neural network is described as follows.

1. Layer 1. Layer 1 contains J groups and each group contains n nodes. Node (i,j) of this layer produces its output, $o_{ij}^{(1)}$, by computing the value of the corresponding Gaussian function, i.e.,

$$o_{ij}^{(1)} = \mu_{ij}(x_i) = g(x_i; m_{ij}, \sigma_{ij})$$

$$= \exp\left[-\left(\frac{x_i - m_{ij}}{\sigma_{ij}}\right)^2\right] \tag{38}$$

for $1 \leq i \leq n$ and $1 \leq j \leq J$.

2. Layer 2. Layer 2 contains J nodes. Node j's output, $o_j^{(2)}$, of this layer is the product of all its inputs from layer 1, i.e.,

$$o_j^{(2)} = \prod_{i=1}^{n} o_{ij}^{(1)} \tag{39}$$

for $1 \leq j \leq J$. Note that Eq.(39) is the firing strength of rule J.

3. Layer 3. Layer 3 contains J nodes. Node j's output, $o_j^{(3)}$, of this layer is the normalized result of $o_j^{(2)}$, i.e.,

$$o_j^{(3)} = \frac{o_j^{(2)}}{\sum_{k=1}^{J} o_k^{(2)}} \tag{40}$$

for $1 \leq j \leq J$.

Figure 4. Architectures of TSK-type fuzzy neural networks. (a) Zero-order. (b) First-order

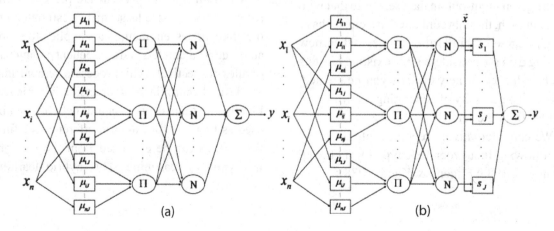

(a)   (b)

4. Layer 4. Layer 4 contains only one node whose output, $o^{(4)}$, represents the result of the centroid defuzzification, i.e.,

$$o^{(4)} = \sum_{j=1}^{J} o_j^{(3)} \times c_j. \qquad (41)$$

Apparently, m_{ij}, σ_{ij}, and c_j are the parameters that can be tuned to improve the performance of the system. We develop a hybrid learning algorithm which combines a recursive SVD-based least squares estimator and the gradient descent method to refine these parameters.

Hybrid Learning Algorithm

We present a hybrid learning algorithm for tuning the parameters m_{ij}, σ_{ij}, and c_j of the fuzzy neural networks efficiently. In particular, the hybrid leaning algorithm consists of a recursive SVD-based least squares estimator and the gradient descent method. The former is used to optimize parameters c_j, while the latter is used to optimize m_{ij} and σ_{ij}.

Suppose we have a total number N of training patterns. An iteration of learning involves the presentation of all training patterns. In each iteration of learning, both the recursive SVD-based least squares estimator and the gradient descent method are applied. We first treat all m_{ij} and σ_{ij} as fixed, and use the recursive SVD-based least squares estimator to optimize c_j. Then we treat all c_j as fixed and use the gradient descent method to refine m_{ij} and σ_{ij}. The process is iterated until the desired approximation precision is achieved.

Recursive SVD-Based Least Squares Estimator

Let $(\vec{p}_v, q_v)$ be the vth training pattern, where $\vec{p}_v = [p_{1v} \ p_{2v} \ \cdots \ p_{nv}]$ is the input vector and q_v is the desired output. Let $v \cdot o^{(4)}$ and $v \cdot o_j^{(3)}$ denote the actual output of layer 4 and the actual output of

node j in layer 3, respectively, for the vth training pattern. By Eq.(41), we have

$$v \cdot o^{(4)} = a_{v1}c_1 + a_{v2}c_2 + \cdots + a_{vJ}c_J \qquad (42)$$

where

$$a_{vj} = v \cdot o_j^{(3)} \qquad (43)$$

for $1 \leq j \leq J$. Apparently, we would like $|q_v - v \cdot o^{(4)}|$ to be as small as possible for the vth training pattern. For all N training patterns, we have N equations of the form Eq.(42). Clearly, we would like

$$J(\mathbf{X}) = \left\| \mathbf{B} - \mathbf{A}\mathbf{X} \right\| \qquad (44)$$

to be as small as possible, where $\mathbf{B}$, $\mathbf{A}$, and $\mathbf{X}$ are matrices of $N \times 1$, $N \times J$, and $J \times 1$, respectively, and

$$\mathbf{B} = [q_1, q_2 \cdots q_n]^T, \qquad (45)$$

$$\mathbf{A} = \begin{bmatrix} a_{11} & a_{12} & \cdots & a_{1J} \\ a_{21} & a_{22} & \cdots & a_{2J} \\ \vdots & \vdots & \vdots & \vdots \\ a_{N1} & a_{N2} & \cdots & a_{NJ} \end{bmatrix} = \begin{bmatrix} \vec{a}_1^{\ T} \\ \vec{a}_2^{\ T} \\ \vdots \\ \vec{a}_N^{\ T} \end{bmatrix}, \qquad (46)$$

$$\mathbf{X} = [c_1, c_2 \cdots c_J]^T \qquad (47)$$

Note that for a matrix $\mathbf{D}$, $\left\| \mathbf{D} \right\|$ is defined to be $\sqrt{trace(\mathbf{D}^T\mathbf{D})}$. As mentioned earlier, we treat m_{ij} and σ_{ij} as fixed, so $\mathbf{X}$ is the only variable vector in Eq.(44). In this case, we can use the techniques based on singular value decomposition (SVD) (Golub & Reinsch, 1970; Golub & Van Loan, 1996) to obtain the optimal solution, $\mathbf{X}^*$, which minimizes Eq.(44).

We derive a recursive SVD-based estimator which only requires the decomposition of a small matrix in each iteration, leading to less demanding in time and space requirements. In this method, training patterns are considered one by one, starting with the first pattern, t=1, until the last pattern, t=N. For each t, we want to find the optimal $\mathbf{X}(t)$ such that

$$J(\mathbf{X}(t)) = \| \mathbf{B}(t) - \mathbf{A}(t)\mathbf{X}(t)\| \qquad (48)$$

is minimized. Note that

$$\mathbf{A}(t) = \begin{bmatrix} \vec{a}_1^{\,T} \\ \vec{a}_2^{\,T} \\ \vdots \\ \vec{a}_t^{\,T} \end{bmatrix}, \qquad (49)$$

$$\mathbf{B}(t) = \begin{bmatrix} q_1 \\ q_2 \\ \vdots \\ q_t \end{bmatrix} \qquad (50)$$

for t =1,2,...,N. Before we proceed, we present a theorem that will be used later.

Theorem 3: Recursive SVD-Based Least Squares Estimator

Minimizing Eq.(48) is equivalent to minimizing

$$\hat{J}(\mathbf{X}(t)) = \| \mathbf{B}'(t) - \mathbf{\Sigma}'(t)\mathbf{V}^T(t)\mathbf{X}(t)\| \qquad (51)$$

where $\mathbf{B}'(t), \mathbf{\Sigma}'(t), \mathbf{V}^T(t)$, and $\mathbf{X}(t)$ satisfy the following equalities:

$$\begin{cases} \mathbf{A}(1) = \mathbf{U}(1)\mathbf{\Sigma}(1)\mathbf{V}^T(1), \\ \begin{bmatrix} \mathbf{\Sigma}'(t-1)\mathbf{V}^T(t-1) \\ \vec{a}_t^{\,T} \end{bmatrix} = \mathbf{U}(t)\mathbf{\Sigma}(t)\mathbf{V}^T(t), \quad t \geq 2 \end{cases} \qquad (52)$$

$$\mathbf{\Sigma}(t) = \begin{bmatrix} \mathbf{\Sigma}'(t) \\ 0 \end{bmatrix}, \quad t \geq 1 \qquad (53)$$

$$\begin{cases} \mathbf{U}^T(1)\mathbf{B}(1) = \begin{bmatrix} \mathbf{B}'(1) \\ \mathbf{B}''(1) \end{bmatrix} \\ \mathbf{U}^T(t)\begin{bmatrix} \mathbf{B}'(t-1) \\ q_t \end{bmatrix} = \begin{bmatrix} \mathbf{B}'(t) \\ \mathbf{B}''(t) \end{bmatrix} \end{cases}, t \geq 2. \qquad (54)$$

Proof:

We prove the theorem in two steps.

1. For t=1. This case is equivalent to the batch SVD-based method with N=1. By referring to the derivation in (Golub & Van Loan, 1996), we have

$$J(\mathbf{X}(1)) = \| \mathbf{B}(1)-\mathbf{A}(1)\mathbf{X}(1) \| = \left\| \begin{bmatrix} \mathbf{B}'(1) - \mathbf{\Sigma}'(1)\mathbf{V}^T(1)\mathbf{X}(1) \\ \mathbf{B}''(1) \end{bmatrix} \right\| \qquad (55)$$

Since $\mathbf{B}''(1)$ is a constant, minimizing $\|\mathbf{B}(1) - \mathbf{A}(1)\mathbf{X}(1)\|$ is equivalent to minimizing $\|\mathbf{B}'(1) - \mathbf{\Sigma}'(1)\mathbf{V}^T(1)\mathbf{X}(1)\|$.

2. For $t \geq 2$. We prove this by induction.
   (a) When t=2, we have

$$J(\mathbf{X}(2)) = \left\| \begin{bmatrix} \mathbf{B}(1) \\ q_2 \end{bmatrix} - \begin{bmatrix} \mathbf{A}(1) \\ \vec{a}_2^{\,T} \end{bmatrix}\mathbf{X}(2) \right\|. \qquad (56)$$

By the case of t=1, we have $\mathbf{A}(1)=\mathbf{U}(1)\mathbf{\Sigma}(1)\mathbf{V}^T(1)$. Therefore,

$$J(\mathbf{X}(2)) = \left\| \begin{bmatrix} \mathbf{B}(1) \\ q_2 \end{bmatrix} - \begin{bmatrix} \mathbf{U}(1)\mathbf{\Sigma}(1)\mathbf{V}^T(1) \\ \vec{a}_2^{\,T} \end{bmatrix} \mathbf{X}(2) \right\|$$

$$= \left\| \begin{bmatrix} \mathbf{U}^T(1)\mathbf{B}(1) \\ q_2 \end{bmatrix} - \begin{bmatrix} \mathbf{\Sigma}(1)\mathbf{V}^T(1) \\ \vec{a}_2^{\,T} \end{bmatrix} \mathbf{X} \right\|$$

$$= \left\| \begin{bmatrix} \mathbf{B}'(1) \\ \mathbf{B}''(1) \\ q_2 \end{bmatrix} - \begin{bmatrix} \mathbf{\Sigma}'(1) \\ 0 \\ \vec{a}_2^{\,T} \end{bmatrix} \mathbf{V}^T(1) \mathbf{X}(2) \right\|$$

$$= \left\| \begin{bmatrix} \mathbf{B}'(1) \\ q_2 \end{bmatrix} - \begin{bmatrix} \mathbf{\Sigma}'(1)\mathbf{V}^T(1) \\ \vec{a}_2^{\,T} \end{bmatrix} \mathbf{X}(2) \right\| \atop \mathbf{B}''(1) \quad (57)$$

Clearly, minimizing $J(\mathbf{X}(2))$ is equivalent to minimizing the following expression:

$$M(\mathbf{X}(2)) = \left\| \begin{bmatrix} \mathbf{B}'(1) \\ q_2 \end{bmatrix} - \begin{bmatrix} \mathbf{\Sigma}'(1)\mathbf{V}^T(1) \\ \vec{a}_2^{\,T} \end{bmatrix} \mathbf{X}(2) \right\|. \quad (58)$$

By Eqs.(52), (53), and (54) with $t=2$, we have

$$M(\mathbf{X}(2)) = \left\| \begin{bmatrix} \mathbf{B}'(1) \\ q_2 \end{bmatrix} - \mathbf{U}(2)\mathbf{\Sigma}(2)\mathbf{V}^T(2)\mathbf{X}(2) \right\|$$

$$= \left\| \mathbf{U}^T \begin{bmatrix} \mathbf{B}'(1) \\ q_2 \end{bmatrix} - \mathbf{\Sigma} \; \mathbf{V}^T \; \mathbf{X} \right\|$$

$$= \left\| \begin{bmatrix} \mathbf{B}'(2) \\ \mathbf{B}''(2) \end{bmatrix} - \begin{bmatrix} \mathbf{\Sigma}'(2) \\ 0 \end{bmatrix} \mathbf{V}^T \; \mathbf{X} \right\|$$

$$= \left\| \begin{matrix} \mathbf{B}'(2) - \mathbf{\Sigma}'(2)\mathbf{V}^T(2)\mathbf{X}(2) \\ \mathbf{B}''(2) \end{matrix} \right\| \quad (59)$$

Similarly, minimizing $M(\mathbf{X}(2))$ is equivalent to minimizing

$$\hat{J}(\mathbf{X}(2)) = \left\| \mathbf{B}'(2) - \mathbf{\Sigma}'(2)\mathbf{V}^T(2)\mathbf{X}(2) \right\|. \quad (60)$$

Therefore, minimizing Eq.(48) is equivalent to minimizing Eq.(51) for $t=2$.

(b) We assume that minimizing Eq.(48) is equivalent to minimizing Eq.(51) for $3 \le t \le k$.

(c) Now we want to prove that minimizing Eq.(48) is equivalent to minimizing Eq.(51) for $t=k+1$. For $t=k+1$, we have

$$J(\mathbf{X}(k+1))$$
$$= \left\| \mathbf{B}(k+1) - \mathbf{A}(k+1)\mathbf{X}(k+1) \right\|$$

$$= \left\| \begin{bmatrix} \mathbf{B}(1) \\ q_2 \\ \vdots \\ q_{k+1} \end{bmatrix} - \begin{bmatrix} \mathbf{A}(1) \\ \vec{a}_2^{\,T} \\ \vdots \\ \vec{a}_{k+1}^{\,T} \end{bmatrix} \mathbf{X}(k+1) \right\| \quad (61)$$

By following the same reasoning path of $t=2$, we conclude that minimizing $J(\mathbf{X}(k+1))$ is equivalent to minimizing the following expression:

$$\left\| \begin{bmatrix} \mathbf{B}'(2) \\ q_3 \\ \vdots \\ q_{k+1} \end{bmatrix} - \begin{bmatrix} \mathbf{\Sigma}'(2)\mathbf{V}^T(2) \\ \vec{a}_3^{\,T} \\ \vdots \\ \vec{a}_{k+1}^{\,T} \end{bmatrix} \mathbf{X}(k+1) \right\|. \quad (62)$$

Similarly, minimizing Eq.(62) is equivalent to minimizing

$$\left\| \begin{bmatrix} \mathbf{B}'(k) \\ q_{k+1} \end{bmatrix} - \begin{bmatrix} \mathbf{\Sigma}'(k)\mathbf{V}^T(k) \\ \vec{a}_{k+1}^{\,T} \end{bmatrix} \mathbf{X}(k+1) \right\|. \quad (63)$$

Moreover, minimizing Eq.(63) is equivalent to minimizing

$$\hat{J}(\mathbf{X}(k+1)) =$$
$$\left\| \mathbf{B}'(k+1) - \mathbf{\Sigma}'(k+1)\mathbf{V}^T(k+1)\mathbf{X}(k+1) \right\| \quad (64)$$

Therefore, we conclude that minimizing Eq.(48) is equivalent to minimizing Eq.(51) for $t \ge 2$.

By combining the cases of $t=1$ and $t \ge 2$, we complete the proof.

The above theorem provides the basis for our recursive SVD-based estimator. Apparently, what we want is to find the optimal $\mathbf{X}^*(N)$ which minimizes

$$J(\mathbf{X}(N)) = \left\| \mathbf{B}(N) - \mathbf{A}(N)\mathbf{X}(N) \right\|. \quad (65)$$

By the theorem, we only need to find the optimal $\mathbf{X}^*(N)$ which minimizes

$$\hat{J}(\mathbf{X}(N)) = \left\| \mathbf{B}'(N) - \mathbf{\Sigma}'(N)\mathbf{V}^T(N)\mathbf{X}(N) \right\|. \quad (66)$$

We obtain $\mathbf{B}'(N)$, $\mathbf{\Sigma}'(N)$, and $\mathbf{V}^T(N)$ by the following recursive procedure:

1. *Step 1*. Set $t=1$ and calculate $\mathbf{U}(1)$, $\mathbf{\Sigma}(1)$, and $\mathbf{V}(1)$ by Eq.(52). Then, get $\mathbf{\Sigma}'(1)$ and $\mathbf{B}'(1)$ by Eqs. (53) and (54).
2. *Step 2*. Increase t by 1. Calculate $\mathbf{U}(t)$, $\mathbf{\Sigma}(t)$, and $\mathbf{V}(t)$ by Eq.(52).

Then, get $\mathbf{\Sigma}'(t)$ and $\mathbf{B}'(t)$ by Eqs. (53) and (54).

3. *Step 3*. If $t=N$, then we are done. Otherwise, go to Step 2.

Let $\mathbf{Y}(N)=\mathbf{V}^T(N)\mathbf{X}(N)$. Eq.(66) becomes

$$\hat{J}(\mathbf{Y}(N)) = \left\| \mathbf{B}'(N) - \mathbf{\Sigma}'(N)\mathbf{Y}(N) \right\|. \quad (67)$$

Apparently, Eq.(67) is minimized by $\mathbf{Y}^*(N)$ such that $\mathbf{B}'(N)-\mathbf{\Sigma}'(N)\mathbf{Y}^*(N)$ is 0, i.e.,

$$\mathbf{\Sigma}'(N)\mathbf{Y}^*(N)=\mathbf{B}'(N). \quad (68)$$

Suppose $\mathbf{\Sigma}'(N)$ we got is an $h' \times J$ diagonal matrix with each component $\mathbf{\Sigma}'(N)_{ij}$ being

$$\mathbf{\Sigma}'(N)_{ij} = \begin{cases} 0 & \text{, if } i \neq j \\ e_i' & \text{, otherwise} \end{cases} \quad (69)$$

where $h' \leq J$. Moreover, let $\mathbf{B}'(N)$ and $\mathbf{Y}^*(N)$ be represented by

$$\mathbf{B}'(N)=[b_1 b_2 \dots b_{h'}]^T, \quad (70)$$

$$\mathbf{Y}^*(N)=[y_1^* y_2^* \dots y_J^*]^T. \quad (71)$$

Then we have

$$y_i^* = \begin{cases} \dfrac{b_i}{e_i'} & \text{, if } i \leq h' \\ 0 & \text{, if } h' \leq i \leq J \end{cases} \quad (72)$$

Therefore, the optimal solution $\mathbf{X}^*(N)$ which minimizes Eq.(65) is

$$\mathbf{X}^*(N)=\mathbf{V}(N)\mathbf{Y}^*(N). \quad (73)$$

Gradient Descent Method

As mentioned, parameters m_{ij} and σ_{ij}, $1 \leq i \leq n$ and $1 \leq j \leq J$, are refined by the gradient descent method. The error function we consider is

$$E = \frac{1}{2N} \sum_{v=1}^{N} (q_v - y_v)^2 \quad (74)$$

where q_v is the desired output and $y_v=v \cdot o^{(4)}$ is the actual output of the vth training pattern. Note that we use the batch BP mode in order to work properly with our recursive SVD-based estimator. By the batch BP mode, weight updating is performed after the presentation of all the training data in an iteration (Haykin, 1999). The learning rule for m_{ij} is

$$m_{ij}^{new} = m_{ij}^{old} - \eta \left(\frac{\partial E}{\partial m_{ij}} \right) \quad (75)$$

where η is the learning rate and

$$\frac{\partial E}{\partial m_{ij}} = \frac{1}{N}\sum_{v=1}^{N}\left\{\left[v\cdot o^{(4)} - q_v\right]\frac{\partial v\cdot o^{(4)}}{\partial m_{ij}}\right\}$$

$$= \frac{1}{N}\sum_{v=1}^{N}\left\{\left[v\cdot o^{(4)} - q_v\right]\frac{c_j - v\cdot o^{(4)}}{\sum_{r=1}^{J}v\cdot o_r^{(2)}}\frac{\partial v\cdot o_j^{(2)}}{\partial m_{ij}}\right\}$$

$$= \frac{1}{N}\sum_{v=1}^{N}\left\{\left[v\cdot o^{(4)} - q_v\right]\frac{[c_j - v\cdot o^{(4)}]v\cdot o_j^{(2)}}{\sum_{r=1}^{R}v\cdot o_r^{(2)}}\frac{\partial\left[-\left(\frac{p_{iv} - m_{ij}}{\sigma_{ij}}\right)^2\right]}{\partial m_{ij}}\right\}$$

$$= \frac{2}{N}\sum_{v=1}^{N}\left\{\left[v\cdot o^{(4)} - q_v\right]v\cdot o_j^{(3)}\frac{[c_j - v\cdot o^{(4)}][p_{iv} - m_{ij}]}{\sigma_{ij}^2}\right\}. \tag{76}$$

Similarly, we have

$$\sigma_{ij}^{new} = \sigma_{ij}^{old} - \eta\left(\frac{\partial E}{\partial \sigma_{ij}}\right) \tag{77}$$

where

$$\frac{\partial E}{\partial \sigma_{ij}} = \frac{2}{N}\sum_{v=1}^{N}\left\{\left[v\cdot o^{(4)} - q_v\right]v\cdot o_j^{(3)}\frac{[c_j - v\cdot o^{(4)}][p_{iv} - m_{ij}]^2}{\sigma_{ij}^{(3)}}\right\} \tag{78}$$

First-Order TSK-Type Fuzzy Neural Networks

For more powerful capabilities of approximation and representation, we can construct a first-order TSK-type fuzzy neural network, with input variables $\vec{x} = [x_1\ x_2\cdots x_n]$ and output variable y, based on the set of J first-order TSK-type fuzzy rules obtained in the structure identification phase, as shown in Figure 4(b). The five layers are called the fuzzification layer (layer 1), the conjunction layer (layer 2), the normalization layer (layer 3), the inference layer (layer 4), and the output layer (layer 5), respectively. The links connecting inputs $\vec{x}$ to layer 1 are weighted by $(m_{ij}, \sigma i_{ij}, 1 \leq i \leq n, 1 \leq j \leq J$, the links connecting inputs $\vec{x}$ to layer 4 are weighted by $b_{0j}, b_{1j}, ..., b_{nj}, 1 \leq j \leq J$, and all the other links are weighted by 1. Note that there are J groups of nodes in Layer 1, each group having n

nodes for a rule. Layers 2–4 all have J nodes, one node for a rule. Layer 5 contains only one node, providing output for the whole system. For any input $\vec{x}$, the function of each layer is described as follows:

1. *Layer 1.* Compute the matching degree to a fuzzy condition involving one variable, i.e.,

$$o_{ij}^{(1)} = \mu_{ij}(x_i) = g(x_i; m_{ij}, \sigma_{ij}) = \exp\left[-\left(\frac{x_i - m_{ij}}{\sigma_{ij}}\right)^2\right]$$

$, 1 \leq i \leq n\ 1 \leq j \leq J.$ (79)

2. *Layer 2.* Compute the firing strength of each rule, i.e.,

$$o_j^{(2)} = \prod_{i=1}^{n} o_{ij}^{(1)}, 1 \leq j \leq J. \tag{80}$$

3. *Layer 3.* Compute the normalized matching degree for each rule, i.e.,

$$o_j^{(3)} = \frac{o_j^{(2)}}{\sum_{k=1}^{J} o_k^{(2)}}, 1 \leq j \leq J. \tag{81}$$

4. *Layer 4.* Compute the conclusion inferred by each fuzzy rule, i.e.,

$$o_j^{(4)} = s_j(\vec{x}) = o_j^{(3)} \times f_j(\vec{x}) =$$
$$o_j^{(3)} \times (b_{0j} + b_{1j}x_1 + b_{2j}x_2 + ... + b_{nj}x_n),$$
$$1 \leq j \leq J \tag{82}$$

5. *Layer 5.* Combine the conclusion of all fuzzy rules and obtain the network output:

$$y = o^{(5)} = \sum_{j=1}^{J} o_j^{(4)}. \tag{83}$$

Apparently, m_{ij}, σ_{ij}, and $b_{0j}, b_{1j}, ..., b_{nj}$ are the parameters that can be tuned to improve the performance of the system. Obviously, the constructed network performs the fuzzy rule-based inference exactly. After the construction of the network, we employ the hybrid learning algorithm developed earlier in this chapter to train the network.

When the antecedent parameters are fixed, the optimization of consequent parameters can be regarded as a special case of linear regression model and SVD-based optimization algorithms can be applied. Let $t_v = (\vec{p}_v, q_v)$ be the vth training pattern, where $\vec{p}_v = [p_{1v} \cdots p_{nv}]$ is the input vector and q_v is the desired output. Let $v \cdot o^{(5)}$ and $v \cdot o_j^{(3)}$ denote the actual output of layer 5 and the actual output of node j in layer 3, respectively, for the vth training pattern. From Eqs.(82) and (83), we have the network output $v \cdot o^{(5)}$ to be

$$v.o^{(5)} = \sum_{j=1}^{J} v.o_j^{(3)} \times$$
$$(b_{0j} + b_{1j}p_{1v} + b_{2j}p_{2v} + \ldots + b_{nj}p_{nv}) \qquad (84)$$

for input pattern t_v. For all N training patterns, we have N equations with the form of Eq.(84). We would like to have the following mean square error (MSE):

$$E = \frac{1}{N} \sum_{v=1}^{N} (q_v - v \cdot o^{(5)})^2$$
$$= \frac{1}{N} \sum_{v=1}^{N} \left[q_v - \sum_{j=1}^{J} v.o_j^{(3)} \times f_j(\vec{p}_v) \right]^2 \qquad (85)$$

to be as small as possible. Let

$$\mathbf{B} = [q_1 q_2 \cdots q_N]^T \qquad (86)$$

$$\mathbf{A} = \begin{bmatrix} a_{11} & a_{11}p_{11} & \cdots & a_{11}p_{n1} & \cdots & a_{1J} & \cdots & a_{1J}p_{n1} \\ a_{21} & a_{21}p_{12} & \cdots & a_{21}p_{n2} & \cdots & a_{2J} & \cdots & a_{2J}p_{n2} \\ \vdots & \vdots & \ddots & \vdots & \ddots & \vdots & \ddots & \vdots \\ a_{N1} & a_{N1}p_{1N} & \cdots & a_{N1}p_{nN} & \cdots & a_{NJ} & \cdots & a_{NJ}p_{nN} \end{bmatrix} \qquad (87)$$

$$\mathbf{X} = [b_{01} b_{11} \cdots b_{n1} \cdots b_{0J} b_{1J} \cdots b_{nJ}]^T \qquad (88)$$

where

$$a_{ij} = v.o_j^{(3)}, 1 \le i \le N, 1 \le j \le J . \qquad (89)$$

Then minimizing Eq.(85) is equivalent to minimizing

$$E_1 = \left\| \mathbf{B} - \mathbf{AX} \right\| \qquad (90)$$

where for a matrix $\mathbf{D}$, $\left\| \mathbf{D} \right\|$ is defined to be $\sqrt{trace(\mathbf{D}^T\mathbf{D})}$. Since we treat all the parameters in the antecedent part to be fixed at this point, $\mathbf{A}$ is fixed and $\mathbf{X}$ is the only variable vector in Eq.(90). Eq.(90) is a special form of linear regression model and the optimal solution, $\mathbf{X}^*$, which minimizes Eq.(90) can be obtained by the recursive SVD-based least squares estimator.

The deviation of learning rules for m_{ij} and σ_{ij} based on gradient descent method is the same as that in Eqs. (75) -(78). Therefore, we have the learning rules for m_{ij} and σ_{ij} as the following equations:

$$m_{ij}^{new} = m_{ij}^{old} - \eta \left(\frac{\partial E_2}{\partial m_{ij}} \right), \qquad (91)$$

$$m_{ij}^{new} = m_{ij}^{old} - \eta \left(\frac{\partial E_2}{\partial \sigma_{ij}} \right),$$
$$1 \le i \le n, 1 \le j \le J \qquad (92)$$

where η is the learning rate, $E_2 = \frac{1}{2} E$, and

$$\left(\frac{\partial E_2}{\partial m_{ij}} \right) = \frac{2}{N} \sum_{v=1}^{N} \left\{ \left[v.o^{(5)} - q_v \right] v.o_j^{(3)} \frac{\left[f_j(\vec{p}_v) - v.o^{(5)} \right]\left[p_{iv} - m_{ij} \right]}{\sigma_{ij}^2} \right\}, \qquad (93)$$

$$\left(\frac{\partial E_2}{\partial \sigma_{ij}} \right) = \frac{2}{N} \sum_{v=1}^{N} \left\{ \left[v.o^{(5)} - q_v \right] v.o_j^{(3)} \frac{\left[f_j(\vec{p}_v) - v.o^{(5)} \right]\left[p_{iv} - m_{ij} \right]^2}{\sigma_{ij}^3} \right\} \qquad (94)$$

An Example

The example concerns the modeling of the following nonlinear function, as shown in Figure 5(a).

$$y = \frac{1}{1 + e^{(-25(x-0.5))}}. \tag{95}$$

We firstly apply SMRG on these training patterns with ρ, τ, σ_0^I, σ_0^O, ε, and θ being 0.30, 0.30, 0.08, 0.10, 0.35, and 0.10, respectively. After the data partitioning stage, 7 clusters are obtained and their locations are shown in Figure 5(b). Note that each contour represents one cluster with its mean indicated by a dot, and the size of a cluster is drawn with radii being $\sqrt{2}\sigma_x$ and $\sqrt{2}\sigma_y$, respectively. From these clusters, we have a rule set R_1 consisting of the following 7 fuzzy rules:

R_1 : IF x IS $g(x;\ 0.0400,\ 0.1074)$ THEN y IS 0.0000;
R_2 : IF x IS $g(x;\ 0.1400,\ 0.1132)$ THEN y IS 0.0002;
R_3 : IF x IS $g(x;\ 0.2600,\ 0.1189)$ THEN y IS 0.0037;
R_4 : IF x IS $g(x;\ 0.4250,\ 0.1392)$ THEN y IS 0.2081;
R_5 : IF x IS $g(x;\ 0.6450,\ 0.1507)$ THEN y IS 0.9289;
R_6 : IF x IS $g(x;\ 0.8300,\ 0.1189)$ THEN y IS 0.9976;
R_7 : IF x IS $g(x;\ 0.9500,\ 0.1131)$ THEN y IS 1.0000

with mean square error (MSE) being 0.0044 for the training data. From these rules, the output for any given input can be computed. For example, when x=0.705, we compute the firing strength

$$g(0.705, 0.400, 0.1074)=0.0000 \tag{96}$$

for R_1. Similarly, we have firing strengths 0.0000, 0.0000, 0.0175, 0.8534, 0.3311 and 0.0092 for R_2, R_3, R_4, R_5, R_6 and R_7, respectively. By centroid defuzzification, we have

Figure 5. Example. (a) Output of the original function. (b) Output of the 7 rules generated by the data partitioning stage of SMRG. (c) Output of the 4 rules generated by the cluster merge stage of SMRG. (d) Output of the 4 rules refined by our HLA.

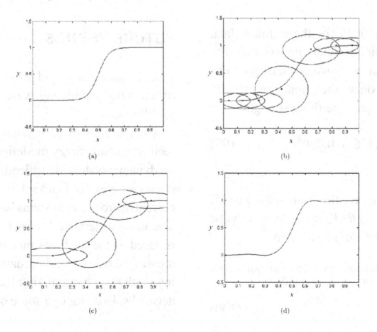

$$\hat{y} = \{0.0000 \times (0.0000) + 0.0000 \times (0.0002) + 0.0000 \times (0.0037) + 0.0175$$
$$\times (0.2081) + 0.8534 \times (0.9289) + 0.3311 \times (0.9976) + 0.0092 \times (1.0000)\}$$
$$/\{0.0000 + 0.0000 + 0.0000 + 0.0175 + 0.8534 + 0.3311 + 0.0092\}$$
$$= 0.9378$$

$$(97)$$

which is an approximation to the desired function value $h(0.705)$:

$$y = h(0.705)$$
$$= \frac{1}{1 + e^{(-25(0.705-0.5))}} = 0.9941. \qquad (98)$$

Figure 5(b) shows the computed output values for all $x \in [0,1]$ with these 7 rules.

The 7 clusters then proceed to the cluster merge stage, and 4 clusters are obtained, as shown graphically in Figure 5(c). Note that the two clusters on the top-right are merged and the three clusters at the bottom-left are merged. This is reasonable since these two parts are fairly flat. Correspondingly, we have a rule set R_2 of the following 4 rules:

R_1 : IF x IS $g(x;\ 0.1600,\ 0.1767)$ THEN y IS 0.0015;
R_2 : IF x IS $g(x;\ 0.4250,\ 0.1392)$ THEN y IS 0.2081;
R_3 : IF x IS $g(x;\ 0.6450,\ 0.1507)$ THEN y IS 0.9289;
R_4 : IF x IS $g(x;\ 0.8850,\ 0.1507)$ THEN y IS 0.9998

with MSE being 0.0055 for the training data. These 4 rules provide another approximation to the original function, as shown in Figure 5(c). For example, we approximate the output y for x=0.705 as follows. We compute the firing strength

$$g(0.705, 0.1600, 0.1767) = 0.0001 \qquad (99)$$

for R_1. Similarly, we have firing strengths 0.0175, 0.8534, and 0.2401 for R_2, R_3, and R_4, respectively. By centroid defuzzification, we have

$$\hat{y} = \{0.0001 \times (0.0015) + 0.0175 \times (0.2081) + 0.8534 \times (0.9289) + 0.2401$$
$$\times (0.9998)\} \ /\{0.0001 + 0.0175 + 0.8534 + 0.2401\}$$
$$= 0.9328$$

$$(100)$$

which is almost identical to Eq.(97) but is computed from only 4 rules.

Next, we build a first-order TSK-type fuzzy neural network corresponding to the rule set R_2. The parameters contained in R_2 are tuned with our HLA. After two iterations, we have a rule set R_3 of the following refined rules:

R_1 : IF x IS $g(x;\ 0.1600,\ 0.1767)$ THEN y IS $f_1(x) = -0.0108 + 0.1603x$;
R_2 : IF x IS $g(x;\ 0.4236,\ 0.1377)$ THEN y IS $f_2(x) = -0.3447 + 0.8710x$;
R_3 : IF x IS $g(x;\ 0.6447,\ 0.1521)$ THEN y IS $f_3(x) = 1.8148 - 1.1979x$;
R_4 : IF x IS $g(x;\ 0.8850,\ 0.1516)$ THEN y IS $f_4(x) = 1.3564 - 0.3678x$

with MSE being 0.0001. The computed output from these refined fuzzy rules for $x \in [0,1]$ is shown in Figure 5(d) which gives a better approximation than Figure 5(b) and (c). For example, to compute the output for x=0.705, we have the firing strengths 0.0001, 0.0154, 0.8546, and 0.2442 for these refined rules, and thus

$$\hat{y} = \{0.0001 \times f_1(0.705) + 0.0154 \times f_2(0.705) + 0.8546 \times f_3(0.705) + 0.2442$$
$$\times f_4(0.705)\} \ /\{0.0001 + 0.0154 + 0.8546 + 0.2442\}$$
$$= \{0.0001 \times (0.1022) + 0.0154 \times (0.2694) + 0.8546 \times (0.9703) + 0.2442$$
$$\times (1.0971)\} \ /\{0.0001 + 0.0154 + 0.8546 + 0.2442\}$$
$$= 0.9884$$

$$(101)$$

which is very close to Eq.(98).

FUTURE TRENDS

For the future trends and possible research issues of neuro-fuzzy modeling, two topics are suggested as follows.

Compared with static neuro-fuzzy modeling, recurrent neuro-fuzzy modeling is more suitable for dynamic system identification since it includes dynamics with feedbacks. Up to now, several recurrent neuro-fuzzy systems have been proposed. The main difference between these approaches is based on the feedback mechanisms. However, most of them do not include data-driven constructing methods for initializing the structures of the networks. Even though some of them do include such initialization methods, they do not consider the time-dependent property of the training data in their initialization processes. In other words, the training data are viewed as time-independent for constructing the initial structure of the recurrent fuzzy neural network with a clustering method as that used in static neuro-fuzzy modeling. This results in a loss of information about the training data. Besides, they still encounter the problem of having to know the number of delayed inputs and outputs in advance. Therefore, maybe some analytic methodologies could be employed to predict a possible order of time-delay and develop a neural network learning algorithm to learn and discover the actual related delayed inputs or outputs. Besides, a data-driven self-clustering method which considers the time-dependent property of the training data should be developed for the initialization of the network structure.

Type-2 neuro-fuzzy modeling (T2NFM) (Mendel, 2007) has attracted a lot of attention in recent years. The main differences between the type-2 and type-1 mentioned in this chapter are the used fuzzy sets and fuzzy logical inference. Compared to the type-1 neuro-fuzzy modeling (T1NFM), the fuzzy membership functions employed in T2NFM are type-2 fuzzy sets proposed by Zadeh (1975). Besides, an additional component named type reduction should be developed to transform type-2 fuzzy sets into type-1 fuzzy sets. Therefore, the T2NFM is more powerful than type-1 one, especially when the uncertainties and vagueness of the considered system are high. However, general T2NFM are computationally intensive because of the calculation of type reduction. Therefore, most of researchers focus on the special case of T2NFM, i.e., interval type-2 neuro-fuzzy modeling (IT2NFM). Up to now, many approaches have been proposed for solving the construction and training of IT2NFM. However, it is still an open problem. Like the issues concerned in T1NFM, the development of efficient approaches for structure identification and parameter identification is necessary and emerging.

CONCLUSION

We have introduced some preliminary and basic concepts about neural networks, fuzzy systems, and neuro-fuzzy systems. Also, some important literatures about neuro-fuzzy system modeling are reviewed and discussed. We also have presented two proposed approaches for solving the most important two problems of neuro-fuzzy system modeling, i.e., structure identification and parameter identification.

For the structure identification, we proposed a similarity-and-merge-based rule generation method. The task of our method is to partition the given input–output dataset into fuzzy clusters, with the degree of association being strong for data within a cluster and weak for data in different clusters. Our method is an incremental one and consists of two stages, data partitioning and cluster merge. In the data partitioning stage, the data are considered one by one and are partitioned into a set of clusters incrementally through input-similarity and output-variance tests. Also, the corresponding membership functions of each cluster are derived. Like other incremental clustering algorithms, the clusters obtained from the data partitioning stage are sensitive to the input order of the training patterns, and maybe some of them are redundant. The influence of these two problems is reduced by the second stage, i.e., the cluster merge stage. In this stage, similar clusters are merged together dynamically through input-similarity, output-similarity, and output-variance tests. Therefore, more clusters are located in the local areas with a highly variant output surface and fewer clusters are located in the areas with less variant output values. The proposed method has several advantages. The information about input and output data subspaces is considered simultaneously for cluster generation and merging. Membership functions match closely with and describe properly the real distribution of the training data points. Redundant clusters are combined, and the sensitivity to the input order of training data is reduced. Besides, generation of the whole set of clusters from the scratch can be avoided when new training data are considered.

For the parameter identification, we proposed a hybrid learning algorithm composed of a recursive SVD-based least squares estimator and the gradient descent method. The former is developed based on the well-known matrix decomposition technique, i.e., singular value decomposition, while the latter is derived based on the gradient descent method. Such a learning algorithm is suitable for refining a zero-order or first-order TSK-type fuzzy system. Firstly, a zero order or first-order TSK-type fuzzy neural network is constructed according to the set of initial fuzzy rules obtained in the structure identification phase. Then, the hybrid leaning algorithm is used to train the network. In each iteration, both the recursive SVD-based least-squares estimator and the gradient descent method are applied. We first treat all antecedent parameters of rules are fixed, and use the recursive SVD-based least-squares estimator to optimize the consequent parameters of rules. Then we treat all consequent parameters as fixed and use the gradient descent method to refine all antecedent parameters. The process is iterated until the desired approximation precision is achieved. Finally, the trained fuzzy neural network can be used as they are for numeric inference, or final fuzzy rules can be extracted from the network for symbolic reasoning. This hybrid learning algorithm has the advantage of alleviating the local minimal problem. Besides, it learns faster, consumes less memory, and produces lower approximation errors than other methods.

Finally, the future trends and possible research issues of neuro-fuzzy modeling are also discussed. Two topics are suggested, i.e., recurrent neuro-fuzzy modeling and type-2 neuro-fuzzy modeling. Apparently, neuro-fuzzy modeling is now still an open problem for research. In the future, we believe that the technique of neuro-fuzzy modeling will be widely applied in more and more real applications.

REFERENCES

Azeem, M. F., Hanmandlu, M., & Ahmad, N. (2003). Structure identification of generalized adaptive neuro-fuzzy inference systems. *IEEE transactions on Fuzzy Systems, 11*(15), 666–681. doi:10.1109/TFUZZ.2003.817857

Berry, M., & Sameh, A. (1989). An overview of parallel algorithms for the singular value and dense symmetric eigenvalue problems. *Journal of Computational and Applied Mathematics, 1*(27), 191–213. doi:10.1016/0377-0427(89)90366-X

Berry, M. W. (1990). *Multiprocessor Sparse SVD Algorithms and Applications*. Doctoral dissertation, The University of Illinois at Urbana-Champaign, Urbana, IL.

Bezdek, J. C. (1981). *Pattern Recognition with Fuzzy Objective Function Algorithms*. New York: Plenum Press.

Golub, G. H., & Reinsch, C. (1970). Singular value decomposition and least squares solutions. *Numerische Mathematik, 14*, 403–420. doi:10.1007/BF02163027

Golub, G. H., & Van Loan, C. F. (1996). *Matrix Computations*. Baltimore: The Johns Hopkins University Press.

Gomm, J. B., & Yu, D. L. (2000). Selecting radial basis function network centers with recursive orthogonal least squares training. *IEEE Transactions on Neural Networks, 11*(2), 306–314. doi:10.1109/72.839002

Gonzalez, J., Rojas, I., Pomares, H., Ortega, J., & Prieto, A. (2002). A new clustering technique for function approximation. *IEEE Transactions on Neural Networks, 13*(1), 132–142. doi:10.1109/72.977289

Gupta, M. M., Ragade, R. K., & Yager, R. R. (1979). *Advances in Fuzzy Set Theroy and Applications*. New York: North-Holland.

Hagan, M. T., Demuth, H. B., & Beale, M. (1996). *Neural Network Design*. Boston: PWS.

Haykin, S. (1999). *Neural Networks – A Comprehensive Foundation*. Upper Saddle River, NJ: Prentice-Hall.

Jang, J.-S. R., & Sun, C.-T. (1995). Neuro-fuzzy modeling and control. *Proceedings of the IEEE, 83*(3), 378–406. doi:10.1109/5.364486

Jang, J.-S. R., Sun, C.-T., & Mizutani, E. (1997). *Neuro-Fuzzy and Soft Computing*. Upper Saddle River, NJ: Prentice Hall.

Jin, Y. (2000). Fuzzy modeling of high-dimensional systems: complexity reduction and interpretability improvement. *IEEE transactions on Fuzzy Systems, 8*(2), 212–221. doi:10.1109/91.842154

Juang, C.-F. (2002). A TSK-type recurrent fuzzy network for dynamic systems processing by neural network and genetic algorithms. *IEEE transactions on Fuzzy Systems, 10*(2), 155–170. doi:10.1109/91.995118

Kasabov, N. K., & Song, Q. (2002). DENFIS: dynamic evolving neural-fuzzy inference system and its application for time-series prediction. *IEEE transactions on Fuzzy Systems, 10*(2), 144–154. doi:10.1109/91.995117

Klir, G. J., & Yuan, B. (1995). *Fuzzy Sets and Fuzzy Logic: Theory and Applications*. Upper Saddle River, NJ: Prentice Hall.

Kosko, B. (1992). *Neural Networks and Fuzzy Systems*. Upper Saddle River, NJ: Prentice Hall.

Kukolj, D., & Levi, E. (2004). Identification of complex systems based on neural and Takagi-Sugeno fuzzy model. *IEEE Transactions on Systems, Man, and Cybernetics. Part B, Cybernetics, 34*(1), 272–282. doi:10.1109/TSMCB.2003.811119

Lee, S.-J., & Ouyang, C.-S. (2003). A neuro-fuzzy system modeling with self-constructing rule generation and hybrid SVD-based learning. *IEEE transactions on Fuzzy Systems, 11*(3), 341–353. doi:10.1109/TFUZZ.2003.812693

Lin, Y., Cunningham, G. A. III, & Coggeshall, S. V. (1997). Using fuzzy partitions to create fuzzy systems from input-output data and set the initial weights in a fuzzy neural network. *IEEE transactions on Fuzzy Systems, 5*(4), 614–621. doi:10.1109/91.649913

Mamdani, E. H., & Assilian, S. (1975). An experiment in linguistic synthesis with a fuzzy logic controller. *International Journal of Man-Machine Studies, 7*(1), 1–13. doi:10.1016/S0020-7373(75)80002-2

Mendel, J. M. (2007). Type-2 fuzzy sets and systems: an overview. *IEEE Computational Intelligence Magazine, 2*(1), 20–29. doi:10.1109/MCI.2007.380672

Nauch, D., Klawonn, F., & Kruse, R. (1997). *Foundations of Neuro-Fuzzy Systems*. New York: John Wiley & Sons.

Nomura, H., Hayashi, I., & Wakami, N. (1992). A learning method of fuzzy inference rules by descent method. In *Proceedings of IEEE International Conference on Fuzzy Systems*, San Diego, CA, (pp. 203–210).

Ouyang, C.-S., Lee, W.-J., & Lee, S.-J. (2005). A TSK-type neurofuzzy network approach to system modeling problems. *IEEE Transactions on Systems, Man, and Cybernetics. Part B, Cybernetics*, *35*(4), 751–767. doi:10.1109/TSMCB.2005.846000

Panella, M., & Gallo, A. S. (2005). An input-output clustering approach to the synthesis of ANFIS networks. *IEEE transactions on Fuzzy Systems*, *13*(1), 69–81. doi:10.1109/TFUZZ.2004.839659

Pedrycz, W., & Card, H. C. (1992). Linguistic interpretation of self-organizing maps. In *Proceedings of IEEE International Conference on Fuzzy Systems*, San Diego, CA, (pp. 371–378).

Roubos, H., & Setnes, M. (2001). Compact and transparent fuzzy models and classifiers through iterative complexity reduction . *IEEE transactions on Fuzzy Systems*, *9*(4), 516–524. doi:10.1109/91.940965

Rumehart, D. E., & McClelland, J. L. (1986). *Parallel Distributed Processing (Two Volumes)*. Cambridge, MA: MIT Press.

Simon, H. D. (1984). Analysis of the symmetric Lanczos algorithm with reorthogonalization methods. *Linear Algebra and Its Applications*, *61*, 101–131. doi:10.1016/0024-3795(84)90025-9

Sudkamp, T., Knapp, A., & Knapp, J. (2003). Model generation by domain refinement and rule reduction. *IEEE Transactions on Systems, Man, and Cybernetics . Part B*, *33*(1), 45–55.

Sugeno, M., & Kang, G. T. (1988). Structure identification of fuzzy model. *Fuzzy Sets and Systems*, *28*(1), 15–33. doi:10.1016/0165-0114(88)90113-3

Sun, Z.-L., Au, K.-F., & Choi, T.-M. (2007). A neuro-fuzzy inference system through Integration of fuzzy logic and extreme learning machines. *IEEE Transactions on Systems, Man, and Cybernetics. Part B, Cybernetics*, *37*(5), 1321–1331. doi:10.1109/TSMCB.2007.901375

Takagi, T., & Sugeno, M. (1985). Fuzzy identification of systems and its application to modeling and control. *IEEE Transactions on Systems, Man, and Cybernetics*, *15*(1), 116–132.

Wang, J. S., & Lee, C. S. G. (2000). Structure and learning in self-adaptive neural fuzzy inference systems. *International Journal on Fuzzy Systems*, *2*(1), 12–22.

Wang, J. S., & Lee, C. S. G. (2002). Self-adaptive neuro-fuzzy inference systems for classification applications. *IEEE transactions on Fuzzy Systems*, *10*(6), 790–802. doi:10.1109/TFUZZ.2002.805880

Wong, C.-C., & Chen, C.-C. (1999). A hybrid clustering and gradient descent approach for fuzzy modeling. *IEEE Transactions on Systems, Man, and Cybernetics. Part B, Cybernetics*, *29*(6), 686–693. doi:10.1109/3477.809024

Wu, S., Er, M. J., & Gao, Y. (2001). A fast approach for automatic generation of fuzzy rules by generalized dynamic fuzzy neural networks. *IEEE transactions on Fuzzy Systems*, *9*(4), 578–594. doi:10.1109/91.940970

Yager, R. R., & Filev, D. P. (1994). Approximate clustering via the mountain method. *IEEE Transactions on Systems, Man, and Cybernetics. Part B, Cybernetics*, *24*(8), 1279–1284.

Yen, J., Wang, L., & Gillepie, C. W. (1998). Improving the interpretability of TSK fuzzy models by combining global learning and local learning. *IEEE transactions on Fuzzy Systems*, *6*(4), 530–537. doi:10.1109/91.728447

Zadeh, L. A. (1965). Fuzzy sets. *Information and Control*, *8*, 338–353. doi:10.1016/S0019-9958(65)90241-X

Zadeh, L. A. (1975). The concept of a linguistic variable and its application to approximate reasoning—I. *Information Sciences*, *8*, 199–249. doi:10.1016/0020-0255(75)90036-5

Chapter 9
Network Based Fusion of Global and Local Information in Time Series Prediction with The Use of Soft-Computing Techniques

Shun-Feng Su
National Taiwan University of Science and Technology, Taiwan

Sou-Horng Li
National Taiwan University of Science and Technology, Taiwan

ABSTRACT

Forecasting data from a time series is to make predictions for the future from available data. Thus, such a problem can be viewed as a traditional data mining problem because it is to extract rules for prediction from available data. There are two kinds of forecasting approaches. Most traditional forecasting approaches are based on all available data including the nearest data and far away data with respect to the time. These approaches are referred to as the global prediction scheme in our study. On the other hand, there also exist some prediction approaches that only construct their prediction model based on the most recent data. Such approaches are referred to as the local prediction schemes. Those local prediction approaches seem to have good prediction ability in some cases but due to their local characteristics, they usually fail in general for long term prediction. In this chapter, the authors shall detail those ideas and use several commonly used models, especially those model free estimators, such as neural networks, fuzzy systems, grey systems, etc., to explain their effects. Another issues discussed in the chapter is about multi-step predictions. From the author's study, it can be found that those often-used global prediction schemes can have fair performance in both one-step-ahead predictions and multi-step predictions. On the other hand, good local prediction schemes can have better performance in the one-step-ahead prediction when compared to those global prediction schemes, but usually have awful performance for multi-step predictions. In this chapter, the authors shall introduce several approaches of combining local and global prediction results to improve the prediction performance.

DOI: 10.4018/978-1-61520-757-2.ch009

INTRODUCTION

Time series data can be seen in many application domains, such as daily indices of stock market, various kinds of weather data, and traces of observations of various dynamic processes and scientific experiments. Ways of finding useful information from time series has been investigated for more than a century. In fact, time series can also be viewed as a kind of database. Thus, those techniques considered for finding information from time series can also be considered as data mining techniques. There are some major tasks are considered by the time series data mining community (Keogh, 2008), such as, indexing (Chakrabarti, *et al*, 2002; Meyer, 2005), clustering (Keogh, *et al*, 2006; Keogh & Pazzani, 1998), classification (Keogh & Pazzani, 1998), Motif Discovery (Abe & Yamaguchi, 2005), Prediction (Forecasting) (Su & Huang, 2003), Association Detection (Das, *et al*, 1998), summarization (Indyk *et al*, 2000), Anomaly Detection (Interestingness/Novelty Detection) (Keogh, *et al*, 2002), Segmentation (Keogh & Pazzani, 1998). In this chapter, we would like to report our study on time series prediction.

In recent decades, neural networks, fuzzy systems and neural-fuzzy systems have been successfully applied to many real-world problems, such as system identification, control, prediction, etc. (Rovithakis, *et al*, 1999; Lin, *et al*, 1999; Hwang, 1999; Cabrera & Narendra, 1999; Takashima, 1989; Tanaka & Sano, 1994). These techniques are referred to as model-free estimators because they build models from data without physical knowledge about the system. In the training process, these techniques treat all data equally. Nevertheless, if the prediction is for time series, it is intuitive to say that the most recent data may carry more information than those data far away from the present. Hence, when a prediction model is constructed based on all training data without preference, the resultant prediction may not be accurate enough because the prediction accuracy may be corrupted by those far away data, which are supposed to have less relationship to the current prediction. Such approaches are referred to as the global prediction schemes in our research.

One may then consider another kind of approach in which the prediction is only based on the most recent data without considering other data. Such a kind of approach in fact is curve-fitting schemes. They are called the local prediction schemes in our research. It is noted that local prediction schemes can also be employed as global prediction schemes by considering all training data as input. However, it is rarely the case, due to its bad performance. As discussed in (Lin, 2000), when it is to predict the value of the next step, good local prediction schemes usually have better performance than global ones do. However, those local prediction schemes only use the most recent information and ignore certain information bearing in the past. Thus, the accuracy of those local prediction schemes may be limited. In (Su, *et al*, 2002), a prediction approach, termed as the Markov Fourier Grey Model (MFGM) is proposed to incorporate global information into local prediction schemes. From those examples shown in (Su, *et al*, 2002), it is evident that MFGM indeed can have the best performances among those existing prediction schemes.

Nevertheless, MFGM is to incorporate global information based on a local prediction scheme, Fourier Grey Model (FGM). As shown later, when the prediction is not one-step ahead prediction, such an approach may have worse performance than traditional global prediction schemes do. Of course, we can simply employ a global prediction scheme to conduct multi-step prediction. But, if we can use both kinds of information, it may have a great chance to obtain a better prediction. In this research, we intend to report our study for fusing global information with local prediction results. Various fusion techniques are introduced and analyzed in this study.

The chapter is organized as follows. After this introduction section, local prediction approaches are introduced in section 2. The considered local prediction schemes are the grey model and FGM. The MFGM is also discussed in this section. Their prediction performances on one-step prediction and multi-step prediction are also illustrated. In section 3, global prediction schemes are then briefly introduced. Two often-used global prediction schemes are considered; they are neural networks and SONFIN. Afterward, the concept of fusing global and local information is introduced in section 4. Various fusion approaches are proposed. Finally, section 5 concludes this chapter.

LOCAL PREDICTION APPROACHES

In this section, we shall introduce various local prediction approaches used in our study. They are GM(1,1), which is a traditional grey model, the Fourier grey model (FGM) (Tan & Chang, 1996), and the **Markov** Fourier grey model (MFGM) (Su & Lee, 1992). In the study, we attempt to investigate the prediction accuracy of those approaches for **multi-step prediction**. How those approaches are implemented for multi-step prediction is also introduced.

Grey Model

The grey system was first introduced by Deng in 1982 (Deng, 1982). A grey system is a system in which the regarded information is partially known and partially unknown in contents. The grey theorem has been widely applied in various disciplines and demonstrated promising results (Hsu, *et al*, 1997; Hsu, *et al*, 1998). Departing from using original training data to create prediction models, the grey theorem uses the so-call accumulated generating operation (AGO) (Deng, 1987) to preprocess the raw data. AGO is to accumulate the data from the first one up to the considered step. Since training data are all assumed to be positive (Su, *et al*, 2002), the data obtained by AGO is always monotonically increasing. A

reasonable model for the accumulated data is an exponential form. This model is the so-call grey model. The most commonly used grey model is GM(1,1), which indicates the model is constructed for a single variable and a first order differential equation is used in matching the data generated by AGO. The detailed algorithm can be found in (Su, *et al*, 2002) and we briefly introduce the algorithm in the following.

Let the raw data series be $[X^{(0)}(1), X^{(0)}(2), ..., X^{(0)}(j), ..., X^{(0)}(n)]$, where $X^{(0)}(j)$ is the datum at time j and n is the number of data used for prediction. Let $X^{(1)} = [X^{(1)}(1), X^{(1)}(2), ..., X^{(1)}(n)]$ be the series generated from the raw data by applying AGO as

$$X(1)(k) = AGO(X^{(0)}(k)) = \sum_{j=1}^{k} X^{(0)}(j). \qquad (1)$$

Assume that $X^{(1)}$ can be modeled by a first-order differential equation as:

$$\frac{dX^{(1)}}{dt} + aX^{(1)} = b, \qquad (2)$$

where a and b are constants to be estimated by using the least square method (Hsia, 1979). Then, the predicted value $\hat{X}^{(1)}(n+1)$ can be obtained as:

$$\hat{X}^{(1)}(n+1) = \left(X^{(0)}(1) - \frac{b}{a} \right) e^{-an} + \frac{b}{a}. \qquad (3)$$

The predicted value for $X^{(0)}(n+1)$ is $\hat{X}^{(0)}(n+1) = \hat{X}^{(1)}(n+1) - \hat{X}^{(1)}(n)$.

In the simulation, the multi-step prediction is considered. We try to model the Grey system with eight points to predict next four data. The above prediction is the so-called *one-step ahead prediction* because the next datum in the time series is predicted. In various applications, we may need more information about future, not only the next datum. When the prediction is for a datum not immediately following the current one, by repeating the above process, $X^{(0)}(n+i)$ can easily be predicted. However, in our early implementation (Lin, 2000), when such a multi-step prediction is conducted by using GM(1,1), the performance is very bad. Thus, we also studied the effects of using the same sampling interval in (Li, 2002). For example, when $i=2$, instead of using $X(n-7)$, $X(n-6)$, $X(n-5)$, $X(n-4)$, $X(n-3)$, $X(n-2)$, $X(n-1)$, $X(n)$, we use $X(n-14)$, $X(n-12)$, $X(n-10)$, $X(n-8)$, $X(n-6)$, $X(n-4)$, $X(n-2)$, $X(n)$ to predict $X(n+2)$. The original time series still has better performance (Li, 2002). In fact, for the global prediction schemes introduced later, the multi-step prediction can also have two different models. Similar to GM(1,1), the original way of prediction can have better accuracy. Thus, in the following study, we still used the original sequence of the data series to conduct multi-step prediction. In our study, the **Mackey-Glass chaotic time series** is considered. The Mackey-Glass chaotic function is

$$\frac{dx(t)}{dt} = \frac{0.2 \cdot x(t-\tau)}{1 + x^{10}(t-\tau)} - 0.1 \cdot x(t) + noise(t) \tag{4}$$

where $\tau=30$ is used here. Figure 1 shows 1000 data of the Mackey-Glass chaotic time series. 1000 data are used. Among them, the first 700 data are used as the training data set and the last 300 data are used as the testing data set. Nevertheless, in the multi-step prediction, only 697 data are used as the training data set and the testing data set also only contains 297 data. The simulation performances are listed in table 1. Two criteria are used for evaluating those approaches. The first is the Absolute Mean Error, AME. The criterion of AME is computed as

$$AME = \frac{1}{n} \sum_{k=1}^{n} \left| X(k) - \hat{X}(k) \right| \tag{5}$$

where $X(k)$ is the actual value at time k, $\hat{X}(k)$ is the predicted value at time k and n is the number of data used for prediction. The second criterion is the Mean Square Error, MSE and is computed as

$$MSE = \frac{1}{n} \sum_{k=1}^{n} \left(X(k) - \hat{X}(k) \right)^2 \tag{6}$$

Figure 1. the original data of Mackey-glass chaotic

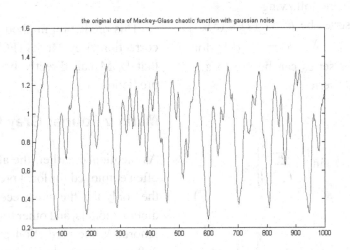

Table 1. The result of predicting the second-step data in different input data order

	MSE	AME
Consecutive data order	0.0017	0.0332
Nonconsecutive data order	0.0146	0.0995

It is clear that the original time series still has a better performance. Thus, in the following study, we still used the original GM(1,1) as the main approach.

Fourier Grey Model (FGM)

As stated in (Bingqian, 1990), GM(1,1) may have worse curve fitting effects while used in more random data and center-symmetry curve cases. Various remedies for GM(1,1) have been discussed in the literate (Deng, 1982; Tan & Lu, 1996; Chen & Tien, 1997; Lin, *et al*, 2001). Many of them are to propose ways of modeling the residual of GM(1,1) so as to increase the accuracy of the grey prediction. In this study, we also incorporate the idea of residual correction to improve the prediction accuracy of GM(1,1). The used approach is the Fourier Grey Model (FGM), which employs a Fourier series to model the residual series obtained from GM(1,1). We shall briefly introduce the FGM algorithm in the following.

Let the residual series be $E_r = \{E_r(2)\ E_r(3)\ldots E_r(n)\}^T$, where $E_r(k) = X^{(0)}(k) - \hat{X}^{(0)}(k)$, for $k=2,3,\ldots,n$. A Fourier series can be use to approximate the residual series as:

$$E(k) = \frac{1}{2} a_0 +$$
$$\sum_{i=1}^{k_a} \left[a_i \cos\left(\frac{i \cdot 2\pi}{T} k \right) + b_i \sin\left(\frac{i \cdot 2\pi}{T} k \right) \right],$$
$$for \quad k = 2, 3, \cdots, n, \tag{7}$$

where $T=n$-1 and $k_a = \left\lfloor (n-1)/2 \right\rfloor - 1$. Here $\left\lfloor (n-1)/2 \right\rfloor - 1$ is the integer portion of $(n-1)/2$.

The least square approach is applied, and the parameters a_0, a_i and b_i for $i=1,2,\ldots,k_a$ in Eq. (7) are estimated as:

$$C=(P^TP)^{-1}P^TE_r, \tag{8}$$

where $C=[a_0 a_1 b_1 a_2 b_2 \ldots a_{ka} b_{ka}]$ and

$$P = \begin{bmatrix} \frac{1}{2} & \cos\left(\frac{2\pi \cdot 2}{T}\right) & \sin\left(\frac{2\pi \cdot 2}{T}\right) & \cos\left(\frac{2 \cdot 2\pi \cdot 2}{T}\right) & \sin\left(\frac{2 \cdot 2\pi \cdot 2}{T}\right) & \cdots & \cos\left(\frac{k_a \cdot 2\pi \cdot 2}{T}\right) & \sin\left(\frac{k_a \cdot 2\pi \cdot 2}{T}\right) \\ \frac{1}{2} & \cos\left(\frac{2\pi \cdot 3}{T}\right) & \sin\left(\frac{2\pi \cdot 3}{T}\right) & \cos\left(\frac{2 \cdot 2\pi \cdot 3}{T}\right) & \sin\left(\frac{2 \cdot 2\pi \cdot 3}{T}\right) & \cdots & \cos\left(\frac{k_a \cdot 2\pi \cdot 3}{T}\right) & \sin\left(\frac{k_a \cdot 2\pi \cdot 3}{T}\right) \\ \vdots & \vdots & \vdots & \vdots & \vdots & & \vdots & \vdots \\ \frac{1}{2} & \cos\left(\frac{2\pi \cdot n}{T}\right) & \sin\left(\frac{2\pi \cdot n}{T}\right) & \cos\left(\frac{2 \cdot 2\pi \cdot n}{T}\right) & \sin\left(\frac{2 \cdot 2\pi \cdot n}{T}\right) & \cdots & \cos\left(\frac{k_a \cdot 2\pi \cdot n}{T}\right) & \sin\left(\frac{k_a \cdot 2\pi \cdot n}{T}\right) \end{bmatrix}$$

Then, the original prediction series can be corrected as:

$$\tilde{X}(1) = X^{(0)}(1) \text{ and } \tilde{X}(1) = X^{(0)}(1)$$
$$\tilde{X}^{(0)}(k) = \hat{X}^{(0)}(k) + E(k) \text{ and }$$
$$\tilde{X}^{(0)}(k) = \hat{X}^{(0)}(k) + E(k), \text{ for } k=2, 3, \ldots, n,$$
$$n+1, n+2, \ldots \tag{9}$$

This prediction method is called the Fourier correction Grey Model (FGM). It is easy to see that FGM can directly be used for multi-step prediction.

Markov Fourier Grey Model (MFGM)

As mentioned earlier, the above approaches are often employed for local prediction. In that case, they only use the most recent data to build prediction models, and other training data are totally ignored in the prediction process. In (Su, *et al*, 2002), an approach was proposed to incorporate global information so that the prediction can be more accurate. The approach is called the Markov–Fourier Grey model (MFGM), which combines FGM and the **Markov** forecasting model (Tan & Lu, 1996).

The algorithm is first to use FGM to model a time series. A residual series then is obtained from FGM. In order to define states for Markov transition matrices, the residual errors are partitioned into k regions called states. In our algorithm, $k=3$. When k is 3, it indicates that the global information may suggest that the current prediction should be moved forward, backward, or stay unchanged. Then, the dimensions of Markov transition matrices are 3×3. For practical reasons, the error partition is not equally divided. The sample mean and standard deviation of the residuals are used to define the partition. Let the sample mean and standard deviation of the residuals be μ and σ, respectively. In our algorithm, the interval $[\mu-2\sigma\ \mu-\sigma/8]$ is state 1, $[\mu-\sigma/8\ \mu+\sigma/8]$ is state 2, and $[\mu+\sigma/8\ \mu+2\sigma]$ is state 3. It should be noted that the actual value might be outside the defined state boundaries. Thus, in our implementation, we have extended the left boundary for state 1 and the right boundary for state 3 to infinite to cover all possible data. Nevertheless, in the approach, the center of each state must be used and then $\mu-2\delta$ or $\mu+2\delta$ is still defined. With those states defined, the state transition in the residual series can be defined and recorded.

Generally, the m-th step state transition matrix is defined as:

$$R^{(m)} = \begin{vmatrix} P_{11}^{(m)} & P_{12}^{(m)} & \cdots & P_{1k}^{(m)} \\ P_{21}^{(m)} & P_{22}^{(m)} & \cdots & P_{2k}^{(m)} \\ \vdots & \vdots & \vdots & \vdots \\ P_{k1}^{(m)} & P_{k2}^{(m)} & \cdots & P_{kk}^{(m)} \end{vmatrix}, \qquad (10)$$

where $P_{ij}^{(m)}$ is the state transition probability from state i to state j after m steps and is obtained as

$$P_{ij}^{(m)} = \frac{M_{ij}^{(m)}}{M_i^{(m)}}, \text{ for } i, j=1,2,\ldots,k, \text{ where } M_{ij}^{(m)} \text{ is the}$$

number of state transitions from state i to state j after m steps and $M_i^{(m)} = \sum_j M_{ij}^{(m)}$. When the effects up to the r-th step are considered, r state transition matrices are defined. Those steps up to the previous r steps may influence the current state and then, in this study those r steps are said to form an influence window. Those transition probabilities indicate the tendency of the state transition and can be used to predict the possible error state for the next step. For example, when the actual residual error of the immediately previous data is located in the interval of state 1, the first row vector of $R^{(1)}$ is then used. When the second previous data is in state 3, then the third row vector of $R^{(2)}$ is used, and so on for all r previous steps. In should be noted that the entries in $R^{(m)}$ are conditional probabilities and the sample size does not affect their meaning but may change the confidence of the obtained probability for different rows. In fact, in the use of those matrices, only one row of $R^{(m)}$ is used for each datum. The confidence difference in different rows plays no role in our approach.

With all r transition probability vectors, the possibilities of a certain error state for the next step are obtained by summing all those probabilities in those r vectors, denoted as $w_1 w_2$ and w_3 (for $k=3$). Define the centers of those three states as $v1\ v2$ and $v3$. Then, the predicted value for the next step is

$$\hat{X}(n+1) = \tilde{X}(n+1) + \lambda_1$$
$$*v1 + \lambda_2 * v2 + \lambda_3 * v3 \qquad (11)$$

where λ_1, λ_2, and λ_3 are the corresponding weights for those three states and $\tilde{X}(n+1)$ is the value predicted by FGM at time step $n+1$. Intuitively, λ_1, λ_2, and λ_3 are proportional to $w_1 w_2$ and w_3. Usually, a normalization approach is employed; that is, $\lambda_i=w_i/(w_1+w_2+w_3)$ for $i=1$, 2, and 3. Other formulations can also be used here (Lin, *et al*, 2001). For simplicity, the normalization approach is used.

The following example is presented for illustration. Consider a simple time series X with sixteen data points listed in the second column of Table 1. Assume that the last datum is unknown and to be predicted from the previous data. First, FGM is constructed to obtain the predicted series $\tilde{X}$ and the errors are calculated. All are listed in Table 2 (the third and the fourth columns, respectively). Three states are defined in this example. The corresponding intervals of those three states are [-0.0177, 0.0097], [0.0097, 0.0133], and [0.0133, 0.0407]. The states of all steps based on their errors are then defined and listed in the last column of Table 2. In this example, the size of the influence window is selected as 5 (i.e. r=5). In this example, there are twelve training data and four data to be predicted from the 13-th to the 6-th one. Then five transition matrices can be obtained. In the multi-step prediction, the one-step predicted value can be obtained by Eq. (11) as

$$\hat{X}(n+1|n) = \tilde{X}(n+1|n) + \lambda_1(n+1)$$
$$\times v1 + \lambda_2(n+1) \times v2 + \lambda_3(n+1) \times v3 \quad (12)$$

where $\hat{X}\left(n+1|n\right)$ and $\tilde{X}\left(n+1|n\right)$ are the predicted values of MFGM and of FGM, respectively, for the $(n+1)$-th step based on the observation at the nth step, and $\lambda_1(n+1)$, $\lambda_2(n+1)$ and $\lambda_3(n+1)$ are the normalized weights generated from Markov transition matrices for the $(n+1)$-th step. When the influence window is 1, the transition matrices shall calculate the probabilities about all possible states in the next step. In the example, the possible probabilities of the next transition states are showed in the first column of Table 3. In the same way, Table 3 shows the transition probabilities of all states when s=2, 3, 4, and 5. Finally, the total probabilities of all states are calculated and the one-step ahead value are obtained and Table 4 shows the results, where EP is the error percentage.

Table 2. The data of the example

n	X	$\tilde{X}$	error	state
1	0.368	0.351	0.017	2
2	0.367	0.343	0.024	3
3	0.374	0.346	0.028	3
4	0.387	0.359	0.028	3
5	0.404	0.381	0.023	3
6	0.420	0.407	0.013	2
7	0.435	0.433	0.002	1
8	0.448	0.435	0.013	2
9	0.457	0.447	0.010	2
10	0.466	0.451	0.015	3
11	0.475	0.481	-0.006	1
12	0.488	0.487	0.001	1
13	0.508	0.498		
14	0.539	0.517		
15	0.584	0.551		
16	0.644	0.604		

Table 3. The transition probability of each state in the influence window in the first-step prediction

s influence window (transition step)	State	Transition probability		
		State1	State2	State3
1(n=12)	1	0.5	0.5	0
2(n=11)	1	0	1	0.667
3(n=10)	3	0.25	0.5	0.25
4(n=9)	2	0.333	0	0.667
5(n=8)	2	0.25	0.75	0
Total possibilities		1.333	2.75	2.251

Table 4. The predicted result in the first-step prediction

	Original data X	FGM	MFGM
Predict data	0.508	0.498	0.512
EP(%)		1.97	0.79

Similarly, the transition matrices for two-step ahead prediction can be obtained. Since the data in the (n+1)-th step is unknown, it is not possible to define the transition matrix for s=1. We simply set R_1=0 for this case. Then, the prediction is still obtained but instead of using Eq. (13), it uses

$$\hat{X}(n+2|n) = \tilde{X}(n+2|n) + \lambda_1(n+2)$$
$$\times v1 + \lambda_2(n+2) \times v2 + \lambda_3(n+2) \times v3 \qquad (13)$$

where $\hat{X}\left(n+2|n\right)$ and $\tilde{X}\left(n+2|n\right)$ are the predicted values of MFGM and of FGM, respectively, for the (n+2)-th step based on the observation at the nth step, and $\lambda_1(n+2), \lambda_2(n+2)$ and $\lambda_3(n+2)$ are the normalized weights generated from Markov transition matrices for the (n+2)-th step. Table 5 shows the transition probabilities of all states and Table 6 is the result of the two-step ahead prediction. Similarly, Table 7 shows the transition probabilities of all states in the three-step ahead value. Here, there are two unknown data and R_1

and R_2 are set to zeros. The predicted result is shown in Table 8. Finally, the four-step ahead prediction is showed in Table 9 and Table 10. From Tables 3 ~ 10, it can be seen that to use the MFGM algorithm have better performances than that of using the FGM algorithm.

When using the MFGM algorithm for multi-step prediction, training data are used to generate possible states for the Markov transition matrices. In the testing phase, the Markov transition matrices are used to generate suitable weights and to predict four future point data. Table 11 shows the prediction performance for the Mackey-Glass chaotic function. From those tables, it seems that the first step prediction can have more accurate prediction in MFGM results, but for multi-step prediction, the performances of using MFGM become worse especially when the prediction step become large. In other words, MFGM is a local prediction scheme in nature and then is not suitable for multi-step prediction.

Table 5. The transition probability of each state in the influence window in the second-step prediction.

Transition Step (n)	state	Transition probability		
		State1	State2	State3
$s=1(n=12)$	1	0	0	0
$s=2(n=11)$	1	0	1	0.667
$s=3(n=10)$	3	0.25	0.5	0.25
$s=4(n=9)$	2	0.333	0	0.667
$s=5(n=8)$	2	0.25	0.75	0
Total possibilities		0.833	2.25	2.251

Table 6. The predicted result in the second-step prediction

	Original data	FGM	MFGM
Predict data	0.539	0.517	0.533
EP(%)		4.08	1.18

Table 7. The transition probability of each state in the influence window in the third-step prediction

Transition Step (n)	state	Transition probability		
		State1	State2	State3
1(n=12)	1	0	0	0
2(n=11)	1	0	0	0
3(n=10)	3	0.25	0.5	0.25
4(n=9)	2	0.333	0	0.667
5(n=8)	2	0.25	0.75	0
Total possibilities		0.583	0.75	0.667

Table 8. The results in the third-step prediction

	Original data	FGM	MFGM
Predict data	0.584	0.551	0.563
EP(%)		5.65	3.57

GLOBAL PREDICTION APPROACHES

In this section, we shall introduce two well-known global prediction approaches, neural networks and SONFIN. Neural networks (Lin & Lee, 1996; Ko-sko, 1992; Hornik, *et al*, 1989) and fuzzy systems (Zadeh, 1973; Pedrycz, 1986; Yager & Filev, 1994; Wang, 1992) are often used to model complicated systems and thus can be used to model time series. These approaches can construct systems directly from the input-output relationship without the use

Table 9. The transition probability of each state in the influence window in the fourth-step prediction

Transition Step (n)	state	Transition probability		
		State1	State2	State3
1(n=12)	1	0	0	0
2(n=11)	1	0	0	0
3(n=10)	3	0	0	0
4(n=9)	2	0.333	0	0.667
5(n=8)	2	0.25	0.75	0
Total possibilities		0.583	0.75	0.667

Table 10. The results in the fourth-step prediction

	Original data	FGM	MFGM
Predict data	0.644	0.604	0.616
EP(%)		6.21	4.32

Table 11. The MSEs for predicting the Mackey-Glass chaotic time series in different step prediction

	First-step	Second-step	Third-step	Forth-step
FGM	7.6263e-004	0.0050	0.0134	0.0256
MFGM	5.3841e-004	0.0049	0.0136	0.0256

of any domain knowledge. Thus, they are often referred to as model-free estimators (Kosko, 1992). In fact, they have also been proven to be universal approximators (Hornik, *et al*, 1989; Kosko, 1992; Cichocki & Unbehauen, 1993) under certain circumstances. In other words, these approaches can approximate virtually any function (Borel measurable) of interest to any desired degree of accuracy (Hornik, *et al*, 1989). The bottom line of these approaches to be universal approximators is that the learning scheme used must work well and then the learning process can actually converge to the desired function. Nevertheless, it is more than often that this bottom line cannot be satisfied in various applications. Hence, various approaches to improve the learning capability have been proposed and discussed in the literature, such as (Bernasconi, 1990; Jacobs, 1988; Battiti,

1992; Leung, *et al*, 1994; Ng, *et al*, 1996; Castillo, *et al*, 1996; Castillo, *et al*, 2000; Hirose, *et al*, 1991; Fahlman & Lebiere, 1991; Huber, 1981). In this research, we shall also consider them as prediction schemes. Since those approaches are to model systems from all available data, they are of course global prediction schemes.

Backpropagation Neural Networks

The most commonly used model-free estimators are multi-layer feedforward neural networks. For this kind of networks, the backpropagation learning algorithm is often used as the learning scheme (Cichocki & Unbehauen, 1993; Lin & Lee, 1996; Chuang, *et al*, 2000). The introduction of backpropagation networks can be found in any textbooks, such as (Cichocki & Unbehauen, 1993;

Lin & Lee, 1996). Here, we briefly introduce the idea. Consider a set of given input-output training patterns, $\{(x^{(k)}, d^{(k)})\}$, for $k=1, 2, \ldots, N$, where $x^{(k)}$ is the input vector for the k-th training pattern, $d^{(k)}$ is the desired output for the input $x^{(k)}$, and N is the number of training patterns. The algorithm is to compute the output $y^{(k)}$ from the network and then to back- propagate the error to modify the weights of the network in a gradient-descent fashion (Su, *et al*, 2002). The cost function is usually defined as

$$E(w) = \frac{1}{2} \sum_{k=1}^{N} |d^{(k)} - y^{(k)}(w)|^2, \qquad (14)$$

where w is the weight vector and $|d^{(k)}-y^{(k)}|$ is the norm of $d^{(k)}-y^{(k)}$ representing the error to be corrected. The above cost function is often referred as the global error function (Cichocki & Unbehauen, 1993; Rumelhart, *et al*, 1986) in that the error function is obtained by summing the errors for all training patterns. Owing to the iterative nature of learning, in backpropagation learning instead of using Eq. (14) as the cost function, the so-called local error function (Cichocki & Unbehauen, 1993; Rumelhart, *et al*, 1986) is used for each training pattern. The local error function for the k-th pattern is:

$$E^{(k)}(w) = \frac{1}{2} |d^{(k)} - y^{(k)}(w)|^2. \qquad (15)$$

When Eq. (14) is used as the error function, it is called the on-line or per-example learning (Cichocki & Unbehauen, 1993) as compared to the batch learning in which Eq. (14) is used. In our research, the per-example learning is employed.

By using Eq. (15) as the cost function, the weight in the connection from the q-th neuron to the i-th neuron of the network for the k-th pattern is updated as (Rumelhart, *et al*, 1986)

$$\Delta w_{iq} = -\eta \frac{\partial E^{(k)}}{\partial w_{iq}}, \qquad (16)$$

where η is the learning constant. Notice that if the batch learning is applied; i.e., Eq. (14) is the cost function used; the updating algorithm in Eq. (16) may need to accumulate errors over all training patterns before the weight is actually changed. Many variations of the above approaches can be seen in the literature. Mainly, those variations are regarding the use of adaptive learning constants (Jacobs, 1988) or different forms of cost functions (Cichocki & Unbehauen, 1993; Huber, 1981; Chuang, *et al*, 2001). Those approaches are aimed at increasing the convergence speed or at avoiding the local minimum problem. Some of them are to provide mechanisms for robust learning (Chuang, *et al*, 2001; Liano, 1996; Chen & Jain, 1994), which is supposed to have fair learning performance when outliers exist. More detailed discussion can be found in (Cichocki & Unbehauen, 1993; Lin & Lee, 1996; Chuang, *et al*, 2000; Rumelhart, *et al*, 1986).

SONFIN

Another popular way of numerically constructing fuzzy systems is to embed the learning concept of neural networks into fuzzy modeling (Chen, 1998; Jang, 1993; Su & Huang, 2003; Lin & Lee, 1991). In these approaches, fuzzy systems are coded into a network structure, and parameters required in fuzzy systems become weights in the network. The backpropagation type of learning is then employed to modify those weights. Since being inspired by and very similar to the learning scheme in neural networks, such a kind of leaning is often referred to as neural-network-based fuzzy systems, adaptive network for fuzzy inference systems, neural fuzzy inference networks, or simply, neural fuzzy networks. In this research, the name, neural fuzzy networks, is used. Neural fuzzy networks are fuzzy systems being equipped with learning scheme often used for neural networks. They can have nice modeling capability in various applications (Jang, 1993; Su & Huang, 2003; Su & Chen, 2004; Lee & Teng, 2000; Su & Yang, 2002). In fact, due to the fulfillment of the minimum disturbance principle (Chen, 1998; Jang, 1993; Su & Chen, 2004; Su & Yang, 2002) in fuzzy systems, neural fuzzy systems are always claimed to have better modeling performance than neural networks do. Most of neural fuzzy networks use all rules of possible combinations of fuzzy labels of input variables. However, if all possible rules are used, the rule number will be extremely large and then the learning performance may seriously be degraded. In order to avoid huge sizes of rules, an approach, called the Self-cOnstructing Neural Fuzzy Inference Networks (**SONFIN**) is proposed in (Juang & Lin, 1998). In the approach, the rules are generated only when necessary. The detailed description can be found in (Juang & Lin, 1998; Chen, 1998).

In the system, the TSK type of fuzzy models is used to define fuzzy rules. Six layers as shown in Figure 2 are defined in the structure. The corresponding meanings of those layers are described as follows. First, the input layer is to simply transmit input data to the next layer. Layer A is to fuzzify the input data into membership degrees for fuzzy labels. Layer B is to define the premise part for fuzzy rules. For example, layer B is to specify "x_1 is A_1^i and x_2 is A_2^i and ... and x_m is A_m^i" for the i-th rule. Layer C is to define the consequence part for fuzzy rules. For the i-th rule, it is to define $y_i = p_{i0} + p_{i1}x_1 + p_{i2}x_2 + ... + p_{im}x_m$. Layer D is to compute the product of the output of layer C and the output of layer B for each rule in fulfilling the TSK fuzzy reasoning for one rule. Finally, the output layer is to compute the sum of the output of layer D. In that structure, layer A together with layer B characterize the behavior of the premise parts of fuzzy rules to obtain the firing strength of fuzzy rules. Layer C together with layer D characterize the behavior of the consequence parts to obtain the output of the network in the sense of the TSK fuzzy reasoning.

Figure 2. The structure of neural fuzzy networks used

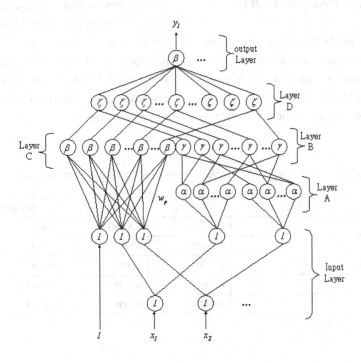

Basically, **SONFIN** is a neural fuzzy network being equipped with the capability of structure learning. **SONFIN** uses training patterns in the input space to generate fuzzy rules. For a new training pattern, it is to check whether it is in the existing rules by measuring the firing strengths of rules. When a new training pattern does not belong to any of the existing rules, then a new rule is generated. When a new rule is generated, the corresponding fuzzy labels are defined according to the first-nearest- neighbor heuristic (Juang & Lin, 1998). Two different ways of tuning parameters in the consequences of TSK fuzzy models can be found in the literature. They are the Recursive Least Square method (RLS) (Juang & Lin, 1998; Jang, 1993) and the traditional backpropagation (BP) learning algorithm (Chen, 1998; Su & Huang, 2003). From our early study (Chen, 1998), the performances of those two approaches are not significantly different. Since the input partition is very large in our study, the BP approach is employed to reduce the computational time.

STUDY OF FUSING APPROACHES FOR MULTI- STEP PREDICTION

Table 12 shows the prediction errors of using various approaches introduced in the above section. Here the used neural network is a simple 3-layer network with 15 hidden neurons. In fact, we have tried various types of network struc-

ture, the reported one have fair performance in all aspects. From the table, it is clearly evident that local prediction schemes usually outperform global prediction schemes in traditional one-step ahead prediction. But, when they are employed for multi-step prediction, local prediction schemes perform badly. It should be noted that the errors of using SONFIN for multi-step predictions are larger than those of using neural networks.

In the following, we shall propose several approaches that not only can have the advantages of local prediction schemes but also can have better prediction performance than global prediction schemes do. The basic idea is to fuse those two types of information so as to generate more accurate predictions. In our research, various fusion techniques are proposed and discussed. In this section, we shall discuss those approaches and present the corresponding prediction results. In this chapter, we proposed to integrate the local and global predictions for time series prediction to have a novel prediction approach. Since model free estimators are considered in our study, those predictions are integrated in a network structure. Thus, it is referred to as network-based fusion approaches. It can be expected that other structures of fusing data may involve requirement of knowledge of those data. Thus, in the chapter, network-based approached are discussed. Several ways of network-based fusing approaches are proposed and their performances are analyzed in this session.

Table 12. MSEs of using various prediction schemes in four different step predictions.

	1st-step	2nd-step	3rd-step	4th-step
Training errors of NN	0.00033	0.00090	0.0041	0.0068
Testing errors of NN	**0.00099**	**0.0024**	**0.0043**	**0.0071**
Training errors of SONFIN	0.00043	0.0015	0.0015	0.0042
Testing errors of SONFIN	**0.00093**	**0.0026**	**0.0047**	**0.0093**
Testing errors of FGM	**0.00076**	**0.0050**	**0.0134**	**0.0256**

Neural Network Based Residual Correction Approach

Even though MFGM has demonstrated good prediction performance for the 1st-step prediction as shown in (Su, *et al*, 2002), in this paper, we propose a neural network based residual correction approach, which can outperform MFGM in all aspects. The idea is to employ a neural network to serve the role of Markov transition matrices in the residual correction scheme. In MFGM, Markov transition matrices are to record the possibilities of state transition of the residual series. In this proposed approach, we employ a neural network to directly model the residual errors of FGM for all training patterns. In other words, the errors of FGM are modeled into a neural network and after training, the network is used to predict possible correcting amount in prediction.

Table 13 shows the training errors and the testing errors for various step predictions. It is clearly evident that not only network based approach can have much better prediction accuracy than MFGM has, but also the proposed approach can have fair prediction accuracies in multi-step prediction. However, it can be seen that in the 4th-step prediction, the testing error is larger than the error predicted by a neural network reported in Table 12. It is because such error correction schemes are to make prediction based on the result obtained from a local prediction scheme, FGM. As mentioned, local prediction schemes cannot have fair performance while used for multi-step prediction. Thus, it is natural to observe bad prediction performance while using error correction prediction schemes for multi-step predictions.

Global Based Neural Network Fusion

In view of the above results, we then attempt to include a local prediction into a global prediction scheme to see whether it can have better prediction accuracy for multi-step predictions. The idea is to make predictions mainly based on a global prediction scheme, but with the inclusion of local prediction information. In this subsection, a traditional backpropagation neural network is employed as the global prediction scheme.

In this study, we simply include a FGM result (local prediction information) as another input in the neural network. In the implementation, we noticed several questions arising in performing such a fusion approach in neural networks. First, in the conducted prediction experiment, there are 8 input data points acting as global information but only one input data point as local information. Since the learning algorithm for neural networks treats all data equally, if all input data are normalized into the same scale, for a given training pattern, its global information carries 8 times of effects on the output generation compared to the effects of the local information. This seems infeasible. Thus, in this study, we propose to multiply the local input data by 8 to increase its weighting effects on the output generation.

Secondly, it is easy to find that the local prediction information is less informative for the 4th step prediction than for the 1st step prediction. Thus, it is desired to give different weighting effects for the local prediction information in different step predictions. In order to realize such a difference, we propose to use different learning rates for the local prediction input and for the original

Table 13. MSEs of using the neural network based residual correction scheme in four different step predictions.

	1st-step	2nd-step	3rd-step	4th-step
Training errors of NN based residual correction	0.00028	0.0012	0.0020	0.0061
Testing errors of NN based residual correction	**0.00031**	**0.0014**	**0.0025**	**0.0093**

data points (global information inputs) in different step predictions. The idea of this approach is somehow like the concept of credit assignment learning (Smalz & Conrad, 1994; Su, *et al*, 2003). This concept is to distribute the learning effects proportional to the importance of the weights. Since a neural network is a parallel distribution processing approach and all kinds of information are mixed into the hidden layer, the learning rate can only be meaningfully different in the input layer. Here we only use different learning rates for weights associated with different inputs in the input layer according to their importance. It is easy to see that there is no definitely way of defining the ratio of learning rates between the global information and the local information. In our study, we propose to use their MSEs as shown in Table I when they are individually used for prediction to define the corresponding learning rate. The relative magnitudes of their MSEs in different step predictions are shown in Table 14.

The prediction results of using the proposed global neural network based fusion approach are shown in Table 15. It is clear that the performances are better than those in the global and those in the local approaches in all types of predictions. Especially, it can be found that the performance of those multi-step predictions are very nice. However, it can also be observed that the error of

the 1st step prediction is still larger than that of MFGM or of the neural network based residual correction approach. It is because this approach is a global prediction based approach.

Global Based SONFIN Fusion

The SONFIN is a model-free approach of which the structure is in terms of fuzzy rules and the training procedure is in terms of parameter learning. It should be noted that SONFIN is different from neural networks in that unlike recognition without definition in neural network learning (Kosko, 1992), SONFIN has already roughly defined its rule characteristics in terms of spatial relationships (Chen, 1998). In this subsection, we attempt to fuse information by using SONFIN in the place of neural networks as in B to see whether the fusion performance can be further improved.

Similar to the neural network fusion, in order to account for different weighting effects, we have adopted two modifications for this fusion approach. First, when a new rule is generated, the initial values of the consequence of the rule are set to be 1 for the FGM variable and 0 for the others to emphasis the FGM prediction initially. The second one the same as that in the above is to tune the learning constants according their corresponding MSE in the learning process.

Table 14. The relative magnitudes of errors for the FGM and for neural networks shown in Table 1

	1st-step	2nd-step	3rd-step	4th-step
Relative magnitude of FGM	0.5656	0.3253	0.2429	0.2165
Relative magnitude of NN	0.4344	0.6747	0.7571	0.7835

Table 15. MSEs of using the global neural network fusion scheme in four different step predictions

	1st-step	2nd-step	3rd-step	4th-step
Training errors of Global NN fusion	0.00055	0.0013	0.0024	0.0047
Testing errors of Global NN fusion	**0.00062**	**0.0015**	**0.0027**	**0.0052**

Table 16 shows the relative magnitudes of SONFIN and of FGM approaches. Those magnitudes are computed from the MSEs shown in Table 12. The performances of predicted by using the global SONFIN based fusion approach for different step predictions are listed in Table 17. It is evident that the SONFIN fusion approach indeed can have better performance for the 1st step prediction but gets worse in multi-step prediction due to the approach of emphasizing the local prediction information in the initial rule construction.

Kalman Filter Based Estimator

In the above, those approaches either use a local prediction scheme or use a global prediction as the backbone to predict the future. It is evident that those approaches have their limitations either in the 1st step prediction or in the 4th step prediction. In our research, we attempt to find another way of fusion approach that can have better performance both for the 1st step prediction and for the multi-step prediction.

Traditionally, a simple way of using different kinds of information is to "average" them or to fuse them. In our early work (Lin, 2000), we simply used a set of pre-determined weights to fuse the values obtained from a global prediction scheme and from a local prediction scheme. The results seemed to be nice. However, in that approach, those pre-determined weights are selected *ad hoc* and we do not think those weights can work well for other cases. A commonly used parameter estimator for data fusion is the Kalman filter (Su & Lee, 1992), which is a linear estimator and the weights are defined based on their variances. We shall briefly introduce the idea in the following.

In our implementation, the used local prediction scheme is FGM and the used global prediction scheme is a neural network. Let the value predicted by FGM be v_f and the value predicted by the neural network is v_n. Since the Kalman filter uses variances to calculate weights for fusing, we need to find ways of defining the variances for those predicted values. In our research, we propose to define the variance as the MSE of the prediction schemes. Then, the Kalman filter estimator can be written as (Su & Lee, 1992)

$$v_k = \frac{E_f^{-1}}{E_f^{-1} + E_n^{-1}} v_f + \frac{E_n^{-1}}{E_f^{-1} + E_n^{-1}} v_n \quad (17)$$

where E_f and E_n are the mean square errors of FGM and of the **neural network**, respectively, for the training data set.

Table 18 shows the MSE of using the Kalman filter estimator to fuse the predicted values of using FGM and of using neural networks. It can be found that the Kalman filter approach has demonstrated

Table 16. The relative magnitudes of errors for the FGM and for SONFIN shown in Table 1

	1st-step	2nd-step	3rd-step	4th-step
Relative magnitude of FGM	0.5482	0.3463	0.2614	0.2671
Relative magnitude of SONFIN	0.4518	0.6537	0.7386	0.7329

Table 17. MSEs of using the global SONFIN fusion scheme in four different step predictions

	1st-step	2nd-step	3rd-step	4th-step
Training errors of Global SONFIN fusion	0.00028	0.00083	0.0017	0.0026
Testing errors of Global SONFIN fusion	**0.00049**	**0.0025**	**0.0052**	**0.0150**

some good results, but the performance is not good enough, especial for cases of the 3rd step prediction and the 4th step prediction. It seems that a linear estimator is not generally suitable for **data fusion** of local and global prediction.

Network Based Estimator

In the above approach, in addition to the assumption of a linear estimator, it also needs to estimate the variances from training data. As can be expected, the performance is not good enough. In this paper, we propose to employ a **model free estimator** to take place of the **Kalman filter**. Here a **neural network** or **SONFIN** can be used here. Thus, this approach is referred to as a network based estimator.

In our implementation, the same case as used in the **Kalman filter**, we use FGM as the **local prediction scheme** and a **neural network** as the global prediction scheme. The fusion network is a **SONFIN**, which will be trained to fuse the predicted values obtained by using **neural network**s and by using FGM model. The performance of using this approach is shown in Table 19. It is clearly evident that this approach not only can have the best **multi-step prediction** among those used approaches, but also the error of the 1st step prediction is also slightly less than that of using networked based residual correction scheme

in this example. In other words, this approach can outperform all other approaches used in all predictions.

CONCLUSION

Various prediction methods and approaches are considered in our studies. Usually, local prediction is more accurate than global prediction while being used for predicting the most recent information, which is referred to as the one-step ahead prediction. In the literature, an approach, c (MFGM) has been proposed to incorporate global information based on local prediction schemes and has been shown to have nice prediction accuracy for one-step ahead prediction. However, when multi-step prediction is considered, MFGM may result in very bad prediction performance. In this study, various fusing methods for combining global and local prediction results are proposed. First, we proposed to use a neural network to take place of Markov transition matrices. The results of using this network based approach indeed are much better than those of using MFGM. However, the performance of multi-step prediction is still not good due to the use of a local prediction scheme as the backbone. We then used a global prediction scheme (neural network or SONFIN) as the backbone and proposed ways of including

Table 18 MSEs of using the Kalman Filter fusion scheme in four different step predictions.

	1st-step	2nd-step	3rd-step	4th-step
Testing errors of KF fusion	0.00049	0.0019	0.0054	0.0089

Table 19 MSEs of using the network based fusion scheme in four different step predictions.

	1st-step	2nd-step	3rd-step	4th-step
Training errors of networked based Fusion	0.00030	0.00088	0.0021	0.0043
Testing errors of networked based Fusion	0.00030	0.00088	0.0024	0.0050

local prediction information. The results shown this approach indeed can have very nice prediction performance in multi-step prediction, but they may not get nice prediction accuracy for one-step ahead prediction. Finally, we considered a simple fusion idea. A commonly used fusion idea is the Kalman filter, which assumes a linear estimator for the fusion function. Its performance indeed demonstrated some advantages, but is not good enough. In this paper, we proposed to use SONFIN to model the fusing relationship from the training data. The prediction results of using this approach are very nice. They are the best of those used approaches for all steps of predictions.

REFERENCES

Abe, H., & Yamaguchi, T. (2005). Implementing an integrated time-series data mining environment – a case study of medical KDD on chronic hepatitis. In *Proceedings of the 1st International Conference on Complex Medical Engineering (CME2005)*.

Battiti, R. (1992). First- and Second-order methods for learning: between steepest descent and Newton's method. *Neural Computation, 4*, 141–166. doi:10.1162/neco.1992.4.2.141

Bernasconi, J. (1990). Learning in neural networks. In R. Lima, R. Streit & R. Vilela Mendes (Eds.), *Dynamics and Stochastic Processes: Theory and Applications*, (LNCS Vol. 355, pp. 42-54). Berlin: Springer.

Bingqian, L. (1990). The grey modelling for central symmetry sequence. *The Journal of Grey System, 2*(2), 95–103.

Cabrera, J. B. D., & Narendra, K. S. (1999). Issues in the application of neural networks for tracking based on inverse control. *IEEE Transactions on Automatic Control, 44*(11), 2007–2027. doi:10.1109/9.802910

Castillo, P. A., Carpio, J., Merelo, J. J., Prieto, A., Rivas, V., & Romero, G. (2000). Evolving multilayer perceptions. *Neural Processing Letters, 12*(2), 115–128. doi:10.1023/A:1009684907680

Castillo, P. A., Merelo, J. J., González, J., Prieto, A., Rivas, V., & Romero, G. (1996). G-Prop-III: Global optimization of multilayer perceptions using an evolutionary algorithm. *Proc. Of the Congress on Evolutionary Computation, 1*, 942-947.

Chakrabarti, K., Keogh, E. J., Pazzani, M., & Mehrotra, S. (2002). Locally adaptive dimensionality reduction for indexing large time series databases. *ACM Transactions on Database Systems, 27*(2), 188–228. doi:10.1145/568518.568520

Chen, C. K., & Tien, T. L. (1997). The indirect measurement of tensile strength by the deterministic grey dynamic model DGDM (1,1,1). *International Journal of Systems Science, 28*(7), 683–690. doi:10.1080/00207729708929428

Chen, D. S., & Jain, R. C. (1994). A robust backpropagation learning algorithm for function approximation. *IEEE Transactions on Neural Networks, 5*(3), 467–479. doi:10.1109/72.286917

Chen, K. Y. (1998). *On the Study of the Learning Performance for Neural Networks and Neural Fuzzy Networks*. Master Thesis, Dept. of Electrical Eng., NTUST, Taiwan, R.O.C.

Chuang, C. C., Su, S. F., & Chen, S. S. (2001). Robust TSK fuzzy modeling for function approximation with outliers. *IEEE transactions on Fuzzy Systems, 9*(6), 810–821. doi:10.1109/91.971730

Chuang, C. C., Su, S. F., & Hsiao, C. C. (2000). The annealing robust backpropagation (ARBP) learning algorithm. *IEEE Transactions on Neural Networks, 11*(5), 1067–1077. doi:10.1109/72.870040

Chuang, C. C., Su, S. F., Jeng, J. T., & Hsiao, C. C. (2002). Robust support vector regression networks for function approximation with outliers. *IEEE Transactions on Neural Networks, 13*(6), 1322–1330. doi:10.1109/TNN.2002.804227

Cichocki, A., & Unbehauen, R. (1993). *Neural Networks for Optimization and Signal Processing.* New York: John Wiley & Sons.

Cichocki, A., & Unbehauen, R. (1993). *Neural Networks for Optimization and Signal Processing.* Hoboken, NJ: John Wiley & Sons.

Das, G., Lin, K., Mannila, H., Renganathan, G., & Smyth, P. (1998). Rule discovery from time series. In *Proceedings of the 4th International Conference on Knowledge Discovery and Data Mining,* (pp. 16–22).

Deng, J. L. (1982). Control problem of grey system. *Systems & Control Letters, 5,* 288–294.

Deng, J. L. (1987). *The Essential Methods of Grey Systems.* Wuhan, China: Huazhong University of Science & Technology Press.

Fahlman, S. E., & Lebiere, C. (1991). *The cascade-correlation learning architecture* (Tech. Rep. *CMU-CS-90-100*). Pittsburgh, PA: Carnegie Mellon University, Dept. of CS.

Hirose, Y., Yamashita, K., & Hijiya, S. (1991). Back-propagation algorithm which varies the number of hidden units. *Neural Networks, 4,* 61–66. doi:10.1016/0893-6080(91)90032-Z

Hornik, K., Stinchcommbe, M., & White, H. (1989). Multilayer feedforward networks are universal approximators. *Neural Networks, 2,* 359–366. doi:10.1016/0893-6080(89)90020-8

Hsia, T. C. (1979). *System Identification: Least Square Method.* Davis, CA: University of California, at Davis.

Hsu, Y. T., Cheng, C. S., & Wu, C. C. (1997). Reliability Evaluations based on Grey Models. *The Journal of Grey System, 9*(1), 25–39.

Hsu, Y. T., Lin, C. B., Mar, S. C., & Su, S. F. (1998). High noise vehicle plate recognition using grey system. *The Journal of Grey System, 10*(3), 193–208.

Huber, P. J. (1981). *Robust Statistics.* New York: John Wiley.

Hwang, C. L. (1999). Neural-network-based variable structure control of electrohydraulic servosystems subject to huge uncertainties without persistent excitation. *IEEE/ASME Transactions on Mechatronics, 4*(1), 50–59. doi:10.1109/3516.752084

Indyk, P., Koudas, N., & Muthukrishnan, S. (2000). Identifying representative trends in massive time series data sets using sketches. In *Proceedings of the 26th International Conference on Very Large Data Bases,* (pp. 363–372).

Jacobs, R. A. (1988). Increased rates of convergence through learning rate adaptation. *Neural Networks, 1,* 295–307. doi:10.1016/0893-6080(88)90003-2

Jang, J. S. R. (1993). Adaptive-network-based fuzzy inference systems. *IEEE Transactions on Systems, Man, and Cybernetics, 23*(3), 665–685. doi:10.1109/21.256541

Jang, J. S. R., Sun, C. T., & Mizutani, E. (1997). *Neuro-Fuzzy and Soft Computing: A Computational Approach to Learning and Machine Intelligence.* Upper Saddle River, NJ: Prentice-Hall.

Juang, C. F., & Lin, C. T. (1998). An on-line self-constructing neural fuzzy inference network and its applications. *IEEE transactions on Fuzzy Systems, 6*(1), 12–32. doi:10.1109/91.660805

Keogh, E. J. (2008). Indexing and mining time series data, *Encyclopedia of GIS 2008,* (pp. 493-497).

Keogh, E. J., Lonardi, S., & Chiu, W. (2002). Finding surprising patterns in a time series database in linear time and space. In *The 8th ACM SIGKDD International Conference on Knowledge Discovery and Data Mining*, (pp. 550–556).

Keogh, E. J., & Pazzani, M. (1998). An enhanced representation of time series which allows fast and accurate classification, clustering and relevance feedback. In *Proceedings of the 4th International Conference on Knowledge Discovery and Data Mining*, (pp. 239–241).

Kosko, B. (1992). *Fuzzy systems as universal approximators.* Paper presented at Proc. IEEE Int'l Conf. On Fuzzy Systems.

Kosko, B. (1992). *Neural Networks and Fuzzy Systems, A Dynamical Systems Approach to Machine Intelligence.* Upper Saddle River, NJ: Prentice-Hall.

Lee, C. H., & Teng, C. C. (2000). Identification and control of dynamic systems using recurrent fuzzy neural network. *IEEE transactions on Fuzzy Systems, 8*(4), 349–366. doi:10.1109/91.868943

Leung, S. H., Luk, A., & Ng, S. C. (1994). Fast convergent genetic-type search for multi-layered network. *IEICE Trans. Fundamentals . E (Norwalk, Conn.), 77-A*(9), 1484–1492.

Li, S. H. (2002). *Neural Network Based Fusion of Global and Local Information in Predicting Time Series.* Master Thesis, Dept. of Electrical Eng., NTUST, Taiwan, R.O.C.

Liano, K. (1996). Robust error measure for supervised neural network learning with outliers. *IEEE Transactions on Neural Networks, 7*(1), 246–250. doi:10.1109/72.478411

Lin, C. B. (2000). *Grey System Applications and Its Utilization in Prediction.* Ph.D Dissertation, Department of Electrical Engineering, National Taiwan University of Science and Technology, Taiwan, R.O.C.

Lin, C. B., Su, S. F., & Hsu, Y. T. (2001). High precision forecast using grey models. *International Journal of Systems Science, 32*(5), 609–619. doi:10.1080/002077201300155791

Lin, C. T., & Lee, C. S. G. (1991). Neural-network-based fuzzy logic control and decision systems. *IEEE Transactions on Computers, 40*(12), 1320–1336. doi:10.1109/12.106218

Lin, C. T., & Lee, C. S. G. (1996). *Neural Fuzzy Systems: A Neural Fuzzy Synergism to Intelligent Systems.* Upper Saddle River, NJ: Prentice Hall.

Lin, F. J., Hwang, W. J., & Wai, R. J. (1999). Supervisory fuzzy neural network control system for tracking periodic inputs. *IEEE transactions on Fuzzy Systems, 7*(1), 41–52. doi:10.1109/91.746304

Meyer, S. C. (2005). Analysis of base flow trends in urban streams, northeastern Illinois, USA. *Hydrogeology Journal, 13*, 871–885. doi:10.1007/s10040-004-0383-8

Ng, S. C., Leung, S. H., & Luk, A. (1996). Evolution of connection weights combined with local search for multi-layered neural networks. *IEEE*, 726–731.

Pedrycz, W. (1986). Structured fuzzy models. *Cybernetics and Systems, 16*, 103–117. doi:10.1080/01969728508927757

Rovithakis, G. A., Gaganis, V. I., Perrakis, S. E., & Christodoulou, M. A. (1999). Real-time control of manufacturing cells using dynamic neural networks. *Automatica, 35*(1), 139–149. doi:10.1016/S0005-1098(98)00139-3

Rumelhart, D. E., Hinton, G. E., & Williams, R. J. (1986). *Learning internal* representations by error propagation. *Parallel Distribution Processing, 1*, 318–362.

Smalz, R., & Conrad, M. (1994). Combining evolution with credit apportionment: A new learning algorithm for neural nets. *Neural Networks, 7*(2), 341–351. doi:10.1016/0893-6080(94)90028-0

Su, S. F., & Chen, K. Y. (2004). Fuzzy hierarchical data fusion networks for terrain location identification problems. *IEEE Transactions on Systems, Man, and Cybernetics. Part B, Cybernetics, 34*(1), 731–739. doi:10.1109/TSMCB.2003.811292

Su, S. F., & Chen, K. Y. (2005). Conceptual discussions and benchmark comparison for neural networks and fuzzy systems. *Differential Equations and Dynamical Systems., 13*(1), 35–61.

Su, S. F., & Huang, S. R. (2003). Applications of model-free estimators to the stock market with the use of technical indicators and non-deterministic features. *Journal of the Chinese Institute of Engineers, 26*(1), 21–36.

Su, S. F., & Lee, C. S. G. (1992). Uncertainty manipulation and propagation and verification of applicability of actions in assembly tasks. *IEEE Transactions on Systems, Man, and Cybernetics, 22*(6), 1376–1389. doi:10.1109/21.199463

Su, S. F., Lin, C. B., & Hsu, Y. T. (2002). A high precision global prediction approach based on local prediction approaches. *IEEE Trans. on Systems, Man, and Cybernetics . Part C: Applications and Reviews, 32*(4), 416–425.

Su, S. F., Tao, T., & Hung, T. H. (2003). Credit assigned CMAC and its application to online learning robust controllers. *IEEE Trans. on Systems, Man, and Cybernetics . Part B: Cybernetics, 33*(2), 202–213.

Su, S. F., & Yang, F. P. (2002). On the dynamical modeling with neural fuzzy networks. *IEEE Transactions on Neural Networks, 13*(6), 1548–1553. doi:10.1109/TNN.2002.804313

Takashima, S. (1989). *100 Examples of Fuzzy Theory Application mostly in Japan*. Trigger.

Tan, C. L., & Chang, S. P. (1996). Residual correction method of Fourier series to GM(1,1) model. *1996 First National Conference on Grey Theory and Applications*, (pp. 93-101).

Tan, C. L., & Lu, B. F. (1996). Grey Markov chain forecasting model. *1996 First National Conference on Grey Theory and Applications*, (pp. 157-162).

Tanaka, K., & Sano, M. (1994). A Robust Stabilization Problem of Fuzzy Control Systems and Its Application to Backing up Control of a Truck-Tailer. *IEEE transactions on Fuzzy Systems, 2*(2), 1–14. doi:10.1109/91.277961

Wang, L. X. (1992). *Fuzzy systems are universal approximators*. Paper presented at Proc. IEEE Int'l Conf. On Fuzzy Systems.

Wang, L. X., & Mendel, J. M. (1992). Generating fuzzy rules by learning from examples. *IEEE Transactions on Systems, Man, and Cybernetics, 22*(6), 1414–1427. doi:10.1109/21.199466

Xi, X., Keogh, E. J., Shelton, C. R., Li, W., & Ratanamahatana, C. A. (2006). Fast time series classification using numerosity reduction. In *Proceedings of the 23rd International Conference on Machine Learning, (ICML 2006)*, (pp. 1033–1040).

Yager, R. R., & Filev, D. P. (1994). *Essentials of Fuzzy Modeling and Control*. Hoboken, NJ: John Wiley & Sons.

Zadeh, L. (1973). Outline of a new approach to the analysis of complex systems and decision process. *IEEE Transactions on Systems, Man, and Cybernetics, 14*(1), 28–44.

Chapter 10
Weights Direct Determination of Feedforward Neural Networks without Iterative BP–Training

Yunong Zhang
Sun Yat-Sen University (SYSU), China

Ning Tan
Sun Yat-Sen University (SYSU), China

ABSTRACT

Artificial neural networks (ANN), especially with error back-propagation (BP) training algorithms, have been widely investigated and applied in various science and engineering fields. However, the BP algorithms are essentially gradient-based iterative methods, which adjust the neural-network weights to bring the network input/output behavior into a desired mapping by taking a gradient-based descent direction. This kind of iterative neural-network (NN) methods has shown some inherent weaknesses, such as, 1) the possibility of being trapped into local minima, 2) the difficulty in choosing appropriate learning rates, and 3) the inability to design the optimal or smallest NN-structure. To resolve such weaknesses of BP neural networks, we have asked ourselves a special question: Could neural-network weights be determined directly without iterative BP-training? The answer appears to be YES, which is demonstrated in this chapter with three positive but different examples. In other words, a new type of artificial neural networks with linearly-independent or orthogonal activation functions, is being presented, analyzed, simulated and verified by us, of which the neural-network weights and structure could be decided directly and more deterministically as well (in comparison with usual conventional BP neural networks).

INTRODUCTION

Benefiting from parallel-processing nature, distributed storage, self-adaptive and self-learning abilities, artificial neural networks (ANN) have been investigated and applied widely in many scientific, engineering and practical fields, such as, classification and diagnosis (Hong & Tseng, 1991; Jia & Chong, 1995; Sadeghi, 2000; Wang & Li, 1991), image and signal processing (Steriti & Fiddy, 1993), control system design (Zhang & Wang, 2001, 2002), equations solving (Zhang, Jiang & Wang, 2002; Zhang & Ge, 2005; Zhang

DOI: 10.4018/978-1-61520-757-2.ch010

& Chen, 2008), robot inverse kinematics (Zhang, Ge & Lee, 2004), regression and identification (Zhang *et al*, 2008).

As we may realize, the feedforward neural network (FNN) based on the error back-propagation (BP) training algorithm or its variants is one of the most popular and important neural-network (NN) models, which has been involved in many theoretical analyses and real-world applications (Hong & Tseng, 1991; Jia & Chong, 1995; Rumelhart, McClelland & PDP Research Group 1986; Wang & Li, 1991; Yu, Chen & Cheng, 1993; Zhang *et al*, 2008). In particular, BP neural networks proposed in mid 1980s (or even earlier, in 1974) is a kind of multilayer feedforward neural network (Rumelhart, McClelland & PDP Research Group 1986; Zhang *et al*, 2008; Zhou & Kang, 2005), of which the error back-propagation algorithm could be summarized simply as

$$
\begin{aligned}
w(k+1) &= w(k) + \Delta w(k) \\
&= w(k) - \eta (\partial E \,/\, \partial w)\big|_{w=w(k)}
\end{aligned}
\tag{1}
$$

where w denotes a vector or matrix of neural weights (and/or thresholds), $k=0, 1, 2, \ldots$ denotes the iteration number during the training procedure, $\Delta w(k)$ denotes the weights-updating value at the kth iteration of the training procedure with η denoting the learning rate (or termed, learning step-size) which should be small enough, and finally we use E to denote the error function that monitors and control such a BP-training procedure.

The above conventional BP neural network and algorithm are essentially a gradient-descent based error-minimization method, which adjusts the neural-network weights (and/or thresholds) to bring the neural-network input/output behavior into a desired mapping as of some specific application task or environment. For better performance (e.g., in terms of the training efficiency and the generalization accuracy), many improved BP algorithms have been proposed since mid 1980s;

see Corwin, Logar & Oldham (1994), Goodman & Zeng (1994), Hong & Tseng (1991), Jenkins (2006), Jia & Chong (1995), Pai (2004), Ren & Zhou (2008), Yu, Chen & Cheng (1993), Zhang, Lin & Tang (2008), Zhang *et al* (2008), Zhou & Kang (2005) and the references therein. Generally speaking, there are two widely-adopted types of improvements. On one hand, BP algorithms could be improved based on standard gradient-descent method (e.g., introducing momentum). On the other hand, numerical minimization techniques could be employed for network training. It is worth pointing out that people usually pay more attention to the iterative learning procedure and algorithms so as to ameliorate the performance of such BP neural networks. However, as researchers (including us) realize and experience quite frequently, the inherent weaknesses of BP-type neural networks are still there! Specifically, BP-type neural networks appear to have the following weaknesses (Hong & Tseng, 1991; Jenkins, 2006; Jia & Chong, 1995; Lippmann, 1987; Looney, 1996; Miller, Arguello & Greenwood, 2004; Wen *et al*, 2000; Wilson & Martinez, 2001; Yeung & Zeng, 2002; Yu, Chen & Cheng, 1993; Yu & Chen, 1995; Zhang, 1999; Zhang *et al*, 2008; Zhou & Kang, 2005):

1) possibility of being trapped into some local minima,
2) difficulty in choosing appropriate learning rates, and
3) inability to design the optimal or smallest NN-structure in a deterministic way.

Since the late 1990s (e.g., Zhang, 1999, 2002), we have asked ourselves the question: Could the above NN problem be solved radically? Based on our ten-year research experience on the neural network topic, as reported here in this chapter, we are now trying to resolve these neural-network weaknesses (i.e., local minima, slow convergence of training, and network-structure uncertainty) while maximizing the neural-network performance, by means of using linearlyindependent or orthogonal activation functions. In addition, different from others' algorithmic improvements on the training procedure, our way of the problem solving exploits some elegant structure-design, parameter-setting, and pseudoinverse-based techniques. These finally lead to our proposed weights-direct-determination and structure-determination method for the feedforward neural networks, which perform in a more efficient, more accurate and more deterministic way.

The remainder of this chapter is thus organized as follows. The section of BACKGROUND provides the related BP discussion and views, including the usage of MATLAB Neural Network Toolbox (Demuth, Beale & Hagan, 2007; Zhou & Kang, 2005) for general comparative purposes as well as in the context of this chapter. After that, the ensuing three sections present the main contents of this chapter; that is, a power-activation feedforward neural network, a Laguerre-orthogonal-basis feedforward neural network, and a Gegenbauer-orthogonal-basis feedforward neural network, of which the neural-network weights and structure all could be determined directly and deterministically. In the section of FUTURE TRENDS, we will discuss future and emerging trends of the neural-network research and its usage in data mining, with several future research opportunities suggested then. Final remarks are given in the conclusion section. Simply put, by conducting this research, we are happy to show that neural-network weights could be determined directly just in one step (i.e., without an iterative BP-training procedure) if linearly-independent and/or orthogonal activation functions are employed, and that so could the neural-network structure be decided more deterministically.

BACKGROUND

In conventional definitions and descriptions (Demuth, Beale & Hagan, 2007; Hong & Tseng,

1991; Jia & Chong, 1995; Rumelhart, McClelland & PDP Research Group, 1986; Wang & Li, 1991; Yu, Chen & Cheng, 1993; Zhang, 1999; Zhou & Kang, 2005), artificial neural networks, consisting of many simple processing-elements (or termed, neurons), could operate in parallel and are capable of handling clean and/or noisy data, fitting known or unknown target functions and recognizing patterns by adjusting the values of the connecting weights between neurons. In addition, it has been thought traditionally by most researchers that the marvelous generalization ability of artificial neural networks could be achieved only by repetitive training and iterative adjusting until particular inputs lead to the specific target outputs.

Figure 1 shows the above-mentioned situation and procedure, where the neural network is trained based on the comparison between the neural-network output and the target-system output (until the neural-network output finally matches the target-system output). Typically, a gradient-based error-minimization training algorithm could be used to adjust the weights, and there are many proofs, theoretically and/or practically, showing that fairly complex neural networks could fit any target function or system with a finite number of discontinuity points.

Moreover, as we know, in the conventional construction of the neural network (e.g., in Figure 1), there are many artificial neurons used of the same kind, with their mathematical model inspired somewhat by biological neurons and nervous systems. For completeness and readability, a simple artificial neuron is shown in Figure 2, where the neuron usually takes in multiple inputs (denoted here as $s_1, s_2, \cdots, s_p$) multiplied correspondingly by the weights (denoted here as $v_1, v_2, \cdots, v_p$), in addition to the threshold effect of neuron bias during such a weighted input-signal summation. Note that, in Figure 2, the activation function (or termed, transfer function) used in BP neural networks is usually log-sigmoid function, tan-sigmoid function and/or linear function, which is, however

Figure 1. Block diagram about conventional BP neural-network training procedure

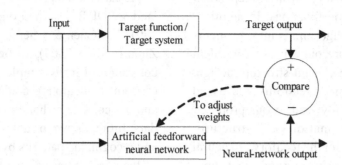

(being a weakness in our eyes), usually of the same kind of activation functions used in BP networks or used in one layer of the BP networks.

With a number of artificial neurons connected, a feedforward neural network could then be constructed. For example, as of our interest in this chapter, a single-input-single-output (SISO) feedforward BP neural network is demonstrated in Figure 3 for illustrative and comparative purposes (which is to be compared in the ensuing sections with our proposed weights-directly-determined neural-network models). In the figure, the input layer has one neuron (using a linear activation function), the hidden layer has *n* neurons (using sigmoid activation functions), and the output layer has one neuron (using a linear activation function).

After the neural network is constructed (e.g., as in Figure 3), an important issue for us is to endow it with the marvelous approximation, generalization and prediction abilities. The usual way to achieve so is by means of the iterative/ repetitive BP training procedure. That is, the neural network can be trained for function approximation, system identification or pattern classification by iteratively adjusting the weights and biases of the neural network for the sake of minimizing the network-output error. According to the error's definition, there are conventionally two ways of implementing the training algorithm: incremental-processing mode (which corresponds to the network-output error for an individual sample pair) or batch-processing mode (which corresponds to the network-output error for all sample pairs, and is adopted in our research often). Besides, as we mentioned previously, most BP training algorithms belong to the gradient-based methods, which perform the weights-adjusting

Figure 2. A simple artificial neuron with an activation function usually of the same kind used in conventional feedforward neural networks and/or of the same kind used in one layer of neurons

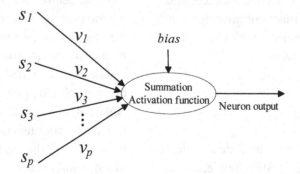

Figure 3. A single-input-single-output feedforward BP neural network with hidden-layer neurons activated by sigmoid activation functions I(·) which are of the same kind throughout the layer

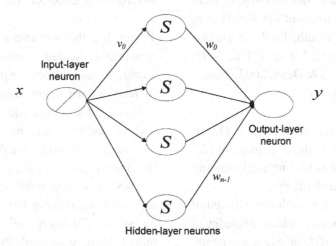

computation backward from the output layer of the neural network to hidden layer and then back to the input layer. There are many variations of the BP algorithm with its basic form depicted in Equation (1). In the MATLAB Neural Network Toolbox (Demuth, Beale & Hagan, 2007; Zhou & Kang, 2005; and the references therein), the BP training algorithms improved from the above standard gradient-descent method include

1) a batch gradient-descent algorithm with momentum (MATLAB routine *traingdm*),
2) variable-learning-rate algorithms (MATLAB routines *traingda* and *traingdx*), and
3) a resilient back-propagation algorithm (MATLAB routine *trainrp*).

In addition, the BP training algorithms more related to numerical optimization techniques include

1) conjugate-gradient algorithms (routines *traincgf*, *traincgp*, *traincgb* and *trainscg*),
2) quasi-Newton BFGS algorithm (MATLAB routine *trainbfg*) with the standard form of Newton's method as
$$w(k+1) = w(k) - H^{-1}(k) * (\partial E / \partial w)\big|_{w=w(k)}$$

where $H(k)$ denotes the Hessian matrix (i.e., the second-order derivative) of the error function $E(w)$ at the kth iteration of the BP training procedure [see also Leithead & Zhang (2007)], and

3) Levenberg-Marquardt algorithm (MATLAB routine *trainlm*) using the approximation to the aforementioned Hessian matrix and using the following Newton-like update:

$$w(k+1) = w(k) - \left(J^T(k)J(k) + \mu I\right)^{-1}$$
$$* (\partial E / \partial w)\big|_{w=w(k)} \tag{2}$$

where $J(k)$ is the Jacobian matrix (i.e., the first-order derivative) of the error function at the kth iteration of the BP training procedure (with μ having an appropriate value).

From the above descriptions about BP neurons and neural networks, a summary about their current limitations and issues is thus provided below (at the end of this section), which is consistent with the brief discussions presented in the previous sections (i.e., at the ABSTRACT and INTRODUCTION parts). The multiple-layer feedforward neural networks are, theoretically, capable of performing linear and nonlinear computations in parallel, and capable of approximating any reasonable target function, pattern and/or system arbitrarily well. However, it is evident to point out that (Chen, Wang & Lin, 2002; Demuth, Beale & Hagan, 2007; Gao & Cong, 2001; Liang & Tso, 2002; Pu, Sun & Zhao, 2006; Su & Deng, 2003; Zhang, 1999; Zhou & Kang, 2005):

1) picking the learning rate η [e.g., in (1)] or the conditioning parameter μ [e.g., in (2)] for a nonlinear-BP-neural-network training procedure is a real challenge;

2) the error surface of a nonlinear BP neural network is quite complex with multiple (even an infinite number of) local minima existing, which may trap the neural-network system, algorithm and users into one of them, thus generating a less correct solution;

3) with an iterative-training nature, the gradient-descent and its variant algorithms are generally slow (i.e., time-consuming), which may take a few days, hours or minutes while generate a less-accurate solution (e.g., with a precision usually worse than 10^{-8}); and that,

4) BP neural networks are quite sensitive to the number of hidden-layer neurons, which is usually hard to decide during a dynamic iterative-training procedure: pruning a neuron (or having fewer neurons) may lead to the occurrence of a larger output error, whereas adding a neuron (or having more neurons) may lead to an over-fitting phenomenon (in addition to a larger computational load and hardware complexity).

POWER-ACTIVATION NN WITH WEIGHTS DIRECTLY DETERMINED

To resolve the weaknesses of the BP neural networks presented in previous sections, in the ensuing three sections we propose a special type of feedforward neural networks, of which the weights and structure could be decided directly and automatically, in a more deterministic way.

The first feedforward-neural-network of this kind is a power-activation neural network (PANN) presented in this section. Different from the usual algorithmic BP-improvements, based on polynomial interpolation and approximation theory (Mathews & Fink, 2004; Mo & Liu, 2003; Zhang & Wang, 2001), we can construct a simple power-activation feed-forward neural network as shown in Figure 4. Specifically speaking, the hidden-layer neurons of the neural network are activated by a group of order-increasing power functions (Zhang & Wang, 2001; Zhang & Ge, 2005; Zhang et al, 2008), while the neurons of input- and output-layers employ linear activationfunctions. In addition, the weights between the input-layer and hidden-layer neurons and all the thresholds of neurons could be fixed to be 1 and 0 respectively, which are shown in Figure 4 clearly. Even so, it could be theoretically proved that this neural-network model is able to learn the given data samples and approximate the unknown target function effectively. Besides, for such approximation ability, the weights connecting hidden-layer to output-layer neurons should be obtained either by means of conventional BP-type training algorithms or by the proposed weights-direct-determination (WDD) method (actually, a pseudoinverse-based method). The WDD method could not only obtain the neural-network weights just in one step which avoids the usually-lengthy BP iterative-training procedure, but also achieve the highest accuracy of approximation in the least squares sense.

PANN Model Description & Theoretical Basis

Now let us come to the details of the power-activation neural network and algorithms. As shown in Figure 4, we could introduce and construct a power-activation feed-forward neural network, of which the input-layer has one neuron using linear activation function $f(x)=x$. The hidden-layer has n neurons which employ a group of order-increasing power functions x^j, $j= 0,1,2,\cdots,n\text{-}1$ (in other words, the $(j+1)$th hidden-layer neuron adopts x^j as its activation function). It is also worth mentioning here that all thresholds of the neural-network are set to be zero, which

further simplifies the neural-network structure and possible hardware-implementation. This power-activation feed-forward neural network can still be considered as a type of BP neural networks, so it could make use of error back-propagation algorithm to be its training rule.

The power-activation feed-forward neural network could be applied to approximating the unknown target function or system $\phi(x)$, which appears frequently in practical problems. Here, x and $\phi(x)$ denote the function's input and output, respectively. In general, the target function $\phi(x)$ is assumed unknown and we could only get a series of functional values $\gamma i=_{\phi}(xi)_c$ corresponding to input $xi\ t_a$ ken from an interval of interest, $[a,b]\subseteq R$. That is, a training-sample dataset $\{(xi,\gamma_i),\ _i=1,2,\ldots,m\}$ can be defined and given in Table 1.

After constructing the neural network (actually before that), we could present a simple theoretical analysis on the approximation ability of the power-

Figure 4. A simple power-activation feedforward neural network with hidden-layer neurons activated by a group of order-increasing power functions which are linearly independent

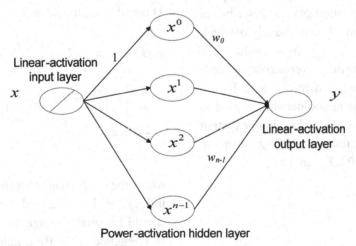

Table 1. Data samples of unknown target function $\gamma = \phi(x)$

Sample-pair input x	X_1	X_2	X_3	...	X_{m-1}	x_m
Sample-pair output $\phi(x)$	γ_1	γ_2	γ_3	...	γ_{m-1}	γ_m

activated feed-forward neural network. Based on the polynomial interpolation and approximation theory (Mathews & Fink, 2004; Mo & Liu, 2003), we could always construct a polynomial function $\phi(x)$ to interpolate and/or approximate the unknown function $\phi(x)$. For this approximation ability, we have the following definition and theorem (Lin, 2007; Zhang et al, 2008).

Definition 1 (Lin*early-Independent Polynomial Approximation*). Assume that, $\phi j(x) \in C[a,b]$ $j=0,1,2,...,n-1$ (in other words, function $\phi(x)$ and every function $\phi j(x)$ of functional sequence $\{\varphi_j(x)\}_{j=0}^{n-1}$ are continuous on closed interval $[a,b]$). Assume that $\{\varphi_j(x)\}_{j=0}^{n-1}$ is a linearly-independent functional sequence on interval $[a,b]$. For polynomial function $\varphi(x) = \sum_{j=0}^{n-1} w_j \varphi_j(x)$ we can minimize $\int_a^b \left(\phi(x) - \varphi(x) \right)^2 dx$ over a group of coefficients $w0, w1, ..., wn-1$. In this sense, polynomial $\phi(x)$ is termed the least-squares approximation (LSA) of unknown target function $\phi(x)$ on the interval of our interest, $[a,b]$.

Theorem 1 (LSA *Existence and Uniqueness*). For unknown target function $\phi(x) \in C[a,b]$, its least-squares approximation $\phi(x)$ (as described in the above definition) could exist uniquely, of which the coefficients $w0, w1, ..., w_n-1$ are solvable.

Now, let us return to the power-activation feed-forward neural network constructed as in Figure 4. Note that, when the neural network is used to approximate unknown target function or system $\phi(x)$, its input-output relation can be given as (in terms of $\phi j(x)=x_j$, $j=0,1,2,...,n-1$):

$$y = \varphi(x) = w_0 x^0 + w_1 x^1 + w_2 x^2 + \cdots + w_{n-1} x^{n-1} \tag{3}$$

which is exactly the least-squares approximation to $\phi(x)$ as described and guaranteed in the above definition and Theorem 1. The approximation ability of the proposed power-activation feed-forward neural network is thus ensured.

PANN Weights-Updating Formulas

For the power-activation feed-forward neural network as shown in Figure 4, its hidden-layer has n neurons, and the weights between hidden-layer and output-layer neurons are defined as wj, j=$0,1,\cdots$,n-1. Then, the neural-network relation between input x and output y could be described as in equation (3). Taking $(x_i, \gamma_i) \mid_{i=1}^m$ as the training-sample pair and defining the batch-processing error (BPE) function as

$$E = \frac{1}{2} \sum_{i=1}^m \left(\gamma_i - \sum_{p=0}^{n-1} w_p x_i^p \right)^2,$$

we could then have the following theorems about the weights-updating formula of the power-activation feed-forward neural network (Zhang *et al*, 2008).

Theorem 2 (*Elementwise Update*). Based on the negative-gradient method, the BP weights-updating formula for the power-activation feed-forward neural network (as established in Figure 4) could be designed as

$$w_j(k+1) = w_j(k) - \eta \frac{\partial E}{\partial w_j} = w_j(k)$$
$$-\eta \sum_{i=1}^m \left(x_i^j \left(\sum_{p=0}^{n-1} w_p(k) x_i^p - \gamma_i \right) \right),$$
$$j = 0, 1, 2, ..., n-1$$

where the iteration number (or to say, the iteration index) $k=0,1,2,3,...$, and the learning rate $\eta>0$ should be small enough so as to guarantee the convergence of the BP training procedure.

Proof. It follows from the above definition of error function E that the partial derivative

$$\frac{\partial E}{\partial w_j} = \sum_{i=1}^m \left(x_i^j \left(\sum_{p=0}^{n-1} w_p x_i^p - \gamma_i \right) \right),$$

which, combined with the standard gradient-descent BP algorithm (1), yields the elementwise weights-updating formula presented in this theorem. The proof is thus complete.

From Theorem 2, we could derive the above weights-updating formula in the further matrix-vector form, i.e., Theorem 3, a more concise one.

Theorem 3 (*Matrixwise Update*). The BP weights-updating formula of the power-activation neural network presented in Theorem 2 could be further reformulated into the following matrix-vector form:

$$w(k+1) = w(k) - \eta X^T \left(Xw(k) - \gamma \right),$$

where the weights vector w, the input activation matrix X (with superscript ^{T} denoting its transpose) and the target-output vector γ are defined respectively as

$$w := \begin{bmatrix} w_0 \\ w_1 \\ \vdots \\ w_{n-1} \end{bmatrix} \in R^n, \ X := \begin{bmatrix} x_1^0 & x_1^1 & \cdots & x_1^{n-1} \\ x_2^0 & x_2^1 & \cdots & x_2^{n-1} \\ \vdots & \vdots & \ddots & \vdots \\ x_m^0 & x_m^1 & \cdots & x_m^{n-1} \end{bmatrix} \in R^{m \times n}, \ \gamma := \begin{bmatrix} \gamma_1 \\ \gamma_2 \\ \vdots \\ \gamma_m \end{bmatrix} \in R^m.$$

Proof. With the weights vector w, the input activation matrix X and the target-output vector γ defined as the above, from the proof of Theorem 2, it could be further shown that $\partial E/\partial w = X^T(Xw - \gamma)$. Then, the matrix-vector form of the weights-updating formula as in Theorem 2 can be given as $w(k+1) = w(k) - \eta(\partial E / \partial w)|_{w=w(k)} = w(k) - \eta X^T (Xw(k) - \gamma)$ for the power-activation feedforward neural network. The proof is thus complete.

PANN Weights Direct Determination

In the previous subsection, we have derived the weights-updating formulas of the power-activation feed-forward neural network (based on the standard negative-gradient BP method).

Theorems 2 and 3 are mathematically equivalent, though Theorem 2 is about the elementwise weights-updating formula while Theorem 3 is its matrix-vector-form equivalence. Remember that, as mentioned previously, for this special-type neural-network model, we can determine the neural-network weights directly (i.e., just in one step and without a lengthy BP iterative-training procedure). Now we show how to do so via the following theorem.

Theorem 4 (*Weights Direct Determination*). Let us define w, X, γ and other parameters to be the same as in Theorem 3. Then, the steady-state optimal weights of the power-activation feed-forward neural network (as shown in Figure 4), $\omega := \lim_{k \to +\infty} w(k)$, could be determined directly as

$$\omega = X^+ \gamma := (X^T X)^{-1} X^T \gamma, \tag{4}$$

where X^+, or rewritten as pinv(X), denotes the pseudoinverse of the input activation matrix X [which equals $(X^T X)^{-1} X^T$ here (Zhang & Ge, 2005) and could be done by calling MATLAB routine "pinv" (Zhang *et al*, 2008)]. Based on the steady-state weights ω in (4), the power-activation feed-forward neural network can approximate optimally the unknown target function $\phi(x)$ in the least-squares sense.

Proof. Look carefully at Theorem 3 and the weights-updating formula of the matrix-vector form, i.e., $w(k+1) = w(k) - \eta X^T (Xw(k) - \gamma)$. In view of the learning rate $\eta > 0$, when the BP neural-network training process reaches its steady state (with k large enough), we have $w(k+1) = w(k) := \omega$. Substituting it into the matrix-vector weights-updating formula yields

$$X^T (X\omega - \gamma) = 0, \tag{5}$$

The direct solution to (5) determines that the steady-state weights of the power-activation neural network are $\lim_{k \to +\infty} w(k) := \omega = X^+ \gamma := (X^T X)^{-1} X^T \gamma$; i.e., equation (4). As guaranteed by Theorems 1 through 3, ω could minimize the BPE function E. The proof is thus completed.

PANN Simulation & Verification

For illustrative and comparative purposes, two examples are taken into consideration and shown below in this simulative study; specifically, a target-function-approximation example (Zhang *et al*, 2007) and a nonlinear-dynamic-system-identification example (Zhang *et al*, 2008).

Example 1 (Target Function Approximation)

As the first example, we can simply choose the target function to be sin(x). Assume that we have the training dataset $\{(x_i, \gamma i_i, \text{ i}=1,2,\ldots,401$ by sampling uniformly over interval [-2,2] with gap size $xi_{+1} - xi_{=} 0.01$, with the function-output measurements obtained correspondingly. Then, the proposed power-activation feedforward neural network with ten hidden-layer neurons (i.e., n=10) is applied, of which the detailed results are demonstrated in Table 2 and Figure 5.

From Table 2, we can see that the power-activation neural network learns much faster (only

Table 2. Performance comparison of power-activation feedforward neural network synthesized by three different weights-learning methods for target function approximation in Example 1

Weights methods	Training process	Runtime (second)	Average error E/m
Element BP	5×10^5 iterations	1.69×10^4	2.29×10^{-3}
Matrix BP	5×10^5 iterations	2.53×10^3	7.06×10^{-4}
Proposed WDD (4)	Directly (in one step)	0.0179	4.32×10^{-16}

Figure 5. Performance comparison of power-activation feedforward neural network synthesized by three different weights-learning methods for target function approximation in Example 1

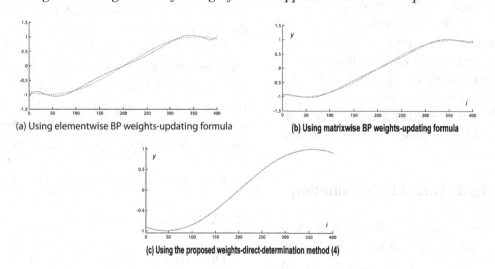

(a) Using elementwise BP weights-updating formula

(b) Using matrixwise BP weights-updating formula

(c) Using the proposed weights-direct-determination method (4)

0.0179 second) which but achieves a much smaller approximation-error (only $4.32 \times 1\text{-}^{-16}$) by using the proposed weights-direct-determination method (4) [i.e., proved in Theorem 4], as compared with the usual situation of using iterative BP training formulas given in Theorems 2 and 3. In addition, Figure 5 shows the performance comparison of the power-activation neural network used in approximating the target function $\sin(x)$, where solid curves in red correspond to the neural-network output y with horizontal axis showing the index number i of the sample dataset. From Figure 5, we can see that the power-activation neural network using weights-direct-determination method (4) can approximate the target function very accurately. In contrast, the network using iterative BP methods has less favorable approximation performance.

Example 2 (Nonlinear Dynamic System Identification)

In order to check and show the system-identification ability of this power-activation feed-forward neural network, we consider the following nonlinear dynamic system:

$$\gamma_{i+1} = (1 + \gamma_i^2)^{-1}(-0.9\gamma_i + x_i). \tag{6}$$

For system-identification purposes, the system input could be chosen as a sinusoidal signal $x_i = 0.75\sin(\pi(i-1)/180)$, $i=1,2,\ldots,400,401$ Starting with initial state $\gamma_1 = 0.1$, we could know (or measure) a sequence of system responses γ_i, $i=1,2,\ldots,401$ which constitutes the system's input-output dataset $\{(x_i, \gamma i_j, i=1,2,\ldots,401\}$, being the same as in Table 2 (m=401).

Training Procedure
The power-activation neural network is assumed again to have ten hidden-layer neurons (i.e., $n=10$). We could train the neural network with the system data $\{(x_i, \gamma i_j, i=1,2,\ldots,401\}$ in the above-

mentioned three ways; namely, an elementwise BP formula, a matrixwise BP formula, and the weights-direct-determination method (4). The training results are shown in Table 3 and Figure 6. From Table 3, we can see that, for the neural network, it is much faster to use the weights-direct-determination method (4) than conventional BP iterative-training algorithms (including both elementwise and matrixwise formulas). The neural-network runtime here is only 0.033 seconds (being the average over ten times), when the weights-direct-determination method (4) is used. In comparison, the training-times corresponding to elementwise and matrixwise algorithms are respectively 61.07 seconds and 15.71 seconds (both with 1500 iterations). Evidently, the weights-direct-determination method illustrates a huge advantage of the computational speed (at least 400 times faster than iterative algorithms in MATLAB environment). Figure 6 shows the comparison between the neural-network output and the dynamic-system response, resulting from a sinusoidal input $xi\_0.75\sin(\pi(i-1)/180)$. In the figure, the dotted blue curves denote the target outputs (i.e., real dynamic-system responses), while the solid red curves correspond to the neural-network outputs. We could observe from Figure 6 that the neural-network output matches roughly well the target-system output, no matter which method we adopt. Table 3 further tells us that the power-activation feed-forward neural network has obtained an average error of 7.86×10^{-5}, 7.86×10^{-5} and 7.82×10^{-5} corresponding to the elementwise BP training formula, matrixwise BP training formula and weights-direct-determination formula (4), respectively.

Such a small difference between the neural output and target output reveals the good system-identification capability of the proposed power-activation neural network. Moreover, the training error obtained by using weights-direct-determination method (4) is a little bit lower than those corresponding to BP iterative formulas in this example. It can thus be summarized that the

Table 3. Training-results comparison of power-activation neural network synthesized by three different weights-learning methods for nonlinear system identification in Example 2 (Zhang, Li, Yi, & Chen, A weights-directly-determined simple neural network for nonlinear system identification, IEEE International Conference on Fuzzy Systems, ©2008 IEEE)

Weights methods	Training process	Runtime (second)	Average error E/m
Element BP	1500 iterations	61.07	7.86×10^{-5}
Matrix BP	1500 iterations	15.71	7.86×10^{-5}
Proposed WDD (4)	Directly (in one step)	0.033	7.82×10^{-5}

Figure 6. Comparison on neural-network output and nonlinear-system response resulting from sinusoidal input $x_i=0.75sin(\pi(i-1)/180)$ (i.e., the training situation in Example 2)

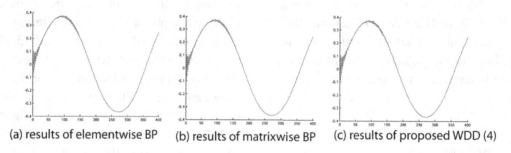

(a) results of elementwise BP   (b) results of matrixwise BP   (c) results of proposed WDD (4)

pseudoinverse-based weights-direct-determination method has better training performance than conventional BP iterative algorithms.

Testing Results

After training, we could exploit the neural network to predict the target-system response resulting from an untrained input, e.g., $x_i=0.75sin(\pi(i-1)/180)$. This could be viewed as some kind of testing on the system-identification ability of this power-activation neural network. As the second column of Table 4 shows, such a testing error is 6.79×10^{-5} on average (for iterative BP formulas), whereas the testing error corresponding to weights-direct-determination method (4) is 6.75×10^{-5} (a little bit lower than the former in this example). This test can also be observed from Figure 7: the power-activation neural network predicts roughly well. Note that we still use a sine signal as the input, but its amplitude is 0.5 instead of 0.75 during the training procedure -- a so-called "different amplitude" testing.

In addition to the above "different amplitude" testing, we could test the system-identification effectiveness of the proposed power-activation neural-network by inputting the sine signals with different phase, with different initial-value γ_1, and with different frequency. The results are shown in the 3rd through 5th columns of Table 4. It reveals that the identification results are acceptably good, even if we take untrained signals as the input. For better understanding and visual effects, we show Figures 7 and 8, of which the sub-graphs correspond to the sinusoidal input-signal with different phase, with different initial-value γ_1, and with different frequency. Note that, because the figure results obtained by the three weights-learning formulas are quite the same in this example, only one group of them is shown in Figure 8. The small difference between the neural-network prediction and target-system response in these testing examples further substantiates the good generalization, prediction and

Table 4. Testing-results comparison of power-activation feedforward neural network synthesized by three different weights-learning methods for nonlinear system identification in Example 2 (Zhang, Li, Yi, & Chen, A weights-directly-determined simple neural network for nonlinear system identification, IEEE International Conference on Fuzzy Systems, ©2008 IEEE)

Weights-learning methods	Input of different amplitude	Input of different phase	Input with different γ_1	Input of different frequency
Element BP	6.79×10^{-5}	8.27×10^{-6}	4.83×10^{-4}	1.34×10^{-4}
Matrix BP	6.79×10^{-5}	8.27×10^{-6}	4.83×10^{-4}	1.34×10^{-4}
WDD (4)	6.75×10^{-5}	7.71×10^{-6}	4.82×10^{-4}	1.33×10^{-4}

Figure 7. Comparison on neural-network prediction and nonlinear-system response resulting from different sinusoidal input $x_i = 0.75\sin(\pi(i-1)/180)$ (i.e., the testing situation in Example 2)

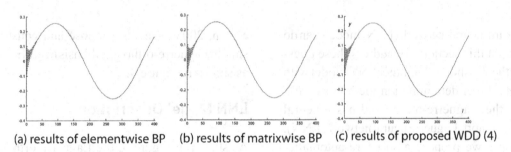

(a) results of elementwise BP   (b) results of matrixwise BP   (c) results of proposed WDD (4)

system-identification abilities of the proposed power-activation neural-network.

PANN Section Summary

Conventional BP feed-forward neural networks have some inherent drawbacks such as slow-convergence and local-minima existence. To improve the BP-type feedforward neural-network performance, people have made a lot of effort in revising the weights-updating algorithms. Different from them, we propose to adopt power activation functions, in addition to some elegant network-settings. The proposed power-activation neural network (PANN), as our first try of this kind, has been established and applied to function approximation and system identification as well. In this section, we have also derived the weights-updating formulas, and more importantly, a weights-direct-determination method for the neural network. The latter method could determine the neural-network weights directly (i.e., just in one step) without lengthy BP iterative-training procedures. Computer-simulation results have substantiated that this power-activation neural network could be applied effectively to function approximation, system identification and prediction, and that its weights-direct-determination method could be much more efficient than the conventional BP-type iterative-training algorithms.

LAGUERRE NN WITH WEIGHTS & STRUCTURAL DETERMINATION

Facing the success of the power-activation feed-forward neural network and its weights-direct-determination method on function approximation and system identification/prediction, we may doubt whether this kind of neural-network-weights direct determination method generally exists in the research fields. How, where, and which more

Figure 8. Comparison on neural-network prediction and nonlinear-system response resulting from different sinusoidal inputs (further testing situations of using WDD method (4) in Example 2)

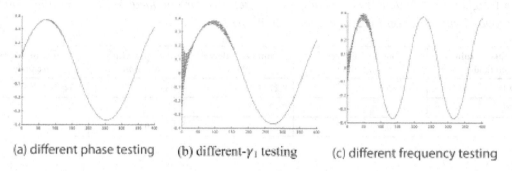

(a) different phase testing (b) different-y_1 testing (c) different frequency testing

feedforward-neural-network (FNN) models can do so? Now, in this section, we address these questions further by showing another FNN model with a weights direct determination method as well; namely, the Laguerre-orthogonal-basis neural network (in short, Laguerre neural network, LNN). In addition, we propose a structure-automatic-determination (SAD) method for this kind of feedforward neural networks which will take the mentioned Laguerre-orthogonal-basis neural network as the presentation basis/example.

Also based on the polynomial interpolation and approximation theory (Kincaid & Cheney, 2003; Lin, 2007; Mathews & Fink, 2004; Mo & Liu, 2003), we can propose and construct a simple Laguerre-orthogonal-basis neural network as shown in Figure 9.

LNN Model Description

As shown in Figure 9, the Laguerre orthogonal basis neural network consists of three layers (Zhang *et al*, 2008). The input and output of the neural network are denoted respectively as x and y. The input- and output-layers each employ one neuron with a linear activation function $f(x){=}x$, while the hidden-layer has n neurons activated by a group of order-increasing Laguerre orthogonal

Figure 9. A simple Laguerre-orthogonal-basis feedforward neural network model with hidden-layer neurons activated by a group of order-increasing Laguerre orthogonal polynomials

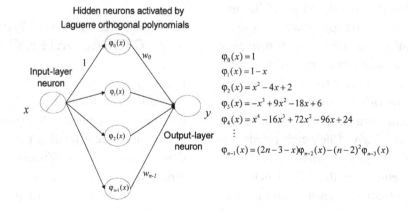

$$\varphi_0(x) = 1$$
$$\varphi_1(x) = 1 - x$$
$$\varphi_2(x) = x^2 - 4x + 2$$
$$\varphi_3(x) = -x^3 + 9x^2 - 18x + 6$$
$$\varphi_4(x) = x^4 - 16x^3 + 72x^2 - 96x + 24$$
$$\vdots$$
$$\varphi_{n-1}(x) = (2n - 3 - x)\varphi_{n-2}(x) - (n-2)^2\varphi_{n-3}(x)$$

polynomials $\varphi_j(x)$, $j=0,1,2,\ldots,n\text{-}1$. Network parameters w_j, $j=0,1,\ldots,n\text{-}1$, denote the connection weights between the hidden-layer and output-layer neurons. Moreover, the connection weights between the input-layer and hidden-layer neurons could all be fixed as 1, and all neuronal thresholds could be fixed as 0 as well. This measure would much simplify the network design, model, computational complexity, and its possible hardware implementation. Besides, even with such constant settings on some weights and all bias, it could still be theoretically proved that this Laguerre-neural-network model is able to learn the given data samples and approximate the unknown target function effectively. It is also worth mentioning that this Laguerre neural network can be viewed as a special type of feedforward BP neural networks and thus could adopt any BP iterative-training algorithm as its training rule.

LNN Theoretical Foundation

After constructing the Laguerre-orthogonal-basis neural network (actually also before that), we have to introduce and present some theoretical analysis and results about the approximation ability of the neural network. By the polynomial interpolation and curve-fitting theory (Kincaid & Cheney, 2003; Lin, 2007; Mathews & Fink, 2004; Mo & Liu, 2003), we could always construct a polynomial function $\varphi(x)$ (i.e., an underlying input-output function of Laguerre-orthogonal-basis neural network) to approximate the unknown target function $\phi(x)$. For this approximation ability, we could have the following definitions and theorem (in addition to the ones presented in the previous section about power-activation neural network, i.e., Definition 1 and Theorem 1). For more details, please refer to Kincaid & Cheney (2003), Lin (2007), Mathews & Fink (2004), Mo & Liu (2003), Zhang *et al* (2008), and the references therein.

Definition 2 (*Orthogonal Polynomial*). Define that $\varphi_j(x)$ is a polynomial of degree j and that

polynomial sequence $\{\varphi_j(x)\}_{j=0}^{n-1}$ is a set of n orthogonal-polynomial functions with respect to some weighting function $\rho(x)$ on a finite or infinite interval $[a,b]$; i.e., for any $i,j \in \{0,1,2,\ldots,n\text{-}1\}$,

$$\int_a^b \varphi_i(x)\varphi_j(x)\rho(x)dx \begin{cases} =0 & i \neq j, \\ >0 & i = j. \end{cases}$$

Then, $\{\varphi_j(x)\}_{j=0}^{n-1}$ is termed as an orthogonal polynomial sequence with respect to weighting function $\rho(x)$ on the interval $[a,b]$.

Definition 3 (*Laguerre Orthogonal Polynomial*). Laguerre orthogonal polynomials could be defined theoretically by the following equation:

$$\varphi_{n-1}(x) = e^x \frac{d^{n-1}\left(x^{n-1}e^{-x}\right)}{dx^{n-1}}, \quad 0 \leq x < +\infty,$$

which is an orthogonal polynomial of degree $n\text{-}1$ with respect to the weighting function $\rho(x)=e^{-x}$ over interval $[0,+\infty)$, with its orthogonal relationship derived as below:

$$\int_0^{+\infty} \varphi_i(x)\varphi_j(x)e^{-x}dx = \begin{cases} 0 & i \neq j, \\ (i!)^2 & i = j. \end{cases}$$

Moreover, the recurrence relation for the Laguerre orthogonal polynomials could be expressed as follows (which is of more practical use as compared to the first equation in this definition):

$$\varphi_{n-1}(x) = (2n - 3 - x)\varphi_{n-2}(x) \\ -(n-2)^2\varphi_{n-3}(x), \quad n = 3, 4, \cdots$$

The first few Laguerre orthogonal polynomials can thus be written down readily as follows:

$$\varphi_0(x) = 1,$$
$$\varphi_1(x) = 1 - x,$$
$$\varphi_2(x) = x^2 - 4x + 2,$$

$$\varphi_3(x) = -x^3 + 9x^2 - 18x + 6,$$
$$\varphi_4(x) = x^4 - 16x^3 + 72x^2 - 96x + 24,$$
$$\cdots \cdots$$

From the mathematical perspective of polynomial curve-fitting, the training of the neural network is essentially the establishment of the best functional approximation, and thus we would like to present and recall the following theoretical foundation (a definition together with the repeated Theorem 1 for readers' convenience) about the approximation ability of the proposed Laguerre-orthogonal-basis neural network.

Definition 4 (*Generalized Polynomial Approximation*). Assume that functions $\phi(x)$, $\varphi_j(x) \in C[a,b]$, $j=0,1,2,\ldots,n-1$, and that $\{\varphi_j(x)\}_{j=0}^{n-1}$ is at least a set of linearly-independent polynomial-functions. For given weighting-function $\rho(xi)$ on interval $[a,b]$, appropriate coefficients $w_0, w_1, \ldots, w_{n-1}$ could be chosen for generalized polynomial $\varphi(x) = \sum_{j=0}^{n-1} w_j \varphi_j(x)$ so as to minimize $\int_a^b \left(\phi(x) - \varphi(x) \right)^2 \rho(x) dx$. Then, generalized polynomial function $\varphi(x)$ is termed the least-square approximation of target function $\phi(x)$ with respect to the weighting-function $\rho(x)$ over the interval of our interest, $[a,b]$.

Theorem 1 (*LSA Existence and Uniqueness, as Repeated for Reading Convenience*). For unknown target function $\phi(x) \in C[a,b] \in C[a,b]$, its least-squares approximation $\varphi(x)$ (as described in the above definition) could exist uniquely, of which the coefficients $w_0, w_1, \ldots, w_{n-1}$ are solvable.

When approximating the unknown target function $\phi(x)$, the relation between the input and output of the Laguerre-orthogonal-basis neural network could be expressed exactly as

$$y = \varphi(x) = w_0 \varphi_0(x) + w_1 \varphi_1(x)$$
$$+ w_2 \varphi_2(x) + \cdots + w_{n-1} \varphi_n(x), \quad (7)$$

of which the approximation ability is well guaranteed by Definitions 2 to 4 and Theorem 1.

LNN Weights Updating & Determination

As discussed previously (actually many times), the weights between the hidden-layer and output-layer neurons could be adjusted iteratively or determined directly so as to approximate the unknown target function effectively. The procedure is termed learning (or training with) the given data samples. Besides, the proposed Laguerre neural network has a weights-direct-determination (WDD) property as well, which can generate the steady-state optimal weights of the neural network directly (or to say, just in one step), avoiding the usually lengthy BP iterative-training procedure. In addition, the WDD property could remove the inherent weaknesses of conventional BP algorithms (e.g., local minima, slow convergence and an uncertain number of hidden neurons).

Now let us show the LNN weights-learning methods. Firstly, take $\{(x_i, \gamma i, i=1,2,\ldots,m\}$ as the training (or termed, sample-pair) data-set, and define the batch-processing error (BPE) as

$$E = \frac{1}{2} \sum_{i=1}^{m} \left(\gamma_i - \sum_{p=0}^{n-1} w_p \varphi_p(x_i) \right)^2,$$

then the weights-updating formula could be described as the following two theorems.

Theorem 5 (*Elementwise Update*). The weights-updating formula based on the standard BP algorithm for the Laguerre-orthogonal-basis neural network can be designed as

$$w_j(k+1) = w_j(k) - \eta \sum_{i=1}^{m} \left(\varphi_j(x_i) \left(\sum_{p=0}^{n-1} w_p(k) \varphi_p(x_i) - \gamma_i \right) \right)$$

where the element index j=0,1,2,...,n-1, iteration index k=0,1,2,3,..., and the learning rate η>0 should be sufficiently small to guarantee the convergence of the iterative training.

Proof. Similar to the proof of Theorem 2, from the definition of the above error E, we have

$$\frac{\partial E}{\partial w_j}\bigg|_{w=w(k)} = \sum_{i=1}^{m}\left(\varphi_j(x_i)\left(\sum_{p=0}^{n-1} w_p\varphi_p(x_i) - \gamma_i\right)\right),$$

which, combined with the standard gradient-descent BP algorithm (1), yields the elementwise weights-updating formula presented in this theorem for the proposed Laguerre-orthogonal-basis neural newtork. The proof is thus complete.

Theorem 6 (*Matrixwise Update*). The elementwise weights-updating formula in Theorem 5 for the Laguerre-orthogonal-basis neural network can be rewritten in the matrix-vector form:

$$w(k+1) = w(k) - \eta X^T\left(Xw(k) - \gamma\right),$$

where the weights vector w, input activation matrix X, and target-output vector γ are defined respectively as

$$w := \begin{bmatrix} w_0 \\ w_1 \\ \vdots \\ w_{n-1} \end{bmatrix} \in R^n, \ X := \begin{bmatrix} \varphi_0(x_1) & \varphi_1(x_1) & \cdots & \varphi_{n-1}(x_1) \\ \varphi_0(x_2) & \varphi_1(x_2) & \cdots & \varphi_{n-1}(x_2) \\ \vdots & \vdots & \ddots & \vdots \\ \varphi_0(x_m) & \varphi_1(x_m) & \cdots & \varphi_{n-1}(x_m) \end{bmatrix} \in R^{m \times n}, \ \gamma := \begin{bmatrix} \gamma_1 \\ \gamma_2 \\ \vdots \\ \gamma_m \end{bmatrix} \in R^m.$$

Proof. Similar to the proof of Theorem 3, based on the above parameters' definition, from the definition of error E and the derivation results of $\partial E/\partial w_j$, we can have the matrix-vector form of $\partial E/\partial w$ as $X^T(Xw-\gamma)$. As an immediate result, the matrix-vector form of the standard BP weights-updating formula in Theorem 5 is then $w(k+1) = w(k) - \eta X^T\left(Xw(k) - \gamma\right)$, which thus completes the proof of this theorem.

Based on the two BP weights-updating formulas, the weights-direct-determination method

can be derived straightforwardly for the Laguerre neural network, i.e., Theorem 7.

Theorem 7 (*Weights Direct Determination*). Define w, X, γ and other parameters the same as in Theorem 6. The steady-state optimal weights of the Laguerre-orthogonal-basis feed-forward neural network (as shown in Figure 9), $\omega := \lim_{k \to +\infty} w(k)$, can be determined directly as

$$\omega = X^+\gamma := (X^TX)^{-1}X^T\gamma, \tag{8}$$

where X^+ or rewritten as pinv(X) equals $(X^TX)^{-1}X^T$. Based on the steady-state weights ω in (8), the Laguerre-orthogonal-basis feed-forward neural network can approximate the unknown target function $\phi(x)$ optimally in the least-squares sense.

Proof. Similar to the proof of Theorem 4, let us consider the limiting (steady-state) situation of the matrix-vector-form BP weights-updating formula, $w(k+1) = w(k) - \eta X^T(Xw(k) - \gamma)$. In view of η>0 and $w(k+1) = w(k) := \omega$ as $k \to +\infty$, we have $X^T(X\omega - \gamma) = 0$, to which the direct solution is evidently $\lim_{k \to +\infty} w(k) := \omega = X^+\gamma := (X^TX)^{-1}X^T\gamma$; i.e., our proposed WDD formula (8). As guaranteed by Definitions 1 through 4 and Theorems 1, 5 and 6, the steady-state weights vector ω could minimize the BPE function E to its global minimum. The proof is now thus completed. $\square$

LNN Structure Automatic Determination

After having derived the above weights-direct-determination formulas (4) and (8), we can thus readily propose and develop a structure-automatic-determination method (also a neural-network algorithm) for this kind of feedforward neural networks we are discussing. Note that, if we only have the iterative BP-type weights-updating formulas, we usually dare not say that some hidden-

Figure 10. A flowchart of the structure-automatic-determination algorithm determining the smallest (optimal) number of hidden-layer neurons under user-specified learning-accuracy ε

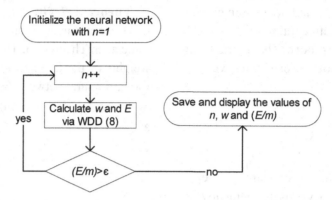

neurons' number is optimal, or even dare not use the words ``determination'', ``deterministic'' and ``determined'' (instead, in this context we may use the less-certain words such as ``estimate'', ``guess''). This, as we have experienced (Zhang, 1999), is because, during a dynamic/iterative BP training procedure, it is even harder to decide the number of hidden-layer neurons in a network, in addition to the intrinsic nonlinearity and sensitivity of conventional BP neural networks. See the BACKGROUND section and the references therein for more discussions on this subtopic.

Our way is different! Based on the aforementioned weights-direct-determination method, we can have the following more-deterministic algorithm to determine the smallest (optimal) number of hidden- layer neurons (corresponding to a user-specified accuracy of learning). Now let us take Laguerre neural network as an example (with a flowchart of the algorithm illustrated in Figure 10).

Step 0: Obtain training data-set $\{(x_i, \gamma_i), i=1,2,\ldots,m\}$, with x_i and γ_i corresponding to the ith input- and output-values of the (unknown) target function $\phi(x_i)$, respectively. Note that γ_i is also termed the expected, desired or target output.

Step 1: Construct the Laguerre neural network. Initialize the number of hidden-layer neurons to

be $n=1$ and limit the maximal number of hidden-layer neurons to be *MaxNueNum* (e.g., 10000). Specify the target (or desired) precision in the sense of the batch-processing error E over m as ε (e.g., 10^{-8}).

Step 2: If $n>MaxNeuNum$, then terminate the algorithm with a notice about the inability failure. Otherwise, compute the neural-network weights w by using weights-direct-determination formula (8) and calculate the actual training error E/m at the present stage (i.e., with n hidden-layer neurons).

Step 3: If the actual training error $(E/m)>\varepsilon$ (i.e., target precision), then update $n=n+1$ and go back to Step 2 to continue the growing algorithm. Otherwise, terminate the algorithm by supplying the smallest number n of hidden-layer neurons, the corresponding weights vector w and the actual training error E/m.

In the above simple structure-automatic-determination algorithm, the neural-network weights direct determination method is the basis, and the optimal number of hidden-layer neurons can thus be decided rapidly and certainly. In the ensuing subsection, we would like to present the computer-simulation results which substantiate further the efficacy and superiority of the proposed Laguerre neural network and its systematic algorithms.

LNN Approximation & Prediction Example

For illustrative purposes, we choose the following target function as our simulation example:

$$\phi(x) = \cos^4 x / (x+1)$$
$$+(x-1) / (2x+1) + e^{-x}.$$

Assume that we have the training data-set $\{(x_i, \gamma i_j, \ i=1,2,\dots,201\}$ by sampling uniformly over interval [0,1] with step-size $x i_{+1} x i = 0.005$. Then, the constructed Laguerre neural network is simulated and compared, of which the detailed results are shown in Table 5 together with Figures 11 and 12 (Zhang e*t al*, 2008).

Table 5. Training and testing results of Laguerre neural network using the proposed weights-direct-determination (WDD) and structure-automatic-determination (SAD) algorithms (Zhang, Zhong, Li, Xiao, & Yi, Growing algorithm of Laguerre orthogonal basis neural network with weights directly determined, Lecture Notes in Artificial Intelligence, ©2008 Springer-Verlag)

Target precision	Training error	Optimal	Runtime (second)	Testing error
$\varepsilon := 10^{-4}$	3.519×10^{-5}	$n \to 4$	0.01326	3.361×10^{-5}
$\varepsilon := 10^{-5}$	7.463×10^{-7}	$n \to 5$	0.01337	6.986×10^{-7}
$\varepsilon := 10^{-6}$	7.463×10^{-7}	$n \to 5$	0.01339	6.986×10^{-7}
$\varepsilon := 10^{-7}$	5.109×10^{-8}	$n \to 6$	0.01379	4.722×10^{-8}
$\varepsilon := 10^{-8}$	6.321×10^{-9}	$n \to 7$	0.01425	5.828×10^{-9}

Figure 11. Training performance of Laguerre neural network (under target precision 10^{-8})

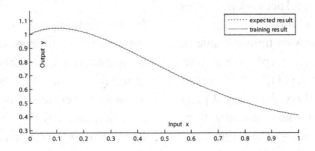

Figure 12. Testing and prediction results of Laguerre neural network (under target precision 10^{-8})

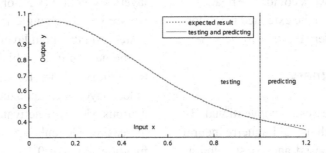

From Table 5, we can see that, under some prescribed accuracy of learning (or termed, target precision), the optimal (smallest) number of hidden-layer neurons can be determined almost immediately and deterministically for the Laguerre-orthogonal-basis neural network by using our proposed weights-direct-determination and structure-automatic-determination algorithms. Besides, to count the average LNN runtime, we have conducted the simulation for 1000 times per target-precision. As we can see from the fourth column of Table 5, it takes only 0.01425 seconds to obtain the optimal number of hidden-layer neurons even when the target precision is 10^{-8}. In addition, the training error E/m in that case is only 6.321×10^{-9}, which reveals the excellent approximation ability of the constructed Laguerre neural network. This is also shown via Figure 11.

It is worth pointing out here that, as for the fifth column of Table 5 about the testing error E/m, we have selected totally $200 \times 5 = 1000$ untrained points $(x_i, \gamma i)$ with boundary-points unconsidered (Leithead & Zhang, 2007) to test the Laguerre neural network. The small (and tiny) testing errors show that this Laguerre neural network possesses very good generalization ability.

Moreover, we could apply the trained Laguerre neural network for predictive purposes, e.g., testing over the untrained interval [1,1.2]. The result is shown in Figure 12, where the interval [0,1] corresponds to the training and generalization-testing interval which is about the trained and untrained points mentioned previously in the fifth column of Table 5. From the figure (especially the untrained interval [1,1.2]), we can see that the Laguerre neural network could have relatively good prediction ability at the extended neighborhood of the training interval.

LNN Section Summary

To remedy the weaknesses of conventional BP neural-network algorithms, a Laguerre neural network has been proposed and constructed as well based on the polynomial interpolation and curve-fitting theory. In addition to the BP-type weights-updating formulas, we have derived and achieved the weights-direct-determination method again, which calculates the optimal connection weights directly (just in one step). Moreover, based on the weights-direct-determination method, we have further proposed a simple but deterministic neural-network growing algorithm (also termed, structure-automatic-determination method), which decides the optimal (smallest) number of hidden-layer neurons efficiently and effectively. The longstanding difficulty about the hidden-layer neurons' number of BP neural-networks appears to be alleviated (and possibly solved) by the proposed neural-network framework and algorithms. Theoretical analysis and simulation results have both substantiated the efficacy of the constructed neural networks by using orthogonal or at least linearly-independent activation functions.

GEGENBAUER NN WITH WEIGHTS & STRUCTURAL DETERMINATION

In this section, one more feedforward-neural-network model is proposed which possesses the aforementioned weights-direct-determination property as well. This neural network is termed as Gegenbauer neural network (GNN) for presentation convenience, in view of the fact that its hidden-layer neurons are being activated by Gegenbauer orthogonal polynomial functions.

The Gegenbauer-neural-network structure is shown in Figure 13, which consists of three layers of neuron(s). For illustrative purposes, we are handling single-input single-output data systems: in the input layer and output layer there is one neuron each, which adopts linear activation function $f(x)=x$ for simplicity. Similarly, the hidden layer of Gegenbauer neural network has n neurons which are activated by a group of order-increasing Gegenbauer orthogonal-polynomial functions $\varphi_j(x)$, $j=0,1,2,\ldots,n$-1 [that is, the $(j+1)$

th hidden-layer neuron adopts $\varphi_j(x)$ as its activation function]. Note that the general mathematical expression of Gegenbauer orthogonal polynomials can be written as (Fang *et al*, 2004; Wu, Zhang & Fang, 2007):

$$\phi_j(x,\lambda) = \sum_{k=0}^{j} \frac{1}{k!(j-k)!} \frac{(2\lambda)_j (2\lambda + j)_k}{(\lambda + 1/2)_k} (\frac{x-1}{2})^k,$$
$$j = 0, 1, 2, \cdots$$

where symbol $(\lambda)_k$ here denotes $\lambda(\lambda+1)\ldots(\lambda+k-1)$. Given $\lambda=4$ in our neural-network scheme, the corresponding expression of $\varphi_j(x)$ of better practical use could be given readily as in the right part of Figure 13. In addition, similar to the definitions before, network-parameter w_j denotes the connection-weight from the $(j+1)$th hidden-layer neuron to the output-layer neuron, with $j \in \{0,1,2,\ldots,n-1\}$. Before proceeding to the weights-&-structure determination method and its related computer-simulation, it is worth pointing out that the approximation ability of Gegenbauer neural network can also be guaranteed by Definitions 1, 2, 4 and Theorem 1.

Similar to the previous two sections (i.e., about PANN and LNN), in this section we could also develop the weights-direct-determination method

for determining the Gegenbauer-neural- network weights (without a lengthy iterative-training procedure). The theorem is the following.

Theorem 8 (*GNN Weights Direct Determination*). The optimal weights of the Gegenbauer-orthogonal-basis feed-forward neural network (as shown in Figure 13) can be determined directly as

$$\lim_{k \to +\infty} w(k) := \omega =$$
$$X^+ \gamma = (X^T X)^{-1} X^T \gamma \qquad (9)$$

where, with most parameters and symbols defined the same as in Theorems 6 and 7, for this Gegenbauer neural network, the related input-activation-matrix X is defined to be

$$X := \begin{bmatrix} \varphi_0(x_1) & \varphi_1(x_1) & \cdots & \varphi_{n-1}(x_1) \\ \varphi_0(x_2) & \varphi_1(x_2) & \cdots & \varphi_{n-1}(x_2) \\ \vdots & \vdots & \ddots & \vdots \\ \varphi_0(x_m) & \varphi_1(x_m) & \cdots & \varphi_{n-1}(x_m) \end{bmatrix} \in R^{m \times n}.$$

Proof. Omitted here and left to readers due to its similarity to the proof of Theorems 4 and 7 but with different input-activation-matrix X. □

Moreover, based on the structure-automatic-determination algorithm (which is also termed

Figure 13. A proposed Gegenbauer-orthogonal-basis feedforward neural network with hidden-layer neurons activated by a group of order-increasing Gegenbauer orthogonal polynomials

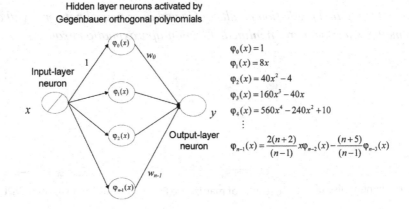

by us more specifically as a structure-growing algorithm, presented in the previous section about LNN with a flowchart shown in Figure 10), we can determine the optimal number of hidden-layer neurons of Gegenbauer neural network in a rapid and certain way. In addition, computer-simulation results are provided below, which substantiate further the effectiveness, efficiency and superiority of the proposed kind of feedforward neural networks (specifically, here, Gegenbauer neural network) and their systematic algorithms (specifically, here, WDD and SAD methods).

Firstly, let us consider the following target-function-approximation problem:

$$\phi(x) = e^{-x}\sin x + \frac{x-1}{x^2+x+1}$$
$$+(1-x)^3 e^{-x^2/2} + \cos^2(3x).$$

The input elements of the training set are taken from interval [-1,0.8] over a sampling gap of 0.01, and the output measurements are correspondingly obtained. GNN simulation results

with n=15 hidden neurons as synthesized by three different weights-learning methods are shown in Table 6, where we can observe again that the neural network learns much faster and achieves a much smaller approximation-error by using the proposed weights-direct-determination method (9), as compared to the situation of using iterative BP training formulas. In addition, for better visual effects, Figure 14 illustrates the performance comparison of Gegenbauer neural network used in approximating and predicting the above-mentioned target function. From Figure 14, we can observe and summarize once again that Gegenbauer neural network using the proposed weights-direct-determination method (9) can approximate and predict the target function quite well in both of the two regions, where [-1,0.8] is the training and testing region, while [0.8,1.3] is the prediction region of which the points have never been used for training purposes. In contrast, though approximating well in the training and testing region with average error E/m=6.53×10^{-7}, the neural network using iterative BP weights-

Table 6. Training-results comparison of Gegenbauer neural network synthesized by three different weights-learning methods for the above nonlinear-function-approximation example

Weights methods	Training process	Runtime (second)	Average error E/m
Element BP	5×10^5 iterations	7.26×10^3	6.53×10^{-7}
Matrix BP	5×10^5 iterations	5.48×10^3	6.53×10^{-7}
Proposed WDD (9)	Directly (in one step)	0.60	2.39×10^{-12}

Figure 14. Training, testing and prediction results of Gegenbauer neural network synthesized by three different weights methods for the above nonlinear-function-approximation example

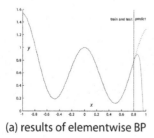 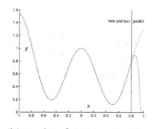 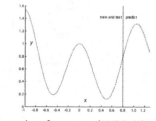

(a) results of elementwise BP   (b) results of matrixwise BP   (c) results of proposed WDD (9)

updating formulas has a much less favorable prediction performance (as seen evidently from the left two sub-graphs of Figure 14).

Secondly, let us take the target function $\phi(x) = xe^{x^2} + \cos(3\pi x)$ as another example. In this simulation example, the number of hidden-layer neurons of Gegenbauer neural network is no longer fixed, but decided by using the proposed structure-automatic-determination (SAD) method. Remember that, as shown in the algorithm flowchart via Figure 10, the SAD method gives the optimal (smallest) number of hidden-layer neurons, which relates to the user-prescribed target precision of learning as well as a specific target function (or to say, data problem) of interest.

See Table 7 for the detailed simulation results of using Gegenbauer network synthesized by WDD and SAD algorithms, where interval [-1,0.75] is used for training and testing purposes, and totally m=176 data points are generated with sampling gap 0.01. From the table, we can observe that, under some prescribed accuracy of learning, the smallest number of hidden-layer neurons can be determined almost immediately (less than a few seconds) and deterministically (without any uncertainty) for the Gegenbauer-orthogonal-basis neural network by using the proposed weights-

direct-determination and structure-automatic-determination algorithms. Besides, it is worth mentioning that the simulation results shown in Table 7 were obtained based on a notebook computer (with an AMD Turion 64 MT-30 CPU and 512MB RAM), and that, as we believe, such small GNN runtime can be further reduced by using desktop computers. Specifically, as seen from the last row of Table 7, it takes only 2.3 seconds to obtain the optimal number of hidden-layer neurons (n=25) so as to achieve the precision of 10^{-20} (what a tiny value!). Moreover, the excellent performance and significance of the proposed GNN, WDD and SAD algorithms can be further demonstrated via Figure 15.

From Figure 15, we can see that, under some prescribed accuracy of learning (also termed, target precision), the optimal (smallest) number of hidden-layer neurons can be determined effectively for Gegenbauer neural network by using the proposed weights-direct-determination and structure-automatic-determination algorithms. For example, to achieve the target precision of ε=10^{-10}, the smallest number of hidden-layer neurons of Gegenbauer neural network is 18, which appears to have made a very good approximation over the training interval [-1,0.75], but predicts less well over the untrained interval [0.75,1].

Table 7. Training and testing results of Gegenbauer neural network using the proposed weights-direct-determination (WDD) and structure-automatic-determination (SAD) algorithms

Target precision	Training error	Optimal	Runtime (second)	Testing error
ε:=10^{-2}	1.677223×10^{-3}	$n \rightarrow 10$	0.020877	1.632841×10^{-3}
ε:=10^{-4}	3.888849×10^{-5}	$n \rightarrow 12$	0.246211	3.767265×10^{-5}
ε:=10^{-6}	4.372885×10^{-7}	$n \rightarrow 14$	0.469056	4.226319×10^{-7}
ε:=10^{-8}	2.675977×10^{-9}	$n \rightarrow 16$	0.692736	2.588702×10^{-9}
ε:=10^{-10}	9.676783×10^{-12}	$n \rightarrow 18$	0.956072	9.402507×10^{-12}
ε:=10^{-12}	2.199565×10^{-14}	$n \rightarrow 20$	1.260809	2.154067×10^{-14}
ε:=10^{-14}	4.308150×10^{-5}	$n \rightarrow 21$	1.514899	4.205626×10^{-15}
ε:=10^{-16}	3.297912×10^{-17}	$n \rightarrow 22$	1.777932	3.266554×10^{-17}
ε:=10^{-18}	3.432296×10^{-20}	$n \rightarrow 24$	2.048795	3.457411×10^{-20}
ε:=10^{-20}	5.489574×10^{-21}	$n \rightarrow 25$	2.322376	5.391438×10^{-21}

Figure 15. Testing and predicting results of Gegenbauer neural network under different target precision of learning and thus with different optimal numbers of hidden-layer neurons

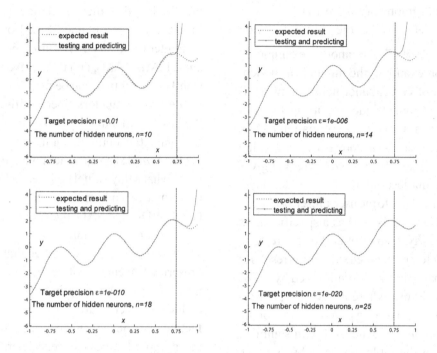

However, as the target precision ε improves (e.g., to be 10^{-20}), the Gegenbauer neural network could now make a very good prediction over such an untrained interval [0.75,1]. This point is shown most evidently in the bottom-right sub-graph of Figure 15. Besides, as a by-product, it might give us some inspirations and supporting evidence about human-beings' learning and intelligence; i.e., the better we learn, the better we predict!

As a section summary about GNN and its algorithms, we would like to point out that the new type of feed-forward neural networks with weights directly determined appears to be an effective way which could remedy the inherent weaknesses of conventional BP-type neural-networks. The Gegenbauer neural network has been proposed, constructed, simulated and substantiated in this section. Similar to our proposed power-activation neural network and Laguerre neural network, this Gegenbauer neural network has been established also based on the polynomial interpolation and

curve-fitting theory. The weights-direct-determination and structure-automatic-determination methods are further proposed and equipped for the Gegenbauer neural network, which can decide the neural-network weights and the optimal number of hidden-layer neurons very efficiently and effectively. The longstanding difficulties about BP neural-networks appear to have been much alleviated via the proposed neural-network design approach. Computer-simulation results have further substantiated the efficacy of the constructed Gegenbauer neural networks on nonlinear functions/systems approximation and prediction.

COMPARISON AMONG PANN, LNN AND GNN

As illustrated individually in previous sections, the three types of feedforward neural networks (i.e., PANN, LNN and GNN) proposed above all have good performance on nonlinear function approximation, system identification and prediction. In this section, according to the insightful review comments, the following comparison results are presented for the three types of neural networks we proposed, in order to see more evidently the superior performance they have.

Let us consider the nonlinear target function as below:

$$\phi(x) = \frac{1}{(1 + x^2 + e^x)\sin(3x - 2)}.$$

Suppose that we have the training data-set $\{(x_i, \lambda i_i, i=1,2,\ldots,201\}$ by sampling uniformly over interval [0,2] with step-size $x i_{+1x} i_- 0.01$. Then, the three constructed feedforward neural networks are simulated and compared, of which the detailed results are shown in Table 8.

As we can see from Table 8, under the same target precisions, the optimal numbers of hidden-layer neurons, runtime (including the training time) and training errors of the three feedforward neural networks are similar (or to say, basically the same, consistent). The similarity (or to say, consistency) may originate from the common basis of the proposed neural network design, i.e., curve-fitting theory (more specifically, polynomial interpolation and approximation theory). A difference among the performance of the three neural networks exists that, to achieve the target

precision of 10^{-9}, LNN needs more hidden-layer neurons (i.e., $n \rightarrow 14$) and has larger training error (i.e., 8.781116×10^{-10}) than PANN and GNN do (which both need 9 hidden-layer neurons and achieve the training error of 3.294184×10^{-10}).

FUTURE TRENDS

Conventional BP feed-forward neural networks have some inherent weaknesses, such as, slow-convergence, local-minima existence and uncertain structure. To improve the BP-type feedforward neural-network performance, people have made a lot of efforts in improving the weights-updating algorithms (or to say, training algorithms). Different from them, we propose to use a group of linearly-independent or orthogonal functions as the neurons' activation functions, together with some elegant network-design and settings. The illustrated PANN, LNN and GNN with WDD and SAD properties are actually our first try of this kind of thoughts, which are all SISO systems and also far from mature. One future and emerging trend of this neural-network research is thus to find more different groups of linearly-independent or orthogonal functions so as to construct more ANN models with the weights-direct-determination property. Another future and emerging trend of this research, as we can see and ``predict'', is evidently to generalize the success from SISO

Table 8. Comparisons among PANN, LNN and GNN using weights-direct-determination (WDD) and structure-automatic-determination (SAD) algorithms for nonlinear function approximation

NN type	Target precision	Optimal	Runtime (second)	Training error
PANN	$\varepsilon := 10^{-5}$	$n \rightarrow 6$	1.186195	3.556888×10^{-6}
	$\varepsilon := 10^{-7}$	$n \rightarrow 8$	1.838504	4.246173×10^{-8}
	$\varepsilon := 10^{-9}$	$n \rightarrow 9$	2.521487	3.294184×10^{-10}
LNN	$\varepsilon := 10^{-5}$	$n \rightarrow 6$	1.315638	3.556888×10^{-6}
	$\varepsilon := 10^{-7}$	$n \rightarrow 8$	1.966896	4.246173×10^{-8}
	$\varepsilon := 10^{-9}$	$n \rightarrow 14$	2.641055	8.781116×10^{-10}
GNN	$\varepsilon := 10^{-5}$	$n \rightarrow 6$	1.322076	3.556888×10^{-6}
	$\varepsilon := 10^{-7}$	$n \rightarrow 8$	2.109997	4.246173×10^{-8}
	$\varepsilon := 10^{-9}$	$n \rightarrow 9$	2.876100	3.294184×10^{-10}

neural-network systems to multiple-input-multiple-output (MIMO) neural-network systems or at least multiple-input-single-output (MISO) neural-network systems. Moreover, any possible applications (such as, used in data mining) of the neural-network models are sincerely welcome as a future research direction as well as a cooperation basis. This suggestion is made in view of the excellent generalization and prediction abilities of the proposed neural-network models. In addition, think the benefits, effectiveness, efficiency and superiority of the neural-network-weights direct determination method and neural-network-structure automatic determination algorithm: there are many possible future and emerging trends/opportunities related to this research that need us to find …

CONCLUSION

As we mentioned at the beginning of this book-chapter, artificial neural networks especially with BP training algorithms have been widely investigated and applied in science and engineering fields. The BP neural-networks and algorithms have long shown a number of inherent weaknesses, such as, 1) the possibility of being trapped into local minima, 2) the difficulty in choosing appropriate learning rates and thus a slow convergence of training, 3) the inability to design the optimal (or smallest) neural-network-structure. As a possible way of resolving such weaknesses of BP neural networks, we asked ourselves a question: could neural-network weights be decided directly without a lengthy and dynamic iterative BP-training procedure? In this chapter with three positive examples (i.e., PANN, LNN and GNN), we have addressed the question roughly. Its answer is YES by means of using linearly-independent or orthogonal activation functions, though we still need work more and work on the MIMO neural-network systems. Based on the proposed weights-direct-

determination method and structure-automatic-determination algorithm, it has been shown that the new kind of feed-forward neural networks can determine their weights and structure more efficiently, certainly and optimally (in comparison with usual conventional BP neural networks). In addition, the excellent generalization and prediction abilities of the proposed neural networks have been demonstrated well in this chapter. Our future research directions may thus lie in the MIMO neural-networks design with a WDD method and their various applications. Besides, before ending this chapter, it is worth mentioning that, as the core of the weights-direct-determination method, the calculation of matrix pseudoinverse generally requires $O(n^3)$ arithmetic operations and $O(n^2)$-level memory/storage. However, based on our research on efficient and economical Toeplitz-computation algorithms proposed for manipulating very large matrices (e.g., with dimension 60000×60000) (Zhang, Leithead & Leith, 2005), we may develop better pseudoinverse-solving algorithms which are expected with $O(n^2)$ arithmetic operations and $O(n)$-level memory/storage or even less.

ACKNOWLEDGMENT

This work is funded by National Science Foundation of China under Grant 60775050 and by the Program for New Century Excellent Talents in University (NCET-07-0887).. Before joining SYSU in 2006, Zhang (http://www.ee.sysu.edu.cn/teacher/detail.asp?sn=129) had been with National University of Ireland at Maynooth, University of Strathclyde, National University of Singapore, Chinese University of Hong Kong, South China University of Technology, and Huazhong University of Science and Technology, since 1992. Zhang (ynzhang@ieee.org) had been supported by those research fellowships and studentships, which inspired this research.

REFERENCES

Chen, Y., Wang, R., & Lin, H. (2002). The application and compare of training algorithms in MATLAB 6.0's neural network toolbox. *Computer and Information Technology, 3*, 1-6/18.

Corwin, E. M., Logar, A. M., & Oldham, W. J. B. (1994). An iterative method for training multilayer networks with threshold function . *IEEE Transactions on Neural Networks, 5*, 507–508. doi:10.1109/72.286926

Demuth, H., Beale, M., & Hagan, M. (2007). Neural network toolbox 5 user's guide. Natick, MA: MathWorks Inc.

Fang, T., Leng, X., Ma, X., & Guang, M. (2004). λ-*PDF* and Gegenbauer polynomial approximation for dynamic response problems of random structures. *Acta Mechanica Sinica, 20*(3), 292–298. doi:10.1007/BF02486721

Gao, X., & Cong, S. (2001). Comparative study on fast learning algorithms of BP networks. *Control and Decision, 16*(2), 167–171.

Goodman, R. M., & Zeng, Z. (1994) A learning algorithm for multi-layer perceptrons with hard-limiting threshold units. In IEEE Workshop of Neural Networks for Signal Processing, (pp. 219-228), Ermioni.

Hong, T. P., & Tseng, S. S. (1991). Trade-off between time complexity and accuracy of perceptron learning. In *IEEE Region 10 International Conference on EC3 - Energy, Computer, Communication and Control Systems: Vol. 2* (pp. 157-161), New Delhi.

Jenkins, W. M. (2006). Neural network weight training by mutation. *Computers & Structures, 84*, 2107–2112. doi:10.1016/j.compstruc.2006.08.066

Jia, J. C., & Chong, C. C. (1995). Distributed normalisation input coding to speed up training process of BP-neural network classifier. *Electronics Letters, 31*(15), 1267–1269. doi:10.1049/el:19950854

Kincaid, D., & Cheney, W. (2003). Numerical analysis: mathematics of scientific computing. Beijing: China Machine Press.

Leithead, W. E., & Zhang, Y. (2007). O(N^2)-operation approximation of covariance matrix inverse in Gaussian process regression based on quasi-Newton BFGS methods. *Communications in Statistics Simulation and Computation, 36*(2), 367–380. doi:10.1080/03610910601161298

Liang, X., & Tso, S. K. (2002). An improved upper bound on step-size parameters of discrete-time recurrent neural networks for linear inequality and equation system. *IEEE Transactions on Circuits and Systems I, 49*(5), 695–698. doi:10.1109/TCSI.2002.1001961

Lin, C. (2007). Numerical analysis. Beijing: Science Press.

Lippmann, R. P. (1987). An introduction to computing with neural nets. *IEEE ASSP Magazine, 4*(2), 4–22. doi:10.1109/MASSP.1987.1165576

Looney, C. G. (1996). Advances in feedforward neural networks: demystifying knowledge acquiring black boxes. *IEEE Transactions on Knowledge and Data Engineering, 8*(2), 211–226. doi:10.1109/69.494162

Mathews, J. H., & Fink, K. D. (2004). Numerical methods using MATLAB. Beijing: Pearson Education Inc.

Miller, D. A., Arguello, R., & Greenwood, G. W. (2004). Evolving artificial neural network structures: experimental results for biologically-inspired adaptive mutations. In *Congress on Evolutionary Computation: Vol. 2* (pp. 2114-2119), Portland, OR.

Mo, G., & Liu, K. (2003). Function approximation methods. Beijing: Science Press.

Pai, G. A. V. (2004). A fast converging evolutionary neural network for the prediction of uplift capacity of suction caissons. In *IEEE Conference on Cybernetics and Intelligent Systems* (pp. 654-659), Singapore.

Pu, C., Sun, Z., & Zhao, S. (2006). Comparison of BP algorithms in MATLAB NN toolbox. *Computer Simulation, 23*(5), 142–144.

Ren, Y., & Zhou, L. (2008). PMSM control research based on particle swarm optimization BP neural network. In *International Conference on Cyberworlds* (pp. 832-836), Hangzhou.

Rumelhart, D. E., McClelland, J. L., & PDP Research Group (1986). *Parallel distributed processing*. Cambridge, MA: MIT Press.

Sadeghi, B. H. M. (2000). A BP-neural network predictor model for plastic injection molding process. *Journal of Materials Processing Technology, 103*, 411–416. doi:10.1016/S0924-0136(00)00498-2

Steriti, R. J., & Fiddy, M. A. (1993). Regularized image reconstruction using SVD and a neural network method for matrix inversion. *IEEE Transactions on Signal Processing, 41*(10), 3074–3077. doi:10.1109/78.277813

Su, G., & Deng, F. (2003). On the improving backpropagation algorithms of the neural networks based on MATLAB language: a review. *Bulletin of Science and Technology, 19*(2), 130–135.

Wang, S. L., & Li, P. Y. (1991). Neural networks for medicine: two cases. In *Electro International Conference* (pp. 586-590), New York.

Wen, J. W., Zhao, J. L., Luo, S. W., & Han, Z. (2000). The improvements of BP neural network learning algorithm, In *International Conference on Signal Processing: Vol. 3* (pp. 1647-1649), Beijing.

Wilson, D. R., & Martinez, T. R. (2001). The need for small learning rates on large problems. In *International Joint Conference on Neural Networks: Vol. 1* (pp. 115-119), New York.

Wu, C., Zhang, H., & Fang, T. (2007). Flutter analysis of an airfoil with bounded random parameters in incompressible flow via Gegenbauer polynomial approximation. *Aerospace Science and Technology, 11*, 518–526. doi:10.1016/j.ast.2007.03.003

Yeung, D. S., & Zeng, X. (2002). Hidden neuron pruning for multilayer perceptrons using a sensitivity measure. In *International Conference on Machine Learning and Cybernetics* (pp. 1751-1757), New York.

Yu, X. H., & Chen, G. A. (1995). On the local minima free condition of backpropagation learning. *IEEE Transactions on Neural Networks, 6*(5), 1300–1303. doi:10.1109/72.410380

Yu, X. H., Chen, G. A., & Cheng, S. X. (1993). Acceleration of backpropagation learning using optimised learning rate and momentum. *Electronics Letters, 29*(14), 1288–1290. doi:10.1049/el:19930860

Zhang, C., Lin, M., & Tang, M. (2008). BP neural network optimized with PSO algorithm for daily load forecasting. In *International Conference on Information Management, Innovation Management and Industrial Engineering: Vol. 3,* (pp. 82-85). Taipei.

Zhang, Y. (1999). *Software implementation of artificial neural networks using JAVA and object oriented programming (OOP) technique*. Unpublished master's thesis, South China University of Technology, Guangzhou.

Zhang, Y. (2002). *Analysis and design of recurrent neural networks and their applications to control and robotic systems*. Unpublished doctoral dissertation, Chinese University of Hong Kong, Hong Kong.

Zhang, Y., & Chen, K. (2008). Global exponential convergence and stability of Wang neural network for solving online linear equations. *Electronics Letters, 44*(2), 145–146. doi:10.1049/el:20081928

Zhang, Y., & Ge, S. S. (2005). Design and analysis of a general recurrent neural network model for time-varying matrix inversion. *IEEE Transactions on Neural Networks, 16*(6), 1477–1490. doi:10.1109/TNN.2005.857946

Zhang, Y., Ge, S. S., & Lee, T. H. (2004). A unified quadratic-programming based dynamical system approach to joint torque optimization of physically constrained redundant manipulators. *IEEE Transactions on Systems, Man, and Cybernetics . Part B, 34*(5), 2126–2132.

Zhang, Y., Jiang, D., & Wang, J. (2002). A recurrent neural network for solving Sylvester equation with time-varying coefficients. *IEEE Transactions on Neural Networks, 13*(5), 1053–1063. doi:10.1109/TNN.2002.1031938

Zhang, Y., Leithead, W. E., & Leith, D. J. (2005). Time-series Gaussian process regression based on Toeplitz computation of $O(N^2)$ operations and $O(N)$-level storage. In *IEEE Conference on Decision and Control* (pp. 3711-3716), Seville.

Zhang, Y., Li, W., Liu, W., Tan, M., & Chen, K. (2007). Power-activation feed-forward neural network with its weights immediately determined. In *Chinese Conference on Pattern Recognition* (pp. 72-77). Beijing: Science Press.

Zhang, Y., Li, W., Yi, C., & Chen, K. (2008). A weights-directly-determined simple neural network for nonlinear system identification. In *IEEE International Conference on Fuzzy Systems* (pp. 455-460), Hong Kong.

Zhang, Y., & Wang, J. (2001). Recurrent neural networks for nonlinear output regulation. *Automatica, 37,* 1161–1173. doi:10.1016/S0005-1098(01)00092-9

Zhang, Y., & Wang, J. (2002). Global exponential stability of recurrent neural networks for synthesizing linear feedback control systems via pole assignment. *IEEE Transactions on Neural Networks, 13*(3), 633–644. doi:10.1109/TNN.2002.1000129

Zhang, Y., Zhong, T., Li, W., Xiao, X., & Yi, C. (2008). Growing algorithm of Laguerre orthogonal basis neural network with weights directly determined. In D.-S. Huang *et al* (Eds.), *International Conference on Intelligent Computing: Vol. 5227. Lecture Notes in Artificial Intelligence* (pp. 60-67), Shanghai. Berlin: Springer-Verlag.

Zhou, K., & Kang, Y. (2005). Neural network models and their MATLAB simulation program design. Beijing: Tsinghua University Press.

226

Chapter 11
The Hopfield–Tank Neural Network for the Mobile Agent Planning Problem

Cha-Hwa Lin
National Sun Yat-sen University, Taiwan

Jin-Fu Wang
National Sun Yat-sen University, Taiwan

ABSTRACT

Mobile agent planning (MAP) is one of the most important techniques in the mobile computing paradigm to complete a given task in the most efficient manner. To tackle this challenging NP-hard problem, Hopfield-Tank neural network is modified to provide a dynamic approach which not only optimizes the cost of mobile agents in a t, but also satisfies the location-based constraints such as the starting and ending nodes of the routing sequence which must be the home site of the traveling mobile agent. Meanwhile, the energy function is reformulated into a Lyapunov function to guarantee the convergence to a stable state and the existence of valid solutions. Moreover, the objective function is designed to estimate the completion time of a valid solution and to predict the optimal routing path. This method can produce solutions rapidly that are very close to the minimum cost of the location-based and time-constrained distributed MAP problem.

INTRODUCTION

In recent years, much research has been carried out into mobile agent in distributed computing. Mobile agent planning (MAP) is one of the most important techniques in the mobile computing paradigm to complete a given task in the most efficient manner (Baek, Yeo, Kim, & Yeom, 2001; Baek, Kim, & Yeom, 2002; Baek, Yeo, & Yeom, 2002; Baek

DOI: 10.4018/978-1-61520-757-2.ch011

& Yeom, 2003; Moizumi, 1998; MAL; Yang, Liu, Yang, & Wang, 2003). If it is possible to acquire the execution performance and the moving time of a mobile agent between sites of the entire network by long-term periodic detection, collection, or compilation statistics, a user can apply these data to plan the sequence the sites should be visited by the mobile agent, enabling which to efficiently complete a task and move among sites in minimum completion time. This scheduling activity is called the mobile agent planning problem. In general, to conduct the mobile agent planning problem, mobile agents must have knowledge of the network conditions so that they can adapt to the network environment and make the best use of the available resources such as the history of network conditions, which can facilitate their tasks in achieving the expected performances.

Moizumi (Moizumi, 1998) explored how mobile agents can efficiently spend their time traveling throughout the network completing distributed information retrieval. The planning problem was to decide in what sequence the sites should be visited in order to complete a task in minimum time, assuming the availability of the network statistics and the directory service. He named this mobile agent planning problem Traveling Agent Problem (TAP) because of its analogous to the traditional TSP problem. He treated the TAP problem as a traditional TSP problem and proved it is NP-complete. Moizumi used dynamic programming to solve the TAP problem in polynomial time by assuming that the network consisted of subnetworks where latencies between machines in the same subnetwork were constant while latencies between machines located in different subnetworks varied.

Baek et al. analyzed the characteristics of mobile agents, identified significant factors in MAP, and presented several useful planning methods. They tackled the number of agents and the execution time of the participating agent for retrieving information from distributed computing environment (Baek, Yeo, Kim, & Yeom, 2001). Using fewer agents could cause lower network traffic and consume less bandwidth, but badly scheduled agent itineraries could cause longer execution time as a result of higher routing cost. The number of agents created for a task could also influence the total routing cost. To reduce the overhead, they suggested two cost-effective mobile agent planning algorithms, BYKY1 and BYKY2. Consider the nodes that present correct information only for some time interval. If an agent is sent and arrives earlier than a specified

update time to gather information, it may retrieve useless or corrupted information. In (Baek, Kim, & Yeom, 2002), they provided Time Planning method and extended versions of the BYKY1 and the BYKY2 algorithms to support the time constrains that reside on the node of the information repository. In (Baek, Yeo, & Yeom, 2002), they proposed a dynamic planning algorithm, named n-ary agent chaining which was based on static mobile agent planning to find a new itinerary taking into account dynamic traffic fluctuations on the network. Mobile agents could change their itinerary dynamically according to current network status using n-ary agent chaining algorithm. Finally in (Baek & Yeom, 2003), they presented an agent planning algorithm called *d*-agent for distributed information retrieval. This algorithm was based on the previous studies, and focused in particular on turn-around time.

Yang et al. (Yang, Liu, Yang, & Wang, 2003) proposed the concept of itinerary graph as a reference for the migration strategies of a mobile agent. The three migration strategies were ideal, one-step, and learning. During the migration of a mobile agent, an itinerary plan, was made according to the migration strategy chosen and requirements of tasks. An itinerary graph was made out of the itinerary plan. An itinerary graphs a directed graph similar to a tree with the root as the home site and the other nodes denoting the sites to be visited by the mobile agent. The father node of a node in the graph was the previous site visited by the mobile agent, and the child node was the next site to be visited. The connection line between two nodes represented the moving route of the mobile agent. Each connection line and each node were weighted according to the requirements or constraints of the task. An optimal solution was speed-optimal, price-optimal, and quality-optimal at the same time. Itinerary graph could describe the migration semantics of mobile agent and reflect the change of network environment status where mobile agent lives. During its travel, mobile agent equipped with itinerary graph can perceive these changes, react quickly, modify its migration path autonomously and accomplish its task according to certain specified criterions. In addition to improve the efficiency, the migration strategies could enhance performance of mobile agent systems by avoiding migration failure resulted from network disconnection or node crashing.

The MAP problem is similar to the conventional Traveling Salesperson Problem (TSP). Both of them are NP-Complete problems (Carey & Johnson, 1979; Mañdziuk, 1996; Moizumi, 1998; Talavan & Yanez, 2002). The main issue for such problems is that it is difficult to find out the optimization solution because the computation would become intractable when the number of the variables increases. Among the various methods, Hopfield-Tank neural network is suggested to solve optimization problems for its potential in fast searching the most optimum solution or local optimum solution by massive parallelism (Hopfield & Tank, 1985; Takeda & Goodman, 1986). In 1985, Hopfield and Tank successfully solved the TSP problems by placing optimization problems in a recurrent neural network, the Hopfield-Tank neural network, with the stable convergence of Lyapunov energy function (Hopfield, 1982; Hopfield & Tank, 1985). However, most applications use such network to solve optimization problems in static environment, but not for mobile agent planning problems in dynamic environment.

In this chapter, a modified Hopfield-Tank neural network and a new energy function are presented to cope with the dynamic temporal features of the computing environment, in particular the server performance and network latency when scheduling mobile agents. The location-based constraint that the starting and ending nodes of the routing sequence which must be the home site of the traveling mobile agent is satisfied. In addition, the energy function is reformulated into a Lyapunov function to guarantee the convergence to a stable state and existence of the valid solutions. We begin with an introduction to the mobile agent, Hopfield neural network, and Hopfield-Tank

neural network in Section 2. The MAP problem statement is described in Section 3. The modified Hopfield-Tank neural network and the new energy function are elaborated in Section 4. Section 5 describes the future trends, and the concluding remarks are drawn in the last section.

BACKGROUND

The mobile agent with the characteristics of moving codes is very suitable for developing distributed computing network application systems. A desired functionality of mobile agent is the agent path planning based on network conditions or other significant planning factors. Section 2.1 describes the characteristics, strength, and application fields of a mobile agent. Nowadays, artificial neural network has been successfully applied in different fields to solve many difficult problems. Hopfield-Tank neural network is an artificial neural network model to solve optimization problems. In this chapter, Hopfield-Tank neural network is used to solve MAP problems. Because Hopfield-Tank neural network (Hopfield & Tank, 1985) is extended from Hopfield neural network (Hopfield, 1982), they are based on the same network architecture and basic operation method. The main differences between the two networks are the distinct energy functions and network construction methods. The basic architecture and concept of Hopfield neural network are presented in Section 2.2. Finally, Section 2.3 introduces the construction of Hopfield-Tank neural network with the example of conventional Traveling Salesperson Problem. For simplicity, we use "neural network" and "neurons" instead of "artificial neural network" and "artificial neurons" in this chapter.

The Mobile Agent

A mobile agent is a software program, which is one of the intelligent agent technologies (Fuggetta, Picco, & Vigna, 1998). Mobile agents are able to migrate from one machine to another to directly access the resources of the destination and execute the tasks of a user or another agent in the heterogeneous network system. After finishing its task, a mobile agent will continue to execute the following tasks, or return the execution result to the user. Mobile agents can move not only codes and executable results, but also the executable status of the program, such as the arguments or variables, or even the whole object of the problem.

Due to the characteristics of the mobile agent that it can move codes to remote machines and directly access the resources of the destination, it can largely reduce unnecessary messages and data in the network, and decrease network traffic overload during task execution. Mobile agents can also execute disconnected operations without keeping connecting to the network. Therefore, when the communication network environment is damaged, the mobile agent is able to keep executing goal task by analyzing and judging autonomously and carries out the next task or sends the result back to the user until the network environment is fixed. Compared to conventional distributed computing that relays on message transmission and coordination, such as the Remote Procedure Call (RPC) or the client/server mode, mobile agent not only has a great efficiency, but also reduces network communication cost in a great deal.

The features of a mobile agent make it very suitable for developing distributed network application system. Lange and Oshimau (Lange & Oshima, 1999) drew a conclusion to collect 7 strengths of the mobile agent: the ability to reduce the network load, to overcome network latency, to encapsulate protocols, to execute asynchronously and autonomously, to adapt dynamically, to be naturally heterogeneous, and to be robust and fault-tolerant. The mobile agent is regarded to be one of the most important next-generation distribution techniques (Chess, Harrison, & Kershenbaum, 1995; Fuggetta, Picco, & Vigna, 1998). As many researchers have paid efforts in the area, several mobile agent systems have been developed (Lange & Oshima, 1998, MAL).

Hopfield Neural Network

Hopfield proposed a recurrent associative artificial neural network called Hopfield neural network (Figure 1) in 1982 (Hopfield, 1982). This architecture is a fully connected network that consists of many neurons linked with one another as illustrated in Figure 1. Every neuron receives input from all the other neurons, and outputs the result into these neurons in the network concurrently. There are m neurons in the network, where V_1, V_2, ..., V_m denote the state values of the neurons, and W_{ij} is the connection weight between neurons i and j. Two constraints are required to set the bidirectional symmetric connection weights, $W_{ij} = W_{ji}$ and $W_{ii} = 0$. After the network sets the initial state values $(x_1, x_2, ..., x_m)$ of the neurons, the state values will be modified iteratively according to the activation function. The process will be repeated until the state values converge to certain stable ones (x_1', x_2', ..., x_m'). The equation below which is an activation function can revise the state value of the ith neuron.

$$V_i^{new} = \begin{cases} 1 & if \sum_j W_{ij} V_j^{old} - \theta_i > 0 \\ V_i^{old} & if \sum_j W_{ij} V_j^{old} - \theta_i = 0 \\ -1 & if \sum_j W_{ij} V_j^{old} - \theta_i < 0 \end{cases}$$

where

V_i^{old} = the original state value of the ith neuron,

V_j^{old} = the original state value of the jth neuron,

V_i^{new} = the modified state value of the ith neuron,

and

θ_i = the bias of the ith neuron.

Figure 1. The architecture of Hopfield neural network

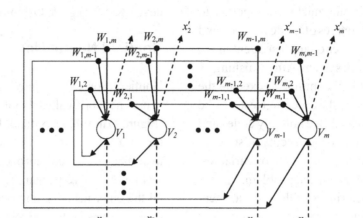

By applying Lyapunov stability theory and finding system-related Lyapunov energy function, the operation of Hopfield neural network can be analyzed and explained. In the field of physics, assume an energy function $E(t)$ represents the energy of system, according to Lyapunov stability theory, if the energy of the system is limited, then the rate of change is always negative, meaning $\frac{\partial E(t)}{\partial t} < 0$. The system energy will reduce as the time passes by, and all the motions in the system are limited until the system converges to a stable state. The system energy then achieves a local minimum.

The energy function that corresponds to Hopfield neural network can be expressed as

$$E = (-\frac{1}{2})\sum_i \sum_j V_i W_{ij} V_j + \sum_j \theta_j V_j$$

where

V_i = the state value of the *i*th neuron. It can only be +1 or -1,

V_j = the state value of the *j*th neuron. It can only be +1 or -1,

W_{ij} = the connection weight between the *i*th neuron and the *j*th neuron, $W_{ij}=W_{ji}$ and $W_{ii}=0$,

and

θ_j = the bias value of the *j*th neuron.

The weight training rule

$$W_{ij} = \sum_p V_i^p \cdot V_j^p$$

where

V_i^p = the *i*th element value of the feature vector of the *p*th training data.

Therefore, if the state values are modified iteratively according to the activation function and the weight training rule, the energy function will converge and achieve a local minimum.

Hopfield showed that given any set of weights and any initial states, the network would eventually converge into a stable state by his parallel relaxation algorithm. The main contribution of Hopfield neural network lies in introducing the research results of the dynamics and statistical mechanics into artificial neural network, and investigating associative memory with Lyapunov energy function. An associative memory is a system which stores mappings of specific input representations to closely resembling output representations. That is to say, a system that "associates" two patterns such that when one is encountered subsequently, the other can be reliably recalled. Besides, Hopfield neural network is also exploited in other application aspects such as the optimization computation (Mañdziuk, J. 1996; Talavan & Yanez, 2002).

The Hopfield-Tank Neural Network

In 1985, J. J. Hopfield and D. W. Tank developed Hopfield-Tank neural network (Hopfield & Tank, 1985). They suggested applying artificial neural network to solve optimization problems, and successfully solved the NP-complete TSP problem.

Hopfield-Tank neural networks are a family of massively parallel architectures that solve difficult problems by the cooperation of highly interconnected but simple computing elements. They can minimize the energy function of a specific problem. The computation complexity will not boost along with the increase of the number of cities when applying Hopfield-Tank neural network to solve the TSP problem. According to the explanations of Takeda (Takeda & Goodman, 1986), Hopfield-Tank network only requires N^2 neurons and a complexity of $O(N^3)$. In this case, the method of the artificial neural network is worth researching due to the significantly reduced computation complexity. But it is worth noticing that the method can only achieve local minimum instead of the best solution.

Hopfield and Tank introduced the neural network for combinatorial optimization problems and solved the TSP problem. The motion equations of the ith neuron were given by

$$\frac{dU_i}{dt} = -\frac{U_i}{\tau} - \frac{\partial E}{\partial V_i}$$

$$V_i = g(U_i) = (\frac{1}{2})(1 + \tanh(\lambda U_i))$$

where

U_i = the input value of the ith neuron,
V_i = the output value of the ith neuron,
E = an energy function,
τ = a constant parameter which can be set to 1 without loss of generality,

and

λ = a constant parameter which determines the slope of the sigmoid function $g()$.

It was shown (Hopfield & Tank, 1985) that the equations of motion for a network with symmetric connections ($W_{ij}=W_{ji}$) always lead to a convergence to stable states, in which the outputs of all neurons remain constant. The stable states of a network were the local minima of the predefined simple Lyapunov-type energy function given by

$$E = (-\frac{1}{2})\sum_i \sum_j V_i W_{ij} V_j + \sum_j \theta_j V_j$$

where

V_i = the state value of the ith neuron. It can only be 0 or 1,
V_j = the state value of the jth neuron. It can only be 0 or 1,
W_{ij} = the connection weight between the ith neuron and the jth neuron,

and

θ_j = the bias value of the jth neuron.

The conditions of $W_{ij}=W_{ji}$ and $W_{ii}=0$ must be always satisfied.

In fact, the operations of Hopfield-Tank network and Hopfield network are the same. What makes the difference is that Hopfield network merely uses simple energy function; whereas, Hopfield-Tank network needs to use suitable energy function in accordance with different applications. Different types of optimization problems require different energy functions. One problem may require several different sub-energy functions corresponding with the constraints. For example, the corresponding energy function for the TSP problem has to include penalty terms to represent problem constraints. In the setting of network architecture, Hopfield-Tank network can set the inner connection weights and bias by using energy function analysis instead of adjusting the inner connection weights by learning massive training data. Therefore, in the process of solving optimization problems by Hopfield-Tank network, a new network model is needed when dealing with a new type of problems.

THE MOBILE AGENT PLANNING PROBLEM

An $N+1$ sites MAP problem consists of a home site H and N remote sites S_1, S_2, ..., S_N (Lin & Wang, 2006; Lin & Wang, 2007). When a mobile agent is sent from the home site to work at N remote sites, it will visit each site exactly once in sequence and return to the home site. There are $N!$ total distinct tours. As server performance and network status dynamically change that can influence the efficiency and the moving time of a mobile agent, they have to be considered to make the completion time the minimum.

An example 4-site 1-agent MAP problem is shown in Figure 2. The home site H is where the user locates. If the user wants to collect data from sites S_1, S_2, and S_3, he or she can assign the mobile agent to visit these three sites. The mobile agent will move to the destined site according to the previously planned schedule whenever it finishes

working in one of the sites. However, during the migration, both server performance and network status are factors dynamically changing in the computing environment. The influences of the two factors are closely related to the completion time of a mobile agent. To illustrate the MAP problem in terms of the above example, we consider the following scenario. Suppose that by long-terms periodical detection, collection, and gathering statistics, it is possible to acquire the data of the server performance at each site and the moving time of a mobile agent between sites. Assume the detection period time is fixed to 300 seconds. Table 1, named the *PoS* table, indicates the server

performance in the time slot T_1 to T_4 of the three sites respectively. Table 2, named the *SoN* table, shows the moving time of a mobile agent in time slot T_1 to T_4 as the mobile agent moves among sites. According to the *PoS* and *SoN* tables, a shortest visiting schedule of the mobile agent can be planned in advance.

Suppose that OCL is the detection time length and x is the moment starting from T_1. Let $T(x)$ be the time slot within contains the moment x, $\tau(x)$ be the starting time of the next time slot for the moment x, $rt(x)$ be the remaining time for the moment x in time slot $T(x)$. Figure 3 shows the relationship between the moment x and the corresponding time slots, where the detection period time length $OCL = 300$ and $x = 360$. Then, $T(x)=2$, $\tau(x)=600$, and $rt(x)=600-x=240$. These values are calculated by the following equations.

$$T(x) = \left\lfloor \frac{x}{OCL} \right\rfloor + 1,$$

$\tau(x)=OCL \cdot T(x),$

$rt(x)=\tau(x)-x.$

In order to correctly calculate the dynamic execution time of a task by a mobile agent at a certain site, the possible time slots which are passed for the execution should be considered.

Figure 2. An example of the MAP problem

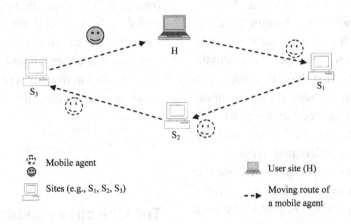

Table 1. The server performance (tasks / s): the PoS table

Time Slot Site	T_1	T_2	T_3	T_4
S_1	0.005556	0.004831	0.004098	0.004525
S_2	0.002924	0.003610	0.003175	0.002681
S_3	0.002083	0.001818	0.002571	0.002433

Table 2. The moving time of the mobile agent (second): the SoN table

Time Slot	T_1				T_2				T_3				T_4			
To From	H	S_1	S_2	S_3	H	S_1	S_2	S_3	H	S_1	S_2	S_3	H	S_1	S_2	S_3
H	0	4	6	3	0	2	4	4	0	3	5	6	0	5	7	5
S_1	4	0	5	2	2	0	3	3	3	0	4	4	5	0	6	4
S_2	6	5	0	7	4	3	0	5	5	4	0	4	7	6	0	4
S_3	3	2	7	0	4	3	5	0	6	4	4	0	5	5	4	0

Figure 3. The relationship between the moment x and the corresponding time slots

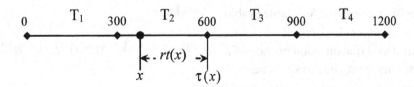

Let rs be the proportion of a task to be completed by a mobile agent at site i during a time slot $T(x)$ given the moment x, and $0 \leq rs \leq 1$. Assume the initial value of rs is 1, which indicates that the mobile agent has not started to work yet. To calculate the execution time, the first thing is to apply the *PoS* table (Table 1) to evaluate if the execution will be completed during a certain time slot. If it can be completed, i.e., $rt(x) \cdot PoS_{i,T(x)} \geq rs$, then the execution time can be calculated according to the *PoS* table. Otherwise, we can recalculate the unfinished rs part, as well as the time cost for a mobile agent to complete the rs part in the next time slot. And then, the remaining time $rt(x)$ is added to this time cost for completing the entire rs part. Thus the execution time for a mobile agent to complete the entire rs part of a task at site i at the moment x is a recursive function and can be expressed as

$$MCS(x,i,rs) = \begin{cases} \dfrac{rs}{PoS_{i,T(x)}} & \text{if } rt(x) \cdot PoS_{i,T(x)} \geq rs \\ rt(x) + MCS(\tau(x), i, rs - rt(x) \cdot PoS_{i,T(x)}) & \text{otherwise} \end{cases}$$

$$(1)$$

Similarly, to calculate the time a mobile agent takes by moving from site i to site j, we have to consider the network status in different time slots while it is moving. Let rm be the unfinished network transmission of a mobile agent when it moves from site i to site j, and $0 \leq m \leq 1$. Assume that the initial value of rm is 1 before the mobile agent starts moving at the moment x. The way to calculate the moving time, firstly, is to check with the *SoN* table to see if it is possible for a mobile agent to finish moving within the remaining time during a time slot. If it is possible, i.e., $rt(x) \geq SoN_{T(x),i,j} \cdot rm$, then we can calculate the execution time in accordance with the *SoN* table (Table 2). Otherwise, we can recalculate the rm value, which is the unfinished transmission portion of a mobile agent moving from site i to sit j when the time period is up of the current time slot as well

as the time cost to complete the rm part in the next time slot. And then, the remaining time $rt(x)$ is added to the time cost for completing the entire rm part. Thus the time cost for a mobile agent to complete the entire rm part when it moves from site i to site j at the moment x is also a recursive function and can be expressed as

$$MCN(x,i,j,rm) = \begin{cases} SoN_{T(x),i,j} \cdot rm & \text{if } rt(x) \geq SoN_{T(x),i,j} \cdot rm \\ rt(x) + MCN(\tau(x), i, j, rm - \dfrac{rt(x)}{SoN_{T(x),i,j}}) & \text{otherwise} \end{cases}$$

$$(2)$$

The Objective Function

The study of the MAP problem seeks to minimize a function with which the completion time of a mobile agent is optimized. By applying (1) and (2), the completion time of a mobile agent can be calculated. Let T_1 be the starting time slot for the mobile agent and 0 be the starting time of T_1. Assume k is the moment that a mobile agent is sent from time slot T_1, $0 \leq k \leq OCL$, where OCL is the detection period length. Suppose that n is the serial number of the nth site visited in a visiting sequence of a mobile agent, where $n \in \{0, 1, \dots, N\}$ and $n = 0$ indicates that the mobile agent is at the home site H. Let $f(n)$ be the moment that a mobile agent arrives site j after leaving the nth site i timed from the beginning of time slot T_1, and $g(n)$ be the moment that a mobile agent finishes a task at the nth site i timed from the beginning of time slot T_1. Then, the objective function can be express as

$$\text{Min}(f(N)-k) \qquad (3)$$

where

$$f(n) = g(n) + MCN(g(n), i, j, 1) \quad 0 \leq n \leq N,$$

$$g(n) = \begin{cases} f(n-1) + MCS(f(n-1), i, 1) & \text{if } 0 < n \leq N \\ k & \text{else } n = 0 \end{cases}$$

Given (3), the time interval for a mobile agent to complete its tour from the beginning of time slot T_1 is $f(N)$. Therefore, the completion time for the mobile agent is $f(N)$-k.

Example

To develop some intuitions, consider a mobile agent passes through S_1, S_2, and S_3, and finally returns to site H in sequence as shown in Figure 2. Assume that $OCL = 300$ and the home site H begins to send out a mobile agent after time slot T_1 started out for 10 seconds, that is k=10. The completion time of the mobile agent can be calculated as follows.

$g(0)$=10

$f(0)$=$g(0)$+$MCN(g(0),H,S_1,1)$=10+4=14

$g(1)$=$f(0)$+$MCS(f(0),S_1,1)$=14+179.99=193.99

$f(1)$=$g(1)$+$MCN(g(1),S_1,S_2,1)$=193.99+5=198.99

$g(2)$=$f(1)$+$MCS(f(1),S_2,1)$=198.99+296.20=495.19

$f(2)$=$g(2)$+$MCN(g(2),S_2,S_3,1)$=495.19+5=500.19

$g(3)$=$f(2)$+$MCS(f(2),S_3,1)$=500.19+419.23=919.42

$f(3)$=$g(3)$+$MCN(g(3),S_3,H,1)$=919.42+5=924.42

Thus, the completion time for the mobile agent is $f(3)$-10=924.42-10=914.42s.

THE MOBILE AGENT PLANNING MODEL

This model intends to solve MAP problems by applying Hopfield-Tank neural network to define new problem status variables, limitations, and goal (Lin & Wang, 2006; Lin & Wang, 2007). In addition, a new energy function is designed to meet constraint requirements and achieve problem goal. The architecture of the network is constructed by the connection weight matrices according to the Lyapunov function which is reformulated based on the energy function. Furthermore, the activation function of state variables in the dynamic network is devised in searching for the valid solutions if the energy function converges. The valid solution with the minimum completion time is the optimal solution.

The State Variables

The completion time for a mobile agent to visit a group of sites and return to the home site is influenced by server performance and network status as time changes. Thus, the state variable method, applied when using Hopfield-Tank network to solve TSP problems, is not suitable for solving MAP problems. A new state variable method should be employed. For the reason that time is sequent, we can divide time into many time slots by using the time length of original network state detection period OCL. Let OCN be the possible number of time slots passed for the mobile agent in a round tour, we define

$$OCN = \left\lceil \frac{\text{the possible completion time} + k}{\text{the time length of detection period}} \right\rceil = \left\lceil \frac{\text{the possible completion time} + k}{OCL} \right\rceil$$

where k is the moment that a mobile agent is sent from time slot T_1. We can estimate OCN by randomly picking up a set of sites as a visiting sequence. Suppose that a random visiting sequence is H, S1, S2, S3, and H. Let OCL=300 s, k=10, and the completion time is 914.42 s. Then

$$OCN = \left\lceil \frac{914.42 + 10}{300} \right\rceil = 4.$$

Let T_1 be the starting time slot when the mobile agent begins to launch at site H. Designing the state variables for the problem in the following way, we can imitate the setting of Hopfield-Tank neural network by changing the visiting sequence of a mobile agent into a sequence of states in which it visits site s within time slot t. Hence, the definition of the state variables of this problem can be: V_{st} shows whether or not the mobile agent is at site s within time slot t. If it is, then $V_{st} = 1$; otherwise, $V_{st} = 0$.

The matrix constructed by variable V_{st} is called a permutation matrix. Consider the example as illustrated in Figure 2, the corresponding permutation matrix is shown in Table 3. Every row represents the visiting status of a site for a mobile agent, and every column is a time slot. From the permutation matrix, it can be observed that a mobile agent will start from site H, visit S_1 and S_2 in T_1, then visit site S_3 in T_2, and finally return to site H in T_4.

The Constraints and Problem Goal

However, the permutation matrix described above has two deficiencies. Firstly, because the starting

and end points of the mobile agent must be the home site H, how to decide the starting and end points of a mobile agent becomes the main problem when using Hopfield-Tank neural network to solve MAP problems. Secondly, Table 3 only shows that a mobile agent visits sites H, S_1, and S_2 in T_1, but it does not show the visiting sequence. Therefore, it requires additional constraints to overcome the difficulty of showing the visiting sequence of a mobile agent. Besides, according to the definition of the problem, other constraints are imposed to achieve the goal of solving the MAP problem by Hopfield-Tank network.

Constraint 1: The Starting and End Points of the Mobile Agent Must Be Site H

Since H must be the starting and end points for a mobile agent, the state values of the corresponding variables are always 1. Thus, the state variables in H-site row of the permutation matrix in the entire Table 3 can be removed as shown in Table 4.

Constraint 2: Visit At Most One Site In Each Time Slot

This constraint merely considers the tour of a mobile agent between sites of the entire network. The sequence of sites visited by a mobile agent in a certain time slot is still not recognizable. For example, assume that the mobile agent visits sites S_1, S_2, and S_3 in sequence. However, from the values of T_1 column in Table 4, although

Table 3. The permutation matrix of state variable V_{st} for a 4-site MAP problem

Time slot Site	T_1	T_2	T_3	T_4
H	1	0	0	1
S_1	1	0	0	0
S_2	1	0	0	0
S_3	0	1	0	0

Table 4. H-site variables and the permutation matrix after the cancellation of H-site row

Starting Site	Time slot Site	T_1	T_2	T_3	T_4	End Site
1	S_1	1	0	0	0	1
	S_2	1	0	0	0	
	S_3	0	1	0	0	

the mobile agent visits S_1 and S_2 in time slot T_1, the sequence of the visiting is not known. The reason of this case is that time slot T_1 ends after the mobile agent starts to work on site S_2. Thus T_1 column shows two sites visited by the mobile agent. Under such circumstances, Hopfield-Tank neural network cannot be applied to find out the minimum completion time for the mobile agent.

To solve this problem, we may rearrange the original detection period *OCL*. Let *k* be the starting moment for the mobile agent and *MCL* be the modified interval of time slot. The basic idea for the modification is that the mobile agent can at most stay in one site within one time slot. Take Table 4 for example, assume that *k*=10 seconds and let *MCL*=180 seconds which is shorter than the original time interval. Then there are seven time slots instead of four time slots as shown in Table 5. In this way, the visiting sequence of the

mobile agent is clearly S_1, S_2, and S_3 as only one state variable has the value of 1 in each time slot of the permutation matrix.

Constraint 3: Visit The Same Site Exactly Once

According to the definition of the problem, the mobile agent can visit each site only once such that only one state variable has the value of 1 in each row of the permutation matrix as shown in Table 6.

Constraint 4: Visit All The N Sites

By definition, the mobile agent can return to the home site H only when it has visited all the *N* sites such that *N* state variables have the value of 1 in the permutation matrix as shown in Table 7.

Table 5. The permutation matrix when time slot length MCL= 180 seconds

Time slot Site	T_1	T_2	T_3	T_4	T_5	T_6	T_7
S_1	1	0	0	0	0	0	0
S_2	0	1	0	0	0	0	0
S_3	0	0	0	1	0	0	0

Table 6. The permutation matrix satisfying Constrain 3

Time slot Site	T_1	T_2	T_3	T_4	T_5	T_6	T_7
S_1	1	0	0	0	0	0	0
S_2	0	1	0	0	0	0	0
S_3	0	0	0	1	0	0	0

Table 7. The permutation matrix satisfying Constrain 4

Time slot Site	T_1	T_2	T_3	T_4	T_5	T_6	T_7
S_1	1	0	0	0	0	0	0
S_2	0	1	0	0	0	0	0
S_3	0	0	0	1	0	0	0

Constraint 5: The Legitimacy of a Tour

The tour of a mobile agent using state variable V_{st} is depicted in Figure 4. Every cell is a state variable and every black directed arrow connecting two state variables represents one of the many segments of the entire tour. A tour segment has two kinds of time costs. The first is the execution time of the mobile agent at one site, and the second is the moving time of the mobile agent from that site to the next site. For example, the time cost of tour segment 2 in Figure 4 is the sum of the execution time of the mobile agent at site S_1 and its moving time from site S_1 to site S_2.

By applying (1) and (2), we can calculate the time cost for the mobile agent to move from site $s1$ to site $s2$ at the moment x by

$$CT(x,s1,s2)=MCS(x,s1,1)+MCN((x+MCS(x,s1,1)),s1,s2,1) \qquad (4)$$

Using (4), we can substitute x by the starting time of a time slot in Table 5, and make Table 8, named the CT table, to represent the time cost of

the mobile agent for executing in site $s1$ and moving from site $s1$ to site $s2$. If $s1 = s2$, then set the value of $CT_{t1,s1,s2}$ in the CT table as 0. Otherwise, if the completion time exceeds the last time slot, then set the value of $CT_{t1,s1,s2}$ as -1. For example, the time cost of tour segment for a mobile agent moves from site S_3 to site S_1 at the moment 10 with $OCL = 300$ can be calculated as follows.

$$CT(10,S_3,S_1)=MCS(10,S_3,1)+MCN((10+MCS(10,S_3,1)),S_3,S_1,1) =290+MCS(300,S_3,0.39593)+ MCN((10+MCS(10,S_3,1)),S_3,S_3,1)$$

$$=507.78+MCN((10+507.78),S_3,S_3,1)$$

$$=507.78+3=510.78$$

The CT table can be used to calculate the time slot in which the mobile agent finishes moving to site $s2$ from site $s1$ at time slot $t1$ by

$$NC(t1, s1, s2) = Round\left(\frac{CT_{t1,s1,s2}}{MCL} + t1\right) \qquad (5)$$

Figure 4. The tour of a mobile agent using state variables

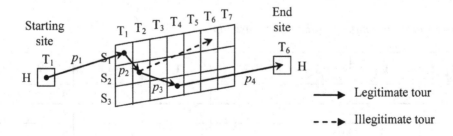

Table 8. The completion time CT() for the mobile agent to move between sites in each time slot (CT Table)

Time Slot	T_1 (10-190)				T_2 (190-370)				T_3 (370-550)			
To From	H	S_1	S_2	S_3	H	S_1	S_2	S_3	H	S_1	S_2	S_3
H	0	4	6	3	0	4	6	3	0	2	4	4
S_1	183.99	0	184.99	181.99	192.49	0	193.49	193.49	209.00	0	210.00	210.00
S_2	336.12	335.12	0	337.12	301.91	300.91	0	302.91	288.45	287.45	0	287.45
S_3	511.78	510.78	512.78	0	503.70	501.70	501.70	0	462.32	460.32	460.32	0

Time Slot	T_4 (550-730)				T_5 (730-910)				T_6 (910-1090)			
To From	H	S_1	S_2	S_3	H	S_1	S_2	S_3	H	S_1	S_2	S_3
H	0	2	4	4	0	3	5	6	0	5	7	5
S_1	238.08	0	239.08	239.08	242.04	0	243.04	241.04	225.99	0	226.99	224.99
S_2	313.11	312.11	0	312.11	348.67	347.67	0	345.67	-1	-1	0	-1
S_3	411.64	411.64	410.64	0	406.37	406.37	405.37	0	-1	-1	-1	0

Time Slot	T_7 (1090-1200)			
To From	H	S_1	S_2	S_3
H	0	5	7	5
S_1	-1	0	-1	-1
S_2	-1	-1	0	-1
S_3	-1	-1	-1	0

For example, the time slot in which the mobile agent finishes moving to site S_1 from site S_3 at time slot T_1 with *MCL* = 180 can be calculated as follows.

$$NC(1, S_3, S_1) = Round\left(\frac{CT_{1,S_3,S_1}}{180} + 1\right)$$
$$= Round\left(\frac{510.78}{180} + 1\right)$$
$$= Round(3.83) = 4$$

This helps in judging the legitimacy of the tour between two consecutive sites of a mobile agent, and controlling the time slot where the mobile agent is in when it finishes visiting a certain site. By rounding off the value of the above calculation,

the predicted time slot in which the mobile agent arrives at the next site for a visit can be collected as shown in Table 9, called the *NC* table. From the table whether the tour of a mobile agent is legitimate can be judged. The value -1 in the table indicates that the time of the move exceeds the last time slot.

Assume that the round circle at the tail of an arrow in Figure 4 connects the state variable V_{s1t1}, and the arrow directs to the state variable V_{s2t2}. Then $s1$ is the starting site and $t1$ is the starting time slot of the mobile agent; whereas $s2$ is the site to be visited by the mobile agent after finishing the job in $s1$, and $t2$ is the time slot in which the mobile agent arrives $s2$. The time cost of that tour segment, known as $CT_{t1,s1,s2}$, can be found in

Table 9. Predicted time slot NC() in which the mobile agent arrives at the next site for a visit in each time slot (NC Table)

Time Slot	T_1 (10-190)				T_2 (190-370)				T_3 (370-550)			
To From	H	S_1	S_2	S_3	H	S_1	S_2	S_3	H	S_1	S_2	S_3
H	1	1	1	1	2	2	2	2	3	3	3	3
S_1	2	1	2	2	3	2	3	3	4	3	4	4
S_2	3	3	1	3	4	4	2	4	5	5	3	5
S_3	4	4	4	1	5	5	5	2	6	6	6	3

Time Slot	T_4 (550-730)				T_5 (730-910)				T_6 (910-1090)			
To From	H	S_1	S_2	S_3	H	S_1	S_2	S_3	H	S_1	S_2	S_3
H	4	4	4	4	5	5	5	5	6	6	6	6
S_1	5	4	5	5	6	5	6	6	7	6	7	7
S_2	6	6	4	6	7	7	5	7	-1	-1	6	-1
S_3	6	6	6	4	7	7	7	5	-1	-1	-1	6

Time Slot	T_7 (1090-1200)			
To From	H	S_1	S_2	S_3
H	7	7	7	7
S_1	-1	7	-1	-1
S_2	-1	-1	7	-1
S_3	-1	-1	-1	7

the *CT* table, and *t2* can also be examined with the *NC* table to see if it is consistent with $NC_{t1,s1,s2}$. If they are equal, then the tour is a legitimate one. Otherwise, it is illegitimate. Consider the state variables $V_{S_2 T_2}$ and $V_{S_3 T}$ of tour segment p_3 in Figure 4 for example. According to the *NC* table, the end time slot of the tour NC_{T_2, S_2, S_3} is T_4, the same as that of the state variable $V_{S_3 T}$. Thus, this tour is legitimate, and the time cost is NC_{T_2, S_2, S_3}. Suppose that the state variable $V_{S_3 T}$ is replaced by V_{S_1, T_6}, as the dotted line arrow. By the *NC* table, the end time slot of NC_{T_2, S_2, S_3} is T_4. However, the end time slot of state variable V_{S_1, T_6} is T_6. Thus the tour is illegitimate and additional constraints should be added to avoid the irrationality of the tour.

Problem Goal: Minimum Completion Time for a Mobile Agent

The problem goal is to find the sequence of the sites being visited to make the completion time of the mobile agent the minimum. In this section the explanation of how to calculate the completion time of the mobile agent by taking advantage of artificial neural network is described.

Consider the example as shown in Figure 4, the moving sequence of the mobile agent is p_1, p_2, p_3, and p_4. The completion time for the mobile agent is the sum of time cost of tour segments $p_1 + p_2 + p_3 + p_4 = CT_{T_1, H, S_1} + CT_{T_1, S_1, S_2} + CT_{T_2, S_2, S_3} + CT_{T_4, S_3, H} = 4.0 + 184.99 + 302.91 + 411.64 = 903.54s$.

This result differs from the actual completion time of the mobile agent, 914.42s as described in section II. It is difficult even to predict the starting and end points of the mobile agent by calculating the time cost between sites in each time slot, let alone the prediction of an actual completion time. We can only have the most approximate value by approaching. The value thus can represent its sequence that is "comparatively" better. The lower the value is, the higher the possibility is to have the minimum routing time.

According to the above discussion, an amount of $N*Q+2$ neurons can help solving the MAP problems where $Q = \left| \dfrac{OCL \cdot OCN}{MCL} \right|$ which is the number of time slots produced after resetting the length of the time slot visited by the mobile agent. OCL is the original length of detection period, OCN is the number of time slots probably passed through by the mobile agent, and MCL is the modified length of the time slot. For example, when $OCL=300$, $OCN=4$, and $MCL=180$, the number of time slots produced would be $Q = \left| \dfrac{300.4}{180} \right| = 7$.

Because a mobile agent visits at most one site in each time slot (Constraint 2), the relation of Q and N is $Q \geq N$. When $N = 3$, $Q = 7$, there are $3*7+2=21$ neurons in total as shown in Figure 4.

The MAP Energy Function

Hopfield-Tank neural networks are a family of massively parallel architectures that solve difficult problems by the cooperation of highly interconnected but simple computing elements. The problem modeled by the network maybe described as an energy function to be minimized. However, such energy function must be consistent with the constraints and goal of the problem. The strategies of designing the energy function that corresponds to MAP problem according to its constraints and goal are discussed and presented. For a more smooth discussion, in the equations below, we set variables $s1$ and $s2$ as two random sites, where $1 \leq s1, s2 \leq N$, and set $t1$ and $t2$ as certain time slots,

where $1 \leq t1, t2 \leq Q$. Consider the permutation matrix as shown in Table 5 for example, the amount of sites $N=3$, and the amount of time slots $Q=7$. The proposed energy function E is expressed in terms of variables E_1, E_2, E_3, E_4, and E_5 to satisfy constraints 2 to 5 and achieve goal of the MAP problem described above, respectively.

Constraint 2: Visit At Most One Site In Each Time Slot

With this constraint, not more than one state variable is allowed to be 1 in the same column of the permutation matrix. This constraint can be expressed as the minimization of

$$E_1 = \frac{1}{2} \sum_{s1} \sum_{t1} \sum_{s2 \neq s1} V_{s1,t1} \cdot V_{s2,t1} \qquad (6)$$

If the values of all the state variables in the permutation matrix agree with this constraint, then the minimum value of E_1 equals 0. Otherwise, E_1 is greater than 0.

Constraint 3: Visit The Same Site Exactly Once

With this constraint, only one state variable is 1 in the same row of the permutation matrix. This constraint can be expressed as the minimization of

$$E_2 = \frac{1}{2} \sum_{s1} \sum_{t1} \sum_{t2 \neq t1} V_{s1,t1} \cdot V_{s1,t2} \qquad (7)$$

If the values of all the state variables in the permutation matrix agree with this constraint, then the minimum value of E_2 equals 0. Otherwise, E_2 is greater than 0.

Constraint 4: Visit All The N Sites

With this constraint, exactly N state variables are 1 in the permutation matrix. This constraint can be expressed as the minimization of

$$E_3 = \frac{1}{2}\left|\left(\sum_{s1}\sum_{t1}V_{s1,t1}\right) - N\right|^2 \qquad (8)$$

If the values of all the state variables in the permutation matrix agree with this constraint, then the minimum value of E_3 equals 0. Otherwise, E_3 is greater than 0.

Constraint 5: The Legitimacy of a Tour

In order to control the legitimacy of the tour of a mobile agent and time cost, *NEAR* array is designed to record the column number (or time slot number) if the column has at least an element with a value of 1 in the permutation matrix. By looking at the data in Table 5, the *NEAR* array will record $near_1$ = T_1, $near_2 = T_2$, $near_3 = T_4$ respectively. The size of this array $L = 3$. This array represents that T_1, T_2, and T_4 are the time slots that a mobile agent visited the sites in sequence.

When considering the legitimacy of the tours between two consecutive sites of a mobile agent, three conditions have to be examined: the distance from the starting site H to the first site, the tour segments between the sites except home site, and the distance from the last site back to site H. Thus, the energy function that agrees with the legitimacy constraint has to reflect these three conditions.

Consider the setting in Figure 4. Assume we have to examine $near_1$ to see if the mobile agent finishes its visit in the current time slot when it moves from site H to site $s1$. The inspection can be defined as

$$\sum_{s1}V_{s1,near_1}\cdot(1 - \delta(NC_{1,H,s1}, near_1)) \qquad (9)$$

where the function $\delta(a,b)$ can be used to judge whether a and b are equal. It can be expressed as follows.

$$\delta(a,b) = \begin{cases} 1 & \text{if } a = b \\ 0 & \text{otherwise} \end{cases}$$

Because the starting time slot of the mobile agent must be the first time slot, we can check if the value of $NC_{1,H,s1}$ in the *NC* table is the same as the value of $near_1$. If it is the same, then the tour is legitimate, and the result of (9) is 0. Otherwise, the tour is illegitimate, and the value is greater than 0.

As for the tour segments between the sites except home site, if the mobile agent is in time slot $near_i$ when it works in site $s1$, then we have to consider two situations. First, if site $s2$ is the site to be visited of the tour, then we have to examine whether $near_{i+1}$ is the time slot in which this tour ends. Second, if site $s2$ is the starting site of the tour, then we have to examine if $near_i$ is the time slot in which this tour ends. The inspection can be expressed as

$$\frac{1}{2}\sum_{s1}\sum_{i}\sum_{s2\neq s1}\left(V_{s1,near_i}\cdot V_{s2,near_{i+1}}\right.$$
$$\cdot\left(1 - \delta(near_{i+1}, NC_{near_i,s1.s2})\right)$$
$$+V_{s1,near_i}\cdot V_{s2,near_{i-1}}$$
$$\left.\cdot\left(1 - \delta(near_i, NC_{near_{i-1},s2,s1})\right)\right) \qquad (10)$$

Thus, if $s2$ is the site to be visited from $s1$, then we can check if the value of $NC_{near_i,s1,s2}$ in the *NC* table is the same as the value of $near_{i+1}$. If $s2$ is the starting site to $s1$, then we can also check if the value of $NC_{near_{i-1},s2,s1}$ in the *NC* table is the same as the values of $near_i$. If the values of state variables can pass the above examinations, then the total tour is a legitimate one, and the value of the energy function is the minimum 0. Otherwise, there are illegitimate tours, and the value is greater than 0.

For the mobile agent that returns from the last site $s1$ to site H, the starting time slot of this move is $near_L$. Under such circumstance, the legitimacy constraint is to check if this move is within the last time slot or not. If it not, then the tour is illegitimate. The inspection is expressed as

$$\sum_{s1} V_{s1,near_L} \cdot \delta(NC_{near_L,s1,H}, -1) \quad (11)$$

Equation (11) indicates that if this move agrees with the legitimacy constraint, then the value of the result equals 0. Otherwise, it is greater than 0.

At this point, we can integrate (9), (10), and (11) into E_4 that can constrain the legitimacy of a tour and be expressed as

$$\begin{aligned}
e_4 &= \sum_{s1} V_{s1,near_i} \cdot \left(1 - \delta(NC_{1,H,s1}, near_i)\right) \\
&+ \frac{1}{2} \sum_{s1} \sum_i \sum_{s2 \neq s1} \left(V_{s1,near_i} \cdot V_{s2,near_{i+1}} \cdot \left(1 - \delta(near_{i+1}, NC_{near_i,s1,s2})\right)\right. \\
&+ V_{s1,near_i} \cdot V_{s2,near_{i-1}} \cdot \left.\left(1 - \delta(near_i, NC_{near_{i-1},s2,s1})\right)\right) \\
&+ \sum_{s1} V_{s1,nrar_L} \cdot \delta\left(NC_{near_L,s1,H}, -1\right)
\end{aligned} \quad (12)$$

Problem Goal: Minimum Completion Time for a Mobile Agent

The method to calculate E_5 for the problem goal is similar to that of deriving E_4 for Constraint 5. The only difference is E_5 is aimed to compute the time cost if the tour is legitimate. If the tour between two consecutive sites is legitimate, then we can add the cost of this tour, according to the CT table, into the total completion time of the mobile agent. If the tour between two consecutive sites is illegitimate, then we ignore it. To attain the goal of the minimum completion time of the mobile agent, we also have to examine the following three conditions: the distance from the starting site H to the first site, the tour segments between the remote sites, and the distance from the last site back to site H.

Consider again the setting in Figure 4. Assume the mobile agent moves from the starting site H to the first site $s1$ and $near_1$ is the time slot when the mobile agent arrives $s1$. We can judge whether the tour is legitimate or not by checking the NC table. If it is legitimate, then add the time cost of this tour into the completion time of the mobile agent. The inspection can be defined as

$$\sum_{s1} CT_{near_i,H,s1} \cdot V_{s1,near_i} \cdot \delta(NC_{1,H,s1}, near_1) \quad (13)$$

As for the tour segments between the sites except home site, if the mobile agent is in time slot $near_i$ when it works in site $s1$, then we have to consider two situations. First, if site $s2$ is the site to be visited of the tour, then we have to examine whether $near_{i+1}$ is the time slot in which this tour ends. Second, if site $s2$ is the starting site of the tour, then we have to examine if $near_i$ is the time slot in which this tour ends. If all the above tour segments are legitimate, then add the time cost of this tour into the completion time of the mobile agent. Otherwise, we ignore it. The inspection can be expressed as

$$\begin{aligned}
\frac{1}{2} \sum_{s1} \sum_i \sum_{s2 \neq s1} &\left(CT_{near_i,s1,s2} \cdot V_{s1,near_i} \cdot V_{s2,near_{i+1}} \cdot \delta\left(near_{i+1}, NC_{near_i,s1,s2}\right)\right. \\
&+ CT_{near_{i-1},s2,s1} \cdot V_{s1,near_i} \cdot V_{s2,near_{i-1}} \cdot \left.\delta\left(near_i, NC_{near_{i-1},s2,s1}\right)\right)
\end{aligned} \quad (14)$$

For the mobile agent that returns from the last site $s1$ to site H, the starting time slot of this move is represented by the variable $near_L$. Under such circumstance, we have to check if this move is within last time slot or not. If it is, then the tour is legitimate. And we can add the time cost of this tour into the completion time of the mobile agent. The inspection can be expressed as

$$\begin{aligned}
\sum_{s1} &CT_{near_L,s1,H} \cdot V_{s1,near_L} \\
&\cdot \left(1 - \delta\left(NC_{near_L,s1,H} - 1\right)\right)
\end{aligned} \quad (15)$$

Finally, we can obtain the information about the time cost corresponding to a given tour when searching for the valid tour with minimum cost for the problem goal of a mobile agent by adding (13), (14), and (15) together as

$$
\begin{aligned}
E_5 &= \sum_{s1} CT_{near_i,H,s1} \cdot V_{s1,near_i} \cdot \delta\left(NC_{1,H,s1}, near_1\right) \\
&+ \frac{1}{2}\sum_{s1}\sum_{i}\sum_{s2\neq s1}\left(CT_{near_i,s1,s2} \cdot V_{s1,near_i} \cdot V_{s2,near_{i+1}} \cdot \delta\left(near_{i+1}, NC_{near_i,s1,s2}\right)\right. \\
&+ CT_{near_{i-1},s2,s1} \cdot V_{s1,near_i} \cdot V_{s2,near_{i-1}} \cdot \delta\left(near_i, NC_{near_{i-1},s2,s1}\right)\right) \\
&+ \sum_{s1} CT_{near_L,s1,H} \cdot V_{s1,near_L} \cdot \left(1 - \delta\left(NC_{near_L,s1,H} - 1\right)\right)
\end{aligned}
$$

(16)

To summarize the discussions about E_1, E_2, E_3, E_4, and E_5, if these variables reach their minimum values and $E_1 = E_2 = E_3 = E_4 = 0$, then the solution must be valid and best. By using weighted method—multiply each function by one coefficient, and add them all—then we can have the energy function E for the Mobile Agent Planning problem as follows.

$$
\begin{aligned}
E &= AE_1 + BE_2 + CE_4DE_4 + FE_5 \\
&= \frac{A}{2}\sum_{s1}\sum_{t1}\sum_{s2\neq s1} V_{s1,t1} \cdot V_{s2,t1} \\
&+ \frac{B}{2}\sum_{s1}\sum_{t1}\sum_{t2\neq t1} V_{s1,t1} \cdot V_{s1,t2} \\
&+ \frac{C}{2}\left[\left[\sum_{s1}\sum_{t1} V_{s1,t1}\right] - N\right]^2 \\
&+ D\sum_{s1} V_{s1,near_1} \cdot \left(1 - \delta\left(NC_{1,H,s1}, near_1\right)\right) \\
&+ \frac{D}{2}\sum_{s1}\sum_{i}\sum_{s2\neq s1}\left(V_{s1,near_i} \cdot V_{s2,near_{i+1}} \cdot \left(1 - \delta\left(near_{i+1}, NC_{near_i,s1,s2}\right)\right)\right. \\
&+ V_{s1,near_i} \cdot V_{s2,near_{i-1}} \cdot \left(1 - \delta\left(near_i, NC_{near_{i-1},s2,s1}\right)\right)\right) \\
&+ D\sum_{s1} V_{s1,near_L} \cdot \delta\left(NC_{near_L,s1,H}, -1\right) \\
&+ F\sum_{s1} CT_{near_1,H,s1} \cdot V_{s1,near_1} \cdot \delta\left(NC_{1,H,s1}, near_1\right) \\
&+ \frac{F}{2}\sum_{s1}\sum_{i}\sum_{s2\neq s1}\left(CT_{near_i,s1,s2} \cdot V_{s1,near_i} \cdot V_{s2,near_{i+1}} \cdot \delta\left(near_{i+1}, NC_{near_i,s1,s2}\right)\right. \\
&+ CT_{near_{i-1},s2,s1} \cdot V_{s1,near_i} \cdot V_{s2,near_{i-1}} \cdot \delta\left(near_i, NC_{near_{i-1},s2,s1}\right)\right) \\
&+ F\sum_{s1} CT_{near_L,s1,H} \cdot V_{s1,near_L} \cdot \left(1 - \delta\left(NC_{near_L,s1,H}, -1\right)\right)
\end{aligned}
$$

(17)

The Connection Weight Matrices

After deriving the energy function E (17), we can build the architecture of the neural network for MAP problem. In order to introduce the connection weight matrix of the network, we have to compare (17) with Lyapunov energy function and rewrite Lyapunov energy function to guarantee the convergence of the neural network (Appendix) as follows.

$$
\begin{aligned}
E &= \frac{-1}{2}\sum_{s1}\sum_{t1}\sum_{s2}\sum_{t2} V_{s1,t1} X_{s1,t1,s2,t2} V_{s2,t2} \\
&+ \sum_{s1}\sum_{t1} \theta_{s1,t1} V_{s1,t1}
\end{aligned}
$$

(18)

where

V_{st} = the state of site s in time slot t

$X_{s1,t1,s2,t2}$ = the connection weight matrix between site $s1$ in time slot $t1$ and site $s2$ in time slot $t2$

and

θs_t = the bias of site s in time slot t.

There are three forms of the connection weight matrix X to construct the architecture of the Hopfield-Tank network for MAP problems. The connection weight matrix X of the tour from starting site H to the first site $s1$ in time slot $t1$ can be defined as

$$
\begin{aligned}
X &= HSW_{s1,t1} = -D \cdot \left(1 - \delta\left(NC_{1,H,s1}, t1\right)\right) \\
&- F \cdot CT_{t1,H,s1} \cdot \delta\left(NC_{1,H,s1}, t1\right)
\end{aligned}
$$

(19)

The connection weight matrix X of the tour among sites except home site can be defined as

$$X = W_{s1,t1,s2,t2} = -A \cdot \delta\left(t1,t2\right) \cdot \left(1 - \delta\left(s1,s2\right)\right)$$
$$-B \cdot \delta\left(s1,s2\right) \cdot \left(1 - \delta\left(t1,t2\right)\right)$$
$$-C$$
$$-D \cdot \lambda\left(t2,t1\right) \cdot \left(1 - \delta\left(t2, NC_{t1,s1,s2}\right)\right)$$
$$-D \cdot \lambda\left(t1,t2\right) \cdot \left(1 - \delta\left(t1, NC_{t2,s2,s1}\right)\right)$$
$$-F \cdot CT_{t1,s1,s2} \cdot \lambda\left(t2,t1\right) \cdot \delta\left(t2, NC_{t1,s1,s2}\right)$$
$$-F \cdot CT_{t2,s2,s1} \cdot \lambda\left(t1,t2\right) \cdot \delta\left(t1, NC_{t2,s2,s1}\right) \tag{20}$$

where $\lambda\left(a,b\right) = \begin{cases} 1 & \text{if } a > b \\ 0 & \text{otherwise} \end{cases}$

The connection weight matrix X of the tour from the last site $s1$ back to site H, can be defined as

$$X = SHW_{s1,t1} = -D \cdot \delta\left(NC_{t1,s1,H}, -1\right)$$
$$-F \cdot CT_{t1,s1,H} \cdot \left(1 - \delta\left(NC_{t1,s1,H}, -1\right)\right) \tag{21}$$

Finally, the bias matrix can be set as

$$\Theta_{s1,t1} = -C \cdot N \tag{22}$$

Example

To understand the features of the connection weight matrix, assume that $s1=2$ and $t1=2$ for a 4-site 1-agent MAP problem as shown in Figure 2. There are three forms of the connection weight matrix X to construct the architecture of the Hopfield-Tank network for MAP problems. The values of each connection weight matrix can be obtained in terms of $\delta(a,b)$ and $\lambda(a,b)$ over the three sites and seven time slots.

The connection weight matrix X of the tour from starting site H to the first site $s1$ in time slot $t1$ can be obtained as

$$HSW_{2,2} = -D \cdot \left(1 - \delta\left(NC_{1,H,s1}, t1\right)\right) - F \cdot CT_{t1,H,s1} \cdot \delta\left(NC_{1,H,s1}, t1\right)$$
$$= -D \cdot \left(1 - \delta\left(NC_{1,H,2}, 2\right)\right) - F \cdot CT_{2,H,2} \cdot \delta\left(NC_{1,H,2}, 2\right)$$
$$= -D \cdot \left(1 - \delta\left(1,2\right)\right) - F \cdot CT_{2,H,2} \cdot \delta\left(1,2\right)$$
$$= -D \cdot \left(1 - 0\right) - F \cdot CT_{2,H,2} \cdot 0$$
$$= -D$$

The connection weight matrix X of the tour among sites except home site can be calculated as

$$W_{2,2,s2,t2} = -A \cdot \delta\left(t1,t2\right) \cdot \left(1 - \delta\left(s1,s2\right)\right)$$
$$-B \cdot \delta\left(s1,s2\right) \cdot \left(1 - \delta\left(t1,t2\right)\right)$$
$$-C$$
$$-D \cdot \lambda\left(t2,t1\right) \cdot \left(1 - \delta\left(t2, NC_{t1,s1,s2}\right)\right)$$
$$-D \cdot \lambda\left(t1,t2\right) \cdot \left(1 - \delta\left(t1, NC_{t2,s2,s1}\right)\right)$$
$$-F \cdot CT_{t1,s1,s2} \cdot \lambda\left(t2,t1\right) \cdot \delta\left(t2, NC_{t1,s1,s2}\right)$$
$$-F \cdot CT_{t2,s2,s1} \cdot \lambda\left(t1,t2\right) \cdot \delta\left(t1, NC_{t2,s2,s1}\right)$$
$$= -A \cdot \delta\left(2,t2\right) \cdot \left(1 - \delta\left(2,s2\right)\right)$$
$$-B \cdot \delta\left(2,s2\right) \cdot \left(1 - \delta\left(2,t2\right)\right)$$
$$-C$$
$$-D \cdot \lambda\left(t2,2\right) \cdot \left(1 - \delta\left(t2, NC_{2,2,s2}\right)\right)$$
$$-D \cdot \lambda\left(2,t2\right) \cdot \left(1 - \delta\left(2, NC_{t2,s2,2}\right)\right)$$
$$-F \cdot CT_{2,2,s2} \cdot \lambda\left(t2,2\right) \cdot \delta\left(t2, NC_{2,2,s2}\right)$$
$$-F \cdot CT_{t2,s2,2} \cdot \lambda\left(2,t2\right) \cdot \delta\left(2, NC_{t2,s2,2}\right)$$

The values of the first term of the connection weight matrix $W_{2,2,s2,t2}$, $-A \cdot \delta(2,t2) \cdot (1 - \delta(2,s2))$, can be obtained and represented by the following table.

Similarly, the values of the second term of the connection weight matrix $W_{2,2,s2,t2}$, $-B \cdot \delta(2,t2) \cdot (1 - \delta(2,s2))$, can be obtained and represented by the following table.

In this same manner, the values of the rest terms of the connection weight matrix $W_{2,2,s2,t2}$ can be calculated. We then obtain

Table 10.

t2 s2	T_1	T_2	T_3	T_4	T_5	T_6	T_7
S_1	0	A	0	0	0	0	0
S_2	0	0	0	0	0	0	0
S_3	0	A	0	0	0	0	0

Table 11.

t2 s2	T_1	T_2	T_3	T_4	T_5	T_6	T_7
S_1	0	0	0	0	0	0	0
S_2	B	0	B	B	B	B	B
S_3	0	0	0	0	0	0	0

$$W_{2,2,s2,t2} = -\begin{vmatrix} 0 & A & 0 & 0 & 0 & 0 & 0 \\ B & 0 & B & B & B & B & B \\ 0 & A & 0 & 0 & 0 & 0 & 0 \end{vmatrix} - \begin{vmatrix} C & C & C & C & C & C & C \\ C & C & C & C & C & C & C \\ C & C & C & C & C & C & C \end{vmatrix}$$

$$-\begin{vmatrix} 0 & 0 & D & 0 & D & D & D \\ 0 & 0 & 0 & 0 & 0 & 0 & 0 \\ D & 0 & D & 0 & D & D & D \end{vmatrix} - F \cdot \begin{vmatrix} CT_{1,1,2} & 0 & 0 & CT_{2,2,1} & 0 & 0 & 0 \\ 0 & 0 & 0 & 0 & 0 & 0 & 0 \\ 0 & 0 & 0 & CT_{2,2,3} & 0 & 0 & 0 \end{vmatrix}$$

The connection weight matrix X of the tour from the last site $s1$ back to site H, can be obtained as

$$SHW_{2,2} = -D \cdot \delta\left(NC_{t1,s1,H}, -1\right) - F \cdot CT_{t1,s1,H} \cdot \left(1 - \delta\left(NC_{t1,s1,H}, -1\right)\right)$$
$$= -D \cdot \delta\left(NC_{2,2,H}, -1\right) - F \cdot CT_{2,2,H} \cdot \left(1 - \delta\left(NC_{2,2,H}, -1\right)\right)$$
$$= -D \cdot \delta\left(4, -1\right) - F \cdot CT_{2,2,H} \cdot \left(1 - \delta\left(4, -1\right)\right)$$
$$= -D \cdot 0 - F \cdot CT_{2,2,H} \cdot \left(1 - 0\right)$$
$$= -F \cdot CT_{2,2,H}$$

Finally, the bias matrix can be obtained as

$$\theta_{2,2} = -C \cdot N = -3 \cdot C$$

where $1 \leq s2 \leq 3$ and $1 \leq t2 \leq 7$.

With the modified Lyapunov energy function to model the system network which solves the MAP, the system may converge to a valid solution which minimizes the energy function E.

The Activation Function

After constructing the architecture of neural networks for solving the MAP problem, we can modify the dynamic neuronal state variables by applying the following equation.

$$V_{s1,t1}^{n+1} = \begin{cases} 1 & \text{if} \quad net_{s1,t1}^{n+1} > 0 \\ V_{s1,t1}^{n} & \text{if} \quad net_{s1,t1}^{n+1} = 0 \\ 0 & \text{if} \quad net_{s1,t1}^{n+1} < 0 \end{cases} \quad (23)$$

where

$$net_{s1,t1}^{n+1} = HSW_{s1,t1} + \sum_{s2}\sum_{t2} W_{s1,t1,s2,t2} \cdot V_{s2,t2}^{n} + SHW_{s1,t1} - \theta_{s1,t1}$$

The above activation function is repeated until the network energy converges without violating any constraints. That is to say, when the values of E_1, E_2, E_3, and E_4 for the general constraints are all 0, the minimal network cost is a solution of the problem.

The MAP Algorithm

The steps of solving MAP problems with the proposed modified Hopfield-Tank neural network are presented as follows.

1. Randomly pick up a tour sequence and calculate the cost for a mobile agent to complete its task to estimate the possible number of time slots *OCN* needed.
2. Set new length of the time slot *MCL* and coefficients *A*, *B*, *C*, *D*, and *F*.
3. Set the values of connection weight matrices *HSW*, *W*, and *SHW*, and bias weight matrix θ according to corresponding formulas, respectively.
4. Initialize the permutation matrix, often randomly, of the neuronal state variables.
5. Modify each neuronal state variable in the neural network by applying the activation function.
6. Repeat step 5 until the energy function *E* converges without violating any constraints or the predefined number of iterations is reached to search for the valid solutions. One of these valid solutions might be the best solution for the MAP problem.
7. Substitute each valid solution into objective function to calculate the completion time of the mobile agent.
8. Output the optimal solution. The one with the minimum completion time is the optimal solution.

Step 2 indicates that many coefficients have to be considered when using neural network to solve MAP problems. Besides, careful setting of the coefficient value is required because it can influence the quality of the solution drastically. However, the setting of the coefficients is lack of a systematic method, and can only rely on experiences and trial-and-error.

FUTURE TRENDS

The application fields of mobile agent mainly include e-commerce, web services, distributed software, information retrieval, systematic control, and network management. Taking advantage of the mobility of the mobile agent, better service quality and network performance can be attained. When these application techniques became more mature, mobile agents will be seen roam among hosts or nodes in the network, communicating and negotiating with other mobile agents in order to complete the tasks of the users. A desired functionality of mobile agent is the agent path planning based on network conditions or other significant planning factors. Mobile agent planning is a well-studied research topic known to perform a distributed computing application in an efficient way. In general, to conduct mobile agent planning problem, mobile agents must have knowledge of the network conditions so that they can adapt to the network environment and make the best use of the available resources such as the history of network conditions, which can facilitate their tasks in achieving the expected performances.

The area of mobile agent planning is moving towards multiple agents and grid computing with geographically dispersed grids. Another important research topic is to enhance the capability of the mobile agent. The mobile agents are expected to equip the ability of perceiving the change of network environment status where they are routing and adapt dynamically to maintain an appropriate number of agents alive to reduce the traffic in the network.

CONCLUSION

Mobile agent planning (MAP) is increasingly viewed as an important technique of information retrieval systems to provide location aware services of minimum cost in mobile computing environment. To solve this difficult problem with complex spatio-temporal constraints, in this chapter, a new model with a new energy function has been introduced and how it can be applied to solve the MAP problem by utilizing Hopfield-Tank neural network is shown. The energy function is reformulated into a Lyapunov function to guarantee the convergent stable state and existence of the valid solution. The connection weights between the neurons and the activation function of state variables in the dynamic network are devised in searching for the valid solutions. Moreover, the objective function is derived to estimate the completion time of the valid solutions and predict the optimal routing path. The primary goal of finding the near-optimum solutions could be achieved in terms of the computation time and the solution quality. The algorithm could be easily modified and applied to solve similar optimization problems in dynamic environment. The spatio-temporal technique presented in this chapter is an innovative approach in providing knowledge applicable to improving the effectiveness of solving optimization problems.

REFERENCES

Baek, J., Kim, G., & Yeom, H. (2002). Cost effective planning of timed mobile agent. In *Proceedings of the international conference on information technology: Coding and computing* (pp. 536–541).

Baek, J., Yeo, J., Kim, G., & Yeom, H. (2001). Cost effective mobile agent planning for distributed information retrieval. In *Proceedings of the 21st international conference on distributed computing systems* (pp. 65–72).

Baek, J., Yeo, J., & Yeom, H. (2002). Agent chaining: An approach to dynamic mobile agent planning. In *Proceedings of the 22nd international conference on distributed computing systems* (pp. 579–586).

Baek, J., & Yeom, H. (2003). d-Agent: an approach to mobile agent planning for distributed information retrieval. *IEEE Transactions on Consumer Electronics*, *49*(1), 115–122. doi:10.1109/TCE.2003.1205463

Carey, M., & Johnson, D. (1979). *Computers and Intractability: A guide to the theory of NP-completeness*. San Francisco, CA: Freeman.

Chess, D., Harrison, C., & Kershenbaum, A. (1995). *Mobile agents: Are they a good idea?* IBM Research Report.

Fuggetta, A., Picco, G. P., & Vigna, G. (1998). Understanding Code Mobility. *IEEE Transactions on Software Engineering*, *24*(5). doi:10.1109/32.685258

Hopfield, J. J. (1982). Neural networks and physical systems with emergent collective computational abilities. *Proceedings of the National Academy of Sciences of the United States of America*, *79*, 2554–2558. doi:10.1073/pnas.79.8.2554

Hopfield, J. J., & Tank, D. W. (1985). 'Neural' computation of decisions in optimization problems. *Biological Cybernetics*, *52*, 141–152.

Lange, D. B., & Oshima, M. (1998). *Programming mobile agents in java—with the java aglet API*. Reading, MA: Addison-Wesley.

Lange, D. B., & Oshima, M. (1999). Seven good reasons for mobile agents: Dispatch your agents, shut off your machine. *Communications of the ACM*, *42*(3), 88–89. doi:10.1145/295685.298136

Lin, C. H., & Wang, J. F. (2006). Solving the Mobile Agent Planning Problem with a Hopfield-Tank Neural Network. In *Proceedings of the 2006 IAENG International Workshop on Artificial Intelligence and Applications,* (pp. 104–114).

Lin, C. H., & Wang, J. F. (2007). The Hopfield-Tank Neural Network Applied to the Mobile Agent Planning Problem. *Applied Intelligence*, *27*(2), 167–187. doi:10.1007/s10489-006-0021-3

MAL. *The Mobile Agent List* (n.d.). Retrieved from http://reinsburgstrasse.dyndns.org/mal/preview/preview.html

Mañdziuk, J. (1996). Solving the Traveling Salesperson Problem with Hopfield—type neural network. *Demonstration Math, 29*(1), 219–231.

Moizumi, K. (1998). *Mobile agent planning problems*. PhD thesis, Thayer School of Engineering, Dartmouth College.

Takeda, M., & Goodman, J. W. (1986). Neural networks for computation: number representations and programming complexity. *Applied Optics, 25*(18), 15. doi:10.1364/AO.25.003033

Talavan, P., & Yanez, J. (2002). Parameter setting of the Hopfield network applied to TSP. *Neural Networks, 15*, 363–373. doi:10.1016/S0893-6080(02)00021-7

Yang, B., Liu, D.-Y., Yang, K., & Wang, S.-S. (2003). Strategically migrating agents in itinerary graph. In *Proceedings of the second international conference machine learning and cybernetics,* (pp. 1871–1876).

Chapter 12

A Novel Neural Fuzzy Network Using a Hybrid Evolutionary Learning Algorithm

Cheng-Jian Lin
National Chin-Yi University of Technology, Taiwan, R. O. C.

Cheng-Hung Chen
National Chin-Yi University of Technology, Taiwan, R. O. C.

ABSTRACT

This chapter presents an evolutionary neural fuzzy network, designed using the functional-link-based neural fuzzy network (FLNFN) and a new evolutionary learning algorithm. This new evolutionary learning algorithm is based on a hybrid of cooperative particle swarm optimization and cultural algorithm. It is thus called cultural cooperative particle swarm optimization (CCPSO). The proposed CCPSO method, which uses cooperative behavior among multiple swarms, can increase the global search capacity using the belief space. Cooperative behavior involves a collection of multiple swarms that interact by exchanging information to solve a problem. The belief space is the information repository in which the individuals can store their experiences such that other individuals can learn from them indirectly. The proposed FLNFN model uses functional link neural networks as the consequent part of the fuzzy rules. This chapter uses orthogonal polynomials and linearly independent functions in a functional expansion of the functional link neural networks. The FLNFN model can generate the consequent part of a nonlinear combination of input variables. Finally, the proposed functional-link-based neural fuzzy network with cultural cooperative particle swarm optimization (FLNFN-CCPSO) is adopted in several predictive applications. Experimental results have demonstrated that the proposed CCPSO method performs well in predicting the time series problems.

INTRODUCTION

Prediction has been widely studied for many years as time series analysis (Box & Jenkins, 1970; Tong, 1990). Traditionally, prediction is based on

DOI: 10.4018/978-1-61520-757-2.ch012

a statistical model that is either linear or nonlinear (Li et al., 1990). Recently, several studies have adopted neural fuzzy networks to predict time series (Cowder, 1990; Kasabov & Song, 2002; Ling et al., 2003). Researchers have discussed that the network paradigm is a very useful model for predicting time series and especially for predicting nonlinear time series.

Soft computing tools, including fuzzy sets, neural networks, and evolutionary algorithms, have been experimentally used to handle real-life ambiguous situations (Bhattacharya et al., 2007; Chu & Tsai, 2007; Karaboga & Basturk, 2008; Kim et al., 2006). Many existing soft computing techniques (Huang et al., 2006; Mitra et al., 2002; Yu, 2007; Zhang et al., 2000) are most widely applied to solve data mining problems especially for classification or prediction. Neural fuzzy networks (Angelov & Filev, 2004; Jang, 1993; Juang & Lin, 1998; Li & Lee, 2003; Lin, 2008; Lin & Chin, 2004; Lin & Lee, 1996; Sun et al., 2003; Takagi & Sugeno, 1985) have become a popular research topic. They bring the low-level learning and computational power of neural networks into fuzzy systems and bring the high-level human-like thinking and reasoning of fuzzy systems to neural networks. In the typical TSK-type neural fuzzy network (Angelov & Filev, 2004; Jang, 1993; Juang & Lin, 1998; Li & Lee, 2003; Lin, 2008; Sun et al., 2003; Takagi & Sugeno, 1985), which is a linear polynomial of input variables, the model output is approximated locally by the rule hyperplanes. However, the traditional TSK-type neural fuzzy network does not take full advantage of the mapping capabilities that may be offered by the consequent part. Introducing a nonlinear function, especially a neural structure, to the consequent part of the fuzzy rules has yielded the NARA (Takagi et al., 1992) and the CANFIS (Mizutani & Jang, 1995) models. These models (Mizutani & Jang, 1995; Takagi et al., 1992) use multilayer neural networks in the consequent part of the fuzzy rules. Although the interpretability of the model is reduced, the representational capability of the model is significantly improved. However, the multilayer neural network has such disadvantages as slower convergence and greater computational complexity. Therefore, we proposed the functional link neural fuzzy network (FLNFN), which uses the functional link neural network (FLNN) (Pao, 1989; Patra, 1999) in the consequent part of the fuzzy rules (Chen et al., 2007). The FLNN is a single layer neural structure that is capable of forming arbitrarily complex decision regions by generating nonlinear decision boundaries. Additionally, using functional expansion effectively increases the dimensionality of the input vector and the hyperplanes that are generated by the FLNN provide a good discrimination capability in input data space.

Training of the parameters is the main problem in designing a neural fuzzy system. Backpropagation (BP) training is commonly adopted to solve this problem. It is a powerful training technique that can be applied to networks with a forward structure. Since the steepest descent approach is used in BP training to minimize the error function, the algorithms may reach the local minima very quickly and never find the global solution.

The aforementioned disadvantages lead to suboptimal performance, even for a favorable neural fuzzy network topology. Therefore, technologies that can be used to train the system parameters and find the global solution while optimizing the overall structure, are required. Recently, many studies (Chatterjee et al., 2005; Huang, 2008; Juang, 2004; Wong et al., 2008) have received increasing attention mainly because they combine the neural fuzzy networks with the learning capabilities of swarm intelligence. Accordingly, a new optimization algorithm, called particle swarm optimization (PSO), appears to be better than the backpropagation algorithm. It is an evolutionary computation technique that was developed by Kennedy and Eberhart in 1995 (Eberhart & Kennedy, 1995; Kennedy & Eberhart, 1995). The underlying motivation for the development of PSO algorithm is the social behavior of animals, such as bird flocking, fish schooling and swarm theory. The major advantages of particle swarm optimization are as follows; 1) it has memory, so knowledge of good solutions is retained by all particles; 2) it has constructive cooperation between particles, particles in the swarm share information between them; 3) it has the fast global searching ability. PSO has been successfully applied to many optimization problems, such as control problems (Abido, 2002; Gaing, 2004; Yoshida et al., 2000) and feedforward neural network design (Cai et al., 2007; Feng, 2006; Juang, 2004; Mendes et al., 2002; Song et al., 2007). However, PSO suffers from the burden of many dimensions, such that its performance falls as the dimensionality of the search space increases. Therefore, Bergh *et al.* (Bergh & Engelbrecht, 2004) proposed a cooperative approach that employs cooperative behavior, called CPSO, which uses multiple swarms to improve upon traditional PSO. However, the CPSO still uses the formula (the local best position of each particle and global best position in the swarm) of the traditional PSO to evolve. The trajectory of each particle in the search space is adjusted according to the local best position of the particle and the global best position in the same search space, but it is unable to yield high diversity of particles to increase search space. That is, it is lacking enough capability to satisfy the requirements of exploration (Mansour et al., 2007; Silva et al., 2002). Therefore, the CPSO may find a suboptimal solution. Additionally, the cultural algorithm (Jin & Reynolds, 1999; Reynolds, 1994) can exploit the information of specific belief space to guide the feasible search space and it can also change the direction of each individual in solution space. Hence, the proposed CCPSO learning method, which combines the cooperative particle swarm optimization and cultural algorithm, to increase global search capacity, is proposed herein to avoid trapping in a suboptimal solution and to ensure that a nearby global optimal solution can be found.

This chapter presents an efficient cultural cooperative particle swarm optimization (CCPSO) for the functional-link-based neural fuzzy network (FLNFN) in several predictive applications. The proposed FLNFN model is based on our previous research (Chen et al., 2007). The FLNFN model, which combines a neural fuzzy network with a functional link neural network, is designed to improve the accuracy of functional approximation. The consequent part of the fuzzy rules that corresponds to an FLNN comprises the functional expansion of input variables. The orthogonal polynomials and linearly independent functions are adopted as functional link neural network bases. The proposed CCPSO is a hybrid method which combines cooperative particle swarm optimization and cultural algorithms. The CCPSO method with cooperative behavior among multiple swarms increases the global search capacity using the belief space. Cooperative behavior among multiple swarms involves interaction by exchanging information with each other to solve a problem. The belief space is the information repository in which the individuals can store their experiences for other individuals to learn from them indirectly. The advantages of the proposed FLNFN-CCPSO method are as follows; 1) the consequent of the fuzzy rules involves a nonlinear combination of input variables. A functional link neural network is used to the consequent part of the fuzzy rules in this chapter. The functional expansion in the FLNFN model can yield the consequent part of a nonlinear combination of input variables; 2) the proposed CCPSO with cooperative behavior among multiple swarms can accelerate the search and increase global search capacity using the belief space; 3) as demonstrated in section 5, the FLNFN-CCPSO method is a more effective controller than the other methods.

The rest of this chapter is organized as follows. Section 2 describes the basic concept of particle swarm optimization, cooperative particle swarm optimization and cultural algorithm. Section 3 presents the structure of the functional-link-based neural fuzzy network. Next, Section 4 presents the cultural cooperative particle swarm optimization method. Section 5 presents the results of the simulation of several predictive applications. Section 6 draws conclusions.

PARTICLE SWARM OPTIMIZATION, COOPERATIVE PARTICLE SWARM OPTIMIZATION AND CULTURAL ALGORITHM

This section describes basic concepts concerning particle swarm optimization, cooperative particle swarm optimization and the cultural algorithm. The specialization property of particle swarm optimization and cultural algorithm is consistent with the learning property of the neural fuzzy network. Therefore, the development of a neural fuzzy network based on particle swarm optimization and the cultural algorithm is valuable.

Particle Swarm Optimization

In 1995, Kennedy and Eberhart introduced the particle swarm optimization algorithm (PSO) (Eberhart & Kennedy, 1995; Kennedy & Eberhart, 1995) in the field of social and cognitive behavior. The PSO is a population-based optimization approach, in which the population is called a swarm. Furthermore, each swarm consists of many particles. In the PSO, the trajectory of each particle in the search space is adjusted by dynamically altering the velocity of each particle. Each particle has a velocity vector $\vec{v}_i$ and a position vector $\vec{x}_i$, which represents a possible solution. Then, the particles move rapidly around and search the solution space using the moving velocity of each particle. Each of these particle positions is scored to obtain a fitness value, based on how to define the solution of problem. The local best position (*Lbest*) of each particle and the global best position (*Gbest*) in the swarm are used to yield a new velocity for each particle:

$$\vec{v}_i(k+1) = \omega * \vec{v}_i(k) + \varphi_1$$
$$* rand() * (Lbest - \vec{x}_i(k))$$
$$+ \varphi_2 * rand() * (Gbest - \vec{x}_i(k)) \qquad (1)$$

where ω, φ_1 and φ_2 are called the coefficient of the inertia term, the cognitive term and the society term, respectively. The term $\vec{v}_i$ is limited to the range $\pm v_{max}$. If the velocity violates this limit, then it is set to the actual limit.

Changing the velocity enables each particle to search around its individual best position and global best position. Based on the updated velocities, each particle changes its position according to,

$$\vec{x}_i(k+1) = \vec{x}_i(k) + \vec{v}_i(k+1). \qquad (2)$$

Figure 1 presents the concept of the updated velocity using Eq. (1) and Eq. (2).

Cooperative Particle Swarm Optimization

The cooperative particle swarm optimization (CPSO) (Bergh & Engelbrecht, 2004) that differs from the traditional PSO is introduced in this subsection. The traditional PSO uses one swarm of particles defined by the *P*-dimension vectors to evolve. The cooperative particle swarm optimization (CPSO) can change traditional PSO into *P* swarms of one-dimension vectors, such that each swarm represents a dimension of the original problem. Figures 2 (a)-(b) show the framework of the traditional PSO and CPSO method. The key point is that, instead of using one swarm (of *I* particles) to find the optimal *P*-dimension vector, the vector is split into its components so that *P* swarms (of *I* particles each) optimize a one-dimension vector. Notably, the function that is being optimized still requires a *P*-dimension vector to be evaluated. However, if each swarm represents only a single dimension of the search space, it cannot directly compute the fitness of the individuals of a single population considered in isolation. A context vector is required to provide a suitable context in which the individuals of a

Figure 1. Diagram of the updated velocity in the PSO

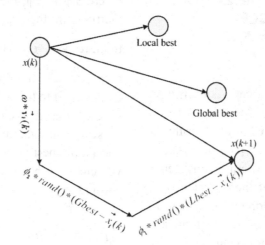

population can be evaluated. To calculate the fitness for all particles in swarm, the other P-1 components in the context vector keep constant values, while the pth component of the context vector is replaced in turn by each particle from the pth swarm. Additionally, each swarm aims to optimize a single component of the solution vector essentially solving a one-dimension optimization problem. Unfortunately, the CPSO still employs just the local best position and the global best position of the traditional PSO to evolution process. Therefore, the CPSO may fall into a suboptimal solution.

Cultural Algorithm

Cultural algorithms (Jin & Reynolds, 1999; Reynolds, 1994) involve acquiring the belief space from the evolving population space and then exploiting that information to guide the search. Figure 3 presents the cultural algorithm components. Cultural algorithms can be described in terms of two basic components - belief space and the population space. The belief space is the information repository in which the individuals can store their experiences for other individuals to learn from them indirectly. In cultural algorithms, the information acquired by an individual can be shared with the entire population, unlike in most evolutionary techniques, in which the information can be shared only with the offspring of individual. The population space comprises a set of possible solutions to the problem, and can be modeled using any population-based approach. The belief space and the population space are linked using a scheme that states rules that govern the individuals of the population space that can contribute to the belief space based on its experiences (according to the acceptance function), and the belief space can influence the new individuals of the population space (according to the influence function).

The acceptance function selects the top 20% individuals that can directly affect the formation of the current belief space. The influence function adopts the normative knowledge containing the intervals for the variables where good solutions have been found, in order to move novel solutions towards those intervals. The following expression shows the influence of the normative knowledge on the variation operators:

$$x_i = \begin{cases} x_i + \left| Rand() \cdot (u - l) \right| & \text{if } x_i < l \\ x_i - \left| Rand() \cdot (u - l) \right| & \text{if } x_i > u \\ x_i + Rand() \cdot (u - l)/m & \text{otherwise} \end{cases}$$

$$(3)$$

Figure 2. Framework of the (a) PSO and (b) CPSO

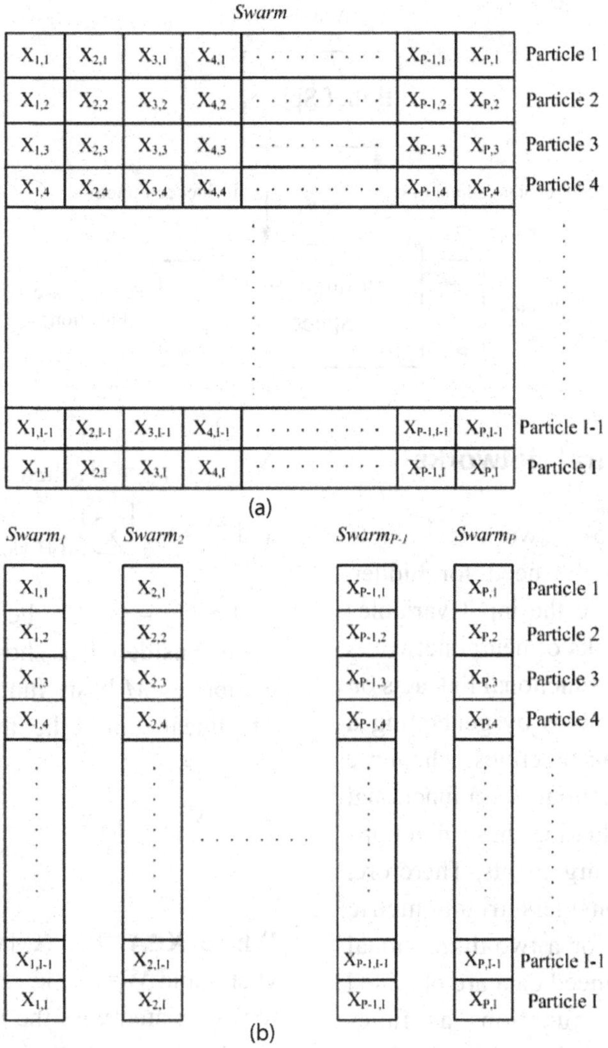

				Swarm			
$X_{1,1}$	$X_{2,1}$	$X_{3,1}$	$X_{4,1}$	· · · · · · · · ·	$X_{P-1,1}$	$X_{P,1}$	Particle 1
$X_{1,2}$	$X_{2,2}$	$X_{3,2}$	$X_{4,2}$	· · · · · · · · ·	$X_{P-1,2}$	$X_{P,2}$	Particle 2
$X_{1,3}$	$X_{2,3}$	$X_{3,3}$	$X_{4,3}$	· · · · · · · · ·	$X_{P-1,3}$	$X_{P,3}$	Particle 3
$X_{1,4}$	$X_{2,4}$	$X_{3,4}$	$X_{4,4}$	· · · · · · · · ·	$X_{P-1,4}$	$X_{P,4}$	Particle 4
$X_{1,I-1}$	$X_{2,I-1}$	$X_{3,I-1}$	$X_{4,I-1}$	· · · · · · · · ·	$X_{P-1,I-1}$	$X_{P,I-1}$	Particle I-1
$X_{1,I}$	$X_{2,I}$	$X_{3,I}$	$X_{4,I}$	· · · · · · · · ·	$X_{P-1,I}$	$X_{P,I}$	Particle I

(a)

$Swarm_1$	$Swarm_2$		$Swarm_{P-1}$	$Swarm_P$	
$X_{1,1}$	$X_{2,1}$		$X_{P-1,1}$	$X_{P,1}$	Particle 1
$X_{1,2}$	$X_{2,2}$		$X_{P-1,2}$	$X_{P,2}$	Particle 2
$X_{1,3}$	$X_{2,3}$		$X_{P-1,3}$	$X_{P,3}$	Particle 3
$X_{1,4}$	$X_{2,4}$		$X_{P-1,4}$	$X_{P,4}$	Particle 4
		· · · · · · ·			
$X_{1,I-1}$	$X_{2,I-1}$		$X_{P-1,I-1}$	$X_{P,I-1}$	Particle I-1
$X_{1,I}$	$X_{2,I}$		$X_{P-1,I}$	$X_{P,I}$	Particle I

(b)

where x_i is the ith variable of the individual; u and l are the upper and lower bounds of all individuals of the belief space, respectively, and m is the number of all individuals of the belief space.

STRUCTURE OF FUNCTIONAL-LINK-BASED NEURAL FUZZY NETWORK

This section describes the structure of functional link neural networks and the structure of the FL-NFN model. In functional link neural networks, the input data usually incorporate high order effects and thus artificially increase the dimensions of the input space. Accordingly, the input representation is enhanced and linear separability is achieved in the extended space. The FLNFN model adopted the functional link neural network generating complex nonlinear combination of input variables as the consequent part of the fuzzy rules. The rest of this section details these structures.

Figure 3. Framework of cultural algorithm

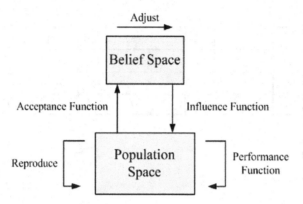

Functional Link Neural Networks

The functional link neural network is a single layer network in which the need for hidden layers is eliminated. While the input variables generated by the linear links of neural networks are linearly weighted, the functional link acts on an element of input variables by generating a set of linearly independent functions, which are suitable orthogonal polynomials for a functional expansion, and then evaluating these functions with the variables as the arguments. Therefore, the FLNN structure considers trigonometric functions. For example, for a two-dimensional input $X=[x_1,x_2]^T$, the enhanced data are obtained by using trigonometric functions as functional expansion $\mathbf{\Phi}=[1,x1\sin(\pi x1),\cos(\pi x1),...$ $,x2\sin(\pi x2),\cos(\pi x2),...]T$. Thus, the input variables can be separated in the enhanced space (Pao, 1989). In the FLNN structure with reference to Fig. 4, a set of basic functions Φ and a fixed number of weight parameters W represent $fW_{(x)}$. The theory behind the FLNN for multidimensional function approximation has been discussed elsewhere (Patra et al., 1999) and is analyzed below.

Consider a set of basic functions $\mathbf{B}=\{\varphi_k \in \Phi(A)\}_{k\in \mathbf{K}}$, $\mathbf{K}=\{1,2,...\}$ with the following properties; 1) $\varphi_1=1$, 2) the subset $B_j = \{\varphi_k \in '\}_{k=1}^M$ is a linearly independent set, meaning that if

$\sum_{k=1}^{M} w_k\varphi_k = 0$, then $w_k=0$ for all $k=1,2,...,M$, and 3) $\sup_j \left[\sum_{k=1}^{j} \|\varphi_k\|_A^2\right]^{1/2} < \infty$.

Let $' = \{\varphi_k\}_{k=1}^M$ be a set of basis functions to be considered, as shown in Fig. 4. The FLNN comprises M basis functions $\{\varphi_1,\varphi_2,....\varphi_M\}\in\mathbf{B}$. The linear sum of the jth node is given by

$$\hat{y}_j = \sum_{k=1}^{M} w_{kj}\varphi_k(\mathbf{X}) \qquad (4)$$

Where $\mathbf{X}\in\mathbf{A}\subset R^N$, $\mathbf{X}=[x_1,x_2,...,x_N]^T$ is the input vector and $\mathbf{W}_j=[w_{1j},w_{2j}...,w_{Mj}]$ is the weight vector associated with the jth output of the FLNN. $\hat{y}_j$ denotes the local output of the FLNN structure and the consequent part of the jth fuzzy rule in the FLNFN model. Thus, Eq. (4) can be expressed in matrix form as $\hat{y}_j = \mathbf{W}_j'$, where $\Phi=[\varphi_1(x),\varphi_2(x),...,\varphi_M(x)]^T$ is the basis function vector, which is the output of the functional expansion block. The m-dimensional linear output may be given by $\hat{\mathbf{y}} = \mathbf{W}_!'$, where $\hat{\mathbf{y}} = [\hat{y}_1,\hat{y}_2,...,\hat{y}_m]^T$, m denotes the number of functional link bases, which equals the number of fuzzy rules in the FLNFN model, and $\mathbf{W}$ is a $(m\times M)$-dimensional weight matrix of the FLNN given by $\mathbf{W}=[\mathbf{w}_1,\mathbf{w}_2,...\mathbf{w}_M]^T$. The jth output of the FLNN is given by $\hat{y}_j' = \rho(\hat{y}_j)$

Figure 4. Structure of FLNN

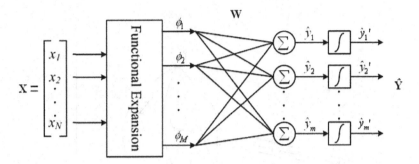

, where the nonlinear function $\rho(\cdot)=tanh(\cdot)$. Thus, the *m*-dimensional output vector is given by

$$\hat{\mathbf{Y}} = \rho(\hat{y}) = f_{\mathbf{W}}(x) \qquad (5)$$

where $\hat{\mathbf{Y}}$ denotes the output of the FLNN.

Structure of FLNFN Model

This subsection describes the functional-link-based **neural fuzzy network** (FLNFN) model, which uses a nonlinear combination of input variables (FLNN). Each fuzzy rule corresponds to a sub-FLNN, comprising a functional link. Figure 5 presents the structure of the proposed FLNFN model. The FLNFN model realizes a fuzzy if-then rule in the following form.

Rule$_j$:

IF x_1 is A_{1j} and x_2 is A_{2j} ... and x_i is A_{ij} ... and x_N is A_{Nj}

THEN $\hat{y}_j = \sum_{k=1}^{M} w_{kj}\varphi_k$

$= w_{1j}\varphi_1 + w_{2j}\varphi_2 + ... + w_{Mj}\varphi_M$

$$\qquad (6)$$

where x_i and $\hat{y}_j$ are the input and local output variables, respectively; A_{ij} is the linguistic term of the precondition part with Gaussian membership function; N is the number of input variables; w_{kj} is the link weight of the local output; φ_k is the basis trigonometric function of input variables;

M is the number of basis function, and *Rule$_j$* is the *j*th fuzzy rule.

The operation functions of the nodes in each layer of the FLNFN model are now described. In the following description, $u^{(l)}$ denotes the output of a node in the *l*th layer.

No computation is performed in layer 1. Each node in this layer only transmits input values to the next layer directly:

$$u_i^{(1)} = x_i . \qquad (7)$$

Each fuzzy set A_{ij} is described here by a Gaussian membership function. Therefore, the calculated membership value in layer 2 is

$$u_{ij}^{(2)} = \exp\left(-\frac{[u_i^{(1)} - m_{ij}]^2}{\sigma_{ij}^2}\right) \qquad (8)$$

where m_{ij} and σ_{ij} are the mean and variance of the Gaussian membership function, respectively, of the *j*th term of the *i*th input variable x_i.

Nodes in layer 3 receive one-dimensional membership degrees of the associated rule from the nodes of a set in layer 2. Here, the product operator described above is adopted to perform the precondition part of the fuzzy rules. As a result, the output function of each inference node is

$$u_j^{(3)} = \prod_i u_{ij}^{(2)} \qquad (9)$$

Figure 5. Structure of proposed FLNFN model

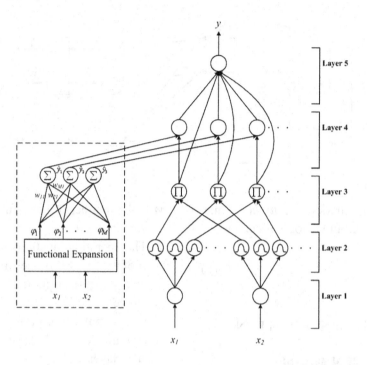

where the $\prod_i u_{ij}^{(2)}$ of a rule node represents the firing strength of its corresponding rule.

Nodes in layer 4 are called consequent nodes. The input to a node in layer 4 is the output from layer 3, and the other inputs are calculated from a functional link neural network that has not used the function $tanh(\cdot)$, as shown in Fig. 5. For such a node,

$$u_j^{(4)} = u_j^{(3)} \cdot \sum_{k=1}^{M} w_{kj}\varphi_k \qquad (10)$$

where w_{kj} is the corresponding link weight of functional link neural network and φ_k is the functional expansion of input variables. The functional expansion uses a trigonometric polynomial basis function, given by $[x_1, sin(\pi x_1), cos(\pi x_1), x_2, sin(\pi x_2), cos(\pi x_2)]$ for two-dimensional input variables.

Therefore, M is the number of basis functions, $M=3 \times N$, where N is the number of input variables. Moreover, the output nodes of functional link neural network depend on the number of fuzzy rules of the FLNFN model.

The output node in layer 5 integrates all of the actions recommended by layers 3 and 4 and acts as a defuzzifier with,

$$y = u^{(5)} = \frac{\sum_{j=1}^{R} u_j^{(4)}}{\sum_{j=1}^{R} u_j^{(3)}} = \frac{\sum_{j=1}^{R} u_j^{(3)}\left(\sum_{k=1}^{M} w_{kj}\varphi_k\right)}{\sum_{j=1}^{R} u_j^{(3)}} = \frac{\sum_{j=1}^{R} u_j^{(3)}\hat{y}_j}{\sum_{j=1}^{R} u_j^{(3)}}$$

$$(11)$$

where R is the number of fuzzy rules, and y is the output of the FLNFN model.

THE CULTURAL COOPERATIVE PARTICLE SWARM OPTIMIZATION FOR THE FLNFN MODEL

This section describes the proposed cultural cooperative particle swarm optimization (CCPSO) method. The CCPSO learning method, which combines the cooperative particle swarm optimization and the cultural algorithm to increase the global search capacity, is proposed to avoid trapping in a suboptimal solution and to ensure the ability to search for a near-global optimal solution.

The CCPSO method is characteristic of the cooperative particle swarm optimization and cultural algorithm. Figure 6 shows the framework of the proposed CCPSO learning method, which is based on a CPSO all of whose parameters are simultaneously tuned using the belief space of the CA. The CCPSO method can strengthen the global search capability. If 50-dimension vectors are used in the original PSO, then the vectors in CCPSO can be changed into 50 swarms of one-dimension vectors. In the original PSO, the particle can exhibit 50 variations in each generation, whereas the CCPSO offers 50x50=2500 different combinations in each generation. Additionally, each position of the CCPSO can be adjusted not only using the belief space which stores the paragons of each swarm, but also by searching around the local best solution and the global best solution. In the aforementioned scheme, the proposed CCPSO method can avoid falling into a suboptimal solution and ensure that the approximate global optimal solution can be found.

The detailed flowchart of the proposed CCPSO method is presented in Fig. 7. The foremost step in CCPSO is the coding of the neural fuzzy network into a particle. Figure 8 shows an example of the coding of parameters of neural fuzzy network into a particle where i and j represent the ith input variable and the jth rule, respectively. In this chapter, a Gaussian membership function is adopted with variables that represent the mean and deviation of the membership function. Figure 8 represents the neural fuzzy network given by Eq. (6), where m_{ij} and σ_{ij} are the mean and deviation of a Gaussian membership function, respectively, and w_{kj} represents the corresponding link weight of the consequent part that is connected to the jth rule node. In this chapter, a real number represents the position of each particle.

The learning process is described step-by-step

Figure 6. Framework of proposed CCPSO learning method

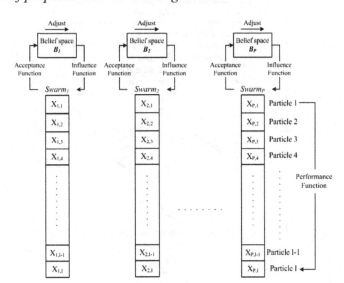

below.

Step 1:Create initial swarms

Before the CCPSO method is applied, every position $x_{p,i}(t)$ must be created randomly in the range [0, 1], where p=1, 2, ..., P represents the pth swarm, i=1, 2, ..., I represents the ith particle, and t denotes the tth generation.

Step 2:Create initial belief space

The belief space is the information repository in which the particles can store their experiences for other particles to learn from them indirectly. Create P belief space, B_p (p = 1, 2, ..., P). Each initial B_p is defined as an empty set.

Step 3:Update every position

○ Step 3.1:Evaluate the performance function of each *Particle*$_i$

The fitness function is used to evaluate the performance function of each particle. The fitness function is defined as follows.

$$F = \sqrt{\frac{1}{D}\sum_{d=1}^{D}(y_d - \bar{y}_d)^2} \qquad (12)$$

where y_d represents the dth model output; $\bar{y}_d$ represents the dth desired output, and D represents the number of input data.

• Step 3.2:Update local best position $L_{p,i}$ and global best position G_p

Figure 7. Flowchart of proposed CCPSO learning method

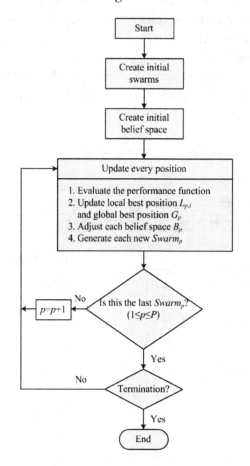

Figure 8. Coding FLNFN model into a particle in the proposed CCPSO

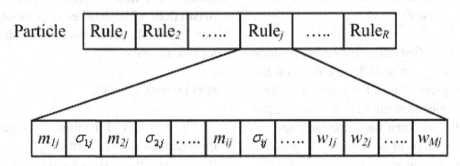

The local best position $L_{p,i}$ is the best previous position that yielded the best fitness value of the *p*th swarm of the *i*th particle, and the global best position G_p is generated by the whole local best position. In step 3.2, the first step updates the local best position. Compare the fitness value of each current particle with that of its local best position. If the fitness value of the current particle exceeds those of its local best position, then the local best position is replaced with the position of the current particle. The second step updates the global best position. Compare the fitness value of all particles in their local best positions with that of the particle in the global best position. If fitness value of the particle in the local best position is better than those of the particles in the global best position, then the global best position is replaced with the current local best position.

$$L_{p,i}(t+1) = \begin{cases} x_{p,i}(t), & if \ F\ (x_{p,i}(t)) \ < F \ (L_{p,i}(t)) \\ L_{p,i}(t), & if \ F\ (x_{p,i}(t)) \ \geq F \ (L_{p,i}(t)) \end{cases}$$
$$G_p(t+1) = \arg\min_{L_{p,i}} F(L_{p,i}(t+1)), \qquad 1 \leq i \leq I$$
$$(13)$$

• Step 3.3: Adjust each belief space B_p using an acceptance function

The first part of step 3.3 sorts these particles in each *Swarm$_p$* in order of increasing fitness. Then, the paragon of each *Swarm$_p$* is put into belief space B_p using an acceptance function. This function yields the number of particles that are

used to adjust each belief space, and is as follows. The number of accepted particles decreases as the number of generations increases.

$$N_{accepted} = n\% \cdot I + \frac{n\%}{t} \cdot I \qquad (14)$$

where *n%* is a parameter that is set by user, and must specify the top performing 20% (Saleem, 2001); *I* is the number of particles, and *t* represents the *t*th generation. The second step adjusts B_p. The interval of belief space BI_p is defined $BI_p = [l_p, u_p] = \{x | l_p \leq x \leq u_p, x \in R\}$, where l_p is the lower bound on belief space B_p and u_p is the upper bound on belief space B_p. Then, the position of each particle in B_p is compared with the lower bound l_p. If the position of the particle is smaller than the lower bound l_p, then the lower bound l_p is replaced with the current position. Furthermore, the position of each particle in the B_p is compared with the upper bound u_p. If the position of the particle is greater than the upper bound u_p, then the upper bound u_p is replaced with the current position. These rules are given below.

$$l_p = \begin{cases} x_{p,i} & if \ x_{p,i} \leq l_p \\ l_p & otherwise \end{cases}$$
$$u_p = \begin{cases} x_{p,i} & if \ x_{p,i} \geq u_p \\ u_p & otherwise \end{cases}$$
$$(15)$$

- Step 3.4:Generate each new $Swarm_p$ using l_p, u_p, $L_{p,i}$, and G_p

In step 3.4, the first step adjusts every position of each $Swarm_p$ using an influence function Eq. (16). This step can change the direction of each particle in solution space, not easily being trapped at a local optimum. Then, the second step updates velocity and position of each particle to generate the each new $Swarm_p$ using Eqs. (17) and (18).

$$x_{p,i}(t) = \begin{cases} x_{p,i}(t) + \left| Rand() \cdot (u_p - l_p) \right| & \text{if } x_{p,i} < l_p \\ x_{p,i}(t) - \left| Rand() \cdot (u_p - l_p) \right| & \text{if } x_{p,i} > u_p \end{cases} \tag{16}$$

$$v_{p,i}(t+1) = w \cdot v_{p,i}(t) + c_1 \cdot Rand() \cdot [L_{p,i}(t+1) - x_{p,i}(t)] \\ + c_2 \cdot Rand() \cdot [G_p(t+1) - x_{p,i}(t)] \tag{17}$$

$$x_{p,i}(t+1) = x_{p,i}(t) + v_{p,i}(t+1) \tag{18}$$

where c_1 and c_2 denote acceleration coefficients; $Rand()$ is generated from a uniform distribution in the range [0, 1], and w controls the magnitude of $v_{p,i}(t)$.

Experimental Results

This section discusses three examples that were considered to evaluate the FLNFN model with the CCPSO learning method. The first example involves predicting a chaotic signal that has been described in (Lin & Lee, 1996); the second example involves predicting a chaotic time series (Cowder, 1990), and the third example involves forecasting the number of sunspots (Ling et al., 2003).

Example 1: Prediction of a Chaotic Signal

In this example, an FLNFN model with an CCPSO learning method (FLNFN-CCPSO) was used to predict a **chaotic signal**. The classical time

series **prediction** problem is a one-step-ahead **prediction**, which has been described in (Lin & Lee, 1996). The following equation describes the logistic function.

$$x(k+1) = ax(k)(1 - x(k)). \tag{19}$$

The behavior of the time series generated by this equation depends critically on parameter a. If $a < 1$, then the system has a single fixed point at the origin, and from a random initial value between [0, 1] the time series collapses to a constant value. For $a > 3$, the system generates a periodic attractor. At $a \geq 3.6$, the system becomes chaotic. In this example, a was set to 3.8. The first 60 pairs (from $x(1)$ to $x(60)$), with initial value $x(1) = 0.001$, were the training data set, while the remaining 100 pairs (from $x(1)$ to $x(100)$), with initial value $x(1) = 0.9$, were the testing data set used to validate the proposed method.

In this example, several particles will be found to minimize the fitness value using the proposed FLNFN-CCPSO method. The learning stage involved parameter learning using the CCPSO method. The coefficient w was set to 0.4. The cognitive coefficient c_1 was set to 1.6, and the society coefficient c_2 was set to 2. The swarm sizes were set to 50. The learning proceeded for 1000 generations, and was repeated fifty times. After 1000 generations, the final average RMS (root mean square) error of the predicted output is about 0.002285. In this example, three fuzzy rules are adopted. They are shown as follows.

$Rule_1$:
$\quad$ IF x is $\mu(0.763596, 19.0781)$
THEN $\hat{y}_1 = -0.846419 + 0.840237x + 0.0103279\cos(\pi x) + 1.61874\sin(\pi x)$
$\quad\quad -0.364635x$

$Rule_2$:
$\quad$ IF x is $\mu(0.235112, 0.307009)$
THEN $\hat{y}_1 = 0.145784 - 0.961044x - 0.146496\cos(\pi x) + 0.857966\sin(\pi x)$
$\quad\quad +6.62004x$

$Rule_3$:
$\quad$ IF x is $\mu(0.771367, 0.351594)$
THEN $\hat{y}_1 = 0.727383 + 0.625871x + 1.00717\cos(\pi x) + 2.25003\sin(\pi x)$
$\quad\quad +0.178136x$

where $\mu(m_{ij}, \sigma i_{ij})$ represents a Gaussian membership function with mean mi_j and deviation σi_j in the ith input variable and the jth rule. Figure 9(a) plots the predictions of the desired output and the model output in 1000 generations of learning. The solid line represents the desired output of the time series, and the notation "*" represents the output of the FLNFN-CCPSO method. Figure 9(b) presents the prediction errors of the proposed method. The experimental results demonstrate the perfect predictive capability of the FLNFN-CCPSO method.

In this example, particle swarm optimization (PSO) (Kennedy & Eberhart, 1995) and cooperative particle swarm optimization (CPSO) (Bergh & Engelbrecht, 2004) were applied to the same problem to show the effectiveness and efficiency of the FLNFN model with the CCPSO learning method. In the PSO and CPSO, the swarm sizes were set to 50. The coefficient w was set to 0.4. The cognitive coefficient c_1 was set to 1.6, and the society coefficient c_2 was set to 2. Three rules were applied to construct the fuzzy model. In the PSO (Kennedy & Eberhart, 1995) and CPSO (Bergh & Engelbrecht, 2004), learning proceeded for 1000 generations, and was performed fifty times.

The performance of the FLNFN model with CCPSO learning was compared with the performance of other methods. First, the performance of the FLNFN-CCPSO method was compared with that of particle swarm optimization (Kennedy & Eberhart, 1995). Figure 9(c) plots the results predicted using particle swarm optimization. Figure 9(d) presents the prediction errors of the particle swarm optimization. Second, cooperative particle swarm optimization (Bergh & Engelbrecht, 2004) is adopted to solve the predictive problem. Figure 9(e) and 9(f) plot the results and the errors of cooperative particle swarm optimization. As presented in Fig. 9, the results predicted by the FLNFN model with the CCPSO learning method are better than those predicting by other methods.

Figure 10 plots the learning curves of the best performance of the FLNFN model with the CCPSO learning method, PSO (Kennedy & Eberhart, 1995) and CPSO (Bergh & Engelbrecht, 2004). This figure indicates that the proposed method converges quickly and yields a lower RMS error than other methods. Computer simulations indicated that the proposed method outperforms other methods. The best performance of the CCPSO was compared with that of the PSO (Kennedy & Eberhart, 1995)

Figure 9. (a) Predictions of the proposed method. (b) Prediction errors of the proposed method. (c) Predictions of particle swarm optimization (Kennedy & Eberhart, 1995). (d) Prediction errors of particle swarm optimization. (e) Predictions of cooperative particle swarm optimization (Bergh & Engelbrecht, 2004). (f) Prediction errors of cooperative particle swarm optimization

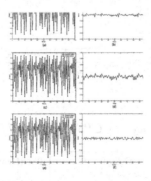

and CPSO (Bergh & Engelbrecht, 2004). Table 1 compares the results. The comparison indicates that the RMS error of training and predicting for the FLNFN-CCPSO method are better than those obtained using other methods.

Example 2: Prediction of Chaotic Time Series

The Mackey-Glass chaotic time series $x(t)$ was generated using the following delay differential equation;

$$\frac{dx(t)}{dt} = \frac{0.2x(t-\tau)}{1+x^{10}(t-\tau)} - 0.1x(t). \tag{20}$$

Crowder (Cowder, 1990) extracted 1000 input-output data pairs $\{x, y^d\}$ using four past values of $x(t)$:

$$[x(t\text{-}18),x(t\text{-}12),x(t\text{-}6),x(t);x(t\text{+}6)] \tag{21}$$

where $\tau=17$ and $x(0)=1.2$. Four inputs to the FLNFN-CCPSO method, corresponded to these values of $x(t)$, and one output was $x(t+\Delta t)$, where Δt is a time interval into the future. The first 500 pairs (from $x(1)$ to $x(500)$) were the training data set, while the remaining 500 pairs (from $x(501)$ to $x(1000)$) were the testing data used to validate the proposed method.

The learning stage entered parameter learning through CCPSO method. The coefficient w was set to 0.4. The cognitive coefficient c_1 was set to 1.6, and the society coefficient c_2 was set to 2. The swarm sizes were set to 50. The learning proceeded for 1000 generations, and was performed fifty times. In this example, three fuzzy rules are applied. They are as follows.

Figure 10. Learning curves of proposed method, PSO (Kennedy & Eberhart, 1995) and CPSO (Bergh & Engelbrecht, 2004)

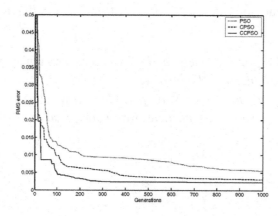

Table 1. Comparison of best performance of CCPSO, PSO and CPSO in Example 1

	CCPSO	PSO(Kennedy & Eberhart, 1995)	CPSO (Bergh & Engelbrecht, 2004)
RMS error (training)	**0.002285**	0.005239	0.003423
RMS error (predicting)	**0.002717**	0.005514	0.003958

Rule$_1$:

IF x_1 is $\mu(0.452959,-5.36833)$ and x_2 is $\mu(-0.10799,0.768855)$
and x_3 is $\mu(-0.850613,-3.60999)$ and x_4 is $\mu(1.09886,0.495632)$
THEN $\hat{y}_1 = 2.20613 + 0.580829x_1 + 0.391061\cos(\pi\,x_1) + 0.332886\sin(\pi\,x_1)$
$-4.68232x_2 - 5.05388\cos(\pi\,x_2) + 1.73753\sin(\pi\,x_2)$
$-0.656754x_3 + 1.71626\cos(\pi\,x_3) + 0.0923789\sin(\pi\,x_3)$
$+4.93925x_4 - 0.416084\cos(\pi\,x_4) + 1.45935\sin(\pi\,x_4)$
$+0.990628x_1\,x_2\,x_3\,x_4$

Rule$_2$:

IF x_1 is $\mu(-0.596747,-0.896165)$ and x_2 is $\mu(0.841226,1.1499)$
and x_3 is $\mu(0.20028,0.310169)$ and x_4 is $\mu(1.01531,0.524704)$
THEN $\hat{y}_1 = 0.683119 + 0.649552x_1 + 1.74121\cos(\pi\,x_1) - 4.32156\sin(\pi\,x_1)$
$+0.200504x_2 - 2.74432\cos(\pi\,x_2) + 1.18918\sin(\pi\,x_2)$
$+0.519391x_3 + 0.641173\cos(\pi\,x_3) + 3.17329\sin(\pi\,x_3)$
$-0.22503x_4 + 0.524293\cos(\pi\,x_4) + 0.685239\sin(\pi\,x_4)$
$-0.127742x_1\,x_2\,x_3\,x_4$

Rule$_3$:

IF x_1 is $\mu(1.03417,0.919468)$ and x_2 is $\mu(-0.115958,1.69308)$
and x_3 is $\mu(-0.114371,1.1357)$ and x_4 is $\mu(-0.152534,0.74255)$
THEN $\hat{y}_1 = 0.58632 - 1.28024x_1 - 0.180169\cos(\pi\,x_1) - 0.470873\sin(\pi\,x_1)$
$-0.530146x_2 - 0.597328\cos(\pi\,x_2) + 0.156929\sin(\pi\,x_2)$
$+0.176057x_3 + 0.0405789\cos(\pi\,x_3) + 1.09262\sin(\pi\,x_3)$
$+0.353992x_4 - 0.437468\cos(\pi\,x_4) - 1.09654\sin(\pi\,x_4)$
$+0.479358x_1\,x_2\,x_3\,x_4$

where $\mu(m_{ij}, \sigma i_{jj}$ represents a Gaussian membership function with mean mi_{ja}nd deviation σi_j in the ith input variable and the jth rule. The final RMS error of the prediction output is about 0.008424. Figure 11(a) plots the prediction outputs of the chaotic time series from x*(501)* to x*(1000),* when 500 training data from x*(1)* to x*(500)* were used. Figure 11(b) plots the prediction errors between the proposed model and the desired output.

In this example, as in example 1, the performance of the FLNFN model with the CCPSO learning method was compared to that of other methods. In the PSO (Kennedy & Eberhart, 1995) and CPSO (Bergh & Engelbrecht, 2004), the parameters are the same as in example 1. Three rules are set to construct the fuzzy model. The learning proceeded for 1000 generations, and was performed fifty times. Figures 11(c) and 11(d) plot the predictions and the prediction errors of particle swarm optimization (Kennedy & Eberhart, 1995). Figures 11(e) and 11(f) plot the predictions

and the prediction errors of cooperative particle swarm optimization (Bergh & Engelbrecht, 2004). Figures 11(g) and 11(h) plot the predictions and the prediction errors of differential evolution (Storn, 1999). Figures 11(i) and 11(j) plot the predictions and the prediction errors of genetic algorithm. Figure 12 plots the learning curves of the best performance of the FLNFN model with CCPSO, PSO (Kennedy & Eberhart, 1995), CPSO (Bergh & Engelbrecht, 2004), differential evolution (DE) (Storn, 1999) and genetic algorithm (GA) (Goldberg, 1989) learning methods. The proposed CCPSO method yields better prediction results than the other methods. Table 2 compares the best performance of the CCPSO was compared with those of PSO (Kennedy & Eberhart, 1995), CPSO (Bergh & Engelbrecht, 2004), differential evolution (DE) (Storn, 1999), and GA (Goldberg, 1989). Table 3 lists the generalization capabilities of other methods (Crowder, 1990; Karr, 1991; Juang et al., 2000). The generalization capabilities were measured by using each model to predict 500 points immediately following the training data set. The results show that the proposed FLNFN-CCPSO method offers a smaller RMS error than other methods.

Example 3: Forecast of the Number of Sunspots

The number of sunspots varied nonlinearly from 1700 to 2004, in non-stationary, and non-Gaussian cycles that are difficult to predict (Ling et al., 2003). In this example, the FLNFN model with the CCPSO learning method was used to **forecast** the number of sunspots. The inputs x_i of the FLNFN-CCPSO method are defined as $x_1(t) = y_1^d(t-1)$ $x_2(t) = y_1^d(t-2)$ and $x_3(t) = y_1^d(t-3)$ where t represents the year and $y_1^d(t)$ is the number of sunspots in the year t. In this example, the number of sunspots of the first 151 years (from 1703 to 1853) was used to train the FLNFN-CCPSO

Figure 11. (a) Prediction results of the proposed method. (b) Prediction errors of the proposed method. (c) Prediction results of particle swarm optimization (Kennedy & Eberhart, 1995). (d) Prediction errors of particle swarm optimization. (e) Prediction results of cooperative particle swarm optimization (Bergh & Engelbrecht, 2004). (f) Prediction errors of cooperative particle swarm optimization. (g) Prediction results of differential evolution (Storn, 1999). (h) Prediction errors of differential evolution. (i) Prediction results of genetic algorithm (Goldberg, 1989). (j) Prediction errors of genetic algorithm

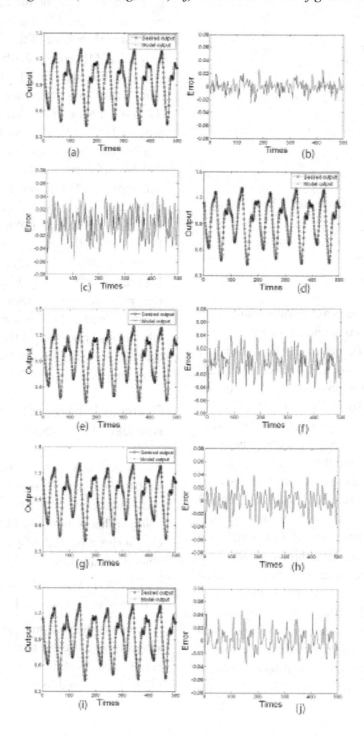

Figure 12. Learning curves of best performance of proposed method, PSO (Kennedy & Eberhart, 1995), CPSO (Bergh & Engelbrecht, 2004), DE (Storn, 1999) and GA (Goldberg, 1989)

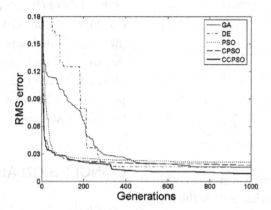

Table 2. Comparison of best performance of CCPSO, PSO, CPSO, DE, and GA in Example 2

	CCPSO	PSO (Kennedy & Eberhart, 1995)	CPSO (Bergh & Engelbrecht, 2004)	DE (Storn, 1999)	GA (Goldberg, 1989)
RMS error (training)	**0.008274**	0.020977	0.017527	0.016165	0.016176
RMS error (predicting)	**0.008424**	0.021054	0.017667	0.016258	0.016341

Table 3. Comparison of performance of various existing models

Method	$RMSE_{Prediction}$
FLNFN-CCPSO	**0.008274**
Back-propagation NN	0.02
Six-order polynomial	0.04
Cascaded-correlation	0.06
Auto regressive model	0.19
Linear predictive	0.55
GA-FLC (Karr, 1991)	0.26
SEFC (Juang et al., 2000)	0.032

method while the number of sunspots of all 302 years (from 1703 to 2004) was used to test the FLNFN-CCPSO method.

The learning stage involved parameter learning by the CCPSO method. The coefficient w was set to 0.4. The cognitive coefficient c_1 was set to 1.6, and the society coefficient c_2 was set to 2. The swarm sizes were set to 50. The learning pro-

ceeded for 1000 generations, and was performed fifty times. In this example, three fuzzy rules are applied. They are as follows.

Rule-1:

$$IF\ x_1\ is\ \mu(0.845312, 0.508771)\ and\ x_2\ is\ \mu(0.90418, 0.451389)$$
$$and\ x_3\ is\ \mu(-0.0895866, 1.06449)$$
$$THEN\ \hat{y}_1 = -3.35896 - 0.436238x_1 + 1.4272\cos(\pi\ x_1) - 0.417788\sin(\pi\ x_1)$$
$$+2.19244x_2 - 0.32409\cos(\pi\ x_2) + 0.2113\sin(\pi\ x_2)$$
$$-1.36183x_3 - 0.480986\cos(\pi\ x_3) + 2.59738\sin(\pi\ x_3) - 0.361671(x_1\ x_2\ x_3)$$

Rule-2:

IF x_1 is $\mu(1.44016,0.616583)$ and x_2 is $\mu(0.314697,7.34735)$
and x_3 is $\mu(2.38597,1.31093)$

THEN $\hat{y}_1 = 1.88537 + 1.78931x_1 + 1.73373\cos(\pi\ x_1) + 2.86658\sin(\pi\ x_1)$
$+4.53188x_2 - 3.75512\cos(\pi\ x_2) - 7.18406\sin(\pi\ x_2)$
$+0.868682x_3 - 0.541793\cos(\pi\ x_3) + 1.52449\sin(\pi\ x_3) + 0.763891(x_1\ x_2\ x_3)$

Rule-3:

IF x_1 is $\mu(0.115385,0.93777)$ and x_2 is $\mu(0.326872,1.02448)$
and x_3 is $\mu(0.984958,0.403378)$

THEN $\hat{y}_1 = 1.56458 + 0.703153x_1 + 0.0115128\cos(\pi\ x_1) - 0.119185\sin(\pi\ x_1)$
$-0.0263568x_2 - 0.681762\cos(\pi\ x_2) + 0.478785\sin(\pi\ x_2)$
$+7.0577x_3 - 0.808627\cos(\pi\ x_3) + 0.462158\sin(\pi\ x_3) + 10.6957(x_1\ x_2\ x_3)$

where $\mu(m_{ij},\sigma i_j)$ represents a Gaussian membership function with mean mi_j and deviation σi_j in the ith input variable and the jth rule. The final RMS error of the forecast output is about 10.337347. Figure 13(a) presents the forecast outputs for years 1703 to 2004, using 151 training data from years 1703 to 1853. Figure 13(b) plots the forecast errors between the proposed model and the desired output.

In this example, as in examples 1 and 2, the performance of the FLNFN model with CCPSO learning method was compared with that of other methods. In PSO (Kennedy & Eberhart, 1995) and CPSO (Bergh & Engelbrecht, 2004), the parameters are the same as in examples 1 and 2. Three rules are used to construct the fuzzy model. The learning proceeded for 1000 generations, and was performed fifty times. Figures 13(c) and 13(d) plot the forecast results and the forecast errors of particle swarm optimization (Kennedy & Eberhart, 1995). Figures 13(e) and 13(f) plot the forecast results and the forecast errors of cooperative particle swarm optimization (Bergh & Engelbrecht, 2004). Figures 13(g) and 13(h) plot the forecast results and the forecast errors of differential evolution (Storn, 1999). Figures 13(i) and 13(j) plot the forecast results and the forecast errors of GA. Figure 14 plots the learning curves of best performance of the FLNFN model with CCPSO, PSO, CPSO, DE and GA learning. The proposed CCPSO learning method yields better forecast results than the other methods. Table 4

presents the best RMS errors of training and forecasting for CCPSO, PSO (Kennedy & Eberhart, 1995), CPSO (Bergh & Engelbrecht, 2004), DE (Storn, 1999), and GA (Goldberg, 1989) learning methods. Table 5 lists the generalization capabilities of other methods (Karr, 1991; Juang et al. 2000). As presented in Table 4 and Table 5, the proposed FLNFN-CCPSO method outperforms the other methods.

CONCLUSION AND FUTURE WORKS

An efficient cultural cooperative particle swarm optimization learning method for the functional-link-based **neural fuzzy network** is proposed in predictive applications. The FLNFN model can generate the consequent part of a nonlinear combination of input variables. The proposed CCPSO method with cooperative behavior among multiple swarms increases the global search capacity using the belief space. The advantages of the proposed FLNFN-CCPSO method are as follows. 1) The consequent of the fuzzy rules is a nonlinear combination of input variables. The functional link neural network is used to the consequent part of the fuzzy rules. The functional expansion in the FLNFN model can yield the consequent part of a nonlinear combination of input variables; 2) the proposed CCPSO with cooperative behavior among multiple swarms can accelerate the search and increase global search capacity using the belief space. The experimental results demonstrate that the CCPSO method can obtain a smaller RMS error than the generally used PSO and CPSO for solving time series prediction problems.

Neural fuzzy networks possess the advantages of both neural networks and fuzzy systems in generating linguistic rules, handling imprecise data, and modeling highly nonlinear decision boundaries. Domain knowledge, in natural form, can be encoded in the network to improve performance. Two advanced topics for the proposed FLNFN-CCPSO method should be addressed in future

Figure 13. (a) Forecast results of the proposed method. (b) Forecast errors of the proposed method. (c) Forecast results of particle swarm optimization (Kennedy & Eberhart, 1995). (d) Forecast errors of particle swarm optimization. (e) Forecast results of cooperative particle swarm optimization (Bergh & Engelbrecht, 2004). (f) Forecast errors of cooperative particle swarm optimization. (g) Forecast results of differential evolution (Storn, 1999). (h) Forecast errors of differential evolution. (i) Forecast results of GA. (j) Forecast errors of GA (Goldberg, 1989)

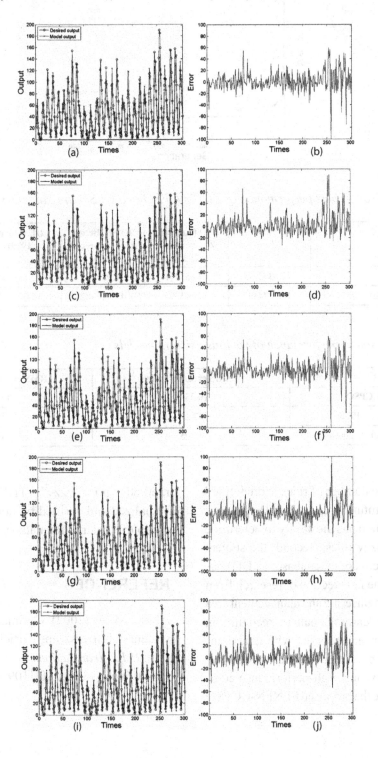

Figure 14. Learning curves of best performance of proposed method, PSO (Kennedy & Eberhart, 1995), CPSO (Bergh & Engelbrecht, 2004), DE (Storn, 1999) and GA (Goldberg, 1989)

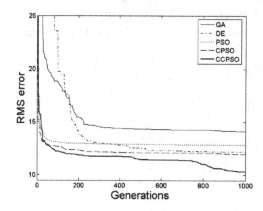

Table 4. Comparison of best performance of CCPSO, PSO and CPSO in Example 3

	CCPSO	PSO (Kennedy & Eberhart, 1995)	CPSO(Bergh & Engelbrecht, 2004)	DE (Storn, 1999)	GA(Goldberg, 1989)
RMS error (training)	**10.336261**	12.853411	11.983985	12.188084	14.143368
RMS error (forecasting)	**14.727455**	17.695794	17.446382	16.075044	19.726994

Table 5. Comparison of performance of various existing models

Method	RMS error (training)	RMS error (forecasting)
FLNFN-CCPSO	**10.3363**	**14.7275**
GA-FLC (Karr, 1991)	12.27	19.81
SEFC (Juang et al., 2000)	11.05	15.05

research. First, the number of rules is predefined in this chapter. In future work, it would be better if the proposed method has the ability to determine the number of fuzzy rules. Second, the subject of knowledge discovery in databases (KDD) has developed from the intersection of research from the construction engineering and management area such as machine learning, pattern recognition, artificial intelligence, reasoning with uncertainties, knowledge acquisition for expert systems, machine discovery, and high-performance computing. We will use the proposed FLNFN-CCPSO method to mine fuzzy IF-THEN rules that can be visualized and verified by domain experts from complex construction databases in future.

REFERENCES

Abido, M. A. (2002). Optimal design of power-system stabilizers using particle swarm optimization. *IEEE Transactions on Energy Conversion, 17*(3), 406–413. doi:10.1109/TEC.2002.801992

Angelov, P. P., & Filev, D. P. (2004). An approach to online identification of Takagi-Sugeno fuzzy models. *IEEE Transactions on Systems, Man, and Cybernetics, 34*(1), 484–498. doi:10.1109/TSMCB.2003.817053

Bhattacharya, A., Abraham, A., Vasant, P., & Grosan, C. (2007). Evolutionary artificial neural network for selecting flexible manufacturing systems under disparate level-of-satisfaction on decision maker. *International Journal of Innovative computing . Information and Control, 3*(1), 131–140.

Box, J. E., & Jenkins, G. M. (1970). *Time Series Analysis, Forecasting and Control.* Holden Day.

Cai, X., Zhang, N., Venayagamoorthy, G. K., & Wunsch, D. C. (2007). Time series prediction with recurrent neural networks trained by a hybrid PSO-EA algorithm. *Neurocomputing, 70*(13-15), 2342–2353. doi:10.1016/j.neucom.2005.12.138

Chatterjee, A., Pulasinghe, K., Watanabe, K., & Izumi, K. (2005). A particle-swarm-optimized fuzzy-neural network for voice-controlled robot systems. *IEEE Transactions on Industrial Electronics, 52*(6), 1478–1489. doi:10.1109/TIE.2005.858737

Chen, C. H., Lin, C. T., & Lin, C. J. (2007). A functional-link-based fuzzy neural network for temperature control. In *2007 IEEE Symposium on Foundations of Computational Intelligence,* Honolulu, HI, (pp. 53-58).

Chu, S. C., & Tsai, P. W. (2007). Computational intelligence based on the behavior of cats. *International Journal of Innovative computing. Information and Control, 3*(1), 163–173.

Cowder, R. S. (1990). Predicting the Mackey-glass time series with cascade-correlation learning. In *Proc. of the 1990 Connectionist Models Summer School,* (pp. 117-123).

Eberhart, R., & Kennedy, J. (1995). A new optimizer using particle swarm theory. In *Proc. of the Sixth International Symposium on Micro Machine and Human Science,* (pp. 39-43).

Feng, H. M. (2006). Self-generation RBFNs using evolutional PSO learning. *Neurocomputing, 70*(1-3), 241–251. doi:10.1016/j.neucom.2006.03.007

Gaing, Z. L. (2004). A particle swarm optimization approach for optimum design of PID controller in AVR system. *IEEE Transactions on Energy Conversion, 19*(2), 384–391. doi:10.1109/TEC.2003.821821

Goldberg, D. E. (1989). *Genetic Algorithms in Search Optimization and Machine Learning.* Reading, MA: Addison-Wesley.

Huang, F. Y. (2008). A particle swarm optimized fuzzy neural network for credit risk evaluation. In *Proc. of the Second International Conference on Genetic and Evolutionary Computing,* (pp. 153-157).

Huang, M. J., Tsou, Y. L., & Lee, S. C. (2006). Integrating fuzzy data mining and fuzzy artificial neural networks for discovering implicit knowledge. *Knowledge-Based Systems, 19*(6), 396–403. doi:10.1016/j.knosys.2006.04.003

Jang, J.-S. R. (1993). ANFIS: Adaptive-network-based fuzzy inference system. *IEEE Transactions on Systems, Man, and Cybernetics, 23,* 665–685. doi:10.1109/21.256541

Jin, X., & Reynolds, R. G. (1999). Using knowledge-based evolutionary computation to solve nonlinear constraint optimization problems: a cultural algorithm approach. In *Proc. of IEEE Congress on Evolutionary Computation,* Washington, DC, (pp. 1672-1678).

Juang, C. F. (2004). A hybrid of genetic algorithm and particle swarm optimization for recurrent network design. *IEEE Trans. on Sys., Man and Cybern. Part B, 34*(2), 997–1006.

Juang, C. F., & Lin, C. T. (1998). An on-line self-constructing neural fuzzy inference network and its applications. *IEEE transactions on Fuzzy Systems, 6*(1), 12–31. doi:10.1109/91.660805

Juang, C. F., Lin, J. Y., & Lin, C. T. (2000). Genetic reinforcement learning through symbiotic evolution for fuzzy controller design. *IEEE Trans. Syst., Man, Cybern. Part B, 30*(2), 290–302.

Karaboga, D., & Basturk, B. (2008). On the performance of artificial bee colony (ABC) algorithm. *Applied Soft Computing, 8*(1), 687–697. doi:10.1016/j.asoc.2007.05.007

Karr, C. L. (1991). Design of an adaptive fuzzy logic controller using a genetic algorithm. In *Proc. of 4th Conf. Genetic Algorithms*, (pp. 450-457).

Kasabov, N. K., & Song, Q. (2002). DENFIS: Dynamic evolving neural-fuzzy inference system and its application for time-series prediction. *IEEE transactions on Fuzzy Systems, 10*(2), 144–154. doi:10.1109/91.995117

Kennedy, J., & Eberhart, R. (1995). Particle swarm optimization. In *Proc. of IEEE Int. Conf. on Neural Networks*, (pp. 1942-1948).

Kim, H., Tan, J. K., Ishikawa, S., Khalid, M., Otsuka, Y., Shimizu, H., & Shinomiya, T. (2006). Automatic judgment of spinal deformity based on back propagation on neural network. *International Journal of Innovative computing . Information and Control, 2*(6), 1271–1279.

Li, C., & Lee, C. Y. (2003). Self-organizing neuro-fuzzy system for control of unknown plants. *IEEE transactions on Fuzzy Systems, 11*(1), 135–150. doi:10.1109/TFUZZ.2002.805898

Li, M., Mehrotra, K., Mohan, C., & Ranka, S. (1990). Sunspot numbers forecasting using neural networks. *Proc. of IEEE Int. Conf. Intelligent Control, 1*, 524-529.

Lin, C. J. (2008). An efficient immune-based symbiotic particle swarm optimization learning algorithm for TSK-type neuro-fuzzy networks design. *Fuzzy Sets and Systems, 159*(21), 2890–2909. doi:10.1016/j.fss.2008.01.020

Lin, C. J. & Chin, C. C. (2004). Prediction and identification using wavelet-based recurrent fuzzy neural networks. *IEEE Trans. Systems, Man, and Cybernetics (Part:B), 34*(5), 2144-2154.

Lin, C. T., & Lee, C. S. G. (1996). *Neural Fuzzy Systems: A Neural-Fuzzy Synergism to Intelligent Systems*. Upper Saddle River, NJ: Prentice-Hall.

Ling, S. H., Leung, F. H. F., Lam, H. K., Lee, Y. S., & Tam, P. K. S. (2003). A novel genetic-algorithm-based neural network for short-term load forecasting. *IEEE Trans. Industrial electornic., 50*(4), 793-799.

Mansour, M., Mekhamer, S. F., & El-Sherif El-Kharbawe, N. (2007). A modified particle swarm optimizer for the coordination of directional overcurrent relays. *IEEE Transactions on Power Delivery, 22*(3), 1400–1410. doi:10.1109/TPWRD.2007.899259

Mendes, R., Cortez, P., Rocha, M., & Neves, J. (2002). Particle swarms for feedforward neural network training. In *The 2002 International Joint Conference on Neural Networks*, (pp. 1895-1899).

Mitra, S., Pal, S. K., & Mitra, P. (2002). Data mining in soft computing framework: a survey. *IEEE Transactions on Neural Networks, 13*(1), 3–14. doi:10.1109/72.977258

Mizutani, E., & Jang, J.-S. R. (1995). Coactive neural fuzzy modeling. In *Proc. of Int. Conf. Neural Networks*, (pp. 760-765).

Pao, Y. H. (1989). *Adaptive Pattern Recognition and Neural Networks.* Reading, MA: Addison-Wesley.

Patra, J. C., Pal, R. N., Chatterji, B. N., & Panda, G. (1999). Identification of nonlinear dynamic systems using functional link artificial neural networks. *IEEE Trans. on Syst., Man, and Cybern. - Part B, 29*, 254–262.

Reynolds, R. G. (1994). An introduction to cultural algorithms. In A.V. Sebald & L.J. Fogel (eds.), *Proc. of the 3rd Annual Conference on Evolutionary Programming,* (pp. 131- 139). River Edge, NJ: World Scientific.

Saleem, S. M. (2001). *Knowledge-based solution to dynamic optimization problems using cultural algorithms.* PhD thesis, Wayne State University, Detroit, Michigan.

Silva, A., Neves, A., & Costa, E. (2002). An empirical comparison of particle swarm and predator prey optimization. *Lecture Notes in Computer Science, 2464,* 103–110. doi:10.1007/3-540-45750-X_13

Song, Y., Chen, Z., & Yuan, Z. (2007). New chaotic PSO-based neural network predictive control for nonlinear process. *IEEE Transactions on Neural Networks, 18*(2), 595–601. doi:10.1109/TNN.2006.890809

Storn, R. (1999). System design by constraint adaptation and differential evolution. *IEEE Transactions on Evolutionary Computation, 3*(1), 22–34. doi:10.1109/4235.752918

Sun, F., Sun, Z., Li, L., & Li, H. X. (2003). Neuro-fuzzy adaptive control based on dynamic inversion for robotic manipulators. *Fuzzy Sets and Systems, 134,* 117–133. doi:10.1016/S0165-0114(02)00233-6

Takagi, H., Suzuki, N., Koda, T., & Kojima, Y. (1992). Neural networks designed on approximate reasoning architecture and their application. *IEEE Transactions on Neural Networks, 3,* 752–759. doi:10.1109/72.159063

Takagi, T., & Sugeno, M. (1985). Fuzzy identification of systems and its applications to modeling and control. *IEEE Transactions on Systems, Man, and Cybernetics, 15,* 116–132.

Tong, H. (1990). *Non-linear Time Series: A Dynamical System Approach.* Oxford, UK: Oxford University Press.

Van den Bergh, F., & Engelbrecht, A. P. (2004). A cooperative approach to particle swarm optimization. *IEEE Transactions on Evolutionary Computation, 8*(3), 225–239. doi:10.1109/TEVC.2004.826069

Wong, J. T., Chen, K. H., & Su, C. T. (2008). Designing a system for a process parameter determined through modified PSO and fuzzy neural network. In *Proc. of the 12th Pacific-Asia Conference on Knowledge Discovery and Data Mining,* (pp. 785-794).

Yoshida, H., Kawata, K., Fukuyama, Y., Takayama, S., & Nakanishi, Y. (2000). A particle swarm optimization for reactive power and voltage control considering voltage security assessment. *IEEE Transactions on Power Systems, 15*(4), 1232–1239. doi:10.1109/59.898095

Yu, W. D. (2007). Hybrid soft computing approach for mining of complex construction databases. *Journal of Computing in Civil Engineering, 21*(5), 343–352. doi:10.1061/(ASCE)0887-3801(2007)21:5(343)

Zhang, Y. Q., Fraser, M. D., Gagliano, R. A., & Kandel, A. (2000). Granular neural networks for numerical-linguistic data fusion and knowledge discovery. *IEEE Transactions on Neural Networks, 11*(3), 658–667. doi:10.1109/72.846737

Chapter 13
Power System Load Frequency Control Using Combined Intelligent Techniques

Yannis L. Karnavas
Technological Educational Institution of Crete, Greece

ABSTRACT

The load frequency control (LFC) is to maintain the power balance in the electrical power system such that the system's frequency deviates from its nominal value to within specified limits and according to practically acceptable dynamic performance of the system. The control strategy evolved may also result in overall high efficiency (fuel saving) and minimum additional equipment to avoid cost, maintenance etc. The supplementary controller i.e. of a diesel or steam turbine generating unit, called the load frequency controller, may satisfy these requirements. The function of the controller is to generate, raise or lower command signals to the speed-gear changer of the prime mover (i.e. diesel engine) in response to the frequency error signal by performing mathematical manipulations of amplification and integration of this signal. The speed-gear changer must not act too fast, as it will cause wear and tear of the engine and, also, should not act too slow, as it will deteriorate system's performance. Therefore, an optimum load frequency controller is required for satisfactory operation of the system. In this Chapter, intelligent controllers for the LFC problem are analyzed and discussed. The use of any single technique or even a combination of genetic algorithms, fuzzy logic and neural networks is explored instead of conventional methods.

INTRODUCTION

Advancing microprocessor technologies have brought automation capabilities to new levels of applications. Load frequency control of power systems (also called automatic generation control – AGC), is one of many important industrial application areas,

which may greatly benefit from such advances. However, development and deployment of such applications are often difficult because of the complex dynamics of actual processes. Conventional control theory is based on mathematical models that describe the dynamic behavior of controlled systems. This is based on the deterministic nature of systems, but its applicability is reduced by computational complexity, parametric and structural uncertain-

DOI: 10.4018/978-1-61520-757-2.ch013

ties, and the presence of nonlinearities. These characteristics often make the controller design complicated and unreliable. A potential solution is offered by shifting the attention from modeling of the process to extracting the control knowledge of human experts. This artificial intelligence approach, implemented in intelligent control systems (ICSs), utilizes the fact that human operators normally do not handle the system control problem with a detailed mathematical model but rather with a qualitative or symbolic description of the controlled system. ICSs have two unique features: ability to make decisions and learning from data or experience. Decision making capabilities provide for the controllers to operate in real-time process-control environments, at both micro and macro levels of system operations. Learning capabilities make it possible for the controllers to adapt their knowledge to specified performance criteria, to reason about potential dynamics of the environment, to predict advantageous features, or even to acquire the needed knowledge.

In this chapter intelligent load frequency controllers which have been developed recently will be demonstrated, which are (most of them) using a combination of fuzzy logic, genetic algorithms and neural networks, to regulate the power output and system frequency by controlling the speed of the generator with the help of fuel rack position control. The aim of these intelligent controllers is to restore the frequency to its nominal value in the shortest time possible whenever there is any change in the load demand. The action of the controllers should be coupled with minimum frequency transient oscillations and zero steady-state error. The design and performance evaluation of the controllers' structure are illustrated with the help of results of relevant case studies applied to single-area or interconnected power systems. It will be clearly shown that this type of controllers exhibit extremely satisfactory performance and overcome the possible drawbacks associated with other conventional techniques.

The chapter is organized as follows: At the next Section, a brief literature review will be reported accompanied by the relevant background and definitions. The electrical power system industry environment will also be discussed. Typical models of a single-area as well as interconnected electrical power systems in the traditional as well as in the open-market environment will be demonstrated to which the associated controllers will be applied. The conventional integral and/or proportional type controller is also reviewed and the reproduction of the results derived from its application to a single area power system is presented. A Section follows, referring to the philosophy of the intelligent controller design. Brief reviews of the main aspects of the three aforementioned modern intelligent techniques are presented. For illustrations purposes, a fuzzy logic controller is also designed and applied to the same single-area power system. In The final Section an effort is made to overcome the drawbacks of the previous methods by incorporating a structure which combines the three modern intelligent methods. The controller developed is actually an on-line neural network, driven by a genetic algorithm based self-learning fuzzy logic controller (NNGAFLC). Some cases of study are being investigated and a comparison is made to show the relative goodness of the control strategy employed.

RELEVANT BACKGROUND AND CONVENTIONAL APPROACHES

Brief Literature Review

Many investigations in the area of automatic generation control of isolated and of interconnected power systems have been reported in the past throughout the last decades A number of control strategies have also been proposed to achieve improved performance. The proportional integral control is successful in achieving zero steady-state error in the system frequency, but it exhibits poor dynamic performance as evidenced by large overshoot and transient frequency oscillations. Moreover, the settling time is relatively large. In the application of optimal control techniques, the controller design is normally based on a fixed parameter model of the system derived by a linearization process. Power system parameters are a function of the operating points. Therefore, as the operating conditions change, system performance with controllers designed for a specific operating point will no longer be suitable. Consequently, the nonlinear nature of the load frequency control problem makes it difficult to ensure stability for all operating points when an integral or a proportional plus integral controller is used. The application of adaptive control theory to the LFC problem has also found acceptance because of its role in eliminating some of the problems associated with classical and modern control. Self-tuning regulators (STR), model reference adaptive control (MRAC) as well as variable structure control (VSC) are used under the heading of adaptive control.

In recent years, modern "intelligent" methods such as artificial neural networks (ANN), fuzzy logic (FL) and genetic algorithms (GA), have gained increasing interest for the LFC problem. Applications of ANNs and generalized neural network (GNN) can be found in literature. The last methods have some deficiencies, such as: large number of neurons in hidden layers for complex function approximation, very large training time required, large number of unknowns (some of them are inaccessible state variables) to be determined for which the use of estimators must be adopted. Applications of FL only and GA based FL control has also been reported. The drawbacks of these methods include fixed parameters of the fuzzy sets of the fuzzy variables as well as large computational time for the rule base to be examined. In other words, the considerable time needed for response when fuzzy set theory is applied makes

the practical realization quite difficult. Finally, very few, but effective, LFC schemes consisting of an overall compination of the above techniques have also been demonstrated. This chapter will illustrate one of these. The reader can find throughout the recent literature analytical details of such implementations.

Electrical Power System Industry

Traditionally, and moreover, what we meet until today in several countries of the world is that, the power system industry has a "vertically integrated utility" structure, which means that the utilities own and handle the generation, transmission, and distribution aspects themselves. In that case, the LFC problem must be formulated accordingly. Figure 1(a) shows the transfer block diagrams for the LFC of a single-area power system along with a new additional signal U(t) that it will be used in the next Sections. Figure 1(b) shows (for illustration purposes) the relevant transfer block diagram of a two-area power system with hydro turbines. The above models, can be expanded appropriately to construct multi-area power systems with different power sources like diesel, steam, gas, wind or hydro units. In this Chapter, for simplicity reasons and without loss of generality, only the single area model will be used for LFC using intelligent techniques, so the following apply only to it. The dynamic model in state-variable form can be obtained from the transfer function model and is given as,

$$\dot{\mathbf{X}} = \mathbf{AX} + \mathbf{BU}, \ \mathbf{Y} = \mathbf{CX} \quad (1)$$

where

$$\mathbf{X} = [\Delta f \, \Delta Pt \, \Delta Pg \, \Delta Pscp]^T, \ \mathbf{U} = [\Delta Pd \, U(t)]^T, \ \mathbf{Y} = [\Delta f] \quad (2)$$

Figure 1. Transfer function models of the LFC for a) single area (steam) power system, b) two area (hydro) power system

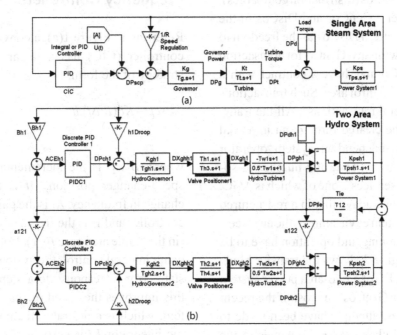

are the state vector and the control vector respectively and,

$$
\mathbf{A} = \begin{bmatrix} -\dfrac{1}{Tps} & \dfrac{Kps}{Tps} & 0 & 0 \\ 0 & -\dfrac{1}{Tt} & \dfrac{Kt}{Tt} & 0 \\ -\dfrac{Kg}{Tg \cdot R} & 0 & -\dfrac{1}{Tg} & \dfrac{Kg}{Tg} \\ -Ki & 0 & 0 & 0 \end{bmatrix} \quad \mathbf{B} = \begin{bmatrix} 0 & 0 & \dfrac{Kg}{Tg} & 0 \\ -\dfrac{Kps}{Tps} & 0 & 0 & 0 \end{bmatrix}^{T}
$$

(3)

$\mathbf{C} = [1\ 0\ 0\ 0]$

are the coefficient matrices.

The nominal parameter values (i.e. gains and time constants of the turbine, governor and power system blocks in per unit), used in literature are shown in Table 1 from which the values of the elements of the system matrices A, B and C may be easily computed. For comparative study between the conventional (pure integral) controller and the intelligent controllers illustrated later, the same values of these parameters are used here.

On the other hand, in the restructured or deregulated environment, vertically integrated utilities no longer exist. The utilities no longer own generation, transmission, and distribution; instead, there are three different entities, viz., GenCos

Table 1. Nominal system parameters for a single-area power system

R [Hz/p.u.MW]	D [p.u.MW/Hz]	Kg	Tg [sec]	Kt
2.4	0.00833	1	0.08	1
Tt [sec]	Kps	Tps [sec]	ΔPd [p.u.MW]	Ki
0.3	1	20	*see text	*see text

(generation companies), TransCos (transmission companies) and DisCos (distribution companies). As there are several GenCos and DisCos in the deregulated structure, a DisCo has the freedom to have a contract with any GenCo for transaction of power. A DisCo may have a contract with a GenCo in another control area. Such transactions are called "bilateral transactions". All the transactions have to be cleared through an impartial entity called an independent system operator (ISO). The ISO has to control a number of so-called "ancillary services", one of which is AGC. So, it is obvious nowadays that in a restructured electric power system environment, the engineering aspects of planning and operation have to be reformulated. Figure 2 shows the transfer block diagram for the LFC of a two-area power system consisting of four GenCos. In most of the recent reported strategies, attempts have been made to adapt well-tested classical LFC schemes to the changing environment of power system operation under deregulation.

Conventional Load Frequency Controllers

Referring to Figure 1(a), a conventional integral controller (CIC) has a linear integral control strategy of the form,

$$\Delta Pscp = -Ki \int (B \cdot \Delta f) dt \qquad (4)$$

where $\Delta Pscp$ is the incremental change in the speed-changer position, Δf is the incremental change in frequency, Ki is the gain of the integral controller and B is the frequency bias parameter (in the single area case $B=1$). With the practice of using integral control, the system has no steady-state error in response to a step input; besides, this improves the speed of response of the system, which is a desirable feature. If the gain of the integrator Ki is sufficiently high, overshoot will occur, increasing sharply as a function of the gain; this is highly undesirable. In the absence of integral control, one can sharply increase the gain

Figure 2. Transfer function models of the LFC for a two area power system consisted of four generation companies, in a deregulated (open market) environment

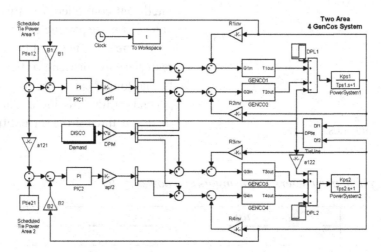

of the closed-loop system and thus improve the system response. However, the system will then display a steady-state error. Even if a compromise is made using a proportional plus integral control, the response is not satisfactory enough and large oscillations occur in the system. Thus, the integrator gain must be set to a level that compromises between fast transient recovery and low overshoot in the dynamic response of the overall system.

Figure 3 depicts the computational results obtained using a CIC and shows the frequency variation after simulating the above mentioned model for different values of integrator gain Ki for 10% and 20% step disturbance in load respectively.

While simulating the model, it is easily seen that for any non-negative value of Ki (except zero) and for any step perturbation, the system is stable (i.e. Δf converges to zero). The critical value of Ki can also be determined from the empirical formula (although it is not proposed to),

$$Ki_{(critical)} = \frac{1}{4TpsKps}\left(1 + \frac{Kps}{R}\right)^2 \tag{5}$$

When the frequency is lower than nominal, the system loses a small component of served load. When it is higher, the system imposes a small additional component onto the connected load. That means that a quality measure must be used in order to compare a controller's overall performance. In this work an integration-absolute-error-time (IAET) criteria of the following form is used, i.e.

$$IAET = J_{fre} = \int_0^{Tsim} \left|\Delta f(t)\right| t \, dt \tag{6}$$

The J_{fre} values obtained are listed in Table 2. It is evident that for $Ki=Ki_{(critical)}$, one gets the most satisfactory system performance.

Figuer3. Frequency variation of single-area power system for different values of integral gain Ki. Step input: (a) ΔPd=0.1 p.u.MW, (b) ΔPd=0.2 p.u.MW

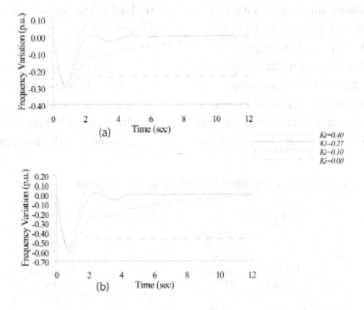

Table 2. J_{fre} values for the two CIC simulation cases

	Ki=0.0	*Ki=0.1*	*Ki(critical)=0.27*	*Ki=0.4*
ΔPd=0.1 p.u.	*1.879*	*0.875*	***0.372***	*0.389*
ΔPd=0.2 p.u.	*3.758*	*1.750*	***0.745***	*0.778*

PHILOSOPHY OF INTELLIGENT CONTROLLER DESIGN

Fuzzy Logic Controller

Fuzzy logic control essentially involves the derivation of a control law from heuristic an imprecise ("fuzzy") rules. While the mathematical models of the power system are available, they tend to be highly nonlinear and therefore the controller design becomes a highly formidable task. Fuzzy logic control has been applied for the design of power system stabilizers and has been shown to give improved performance than conventional controllers.

Figure 4 schematically depicts a typical closed-loop fuzzy control system. The reference signal and plant output, which are crisp values but non-fuzzy variables, must be fuzzified by a fuzzification procedure. Similarly, the fact that the controlled plant can not directly respond to fuzzy logic controls accounts for why the fuzzy logic control signal generated by the fuzzy algorithm must be defuzzified by defuzzification before applied to control the plant. A rule base consists of a set of fuzzy rules. The data base contains membership functions of fuzzy subsets. A fuzzy rule may contain fuzzy variables, fuzzy subsets characterized by membership functions and a conditional statement. The fuzzy control algorithm consists of executing an ordered sequence of fuzzy rules by the concepts of fuzzy implication and the compositional rules of inference. Essentially, a FLC is a deterministic model-free, non-linear and robust controller.

FLC Design Procedure Overview

For the LFC problem one encounters a situation where the system is not amenable to conventional output feedback in all operating regions. Therefore the possibility of using a fuzzy logic load frequency controller (FLLFC) will be explored for this purpose. Next are outlined the steps involved in the pertinent controller design (refer to Figure 4):

1) *Fuzzification*: where precise numerical values obtained by measurements are converted to membership values of the various linguistic variables (e.g. "Positive Small"). For the FLLFC, the inputs are the frequency

Figure 4. Block diagram of a typical closed-loop fuzzy control system

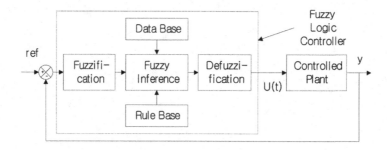

variation (error) and the change in error defined as:

$$e_t = f_{nom} - f_t = \Delta f$$
$$ce_t = e_t - e_{t-1} = \Delta e_t \qquad (7)$$

with the sampling interval could be chosen as 1ms.

The inputs are categorized as belonging to the various linguistic variables with their corresponding membership values. The membership functions are shown in Figure 5. The membership value of an input x in a particular linguistic variable R is denoted by $\mu[R(x)]$. The FLLFC parameters are shown in Table 3.

2) *Fuzzy Control*: where the heuristic rules of the knowledge base are used to determine the (fuzzy) controller action. For example the FLLFC employs a rule: IF e_t is ZeRo AND

Δe_t is Positive Small THEN controller action ($U(t)$) is Positive Small. The part "e_t is ZeRo AND Δe_t is Positive Small" defines another linguistic variable. Though it is possible to derive a membership value for this variable in many possible ways the rule that it have been chosen (due to its simplicity) is

$$\mu A_{\cap B}(x,y) = \min(\mu A(_x), \mu B(_y)) \qquad (8)$$

In the above example A="ZeRo", B="Positive Small", $A \cap B$ ="ZeRo AND Positive Small", x=et, y=cet. The combinations chosen to be examined and the corresponding (fuzzy) controller actions are shown in Table 4.

3) *Defuzzification*: It should be noted that various rules (n) may be in operation for a certain set of (e_t, ce_t), each recommending possibly different fuzzy controller actions. These have to be combined in a certain way to obtain a precise numerical output corresponding to

Figure 5. Triangular type membership function for each fuzzy subset

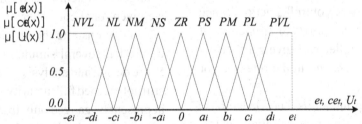

Table 3. Parameters corresponding to membership functions (refer to Fig. 5)

	Case 1				Case 2				Case 3		
	e	*ce*	*u*		*e*	*ce*	*u*		*e*	*ce*	*u*
a	0.05	0.0005	0.05	*a*	0.05	0.002	0.05	*a*	0.35	0.37	0.40
b	0.10	0.00125	0.10	*b*	0.10	0.004	0.10	*b*	0.89	0.63	0.51
c	0.20	0.0025	0.30	*c*	0.20	0.008	0.30	*c*	1.00	1.00	1.00
d	0.40	0.0050	0.50	*d*	0.40	0.012	0.50	*d*	-	-	-
e	0.80	0.0100	0.80	*e*	0.80	0.020	0.80	*e*	-	-	-
		(a)				*(b)*				*(c)*	

Table 4. Combination of inputs and corresponding FLLFC action

ce/e	NVL	NL	NM	NS	ZR	PS	PM	PL	PVL
NVL	PVL	PVL	PL	PL	PM	PM	PS	PS	ZR
NL	PVL	PL	PL	PM	PM	PS	PS	ZR	NS
NM	PL	PL	PM	PM	PS	PS	ZR	NS	NS
NS	PL	PM	PM	PS	PS	ZR	NS	NS	NM
ZR	PM	PM	PS	PS	ZR	NS	NS	NM	NM
PS	PM	PS	PS	ZR	NS	NS	NM	NM	NL
PM	PS	PS	ZR	NS	NS	NM	NM	NL	NL
PL	PS	ZR	NS	NS	NM	NM	NL	NL	NVL
PVL	ZR	NS	NS	NM	NM	NL	NL	NVL	NVL

the actual controller action. The well known center of gravity defuzzification method it is also used because of its simplicity:

$$\Delta u = \sum_{j=1}^{n} \mu_j u_j \Big/ \sum_{j=1}^{n} \mu_j \qquad (9)$$

where μ_j is the membership value of the linguistic variable recommending the fuzzy controller action and u_i is the precise numerical value corresponding to that fuzzy controller action. Since the FLLFC action corresponds to an increment Δ_u, this type of controller will give zero steady state error for a step change in the reference or any step disturbance.

The membership functions, knowledge base and method of defuzzification essentially determine the controller performance. As mentioned before, their choice is heuristic, though a rough estimate of the parameter values can be obtained from our knowledge of steady state characteristics and simulated open-loop behaviour. These have to be tuned after evaluation of the performance using repetitive simulation.

The FLLFC offers many more tunable parameters than the CIC or even a PID type controller. Moreover, since the final output $U(t)$ is a combination of the recommended actions of many rules (which themselves operate on combinations of the inputs (e_t, ce_t)), the controller is more robust to changes in system or controller parameters than a conventional controller.

To demonstrate the efficiency of the FLLFC controller, several simulations were performed. Since design and analysis of fuzzy controllers has still not reached full maturity, the performance can at present be gauged only from simulation. Three cases are examined in this Section considering the FLLFC parameters as well as the combinations and corresponding (fuzzy) controller actions the so called fuzzy associative matrix (FAM):

Table 5. Examined cases of relevant fuzzy associative matrices

	FAM used	Parameters used
Case 1	See Table 4 (outer section).	See Table 3 (a).
Case 2	See Table 4 (outer section).	See Table 3 (b).
Case 3	See Table 4 (inner section).	See Table 3 (c).

Figure 6. Frequency variation of single-area power system with step input change $\Delta Pd=0.1\ p.u.MW$. (a) Case 1, (b) Case 2, (c) Case 3

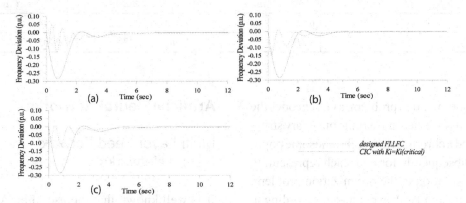

A step load disturbance of $\Delta Pd=0.1$p.u. is applied and the system output frequency (Δf) is observed. The corresponding simulation results (Figure 6) indicate that the FLLFC is relatively insensitive to operating point variations and is not unstable in a wide operating region. The response time of the FLLFC is however somewhat slower than the CIC.

Referring to Figure 1(a) and Figure 4 the control signal $U(t)$ variation which is actually the output of the FLLFC is shown in Figure 7. Furthermore, the IAET criteria gives the values shown in Table 6. From the results it is obvious that the FLLFC is highly dependent on the data base parameters. Case 3 exhibits quite better performance although 5 fuzzy sets have been used for each linguistic variable and only 12 rules (instead of 9 fuzzy sets and 81 rules in Cases 1 and 2).

That means that an initial tuning in the design of a FLC as well as an algorithm to change continuously the data base parameters is needed. This will be explored by the incorporation of a GA. So far, the $Ki_{(critical)}$ case of the CIC simulation results along with the Case 3 of the FLLFC design will be kept to compare them with the NNGAFLC development.

GENETIC ALGORITHMS

A GA is a global search technique based on the operations of natural genetics and a Darwinian survival-of-the-fittest with a randomly structured information exchange. GA related research has received increasing interest owing to its advantages over conventional optimization techniques.

Figure 7. Control signal U(t) variation (output of designed FLLFC)

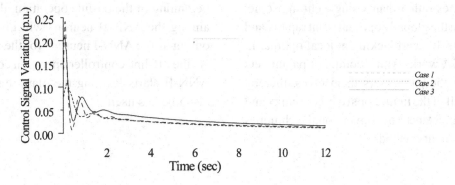

Table 6. Jfre values for the three FLLFC simulation cases

	Case 1	Case 2	Case 3
$\Delta Pd=0.1$ p.u.	0.162	0.156	**0.144**
$\Delta Pd=0.2$ p.u.	0.317	0.302	**0.295**

Given an optimization problem, a GA encodes the parameters concerned into a finite bit binary string that is called a chromosome. A chromosome population is subsequently formed, each representing a possible solution to the optimization problem. Each chromosome is then evaluated according to its fitness function.

Three basic operators "reproduction", "crossover" and "mutation", i.e. similar to genetic evolution, are then performed. The reproduction task randomly selects a new generation of chromosomes. The crossover involves exchanging parts of two chromosomes. With the crossover operation, more chromosomes are generated. The genetic search space is thus extended and more complete. Mutation is the random alteration of the bits in the string. For the binary representation, mutation task simply flips the state of a bit from 1 to 0, or vice versa. The mutation operation is usually associated with helping to re-inject any information that may be vital to the performance of a search process. Elitism, is the procedure where the best individual is replicated into next generation. Finally, the string having the largest value of fitness function is found and, the, decoded to obtain the actual parameters (i.e. of a fuzzy logic controller).

A GA, capable of searching for a population of chromosomes rather than a single chromosome, can arrive at the globally optimal point rapidly and simultaneously avert locking at local optima. In addition, GA works with a coding of parameters rather than the parameters themselves, thereby freeing itself of the limitations (e.g. continuity and derivative existence) of conventional techniques such as gradient methods.

Artificial Neural Networks

Multi-Layer Feed Forward Neural Networks

It is well known that the use of an ANN offers a significant speed advantage, due to its parallel nature, and could be implemented in real-time while the implementation of a complicated conventional controller is not always possible in real-time. Many of the ANNs applications in control areas involve learning the control system dynamics and incorporating them, in some way to the overall system controller. The approaches differ in the methods used for such incorporation, the learning and adaptation of the ANN. One approach is to train the ANN off-line to learn the system dynamics and employ it as a feed-forward controller as shown in Figure 8a. In another approach the ANN is employed as a replacement for the plant dynamics evaluation inside the model-based control algorithm as shown in Figure 8b. In this Chapter, a combination of these two approaches will be used. Actually, two identical ANNs (ANN-I, ANN-II) will be employed. The first one is trained off-line, using the input and output of the FLLFC driven by the GA, and the second one is acting like on-line controller. At the beginning of the on-line operation, the synapses among the ANN-II neurons will give the same output as the ANN-I neurons for the same input. As the off-line controller operation continues the ANN-II starts learning the plant dynamics and also updates itself.

Figure 8. (a) ANN as a feed-forward controller, (b) ANN as an adaptive controller

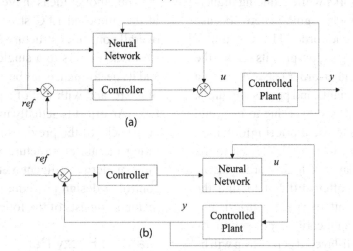

(a)

(b)

Higher-Order Feed-Forward Networks

Multi-layered perceptron (MLP) networks using the back-propagation learning rule or its variants have been successfully applied to applications involving pattern classification and function approximation as well as control schemes of power systems. Unfortunately, the training speeds for multi-layered networks are extremely slower than those for feed-forward networks comprising of a single layer of threshold logic units, and using the perceptron, ADALINE or Hebbian type learning rules. Moreover, these networks converge very slowly in typical situations dealing with complex and nonlinear problems, and do not scale well with problem size.

Higher-order correlations among the input components can be used alternatively to construct a higher-order network to yield a nonlinear discriminant function using only a single layer of cells. The building block of such networks in the higher-order processing unit (HPU), defined as a neural processing unit that includes higher-order input correlations, and its output, y, is given by:

$$y = \sigma\left(\sum_j w_j x_j + \sum_{j,k} w_{jk} x_j x_k + \sum_{j,k,l} w_{jkl} x_j x_k x_l + \cdots\right)$$

(10)

where $\sigma(x)$ is a nonlinear function of input x, x_j is the j-th component of x, and $w_{jkl}\ldots$ is an adjustable weight from product of inputs x_j, x_k, x_l ... to the HPU. If the input is of dimension N, then a k-th order HPU needs a total of

$$\sum_{i=0}^{k}\binom{N+i-1}{i}$$

weights if all products of up to $k <= N$ components are to be incorporated. A single layer of HPU (SLHPU) network is one in which only one layer of mapping from input to output using HPUs is considered. The order of a SLHPU network is the highest order of any of the constituent HPUs. Thus output of the k-th order SLHPU is a nonlinear function of up to the k-th order polynomials. Since it does not have hidden units as in sigma-pi network, reliable single layer learning rules such as perceptron, ADALINE, or Hebbian type rules can be used. However, to accommodate all higher-order correlations, the number of weights required increases combinatorially in the dimensionality of the inputs. Limiting the order of the network leads to a reduction in the classification capability of the network. There have been many approaches which maintain the powerful discrimination capability of higher-order networks while reducing higher-order terms. For example, sigma-pi networks use a hidden layer of higher-order TLUs. A multi-layering strategy using sigma-pi units retains the full capability of a higher-order network using a smaller number of weights and processing units, but its learning speed is slower due to layering. Another approach is to use a priori information to remove the terms which are irrelevant to the problem in a single layer of higher-order TLUs. However since it is often difficult to find the properties of input pattern space a priori, this strategy has limited applications. For simplicity reasons classical multi-layered perceptron will be implemented through the next Section, although it has been found that a higher-order feed-forward neural network would be preferable due to its superior performance.

Overall Load Frequency Intelligent Controller Scheme

In this Section the use of a combination of genetic algorithms, fuzzy logic and neural networks is explored instead of conventional methods for the LFC problem. Also, a controller based on a combination of the aforementioned techniques will be illustrated. The following ideas were formulated in order to overcome the deficiencies of the previous mentioned conventional and adaptive controllers:

- The off-line use of a GA for the continuous determination of the parameters of a FLC as well as of the conventional integral controller's gain.
- The off-line use of a FLC to attain satisfactory control in a wide area of operating conditions. An ANN is also incorporated here to capture system dynamics.
- The on-line use of a suitably pre-trained/re-trained ANN for instantaneous controller response.

The above ideas have been incorporated in the proposed LFC structure developed. The overall controller structure design applied in the simulation refers to a single-area power system and its performance has been compared with that of a CIC and with that of a previously presented FLC. An effort is actually made to overcome the drawbacks of the previous methods by incorporating the above structure which combines the three modern intelligent methods. The presented controller design procedure owing to the above features consists of the following parts:

Stage 1: Fuzzy Part

It is shown that the output $U(t)$, of the FLLFC, can be expressed in terms of e, ce and the parameters a_e, b_e,..., a_{ce}, b_{ce},..., a_u, b_u.... Therefore, the performance of the control system primarily relies on the shapes of the membership functions. However, to apply fuzzy control, the values of the above parameters must be initially determined in an optimal manner. Therefore, a performance index must be defined as well as an algorithm to search for the optimal values of the above parameters. Herein, the performance index is defined as the reciprocal of the summation of the sum of both the weighted absolute of error and the weighted absolute of change of error, i.e.,

$$F = 1 \bigg/ \sum_{j=1}^{npop} \left(w_1 \left| e_j \right| + w_2 \left| ce_j \right| \right) \qquad (11)$$

where w_1 and w_2 are performance weights, and the larger magnitude of weight is related to the corresponding transient response which is of more relevant concern. In this manner, large values of the fitness function F indicate a better performance. In searching for the optimal values of a, b,... parameters that maximize the fitness function, a suitable algorithm must be adopted which can satisfy the following requirements: a) the ability to handle non-linearity such as those of the yielded fuzzy rules, b) the ability to generate an optimal solution rapidly without being stuck at a local optima.

Stage 2: GA Part

In a previous paragraph it was clearly illustrated why a GA satisfies the above requirements and can obviously be applied to search for the optimal values of a_e, b_e,..., a_{ce}, b_{ce},..., a_u, b_u... of the designed FLLFC. Moreover, the CIC's gain Ki will be searched also by the GA. In the application, the first step involves encoding the values of a_i, b_i, Ki into a binary string of fixed-length, in which the length of the string is determined by compromising the resolution accuracy and computational speed. Without loss of generality, assume there are N bit for each value of a_e, b_e,..., a_{ce}, b_{ce},..., a_u, b_u..., Ki respectively. In this manner, the values of a_e, b_e,..., a_{ce}, b_{ce},..., a_u, b_u..., Ki, which determine the shape of the corresponding membership functions are transformed into a string that has $3N+3N+N=7N$ bit as follows:

$$S = \underbrace{S_1}_{a1} \underbrace{S_2}_{b1} \underbrace{S_3}_{a2} \underbrace{S_4}_{b2} \underbrace{S_5}_{a3} \underbrace{S_6}_{b3} \underbrace{S_7}_{Ki}, \text{ and } S_i = \underbrace{00...001}_{N \text{ bit}}$$

$i=1...7$ \hfill (12)

where S represents the chromosome in the GA solution and S_i a parameter representation. In addition to encoding the parameters, several important genetic parameters in the GA searching procedure must be chosen, i.e. the generation number, population size, crossover rate, mutation rate etc. The parameters used in this work are shown in Table 7.

The details of the proposed GA-based fuzzy controller design procedure are summarized as follows:

- Step 1: Determine the number of fuzzy subsets for fuzzy variables e_t, ce_t, $U(t)$ (Figure 5) and the fuzzy control decision table (Table 4).
- Step 2: Define the fitness function as given in eq.(11).
- Step 3: Determine the generation number, population size, the crossover rate and the mutation rate.
- Step 4: Give the range and length of bits strings for a_e, b_e,..., a_{ce}, b_{ce},..., a_u, b_u... and Ki, produce an initial generation of chromosomes in a random manner.
- Step 5: Calculate the error e_t and change of error ce_t. Execute fuzzification, fuzzy inference, defuzzification phases and fuzzy

Table 7. Typical genetic algorithm parameters

Parameter	Value
Maximum no of generations *	*1*
No of population size	*100*
Uniform crossover	*Yes*
Crossover propability	*0.5*
Elitism	*Yes*
Mutation propability	*0.01*
Creep mutations	*Yes*
Creep mutation propability	*0.02*
(*) single function evaluation	

control law for all populations in this generation. Meanwhile, evaluate the fitness values of all populations in this generation.

- Step 6: Reproduce a new generation by the roulette wheel selection.
- Step 7: Crossover the pair of populations in the new generation according to the crossover rate determined in Step 3.
- Step 8: Mutate the populations in the new generation according to the mutation rate determined in Step 3.
- Step 9: Reserve the population having the largest fitness value in the old generation to the new generation.
- Step 10: Decode the chromosome (represented by a binary string) having the largest fitness value into its corresponding values of a_e, b_e,..., a_{ce}, b_{ce},..., a_u, b_u... and Ki.
- Step 11: Replace the old values of a_e, b_e,..., a_{ce}, b_{ce},..., a_u, b_u... with the new ones.
- Step 12: Repeat Steps 5 to 11 while training the ANN-I.

Stage 3: ANN Part

As it is mentioned before there are many types of neural networks but, for simplicity reasons, in this application, the multilayer feed-forward neural network (MLFFN) was adopted, which learns using the back propagation algorithm. Such networks are designed to learn non-linear function mappings and their "trainability" allows on-line learning of the changing system behavior. The employment of the MLFFN is to evaluate in real time the dynamics of the power generating system under study. The used ANN architecture is shown in Figure 9. The neural network present output $U(t)$ and CIC's gain Ki can be determined from the current values e_t, ce_t, the past value of error (e_{t-1}, ce_{t-1}) and the past value of $U(t)$.

ANNs are characterized by their topology, that is, by the number of interconnections, the node characteristics that are classified by the type of nonlinear elements used, and the kind of learning rules implemented. A MLFFN is a layered network consisting of an input layer, an output layer, and at least one layer of nonlinear processing elements. The nonlinear processing elements, which sum the incoming signals and generate output signals according to some predefined functions, are called neurons or nodes. The neural network developed was three-layer feed-forward network. The standard back propagation algorithm with momentum as proposed in literature was used to train the network off-line. Along with the following bipolar sigmoidal transfer function for the hidden neurons,

Figure 9. Used ANN architecture

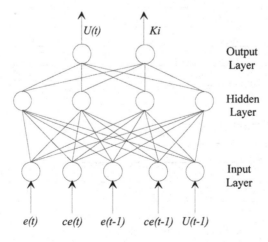

$$y_i = \left(2 \middle/ 1 + e^{-\beta_{x_i}}\right) - 1 \qquad (13)$$

where x_i is the input and y_i is the output for the ith neuron in the network hidden layer. Here, β affects the steepness of the curve. High values of β give a steplike curve and lower ones give a smoother curve. The gradient descent method was used to search for the optimal settings of the weights. During the off-line training the weights in the ANN were updated using the delta rule. Application of the delta learning rule eliminates the problem of the structured presentation of the training set by accumulating the weight changes over several training presentations and making the application all at once. Different learning rates, η, and momentum rates, α, were used between con-

secutive layers to achieve the most rapid learning. Experiments showed that using a lower learning rate for the layers near the output node than those near the input node gave a better learning capability. Further improvement in the learning capability was achieved by using a lower learning rate when the system reached a state where its total mean square error was decreasing at a very slow rate. The parameters used for ANN-I and ANN-II is given in Table 8.

Application and Results

The dynamic subsystems, i.e., the power system, the FLLFC and the GA are interfaced with each other as shown in Figure 10. The designed NN-GAFLC applied to the single-area power system (Figure 1a) and some cases of interest are being

Table 8. ANN-I and ANN-II parameters used

Parameter	Value
No of layers	3
No of neurons (input, hidden, output)	5,4,2
Steepness parameter β	0.2
Learning rate n (off-line)	Started 0.9, reduced to 0.3
Learning rate n (on-line)	Fixed at 0.6
Momentum rate α (off-line)	Started 0.6, reduced to 0.1
Momentum rate α (on-line)	Fixed at 0.3

Figure 10. Overall structure of the illustrated controller (NNGAFLC)

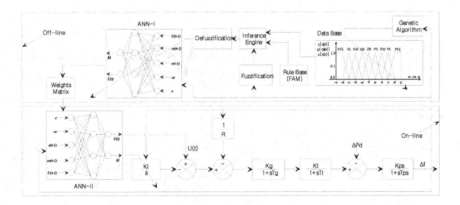

investigated. The effect of power system parameter uncertainty has been carried out also. The cases studied are summarized below:

- Case 1: Step input change $\Delta Pd=0.1$ p.u.MW.
- Case 2: Step input change $\Delta Pd=0.2$ p.u.MW.
- Case 3: Step input change $\Delta Pd=0.15$ p.u.MW and 50% increase to Tt and R.
- Case 4: Step input change $\Delta Pd=0.15$ p.u.MW and 50% decrease to Tt and R.

In all above cases the power system parameters are given in Table 1. In all above cases the weight matrix is copied from ANN-I to ANN-II every 250 ms.

The results (frequency variation) for the above four cases are: for Cases 1 and 2 are shown in Figure 11 and for Cases 3 and 4 in Figure 12. From these figures it is clear that the designed NNGA-FLC gives the overall best results, the FLLFC gives the second best results by comparison to the associated ones of the ones of the CIC (with $Ki= Ki_{(critical)}$). These results, also, show that the behaviour of the demonstrated controller is more "nervous" when the generation rate constraint (GRC) of the turbine (not examined here) was not taken into account. In the opposite case the behaviour of the controller becomes smoother

Figure 11. Frequency variation of single-area power system. Step input: (a) $\Delta Pd=0.1$ p.u.MW, (b) $\Delta Pd=0.2$ p.u.MW

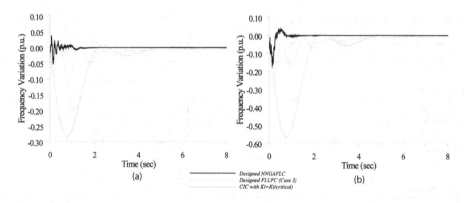

Figure 12. Frequency variation of single-area power system with step input $\Delta Pd=0.15$ p.u.MW. (a) R and Tt 50% decreased, (b) R and Tt 50% increased

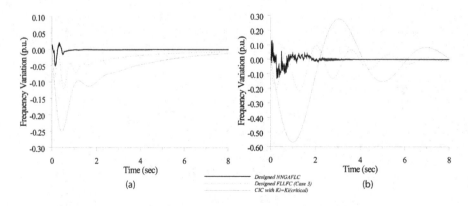

even if the disturbance is larger and GRC is considered. This in fact proves the general ability of ANNs to cope with non-linearities. It should be noted, however, that for the shake of restoring the system frequency to its nominal value in the shortest time possible, one allows greater number of oscillations in the Δf deviation.

Due to space limitations, the time variations of the values of the FLC data base parameters along with the on-line integral gain time variation will not be shown. It is stated though, that, one can see from these variations that the final values of the parameters $a_e, b_e, ..., a_{ce}, b_{ce}, ..., a_u, b_u ...$ and Ki are quite the same with the corresponding values of Case 3 (Table 3) of the designed FLLFC discussed in a previous Section. They are also the same with those ones that formed one of the starting GA's chromosome population. This means that the GA finally reaches an optimal parameter combination but this combination was not optimal before. The latter, points out the need of adopting a well-tuned suitable search algorithm for the overall controller's parameters identification. The effect

of parameter uncertainty has also been carried out. Figure 12 shows the frequency variation for the following two cases: (a) 50% increase in *Tt* and 50% increase in *R* and (b) 50% decrease in *Tt* and 50% decrease in *R*. Furthermore, The control signal *U(t)* variation for Cases 1 and 2 is also shown in Figure 13.

Finally, The associated values of the IAET criterion for the examined cases give the values shown in Table 9 (along with the corresponding values of Table 2 and Table 6), which also leads to the same conclusions.

CONCLUSION

It is a fact nowadays that in a demanding (restructured or not) electric power system environment, the engineering aspects of planning and control are of main importance. Emerging trends lead to absolute reformulation of the strategies followed until today. Summarizing the previous Sections it can be said that intelligent load frequency control

Figure 13. Control signal U(t) variation (output of on-line ANN-II of designed NNGAFLC). Step input: (a) ΔPd=0.1 p.u.MW, (b) ΔPd=0.2 p.u.MW

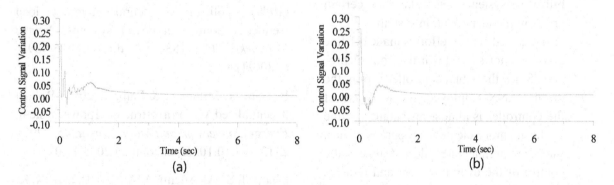

Table 9. Comparison of the Jfre values of the designed controllers

	CIC with $Ki_{(critical)}$	FLLFC (Case 3)	NNGAFLC
ΔPd=0.1 p.u.	0.372	0.144	**0.0117**
ΔPd=0.2 p.u.	0.745	0.295	**0.0351**

concepts are becoming a promising feature to those environments. These concepts mainly based on the following three optional approaches: a) expert systems as adaptive elements in a control system, b) fuzzy calculations as decision-producing elements in a control system, c) neural nets as compensation elements in a control system. LFC structures based on intelligent methods were developed and applied successfully in this chapter. The main advantages of these structures may be summarized as follows:

- The main feature of all AGC controllers used in practice is retained, that is, the feedback is based only on the error and the change in error of frequency measurements, instead on the state variables of the system. This means that measurements of all system state variables are not needed, and that only the measurement of the system frequency suffices.

- The adaptation property helps the controller to stabilize the plant especially when the parameters may vary widely and abruptly. Whereas, the robustness property of the FLC and the search ability of the GA, makes it possible for the controller to stabilize the system even if there are certain errors in the identification system.

- The required control effort is made off-line and does not slow down the control process. Since the actual controller is only the on-line ANN employed, the response of the controller is almost instantaneous due to the memory-element properties it has. Such an architecture 'decentralizes' the control of the overall system and reduces the amount of information to be exchanged between the plant and the controller. This makes possible the implementation of the controller.

- The more economic operation of the power system, since the loss of served load and the imposed excess of load are much smaller.

The various simulation results indicate clearly that the presented power system LFC has by far superior performance and stability properties compared to the corresponding ones of conventional controllers.

REFERENCES

Abdel-Magid, Y. L., & Dawoud, M. M. (1997). Optimal AGC tuning with genetic algorithms. *Electric Power Systems Research, 38*, 231–238. doi:10.1016/S0378-7796(96)01091-7

Aditya, S. K., & Das, D. (2003). Design of load frequency controllers using genetic algorithms for two area interconnected hydro power system. *Electric Power Components and Systems, 31*(1), 81–94. doi:10.1080/15325000390112071

Al-Hamouz, Z. M., & Abdel-Magid, Y. L. (1993). Variable Structure Load Frequency Controllers for Multiarea Power Systems. *Electrical Power & Energy Systems, 15*(5), 293–300. doi:10.1016/0142-0615(93)90050-W

Beaufays, F., Abdel-Magid, Y., & Widrow, B. (1999). Application of neural network to load frequency control in power systems. *Neural Networks, 7*(1), 183–194. doi:10.1016/0893-6080(94)90067-1

Bevrani, H., Mitani, Y., & Tsuji, K. (2004). Robust decentralized AGC in a restructured power system. *Energy Conversion and Management, 45*, 2297–2312. doi:10.1016/j.enconman.2003.11.018

Bhatti, T. S., Al-Ademi, A. A. F., & Bansal, N. K. (1997). Load frequency control of isolated wind diesel hybrid power systems. *Energy Conversion and Management, 38*(9), 829. doi:10.1016/S0196-8904(96)00108-2

Chang, C. S., Fu, W., & Wen, F. (1998). Load frequency controller using genetic algorithm based fuzzy gain scheduling of PI controller. *Electric Machines and Power Systems, 26,* 39–52. doi:10.1080/07313569808955806

Chaturvedi, D. K., Satsangi, P. S., & Kalra, P. K. (1999). Load frequency control: a generalised neural network approach. *Electrical Power & Energy Systems, 21,* 405–415. doi:10.1016/S0142-0615(99)00010-1

Christie, R., & Bose, A. (1996). Load-frequency control issues in power systems operation after deregulation. *IEEE Transactions on Power Systems, 11,* 1191–1200. doi:10.1109/59.535590

Christie, R. D., Wollenberg, B. F., & Wangensteen, I. (2000). Transmission management in the deregulated environment. *Proc. IEEE Special Issue on The Technology of Power System Competition, 88*(2), 170–195.

Cohn, N. (1986). *Control of generation and power flow on interconnected systems.* New York: Wiley.

De Jong, K. (1980). Adaptive system design: a genetic approach. *IEEE Transactions on Systems, Man, and Cybernetics, SMC-10*(9), 1566–1574.

Delfino, B., Fornari, F., & Massucco, S. (2002). Load-frequency control and inadvertent interchange evaluation in restructured power systems. *Proc. IEE in Generation, Transmition & Distribution, 149*(5), 607–614.

Djukanovic, M., Novicevic, M., Sobajic, D. J., & Pao, Y. P. (1995). Conceptual development of optimal load frequency control using artificial neural networks and fuzzy set theory. *Int. J. of Eng. Intelligent Systems for Electrical Engineering and Communication, 3*(2), 95–108.

Djukanovic, M. B., Dobrijevic, D. M., Calovic, M. S., Novicevic, M., & Sobajic, D. J. (1997). Coordinated stabilizing control for the exciter and governor loops using fuzzy set theory and neural nets. *Electrical Power & Energy Systems, 19*(8), 489–499. doi:10.1016/S0142-0615(97)00020-3

Donde, V., Pai, M. A., & Hiskens, I. A. (2001). Simulation and optimization in an AGC system after deregulation. *IEEE Transactions on Power Systems, 16*(3), 481–489. doi:10.1109/59.932285

Elgerd, O. I. (1982). *Electric Energy Systems Theory, an Introduction.* New Delhi, India: Tata McGraw-Hill.

Elgerd, O. I., & Fosha, C. E. (1970). Optimum megawatt frequency control of multi-area electric energy systems. *IEEE Trans. on PAS, PAS-89,* 556–563.

Fleming, P. J., & Fonseca, C. M. (1993). *Genetic algorithms in control systems engineering.* Research Report No. 470. Sheffield, UK: University of Sheffield, Dept. of Automatic Control and Systems Engineering.

Goldberg, D. E. (1989). *Genetic algorithms in search, optimization and machine learning.* Reading, MA: Addison-Wesley.

Green, R. K. (1996). Transformed Automatic Generation Control. *IEEE Transactions on Power Systems, 11*(4), 1799–1804. doi:10.1109/59.544645

Grefenstette, J. J. (1986). Optimization of control parameters for genetic algorithms. *IEEE Transactions on Systems, Man, and Cybernetics, SMC-16,* 122–128. doi:10.1109/TSMC.1986.289288

Hassan, M. A., Malik, O. P., & Hope, G. S. (1991). A fuzzy logic based stabilizer for a synchronous machine. *IEEE Transactions on Energy Conversion, 6*(3), 407–413. doi:10.1109/60.84314

Hicks, G. V., Jeyasurya, B., & Snow, W. F. (1997). *An investigation of automatic generation control for an isolated power system, IEEE PES Winter Meeting*, (pp. 31-34).

Hiyama, T. (1989). Application of rule based stabilizer controller to electric power system. *IEEE Proceedings . Part C, 136*(3), 175–181.

Holland, J. H. (1975). *Adaptation in Nature and Artificial Systems*. Ann Arbor, MI: University of Michigan Press.

Hunter, R., & Elliot, G. (1994). *Wind-Diesel Systems: A Guide to the Technology and Its Implementation*. Cambridge, UK: Cambridge University Press.

Ilic, M., Galiana, F., & Fink, L. (Eds.). (1998). *Power Systems Restructuring: Engineering & Economics*. Boston: Kluwer Academic Publishers.

Jaleeli, N., VanSlyck, L. S., Ewart, D. N., Fink, L. H., & Hoffmann, A. G. (1992). Understanding Automatic Generation Control. *IEEE Transactions on Power Systems, 7*(3), 1106–1122. doi:10.1109/59.207324

Karnavas, Y. L. (2005). AGC tuning of an interconnected power system after deregulation using genetic algorithms. In *Proc. of the 5th WSEAS International Conference on Power Systems and Electromagnetic Compatibility (PSE '05),* Corfu Island, Greece, (pp. 218-223).

Karnavas, Y. L. (2005). On the optimal control of interconnected electric power systems in a restructured environment using genetic algorithms. *WSEAS Transactions on Systems Journal, 4*(8), 1248–1258.

Karnavas, Y. L. (2006). On the optimal load frequency control of an interconnected hydro electric power system using genetic algorithms. In *Proceedings of the 6th IASTED International Conference on European Power and Energy Systems (EuroPES'06),* Rhodes, Hellas, Cd Ref. No 521-099.

Karnavas, Y. L., & Pantos, S. (2008). Performance Evaluation of Neural Networks for μC Based Excitation Control of a Synchronous Generator. In *Proc. of the 18th International Conference on Electrical Machines (ICEM'08)*, Vilamura, Portugal, CD Paper ID 885.

Karnavas, Y. L., & Papadopoulos, D. P. (2000). Excitation control of a power generating system based on fuzzy logic and neural networks. *European Transactions on Electrical Power, 10*(4), 233–241.

Karnavas, Y. L., & Papadopoulos, D. P. (2002). AGC for autonomous power station using combined intelligent techniques. *Int. J. Electric Power Systems Research, 62,* 225–239. doi:10.1016/S0378-7796(02)00082-2

Karnavas, Y. L., & Papadopoulos, D. P. (2002). A genetic-fuzzy system for the excitation control of a synchronous machine. In *Proc. of the 15th International Conference in Electrical Machines (ICEM'02)*, Bruges, Belgium, CD paper Ref. No. 204.

Karnavas, Y. L., & Papadopoulos, D. P. (2003). Power generation control of a wind-diesel system using fuzzy logic and pi-sigma networks. In *Proc. of the 12th International. Conference on Intelligent Systems Application to Power Systems (ISAP '03),* Lemnos Island, Greece, Cd ref. no. 078.

Karnavas, Y. L., Polyzos, N. P., & Papadopoulos, D. P. (2006). On the design of a remote intelligent excitation controller for a synchronous generator. In *Proc. of the 17ᵗʰ International Conference in Electrical Machines (ICEM'06)*, Chania, Crete, Hellas, CD paper Ref. No. 063.

Kumar, A., Malik, O. P., & Hope, G. S. (1985). Variable-structure-system control applied to AGC of an interconnected power system. *IEE Proceedings Part C, 132*(1), 23–29.

Kumar, J., Ng, K. H., & Sheble, G. (1997). AGC simulator for price-based operation-part I: A model. *IEEE Transactions on Power Systems, 12*(2), 527–532. doi:10.1109/59.589593

Lee, C., & Maxwell, T. (1987). Learning, invariance, and generalization in high-order neural network. *Applied Optics, 26*(23).

Lee, C. C. (1990). Fuzzy logic in control systems – Parts I and II. *IEEE Transactions on Systems, Man, and Cybernetics, 20*(2), 404–435. doi:10.1109/21.52551

Lin, C. Y., & Hajela, P. (1992). Genetic algorithms in optimization problems with discrete and integer design variables. *Engineering Optimization, 19*(4), 309–327. doi:10.1080/03052159208941234

Lippmann, R. P. (1989). Pattern classification using neural networks. *IEEE Communications Magazine*, 47–64. doi:10.1109/35.41401

McClelland, J., & Rumelhart, D. (1987). *Parallel Distributed Processing* (Vol.1). Cambridge, MA: The MIT Press.

Minsky, M., & Papert, S. (1969). *Perceptrons*. Cambridge, MA: The MIT Press.

Nanda, J., & Kaul, B. (1978). Automatic generation control of an interconnected power system . *IEE Proceedings, 125*(5), 385–390.

Narendra, K. S., & Parthasarathy, K. (1990). Identification and control of dynamical systems using neural networks. *IEEE Transactions on Neural Networks, 1*(1), 4–27. doi:10.1109/72.80202

Nobile, E., Bose, A., & Tomsovic, K. (2000). Bilateral market for load following ancillary services. In *Proc. Power Energy Systems Summer Power Meeting*, Seattle, WA.

Ogata, K. (1970). *Modern control engineering*. Upper Saddle River, NJ: Prentice Hall.

Pan, C. T., & Lian, C. M. (2005). An adaptive controller for power system load frequency control. *IEEE Transactions on Power Systems, 4*(1), 122–128. doi:10.1109/59.32469

Papadopoulos, D.P., & Amanatidis. (1984). Frequency deviations of steam turbogenerator in isolated operation with representative governor and turbine models. In *Proc. of the International Conference on Electrical Machines (ICEM'84)*, Lausanne, Switzerland, Part 3, (pp. 979-982).

Reid, M. B. (1989). Rapid Training of Higher-order Neural Networks for Invariant Pattern Recognition. In [), Washington D.C.]. *Proceedings of IJCNN, 1*, 689–692.

Rumelhart, D. E., & McClelland, J. L., & the PDP Research Group. (1986). *Parallel distributed processing: explorations in the microstructure of cognition, Vol. 1: Foundations*. Cambridge, MA: MIT Press, Brandford Books.

Schultz, W. C., & Rideout, V. C. (1961). Control system performance measures: past, present and future. *I.R.E. Transactions on Automatic Control, AC-6*(22), 22–35.

Scoot, G. W., Wilreker, V. F., & Shaltens, R. K. (1984). Wind turbine generator interaction with diesel generators on an isolated power system. *IEEE Trans. on PAS, 103*(5), 933.

Sheble, G. B. (1999). *Computational Auction Mechanisms for Restructured Power Industry Operation*. Boston: Kluwer Academic Publishers.

Shin, Y., & Ghosh, J. (1991). The pi-sigma network: An efficient higher-order neural network for pattern classification and function approximation. In [], Seattle.]. *Proceedings of IJCNN, 1*, 13–18.

Stankovic, A. M., Tadmor, G., & Sakharak, J. A. (1998). On robust control analysis and design for load frequency regulation. *IEEE Transactions on Power Systems, 13*(2), 449–455. doi:10.1109/59.667367

Tripathy, S. C., Chandramohanan, P. S., & Balasubramanium, R. (1998). Self tuning regulator for adaptive load frequency control of power system. *The Journal of Institution of Engineers (India), EL79*, 103–108.

Tripathy, S. C., Kalantor, M., & Balasubramanian, R. (1992). Stability Simulation and Parameter Optimization of a Hybrid Wind-Diesel Power Generation System. *International Journal of Energy Research, 16*, 31. doi:10.1002/er.4440160105

Wu, C. J., & Huang, C. H. (1997). A hybrid method for parameter tuning of PID Controllers. *Journal of the Franklin Institute, JFI, 334B*, 547–562. doi:10.1016/S0016-0032(96)00094-4

Xu, X., Mathur, R. M., Jiang, J., Roger, G. J., & Kundur, P. (1996). Modeling of generators and their controls in power system simulations using singular perturbations. *IEEE Transactions on Power Systems, 1*(1), 109–114.

Yang, T. C., Cimen, H., & Zhu, Q. M. (1998). Decentralized load-frequency controller design based on structured singular values. *IEEE Proc. in Generation . Transmission & Distribution, 145*(1), 7–14. doi:10.1049/ip-gtd:19981716

Zadeh, L. A. (1965). Fuzzy sets. *Information and Control, 8*, 338–353. doi:10.1016/S0019-9958(65)90241-X

APPENDIX

Table 10. List of Symbols

f, f_{nom}, f_t	power system frequency, nominal value, value at sampling instant t
Pt	output signal of turbine block
Pg	output signal of governor block
$Pscp$	speed changer position signal
$U(t)$	additional signal input to the existing integral controller structure
Kps, Tps	gain and time constant of power system block
Kt, Tt	gain and time constant of turbine block
Kg, Tg	gain and time constant of governor block
Ki, Kp	integral and proportional gains of a PI structure controller
R	governor droop parameter
X, Y, U	state and output variable, and control vector of a model in state-space form
A, B, C	system matrices of a dynamic model in state-space form
$[]^T$	transpose of a matrix/vector
B	frequency bias parameter
J	performance index
e_t, ce_t	error, change in error (at sampling instant t)
$\mu[R(x)]$	membership function value of fuzzy variable R for an input point x
$a_e..., b_e...$	coordinate parameters of the fuzzy variables
u	output (defuzzified) value of the fuzzy controller
F	fitness function of the genetic algorithm
$w1, w2$	weight values used by the fitness function
S	chromosome representation
Sj	the jth gene of chromosome S
x_i^j, y_i^j	input and output signal value of the ith neuron element of the jth layer
β	steepness parameter (saturation degree) of a neural network element
n	learning rate of a neural network element
a	momentum rate of a neural network element

Chapter 14
Computational Intelligence Clustering for Dynamic Video Watermarking

Daw-Tung Lin
National Taipei University, Taiwan

Guan-Jhih Liao
Chun Hua University, Taiwan

ABSTRACT

Multimedia products today broadcast over networks and are typically compressed and transmitted from host to client. Adding watermarks to the compressed domain ensures content integrity, protects copyright, and can be detected without quality degradation. Hence, watermarking video data in the compressed domain is important. This work develops a novel video watermarking system with the aid of computational intelligence, in which motion vectors define watermark locations. The number of watermark bits varies dynamically among frames. The current study employs several intelligent computing methods including K-means clustering, Fuzzy C-means clustering, Swarm intelligent clustering and Swarm intelligence based Fuzzy C-means (SI-FCM) clustering to determine the motion vectors and watermark positions. This study also discusses and compares the advantages and disadvantages among various approaches. The proposed scheme has three merits. First, the proposed watermarking strategy does not involve manually setting watermark bit locations. Second, the number of embedded motion vector clusters differs according to the motion characteristics of each frame. Third, the proposed special exclusive-OR operation closely relates the watermark bit to the video context, preventing attackers from discovering the real watermark length of each frame. Therefore, the proposed approach is highly secure. The proposed watermark-extracting scheme immediately detects forgery through changes in motion vectors. Experimental results reveal that the watermarked video retains satisfactory quality with very low degradation.

DOI: 10.4018/978-1-61520-757-2.ch014

INTRODUCTION

Video largely transmits in digitalized format owing to Internet pervasiveness and accelerated development of digital multimedia technology. Multimedia content now broadcasts over networks, and is generally compressed and transmitted from host to client. However, illegal tampering with the original video contents is possible. Determining suspect video validity is extremely difficult, necessitating high quality video authentication methods. Adding watermarks to the compressed domain guarantees content integrity and protect copyright, and can be detected without degrading quality (Cox, Miller, & Bloom, 2001; Pan, Huang, Jain, & Fang, 2007). Variable Length Coding (VLC) is the basis for the earliest compressed domain watermarking (Bhattacharya, Chattopadhyay, & Pal, 2006; Huffman, 1952; Ziv & Lempel, 1978). Hartung and Girod (1998) presented a compressed domain watermarking method for content protection. They provide an effective and precise copyright protection and content authentication scheme using spread spectrum. Each watermark bit can be embedded at different spectrums by side information. Watermarks also hide in the DCT coefficients and apply to various video compression standards, such as MPEG2, MPEG4, ITU-T and H.26x (Biswas, Das, & Petriu, 2005; Zhang, Ho, Qui, & Marziliano, 2007). Lu and Liao (2001) has adopted the wavelet transform (DWT) to accomplish information hiding without losing visual quality. Chan *et al.* (2005) proposed a video watermarking technique in compressed domain based on hybrid DWT and audio information to secure the watermarking system. The watermarks are embedded in the plain bit of DWT coefficients. Kong *et al.* (2004) developed an object-based watermarking scheme for image and video, based on a blind object watermarking scheme, using the shape adaptive-discrete wavelet transform (SA-DWT).

Jordan *et al.* (1997) presented a compressed domain watermarking method that adopts motion vector as side information. A decision method determines motion vector change. These modified motion vectors have few altered bits. Watermarks can be retrieved from the motion vectors following motion compensation, even after decompression. Researchers have proposed some improvements to Jordan's approach (Fang, 2004; Zhang, Li, & Zhang, 2001), that strengthen the watermark and reduce quality degradation. All such methods select the motion vector according to motion vector magnitude, and the watermark positions from the phase angles of the motion vectors. Kung *et al.* (2003) developed a method to embed watermarks by verifying motion vector parity. Lu *et al.* (2006) proposed a method to choose motion vectors with different components. The result of the XOR operation of the least significant bits of these components and watermark bit is embedded into the quantized DCT coefficients of the macro-block in the following I-frame. Wang *et al.* (2001) presented a method for specifying the watermark position by Principal Component Analysis (PCA). The method categorizes the high-motion region of the frame, and then adds watermarks to the video.

Our previous study proposed a novel video watermarking scheme that adopts motion vectors to define where to embed the watermarks, and the number of watermark bits varies dynamically among frames (Lin & Liao, 2008a). Fuzzy C-means (FCM) clustering is utilized to select the motion vectors and the watermark positions. The number of embedded motion vector clusters differs depending on the motion characteristics of each frame. Therefore, the proposed scheme is highly secure, and retains satisfactory quality with very low degradation. To set the appropriate motion vector, and to enhance adapting motion vector classification, we further proposed an FCM clustering approach based on swarm intelligence to categorize the motion vectors according to video motion characteristics of each frame (Lin & Liao, 2008b). The EM algorithm is also a well known clustering method for computing maximum likelihood estimation to group data especially for incomplete data (Dempster, Laird, & Rubin, 1977).

This investigation further presents, discusses and compares the advantages and disadvantages among various intelligent computing methods including K-means, Fuzzy C-means, Swarm intelligent clustering and Swarm intelligence based Fuzzy C-means (SI-FCM) clustering to determine the motion vectors and watermark positions. These four algorithms are common unsupervised clustering methods. The classification results rely on data characteristics. Their dynamic clustering characteristics fit our need of content dependent watermarking and enhance embedding security. The remainder of this chapter is organized as follows. Section 2 introduces the intelligent computing approaches to determine the motion vector and watermark position. Section 3 presents the proposed video watermarking method and describes how the intelligent computing techniques are cooperated. Section 4 analyzes the experimental results, and compares them with those of other clustering schemes. Conclusions are finally drawn in Section 5.

APPLYING COMPUTATIONAL INTELLIGENCE CLUSTERING METHODS TO VIDEO WATERMARKING

Clustering is one of the most common techniques to divide input data into groups. Clustering focuses mainly on discerning input data similarity and retrieving data points representing each group. Clustering involves splitting a set of patterns into a number of classes that are homogeneous with regard to the suitable similarity measure, such that it classifies similar patterns into the same clusters. Depending on the partition structure, two different kinds of clustering techniques are often employed, namely, hard clustering and soft clustering methods. This study discusses

and compares the advantages and disadvantages among various intelligent computing methods including K-means, Fuzzy C-means, Swarm intelligent clustering and Swarm intelligence based Fuzzy C-means (SI-FCM) clustering technique in order to find and embed watermarks by selecting a higher motion vector class in the compressed video inter-frames. This work adopts intelligent computation clustering techniques by normalizing motion vectors in a frame as input data, and then selecting some clusters to perform high-motion vector classification. A watermark is embedded in any motion vector that belongs to the high motion class. Changing the number of clusters can control the number of watermark bits, thus maintaining the watermark position in the high motion vector class. Altering the motion vector also modifies the cluster values and input data distribution. Intelligent computation clustering clearly identifies the frame parts that move rapidly or slowly without needing extra *a priori* information.

K-Means Clustering

MacQueen proposed K-means clustering in 1967 [7]. K-means clustering algorithm separates data points into k groups and is a very popular method for general clustering. In K-means, clusters are represented by the mass centers of their members. The K-means algorithm of alternating between assigning cluster membership for each data vector to the nearest cluster center and computing the center of each cluster as the centroid of its member data vectors is equivalent to finding the minimum of a sum-of-squares cost function using coordinate descend (Zha, Ding, Gu, He, & Simon, 2001).

Let $X = \{x_1, x_2, ..., x_n\}$ be a set of data points of R^d. After seeding data with a set of k centers of $c_1, c_2, ..., c_k$ in R^d, the K-means algorithm partitions data points into clusters by assigning c_i to the set of points in X that are closer to c_i than the other center c_j, for all $i \neq j$. Then the new center is updated by computing the mass of all points in each cluster. All data points in X repetitively classify themselves to their closest centers until no point changes clusters (Arthur & Vassilvi, 2006). Although the K-means algorithm can easily implement to our system, some drawbacks may degrade the results of motion vector selection. These drawbacks include difficult selection of the initial k number, ambiguous distinguishing data point in the boundary region, and sensitive initial center selection.

Fuzzy C-Means Clustering and Thresholding

Classical clustering techniques explicitly assign each datum to one cluster. Fuzzy clustering analysis breaks this restriction by permitting gradual memberships, and thus can be adopted to classify data into more than one cluster simultaneously. Bezdek (1973) presented FCM in 1973 to improve the accuracy of K-mans classification by applying fuzzy logic. The FCM attempts to identify cluster centers (centroids) that minimize a dissimilarity function. To facilitate fuzzy partitioning, the membership matrix (U) is randomly initialized as $\sum_{i=1}^{c} u_{ij} = 1,\ \forall j = 1,...,n$, where u_{ij} denotes the relation matrix of current data point j to each centroid i.

The dissimilarity function adopted in FCM depicts as Equation (1):

$$J\left(U, c_1, c_2, ..., c_c\right) = \sum_{i=1}^{c} J_i = \sum_{i=1}^{c} \sum_{j=1}^{n} u_{ij}^m d_{ij}^2, \quad (1)$$

where $0 \leq u_{ij} \leq 1$; c_i denotes the centroid of cluster i, d_{ij} indicates the Euclidian distance between the ith centroid c_i and the jth data point and $m \in [1, \infty]$ represents a weighting exponent. Two conditions given in Equations (2) and (3) need to be checked

to reach the minimum of dissimilarity function:

$$c_i = \frac{\sum_{j=1}^{n} u_{ij}^m x_j}{\sum_{j=1}^{n} u_{ij}^m}, \quad (2)$$

$$u_{ij} = \frac{1}{\sum_{k=1}^{c} \left(\frac{d_{ij}}{d_{kj}}\right)^{2/(m-1)}}, \quad (3)$$

where x_j denotes data point x with index j; n is the total number of data point, and m represents the coefficient of dissimilarity function. Consider the case where $m = 2$ for our method, and d_{ij} denotes the distance from data point j to cluster center i. The FCM moves the cluster centers to the appropriate location within a data set by iteratively updating the cluster centers and the membership grades for each data point. The detailed FCM algorithm proposed by Bezdek (Bezdek, 1973) is listed in Appendix A.1.

By iteratively updating the cluster centers and the membership grades for each data point, FCM iteratively moves the cluster centers to the appropriate location within a data set. However, FCM does not guarantee converging to an optimal solution, since it initializes the cluster centers (centroids) randomly using matrix U. FCM performance depends on initial centroid selection. For a robust approach, we may either adopt an algorithm to determine all of the centroids (e.g. arithmetic means of all data points) or execute the FCM algorithm several times starting with different initial centroids.

Previous works have defined a threshold to perform classification (Fang, 2004, Lin & Liao, 2008a). To evaluate and analyze inter-frame motion distribution in the FCM clustering technique, the total cluster number m must be obtained from previous information or perceptual knowledge. In other words, determining an appropriate cluster number without any side information is difficult. However, we can calculate the distance between the input nodes and their corresponding cluster centers to obtain a better cluster number. We compute the total sum of Euclidean distances between input feature vectors and their corresponding centroid as shown in Equation (4).

$$W_m = \sum_{i=1}^{k} \sum_{j=1}^{n} d(c_i, x_j),$$ (4)

where W_m is defined as the within cluster distance for m clusters, k denotes the total number of centroids and n is the number of input data. $d(c_i, x_j)$ represents the Euclidean distance between input node x_j and its corresponding centroid c_i. The large W_m indicates longer distance between input and centroid. When cluster numbers increase, cluster members will be closer to their centroid. Consequently, W_m will be smaller than the previous value. The W_m will be more stable when the cluster number is large enough. Figure 1 shows the general distribution of within cluster distance where the curve of W_m is steep when the cluster number is small. The curve will be smoother and more stable with increased cluster numbers, so we want to find a key point where the curve turns from steep to smooth. We determine this point based on Equation (5) (Lee & Huang, 1999).

$$\frac{W_{m-1} - W_m}{W_m - W_{m+1}} > T,$$ (5)

where T is the threshold value by experiments and is set to 10 according to the characteristics of video clips (Lin & Liao, 2008a). Equation (5) is evaluated until it satisfies the inequality, then m is the desired cluster number. After performing FCM clustering, this method chooses $\lceil n / 2 \rceil$ clusters with larger centroid magnitudes and embeds the watermarks into the corresponding motion vectors.

The current work experimentally calculates these threshold values, and updates them according to the motion distribution in the frame. However, these methods have some drawbacks. First, the thresholds differ due to scene changes in the video sequences and need to be determined precisely. Second, the threshold value changes significantly if the motion vector is adjusted. No additional information about motion vector distribution changes is available.

Figure 1. The variation of within cluster distance with different numbers of clusters

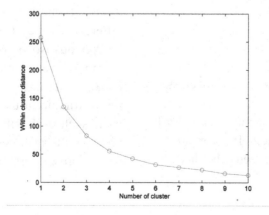

Swarm Intelligence Clustering Algorithm

The swarm intelligence clustering algorithm is based on a basic model proposed by Deneubourg *et al.* (Deneubourg, Goss, Franks, Sendova-Franks, Detrain, & Chrétien, 1991). Swarm intelligence exhibits several notable properties including flexibility, robustness, decentralization and self organization. Swarm intelligence designs algorithms or distributed problem-solving devices in terms of the collective behavior of social insect colonies. A clustering algorithm based on swarm intelligence has three basic procedures, shown in Appendix A2.

Combining Swarm Intelligence and FCM Clustering

The swarm-intelligence-based algorithm provides a relevant partition of data without any knowledge of initial cluster centers. An object that is a poor fit to a heap can take a long time to be transported to a better heap/cluster. The second step considers the heaps formed by the first step, and moves the whole heap onto the 2D board. The ants carry an entire heap of objects. The algorithm for picking up a heap is the same as that for the objects. Ants pick up the heap with a constant probability P_{load}. Ants drop a heap H_1 onto another heap H_2 as long as:

$$\frac{D(O_{center}(H_1), O_{center}(H_2))}{D_{max}} < T_c, \quad (6)$$

where T_c denotes the threshold of creating a heap.

Two heaps H_1 and H_2 can merge to form a single heap H_3, and cannot be separated. The number of heaps continues to decrease as the number of iterations rises. The algorithm of swarm intelligence based on FCM clustering is proposed below.

- Step 1. Perform swarm intelligence computation for input data (motion vectors).
- Step 2. Take the total number of heaps after swarm intelligence clustering as the initial clusters for FCM clustering.
- Step 3. Take the centers of mass of all the objects in the swarm intelligence heaps as the initial FCM cluster position.
- Step 4. Adopt the cluster centers obtained in step 3, and the cluster number in step 2 for FCM clustering.
- Step 5. Classify the data by the FCM clustering algorithm.

PROPOSED VIDEO WATERMARKING SCHEME

This section describes the proposed procedures of video watermark embedding and extraction schemes.

Watermark Embedding Procedure

This study presents a watermarking system for embedding motion vectors in compressed domain video bit streams. This system first extracts motion vectors from a frame by various intelligent computational clustering methods to select the appropriate cluster centroid of each motion vector. The proposed embedding strategy is then performed to alter the vertical or horizontal component of the motion vector. The motion vectors in the inter-frame are represented as (x, y), where x and y indicate the horizontal and vertical coordinator of motion vector, respectively. The values of the x and y coordinates can be either positive or negative. The proposed motion vector selection scheme is only concerned with the magnitude of the motion vector. Therefore, it utilizes the absolute vales of x and y as inputs to the clustering algorithm. The procedure for transferring the motion vector for clustering is described in detail in our previous work (Lin & Liao, 2008a).

To measure and analyze the inter-frame motion distribution in K-means and FCM clustering techniques, the total number of clusters must be calculated from previous information or perceptual knowledge. Restated, the appropriate cluster number is hard to determine. However, the swarm intelligence FCM algorithm (described in Section 2.4) can apply to the normalized motion vector data objects. After performing clustering, watermarks are embedded into the motion vectors of $\lceil n/2 \rceil$ clusters with larger centroid magnitudes; where n is the total cluster. Next, a new motion vector table is built for further watermarking once these motion vector clusters are selected. The motion vector table comprises horizontal and vertical components which are the components of selected motion vectors. Each component of the motion vector table is an 8-bit signed binary presentation $B(i,j)$ of the motion vector horizontal or vertical component, where j denotes the bit number of the component value of the selected motion vector i. Thus, $j = 1$ and $j = 8$ are the most significant bit (MSB) and the least significant bit (LSB), respectively. Additionally, the order of the motion vector table is defined according to a random sequence generated from a private key and a pseudo-random number generator (Lin & Liao, 2008a). Motion vectors belonging to high motion vector clusters, as determined by the clustering algorithms illustrated in Section 2, are then selected.

Once the motion vectors are selected for embedding watermarks, the algorithm decides whether to embed the watermark into the vertical or horizontal component of the motion vectors. The selection criterion is according to angle θ calculated by Equation (7) and rules recommended by Fang (Fang, 2004).

$$\theta = \tan^{-1}\left(\frac{\left\lfloor \frac{MVX}{2} \right\rfloor}{\left\lfloor \frac{MVY}{2} \right\rfloor}\right), \quad (7)$$

where MVX and MVY denote the horizontal and vertical component, respectively, of the selected motion vector. If their floor values are both zero, then no embedding is performed for the selected motion vector. Otherwise, the LSB of the horizontal part (MVX) or vertical part (MVY) of the motion vector table is altered according to the strategy shown in Table 1, where WM_i denotes the watermark bit for the ith motion vector listed in the motion vector table. The watermark bit (WM_i) of the ith motion vector is generated by the following XOR operation:

$$WM_i = B(i,5) \oplus B(i+1,6) \oplus B(i+2,7) \oplus B(i,8) \quad (8)$$

where $B(i,5)$ represents the $5th$ bit of the ith motion vector component, and $B(i + 1, 6)$ indicates the $6th$ bit of the $(i + 1)th$ motion vector, etc..

Table 1. LSB modification rules for motion vector component

LSB	WMi	Positive/zero component		Negative component	
		$0° \leq \theta < 90°$ or $180° \leq \theta < 270°$	$90° \leq \theta < 180°$ or $270° \leq \theta < 360°$	$0° \leq \theta < 90°$ or $180° \leq \theta < 270°$	$90° \leq \theta < 180°$ or $270° \leq \theta < 360°$
0	0	N/A	N/A	N/A	N/A
0	1	$MVX=MVX+1$	$MVY=MVY+1$	$MVX=MVX-1$	$MVY=MVY-1$
1	1	$MVX=MVX-1$	$MVY=MVY-1$	$MVX=MVX+1$	$MVY=MVY+1$
1	0	N/A	N/A	N/A	N/A

Figure 2. Watermark embedding procedure

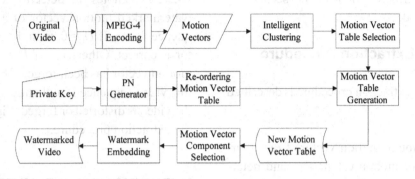

If the resultant $WM_i = 0$ then no action is taken. Otherwise, the LSB is modified as follows. Check the sign bit $B(i,1)$. If $B(i,1) = 0$, then the motion vector value is 0 or positive. Then, the motion vector component is modified based on the rules listed in Table 1. Sign bit $B(i,1) = 1$ signifies that the motion vector value is negative. Thus, the selected motion vector component is modified based on the rules listed in Table 1. Figure 2 illustrates the embedding process in detail. The watermark embedding process can be structured during video encoding and summarized as follows.

- Step 1. Get motion vectors from the inter-frame and determine the number of motion vector clusters in each frame using the clustering method.
- Step 2. Select the motion vectors from half of the clusters with high motion vector magnitudes.
- Step 3. Build motion vector table and represent its horizontal and vertical component in an 8-bit signed binary format. Then re-order the table by a random sequence based on the private key input from user.
- Step 4. Decide which part of the motion vector is to embed the watermark.
- Step 5. Perform the even parity operation corresponding to bit position of the motion vector.
- Step 6. Perform watermark embedding in the LSB.

The reliability and quality of the watermarked video is a tradeoff. Embedding more places with watermarks improves video security, but may also degrade video quality. Suppose there are n macroblocks in an inter-frame. Given a normal distribution pseudo-random generator (in Step 3), Equation (9) shows the total number ($Talt$) of possible combinations of watermark embedding, in which C_n^k denotes the combination of k out of n macroblocks chosen by hacker and 2^k means the possible even or odd parity patterns of these k motion vectors.

$$T_{alt} = \sum_{k=1}^{n} C_n^k 2^k = C_1^n 2 + C_1^n 2^2 + \cdots$$
$$+ C_{n-1}^n 2^{n-1} + C_n^n 2^n = 3^n - 1 \approx 3^n$$
$$(9)$$

Consequently, the probability of a random correct guess without motion vector reordering is $1/T_{alt} \approx 1/3^n$, where n is the total number of macroblocks in an inter-frame. For CIF format video (n=396), the probability of a successful guess to attack the proposed watermarking method without motion vector reordering is as low as $1/3^{396} \approx 10^{-189}$. The probability of a correct guess reduces by a factor of $k!$ after applying random reordering. Furthermore, the number of k is determined by the clustering algorithm based on the motion characteristics of each single frame and thus k may vary in different frames. The security is further improved.

Watermark Extraction Procedure

The watermark extraction procedure is described as follows.

- Step 1. Obtain motion vectors from interframe after motion estimation, and determine the number of motion vector clusters based on the intelligent computational clustering method. Choose motion vectors with large magnitude clusters.
- Step 2. Construct the motion vector table and present it in 8-bit signed format, and re-order the table based on the private key as described in the proposed embedding procedure (see Section 3.1).
- Step 3. Determine the part of the table in which to embed the watermark by intelligent computational clustering.
- Step 4. Perform the parity check by Equation (10).

$$D_i = B(i,8) \oplus B(i,5) \oplus B(i+1,6) \oplus B(i+2,7)$$
$$(10)$$

where D_i denotes the detection value of the *ith* watermarked motion vector of a test video sequence frame. If $D_i = 0$, then the *ith* motion vector is correct. Otherwise, if $D_i = 1$, then the *ith* motion vector has been forged. If all $D_i = 0$, then this video sequence is authenticated. Otherwise, the video is distorted or forged. Figure 3 displays the extraction procedure.

EXPERIMENTAL RESULTS

To evaluate and compare the effectiveness of various clustering strategies, this work tests eight CIF (352×288) format video clips, namely Akiyo, Coastguard, Container, Foreman, Hall, Motherdaughter, News and Silent, as displayed in Fig. 4. The total number of frames in each test video clip is 300. In order to find the high motion region in the inter frame, motion vector magnitude is an important selection criterion. Figure 5 shows the distribution of the motion vector magnitude of test video clips. Observations from statistics in Fig. 5 show that the distribution varies and depends on video content characteristics. Almost all motion vector magnitudes in the Akiyo video clip are less than 5 (see Fig. 5(a)), since the video clip displays less movement. However, "Forman" has wide distribution of the motion vector magnitude indicating considerable motion in the entire video

Figure 3. Watermark extraction procedure

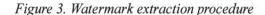
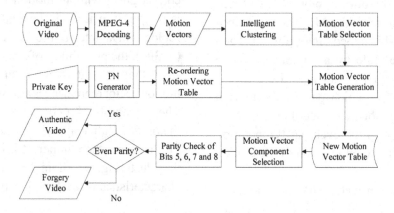

Figure 4. Eight test video clips, Akiyo, Coastguard, Container, Foreman, Hall, Mother-daughter, News and Silent

Figure 5. Distribution of the motion vector magnitudes of eight test video clips: (a) Akiyo, (b) Coastguard, (c) Container, (d) Foreman, (e)Hall, (f) Mother-daughter, (g)News, and (h) Silent

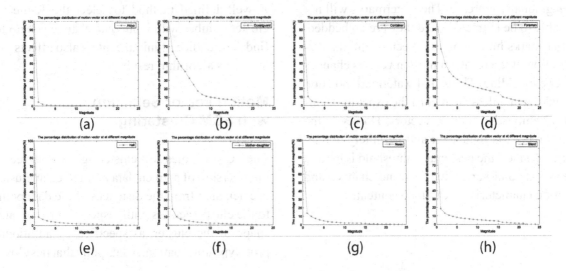

sequence.

This research measures the quality of watermarking video clips based on the PSNR (Peak Signal-to-Noise Ratio) criterion, and evaluates the deviation. The PSNR formula is defined as $PSNR = 10\log(f_{max}^2 / MSE)$, where f_{max} denotes the maximum of the video gray level (generally 255), and MSE represents the mean square error of the original image frame and the recovered image frame ($MSE = \frac{1}{m \times n}\sum_{i=0}^{m-1}\sum_{j=0}^{n-1}\left(\alpha_{ij} - \beta_{ij}\right)^2$). α_{ij} denotes the pixel value at location (i, j) of the original image, and β_{ij} indicates the pixel value

at location (i, j) of the recovered image with size m by n. The PSNR deviation (ε) between the original video and the watermarked video is given by $\varepsilon = \frac{\left| PSNR - PSNR'\right|}{PSNR} \times 100\%$, where $PSNR$ and $PSNR'$ denote the $PSNR$ values of the video before and after embedding, respectively. The video clips were tested with various clustering techniques to select the motion vector (watermark position selection), including K-means, FCM, thresholding FCM and swarm-intelligence-based FCM. This section analyzes the results.

Motion Vector Selection with Fixed Percentage

First, this study examines visual quality of the embedded video clip by selecting the fixed percentage of motion vectors in each inter-frame for watermark embedding. The current work sorts motion vectors in each frame in descending order, then chooses the fixed percentage of motion vectors with larger magnitude for watermark embedding. Table 2 shows the experimental results of the *PSNR* value with different percentages. Observations from Table 2 show the visual quality varies with different percentage values and the change in *PSNR* is not consistent when percentage values gradually increase. The watermarks will not be able to be extracted once they are embedded. Watermarks hide in motion vectors and the distribution of the resultant motion vectors changes after embedding. The actual watermark position is unknown unless we record the exact locations of all embedded motion vectors. However, the extra record is redundant and definitely not secure. Besides, the percentage threshold is hard to determine and varies due to scene changes and motion characteristics of video content.

Motion Vector Selection with K-means Clustering

The current study investigates visual quality of the embedded video using K-means clustering based on video watermarking. Table 3 presents the PSNR values employing a K-means algorithm with different cluster numbers, with the initial clusters randomly chosen from motion vectors. The average derivation of eight test video clips is 0.49%. Table 4 shows the average training iterations using the K-means clustering algorithm with different motion vector clusters. Although K-means is easy to implement and has less training iteration, it is not suitable for the proposed system. A well-defined method to select the K-means cluster number with input data change is hard to find. The choice of initial centers also affects the K-means algorithm result.

Motion Vector Selection with FCM Clustering

The FCM enables soft clustering. The degree of membership of a given data point to each cluster is calculated from the distances of the data point to the cluster centers with respect to the size and shape of the cluster, as specified by additional prototype information. A data point that lies closer

Table 2. PSNR values of test videos using fixed percentage of the motion vector watermark embedding scheme

Video clip	MPEG4 PSNR	Percentage of motion vectors					
		30%	40%	50%	60%	70%	80%
Akiyo	41.86	41.62	41.62	41.64	41.76	41.56	41.53
Coastguard	33.02	32.91	32.91	32.69	32.96	32.91	32.66
Container	37.78	37.48	37.47	37.62	37.49	37.51	37.62
Foreman	35.38	35.26	35.20	35.05	35.07	34.29	34.49
Hall	38.76	38.72	38.72	38.73	38.73	38.70	38.70
Mother-daughter	40.11	39.89	39.69	39.87	39.80	39.44	39.64
News	39.69	39.49	39.41	39.27	39.37	39.45	39.42
Silent	38.84	38.80	38.80	38.79	38.83	38.58	38.76

Table 3. PSNR values of test videos using different numbers of clusters embedded by the K-means based video watermarking scheme

Video clip	MPEG4 PSNR	# of clusters				Average	Deviation
		2	3	4	5		
Akiyo	41.86	41.65	41.55	41.60	41.62	41.61	0.60%
Coastguard	33.02	32.98	32.98	32.97	32.96	32.97	0.15%
Container	37.78	37.52	37.56	37.56	37.54	37.54	0.64%
Foreman	35.38	35.34	35.35	35.37	35.41	35.37	0.03%
Hall	38.76	38.71	38.67	38.71	38.72	38.70	0.15%
Mother-daughter	40.11	39.97	40.11	39.99	39.97	40.01	0.25%
News	39.69	39.53	39.59	39.66	39.59	39.59	0.25%
Silent	38.84	38.45	38.54	38.57	38.45	38.50	0.88%

Table 4. Average training iterations using different numbers of K-means motion vector clusters

Video clip	# of clusters			
	2	3	4	5
Akiyo	1.61	1.90	1.89	1.92
Coastguard	3.13	3.82	5.60	5.01
Container	2.84	3.59	4.08	4.46
Foreman	3.70	4.74	5.97	6.79
Hall	4.38	6.38	7.51	7.19
Mother-daughter	3.12	4.99	6.38	6.49
News	4.04	4.74	6.14	7.09
Silent	4.10	6.85	7.88	8.52

Table 5. PSNR values of test videos using different numbers of clusters embedded with watermarks using FCM

Video clip	MPEG4 PSNR	clusters				Average	Deviation
		2	3	4	5		
Akiyo	41.86	41.51	41.60	41.63	41.64	41.51	0.83%
Coastguard	33.02	32.86	32.90	32.97	32.95	32.92	0.30%
Container	37.78	37.53	37.53	37.59	37.50	37.53	0.64%
Foreman	35.38	34.99	34.72	35.20	35.11	35.00	1.06%
Hall	38.76	38.71	38.74	38.75	38.75	38.73	0.06%
Mother-daughter	40.11	39.96	40.00	39.99	39.92	39.96	0.36%
News	39.69	39.58	39.61	39.62	39.51	39.58	0.27%
Silent	38.84	38.81	38.72	38.87	38.85	38.81	0.08%

Table 6. Average training iterations using the FCM clustering method

Video clip	# of clusters			
	2	**3**	**4**	**5**
Akiyo	5.26	6.85	11.49	20.03
Coastguard	21.60	28.84	29.90	33.26
Container	12.60	24.69	27.91	27.27
Foreman	21.81	30.23	38.43	46.29
Hall	21.07	35.73	39.25	39.72
Mother-daughter	16.82	25.96	32.43	33.88
News	22.01	28.75	35.39	35.74
Silent	18.26	31.08	40.63	42.17

to the centre of a cluster has a higher degree of membership. Table 5 illustrates PSNR values with different initial cluster numbers using FCM clustering. Table 6 indicates the average training iterations of the corresponding cluster number for each video clip. The FCM advantage is that the result of data classification is independent of the choice of initial centers. This section discusses Fuzzy C-Means (FCM) with constant cluster number, which requires the values for cluster number and initial cluster position. Thus, several values of cluster number need to be calculated, and then evaluated by a validity measure.

Motion Vector Selection with Thresholding FCM

The limitation of FCM is that it is based on the hill climbing heuristic with prior knowledge of cluster numbers, which is significantly sensitive to cluster center initialization. Researchers have studied a novel thresholding FCM approach to solve the problem of determining an appropriate cluster number without any side information (Lin & Liao, 2008a). The experiments were performed

with $T = 0.1$ and the maximum number of clusters was set to 10. Table 7 shows the results of PSNR, the average cluster number, and the average training iteration using the thresholding FCM scheme. Some experiments were performed to discover a suitable T by calculating the within-cluster distance using different numbers of clusters in the frame. Figure 6 evaluates the within cluster distance curve from different frames of the test video clip Foreman. According to Equation (5), T should be set at the key point where the curve slope turns from steep to smooth. However, the curves do not generally descend in the same manner. Figure 6 implies the value of T changes based on motion vectors in the frame and single frame characteristics. Thus, the within-cluster distance is not restricted, and has a wide range of values in our experimental results. The variety of within cluster distance makes the appropriate T difficult to determine.

Figure 6. The within cluster distance curve obtained from different frames in the Foreman video clip: (a) frame #0, (b) frame #2, (c) frame #6, (d) frame #9, (e) frame #16, and (f) frame #19

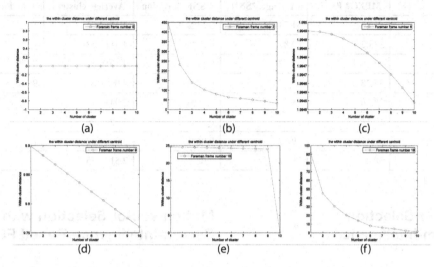

Table 7. Average PSNR and training iteration of the thresholding FCM clustering watermarking scheme

Video clip	MPEG4 PSNR	Average PSNR	PSNR deviation	Average clusters	Training iteration
Akiyo	41.86	41.61	0.60%	2.35±1.07	7.67
Coastguard	33.02	32.92	0.32%	2.49±0.56	24.51
Container	37.78	37.64	0.39%	2.16±0.82	25.10
Foreman	35.38	35.10	0.79%	2.24±0.66	27.68
Hall	38.76	38.75	0.02%	2.11±0.71	34.09
Mother-daughter	40.11	39.97	0.35%	2.18±0.56	26.62
News	39.69	39.59	0.26%	2.21±0.40	27.80
Silent	38.84	38.82	0.06%	2.10±0.42	32.00

Table 8. The average motion vector cluster number using swarm intelligence with different training iterations

Video clip	Iteration					Average clusters
	1000	1500	2000	2500	3000	
Akiyo	32.35	30.89	35.38	32.09	30.09	32.16±2.01
Coastguard	62.49	65.59	65.43	65.99	65.22	64.94±1.40
Container	43.96	41.45	39.39	43.08	48.53	43.28±3.41
Foreman	52.31	55.70	53.20	51.51	51.24	52.79±1.80
Hall	33.19	37.55	31.58	35.38	37.13	34.96±2.56
Mother-daughter	43.19	45.56	42.23	42.73	38.39	42.42±2.59
News	37.09	39.62	33.23	33.62	36.49	36.01±2.64
Silent	32.09	33.38	33.89	29.36	32.52	32.25±1.76

Table 9. Average PSNR values using SI-FCM

Video clip	MPEG4 PSNR	Average PSNR	PSNR deviation	Average clusters	Maximum clusters
Akiyo	41.86	41.73	0.31%	2.37±2.07	10
Coastguard	33.02	32.87	0.45%	4.31±1.63	7
Container	37.78	37.77	0.41%	3.19±0.52	8
Foreman	35.38	35.17	0.58%	4.09±0.67	9
Hall	38.76	38.75	0.02%	2.94±1.71	4
Mother-daughter	40.11	39.95	0.39%	3.18±1.66	8
News	39.69	39.67	0.06%	3.09±1.22	7
Silent	38.84	38.81	0.08%	2.51±0.75	7

Motion Vector Selection Using Swarm-Intelligence

Swarm intelligence provides a clustering method without any extra information. Swarm intelligence exhibits several notable properties including flexibility, robustness, decentralization and self organization. Swarm intelligence designs algorithms or distributed problem-solving devices in terms of the collective behavior of social insect colonies. The current work implements this algorithm as the clustering method for motion vector selection. The following parameters are employed in the swarm intelligence algorithm: number of ants 132; board size 40 by 40; slope $k = 0.1$; radius $r = 3$; $\alpha = 8$; $T_{remove} = 2:0$; $T_{create} = 3$; $P_{destory} = 0.3$; $P_{load} = 0.5$; $T_{createforheap} = 0:001$; and training iteration 1000. However, we discovered that the classification result is not stable. It depends on the number of iterations. Table 8 records simulation results of the average motion vector cluster number with different training iteration settings. Selection of the similarity coefficient effects the classification result. If the swarm similarity coefficient is too large, the dissimilar data objects will cluster together, and the algorithm will converge quickly. Whereas if swarm similarity coefficient is too small, similar data objects will not gather, yet the algorithm will converge slowly.

Motion Vector Selection with Swarm-Intelligence-Based FCM

Swarm intelligence provides the initial FCM cluster number and position. This investigation adopts swarm intelligence based on the FCM approach mentioned in Section 2.4 to specify the motion vector clusters with relative high magnitude for video watermark embedding. The total number of heaps become the initial FCM cluster number, and the centers of mass of all the objects in the heaps become the initial FCM cluster position. This study utilizes the FCM algorithm based on the initial cluster number and initial cluster centroid generated from swarm intelligence computing. Table 8 shows the PSNR values using swarm intelligence based on FCM. Table 9 displays the experimental results of the average PSNR values with the SI-FCM clustering watermarking scheme.

SUMMARY

This work presents and implements a novel watermarking embedding scheme on a compressed MPEG-4 video sequence that adopts various intelligent computation clustering methods to specify watermark locations, and the number of watermark bits varies dynamically among frames. This study then employs a parity checking algorithm to determine whether the motion

Table 10. Advantages and disadvantages of the clustering approaches discussed in this study

Method	Advantage	Disadvantage
Fixed Percentage Thresholding	Very easy to implement.	The threshold is hard to determine. This method is not adaptive.
K-means	Simple computation. The classification result changes dynamically based on the content characteristics of the video sequence.	Need to select an appropriate cluster number k. The clustering result is sensitive to the setting of initial cluster centers. Hard classification for data points.
Fuzzy C-Means	The clustering result is more stable. The classification result changes dynamically based on the content characteristics of the video sequence.	Need to select an appropriate cluster number.
Thresholding Fuzzy C-means	Improve FCM clustering method. The clustering result is more stable. The classification result changes dynamically based on the content characteristics of the video sequence.	Need to determine the threshold T. The within cluster distance curve may not descend in the same manner for different video frames.
Swarm intelligence Clustering	Automatic clustering scheme. The classification result changes dynamically based on the content characteristics of the video sequence.	The similarity coefficient affects the classification result. Need to set up a lot of parameters. The training result may not be stable.
Swarm intelligence based FCM Clustering	Automatic clustering scheme which provides number of cluster and initial centers. Stable training result. The classification result changes dynamically based on the content characteristics of the video sequence.	High computation complexity.

Table 11. The comparison of average video quality degradation (PSNR deviation) of various clustering methods

Method	K-means	FCM	ThresholdingFCM	SI-FCM
Average Deviation	0.49%	0.45%	0.35%	0.29%

vector should be embedded. Altering the least significant bit (LSB) with the proposed parity operation mechanism then modifies the corresponding motion vectors. Finally, the watermark is embedded. In the decoder, the watermark is extracted from the motion vector of these positions where the watermarks are embedded, followed by determining whether the suspicious video is authenticated. Where the distributed video has been illegally modified, the proposed method can authenticate stego-video originality without the original video while maintaining an acceptable fidelity. Additionally, embedding watermarks in motion vectors has the advantage of low degradation of video quality. Moreover, the original video

is not needed during authentication. The proposed method can be implemented for the compressed video offline without altering the existing codec and viewers.

Earlier methods required fixing and defining watermark bit locations before embedding. The current method develops an automatic clustering technique to choose the motion vectors and watermark positions. The number of embedded motion vector clusters also varies according to the motion attributes of each frame. Diversified intelligence computation schemes perform video watermarking, including K-means clustering, Fuzzy C-means clustering and Swarm intelligence based Fuzzy C-means (SI-FCM) clustering, providing different views from the conventional thresholding method in motion vector selection. Table 10 summarizes the advantages and disadvantages of clustering approaches discussed in this study. Table 11 compares video quality deviations of various watermarking schemes based on different clustering algorithms. The simulation results reveal that the video watermarking approach involving swarm-intelligence FCM clustering outperforms the other methods. The overall performance retains satisfactory quality with 0.29% degradation.

REFERENCES

Arthur, D., & Vassilvi, S. (2006). How Slow is the K-means Method? In *Proceedings of the 22th Annual Symposium on Computational Geometry* (pp. 144-153).

Bezdek, J. C. (1973). *Fuzzy mathematics in pattern classification*. Master's thesis, Cornell University, Ithaca, NY.

Bhattacharya, S., Chattopadhyay, T., & Pal, A. (2006). A survey on different video watermarking techniques and comparative analysis with reference to H.264/AVC. In *Proceedings of IEEE Tenth International Symposium on Consumer Electronics* (pp. 1-6).

Bin, W., Yi, Z., Shaohui, L., & Zhongzhi, S. (2002). CSIM: A document clustering algorithm based on swarm intelligence. In *Proceedings of the 2002 Congress on Evolutionary Computation, Vol. 1,* (pp. 477-482).

Biswas, S., Das, S. R., & Petriu, E. M. (2005). An adaptive compressed MPEG-2 video watermarking scheme. *IEEE Transactions on Instrumentation and Measurement, 54*(5), 1853–1861. doi:10.1109/TIM.2005.855084

Chan, P. W., Lyu, M. R., & Chin, R. T. (2005). A novel scheme for hybrid digital video watermarking: approach, evaluation and experimentation. *IEEE Trans. on Circuits and Systems for Video Technology, 15*(12), 1638–1649. doi:10.1109/TCSVT.2005.856932

Cox, I., Miller, M., & Bloom, J. (2001). *Digital Watermarking*. San Francisco: Morgan Kaufmann.

Dempster, A. P., Laird, N. M., & Rubin, D. B. (1977). Maximum likelihood from incomplete data via the EM algorithm. *Journal of the Royal Statistical Society. Series A (General), 39*(1), 1–38.

Deneubourg, J. L., Goss, S., Franks, N., Sendova-Franks, A., Detrain, C., & Chrétien, L. (1991). The dynamics of collective sorting robot-like ants and ant-like robots. In *Proceedings of the first international conference on simulation of adaptive behavior on From animals to animates table of contents,* (pp. 356-363).

Fang, D. Y. (2004). *Information hiding in digital video with phase angle of motion vector.* Master's thesis, Dept. of Computer and Information Science, National Tsing Hua University, Hsinchu, Taiwan.

Hartung, F., & Girod, B. (1998). Watermarking of uncompressed and compressed video. *Signal Processing, 66*(6), 283–301. doi:10.1016/S0165-1684(98)00011-5

Huffman, D. A. (1952). A method for the construction of minimum redundancy codes. *Proc. IRE, 40*(10), 1098-1101.

Jordan, F., Kutter, M., & Ebrahimi, T. (1997). Proposal of a watermarking technique for hiding/retrieving data in compressed and decompressed video. *ISO/IEC Doc. JTC1/SC29/WG11 MPEG97/M2281.*

Kanade, P. M., & Hall, L. O. (2003). Fuzzy ants as a clustering concept. In *Proceedings of the 22nd International Conference of the North American Fuzzy Information Processing Society,* (pp. 227-232).

Kong, X., Lui, Y., Lui, H., & Yang, D. (2004). Object watermarks for digital images and video. *Image and Vision Computing, 22*(8), 583–594. doi:10.1016/j.imavis.2003.09.016

Kung, C. H., Jeng, J. H., Lee, Y. C., Hsiao, H. H., & Cheng, W. S. (2003). Video watermarking using motion vector. In *Proceedings of the 16th IPPR Conference on Computer Vision Graphics and Image,* (pp. 547-551).

Lee, J. D., & Huang, Z. X. (1999). Automatic color image segmentation with fuzzy C-means algorithm. In *Proceedings of the National Computation Symposium,* (pp. 99-106).

Lin, D.-T., & Liao, G.-J. (2008a). Embedding watermarks in compressed video using fuzzy c-means clustering. In *Proceedings of the IEEE International Conference of System Man and Cybernetics,* (pp. 1053-1058).

Lin, D.-T., & Liao, G.-J. (2008b). Swarm Intelligence Based Fuzzy C-Means Clustering for Motion Vector Selection in Video Watermarking. *International Journal of Fuzzy Systems, 10*(3), 185–194.

Lu, C.-S., & Liao, H.-Y. M. (2001). Multipurpose watermarking for image authentication and protection. *IEEE Transactions on Image Processing, 10*(10), 1579–1592. doi:10.1109/83.951542

Lu, Z. M., Li, Y. N., Wang, H. X., & Sun, S. H. (2006). Multipurpose video watermarking algorithm in the hybrid compressed domain. *IEEE Proceedings of Information Security, 153*(4), 173–182. doi:10.1049/ip-ifs:20060034

MacQueen, J. B. (1967). Some methods for classification and analysis of multivariate observations. In *Proceedings of the Fifth Symposium on Math, Statistics, and Probability* (pp. 281-297).

Monmarche, N., Slimane, M., & Venturini, G. (1999). AntClass: discovery of clusters in numeric data by an hybridization of an ant colony with the K-means algorithm. *Internal Report,* 1-21.

Pan, J. S., Huang, H. C., Jain, L. C., & Fang, W. C. (2007). *Intelligent Multimedia Data Hiding: New Directions.* Berlin: Springer.

Wang, R., Cheng, Q., & Huang, T. (2001). Identify regions of interest (ROI) for video watermark embedment with principle component analysis. In *Proceedings of the eighth ACM international conference on Multimedia* (pp. 459-461).

Zha, H., Ding, C., Gu, M., He, X., & Simon, H. D. (2001). Spectral relaxation for K-means clustering. In *Neural Information Processing Systems vol.14* (pp. 1057-1064).

Zhang, J., Ho, A. T. S., Qui, G., & Marziliano, P. (2007). Robust video watermarking of H.264/AVC. *IEEE Transactions on Circuits and Systems, 54*(2), 205–209. doi:10.1109/TC-SII.2006.886247

Zhang, J., Li, J., & Zhang, L. (2001). Video watermark technique in motion vector. In *Proceedings Xiv Brazilian Symposium Computer Graphics and Image Processing* (pp. 179-182).

Ziv, J., & Lempel, A. (1978). Compression of individual sequences via variable-rate coding. *IEEE Transactions on Information Theory, 24*(5), 530–536. doi:10.1109/TIT.1978.1055934

APPENDIX

A. 1 FCM algorithm (Bezdek, 1973):

- Step 1. Randomly initialize the membership matrix U with constraint $\sum_{i=1}^{c} u_{ij} = 1, \; \forall j = 1, \ldots, n$.
- Step 2. Calculate the centroid c_j using Equation (1.2).
- Step 3. Compute the dissimilarity between centroid and data points using Equation (1.1). Stop, if its improvement over previous iteration is below a threshold.
- Step 4. Compute a new U using Equation (1.3). Go to Step 2.

A. 2 Swarm Intelligence Clustering algorithm (Bin, Yi, Shaohui, & Zhongzhi, 2002):

- Step 1. Randomly project data objects onto low dimension space, usually a plane.
- Step 2. Perceive the swarm similarity of current object within the local region and compute the picking-up or dropping probability by a probability conversion function (Monmarche, Slimane, & Venturini, 1999), and then act according to the resultant picking-up or dropping probability. Clusters are visually formed through a simple agent's (ant's) collective action.
- Step 3. Accumulate the clustering results from the plane using a recursive algorithm. Initially, objects are randomly projected to a discrete 2D board which can be viewed as a matrix of m by m cells. Ants can easily travel from one end of this matrix to the other. The size of the board depends on the number of objects. This m by m matrix is clustered using $m^2 = 4n$, where n represents the total number of objects to be clustered. The ants are scattered randomly throughout the board. Generally, the system has $n=3$ ants which collect and move objects to form heaps. A heap is defined as a collection of two or more objects located in a single cell. The following parameters are defined for a heap H with n_H objects and are used to construct heuristics for the clustering algorithm (Kanade & Hall, 2003):

1. The maximum distance between two s-dimensional objects in the heap H.

$$D_{max}\left(H\right) = \max_{X_i, X_j \in H} D\left(X_i, X_j\right),$$ (1.1)

where D denotes the Euclidean distance between the objects, X_i and X_j.

2. The center of mass of all the objects in the heap is given by

$$O_{center}\left(H\right) = \frac{1}{n_H} \sum_{O \in H} O_i$$ (1.2)

3. The most dissimilar object in the heap Odissim (H). This is the object that is the farthest from the center of the heap.

4. The mean distance between the objects of H and the center of the mass of the heap

$$D_{mean}(H) = \frac{1}{n_H} \sum_{O_i \in H} D\left(O_i, O_{center}(H)\right),$$ (1.3)

5. Swarm similarity is the integrated similarity of a data object with other data objects within its neighborhood (Bin, Yi, Shaohui, & Zhongzhi, 2002). Equation (1.4) shows a basic formula for measuring the swarm similarity.

$$f(O_i) = \sum_{O_j \in Neigh(r)} \left[1 - \frac{d(O_i, O_j)}{\alpha} \right],$$ (1.4)

where *Neigh*(r) denotes the local region, and is generally a circular area with a radius r and d (O_i, O_j) denotes the distance of the data object O_i and O_j in the attribute space, typically the Euclidean distance or cosine distance. The parameter α is defined as the swarm similarity coefficient, and is a key coefficient that directly influences the number of clusters and convergence of the algorithm.

6. Probability conversion function is a function that converts the swarm similarity of a data object into picking up or dropping probability for a simple agent. The pick probability and drop probability of the object O_i are two lines with slope *k*, shown in Equations (1.5) and (1.6).

$$P_P(i) = \begin{cases} 1 & f(O_i) \leq 0 \\ 1 - kf(O_i) & 0 < f(O_i) \leq 1/k \\ 0 & f(O_i) > 1/k \end{cases},$$ (1.5)

$$P_d(i) = \begin{cases} 1 & f(O_i) \geq 1/k \\ kf(O_i) & 0 < f(O_i) < 1/k \\ 0 & f(O_i) \leq 0 \end{cases}.$$ (1.6)

Section 3
Data Mining

Chapter 15
Data Mining Meets Internet and Web Performance

Leszek Borzemski
Wroclaw University of Technology, Poland

ABSTRACT

Data mining (DM) is the key process in knowledge discovery. Many theoretical and practical DM applications can be found in science and engineering. However there are still such areas where data mining techniques are still at early stage of development and application. In particular, an unsatisfactory progress is observed in DM applications in the analysis of Internet and Web performance issues. This chapter gives the background of network performance measurement and presents our approaches, namely Internet Performance Mining and Web Performance Mining as the ways of DM application to Internet and Web performance issues. The authors present real-life examples of the analysis where explored data sets were collected with the aid of two network measurement systems WING and MWING developed at our laboratory.

INTRODUCTION AND MOTIVATION

Web performance is an important research area and a hot topic in Internet community. Many software resources are mirrored on hundreds of servers on the Internet. Using a nearby (in the sense of network distance) server would probably speed up the download, and reduce the load on central servers as well as on the Internet as a whole. Our ultimate aim is the development of a system that would have measure

user perceived data transfer performance between the known (observed) or unknown (non-observed) Web servers and user desktop, as well as to provide network throughput predictions on the minute-by-minute, hour-by-hour and day-by-day basis.

The particular motivation of this work is to show our approach for providing Web performance predictions by means of data mining techniques. We concentrate essential issues in the context how we apply data mining to Web performance prediction, with emphasis on the applicability to real-world problems.

DOI: 10.4018/978-1-61520-757-2.ch015

Data mining (DM) is the key process in knowledge discovery in science and engineering. Many pure theoretical and practical DM applications can be found in the literature and real-life applications. However, we notice unsatisfactory progress in the application of DM in the analysis of Internet and Web performance issues, and we hope that our contribution fills this research gap to some extent at least.

Time is the key aspect of performance evaluation of acceptable Internet and Web service levels to end users. Networks always add a delay which is more or less significant in data delivering between network nodes but it always occurs. Sometimes the delay can be estimated accurately but when a significant and changing delay occurs in the data transmission, the user application performance may suffer seriously. This degradation may cause different impacts depending on the way how the application works, including total breakdown.

The ultimate goal is to build an advanced access to Internet providing a means whereby users (whether human or machine) improve likelihood that they use network at good performance. We propose to deploy a new Internet service called Network Monitoring Broker (NMB) which would measure network performance, describe network characteristic and publish the forecasts of network behavior, especially for automatic Internet resource selection for a user domain (e.g. particular local area network).

NMB infrastructure would be established at each of the nodes of the virtual organization and can be organized in the likeness of the intermediary servers that mediate the interaction between clients and servers of the World Wide Web (Borzemski, 2007). Such service could be used in Grids and computing cloud metacomputing infrastructures to analyze current and historical data transfer performance deliverable at the application level for a set of network resources to characterize future throughput of network paths in order to find best predictions at specified action periods.

Nowadays we have developed WING (Borzemski & Nowak, 2004b) and MWING (Borzemski et al., 2007a) active measurement infrastructures to be used by the broker to measure Internet and Web in well-designed and controlled active performance experiments. We have also developed own decision-making forecasting methodology and algorithms to solve performance prediction problem formulated in our research. The broker performs Internet/Web performance forecasting using data mining methods and algorithms9. D. Barelos, E. Pitoura, G. Samaras, Mobile agents procedures: metacomputing in Java, in: Proceedings of the ICDCS Workshop on Distributed Middleware (in conjuction with the 19th IEEE International Conference on Distributed Computing Systems (ICDCS99)), Austin, TX, June 1999..

Our approach is to provide the network performance prediction service which would work similar to weather forecasting system. Network data transfer quality prediction is made in two basis steps. The first step consists of clustering the historical network performance measurements to determine classes of network behavior (the weather). These classes may be described by many measurable network parameters – in this work we use two fundamental network performance measures: *round-trip time* of data packets and *throughput* of data transfer. Each measurement is also characterized by a *time stamp* denoting the date and time at which a measurement occurred. Additional non-measurable features but also related to the event can be taken into account. Among them there is topological information such as geo-spatial parameters for users and servers, Autonomous System affiliation, routers and Autonomous Systems on user-to-server and server-to-user routes (Borzemski & Nowak, 2008).

The second step in the forecasting process consists of the determination the decision trees to descript and generalization of previously network behavior classes. The leaves represent classifications and branches represent conjunctions of features that lead to those classifications. In this chapter the only features considered in decision-making at interior nodes are date and time.

Data mining methods and techniques can be applied to discover useful knowledge from the World Wide Web data. This research field is generally called *Web mining*. It focuses on four main research directions, namely: *Web content mining*, *Web usage mining*, *Web structure mining* and *Web user profile mining*. Various works have been devoted either to theoretical or practical issues of the Web. In Web mining we analyze such data sources as Web documents stored on Web pages (usually text and graphics), data logs available from Web servers (containing access history such as Internet Protocol (IP) user addresses, access date and time and object characterization), data describing Web structure (i.e. HTML and XML tags) and Web users profile data. Web content mining discovers what Web pages are about and reveals new knowledge from them. Web usage mining concerns the identification of patterns in user navigation through Web pages and is performed for the reasons of service personalization, system improvement, and usage characterization. Web structure mining investigates how the Web documents are structured, and discovers the model underlying the link structures of the WWW. Web user profile mining discovers user's profiles to find user preference to adopt Web sites.

The application of data mining to the analysis of time-related network performance problems needs new data sources, new mining methodologies and new actionable ways of knowledge discovering. These data mining applications open new possibilities for common network users, administrators, system designers as well as for Internet and Web systems research.

In this chapter we present a methodological review of data mining issues and opportunities for building Internet and Web performance knowledge. The aim is to present today's achievements in the field as well as to show possible directions of future research. We describe opportunities

related to performance knowledge in real-life practice and discuss our taxonomy of problems and solutions undertaken in the field. We present real-life examples of data mining applications in problems related to Internet and Web performance prediction.

In particular, we present our concepts of Web and Internet domain-driven data mining dimensions called *Web performance mining* (WPM) and *Internet performance mining* (IPM). WPM has been defined to characterize the performance from the perspective of the WWW end-users (i.e. Web clients, more specifically, the WWW browsers) in the sense of the data transfer throughput achievable in Web transactions that are performed between WWW browsers and Web servers to get Web resources such as Web pages and embedded text and image files. In particular, we propose the easy-to-use classification-based predictive model describing performance as perceived by Web clients. IPM has been introduced to characterize performance patterns at the IP layer of the Internet communication model. Both data mining approaches need to setup, deploy, plan and perform active measurement experiments and tools matching on one hand the domain and user expectations, and on the other hand data mining requirements. We discuss Internet and Web active measurement principles and limitations in the context of data mining and present WING and MWING active measurement systems.

Our motivation is also the use a general domain-independent data mining system instead of domain specific software. We clime that the analysis we perform can be effectively and friendly performed using general and conventional stand-alone domain-independent data mining systems. General data mining systems may have advantages including their productivity proved in many domain applications. We are using in our research the IBM Intelligent Miner for Data (IBM, 2008), and Microsoft SQL Server 2005 (Microsoft, 2008) which are one of the software leaders among high-end commercial data mining tools. They are feasible and friendly frameworks for deploying data mining applications for different domains with the minimum user skills required. Normal usage of them needs only a domain expert. It is assumed that the mining expert is needed only for the development of the mining scenarios. Systems use proven mining algorithms to make possible to address a wide range of problems, including clustering, associations, sequential patterns, similar time sequences and classification.

The rest of the chapter is organized as follows. First we present background information concerning the Internet and Web performance problem.. Further section presents our approach and shows our proposition how to measure Web performance and evaluate it using data mining analysis. We discuss research challenges in studying Internet and Web related problems using data mining methodology and tools. Subsequent part presents the real-life case studies of our research in the field. Finally, concluding remarks are presented.

NETWORK BACKGROUND

In this section we present the general information about the communication model valid in Internet and locate the prediction problem we deal with. We also give the motivation of our research and research challenges. As our work is related to three classes of previous efforts: (i) throughput prediction, (ii) network measurement, and (iii) data mining application in Internet and Web, we include an appropriate literature review.

Internet has the communication model based on the multi-layer architecture (Figure 1). In the architectural model of Internet we distinguish two main subsystems we deal with, namely the network communication subsystem and application communication subsystem (Comer, 2008; Crovella & Krishnamurthy, 2006; RFC1945, 2008). For the simplicity, we consider that the upper layer is devoted to World Wide Web and omit two lowest layers, namely Network interface and Physical layers related to hardware specific solutions. The network communication subsystem is the bottom part of the communication model whereas the application communication subsystem is its upper part. The lower subsystem we call the *Internet Layer*. It includes the TCP/IP (Transmission Control Protocol/Internet Protocol), an industry-standard suite of network protocols which is responsible for the reliable and as fast as possible end-to-end data transfer. The upper subsystem we call the *Web Layer*. It comprises the popular HTTP protocol (HyperText Transfer Protocol) which is used to gain World Wide Web (WWW) resources.

When discussing Internet and Web performance problems we should take into account that both subsystems are working independently of each other doing the best efforts only but relying on lower layer services. The application layer utilizes the lower layer having no control what is going inside it. In addition, modern Web applications are multi-tiered what can influence on performance issues, as well.

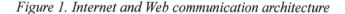

Figure 1. Internet and Web communication architecture

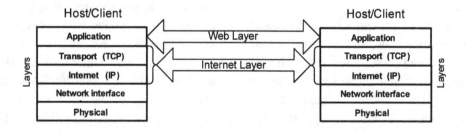

Network Measurements

To understand network performance we need to measure it. Several such efforts are thoroughly reported by CAIDA (CAIDA, 2008) and SLAC (SLAC, 2008) which are the top websites in network measurement. Many measurement initiatives and projects have been launched on the Internet (Brownlee et al., 2001; Crovella & Krishnamurthy, 2006; Claffy et al., 2003; Dovrolis, 2005; Faloutsos et al., 1999; Keynote, 2008; MOME, 2008; Prasad et al., 2003; Watson et al., 2004; Wolski, 1998; Yousaf & Welzl, 2005). There are network measurements projects aimed at dealing with the performance problem related rather to the whole Internet or a significant part of it, where very large amounts of measured data regarding, for instance, network delay among several node pairs over a few hours, days or months are collected. For these purposes the specific measurements and data analysis infrastructures are used. As they are mainly devoted for large Internet-based projects configured with rather complex measurement infrastructures, they cannot help end users. Regarding performance they are referring to IP layer mostly. However only a few of them provide network performance forecasting we are soliciting for.

In our research we use both well known personal measurement tools such as ping or traceroute (commonly used network tools), as well as new tools developed in our laboratory with the aim to deal with the problems of network performance forecasting for the end-users needs. Web specific active measurements tools from another group of solutions. Our research is focused on measuring of Web performance as perceived by end-users. Different HTTP measurement and visualization tools have been widely discussed and compared in our earlier works (Borzemski, 2006a; Borzemski, 2008). We have found that probably the Keynote (Keynote, 2008) professional service is the most advanced benchmarking service that measures Web site's performance and availability perceived

from measurement servers localized in many locations all over the world. However to match our research goals we had to develop own measurement systems.

Passive and Active Measurements

Different performance evaluation principles and practices are used in existing networks. The nature of the network, the possibilities to perform the measurements and the aim of the measurements give the key decision choices how we need to design and conduct Internet and Web measurement experiments.

The main diversification is to measure Internet and Web by means of either passive or active experiments. Active methods rely on sending from the source node probe traffic along one or more network paths and observing it at destination node(s) to evaluate traffic quality. Active measurements allow studying host and service availability, routes of transmitted packets, packet delay, packet loss, and packet inter-arrival jitter. To run such experiments we need to measure network at both ends. To make the experiment easier, active measurements can be sometimes done also in a loop mode, i.e. probe traffic is send to the destination node and back again. Then the destination node is used only to give an answer according to the service used. Active measurements are invasive designs as they require injecting test packets (probes) into the network. The end-to-end nature of active measurement system makes it suitable in the Grids, overlay networks and peer-to-peer networks.

Network administrators and common users often use traditional active measurement tool such as *ping* to determine round-trip delays and server reachability. Slightly more complex is *traceroute* tool. These tools use specific ICMP (Internet Control Message Protocol) protocol, one of the core protocols of the Internet layer. Recent development in active Internet measurement tools includes H.323 Beacon (Calyam, 2004), OWAMP

(RFC4656, 2008), Iperf (Schroder, 2008), Pathchar (Downey, 1999), and Pathload (Jain & Dovrolis, 2002). H.323 Beacon is a tool that can be used to measure, monitor and qualify the performance of an H.323 audio and video-conferences session. It can help in problem troubleshooting before, during or after H.323 session. OWAMP is a command line client application used to determine one-way latency between hosts. Iperf is a tool to measure maximum TCP bandwidth, allowing the tuning of various parameters and characteristics of UDP protocol. UDP is User Datagram Protocol in the Internet transport protocol suite used for transportation of short messages called datagrams, for the needs of the Domain Name System (DNS) and streaming media applications such as IPTV, Voice over IP. Pathchar is a tool that measures the characteristics of links along an Internet path (latency, bandwidth, queue delays). Pathload is also a measurement tool for end-to-end available bandwidth.

Grid users can use one of the special forecasting services, such as well-known Network Weather Service (NWS) (Baker et al., 2002; Wolski 1998). NWS is a distributed measurement framework that aims to provide short-term forecasts of dynamically changing performance characteristics of a distributed set of Internet hosts. It measures, among other parameters, the end-to-end network latency and network bandwidth. NWS measures available bandwidth by transferring a sample block of data and measuring the time taken for the transfer. But this measurement may not be representative for long-term transfers. The reason is that a TCP connection may be in so called slow start phase for a large part of the sample transfer. NWS can periodically monitor and dynamically forecast short-term expected performance of the network path between hosts. In order to calculate expected performance it runs all the time and instantaneously gathers readings of performance conditions from a set of monitors. Unfortunately, NWS runs only in UNIX operating system environments and does not support long-term forecasts.

Passive methods are used when we want to collect real-life traffic at one or more points on a network. Then we use protocol sniffers which capture the traffic and analyze it, e.g. in the scope to filter out unnecessary information and to build traffic statistics. Passive measurements are also referred to as network monitoring.

By combining active and passive measurement techniques, we are able to reduce the need for invasive measurements of the network without sacrificing measurement goals. Our network measurement infrastructures WING and MWING discussed later on are in fact such combined developments.

Sound and Rational Measurements

Measurements can merely report the network state at the time of the measurement. Nevertheless they are effectively used by various protocols to test and monitor current performance and to take necessary action when changes are detected.

When the relevant network properties exhibit to be constant over observed network life-time span, then the measurements can be also a useful guide to the future. The concept of constant network parameters is especially more useful for coarser time scale than for fine time scales. This problem was investigated in real-time experiments by Zhang et al. (2001) and it was shown that in general the round trip packet delay, as measured by the Round-Trip-Time, appears well described as steady on time scale of 10-30 minutes.

Many crucial problems can be encountered while preparation, conducting and analyzing network measurements, and sound measurement is required for avoiding and overcoming error and inaccuracy based pitfalls (Allman & Paxson, 2008; Allman et al, 2008; Brownlee & Claffy, 2004; Duffield, 2004; Krishnamurthy & Willinger 2008; Paxon, 2004; Roughan; 2006). The measurements should be calibrated by examining outliers and tested for consistence. The utilities and measurement systems have to provide reliable and valid measurement taking. The possibility of making reproduction of measurements and analysis must be available for the community. Datasets in Internet archives must be associated with meta-data describing the measurements that may improve the understanding of them and studied problems (MOME, 2008).

Network measurements should obviously have their well defined goal, as in all experiment-based research in other research fields. However due to the complexity of network architecture and functioning, the specific network measurement infrastructure is usually needed for each specific problem investigated, including performance prediction projects. In network measurements we may have to collect and access so large data files that can be almost non-tackleable. Moreover, measurement data bases can be distributed but must be jointly processed. The network behavior can be very unrepeatable and dynamic so we often need real-time processing. Therefore to follow all requirements we must use the designed experiments that match the goals we want to achieve in particular study.

And last but not least, we would like to comment the specificity of the application of data mining in considered research domain. Data mining is the main extraction stage in knowledge discovery in databases (KDD) concept. KDD consists in processing a huge volume of data in order to extract useful and reusable knowledge units from supplied data. The extraction process is based on data mining methods and algorithms. A typical KDD system has four key components: the database, domain knowledge (provided by an expert), data mining methods and algorithms, and user-machine interface helping in interactions with the system, including visualization of the results of mining analysis. This scheme assumes an important role of the user and his/her direct interactivity in KDD. As our ultimate aim is to develop the decision support system working in an automatic mode in Internet as an autonomous

network service (Borzemski, 2007), therefore we are concerned with the development of automatic and script-based data mining analysis, including domain ontology processing and domain problem-solving.

The application of data mining to network performance analysis is basically understandable, but there is more or less nuance concerning one of the KDD principles. Namely, in data mining we consider databases with unknown information and rules. Most data sets used in traditional data mining are well structured like tables. Web mining explores unstructured data such as Web pages. In both situations data sets are originated independently of the analysis phase and they are as they are. However in network measurement where we use designed experiments, data sets are collected under user control. Good examples of controlled attributes are the sampling rate/time and sampling distribution to be chosen in traffic measurement, which are in fact planned by domain expert to obtain usable and interpretable measurements in a suitable experimental plan (design). The experimental design should also take into account time and cost limits as well as other requirements that may influence on the proper experiment completion.

There are also some ethical problems, as networking allows users to share resources and communicate with one another. But scientists, network administrators and casual users, as well who are interested in network measurements would always weight out possible *pros and cons* of proposed measurements.

We should also take into account that network communication is very complex to study, and we are faced with a large number of factors that can affect the result itself and its quality. These factors are often so interrelated and coiled, that it is impossible to delete inert factors in an elegant (that is theoretically proven) way using well documented methodology. In such situations we need to make use of rational and empirically proved processes of network measurement.

The knowledge discovered by the application of data mining should be both practically useful and scientifically rigorous. However, very often in the literature the obtained knowledge cannot be directly used in practice. This problem has very practical importance as it is connected with the need for end-user acceptance of data mining. Therefore, data mining must create an actionable knowledge. Developed DM-based solutions should deeply rely on the incorporating domain knowledge into data mining. This problem is seen by many authors in different practical data mining applications (Cao & Zhang, 2007; Pechenizkiy et al., 2005; Puuronen et al., 2006; Sinha & Zhao, 2008; Wang & Wang, 2007).

Internet Layer Performance

The Internet performance mining can use various performance metrics available at IP layer. Here we consider the performance metrics which in our opinion refer to the Internet performance problems at the most extent and can be evaluated in our experiments.

The Internet Layer performance can be measured by the *network latency* which is the amount of time it takes for a packet to be transmitted across a network between two hosts. It is composed of host, distance, forwarding and protocol delays. Network latency has a unidirectional property. It is evaluated by the *One-way-Trip Time* (OTT) (RFC4656, 2008). In many network operations we employ one-way data transfer and the transfer characteristic in the one direction is more significant than in reverse direction.

OTT measurement requires time synchronization of both sides therefore we usually consider the evaluation of Internet performance by means of the *Round-Trip Time* (RTT) which is defined as the time needed to send the IP packet from the source host to a target server and back again. RTT evaluates total two-way latency characterizing the network path between source and target hosts. However we should remember that it is very

common in networks to have a different traffic path on both parts of a round-trip, which makes using round-trip metrics alone not as useful as one-way metrics.

The most popular way of obtaining an estimation of RTT is to use the ping utility program that employs host-to-host datagram ICMP protocol for packet sending and echoing. This kind of Internet measurement is typically used, e.g. by programs to download files as a means to choose among many servers containing required file that one with the least RTT value to download file from there. The real-life experiments showed many times that the RTT-to-transfer time relationship is no so straightforward because of a long-tail distribution characteristics. In (Borzemski & Nowak, 2004a) we considered RTT to data transfer time relationship in the context of their median values and obtained useful transfer time prediction results.

Internet Data Sources

The most popular data sources used in the analysis of Internet layer include packet traces which consist of time-stamped records of packets observed in certain passive experiment made at certain time interval and at certain network place. This kind of data can be collected e.g., at both ends of end-to-end path to analyze quality of network service. Such data sets can be obtained using one of known packet capturing software, such as *tcpdump*. Another data sets used in the analysis of the communication subsystem include flow traces in which we can identify the pairs of IP addresses and TCP port numbers of both ends, observed in certain measurement point (network node). Also these repositories may store information about packet transfer quality such as packed delay, packet loss ratio, to investigate quality of service.

In case of performance analysis we usually need to plan and conduct an active experiment. To measure RTT we use *ping* utility available as operating system command. Routing information is collected by means of *traceroute* and *reverse traceroute* services. Both use ICMP protocol. Truly speaking ICMP packets (Wenwei et al., 2007) are sent to check server reachability and network routing at the communication layer of Internet.

The routing information shows which routers are visited by communication packets when traversing the network route between end hosts. Then the route is characterized by the number of hops that are counted on the route, as well as the IP information about all visited network nodes, including both end hosts and all intermediary nodes. The route to the target server is measured by means of traceroute whereas the return route is measured by reverse traceroute. Sample routing information from traceroute is illustrated in Table 1. From the end-user point of view the reverse tracerouting would be more valuable if we evaluate performance for data files downloading to the client's location. Traceroute based pinging is available in our operating systems whereas the reverse traceroute requires specific installation of this service on the target servers. This is not a common administrator task to do that, so in Internet measurements we must take advantage of the traceroute servers listed for example at SLAC website (SLAC, 2008).

The collected information by ping and traceroute can be incomplete and both utilities are often considered by network administrators as unreliable network measurement tools. This is due to the way how they operate and how network administrators configure their networks. Both utilities use the ICMP packets that may be not serviced or even are filter out by hosts and intermediate communication nodes due to local security or performance rules. This can be true especially in WWW network because many Web servers block ping service and do not respond for ICMP packets. These packets can also be blocked by firewalls. Furthermore, the routers often provide different prioritizing for ICMP packets than for "normal" traffic, e.g. for TCP sessions in HTTP transfers (Wenwei et al., 2007).

However we think that this features of collected data which is maybe not usable when the statistics based analysis is to be performed, is not a problem when applying data mining.

The second data source for exploratory analysis can be the TCP protocol used for data transmission at Internet Layer. Simple HTTP protocol relies on TCP functionality. TCP carefully keeps track of the data it sends and what happens to it. TCP rearranges data according to needed sequence and provides ordered data transfer, retransmits lost data and discards duplicate data. Protocol is error free and provides flow and congestion control to guarantee reliable delivery.

Flow control mechanism manages the rate at which data is sent so that it does not overwhelm

Table 1. Sample routing information from traceroute

```
Traceroute from icfamon.rl.ac.uk to 156.17.130.48 ()
traceroute to 156.17.130.48 (156.17.130.48), 30 hops max, 38 byte packets
1 130.246.132.254 (130.246.132.254) 1.936 ms 1.822 ms 1.953 ms
2 fw1.routers.net.rl.ac.uk (130.246.80.5) 0.192 ms 0.297 ms 0.168 ms
3 ral-bar.ja.net (146.97.40.73) * 0.487 ms *
4 pos13-0.read-scr.ja.net (146.97.35.81) 0.796 ms 0.901 ms 0.765 ms
5 pos1-0.lond-scr.ja.net (146.97.33.33) 2.110 ms 2.057 ms 1.915 ms
6 geant-gw.ja.net (146.97.35.130) 2.170 ms
7 * * janet.uk1.uk.geant.net (62.40.103.149) 2.347 ms 2.478 ms 2.330 ms
8 uk.se1.se.geant.net (62.40.96.125) 37.334 ms 37.329 ms 37.336 ms
9 * * *
10 z-poznan-gw-e3.wroclaw.pol34.pl (212.191.127.90) 537.462 ms 527.329 ms *
11 elek-a254.wask.wroc.pl (156.17.254.220) 188.082 ms 302.281 ms 189.032 ms
12 kwarc.ists.pwr.wroc.pl (156.17.30.107) 256.616 ms 262.427 ms 317.957 ms
13 Szafir.ists.pwr.wroc.pl (156.17.130.48) 352.169 ms 448.130 ms 472.559 ms
```

the device that is receiving it. The flow control is achieved by implementing sliding window mechanism which basically dynamically tells (by increasing or reducing window size) the communicating parties (client and server) how many bytes one partner is willing to receive at one time from another partner. Thus the server and client ensure that the other device sends data just as fast as the recipient can deal with it. There are also acknowledges (ACKs) the server must send back to the client to indicate that the data was received.

Various implementations of TCP protocol differently use distinct TCP mechanisms. Congestion control is concerned with the slow start, congestion avoidance, fast retransmissions, and fast recovery protocol activities. Current TCP implementations always perform *slow start* procedure. When a new connection is established the transmission may start with the size of one data segment. Each time an ACK is received, the number of data segments that can be sent is increased by one. When each of those two segments is acknowledged, the transmission window is increased to four. The transmission window called *congestion window* would be increased exponentially, however it is not a true as the server may delay return acknowledgement, for example, by sending one ACK for every two data segments. Each implementation of TCP stack can manage this in different way. Nevertheless, the network has its capacity limit which is observed by the client by packet discarding made by Internet routers. Then the transmission window must be decreased. The congestion avoidance mechanism is activated to improve transfer between communicating parties relaying on networks with different capacities (e.g. a client localized on fast local area network and a server localized on slow wide are network).

Congestion avoidance mechanism and slow start algorithms (however often implemented together) are different algorithms with the same goal. Congestion avoidance is based on the lost packets. The receiver observes the effect of packet loss

by the receipt of duplicate ACKs and occurrence of timeouts. If it occurs then TCP decreases its transmission speed and starts slow start again.

Fast Retransmit is made by TCP when it has to send an immediate acknowledgment in case of receiving an out-of-order data segment. This ACK should not be delayed. Fast Recovery allows starting the congestion avoidance mechanism without slow start. This improves high speed transmissions.

TCP transfer depends on many parameters of protocol implementation, connection behavior during transmission and performance factors that refer directly to client and server functioning. In real-life network experiments we have no ability to go too deeply into protocol, client and server inside design and implementation. Moreover this information is available from three different sources, namely client's side, network and server's side.

In our analysis, as we are concerned on the user's performance view we analyze only these parameters that can be measured and monitored or calculated during file transfers at the client's side. The parameters taken into account in our TCP prediction performance research will be presented in the case study.

TCP Throughput Prediction

TCP protocol throughput prediction is a key issue in current network-based computing. Recent developments in novel computing ideas and paradigms, such as Cloud (Grossman et al., 2009) and Grid computing (Baker et al., 2002; NGG, 2008) are based on using resources as distributed data store providing a transparent access to data wherever it is stored. Data is replicated both for reliability and performance reasons. Then we have to solve the replica selection problem (Rahman et al., 2008) which consists in the question of which replica can be fetched most efficiently. Such replica is the best replica. To select the best replica, we need the predictions of end-to-end transfer times for possible transfers to all candidate servers. By selecting the best replica, the data transfer time can be minimized.

However best replica selection is formulated in the literature as the problem in which all replica servers are monitored all the time and performance historical logs for every end-to-end path are available for estimation of the predicted value of transfer time. The problem is going to be complicated when there is the need to predict the throughput on the end-to-end connection which is still unknown, and any historical performance logs are not available. Is this a real-life problem? Of course it is. For instance, the question is how to predict the performance of Web in case of still "unseen" Web server?

Borzemski and Nowak (2008) discuss that problem and present a solution based on the knowledge about client-to-unseen-server network path meta-data and historical performance measurements carried out to the set of known Web servers. Their model employs Autonomous System topological information to predict performance for unknown Web server. The authors presented the metrics estimating the proximity distance between autonomous systems in Internet from the client's point of view. This distance metrics was used in the nearest neighbor server selection. The nearest neighbor server's performance approximately roughly estimates the performance of unknown server. The proposed prediction algorithm was evaluated using real-life Web measurements and it was shown its good predictive performance and simplicity in calculations.

Transfer time prediction may be of pivotal importance to user's satisfaction, especially, when big-size files are transferred. Transfers in grids, movie downloading may take several minutes or even hours. This time is mainly affected by network conditions (network weather) which in turn be reflected in poor or good TCP throughput. TCP prediction is important for Web transfers as the TCP data transfers are originated by HTTP clients (i.e. Internet browsers) and serviced by HTTP servers (i.e. WWW servers). HTTP based transfers are often short-lived as GET requests are issued for small sized objects many times. As the whole client-to-server communication is organized into Web transactions to get a Web page, the users perceive Web performance through complete Web page downloading. Usually, Web pages have its skeleton (base page) and some number of embedded objects. Embedded objects can be of different sizes and may be stored on different servers.

Data transfer prediction problem defined for short-time transfers performed at HTTP layer has an interest in literature (Tan & Jarvis, 2006; Mellia et al., 2002; Sikdar et al., 2001; Weigle et al., 2005;). More research is in the field of the prediction of bulk transfers (Barford et al., 2007; Claffy et al., 2003; Dovrolis, 2005; Huang & Subhlok, 2005; Rahman et al., 2008; Swany & Wolski, 2002; Vazhkudai & Schopf, 2003). Swany and Wolski (2002) built multivariate predictors by constructing cumulative distribution functions of past history and deriving predictions from them as an alternative to regressive models. Vazhkudai and Schopf (2003) used regression techniques to predict large data transfers and proposed several univariate and multivariate linear regression predictors that can use multiple data sources to improve the accuracy of the predictions using regression models have been developed for grid computing in the context of replica selection in Data Grids. The authors observed that multivariate predictors offer considerable benefits when compared with univariate predictors. Claffy et al. (2003) and Dovrolis (2005) proposed four measurement methods, namely: Variable Packet Size Probing (VPS), Packet Pair/Train Dispersion (PPTD), Self-Loading Periodic Streams (SloPS), and Trains of Packet Pairs (TOPP). In general, they are based on sending packets of a given size in a specifically scheduled manner and calculation of the predicted bandwidth by using inter-arrival times of the returned packets, that is TCP acknowledgement packets. The problem is that they assume that the routers and other network appliances queue arriving packets in the First-Come-First-Served (FCFS) manner what is not always necessarily true. Huang and Subhlok (2005) made use of some knowledge on TCP flow patterns to predict future TCP throughput. The authors differentiated the behavior of TCP transfers taking into account the pattern of changes of the throughput. The throughput is measured in the intervals of RTT, next this constitutes the time series of throughput values that is analyzed to make a forecast. When the file transfer time series resembles a known TCP pattern, this information is utilized for prediction.

INTERNET AND WEB MINING BACKGROUND

Interest in data mining is motivated by the growth of computerized data sets and by the high potential value of patterns discovered in available data collections. We can uncover various data mining applications in science, engineering, business, industry, and medicine (Bhatia et al., 2007; Bose & Mahapatra, 2001; Chakrabarti, 2003; Chen et al., 1996; Chu et al., 2008; Czyzowicz et al., 2003; Fürnkranz, 2005; Mahanta et al., 2008; Manganaris et al., 2000; Wu & Yen, 2008; Zhang et al., 2003). Today's typical application of data mining to Web related issues is Web mining (Borzemski & Druszcz, 2006; Chakrabarti, 2003; Cho et al., 2002; El-Ramly & Stroulia, 2004; Facca & Lanzi, 2005; Grossman et al, 2001; Han & Chang, 2002; Lee & Yen, 2008; Li et al., 2008; Nasrouri et al., 2006; Pandey & Mishra, 2006; Spiliopoulou, 2000; Spiliopoulou & Pohle, 2001; Srivastava et al., 2000; Sterne, 2002; Tan & Kumar, 2002; Velásquez & Palade, 2007; Wang et al., 2005; Xing & Shen, 2004; Zhang & Dong, 2002; Zhang et al., 2007; Zhang & Yin, 2008).

Web mining focuses on four main research areas, namely: *Web content mining, Web usage mining, Web structure mining* and *Web user pro-*

file mining. Web mining uses such data sources as Web documents (usually text and graphics), Web data logs in Extended Log File format (W3C, 2008) available from Web servers (containing Internet Protocol (IP) addresses, access date and time, object characterization), data describing the Web structure (i.e. HTML and XML tags), and Web user profile data. Web content mining discovers what Web pages are about and reveals new knowledge from them. Web usage mining concerns the identification of patterns in user navigation through Web pages and is performed for the reasons of service personalization, system improvement, and usage characterization. Web structure mining investigates how the Web documents are structured, and discovers the model underlying the link structures of the WWW. Web user profile mining discovers user's profiles based on users' behavior on the Web.

Data mining and knowledge discovery may have a potentially great impact on computer network development and exploitation what we can see even in first early works (Faloutsos & Faloutsos, 2002; Faloutsos et al., 1999; Garofalakis & Rastogi, 2002; Hellerstein et al., 2001). However this research did not deal with the performance problems which are usually treated by analytical and simulation modeling supported by classical statistical data analysis.

Data Sources

Web data sources can be server-side and client-side. They store and report Web activity in very different ways. They collect different information and may not always match. Both data sources can be effectively used in Web mining according to particular study needs (Pabarskaite & Raudys, 2007; Wu et al., 2004). Considering the taxonomy of passive and active network measurements they are experiments in which we only passively collect data without any possibility to control the experiment to gain its usefulness in Web performance analysis.

Web servers store records of the traffic and information requests in server-side log files. These log files include information on resources accessed, errors, processing times, users' IP addresses as well as other data describing user and server operating environments.

Web servers provide logs in either the common log format CLF or a proprietary format. Each CLF record in this log has the following structure: remotehost rfc931 authuser [date] request status bytes, where remotehost is the IP address or name of the client (remote host), rfc931 is remote log name of user (almost always "-" meaning "unknown"), authuser is the authenticated username, date is the date and time of the completion of the request, request - first line of the request including the HTTP method and URL, status - HTTP response status code (200, 304, ...), and bytes is the number of bytes in the response.

CLF (W3C, 2008) files can be analyzed by common analysis tools but unfortunately the information about each server transaction is not enough in many cases.

Some of these needs are met by the W3C Extended Log File format which contains the following fields (W3C, 2008): Date, Time, Client IP Address, User Name, Service Name and Instance Number, Server Name, Server IP Address, Server Port, Method, URI Stem, URI Query, HTTP Status, Win32 Status, Bytes Sent, Bytes Received, Time Taken, Protocol Version, Host, User Agent, Cookie, Referrer, and Protocol Substatus.

The extended log file format gives description about the following events: the date on which the activity occurred; the time, in coordinated universal time (UTC), at which the activity occurred; the IP address of the client that made the request; the name of the authenticated user who accessed your server; the Internet service name and instance number that was running on the client; the name of the server on which the log file entry was generated; the IP address of the server on which the log file entry was generated; the server

port number that is configured for the service; the requested action, for example, a GET method; the target of the action, for example, Default. htm; the query, if any, that the client was trying to perform; the HTTP status code; the Windows status code (implementation for Windows); the number of bytes that the server sent; the number of bytes that the server received; the length of time that the action took, in milliseconds; the protocol version - HTTP or FTP - that the client used; the host header name; the browser type that the client used; the content of the cookie sent or received; the site that the user last visited, and the substatus error code, respectively. This format permits control over the data records in log file, supports the needs of proxies, clients and servers in a common format, provides robust handling of character escaping issues, allows exchange of demographic data, and allows summary data to be expressed.

Client-side logging data can also be taken into account in Web usage analysis. This is rather limited source of performance knowledge as it is closely related to the activity of particular users, and requires placing a small invisible JavaScript on every Web page that is to be tracked. Also users' browsers must be cookie unable. As users access such page this code places standard cookies on users' computers and the users can be tracked in real-time this way.

However, none of these logs are not suitable for our aim as they do not contain systematically collected performance information how HTTP protocol uses the TCP network from the perspective of user-side. What information (data format) is needed in our predictive analysis is shown in Figure 2. It is not available in any of known Web log formats. To obtain information in proposed in Figure 2 data format we need to develop a particular performance related experiment design as well as a specific active measurement infrastructure that could be installed at user-side.

Figure 2. Time parameters of Web transaction

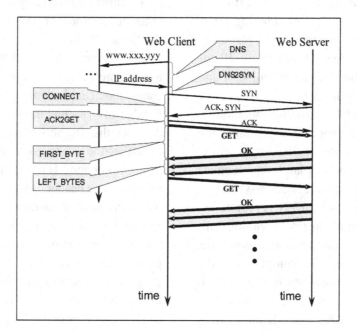

Data Preparation

Data exploration is a multistage process, which discovers and evaluates appropriate problems to find solutions and produce meaningful and actionable results for decision making. In data exploration we can distinguish the following phases: exploration of the problem space, exploration of the solution space, specification of implementation method and mining the data (Pyle, 1999). Data mining which is a key phase in data exploration starts with data preparation step. Data preparation is a necessary and crucial step in data mining and it can possibly take even 60% of total time to complete. Fifteen percent of the relative importance to success of data mining project comes from the data preparation step (Pyle, 1999). After preparing data we can continue data mining by means of data surveying and finally, data modeling.

Generally, data preparation includes techniques concerned with analyzing raw data so as to yield quality data, mainly including data collecting, data integration, data transformation, data cleaning, data reduction, and data discretization. Web

and Internet data sources may require among commonly used data preparation methods, the specific data preparation techniques which are closely related to the domain which is under study. Many of them, mostly heuristic, need the implementation and usage of additional analysis tools (Cooley, Mobasher & Srivastava, 1999; Zhang, S. et al., 2003), designed usually with the help of scripting languages, such as Pearl (Pearl, 2009) and Python (Python, 2009).

Preparation of Web server log files for mining may require removal of irrelevant and duplicate requests, resolving IP addresses into host names, definition of session, removal of robot requests, and differentiation of individual users staying behind the same proxy and NAT information, and many other specific data preparation. Although some particular analysis need may require, for example, not to remove robot requests, but to identify these requests as it was done in (Tan & Kumar, 2002). Data preparation is usually closely related to the problem and solution under consideration, and should be individually designed and performed in each mining case.

To illustrate the data preparation problem in Web mining, let us consider our work that has been done for Web server logs collected during the FIFA Cup in 1998. We used FIFA logs to discover usage profiles (Borzemski & Druszcz, 2006). The discovered profiles may be used, for example, to personalize a Web site and to deploy Web recommendation systems.

The FIFA logs available on the network have been initially prepared by HP Lab researchers (Arlit & Jin, 2000) from the real raw Web logs collected from 30 April to 26 July of 1998. During this period 1,352,804,107 HTTP requests were collected on thirty HTTP servers distributed globally over four locations: Paris, France; Plano, Texas, U.S.; Herndon, Virginia, U.S., and Santa Clara, California, U.S.

The logs from these servers were merged into a single sequence of requests sorted by the time of receiving of the request. The created set of data was not suitable for further analyses because of the size. Therefore it was divided into segments containing entries from one day. Data referring to one day were additionally segmented into partitions, each including seven millions requests at most.

The row source data available on the network (Arlit & Jin, 2000) was not suitable for our Web usage mining because it contained some extra and redundant information that had to be filtered out. This data file had to be cleaned before mining and prepared to be used by specific data mining software package. Four-stage data preparation procedure implemented by a means of Pearl scripts has been developed.

Stage 1

In Web usage analysis we are interested only in the main document entries. Therefore, we need to select the file entries referring to the main documents. Each Web log keeps information about individual objects/files instead of direct information about the Web documents (pages) containing theses objects. In case of requesting Web page containing e.g. images, sounds or films, we obtain in log the entries referring to the main document (usually with *html* or *htm* extension), as well as entries related to all objects embedded in that document.

However, we have found that some entries that could be classified as the main documents were retrieved multiple times together with other one. They were named in the following way: *nav_inet. html*, *nav_top_inet.html*, and *splash_inet.html*. Because the page map of the site was not available at the moment of our analysis, we could not exactly define the role of these entries. But after further analysis of the names of files and their addresses we discovered that this situation could be due to the frame structure used in the construction of the main documents. Hence, we could delete them as they did not add any new information in Web usage analysis. Therefore, the filtering script selected entries referring to documents with the *htm* or *html* extensions, with the exclusion of *nav_inet. html*, *nav_top_inet.html*, *splash_inet. html* documents.

Stage 2

Next, we have to identify the users and user sessions. The users were recognized on the basis of the user unique identifiers. Each identifier in a data file prepared by Arlit and Jin (2000) referred to the original user IP address and was generated by them make the log compact, and to protect user privacy. We could not know these IP addresses. Therefore, we defined user sessions in another way, taking into account the idle time between consecutive requests. The session was assumed to be a new one if the idle time is greater than some assumed threshold. The threshold idle time value was set to 30 minutes and was determined as the compromise between the number of possible sessions and their lengths within the request partitions, each including seven millions requests.

Stage 3

As it was already mentioned, the user identification in analyzed FIFA Web log is based on the IP address used in the request. Such a solution does not fully guarantee the correct user identification because a single IP address can be used by many users. This is due to the proxy server and NAT (Network Address Translation) technologies widely used in Internet. To determine entries for the individual users, we had to reject Proxy server and NAT entries. Such users were recognized in our analysis as ones with too many open documents in the same session. Therefore, the users with more then 15 open documents were classified as proxy users and appropriate entries were filter out from the log.

Stage 4

At this stage, our Pearl scripts filled the log in some additional information required in further mining such as the day number, the session number, and the request number in the session, as well as the session length. Finally, due to the requirements of mining algorithms, each one-day log was formatted into two relational tables: (i) type_1 table with the records containing all data referring to a single request, and (ii) type_2 table containing in a single record the whole sequence of requests from a user in a single session. Type_1 tables were utilized when discovering association rules and revealing sequence patterns. Type_2 tables were used in clustering.

In the cases presented further in this chapter we show how some specific data preparation issues were solved.

Web Layer Performance

In case of Web, typically we deal with the HTTP traces collected in passive Web measurements at some network point which is usually located in Web server. HTTP traces are usually captured in Web server logs which are the primary data sources in Web mining.

Web performance is extremely difficult to study in an integrated way. Web layer performance we may consider either at client or server side. It has never been easy to determine whether slow responses from Web servers are due to either network problems or end-system problems on both sides, and both. Most of these performance problems are transient and very complex in the relationships between different factors that may influence each other; therefore we cannot exactly diagnose and isolate their key sources. Cardellini et al. (2002) presenting solutions for HTTP requests distribution argued that almost 60% latency, as perceived by end-users at their microscopic level, refers to the end-to-end path network latency. Thus understanding the network performance problems to evaluate Web layer behavior is very important.

At first, we can use RTT-like metrics, but determined at the Web layer. Secondly, we need to use more powerful performance metrics which could be the data transfer throughput achievable at Web layer when Web pages are retrieved. Thus we need a measurement tool to monitor TCP transfers invoked by HTTP protocol. This knowledge is not directly known in current client and server developments.

Ping-based technique accomplished at Internet layer is useless at Web layer and we need another method for network latency estimation that would be done at HTTP layer. Our proposal is based on the analysis of the communication process which is performed at this layer between Web client and Web server. Web uses TCP protocol for data delivery. TCP connections are established by Web clients and we propose to use the estimation technique based on the measurements of time spacing between the SYN packet sent by the client and the SYN-ACK packet received by the client in response from destination Web server. Although this delay is not strictly the RTT of the path, it is a good estimation of the RTT from the perspective of

Web client. Note, that this kind of network latency estimation is used by the TCP protocol itself. To estimate the effective throughput of the TCP connection we measure time spacing between the first byte packet and the last byte packet of the object received by the client using that connection. The proposed measurement scheme of network latency and throughput is realized in WING and MWING systems which we describe later on.

Predictive Data Mining

The prediction of Internet and Web performance has been always a challenging and topical issue (Abusina et al., 2005; Arlit et al., 2005; He et al., 2007; Vazhkudai & Schopf, 2002; Vazhkudai & Schopf, 2003). The aim of predictive analysis is to explore current and past historical data to find a model to make predictions about future events. In Internet and Web the predictive models often perform calculations in real-time, in order to guide needed decision, what states additional requirements against approaches that can be applied in the area, which can be generally stated as the applicability of proposed methods and solutions in real-life networks. Predictive models can be built by means of various techniques from statistics and data mining. Former methods are discussed in TCP throughput section of this chapter. Here we deal with the latter methods.

The users may need both short-term and long-term network performance forecasts. Short-term forecasting requires instantaneous measuring of network performance to have available information on the most current network behavior. In long-term forecasting we usually analyze historical information available in prediction window, which can often move in time and change in its size.

Different predictive analysis schemes have been devised in the literature and practical applications, from straightforward to complex ones. Disregarding the discussion performed among statisticians and data miners about taxonomy and

originality of predictive data analysis methods; basically, we can consider data mining based methods that include regression and machine learning techniques such as Neural Networks (NN), Support Vector (learning) Machines (SVMs), K-Neighbor Classifiers, Naïve Bayes, Time Series, Classification and Regression Trees (CART), Regression Methods. Among them we are especially interested in multivariate data analysis techniques that are able to take into account multiple analysis inputs and make the prediction using all of them. They should be actionable, simply, reasonable, as fast as possible and precise in prediction decisions.

Examples of this research are current works on the prediction of large file transfer. Barford et al. (2007) used active measurements and collected history-based data as inputs to Support Regression Vector (SRV) method to construct a prediction. The input parameters include queuing information, available bandwidth and packet loss. However the queuing measurement implies administrative access to the server and/or routers on the way what is not a realistic assumption on the Internet. Rahman et al. (2008) compared neural network and multi-regression based file transfer prediction methods in replica selection in data Grid environment. The predicted transfer time was used as an estimate of transfer bandwidth of different sites that hold replica currently, and helped in selecting the best replica among different sites. They showed that the neural network predictive technique estimates the transfer time among sites more accurately than the multi-regression model.

Two specific prediction techniques have been successfully used in our prior research on Internet and Web performance prediction, namely the Transfer Regression and classification trees. Transfer Regression (TR) algorithm was invented by Pednault (Pednault, 2006) and nicely implemented in the IBM DB2 Intelligent Miner data mining software (IBM, 2008). TR algorithm joins efficiency, non-parametrization and automatization of decision trees with the flexibility of neural networks. Regression analysis is value-based and we are able to predict the value of the dependent variable in a response of independent variables. These methods build the regression models showing the relationship between the dependent variable and a set of independent variables. We used TR algorithm in the prediction of the TCP throughput in transfers of data big files (Borzemski & Starczewski, 2009).

Classification algorithms are class-based. Using classification trees we can predict a class from the set of available and previously defined classes on the basis of the analysis of the classification tree that are formed by a collection of rules based on values of certain variables in the modeling data set. Classes are to be defined and known before classification. We used clustering mining function to define classes. In our approach, the classification algorithms use classes which define the characteristic behavior of chosen variables related to network conditions.

PROPOSED MODEL OF WEB TRANSACTION

This section presents our model of client-to-server interaction at Web layer. Although a client issues one request at a time for a Web page, he or her usually causes multiple client-to-server interactions because retrieving one Web page will impose, on the average, 1+n accesses on the WWW server (1 access to get the HTML base file and n accesses to get n embedded resources). All these interactions are refereed to us as HTTP requests, or simply as requests. These accesses are organized in *Web transactions*.

Figure 2 shows a timeline chart of a simple Web transaction (Borzemski 2006a) we define and take into account in our Web measurement schema and further prediction analysis. The Web transactions can be freely complex, though they are always composed from the basic client-to-server communication patterns as shown in Figure 2. Web page has skeleton and possible objects

embedded. They can be downloaded from different servers; the redirection occurs during the browsing phase. The client's browser may also employ more advanced HTTP protocol functions such as connection persistency and pipelining to speed up page downloading.

HTTP protocol uses TCP protocol connections while Web page retrieval. A typical TCP transfer experiences three phases: the connection establishment phase, the slow start phase and the steady state phase (Comer, 2008). The connection is established after sending the SYN packet and receiving the SYN+ACK packet. During the measurement we obtain full knowledge about receiving packets, packet losses, and retransmissions.

Web transaction starts with IP address determination. IP address can be obtained from local cache memory or from Internet's Domain Name Service (DNS) which is responsible for mapping the server domain names into actual IP addresses. Sometimes, this operation may take much time and deeply influence on the whole Web transaction. After DNS time the browser is able to operate immediately with the target server but sometimes it waits DNS2SYN time. After that there is the time to open the TCP connection which is required for client-to-server data transfer. This connection is used for sending control messages and data stored in packets.

The connection begins when a client sends the connection packet SYN, and ends when the connection is established, that is, when the server receives SYN+ACK packet from the client. The client cooperates with the server in so-called three-way handshaking mechanism. The elapsed time between transmitting the SYN to the server and receiving the SYN response is the connection delay which we call the CONNECT time. CONNECT time is the RTT between client and server. Now the TCP connection is ready for data transmitting. This is the browsing phase of Web transaction.

Data transfers are initiated by the browser by sending successive GET requests. There can be another delay in browser action, namely ACK2GET time, which is the time spending by the browser after receiving ACK respond and up to sending first GET request. The GET request can be for a base page (HTML) or an object embedded in a page. The FIRST_BYTE is the time between the sending of GET request and the reception of the first packet including requested Web resource. The LEFT_BYTES is the time spent for downloading the rest (if any) of the requested object. Further GET requests are issued by the browser according to the Web base page definition, and conditions how the browser and server employ TCP connections.

It is worth to mention that in our Web transaction model, unlike to other developments in the field (Hasegawa et al., 1999; Tan & Jarvis, 2006), we take into account DNS2SYN and ACK2GET times as Web transaction components.

We should take into account the periodic character of Internet. This was evidenced many times by web and network logs. Hellerstein et al. (2001) showed that the number of HTTP operations per second is non-stationary, and its five-minute mean changes with time-of-day and day-of-week. It was also showed that time-of-day explains 53% of the variability in the raw data of HTTP transactions whereas adding day-of-week and month we reach only 64% of the variability in the data.

We should also be conscious that many network and non-network events may effect on path performance. Most of them are beyond our control and knowledge, however some knowledge of these events should be included in a knowledge-based data mining. However until now this knowledge is not taken into account. We use only the knowledge which can be derived from the measurement data.

WING AND MWING MEASUREMENT SYSTEMS

To monitor Web transactions and to perform other types of network measurements we have developed two measurement systems: WING (Borzemski, 2006a; Borzemski & Nowak, 2004b) and MWING (Borzemski et al., 2007).

WING

The WING (Web pING) has been developed for visualization and performance analysis of Web transactions. The emphasis in the WING project was to develop a Web measurement system for supporting real-life usage of Internet browsers such as Microsoft's Internet Explorer, Firefox or Opera. The main WING location is Wroclaw University of Technology (WUT) campus computer network, Wrocław, Poland. Thus system perceives Web performance from the perspective of WUT users.

WING (Figure 3) measures, visualizes and stores all Web page download time components defined in Figure 2. WING supports IP, TCP, and UDP, DNS and HTTP protocols, logging a dozen parameters of HTTP transactions and TCP connections, thus facilitating a much deeper analysis. The information about lost and repeated packets is stored, as well.

WING works like a sonar-location system, sending requests for target Web page and waiting for the answer. The answer is monitored on local network and tracing is done on the raw IP packages level. WING controller monitors and time stamps of all the browser's actions, determines the end of the Web page uploading, and pre-process gathered data into the format convenient for fur-

Figure 3. WING architecture

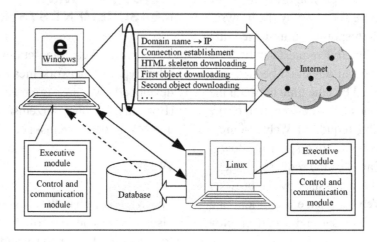

ther statistical and data mining analysis, as well as for visualization. After tracing, the browsing time chart is reconstructed, the result Web page is returned to the client and displayed by user's browser. The design of local monitoring is based on the TCPdump protocol packet capture program that allows recording of network traffic that flows through network. Data is stored in a relational DB2 database (IBM, 2008).

WING can be used to perform either instant or periodic measurements. In instant mode WING downloads to WING's location a target Web page which was asked by the user. In this mode the system returns to the user a Web page showing an HTTP timeline chart of the target Web page as well as detailed, and some aggregated information about target downloading to WING's location. In periodic measurements WING targets Web pages on the basis of given list of URL addresses, and a programmable time schedule. Data are collected in a relational database. The periodic mode was used by us to collect datasets to data mining performance analysis (see Cases 2 and 3).

The details of design and functioning of WING system, as well as sample usages, the reader can find in our previous papers (Borzemski & Nowak, 2004a; Borzemski & Nowak, 2004b; Borzemski, 2006a, Borzemski, 2008).

MWING

MWING (Multiagent WING) is our newest system developed for distributed network measurements (Borzemski et al., 2007). MING general architecture is shown in Figure 4. It follows a multi-agent design paradigm to obtain the ability to locate and run measurement agents (sensors) wherever we need – the only local requirement is to build an agent's program capable to run under Linux operating system.

System consists of the controller component OpHost and Agent Sets. OpHost is a unique system node that features some central functions to the whole system. OPHost consists of the DataBase component organizing a central database, Web Applications component enabling user interface to the system, Operation Services component managing connectivity and data synchronization between OPHost and agents, and DB Synch component synchronizing central and local databases. Each Agent Set include the following components: Scheduler, HeartBeat, Operation Controller, Local DataBase, NTP Synch and Measurement Operation. Scheduler activates measurements according to schedules programmed according to the experiment needs. HeartBeat provides means to verify the continual operation of an agent. Operation Controller orchestrates local actions.

Figure 4. MWING architecture

Local DataBase organizes a local database. NTP Synch synchronizes an agent activity with a global network time to allow synchronized measurements performed by different agents. Measurement Operation orchestrates all measurement events constituting an experiment and gathers raw measurement results.

Agent's functionality is fully open and is defined by individual agent's functional specification. An agent can measure the network actively or passively. It can define and use own network measures. Agents can perform independent or coordinated measurements. Agents can collect and aggregate data locally or in a central localization which is developed for this purpose. Of course, agents can react on local conditions. The experiment plans of each MWING agent as well as the plan of the whole experiment can be freely programmed.

Now we are focused on the distributed measurement project to collect data for the time and spatial analysis showing how the same Web servers are perceived from different Internet locations.

REAL-LIFE EXPLORATORY CASES

We have explored Internet and Web performance issues in various real-life cases. In this section

we present 2 examples from our research. First example presents IPM analysis whereas the second shows WPM case.

Case 1

Experiment Setup

In Internet Performance Mining we exploited data measurable at the communication layer including the Round-Trip Time (RTT) and routing information (Borzemski, 2007). RTT tells us how long a network packet goes from a source to target host and back again. Routing information shows which routers have been visited while transmission.

The network performance was studied on the basis of traceroute and reverse traceroute measurements conducted between WUT location and the following target servers: icfamon.dl.ac.uk, www. sdsc.edu, umaxp1.physics.isa.umich.edu, alf.nbi. dk, katherine.physics.umd.edu, v2.ph.gla.ac.uk, cgi.cs.wisc.edu, and netdb3.es.net. The servers were probed every half an hour over 46 weeks in 2003/2004 (Borzemski, 2004). The source host named szafir.ists.pwr.wroc.pl with IP address 156.17.130.49 run in WUT computer network. The measurements were done and collected by the IBM RISC/6000 F80 computer running AIX 4.3.3 and DB2 8.1 database. Here we show the measurement results obtained for the destination host at the Glasgow University in Scotland named v2.ph.gla.ac.uk and available at the time of measurements at IP address 194.36.1.69.

Data Source and Data Preprocessing

Data mining was done using the IBM Intelligent Miner for Data 8.1 (IBM, 2008) and DB2 8.1 database. The traces were stored in dedicated table in relational database. A row (record) of relational table contained: either the IP address, the IP path hop count and the RTT to the destination, or the IP address, the IP path hop count and RTT of intermediate routers that responded on the path traversed by the probe packets from the source to the destination host. Each record was stamped by the time of the day, day of the week, day of the month and month of the year of the probe.

The initial preprocessing involved cleansing raw data and raw data transformations to prepare data for further processing. Only non-error transactions were used in data mining. Data was checked to avoid missing and invalid field values. Missing RTT and HOP values were estimated as averages. After the cleaning phase we obtained the database with 5004 records. Each record had the following fields: the time stamp of the measurement, the hour of day (HOUR $\in$ {0, 1, 2, 3,..., 23}), the day of week (DAY $\in$ {1, 2, 3, 4, 5, 6, 7}, where 1 denotes Monday and so on), the length of the path between source host (156.17.130.49) and destination host (194.36.1.69), i.e. the number of hops (HOP $\in$ {1, 2,...,30}) as well as three samples of the average RTT. The value of RTT used in further analysis was the average value calculated from these three samples.

In preprocessing phase we had to make a domain based data preanalysis. First, we made the discretization of continuous variable RTT. The quantiles (buckets) for the discretization of RTT data were automatically generated in an automated fashion by Intelligent Miner based on the standard deviation width technique. This method worked

well and the result was satisfactory. Intelligent Miner built an equal-width data-driven even partitioning for a range of continuous variable between two cut-points Low and High that stood out two end quantiles: (-∞ - Low] and [High - +∞). Both ends intervals might contain the outliers to filter out. The values of the RTT at the intermediate cut-points were determined and data was divided into equal-width N quantiles. Therefore the whole variable range was always divided into $N+2$ quantiles. Cut-points were well-established values, such as 25, 50, 75 or 100 because a range [50 - 75] looked more natural than [51.80 − 75.92]. In the sample of 5004 records the whole range of possible RTT values was discretized into 18 quantiles using the following breakpoints: 25, 50, 75, 100, 125, 150, ..., 375, 400, and 425 ms. RTT values were limited by the value 10.000 ms which was used to mark of situation that the host/router did not respond before the time limit specified by the traceroute tool.

The following three intervals to interpret the RTT behaviors were categorized: *Low* if RTT < 50 ms, *Medium* if 50 ms $\leq$ RTT $\leq$ 150 ms and *High* if RTT > 150 ms. The best weather is when RTT is low, fine and acceptable when medium, and bad when high.

Mining Algorithms

The performance prediction method we suggest to use in this case is based on the use, one after another, of two data mining techniques. We use a clustering data mining function followed by classification function in such a way that the results of clustering are the inputs to classification. Some constraint in our analysis was the assumption we have made, namely we can use only algorithms implemented in Intelligent Miner for Data software.

Our Web performance mining methodology in presented case assumed that by means of clustering function we can segment measurement data into groups which were classes of the network behavior whereas the classification can build a decision-making structure (that is a decision tree) based on past measurements to make classification decisions for unseen future cases.

Clustering addresses segmentation problems and assigns data records described by a set of attributes into a set of groups of records called "clusters". This process is performed automatically by clustering algorithms that identify the distinguishing characteristics of the dataset and then partition the space defined by the dataset attributes along natural cleaving boundaries.

One of the disadvantages of cluster models is that there are no explicit rules to define each cluster and there is no clear understanding of how the model assigns data to clusters. The clustering result cannot be easily used in advising to use particular Internet path. Therefore, we employ the classification mining function in the next step of building the model.

Clustering is one of the most important methods of the data exploration. It complies both as the independent method for the purpose to insight into the data, as well as the stage of the preprocessing with further algorithms and analyses. IBM Intelligent Miner for Data has implemented two clustering methods: *Demographic Clustering* and *Neural Clustering* (IBM, 2008).

The clustering based on the demographic function creates clusters across iterative comparing of the value in every following data record with values of data records from earlier formed clusters. The given data record is credited to this group whose elements are most similar to him alone. The number of clusters can be fixed themselves automatically, though the user can define their maximum number.

The clustering based on neural networks uses the Kohonen Feature Map neural network which belongs to self-organizing networks in which the learning takes place without supervision. This kind of clustering algorithm was used to find the groups of similar measurement results in our input mining base.

The clustering algorithm may have several passes. We restricted the number of passes to 20. Specifying multiple passes through the input data improves the quality of the generated clusters but also extends the processing time required to perform clustering. We also restricted the number of clusters to be generated up to 16 in order to find accurate and homogenous groups of objects and simultaneously avoiding the production of too many small clusters.

In the second mining stage we considered the use of two classification mining functions available in IBM's system, namely *Tree-Induction* algorithm and *Neural Classification* function. In our opinion the human understanding of the learned rules is a crucial aspect of data mining. Also we think that the mining results must be actionable. Therefore, we prefer to use the decision tree approach. A tree can be easily converted to a rule set by traversing each path from the root to each leaf node. Moreover, unlike neural networks, trees are easy to understand and modify.

Therefore in the next mining step we proposed to build the decision tree. CART-like Tree-Induction algorithm as implemented in Intelligent Miner was used as a technique for creation rules distinguishing between clusters for new observations. A particular feature of CART is that decision rules are represented via easy for interpretation and implementation binary trees.

Results and Discussion

Table 2 shows a part of the clustering result. In the textual description of the clustering results the discrete numerical fields DAY, HOUR and HOP are described by their moral values counted among all records belonging to the cluster. IM4D uses the term "predominantly" for showing the highest frequency value.

General statistical analysis showed that for 61% of all records the RTT was medium and HOP was predominantly 20. The analysis showed that 17% of records exhibited high RTT. They

Table 2. Textual overview of first ten top clusters

Cluster	Size (%)	Cluster Description
14	7.93%	RTT is high, DAY is predominantly 3, HOP is predominantly 19 an HOUR is predominantly 16.
3	7.79%	DAY is predominantly 1, HOUR is predominantly 2, HOP is predominantly 20 and RTT is medium.
7	7.69%	DAY is predominantly 1, HOUR is predominantly 9, HOP is predominantly 20 and RTT is medium.
12	7.05%	DAY is predominantly 7, HOUR is predominantly 23, RTT is medium and HOP is predominantly 20.
8	6.97%	DAY is predominantly 7, HOUR is predominantly 15, RTT is medium and HOP is predominantly 20.
4	6.91%	DAY is predominantly 7, HOUR is predominantly 11, RTT is medium and HOP is predominantly 20.
0	6.89%	DAY is predominantly 7, HOUR is predominantly 1, RTT is medium and HOP is predominantly 20.
6	6.29%	DAY is predominantly 3, HOUR is predominantly 7, RTT is medium and HOP is predominantly 19.
1	6.20%	DAY is predominantly 5, HOUR is predominantly 5, HOP is predominantly 20 and RTT is medium.
5	6.18%	DAY is predominantly 4, HOUR is predominantly 7, RTT is medium and HOP is predominantly 19.

were grouped into Clusters 14 (the biggest one), Cluster 15 and Cluster 2. For these clusters HOP was predominantly 19, i.e. one hop less than on average. 12.5% of records was characterizing by HOP=19 and medium RTT. For 9.5% of records RTT was medium and HOP was predominantly 21 (Clusters 10 and 11), i.e. one hop more than on average.

Cluster 14 which was the biggest one (7.93% of total population) included the set of records where RTT was high (modal value is 200-225 ms), DAY was predominantly 3, HOP was predominantly 19, and HOUR was predominantly 16.

Cluster 3 (7.79%), the second biggest cluster, featured the set of records where DAY was predominantly 1, HOUR was predominantly 2, HOP was predominantly 20, and RTT was medium (modal value is 50-75 ms).

More details about clusters can be derived from data, for instance, for Cluster 14. Namely, about 42% of measurements belonging to that cluster were performed on Wednesday (DAY=3), and 39% on Thursday (DAY=4). The measurements

were performed mostly between 12:00 and 23:00 (98%) with the predominant hour 16:00 (12%). The other 2% of records included the remaining twelve values of the HOUR field. Cluster 14 characterized bad network conditions as RTT was high. RTT>150 ms was for 89% of records in this cluster. The interval 200 - 225 ms had the highest frequency (14%). Each of the RTT ranges 175-200, 275-300, 300- 325 ms included 12% of records. Clusters 2 and 15 had similar RTT characteristics.

Each cluster defines a class of network behavior. The description of clusters shows how the clusters differ from each other and from the total population. However, that clustering result is not easy for use as a decision guide. To improve predictive decision-making, we employ the classification mining function in the next step of building the model.

The obtained decision tree consists of well-defined rules, which could be easily applied to the decision making how to use the network. Terminal nodes represent classes of network behavior, i.e.

clusters obtained in the previous mining phase. To reach specific class we can traverse down paths through the tree, starting from the root node, and process the test outcomes in intermediate internal nodes, so that the terminal node is the result of forecasting. Each such path defines the *if-then* rule that is easy to understand and implement in real-life decision-making.

Returning to our case, for example, if the user would plan to transfer data on Saturdays or Sundays morning between 6 and 11 o'clock then he or she might expect fine network behaviour because such network behavior forecast could be read from the following rule: *If (DAY ≥ 5.5) and (HOUR < 11.5) and (HOUR ≥ 5.5) then* Cluster = 4. Such conclusion can be derived from cluster characterization - Cluster 4 is characterized by medium RTT which is a fine network behavior by assumption.

Further analysis showed that we can extract the general decision rule characterizing high and medium behavior for studied Internet path, namely:

If [(DAY = 3) *and* (11.5 ≤ HOUR < 16.5)]
or [(DAY = 4) *and* (15.5 ≤ HOUR < 19.5)]
then RTT = High *else* RTT = Medium.

In the context of the classification accuracy measure our classifier was evaluated quite positively as we validated the classification accuracy by new samples at level 67-74% in accordance to dataset division into training and test set. We also evaluated our approach whether the decision was actionable? Our database naturally is continuously expanding which can invalidate discovered patterns and introduce new ones. Therefore we studied two history-based re-execution schemes, namely an *incremental window* and *moving window*. The former scheme assumes that at each re-execution point a dataset includes whole historical data available. The latter scheme consists in the analysis of historical data available within a time window ending at re-execution point.

In incremental window data mining we used one week increment. Thus the dataset size varied from 1 to 46 weeks. The result showed that more data give better classification, achieving around 92% for ten last re-executions. For small datasets the prediction accuracy fluctuates what is can be the result of changes in the network behavior, whereas these changes were not so influential and we observed the "smoothing" effect at the reasonable level of the prediction accuracy.

After analyzing all window sizes in moving window scheme we have found that four week window gives pretty high accuracies, on average, 91% (RTT) and 96% (HOP). Bigger windows did not significantly improve the result and might be too long for justified network monitoring. Very small window (one week) was not enough for prediction.

Case 2

Experiment Setup

In this example of Web performance mining analysis we show the classification-based predictive model describing performance as perceived by Web clients (Borzemski, 2006b).

In compliance with our assumptions, the research had to be subjected a group of dispersed on the Internet WWW servers. To simplify determination of throughput and to limit the errors one decided that from every server would be gained a resource about the same size. One assumed that the size of the resource should be so, that the time of the transmission makes possible to determine the throughput and simultaneously the transmission would not burden excessively the network and servers.

Queries for such resource were carried out by means of Google search engine. Among different proposals on finding dispersed servers fulfilling our criteria, we have chosen repositories of RFC (*Request for Comments*) documents, *as a* result from the following reasons. RFCes are mainly published in text files, therefore every one is the separate Web resource. The file size one can earlier know from the IETF (*Internet Engineering Task Force*) catalogue. Finally, these kinds of documents are accessed rather by a limited number of users, so one can expect that they can be usually found on non-overloaded servers.

The most popular and accessible on the maximum quantity of servers was RFC2616 document containing the specification of the protocol HTTP/1.1. However, because of too large size of this document, we have chosen the file RFC1945. txt about the size of 137582 bytes and containing the specification of the protocol HTTP/1.0. File rfc1945.txt is large enough (its original size is 137582 bytes) to estimate average transfer rate, and yet not too large to overload Internet links and target Web servers. We have found this file on 209 Web servers. Trial measurements showed that some of 209 servers were dead because the DNS service could not resolve IP address based on server's URL. Other problems were due to the lack of HTTP functionality available on the TCP port specified by given URL or the absence of specified file at given URL. We also omitted servers reporting files with the same name but with a different than assumed size. Finally, we obtained the set of 83 servers localized in the following Internet domains: US, NL, AT, AU, BE, CA, CH, CN, UK, PH, CZ, DE, FI, FR, HU, IT, JP, KR, NO, NZ, ZA, ID, PL, PT, RU, SE, SK, TW, GB, and UK. More than 20% of them were in US. In this chapter we use data collected through almost one year period in 2002/2003 when these servers were probed from WUT location at regular intervals of 2h 40 minutes, i.e. ten times a day over 24-hour period.

More information about the experiment testbed and statistical data analysis of the measurements was given in (Borzemski and Nowak 2004b). The same experiment and collected data were used in the mining analysis aiming at the comparison of the predictive modeling capabilities of IBM Miner for Data and Microsoft SQL Server 2005 data mining software systems (Borzemski et al., 2008).

Data Source and Data Preprocessing

For each transaction we measured 20 attributes, including: DATETIME – date and time of probing, CONNECT – time interval for setting the TCP connection with Web server (this is RTT), DNS – time interval for IP address resolving, FIRSTBYTE – time between the end of issuing HTTP request to Web server and the beginning of obtaining of the first data packet, REDIRECTS – time between start of measurement and automatic redirection, INDEXFILE – time interval needed for HTML skeleton download, START_MS – time interval between the start of probing and sending a packet, IP_ADDRESS – IP address of Web server which was probed, PACKET_OK – number of received correct packets, PACKET_NOK – number of received incorrect packets, DNS2SYN – time between the end of DNS communication and start of the TCP connection to the Web server, ACK2GET – time between receiving the acknowledgement of the connection establishment and issuing a HTTP request, THROUGHPUT – throughput in kilobits per second, AVG_PING – average RTT based on three probes, WEEKDAY – day of the week when probing is taken, HOUR – hour when probing was taken, and ERROR_CODE – bit flag for indicating probing error. In addition, SLOT_ID identify the target server.

Row measurements were stored in MS Access relational table which contained about 350.000 rows. By SQL queries we selected the rows related to RFC1945.txt file request from these 83 servers. Next, the set of attributes have been reduced to six attributes: SLOT_ID, DATETIME, FIRSTBYTE, CONNECT, THROUGHPUT, and ERROR. Sample measurements are shown in Table 3.

The data needed further analysis and preparation. We have found that for certain servers some data records concerning of the same timestamp were stored more than once, one after another. For instance, server #88 from California, U.S.

Table 3. Fragment of relational table after attribute reduction

SLOT_ID	DATETIME	ERROR_CODE	FIRSTBYTE	RTT	THROUGHPUT
181	30-09-02 15:39	1	369745	362887	31.57
181	30-09-02 18:19	1	364848	359171	31.56
181	30-09-02 20:59	1	363174	356913	31.73
181	30-09-02 23:40	0			
181	01-10-02 2:31	1	368202	356834	31.86
181	01-10-02 5:07	1	456414	448271	27.19
181	01-10-02 5:53	1	365686	366146	31.66
181	01-10-02 7:47	1	3412469	359033	5.26
181	01-10-02 10:28	1	375606	370605	30.18
181	01-10-02 13:11	0			

had 100% of measurements stored twice. Using a simple SQL query we deleted from the table about 9 thousand of such unnecessary data records.

Analysing our data we also noticed the following undesirable regularity. For many servers within a period from the beginning of April and to the middle of May 2003 there appeared the continuous gap in the data that is one noted errors in measurement in this period (ERROR_CODE=0). In the face of such situation the doubt came into being, that this regularity can concern every server, what would be an unfavourable phenomenon. There were too many data to complement and this data would disturb the results of further exploration. Therefore we need to check whether to omit this data or not.

To confirm or to reject our hypothesis, we used clustering function of the IBM Intelligent Miner for Data. Neural clustering was made using SLOT_ID, ERROR_CODE, and MONTH attributes and all data records prepared up to that moment. System discovered 3 clusters, where one of them (26% of total population) included all erroneous records featured all servers. This concluded that there was a failure of local network, Internet connection or workstation issuing Web page requests. Therefore we had to delete all faulty measurements and consider which data record may be used in further analysis. Additional manual analysis showed that

data from the first seven months is reliable enough and could be used in data mining analysis.

The above lessons learned that the automatic network measurement infrastructure need to be developed taking into account many different events that may suddenly occur, even those which cannot be anticipated before. Experiences with WING helped to develop new mechanisms to make measurements reliable and stable. They were implemented in MWING system.

In further data preparation and transformation we digitized TIME-OF-DAY into 9 equal-width intervals: [00:00-02:40,..., 21:20-00:00]), DAY-OF-WEEK into equal-width 7 intervals with Sunday as the start of the week (Borzemski, 2006b), RTT into non-equal-width 7 bins with breakpoints: [0, 46, 56, 70, 90, 130, 165, 200 ms], and categorized THROUGHPUT by text labels: low, medium, high, where medium is for 180-260 KB/s.

Mining Algorithms

The general objective of creating the decision-making model is to use it to predict RTT and throughput behavior most probable to achieve in the future. We assumed that the only a priori information that characterizes future events is the DAY-OF-WEEK and the TIME-OF-DAY.

The data mining followed the exploration methodology presented in Case 1 which generally assumes two mining stages, namely clustering to group measurement records into classes, which are further used in the classification stage. In clustering we use the following active attributes: RTT, TROUGHPUT, DAY-OF-WEEK and TIME-OF-DAY. After clustering we explore classification using the results of clustering as the inputs in decision tree deployment. Classification is made by means of CART-like decision tree method.

Results and Discussion

We have got 16 clusters that were described in a similar textual form as clusters derived in Case 1. For instance the biggest cluster included 17.73% of population and was defined by the set of records characterizing very good network weather on Sunday mornings. The description of that cluster was the following: DAY-OF-WEEK was predominantly 2 (that is Monday because the week started on Sunday), TIME-OF-DAY was predominantly 3 (that is time interval 5:20 a.m.-7:40 a.m.), RTT was predominantly 1 (that is less than 47 ms) and THROUGHPUT was High (that is more than 260 KB/s).

The decision tree built on this data set using CART method decision tree showed 75% classification accuracy. Sample decision rules from that decision tree built for the server #161 have the following pattern:

IF (TIME<4.5) AND (DAY≥3.5) AND (TIME≥ 3.5) AND (DAY<4.5) THEN CLUSTER_ID=4.

This rule says that, if we download Web resources between 00:00 a.m. and 10:40 a.m. (TIME<4.5) on Wednesday, Thursday, Friday or Saturday (DAY≥3.5), and when this is done after 8:00 a.m. (TIME≥ 3.5), and on Sunday, Monday, Tuesday or Wednesday (DAY<4.5) then we can expect network behavior described by cluster #4. Cluster #4 has been described as grouping records

where DAY-OF-WEEK is predominantly 4 (that is Wednesday), TIME-OF-DAY is predominantly 5 (that is time interval 10:20-13:00), RTT is predominantly 2 (that is 47-55 ms) and THROUGHPUT is medium (that is 180-260 KB/s). 9.41% of record belonged to cluster #4.

Incremental and moving window data mining was also made as in this case. We have found that the interval of six weeks of continuous measurements is a good proposal as the moving window for mining purposes. Less number of measurements caused too much variability in predictions whereas bigger windows showed the "smoothing" effect as discussed in Case 1. This effect causes that we are not able to distinguish clearly different network behavior states.

CONCLUSION

We presented a data mining approach for Internet and Web predictive performance problems. Based on real-life case studies we can summarize that the approach can highlight dependencies in measured data and provide the results that can improve our understanding of studied performance issues. The usefulness of the output of performance evaluation in Internet and Web area is influenced by meta-data not taken into account in the analysis. Therefore further analysis including meta-data remains crucial.

ACKNOWLEDGMENT

This work was supported by the Polish Ministry of Science and Higher Education under Grant No. N516 032 31/3359 (2006-2009).

REFERENCES

W3C. (2008). *Extended Log File Format*. Retrieved October 10, 2008, from http://www. w3.org/TR/WD-logfile

Abusina, Z. U. M., Zabir, S. M. S., Asir, A., Chakraborty, D., Suganuma, T., & Shiratori, N. (2005). An engineering approach to dynamic prediction of network performance from application logs. *Int. Network Mgmt, 15*(3), 151–162. doi:10.1002/nem.554

Allman, M., Martin, L., Rabinovich, M., & Atchinson, K. (2008). On community-oriented Internet measurement. In *Proceedings 9th International Conference, PAM 2008, Passive and Active Measurement Conference,* (LNCS vol. 4979, pp. 112-121). Berlin: Springer.

Allman, M., & Paxson, V. (2008). A Reactive Measurement Framework, In *Proceedings 9th International Conference, PAM 2008, Passive and Active Measurement Conference,* (LNCS vol. 4979, pp. 92-101). Berlin: Springer.

Arlit, M., & Jin, T. (2000). A Workload Characterization Study of the 1998 Word Cup Web Site. *IEEE Network*, (May/June): 30–373. doi:10.1109/65.844498

Arlit, M., Krishnamurthy, B., & Mogul, J. C. (2005). Predicting short-transfer latency from TCP arcane: A trace-based validation. In *Proceedings of International Measurement Conference* (pp. 119-124). USENIX Association.

Baker, M., Buyya, R., & Laforenza, D. (2002). Grids and grid technologies for wide-area distributed computing. *Software, Practice & Experience, 32*(15), 1437–146. doi:10.1002/spe.488

Barford, P., Mirza, M., & Zhu, X. (2007). A machine learning approach to TCP throughput prediction . *ACM SIGMETRICS Performance Evaluation Review, 35*(1), 97–108. doi:10.1145/1269899.1254894

Bhatia, M., Singh, H., & Kumar, N. (2007). A proposal for the management of mobile network's quality of service (QoS) using data mining methods. In *Proceedings of Wireless Communications, Networking and Mobile Computing Conference* (pp. 1-5).

Borzemski, L. (2004). Data mining in evaluation of Internet path performance. In *Proceedings of the 17th International Conference on Industrial and Engineering Applications of Artificial Intelligence and Expert Systems,* (LNCS vol. 3029, pp. 643-652). Berlin: Springer.

Borzemski, L. (2006a). Testing, measuring and diagnosing Web sites from the user's perspective. *International Journal of Enterprise Information Systems, 2*(1), 54–66.

Borzemski, L. (2006b). The use of data mining to predict Web performance. *Cybernetics and Systems, 37*(6), 587–608. doi:10.1080/01969720600734586

Borzemski, L. (2007). Internet path behavior prediction via data mining: Conceptual framework and case study. *J. UCS, 13*(2), 287–316.

Borzemski, L. (2008). Measuring of Web performance as perceived by end-users. In A. Gunasekaran (Ed.), *Techniques and tools for the design and implementation of enterprise information systems* (pp. 293-325). Hershey, PA: IGI Publishing.

Borzemski, L., Cichocki, Ł., Fraś, M., Kliber, M., & Nowak, Z. (2007). MWING: A multiagent system for Web site measurements. In *Proceedings of the First AMSTA KES International Symposium,* (LNCS Vol. 4496, pp. 278-287). Berlin: Springer.

Borzemski, L., & Druszcz, A. (2006). Lessons from the application of domain-independent data mining system for discovering Web user access patterns. In *Proceedings of the 10th International Conference on Knowledge-Based & Intelligent Information & Engineering Systems,* (LNCS Vol. 4253, pp. 789-796). Berlin: Springer.

Borzemski, L., Kliber, M., & Nowak, Z. (2008). Application of data mining algorithms to TCP throughput prediction in HTTP transactions. In *Proceedings of the 21st International Conference on Industrial, Engineering and Other Applications of Applied Intelligent Systems*, (LNCS Vol. 5027, pp. 159-168). Berlin: Springer.

Borzemski, L., & Nowak, Z. (2004a). An empirical study of Web quality: Measuring the Web from the Wroclaw University of Technology campus. In *Engineering Advanced Web Applications* (pp. 307-320). Princeton, NJ: Rinton Publishers.

Borzemski, L., & Nowak, Z. (2004b). WING: A Web probing, visualization and performance analysis service. In *Proceedings of the 4th International Conference on Web Engineering*, (LNCS Vol. 3140, pp. 601-602). Berlin: Springer.

Borzemski, L., & Nowak, Z. (2008). Using Autonomous System topological information in Web server performance prediction. *Cybernetics and Systems*, *39*(7), 751–767. doi:10.1080/01969720802257980

Borzemski, L., & Starczewski, G. (2009). Application of transform regression to TCP throughput prediction. In *Proceedings of the 1th Asian Conference on Intelligent Information and Database Systems ACIIDS 2009*, (pp. 28-33). Los Alamos, CA: IEEE Press.

Bose, I., & Mahapatra, R. K. (2001). Business data mining - a machine learning perspective. *Information & Management*, *39*, 211–225. doi:10.1016/S0378-7206(01)00091-X

Brownlee, N., & Claffy, K. C. (2004). Internet measurement. *IEEE Internet Computing*, *8*(5), 30–33. doi:10.1109/MIC.2004.41

Brownlee, N., Claffy, K. C., Murray, M., & Nemeth, E. (2001). Methodology for passive analysis of a university Internet link. *Passive and Active Measurement Workshop*, Amsterdam, April 22-24. Retrieved October 10, 2008, from http://www.ripe.net/pam2001/program.html

CAIDA. (2008). *The Cooperative Association for Internet Data Analysis*. Retrieved 10 October 2008, from http://www.caida.org

Calyam, P., Sridharan, M., Mandrawa, W., & Schopis, P. (2004). Performance measurement and analysis of H.323 Traffic. In *Proceedings of the Passive and Active Network Measurement Workshop*, (LNCS vol. 3015, pp. 137-146). Berlin: Springer.

Cao, L., & Zhang, C. (2007). The evolution of KDD: Towards domain-driven data mining. *International Journal of Pattern Recognition and Artificial Intelligence*, *21*(4), 677–692. doi:10.1142/S0218001407005612

Cardellini, V., Casalicchio, E., Colajanni, M., & Yu, P. S. (2002). The state of the art in locally distributed Web-server systems. *ACM Computing Surveys*, *34*(2), 263–311. doi:10.1145/508352.508355

Chakrabarti, S. (2003). *Mining the Web: Analysis of Hypertext and Semi Structured Data*. San Francisco, CA: Morgan Kaufmann.

Chen, M. Han, S., J., & Yu, P. S. (1996). Data mining: An overview from a database perspective. *IEEE Transactions on Knowledge and Data Engineering*, *8*(6), 866–883. doi:10.1109/69.553155

Cho, Y. H., Kim, J. K., & Kim, S. H. (2002). A personalized recommender system based on Web usage mining and decision tree induction. *Expert Systems with Applications*, *23*, 329–342. doi:10.1016/S0957-4174(02)00052-0

Chu, B.-H., Lee, Ch.-E., & Ho, Ch.-S. (2008). An ontology-supported database refurbishing technique and its application in mining actionable troubleshooting rules from real-life databases. *Engineering Applications of Artificial Intelligence, 21*, 1430–1442. doi:10.1016/j.engappai.2008.04.015

Claffy, K., Dovrolis, C., & Murray, M. (2003). Bandwidth estimation: metrics, measurement techniques, and tools. *IEEE Network, 17*(6), 27–35. doi:10.1109/MNET.2003.1248658

Comer, D. (2008). *Computer Networks and Internets,* (5ᵗʰ Ed.). Upper Saddle River, NJ: Prentice Hall.

Cooley, R., Mobasher, B., & Srivastava, J. (1999). Data preparation for mining World Wide Web browsing patterns. *Journal of Knowledge and Information System, 1*(1), 5–32.

Crovella, M., & Krishnamurthy, B. (2006). *Internet Measurement: Infrastructure, Traffic, and Applications*. New York: John Wiley & Sons.

Czyzowicz, J., Kranakis, E., Krizanc, D., Pelc, A., & Martin, M. V. (2003). Enhancing hyperlink structure for improving Web performance. *Journal of Web Engineering, 1*(2), 93–127.

Dovrolis, C. (2005). End-to-end available bandwidth estimation. In *Proceedings of the ACM SIGMETRICS International Conference on Measurement and Modeling of Computer Systems,* (pp. 265–276).

Downey, A. B. (1999). Using pathchar to estimate Internet link characteristics. *SIGCOMM Comput. Commun. Rev., 29*(4), 241–250. doi:10.1145/316194.316228

Duffield, N. (2004). Sampling for passive Internet measurement: A review. *Statistical Science, 19*(3), 472–498. doi:10.1214/088342304000000206

El-Ramly, M., & Stroulia, E. (2004). Analysis of Web-usage behavior for focused Web sites: a case study. *Journal of Software Maintenance and Evolution: Research and Practice, 16*(1-2), 129–150. doi:10.1002/smr.286

Facca, F., & Lanzi, P. (2005). Mining interesting knowledge from weblogs: A survey. *Data & Knowledge Engineering, 53*, 225–241. doi:10.1016/j.datak.2004.08.001

Faloutsos, M., & Faloutsos, Ch. (2002). *Data-Mining the Internet: What We Know, What We Don't, and How We Can Learn More*. Full day Tutorial ACM SIGCOMM 2002 Conference, Pittsburgh.

Faloutsos, M., Faloutsos, P., & Faloutsos, C. (1999). On power-law relationships of the Internet topology. In *Proceedings of SIGCOMM* (pp. 251-262).

Fürnkranz, J. (2005). Web mining. In *Data Mining and Knowledge Discovery Handbook,* (pp. 899-920). Berlin: Springer.

Garofalakis, M., & Rastogi, R. (2002). *Network data mining and analysis: The NEMES project,* (LNCS vol. 2336, pp. 1-12). Berlin: Springer.

Grossman, R. L., Gu, Y., Sabala, M., & Zhang, W. (2009). Compute and storage clouds using wide area high performance networks. *Future Generation Computer Systems, 25*, 179–183. doi:10.1016/j.future.2008.07.009

Grossman, R. L., Kamath, Ch., Kegelmeyer, P., Kumar, V., & Namburu, R. R. (Eds.). (2001). *Data Mining for Scientific and Engineering Applications*. Boston: Kluwer Academic Publishers.

Han, J., & Chang, K. Ch.-Ch. (2002). Data mining for Web intelligence. *Computer,* (Nov): 54–60.

Hasegawa, G., Murata, M., & Miyahara, H. (1999). Performance evaluation of HTTP/TCP on asymmetric networks. *International Journal of Communication Systems, 12*(4), 281–296. doi:10.1002/(SICI)1099-1131(199907/08)12:4<281::AID-DAC402>3.0.CO;2-W

He, Q., Dovrolis, C., & Ammar, M. (2007). On the predictability of large transfer TCP throughput. *Computer Networks, 51*(14), 3959–3977. doi:10.1016/j.comnet.2007.04.013

Hellerstein, J., Zhang, F., & Shahabuddin, P. (2001). A statistical approach to predictive detection. *Computer Networks, 35*(1), 77–95. doi:10.1016/S1389-1286(00)00151-1

Huang, T., & Subhlok, J. (2005). Fast pattern-based throughput prediction for TCP bulk transfers. In *Proceedings of the Fifth IEEE International Symposium on Cluster Computing and the Grid* (pp. 410-417).

IBM. (2008). *DB2 Intelligent Miner*. Retrieved October 10, 2008, from http://www.ibm.com

Jain, M., & Dovrolis, C. (2002). Pathload: A measurement tool for end-to-end available bandwidth. In *Proceedings of Passive and Active Measurements (PAM) Workshop* (pp. 14-25).

Keynote. (2008). *Web benchmarking service*. Retrieved October 10, 2008, from http://www.keynote.com

Krishnamurthy, B., & Willinger, W. (2008). What are our standards for validation of measurement-based networking research? *ACM SIGMETRICS Performance Evaluation Review, 36*(2), 64–69. doi:10.1145/1453175.1453186

Lee, Y.-S., & Yen, S.-J. (2008). Incremental and interactive mining of web traversal patterns. *Information Sciences, 178,* 287–306. doi:10.1016/j.ins.2007.08.020

Li, X., Song, L., & Garcia-Diaz, A. (2008). Adaptive web presence and evolution through web log analysis. *International Journal of Electronic Customer Relationship Management, 2*(3), 195–214. doi:10.1504/IJECRM.2008.020408

Mahanta, A. K., Mazarbhuiya, A. F., & Baruah, H. K. (2008). Finding calendar-based periodic patterns. *Pattern Recognition Letters, 29,* 1274–1284. doi:10.1016/j.patrec.2008.01.020

Manganaris, S., Christensen, M., Zerkle, D., & Hermiz, K. (2000). A data mining analysis of RTID alarms. *Computer Networks, 34,* 571–577. doi:10.1016/S1389-1286(00)00138-9

Mellia, M., Stoica, I., & Zhang, H. (2002). TCP model for short lived flows. *IEEE Communications Letters, 6*(2), 85–87. doi:10.1109/4234.984705

Microsoft. (2008). *Microsoft SQL Server*. Retrieved October 10, 2008, from http://www.microsoft.com

MOME. (2008). *MOnitoring and MEsurement project*. Retrieved October 10, 2008, from http://www.ist-mome.org

Nasrouri, O., Rojas, C., & Cardona, C. (2006). A framework for mining evolving trends in Web data streams using dynamic learning and retrospective validation. *Computer Networks, 50,* 1488–1512. doi:10.1016/j.comnet.2005.10.021

NGG. (2008). *Future for European Grids: Grids and Service Oriented Knowledge Utilities - Vision and Research Directions 2010 and Beyond*. The 3rd report of the NGG Expert Group. Retrieved October 10, 2008, from ftp://ftp.cordis.europa.eu

Pabarskaite, Z., & Raudys, A. (2007). A process of knowledge discovery from Web log data: Systematization and critical review. *Journal of Intelligent Information Systems, 28,* 79–104. doi:10.1007/s10844-006-0004-1

Pandey, S. K., & Mishra, R. B. (2006). Intelligent Web mining model to enhance knowledge discovery on the Web. In *Proceedings of the 7th Parallel and Distributed Computing, Applications and Technologies International Conference,* (pp. 339-343).

Paxson, V. (2004). Strategies for sound Internet measurement. In *Proceedings of ACM SIG-COMM Internet Measurement Conference,* (pp. 263 – 271).

Pechenizkiy, M., Tsymbal, A., & Puuronen, S. (2005). Knowledge management challenges in knowledge discovery systems. In *Proceedings of the 16th International Workshop on Database and Expert Systems Applications,* (pp. 433-437).

Pednault, E. (2006). Transform regression and the Kolmogorov superposition theorem, In *Proceedings of the Sixth SIAM International Conference on Data Mining,* (pp. 35-46).

Prasad, R. S., Murray, M., Dovrolis, C., & Claffy, K. C. (2003). Bandwidth estimation: Metrics, measurement techniques, and tools. *IEEE Network, 17*(6), 27–35. doi:10.1109/MNET.2003.1248658

Puuronen, S., Pechenizkiy, M., & Tsymbal, A. (2006). Data mining researcher, who is your customer? Some issues inspired by the information systems field. In *Proceedings of the 17th International Conference on Databases and Expert Systems Applications,* (pp. 579-583).

Pyle, D. (1999). *Data Preparation for Data Mining.* San Francisco, CA: Morgan Kaufmann Publishers, Inc.

Python. (2009). *Python Programming Language - Official Website.* Retrieved February 10, 2009, from http://www.python.org/

Rahman, R. M., Alhajj, R., & Barker, K. (2008). Replica selection strategies in data grid. *Journal of Parallel and Distributed Computing.* doi:. doi:10.1016/j.jpdc.2008.07.013

RFC1945. (2008). Hypertext Transfer Protocol - HTTP/1.0. *Request for Comments: 1945.* Retrieved October 10, 2008, from http://www.ietf.org/rfc/rfc1945.txt

RFC4656. (2008). A One-way Active Measurement Protocol (OWAMP). *Request for Comments: 1945.* Retrieved October 10, 2008, from http://www.ietf.org/rfc/rfc4656.txt

Roughan, M. (2006). A comparison of Poisson and uniform sampling for active measurements. *IEEE Journal on Selected Areas in Communications, 24*(12), 2299–2312. doi:10.1109/JSAC.2006.884028

Schroder, C. (2008). *Measure Network Performance: iperf and ntop.* Retrieved October 10, 2008, from http://www.enterprisenetworkingplanet.com/netos/article.php/3658331

Sikdar, B., Kalyanaraman, S., & Vastola, K. S. (2001). An integrated model for the latency and steady-state throughput of TCP connections. *Performance Evaluation, 46*(2-3), 139–154. doi:10.1016/S0166-5316(01)00048-7

Sinha, A. P., & Zhao, H. (2008). Incorporating domain knowledge into data mining classifiers: An application in indirect lending. *Decision Support Systems.* Available online 16 July 2008, doi:10.1016/j.dss.2008.06.013

SLAC. (2008). *Stanford Linear Accelerator Center. Network Monitoring Tools.* Retrieved October 10, 2008, from http://www.slac.stanford.edu/xorg/nmtf/nmtf-tools.html

Spiliopoulou, M. (2000). Web usage mining for Web site evaluation. *Communications of the ACM, 43*(8), 127–134. doi:10.1145/345124.345167

Spiliopoulou, M., & Pohle, C. (2001). Data mining for measuring and improving the success of Web sites. *Data Mining and Knowledge Discovery, 5,* 85–114. doi:10.1023/A:1009800113571

Srivastava, J., Cooley, R., Deshpande M. & Tan, P. N. (2000). Web usage mining: Discovery and applications of usage patterns from Web data. *2000 SIGKDD Explorations, 1*(2), 12-23.

Sterne, J. (2002). *Web Metrics: Proven Methods for Measuring Web Site Success.* Toronto: John Wiley &Son, Inc. Canada.

Swany, M., & Wolski, R. (2002). Multivariate resource performance forecasting in the network weather service. In *Proceedings of the IEEE/ACM SC2002 Conference,* (pp. 1-10).

Tan, G., & Jarvis, S. A. (2006). Prediction of short-lived TCP transfer latency on bandwidth asymmetric links. *Journal of Computer and System Sciences, 72*(7), 1201–1210. doi:10.1016/j.jcss.2006.01.006

Tan, P. N., & Kumar, V. (2002). Discovery of the Web robot sessions based on their navigational patterns. *Data Mining and Knowledge Discovery, 6,* 9–35. doi:10.1023/A:1013228602957

Vazhkudai, S., & Schopf, J. M. (2002). Predicting sporadic grid data transfers. In *Proceedings of 11th International Symposium on High Performance Distributed Computing HPDC-11,* (pp. 188-196).

Vazhkudai, S., & Schopf, J. M. (2003). Using regression techniques to predict large data transfers. *International Journal of High Performance Computing Applications, 17*(3), 249–268. doi:10.1177/1094342003173004

Velásquez, J. D., & Palade, V. (2007). A Knowledge Base for the maintenance of knowledge extracted from web data. *Knowledge-Based Systems, 20*(3), 238–248. doi:10.1016/j.knosys.2006.05.015

Wang, H., & Wang, S. (2007). Making data mining relevant to business. In *Proceedings of Wireless Communications, Networking and Mobile Computing Conference,* (pp. 5516-5518).

Wang, X., Abraham, A., & Smith, K. A. (2005). Intelligent web traffic mining and analysis. *Journal of Network and Computer Applications, 28,* 147–165. doi:10.1016/j.jnca.2004.01.006

Watson, D., Malan, G. R., & Jahanian, F. (2004). An extensible probe architecture for network protocol performance measurement. *Software, Practice & Experience, 34,* 47–67. doi:10.1002/spe.557

Weigle, M. C., Jeffay, K., & Smith, F. D. (2005). Delay-based early congestion detection and adaptation in TCP: impact on web performance. *Computer Communications, 28*(8), 837–850. doi:10.1016/j.comcom.2004.11.011

Wenwei, L., Dafang, Z., Jinmin, Y., & Gaogang, X. (2007). On evaluating the differences of TCP and ICMP in network measurement. *Computer Communications, 30,* 428–439. doi:10.1016/j.comcom.2006.09.015

Wolski, R. (1998). Dynamically forecasting network performance using the network weather service. *Cluster Computing, 1*(1), 119–132. doi:10.1023/A:1019025230054

Wu, E. H. C., Ng, M. K., & Huang, J. Z. (2004). On improving Website connectivity by using Web-log data streams. In *Proceedings of DASFAA 2004 Conference,* (pp. 352-364).

Wu, S.-Y., & Yen, E. (2008). Data mining-based intrusion detectors. *Expert Systems with Applications.* doi:.doi:10.1016/j.eswa.2008.06.138

Xing, D., & Shen, J. (2004). Efficient data mining for Web navigation patterns. *Information and Software Technology, 46*(1), 55–63. doi:10.1016/S0950-5849(03)00109-5

Yousaf, M., & Welzl, M. (2005). *A reliable network measurement and prediction architecture for grid scheduling.* Paper presented at the 1st IEEE/IFIP International Workshop on Autonomic Grid Networking and Management AGNM'05, Barcelona 28th October, 2005.

Zhang, D., & Dong, Y. (2002). A novel Web usage mining approach for search engines. *Computer Networks*, *39*, 303–310. doi:10.1016/S1389-1286(02)00211-6

Zhang, S., Zhang, C., & Yang, Q. (2003). Data preparation for data mining. *Applied Artificial Intelligence*, *17*, 375–381. doi:10.1080/713827180

Zhang, X., Edwards, J., & Harding, J. (2007). Personalised online sales using web usage data mining. *Computers in Industry*, *58*(8-9), 772–782. doi:10.1016/j.compind.2007.02.004

Zhang, X., & Yin, X. (2008). Design of an information intelligent system based on Web data mining. In *Proceedings of International Conference on Computer Science and Information Technology,* (pp. 88-91). Los Alamos, CA: IEEE Press.

Zhang, Y., Duffield, N., Paxson, V., & Shenker, S. (2001). On the constancy of Internet path properties. In *Proceedings of the 1st ACM SIGCOMM Workshop on Internet Measurement* (pp. 197-211).

Chapter 16
Predicting Similarity of Web Services Using WordNet

Aparna Konduri
University of Akron, USA

Chien-Chung Chan
University of Akron, USA

ABSTRACT

As vast numbers of web services have been developed over a broad range of functionalities, it becomes a challenging task to find relevant or similar web services using web services registry such as UDDI. Current UDDI search uses keywords from web service and company information in its registry to retrieve web services. This method cannot fully capture user's needs and may miss out on potential matches. Underlying functionality and semantics of web services need to be considered. This chapter introduces a methodology for predicting similarity of web services by integrating hierarchical clustering, nearest neighbor classification, and algorithms for natural language processing using WordNet. It can be used to facilitate the development of intelligent applications for retrieving web services with imprecise or vague requests. The authors explore semantics of web services using WSDL operation names and parameter names along with WordNet. They compute semantic interface similarity of web services and use this data to generate clusters. Then, they represent each cluster by a set of characteristic operations to predict similarity of new web services using nearest neighbor approach. The empirical result is promising.

INTRODUCTION

Web Services offer a promise for integrating business applications within or outside an organization. They are based on Service Oriented Architecture (SOA) (Barry, 2003) that provides loose coupling between software components via standard interfaces. Web Services expose their interfaces using

Web Service Description Language (WSDL) (Christensen, Curbera, Meredith, & Weerawarana, 2001). WSDL is an XML based language and hence platform independent. A typical WSDL file provides information such as web service description, operations that are offered by a web service, input and output parameters for each web service operation. Web Service providers use a central repository called UDDI (Universal Description, Discovery and Integration) (Clement et al., 2004) to advertise and

DOI: 10.4018/978-1-61520-757-2.ch016

publish their services. Web Service consumers use UDDI to discover services that suit their requirements and to obtain the service metadata needed to consume those services. Users that want to use a web service will utilize this metadata to query the web service using SOAP (Simple Object Access Protocol) (Mitra, 2003). SOAP is a network protocol for exchanging XML messages or data. Since SOAP is based on HTTP/HTTP-S, it can very likely get through network firewalls. The advantages of XML and SOAP give web services their maximum strength.

With web applications and portals getting complex and rich in functionality, many users are interested in finding similar web services. Users might want to compose two operations from different web services to obtain complex functionality. Also, users might be interested in looking at operations that take similar inputs and produce similar outputs. Let us say, web service *A* has an operation GetCityNameByZip that returns city name by zip code, web service *B* has an operation GetWeatherByCityName that returns weather by city name and web service *C* has an operation GetGeographicalLocationBasedOnZip that returns city name, longitude, latitude and altitude of a location by zip code. Operations from web services *A* and *B* are related, i.e., output from one operation can be used as an input to another. So, these operations can be composed to obtain weather by city name. Operations from web services *A* and *C* are similar. They take similar inputs. Outputs are also similar, i.e., output of operation from web service *C* is fine grained when compared to output of operation from web service *A*.

As more and more web services are developed, it is a challenge to find the right or relevant web services quickly and efficiently. Currently, UDDI supports keyword match just based on web service data entries in its registry. This might potentially miss out on some valid matches. For example, searching UDDI with keywords like zip code may not retrieve web service with postal code information.

Semantics of a web service in terms of the requirements and capabilities of a web service can be really helpful for efficient retrieval of web services. WSDL does not have support for semantic specifications. A lot of researches are done on annotating web services through special markup languages to attach semantics to a web service. Akkiraju et al. proposed WSDL-S to annotate web services (Akkiraju et al., 2005). Cardoso and Sheth used DAML-S (Cardoso & Sheth, 2003). DAML-S was used as annotations to compose multiple web services by (Ankolekar, Burstein, Hobbs, Lassila, Martin, McIlraith, Narayanan, Paolucci, Payne, Sycara, & Zeng, 2001). The OWL-S introduced by (Martin et al., 2004) was used by Ganjisaffar et al. as annotations to compute similarity between web services (Ganjisaffar, Abolhassani, Neshati, & Jamali, 2006), and a semantics-based composition-oriented discovery of web services based on OWL-S was introduced in (Brogi, Corfini, & Popescu, 2008). The main challenges of ontology-based approach are that manual annotation is a time consuming task and how to deal with discrepancies between ontologies.

Another line of research has been done to automate the process of discovery or composition of relevant web services in response to a given query based on the contents of WSDL files. Normally, heuristics are used to infer the functionality or semantics of a web service based on its description, operations along with parameters that these operations take. Wang and Stroulia have used vector space model enhanced by WordNet (Fellbaum, 1998) to perform semantic structure matching for assessing web service similarity (Wang & Stroulia, 2003a, 2003b). Dong et al. built a web search engine called Woogle based on agglomerative clustering of WSDL descriptions, operations and parameters (Dong et al., 2004). Wu and Wu provided a suite of similarity measures to assess the web service similarity (Wu & Wu, 2005). Kil et al. proposed a flexible network model for matching web services (Kil, Oh, & Lee, 2006). A kernel based web services matching mechanism for service discovery and integration was described by (Yu et al., 2007). A tensor space model and rough set ensemble classifier were used to represent and classify web services (Saha et al., 2008).

The objective of this work is to introduce a methodology for predicting similar web services using semantics of WSDL operations and parameters along with WordNet. WordNet is a lexical database that groups words into synsets (synonym sets) and maintains semantic relations between these synsets. WordNet was used in the works of (Wang & Stroulia, 2003b; Wu & Wu, 2005; Kokash, 2006) where they have introduced their own lexical similarity measures. In our work, we used the similarity measure introduced by (Wu & Palmer, 1994), which has been revised by Resnik (Resnik, 1999) and implemented in the WordNet library (Simpson & Dao, 2005). We consider only interface similarity of web services as in (Wu & Wu, 2005; Kokash, 2006), and complex data types are flattened as in (Kil, Oh, & Lee, 2006).

Since there is no publicly available web services dataset, we evaluated our study using a set of WSDL files downloaded from the Internet. The general structure of our approach is as follows: first, we organized web service descriptions, operation names and parameter names from WSDL into three separate Excel files respectively. We used popular natural language pre-processing techniques like Stop Words Removal and Stemming to remove unnecessary and irrelevant terms from the data. Then we compute interface similarity measures based on WordNet to assess the similarity between web services. Once we obtain a similarity matrix of web services, we use hierarchical clustering (Murtagh, 1985) to group or cluster related web services. We represent a cluster by a set of characteristic operations, i.e., for each web service in a cluster; take one characteristic operation that has maximum similarity to operations of other web services in the same cluster. This cluster representation is then used as

a basis for predicting similarity of any new web services to the clusters using the nearest neighbor approach.

The remaining sections of this chapter are organized as follows. Section 2 provides key information on similarity computation of web services. Section 3 presents data collection and pre-processing. In Section 4, we discuss WordNet based semantic similarity. It starts with an overview of WordNet, its organization and use for word sense disambiguation and explains similarity computation measures. Section 5 describes clustering of training set of web services using hierarchical clustering approach, cluster representation and prediction of similarity for web services in the test dataset. Section 6 discusses application setup and results. Conclusions are given in Section 7, followed by references.

SIMILARITY OF WEB SERVICES

A web service is associated with a WSDL file which contains the information of the service name, description, and a set of operations that take input parameters and return output parameters. Typically, a web service is published by registering its WSDL file and a brief description of its features in UDDI registries. Users of web services can search the UDDI registries to find services that meet their requirements. In general, it is challenging to develop a search engine for web services, because the users' queries may not be specified in exact terms and the names and documentation used in WSDL files may be ambiguous and sometimes fragmented. Instead of considering the general web service search problem, we consider only the fundamental issue of determining similarity of web services based on the contents of WSDL files. In the following, we will give a brief review of approaches for determining similarity of web services.

Lexical Similarity of Web Services

Lexical similarity between words indicates how closely their underlying concepts are related. Measures for determining textual similarity have been studied in information retrieval. One popular method is the vector space model with Term Frequency and Inverse Document Frequency (TF/IDF) weighting method for determining the importance of a term in a document (Salton et al., 1975). Terms of a WSDL file can be extracted from words in the file. However, terms in a WSDL file are not as dense as in a typical document; therefore, term-frequency method alone may not work well. One way to enhance the vector space model is by adding the stems of original words, the stems of synonyms for all word senses, and the stems of hypernyms, hyponyms, and their siblings extracted from the WordNet database (Wang & Stroulia, 2003b). Another approach proposed in (Kokash, 2006) is to expand the query and WSDL descriptions with synonyms from WordNet, and then word tuples are compared by using the TF/IDF measure.

Another way to determine lexical similarity without using the WordNet database was introduced by Dong et al. (Dong et al., 2004). The basic idea is to group terms such as parameter names frequently occurred together as semantically meaningful concepts if their frequency of co-occurrence satisfies certain threshold. It is similar to the A-Priori algorithm in association rules (Agrawal et al., 1993). In addition, frequent and rare terms are not clustered, since empirical observations in Information Retrieval suggest that it leads to the best performance in automatic query expansion (Jones, 1971) by not clustering high frequent terms and over-fitting can be avoided by not clustering rare terms. To determine term similarity, each term is mapped to its corresponding concept in the collection of semantically meaningful concepts, and then TF/IDF measure is applied.

In this work, lexical similarity is based on the Least Common Subsumer (LCS) of concepts in the WordNet conceptual hierarchies. The measure was used in (Wu & Palmer, 1994) and revised by (Resnik, 1999). The detail will be given in Section 4.

Structure Similarity of Web Services

Lexical similarity alone is insufficient for determining similarity of web services, because it does not take into the consideration of the structure of a web service. There are three parts of a web service, namely, service name and its description, operation names and their descriptions, and input/output descriptions including parameter names, data types, and arities. In Dong et al. (Dong et al., 2004), a linear combination is used to combine similarities from the three parts of a web service, and a weight is assigned to each part based on its relevance to the overall similarity. Another way to measure the structure similarity of web services is based on the interface of operations as suggested in (Wu & Wu, 2005; Kokash, 2006). Interface similarity between web services is computed by identifying the pair-wise correspondence of their operations that maximizes the sum total of the matching scores of the individual pairs. There are other web service structural similarity measures such as attribute similarity and Quality of Service similarity (Wu & Wu, 2005). In this work, we consider only the interface similarity of web services. More precisely, similarity between web services S_1 with m operations and S_2 with n operations is given by the following formula:

$$Sim_{Interface}(S_1, S_2) = \sum_{i=1}^{m} Max \sum_{j=1}^{n} Sim_{Operation}(O_{1i}, O_{2j}) \qquad (1)$$

where O_{1i} represents an operation from web service S_1 and O_{2j} represents an operation from web service S_2.

To illustrate interface similarity, let us consider the example shown in Figure 1. Here web service 1 has 2 operations, operation 11 and operation 12.

Web service 2 has 3 operations, operation 21, operation 22 and operation 23. We match operation 11 to operation 21, operation 22 and operation 23 and pick the matching that gives maximum similarity. Similarly, we match operation 12 to operations in web service 2. Then we sum up the maximum similarity values from both these matching pairs to give the similarity between web services.

Likewise, the similarity of operation pairs is calculated by identifying the pair-wise correspondence of their input/output parameter lists that maximizes the sum total of the matching scores of the input/output individual pairs. Similarity between web service operation O_1 with m input parameters and u outputs; and web service operation O_2 with n input parameters and v outputs can be given by the following formula:

$$Sim_{Operation}(O_1,O_2)$$
$$= \sum_{i=1}^{m} Max \sum_{j=1}^{n} Sim_{Input}(I_{1i},I_{2j})$$
$$+ \sum_{i=1}^{u} Max \sum_{j=1}^{v} Sim_{Output}(P_{1i},P_{2j}) \qquad (2)$$

Here I_{1i} and I_{2j} stand for input parameters of web service operation O_1 and web service operation O_2 respectively, P_{1i} and P_{2j} stand for outputs of web service operation O_1 and web service operation O_2 respectively, x_{ij} indicates the weight and it is

set to 1 while matching input parameters I_{1i} with I_{2j}, and y_{ij} is the weight and it is set to 1 while matching outputs P_{1i} with P_{2j}.

Parameter name similarity is computed by the lexical similarity of their names. Similarity between Input parameter I_1 of Operation O_1, belonging to web service S_1 and Input parameter I_2 of Operation O_2, belonging to web service S_2 can be given by the following formula:

$$Sim_{Parameter}(I_1,I_2)=Sim_{Lexical}(I_1,Name,I_2,Name) \qquad (3)$$

Likewise, lexical similarity can be computed for outputs of operations O_1 and O_2.

Since number of operations and in turn its parameters are not constant across web services, we normalized the similarity measures. For example, let us say web service A has 3 operations and web service B has 5 operations. Similarity between web services is computed according to the formula for interface similarity and then normalized by dividing by 3 (number of operations in A). This is done to normalize the effect of number of operations across all web services. Similarly, we normalized input and output parameters of operations.

Next two sections explain how web service data was collected and how WordNet was used along with the formulae mentioned in this section for similarity computations.

Figure 1. Matching of web service operations

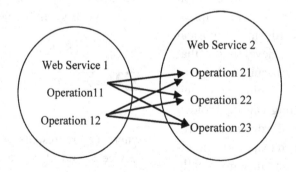

DATA PRE-PROCESSING

There is no publicly available web services data-set. So, we downloaded a set of web services in five domains from *xmethods.net* website. WSDL data from these web services is then organized into three excel files, one for web service name and description, one for web service operation names and another for web service input and output parameter names. Tables 1, 2 and 3 show the format of Excel files. Web service ID in these tables represents a unique numeric identifier for each web service. This is similar to ID column in a database table represents a unique numeric identifier for each web service.

Operation ID in Tables 2 and 3 represents a numeric identifier for each web service operation. Direction in Table 3 indicates whether it is an input parameter 'I' or an output parameter 'O'.

We use parameter flattening similar to that described in (Kil, Oh, & Lee, 2006) when we come across complex data structures for input parameters. For example, if the input parameter of web service operation is a data structure named "PhoneVerify" that contains Phone Number field. Then we take Phone Number as input parameter instead of PhoneVerify.

The three Excel files are then fed as inputs to web service pre-processing module. This module is a third party software downloaded from (Simpson & Dao, 2005). It internally removes Stop Words, uses stemming for preprocessing the data.

Stop Words Removal

A document is a vector or bag of words or terms. Stop Words are a list of words that are insignificant and can be easily removed from a document

Table 1. Format of Excel file with web service descriptions

WS ID	Name	Text Description	WSDL Name	URL
1	US Zip Validator	Zip code validator	USZip	http://www.webservicemart.com/uszip.asmx
2	Phone Number Verification service	Phone number verifier	Phone3T	http://www.webservicemart.com/phone3t.asmx

Table 2. Format of Excel file with web service operations

Web service ID	Operation ID	Name
1	1	ValidateZip
2	1	PhoneVerify

Table 3. Format of Excel file with web service operation parameters

Web service ID	Operation ID	Parameter Name	Direction
1	1	ZipCode	I
1	1	ValidateZipResult	O
2	1	PhoneNumber	I
2	1	PhoneVerifyResult	O

or a sentence or phrase. To achieve this, program is presented with a list of stop words that can be removed. Examples of stop words can be a, an, about, by, get etc. For a web service operation like GetWeatherByZip, significant words are 'Weather' and 'Zip'. 'Get' and 'By' do not convey a lot of meaning and can be safely removed.

Stemming

Normally, terms that originate from a common root or stem have similar meanings. For example, the following words have similar meanings.

- INTERSECT
- INTERSECTED
- INTERSECTING
- INTERSECTION
- INTERSECTIONS

Key idea is to represent such related term groups using a single term, here INTERSECT by removing various suffixes like –ED, -ING, -ION, -IONS. This process of representing a document with unique terms is called Stemming. Stemming reduces the amount and complexity of the data while retrieving information. It is widely used in search engines for indexing and other natural language processing problems.

Porter Stemming Algorithm (Porter, 1980; van Rijsbergen, Robertson, & Porter, 1980) is one of the most popular stemming algorithms. The basic idea is to take a list of suffixes and the criterion during which a suffix can be removed. It is simple, efficient and fast.

Once WSDL data is pre-processed using stemming and stop words removal, WordNet is used in similarity computation of web services. More details on WordNet and similarity computation can be found in the next section.

WORDNET BASED SEMANTIC SIMILARITY

This section provides an overview of WordNet and how WordNet is used for computing semantic similarity of web services.

WordNet

WordNet is an electronic lexical database (Fellbaum, 1998; Fellbaum, 2007) that uses word senses to determine underlying semantics. It differs from the traditional dictionary in that, it is organized by meaning, so words in close proximity are related. WordNet entries are organized as mapping of words and its concepts.

A single concept is represented by a set of multiple synonym words called synonym set or synset. For example, {Comb, Brush} are synonyms. Also, a single word can represent multiple concepts (polysemy). For example, Brush can mean Sweep, Clash, Encounter etc.

Organization of WordNet

WordNet organizes synsets of nouns and verbs as hypernyms and hyponyms (Fellbaum, 2007). For example, animal is a hypernym of cow and cow is a hyponym of animal. Beyond this hypernym /hyponym relation, WordNet also provides relations such as Meronymy/holonymy (part/whole), is-made-of, is-an-attribute-of etc. Also, each concept is quantified by a short description called "gloss". All these relations result in a large interconnection network. The logical structure of WordNet is shown as in Figure 2.

Word Sense Disambiguation

In general, a word can have multiple meanings or make different senses in the context where it

Figure 2. The logical structure of WordNet

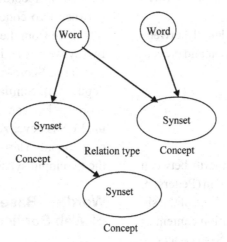

is used. The object of word sense disambiguation is to determine the correct sense of a word. Many algorithms have been developed for this purpose. In the present work, we use Lesk algorithm (Lesk, 1986; Pedersen, 2005). The following steps can summarize it:

1. Retrieve from Machine Readable Dictionary all sense definitions of the words to be disambiguated.
2. Determine the definition overlap for all possible sense combinations
3. Choose senses that lead to highest overlap

For example, to disambiguate PINE CONE using the example introduced by Christiane Fellbaum (reproduced from (Fellbaum, 1998) with author's permission),

PINE has these 2 senses

1. Kinds of evergreen tree with needle-shaped leaves
2. Waste away through sorrow or illness

CONE has these 3 senses

1. Solid body that narrows to a point

2. Something of this shape whether solid or hollow
3. Fruit of certain evergreen trees

Determine all possible combination of senses and their scores as:

Pine#1 ∩ Cone#1 = 0
Pine#2 ∩ Cone#1 = 0
Pine#1 ∩ Cone#2 = 1
Pine#2 ∩ Cone#2 = 0
Pine#1 ∩ Cone#3 = 2
Pine#2 ∩ Cone#3 = 0

Then, we can conclude that Pine1 and Cone3 are highly related.

Determine Word Sense Using WordNet

One idea to determine word sense in a given context by using WordNet is to look for all the paths from the context to the word and take the shortest one as the right sense. A detailed explanation of the adapted Lesk algorithm using WordNet can be found in (Banerjee & Pedersen, 2002; Banerjee & Pedersen, 2003). To elucidate this, consider the following example that is reproduced from

(Simpson & Dao, 2005) with author's written permission:

In Figure 3, we observe that the length between car and auto is 1, car and truck is 3, car and bicycle is 4, and car and fork is 12.

Measure Words Similarity Using WordNet

There are six measures to obtain similarity between words using WordNet. As described in (Pedersen, Patwardhan, & Michelizzi, 2004), three of the six measures are based on the information content of the Least Common Subsumer (LCS) of concepts. Information content is a measure of the specificity of a concept, and the LCS of concepts A and B is the most specific concept that is an ancestor of both A and B. Three similarity measures are based on path lengths between a pair of concepts.

In Figure 3, the LCS of {car, auto} and {truck} is {automotive, motor vehicle}, since the {automotive, motor vehicle} is more specific than the common subsumer {wheeled vehicle}.

In the present study, we use Wu and Palmer similarity measure introduced in (Wu & Palmer, 1994). The measure was revised by Resnik (Resnik, 1999), and the implementation used in our study was downloaded from (WordNet Simi-

larity lib). According to this measure, similarity between two concepts is the path length to the root node from the LCS of the two concepts. For two synsets S_1 and S_2, it is given by the formula: Similarity Score = 2*depth (LCS) / (depth (S_1) + depth (S_2)). Similarity score is in the range $0 <$ score $<= 1$. It can never be zero because depth of the LCS is never zero where the depth of the root of taxonomy starts with one. The score is one if the two input synsets are the same.

WordNet Based Similarity of Web Services

As we know from Section 2, parameter similarity is determined by the lexical similarity of parameter names. We use 3rd party similarity computation software module from (Simpson & Dao, 2005) along with WordNet for this purpose. Figure 4 illustrates the flowchart for the pre-processing and similarity computation that we used in this study. Once parameter similarity is obtained, then we compute operation similarity and web service similarity using the formulae mentioned in Section 2. Similarity matrix for web services thus computed is used as basis for clustering or grouping similar web services.

Figure 3. Illustration of WordNet structure

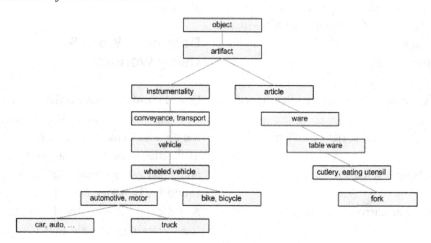

CLUSTERING AND CLASSIFICATION OF WEB SERVICES

Clustering is the process of partitioning data into groups of similar objects or clusters. It is an unsupervised learning technique that is widely used in Artificial Intelligence, Data mining etc. It aims to discover patterns taking into account the entire data. There are no pre-defined conditional and decision variables. Members within a cluster are more similar or related to each other and different from members of other clusters.

Clustering is used in our work to identify related or similar web services. There are many different approaches to clustering. In the present work, we use agglomerative or bottom-up Hierarchical Clustering method. In this method, initially each web service is treated as belonging to a cluster. Then we use similarity matrix of web services in the training dataset to determine the nearest neighbors. Nearest clusters are then merged into one cluster. This process is repeated and in the end all the web services merge to a single cluster.

Figure 4. WordNet based similarity computation

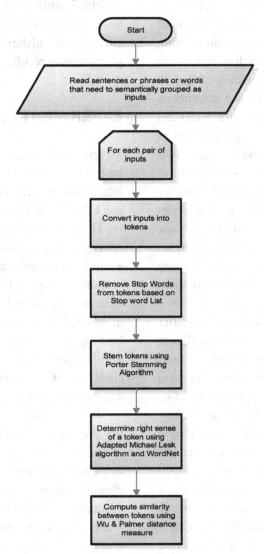

We used adapted version of Hierarchical Clustering program available at (Murtagh, 2002) for clustering web services. We employed a couple of approaches to use this clustering information to predict similarity of web services in the test dataset.

Classification of Web Services

First, we tried to generate rules from the generated clusters using rule-based algorithm BLEM2 (Chan & Santhosh, 2003). Web service operation name and parameter names are taken as condition attributes and cluster number as the decision attribute. Since the number of parameters is not constant across all web services, we have to treat some of the attributes as don't cares in the training set. To illustrate this, let us take web service 1 with operation *A* and web service 2 with operation *B*. Also, assume that operation *A* has 5 parameters (4 input parameters and 1 output parameter) and operation *B* has 3 parameters (2 input parameters and 1 output parameter). We take the maximum number of parameters of all web service operations, here 5, as condition attributes. So, when we represent operation *B* we take its 3 parameters as condition attributes and treat rest of the columns, as don't cares. As expected, this kind of training set would cause problems for most classifier learning algorithms, because too many don't cares entries are artificially inserted into the training set.

Since classification from rule-based classifier did not yield good results, we tried a different approach to predict similarity of web services in the test dataset. Initially, we represent each cluster by a set of characteristic operations of its member web services. To obtain this set of characteristic operations, i.e., for each web service in a cluster; take one characteristic operation that has maximum similarity to operations of other web services in the same cluster. For example, say a cluster has grouped two web services "Electronic Directory Assistance" and "Weather by City". "Electronic Directory Assistance" has three operations namely ResidentialLookup, BusinessLookup, LookupByAddress. "Weather by City" has two operations namely GetWeatherByCity, GetWeatherByCityXml. If similarity between ResidentialLookup and GetWeatherByCity is the highest, then we represent the cluster by these two most similar operations (one operation per web service). If a cluster has only one web service, then we take one web service operation that is very dissimilar to operations of web services in other clusters. This cluster representation is then used as a basis for predicting similarity of any new web services to the clusters using the nearest neighbor approach. To elucidate, we compute interface similarity between operations of each test web service and characteristic operations of clusters and find the nearest cluster. This approach yielded good results.

EXPERIMENTAL RESULTS

To setup the application, first WordNet needs to be installed. WordNet can be downloaded from http://wordnet.princeton.edu/obtain website. We use C#. NET to implement our application.

There is no publicly available web services dataset on the Internet. So, we have downloaded a small set of web services from XMethods.net website. It was tedious to dig through WSDL files and organize data into three excel files as mentioned in Section 3. Table 4 represents our training set of web services. Our clustering algorithm generated 5 clusters based on interface similarity of these web services. These clusters are represented in Figure 5.

We came up with a novel idea of representing the clusters by the most similar operations (1 operation per web service) of web services in that cluster. If there is only one web service in a cluster, then we select an operation that is very dissimilar to operations in other clusters. Table 5 lists the characteristic operations for clusters represented in Figure 5.

Table 4. Training dataset

Web service ID	Name	Text Description
1	US Zip Validator	Zip code validator
2	Phone Number Verification service	Phone number verifier
3	StrikeIron Foreign Exchange Rates	Current and historical foreign exchange rates
4	U.S. Yellow Pages	Access to yellow pages listings for 17 million U.S. businesses
5	City and State by ZIP	Finds the City and State for a given ZIP code
6	Electronic Directory Assistance	white pages
7	Weather by City	Enter a city name and instantly receive the current day's weather report.
8	Forecast by ZIP Code	Enter a U.S. ZIP code and instantly receive the 10-day weather forecast.

Figure 5. Clusters obtained from training data

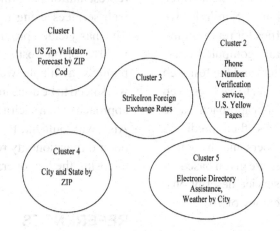

Table 5. Clusters and their characteristic operations

Cluster #	Operation	Web Service
1	ValidateZip	US Zip Validator
1	GetForecastByZip	Forecast by ZIP Code
2	PhoneVerify	Phone Number Verification service
2	ReversePhoneLookup	U.S. Yellow Pages
3	GetAllLatestRatesToUSD	StrikeIron Foreign Exchange Rates
4	GetCityStateByZip	City and State by ZIP
5	GetWeatherByCityXml	Weather by City
5	ResidentialLookup	Electronic Directory Assistance

Table 6. Test web services and nearest clusters

Test Web Service	Nearest cluster #	Web Services in Cluster	Actual Cluster #
FastWeather	1	US Zip Validator, Forecast by ZIP Code	1
Currency Convertor	3	StrikeIron Foreign Exchange Rates	3
StrikeIron Reverse Phone Residential Intel	5	Weather by City, Electronic Directory Assistance	5
DOTS Yellow Pages	3	StrikeIron Foreign Exchange Rates	2
PHONEval	2	Phone Number Verification service	2
Levelsoft GeoServices Global Weather Service	2	Phone Number Verification service	1
Zip Codes	1	US Zip Validator, Forecast by ZIP Code	1
StrikeIron ZIP Code Information	4	City and State by ZIP	4

We downloaded a set of web services to test our idea. We organized the WSDL data into three files as mentioned in Section 3. Similarly, we created another set of three files for representing the clusters. Then our program computed interface similarity between clusters and the test web services and found closest cluster to each test web service based on nearest neighbor approach. Table 6 represents test web services, their predicted nearest clusters, cluster members and the actual clusters. Actual cluster values are given based on semantic similarity of web service descriptions. Our approach yielded an accuracy of 70%.

CONCLUSION

We introduced an approach for finding similar or related web services by taking into account semantic similarity based on WordNet. It can be used as an add-on to any web service search engine with UDDI repository. We used semantics of WSDL along with WordNet to compute similarity between various web services. For web services in the training set, we computed similarities and clustered the data using hierarchical clustering. Next, we represented each cluster by a set of char-

acteristic operations. Then we used these cluster representations to evaluate similarity of any new web services using nearest neighbor approach. This has yielded promising results and accuracy is 70% for our test data. At present, there is no publicly available web services dataset. More work need to be done in future with evaluating our approach, when such a dataset becomes available. Also, we would like to compare our approach with other dimensionality reduction techniques while choosing the key operations of a cluster.

REFERENCES

Agrawal, R., Mannila, H., Srikant, R., Toivonen, H., & Verkamo, A. (1996). Fast discovery of association rules. In U.M. Fayyad, G. Piatetsky-Shapiro, P. Smyth, & R. Uthurusamy, (Eds.), *Advances in Knowledge Discovery and Data Mining* (pp. 307–328). Cambridge, MA: AAAI/MIT Press.

Akkiraju, R., et al. (2005). *Web Service Semantics: WSDL-S*. W3C member submission. Retrieved from www.w3.org/SubmissionWSDL-S/

Ankolekar, A., Burstein, M., Hobbs, J., Lassila, O., Martin, D., McIlraith, S., et al. (2001). DAML-S: Semantic Markup for Web Services. In *Proceedings of the International Semantic Web Working Symposium* (SWWS) (pp. 39–54). Stanford University, California.

Banerjee, S., & Pedersen, T. (2002). An Adapted Lesk Algorithm for Word Sense Disambiguation Using WordNet. In *Proceedings of the Third International Conference on Computational Linguistics and Intelligent Text Processing* (LNCS Vol. 2276, pp. 136–145). Retrieved from http://www.d.umn.edu/~tpederse/Pubs/cicling2002-b.ps

Banerjee, S., & Pedersen, T. (2003). Extended gloss overlap as a measure of semantic relatedness. In *Proceedings of the 18th International Joint Conference on Artificial Intelligence,* (pp. 805–810), Acapulco, Mexico, 9–15 August, 2003. Retrieved from http://www.d.umn.edu/~tpederse/Pubs/ijcai03.pdf

Barry, D. K. (2003). *Web Services and Service-Oriented Architectures: The Savvy Manager's Guide*. San Francisco, CA: Morgan Kaufmann Publishers.

Borgi, A., Corfini, S., & Popescu, R. (2008). Semantics-Based Composition-Oriented Discovery of Web Services. *ACM Trans. on Internet Technol., 8*(4), Article 19. DOI = 10.1145/1391949.1391953 http://doi.acm.org/10.1145/1391949.1391953

Cardoso, J., & Sheth, A. (2003). Semantic e-Workflow Composition. *Journal of Intelligent Information Systems, 21*(3), 191–225. doi:10.1023/A:1025542915514

Chan, C.-C., & Santhosh, S. (2003). Blem2: Learning Bayes' Rules From Examples Using Rough Sets. *NAFIPS 2003, 22nd Int. conf. of the North American Fuzzy Information Processing Society* (pp. 187–190), July 24 – 26, Chicago.

Christensen, E., Curbera, F., Meredith, G., & Weerawarana, S. (2001). *Web Services Description Language (WSDL) 1.1*. W3C Recommendation. Retrieved from http://www.w3.org/TR/2001/NOTE-wsdl-20010315

Clement, L., et al. (Eds.). (2004). *UDDI Version 3.0.2*. http://uddi.org/pubs/uddiv3.0.2-20041019.htm

Dong, X., et al. (2004). Similarity Search for Web Services. In *Proceedings of 2004 VLDB Conference* (pp. 372–383). Toronto, Canada. Retrieved from www.vldb.org/conf/2004/RS10P1.PDF

Fellbaum, C. (1998). *WordNet: An Electronic Lexical Database*. Cambridge, MA: MIT Press.

Fellbaum, C. (2007). *WordNet: Connecting words and concepts*. Retrieved from http://colab.cim3.net/file/work/SICoP/2007-02-06/WordNet02062007.ppt

Ganjisaffar, Y., Abolhassani, H., Neshati, M., & Jamali, M. (2006). A Similarity Measure for OWL-S Annotated Web Services. In *2006 IEEE/WIC/ACM International Conference on Web Intelligence* (pp. 621–624).

Jones, K. S. (1971). *Automatic Keyword Classification for Information Retrieval*. North Haven, CT: Archon Books.

Kil, H., Oh, S.-C., & Lee, D. (2006). On the Topological Landscape of Web Services Matchmaking. In *VLDB Int'l Workshop on Semantic Matchmaking and Resource Retrieval (SMR06)*, Seoul, Korea.

Kokash, N. (2006). A comparison of web service interface similarity measures. *STAIRS 2006 - Proceedings of the Third Starting AI Researchers' Symposium: Frontiers in Artificial Intelligence and Applications* (pp. 220–231), Riva del Garda, Trentino, Italy. Amsterdam: IOS Press.

Lesk, M. (1986). Automatic sense disambifuation using machine readable dictionaries: how to tell a pine cone from an ice cream cone. In *Proceedings of the 1986 SIGDOC Conference* (pp. 24–26).

Martin., et al. (2004). *OWL-S: Semantic Markup for Web Services*. Retrieved from http://www.w3.org/Submission/OWL-S/

Mitra, N. (Ed.). (2003). *SOAP Version 1.2 Part 0: Primer*. W3C Recommendation, 2003. Retrieved from http://www.w3.org/TR/2003/REC-soap12-part0-20030624/

Murtagh, F. (1985). *Multidimensional Clustering Algorithms*. Heidelberg, Germany: Physica-Verlag.

Murtagh, F. (2002). *Multivariate data analysis software and resources*. Retrieved from http://astro.u-strasbg.fr/~fmurtagh/mda-sw

Pedersen, T. (2005). Word sense disambiguation. *The AAAI 2005 Tutorial Advances in Word Sense Disambiguation*, Pittsburgh, PA., July 9, 2005. Retrieved from http://www.d.umn.edu/~tpederse/WSDTutorial.html

Pedersen, T., Patwardhan, S., & Michelizzi, J. (2004). WordNet:Similarity -- Measuring the relatedness of concepts. *Demonstrations of the Human Language Technology Conference of the North American Chapter of the Association for Computational Linguistics* (pp. 267–270), Boston, Mass., 2–7 May 2004. Available online at http://www.cs.utah.edu/~sidd/papers/PedersenPM04b.pdf

Porter, M. F. (1980). An algorithm for suffix stripping. *Program, 14*(3), 130–137.

Resnik, P. (1999). Semantic similarity in a taxonomy: an information based measure and its application to problems of ambiguity in natural language. *Journal of Artificial Intelligence Research, 11*, 95–130.

Saha, S., Murthy, C. A., & Pal, S. K. (2008). Classification of web services using tensor space model and rough ensemble classifier. *ISMIS 2008,* (Berlin: Springer-Verlang). *LNAI, 4994*, 508–513.

Salton, G., Wong, A., & Yang, C. S. (1975). A vector space model for automatic indexing. *Communications of the ACM, 18*(11), 613–620. doi:10.1145/361219.361220

Simpson, T., & Dao, T. (2005). *WordNet-based semantic similarity measurement*. Retrieved from http://www.codeproject.com/cs/library/semantic-similaritywordnet.asp van Rijsbergen, C.J., Robertson, S.E., & Porter, M.F. (1980). *New Models in Probabilistic Information Retrieval*. British Library Research and Development Report, no. 5587. London: British Library.

Wang, Y., & Stroulia, E. (2003a). Flexible interface matching for web-service discovery. In *Proceedings of the 4th Int. Conf. on Web Information Systems Engineering (WISE) 2003* (pp. 147–156), December 10–12, 2003.

Wang, Y., & Stroulia, E. (2003b). Similarity structure matching for assessing web-service similarity. In *ICSOC 2003,* (LNCS Vol. 2910, pp. 194–207). Berlin: Springer-Verlag.

WordNet Similarity lib. (n.d.). Retrieved from http://search.cpan.org/src/SID/WordNet-Similarity-1.04/lib/WordNet/Similarity/wup.pm

Wu, J., & Wu, Z. (2005). Similarity-based Web service matchmaking. In *Proceedings of 2005 IEEE International Conference on Services Computing* (Vol. 1, pp. 287–294).

Wu, Z., & Palmer, M. (1994). Verb semantics and lexical selection. In *Proceedings of the 32nd Annual Meeting of the Associations for Computational Linguistics* (pp. 133–138).

Yu, J., Guo, S., Su, H., Zhang, H., & Xu, K. (2007, May 8-12). A kernel based structure matching for web services search. [Banff, Alberta, Canada.]. *WWW, 2007*, 1249–1250.

Chapter 17
Finding Explicit and Implicit Knowledge:
Biomedical Text Data Mining

Kazuhiro Seki
Kobe University, Japan

Javed Mostafa
University of North Carolina at Chapel Hill, USA

Kuniaki Uehara
Kobe University, Japan

ABSTRACT

This chapter discusses two different types of text data mining focusing on the biomedical literature. One deals with explicit information or facts written in articles, and the other targets implicit information or hypotheses inferred from explicit information. A major difference between the two is that the former is bound to the contents within the literature, whereas the latter goes beyond existing knowledge and generates potential scientific hypotheses. As concrete examples applied to real-world problems, this chapter looks at two applications of text data mining: gene functional annotation and genetic association discovery, both considered to have significant practical importance.

INTRODUCTION

With the help of high throughput gene analysis and increasing computing power, the amount of data produced in biomedicine is rapidly growing, making it one of the most attractive domains for the exploration of data mining techniques. Among various types of data, such as DNA sequences, medical images, and clinical records, that could be mined for interesting knowledge and discoveries, this chapter focuses on textual resources, specifically, the biomedical literature, and discusses two different types of **text data mining** (TDM).

Medline, the world largest bibliographic database in life science, currently contains bibliographies for over 17 million articles, and 2000–4000 new records are added each day. Both the volume and the pace of the publications exceed the capacity of any individuals, which calls for the aid of intelligent information processing techniques, i.e., TDM. There are roughly two types of TDM with respect to the

DOI: 10.4018/978-1-61520-757-2.ch017

goals they pursue. One focuses on the information explicitly stated in text and attempts to extract and organize it for better information access. This type of TDM has been extensively studied in recent years and includes, for example, information retrieval (IR) (Hersh, 2004), information extraction (IE) (Hobbs, 2002), and automatic summarization (Reeve et al., 2007). The other type of TDM is not bound to explicit or existing information but targets implicit information, or heretofore unknown knowledge (Hearst, 1999), that could be revealed by synthesizing fragments of information extracted from a large volume of textual data. This type of TDM is called **hypothesis discovery** and was initiated by Swanson (1986b) in the 1980's. We will see more concrete examples for each type of TDM throughout this chapter.

BACKGROUND

There have been numerous efforts in biomedical TDM dealing with explicit information (Ananiadou et al., 2006; Cohen and Hersh, 2005; Shatkay, 2005). One of the earliest and most successful attempts in this type of TDM is named-entity (NE) recognition, the first step to IE, mainly targeting genes and proteins (Fukuda et al., 1998; Seki and Mostafa, 2005b; Hsu et al., 2008). NE recognition in biomedicine is largely different from other domains tackled earlier, such as newspaper articles, in a sense that biomedical NEs have surprisingly many synonyms and writing variants. This issue is essential in dealing with biomedical text and heavily affects the performance of TDM systems as we will see in the next section.

For biomedical IR, the Genomics Track (Hersh and Bhuptiraju, 2003; Hersh et al., 2004, 2005, 2006, 2007) at the Text REtrieval Conference (TREC) was undoubtedly the most significant strides made in the history. The track was a five-year project held between 2003 and 2007 and tackled various types of IR tasks, including Ad Hoc retrieval and passage retrieval, as well as other

IE oriented tasks. While the track was successful, having attracted the largest number of research groups world-wide among the TREC tracks, there is still much room for improvement, especially for the passage retrieval challenged in 2007 which, given a user query, required to return passages containing relevant named entities of a certain type within the context of supporting text.

Another task from the Genomics Track that is pertinent to TDM (in broader sense) is Gene Ontology (GO) annotation via automatic text analysis. The following provides some background of the task since this will be one of the main focuses in this chapter.

After the completion of the Human Genome Project, the major activities in molecular biology have shifted to understanding the precise functions of individual genes. The consequence in part is the increasing, large number of publications that one cannot digest. To provide direct access to the information regarding gene functions buried in natural language text, three model organism databases created controlled vocabularies, namely, the Gene Ontology (GO), to annotate genes with their functions. GO is structured as directed acyclic graph (DAG) under three top level nodes, Molecular Function (MF), Cellular Component (CC), and Biological Process (BP), as shown in Figure 1.

While GO annotation allows uniform queries across different databases, manually annotating GO terms is labor-intensive and costly due to the voluminous and specialized contents. This resulted in a demand to automate GO annotation, which was the main objective of the GO annotation task at the TREC Genomics Track and, independently, the BioCreative challenge (Blaschke et al., 2005), another important workshop targeting biomedical TDM. The next section will describe in detail how GO annotation can be effectively done in a standard categorization framework coupled with gene-centered document representation.

For biomedical hypothesis discovery, also known as **literature-based discovery** or LBD,

Figure 1. Fragment of Gene Ontology

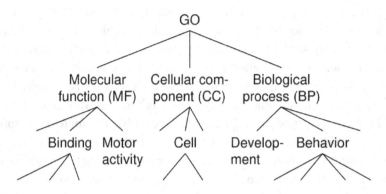

Swanson and his colleagues have conducted a series of pioneering work (Swanson, 1986a, 1986b; Swanson and Smalheiser, 1997; Swanson et al., 2006). He argued that there were two premises logically connected but the connection had been unnoticed due to the overwhelming publications and over-specialization. To instantiate the idea, he manually analyzed numbers of articles and identified premises or explicit information that "Raynaud's disease is characterized by high platelet affregability, high blood viscosity, and vasoconstriction" and "dietary fish oil reduces blood lipids, platelet affregability, blood viscosity, and vascular reactivity." These premises together suggest a hypothesis or *implicit* information that "fish oil may be effective for clinical treatment of Raynaud's disease," which was later supported by experimental evidence.

Based on the groundwork, Swanson and other researchers have developed computer programs to aid hypothesis discovery (Lindsay and Gordon, 1999; Srinivasan, 2004; Swanson and Smalheiser, 1997; Weeber et al., 2003). For instance, Weeber et al. (2003) implemented a system, called DAD-system, taking advantage of a natural language processing tool. The key feature of DAD-system is the incorporation of the UMLS Metathesaurus[1] for knowledge representation. An advantage of using the thesaurus is that irrelevant concepts can be excluded from further exploration if particular *semantic types* under which each Metathesaurus

concept is categorized are given. Independently, Srinivasan (2004) developed another system, called Manjal, also leveraging the Metathesaurus. As opposed to the previous work, however, Manjal relies solely on MeSH[2] terms assigned to Medline records, disregarding all textual information.

More recently, there is some work conceptually related to Swanson's hypothesis discovery but taking a more data-intensive, target-oriented approach. While Swanson's work focused on finding hidden knowledge, where article citations were carefully analyzed to ensure that discovered knowledge was indeed unknown, this type of work focuses more on finding prominent associations between certain types of biomedical entities. For example, Perez-Iratxeta et al. (2005) and Ozgur et al. (2008) independently developed an approach to identifying gene-disease associations. Perez-Iratxeta et al. utilized co-annotation of certain types of MeSH terms to relate phenotypes and chemicals and applied DNA sequence comparison to locate candidate causative genes. On the other hand, Ozgur et al. employed network analysis techniques to identify "central" genes as candidates in a gene network specifically build for an input disease. Both exploited literature data (or their associated meta data) as the knowledge sources. The next section describes, along this line, an approach to gene-disease association discovery as an extension of IR.

BIOMEDICAL TDM

This section describes two independent biomedical TDM projects, one aiming at automatic GO annotation within a standard classification framework and the other generating hypotheses between hereditary diseases and their causative genes in an extended IR model. The former is regarded as the broader sense of TDM, attempting to abstract the explicit information found in journal articles into controlled GO terms, whereas the latter is an instance of the more restricted sense of TDM, predicting implicit genetic associations.

Automatic Gene Ontology Annotation

Given a pair of a gene and an article in which the gene appears, GO annotation can been posed as a traditional text categorization problem to assign one or more predefined classes (i.e., GO terms) to the input (i.e., the gene-article pair). Here, an important difference to note is that GO annotation needs to be done not for each article—as opposed to traditional text categorization—but for each gene-article pair. In other words, when multiple genes appear in an article, each pair article, gene needs to be treated as a "document" or "text" in the sense of text categorization.

Below, we only consider top-level three GO terms, called GO domains, as classes under which an input gene-article pair is to be categorized, following the task definition at the Genomics Track.

Gene-Centered Document Representation

As described above, GO annotation aims to assign one or more classes (GO domains) to each input gene-article pair. A natural way to treat it as text categorization is to represent each gene-article pair as a unique document. There are at least several options as to how to accomplish this task.

The simplest would be to use the whole article irrespective of a given gene. This approach yields the same document representation for any gene coupled with the article, which is not desirable since each gene generally has different functions. Thus, a more reasonable approach would be to employ gene-specific document representation. This section describes such an approach, which has been proven effective for GO annotation. In essence, it extracts only text fragments containing a given gene and uses a set of the extracted text fragments to represent the article, gene pair. Due to the variety of ways to refer to a unique gene, however, the representation needs to be built with care through *gene name expansion* and *gene name identification*, explained next.

Gene name expansion associates given gene name with its synonyms. Gene (or protein) names are known to have many types of synonyms including aliases, abbreviations, and symbols (Sehgal and Srinivasan, 2006), which need to be considered in identifying gene-bearing text fragments. For instance, *membrane associated transporter protein* can be referred to as *underwhite, dominant brown, Matp, uw, Dbr, bls, Aim1*, etc. Fortunately, there are several knowledge resources, such as the Entrez Gene database (Maglott et al., 2005), from which one can obtain a large list of gene synonyms. It is also possible to obtain a certain type of synonymous names in a given article itself since gene name abbreviations often appear immediately following the official names (Schwartz and Hearst, 2003).

After applying gene name expansion, the next step is to find text fragments mentioning a gene in question through *gene name identification*. Here, a problem is that, besides synonyms, gene names often have many variants resulted from inconsistent use of special symbols, white space, and capital and small letters (Cohen et al., 2002; Cohen, 2005; Fang et al., 2006; Morgan et al., 2007). Such writing variations can be tolerated via *normalization* and *approximate matching* steps. For the former, heuristic rules like the followings are often utilized to normalize *both* gene names and text.

- Replace all special symbols (non-alpha-numeric characters) with space (e.g., NF-kappa → NF kappa)
- Insert space between different character types, such as alphabets and numerals (e.g., Diet1 → Diet 1)
- Insert space between Greeks and other words (e.g., kappaB → kappa B)
- Lowercase all characters

For the latter, *approximate name matching*, we describe a simple word-overlap score defined below, which can deal with unconventional word orders and insertions/deletions, between the target gene name (denoted as *canon*) and its actual occurrence in text (denoted as *variant*).

$$\text{Overlap}(canon, variant) = \frac{M - \alpha \cdot U}{N + \beta} \quad (1)$$

M and *U* denote the number of matching and unmatching words, respectively, α is a penalty for unmatching words, *N* is the number of words composing the gene name, and β penalizes shorter gene names. If any *variant* found in a paragraph had a score exceeding a predefined threshold, the paragraph is used as a part of the "document" to represent the article, gene pair.

So far, we have collected a set of paragraphs deemed pertinent to a given gene from a given article. By regarding the set of paragraphs as a document, the next steps can simply follow a standard text categorization procedure, namely, feature selection, term weighting, and then classification. There are many possible choices for each stage from the machine learning literature, and here we arbitrarily choose chi-square statistic (Yang and Pedersen, 1997), TFCHI (Debole and Sebastiani, 2003), and *k* nearest neighbors (*k*NN) (Yang and Liu, 1999), respectively, each widely used for text categorization.

Experiments

Using the data set from the Genomics Track 2004 GO annotation task (Cohen and Hersh, 2006), this section reports the performance of the classification framework coupled with gene-centered representation described in the previous section. The data set consists of 504 full-text articles for training and 378 for test, and each article is associated with one or more genes and each gene is manually annotated with one or more GO domains (MF, BP, and CC) or negative. The training data were used for tuning parameters including the number of *k* neighbors and per-class thresholds. In the following experiments, a gene name synonym dictionary was automatically created from SWISS-PROT (O'Donovan et al., 2002) and LocusLink[3] (Pruitt and Maglott, 2001), containing 493,473 entries.

Table 1 compares the result produced by the approach described above (referred to as "GCR") and the representative results from the TREC official evaluation. Despite its simplicity, GCR performed quite well. Incidentally, the "Best" in TREC was also obtained by the same approach as GCR (Seki and Mostafa, 2005a). The improvement is due to some corrections in our codes for feature selection and classification. The key for the strong performance lies in careful consideration of the various forms of gene mentions in the document representation stage. The following takes a closer look at their contribution.

In the gene-centered document representation stage, there are many alternatives that could be chosen instead of what have been described in the previous section. Here, we provide several empirical observations for the following alternative configurations to shed light on the impact of the corresponding factors in automatic GO annotation.

- Gene name identification: In the original framework, the paragraphs likely to contain the target gene were identified using

Table 1. The TREC official results and our result for GO annotation on the test data set

		Prec	**Recall**	F_1
TREC	Best	0.441	0.769	0.561
	Worst	0.169	0.133	0.149
	Mean	0.360	0.581	0.382
GCR		0.501	0.707	0.586

approximate word matching. An alternative is to perform exact word matching instead, which would improve the precision of gene name identification but may hurt GO annotation by lowering recall.

- Gene name expansion: In the original framework, gene names were expanded based on an automatically compiled name dictionary. Similar to the case of gene name identification, an alternative is not to apply gene name expansion, sticking to given gene names.
- Unit of extraction: In the original framework, paragraphs were used as the unit of extraction. Other alternatives include:
  - Only the sentence containing the target gene (denoted as *G*)
  - In addition to *G*, an immediately succeeding sentence (denoted as *G+S*)
  - In addition to *G+S*, an immediately preceding sentence (denoted as *P+G+S*)

- The entire article irrespective of the target gene (denoted as *ART*)

The original framework focusing on paragraphs can be placed somewhere between *P+G+S* and *ART*.

Table 2 summarizes the system performance in F_1 for each configuration described above, where the training data were classified using leave-one-out cross-validation, while the test data were classified using the training data as before. The bottom row "Default" corresponds to TFCHI in Table 1 but shows higher F_1 since class-specific threshold for *k*NN was optimized on *evaluation data* themselves to compare possible maximum performance in each different configuration. From these experiments, the following observations can be made.

- **Gene name identification:** Using exact word matching for gene name identification severely deteriorates the performance

Table 2. Results for deletion experiments. Numbers in parentheses in column "Average" indicate percent increase/decrease relative to "Default"

System Component		Training	Test	Average
Gene name identification	Exact	0.368	0.417	0.393(-31.5%)
Gene name dictionary	Unused	0.434	0.465	0.450(-21.7%)
	G	0.519	0.609	0.564(-1/7%)
	G+S	0.525	0.612	0.569(-1.0%)
Unit of extraction	*P+G+S*	0.528	0.615	0.572(-0.4%)
	ART	0.499	0.585	0.542(-5.6%)
Default		0.528	0.620	0.574

both on the training and test data sets. This result indicates, as anticipated, that gene names are often written in slightly different forms from their canonical ones (i.e., database entries). Thus, a flexible name matching scheme such as the one described here is needed to locate gene name occurrences.

- **Gene name dictionary:** Disabling the gene name dictionary also decreased F_1 score both on the training and test data by 21.7% on average. It indicates the wide use of gene name synonyms and the importance of gene name expansion. It is also interesting to note that even an automatically created dictionary, which is inevitably noisy and not suitable for NE recognition, can be very beneficial.

- **Unit of extraction:** There is a trend that F_1 gradually increases from G (sentence containing the target gene) to $P+G+S$ (G plus immediately preceding and succeeding sentences) and then decreases when the entire article was used (i.e., *ART*). Thus, extracting paragraphs, which is somewhere between $P+G+S$ and *ART*, appears to be near optimum, although the difference from G, $G+S$, or $P+G+S$ is not quite significant.

An important question for TDM is the utility of different kinds of textual data for an intended task. As opposed to often-used Medline data whose textual contents are basically only titles and abstracts, the Genomics Track data set used in the above experiments are rich, composed of full-text articles in SGML format, where section blocks are also explicitly indicated. Because individual sections have different focuses and convey different types of information, their importance for GO annotation is expected to be different. One can examine the utility of different sections by using only one section at a time from which gene-bearing paragraphs are extracted. Figure 2 presents the results of such an experiment,

comparing different sections in terms of the performance of GO annotation. The experiment revealed that using only "Result" sections achieved $F_1 = 0.524$, which is almost as good as using all sections (0.543), followed by "Abstract" (0.466), "MeSH" (0.427), and so on. This result makes sense because Result sections generally report on empirical findings that would be relevant to GO annotation. Interestingly, using "Method" sections alone yielded the worst $F_1 = 0.286$; even worse than using only titles (0.398).

Genetic Association Discovery

The previous section looks at an instance of TDM in a broader sense, automatic GO annotation, which in essence abstracts and generalizes the knowledge explicitly described in natural language text. In contrast, this section describes an approach to discovering unknown or implicit associations between genes and hereditary diseases. For modeling genetic associations, this approach employs a formal IR model, specifically, the inference network (Metzler and Croft, 2004; Turtle and Croft, 1991).

Inference Network for Genetic Associations

The original inference network IR model, in its simplest form, consists of three layers of nodes, i.e., a user query, terms, and documents, connected in this order. In genetic association discovery where we wish to find candidate genes for a certain disease, a disease d can be seen as a query and genes g as documents by an analogy with IR. Intermediate nodes connecting genes and disease then could be, for example, gene functions f and phenotypes p characterizing genes and a disease, respectively. The structure of this inference network adapted to genetic associations is illustrated in Figure 3. Here, it is much easier to deal with gene functions and phenotypes by transforming them to some standard terminology rather than free form

Figure 2. Results produced by individual sections. "All" used all the sections. Percentages above bars indicate the respective proportions to "All"

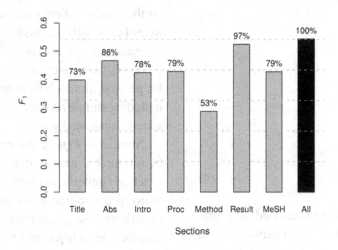

of natural language text. For this purpose, gene functions can be represented by GO terms as we have seen in the previous section, and phenotypes by MeSH terms categorized under the C category (Perez-Iratxeta et al., 2002).

Given the inference network, disease-causing genes can be predicted based on the probability $P(d|G)$ defined below, which quantifies how much a set of candidate genes G increases the belief in the development of disease d.

$$P(d \mid G) = \sum_i \sum_j P(d \mid p_i) \times P(p_i \mid f_j) \times P(f_j \mid G) \quad (2)$$

In Equation (2), p_i and f_j are binary random variable representing the states (active or inactive) of phenotype p_i and gene function f_j, respectively. Applying Bayes' theorem and some elementary manipulations to the equation yields

Figure 3. Inference network to model gene-disease associations

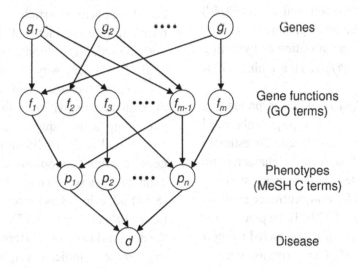

$$P(d \mid G) \propto \sum_i \sum_j \left[\frac{P(p_i \mid d)}{P(\bar{p_i} \mid d)} \times \frac{P(f_j \mid p_i)P(\bar{f_j} \mid \bar{p_i})}{P(\bar{f_j} \mid p_i)P(f_j \mid \bar{p_i})} \times F(p_i) \times F(f_j) \times P(f_j \mid G) \right]$$

(3)

where

$$F(p_i) = \prod_{h=1}^{m} \frac{P(\bar{f_h} \mid p_i)}{P(\bar{f_h} \mid \bar{p_i})},$$

$$F(f_j) = \prod_{k=1}^{n} \frac{P(f_j)P(f_j \mid \bar{p_k})}{P(\bar{f_j})P(\bar{f_j} \mid \bar{p_k})}.$$

(4)

The first factor of the right-hand side of Equation (3) represents the interaction between d and p_i, and the second factor represents the interaction between p_i and f_j, which takes the form of odds ratio. The third and fourth factors represent the main effects of p_i and f_j, respectively. The last factor, for simplicity, takes either 0 or 1, indicating whether f_j is a function of any gene contained in G.

Probability Estimation

Given the final model derived in the previous section, our next task is to estimate the probabilistic parameters involved in Equation (3). Among many types of evidence we could utilize, this section describes one possible solution to exploit the abundant biomedical literature. While the following focuses on estimation methods for $P(p \mid d)$ and $P(f \mid p)$, most of the other parameters can be easily obtained by marginalization or by noting that $P(\bar{f} \mid p)$ equals $1 - P(f \mid p)$ as p is a binary random variable.

The probability $P(p \mid d)$ can be interpreted as a degree of belief that a phenotype p is observed when a disease d has developed. To estimate the probability, we first identify characteristic phenotypes for d based on chi-square statistic, a measure often used for co-occurrence analysis (Manning and Schütze, 1999). To be precise, for given d, a Medline search is conducted using d as a query, and all the MeSH C terms assigned to

the retrieved articles are extracted as phenotypes. Then only those with high χ^2 (computed based on the number of retrieved articles with/without MeSH C terms being assigned) are considered as characteristic phenotypes p for d. As estimates of $P(p \mid d)$, here we reuse χ^2 divided by the max χ^2 for given d, although there are other possibilities, including simple relative frequencies of retrieved articles annotated with p.

Similar to $P(p \mid d)$, the probability $P(f \mid p)$ can be interpreted as a degree of belief that a gene function f underlies a phenotype p. Because there is no direct source to be used as training data to estimate the probability, here we attempt to construct *weakly labeled* training data based on database coannotation as follows. We know, from Medline records, those articles assigned any MeSH C terms and, independently, we know from the Entrez Gene database those articles referenced to by gene entries. Since the articles both annotated by MeSH and referenced to by Entrez Gene (i.e., the intersection of two circles in Figure 4) are associated with particular phenotypes and gene functions, their possible associations may be reported in the article contents.

A common technique to identify such possible associations is to look at co-occurrences of two concepts, i.e., MeSH C terms and GO terms. However, a shortcoming of the approach in this particular case is that MeSH terms do not literally appear in articles and neither do GO terms despite the fact that they are associated with the articles (Camon et al., 2005; Schuemie et al., 2004). One way to mitigate the problem is to expand a concept and represent it by a set of related terms, which is similar to the idea of expanding a user query, called *query expansion*, found in the IR literature. For example, a gene function "endoplasmic reticulum" can be expanded to a set of (weighted) terms {granular (8.54), adhering (8.54), microscopy (7.98), cavities (7.98), cisternae (7.73), . . .} extracted from the description of the GO term, where the figures in parentheses indicate weights calculated based

Figure 4. Coannotated articles (the intersection of two circles) as weakly labeled training data

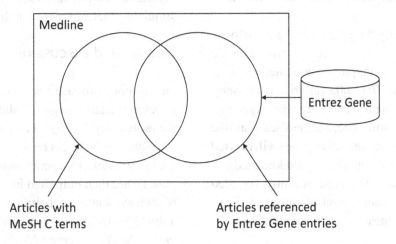

on inverse document frequencies (IDF) (Sparck Jones, 1972) by regarding GO term descriptions as documents. Similarly, MeSH C terms can be expanded into a set of related terms extracted from their scope notes. In the following, these related terms collectively representing a concept are referred to as *proxy terms*.

With the expanded concepts, one can apply the co-occurrence-based approach for estimating $P(f|p)$. As a first step, we define the strength of the association between a gene function f and a phenotype p within an article a as

$$S(f,p;a) = \sum_{C(t_f, t_p; a)} \frac{w(t_f) \cdot w(t_p)}{\left| \Pr oxy(f) \right| \cdot \left| \Pr oxy(p) \right|} \quad (5)$$

where t_f and t_p denote any proxy terms for f and p, respectively, $C(t_f, t_p; a)$ denotes a set of all co-occurrences of t_f and t_p within a, and $w(\cdot)$ returns the weight of the argument. The denominator is the product of the proxy sizes used as a normalizing factor. As a term weight, one can use the IDF values mentioned above or other arbitrary weighting schemes. In the following experiments, we adopted a TFIDF-like weighting scheme. The association scores $S(f, p; a)$ are computed for each training article and are accumulated over the entire training data. Finally, we define the probability

$P(f|p)$ as the relative value of the accumulated association score.

Experimental Setup

A major difficulty in evaluating a hypothesis discovery system is to validate discovered hypotheses because by definition the hypotheses are not known to be true or false. One possible solution to the problem is to separate existing knowledge into older and newer sets and to use only the former for parameter estimation and only the latter as future discovery to target. The following describes the procedure to create such a benchmark data set from a publicly available database, in particular, the genetic association database (GAD).[4] GAD is a manually-curated archive of human genetic studies, containing pairs of gene and disease that are known to have causative relations.

1. Associate each gene-disease pair with the publication date of the article from which the entry was populated. The date can be seen as the time when the relation became public knowledge.

2. Group gene-disease pairs by disease names. As GAD deals with complex diseases, a single disease may be paired with multiple genes.

3. For each pair of a disease and its causative genes,

   (a) Identify the gene whose relation to the disease was most recently reported based on the publication date. If the date is after 7/1/2003 (arbitrarily chosen), the gene will be used as the target, i.e., new knowledge, and the disease and the rest of the causative genes will be used as system input, i.e., old knowledge.

   (b) Remove the most recently reported gene from the set of causative genes and repeat the previous step 3a.

The separation of the data by publication dates ensures to simulate gene-disease association discovery. This procedure resulted in 257 future discoveries of genetic associations categorized under six disease classes: *Cancer, Cardiovascular, Immune, Metabolic, Psych*, and *Unknown*. In the following experiments, the *Cancer* class (containing 45 associations) was used for system development and parameter tuning.

For parameter estimation, training data were collected from the TREC Genomics Track 2004 (Hersh et al., 2004) Ad Hoc retrieval data set, which is a subset of the Medline records created between the years 1994 and 2003. In the data set, there are 29,158 records that can be used as training data such that 1) they are assigned at least one MeSH C term, 2) they are referenced to by at least one Entrez Gene entry, 3) the Entrez Gene entries are not the target causative genes to avoid possible direct evidence, and 4) the Medline records have publication dates before 7/1/2003 to simulate genetic association discovery.

Results and Discussion

Given input (disease name d, known causative genes, and a target region in the human genome), the probability $P(d|G)$ is computed for each gene g residing in the target region, where G is a set of the known causative genes plus g. The candidate genes g are then outputted in a descending order of their associated probabilities as system output. Table 3 shows the system performance in *area under the ROC curve* (AUC) for the approach described in the previous section, denoted by "w/ text" and an alternative approach, denoted by "w/o text", which was produced by setting $S(f, p; a)$ constant disregarding article contents.

Both "w/o text" and "w/ text" achieved significantly higher AUC than 0.5 (corresponding to random guess), indicating the validity of the general framework adapting the inference network for unknown genetic association discovery. Comparing the two schemes, AUC for "w/ text" improved by 4.6% over that for "w/o text", which suggests the overall benefit of textual data to acquire more precise associations between concepts. It should be also mentioned, without proxy terms, that the overall AUC by "w/ text" decreased to 0.682 (not shown in the table), verifying their effectiveness.

The experiment above was conducted using Medline records which have only titles and abstracts as textual data from the main contents.

Table 3. System performance in AUC for different disease classes. The figures in the parentheses indicate percent increase/decrease over "w/o text"

	Cardiovascular	Immune	Metabolic	Psych	Unknown	Overall
w/o text	0.677	0.686	0.684	0.514	0.703	0.682
w/ text	0.737	0.668	0.623	0.667	0.786	0.713
	(8.9%)	(-2.6%)	(-9.0%)	(29.8%)	(11.7%)	(4.6%)

Here, an important question for TDM targeting literature data is whether full text is of any help for a given problem at hand. To answer the question, the same approach "w/ text" was tested with full text articles for parameter estimation. For this experiment, we used the full-text collection from the TREC Genomics Track 2004 categorization task (Hersh et al., 2004). Among the 11,880 full-text articles contained in the data set, it turned out that there were only 679 articles which satisfied the four conditions mentioned in the Experimental Setup section. Table 4 summarizes the results obtained based on full-text articles ("full text") and only on titles and abstracts ("abstract"). For fair comparison, we used only 679 abstracts corresponding to the 679 full texts. Note that these results are not directly comparable with the previous results due to the very different training data size. Examining each disease class, it is observed that the use of full-text articles lead to a large improvement over using abstracts except for the *Immune* class. Overall, the improvement achieved by full texts is 5.1%, indicating the advantage of full text articles.

Lastly, we look at one possible approach to effectively utilizing domain dependent knowledge resources for hypothesis discovery, specifically, domain ontologies. Reflecting the importance of the field, there are numbers of high-quality and comprehensive knowledge resources in the biomedical domain, which could enhance hypothesis discovery systems. While the genetic association discovery framework and the methodology described in this chapter already incorporates/utilizes such knowledge resources, i.e., GAD, Entrez Gene, GO, and MeSH, the use of the latter two was limited as representation of individual concepts without considering their semantic relations. As we have seen in Figure 1, GO has a hierarchical structure representing semantic relations among concepts, and so does MeSH. One can incorporates these additional information into the discovery framework by many possible ways. A simple approach would be to propagate associations between gene functions and phenotypes according to their hierarchical structures. A rational behind is that, for example, a gene function g would be related to a phenotype f if g's parents/children in the hierarchy are related to f.

The intuition above can be formalized as follows. Let A denote an adjacency matrix with a_{ij} being $P(f_j|p_i)$, and let A' denote the updated matrix. Then, A' can be expressed as $A' = W^{(p)}AW^{(f)}$, where $W^{(p)}$ denotes an $n \times n$ matrix with $w_{ij}^{(p)}$ specifying a proportion of a probability to be transmitted from p_j to p_i. Similarly, $W^{(f)}$ is an $m \times m$ matrix with $w_{ij}^{(f)}$ specifying a proportion transmitted from f_i to f_j. For instance, if we equally split the amount of probability among its children (or parents), $w_{ij}^{(p)}$ can be defined as follows.

$$
w_{ij}^{(p)} = \begin{cases} 1 & \text{if } i = j \\ \dfrac{1}{\# \text{ of children of } p_j} & \text{if } p_i \text{ is a child of } p_j \\ \dfrac{1}{\# \text{ of parents of } p_j} & \text{if } p_i \text{ is a parent of } p_j \\ 0 & \text{otherwise} \end{cases}
\tag{6}
$$

Table 4. System performance in AUC based on the training data of 679 articles. The figures in the parentheses indicate percent increase/decrease over "abstract"

	Cardiovascular	Immune	Metabolic	Psych	Unknown	Overall
Abstract	0.652	0.612	0.566	0.623	0.693	0.643
Full text	0.737	0.590	0.640	0.724	0.731	0.676
	(13.0%)	(-3.6%)	(13.0%)	(16.2%)	(5.5%)	(5.1%)

Similarly, $w_{ij}^{(f)}$ can be defined by replacing i and j in the right-hand side of Equation (6). Note that one can iteratively apply Equation (6) to take advantage of more distant relationships than direct children/parents. This propagation would help to mitigate data sparseness attributed to insufficient training data.

Figure 5 shows the results when the simple propagation policy implemented by Equation (6) is iteratively applied (up to twice) for the "w/ text" approach in Table 3 and "full text" in Table 4. Remember that the latter is also based on "w/ text" for estimating $P(f|p)$ but uses a smaller number of full-text articles. This experiment used only child-to-parent relations in the GO hierarchy without using the MeSH hierarchy as using MeSH rather deteriorated the overall performance.

For both cases, "w/ text" and "full text", the effect of the propagation was somewhat mixed for different disease classes. The overall AUC at the right-most bars labeled as "All" improved slightly for "w/ text" and more clearly for "full text" (+4.0%) as the number of iterations increased. The difference is presumably due to the fact that the associations learned from the small number of full text articles are sparser than those from a large number of abstracts, and thus the propagation was more effective for the former.

FUTURE TRENDS

Although both types of TDM, broader and narrower, utilize textual data, they are distinctive in their intended goals and consequently have developed in mostly separate research communities. The research in hypothesis discovery, conducted by Swanson and the followers, has relied on rather simple term co-occurrences and/ or MeSH co-annotations to link two concepts, where knowledge sources were limited to those found in the analyzed articles. The genetic association discovery framework described in the previous section, too, is limited in that respect, although it incorporates external resources, such as the Entrez Gene database and Gene Ontology. On the other hand, there has been a continuously active research area to extract information from textual resources, namely, the broader sense of TDM, which could enhance a variety of knowledge processing/management systems. A natural direction to pursue would be then to exploit the fruits of these research efforts in a complementary manner to benefit each other. One such scenario is illustrated below.

Since current manual GO annotation is overly slow, genes in any given model organism database are thought to be underannotated to a large extent. This hurts the representation of genes in the gene-disease inference network shown in Figure

Figure 5. System performance before and after propagating associations using the GO hierarchy

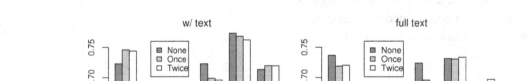
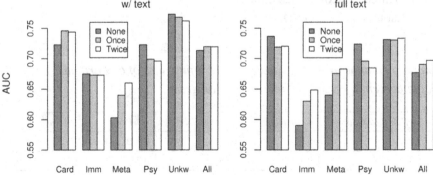

3. Automatic GO annotation could compensate for the problem by providing "new" gene functions which have not been annotated but already reported in the literature. The additional gene functional annotation enables richer representation of individual genes, which in turn could lead to more reliable estimation of gene-disease associations with wider coverage. Conversely, the inference network, specifically the intermediate bipartite network linking gene functions and phenotypes, could help GO annotation. One could identify similar genes in terms of phenotypes, which, similar to the idea of orthologs (Stoica and Hearst, 2006), could be used for spotting likely candidates of gene functions.

CONCLUSION

This chapter looked at two different types of biomedical TDM and, for each, presented a concrete example applied for practical problems in the domain with experiments on real-world data. One type of TDM aims to abstract explicit information described in natural language text, and the other intends to discover implicit knowledge, called hypotheses. For the former, we described an approach to automatic GO domain annotation based on a standard text categorization framework with careful consideration of the specialized terminology. The significance of the approach was not a particular classification technique but came from the document representation, i.e., the effective summary of articles centered on a gene under consideration. In fact, a series of experiments demonstrated that a flexible gene name matching scheme used in conjunction with a gene name dictionary was crucial for GO annotation. Subsequently, for the more restricted sense of TDM, we described an application of the inference network IR model to genetic association discovery and suggested an evaluation methodology where a benchmark data set was systematically created for simulating

hypothesis discovery. In addition, the potential benefits of utilizing the rich knowledge resources, including full-text articles and ontologies, were discussed along with actual experiments.

In conclusion, biomedicine is an attractive domain for the exploration of data mining given the rich, heterogeneous data available. Especially, literature data are unique in that they represent the accumulation of knowledge we have ever discovered but have been severely underused, partly due to the difficulty to access the information contained therein. Now that more and more resources including full-text archives[5] and natural language processing tools[6] are becoming available, the time appears to have ripened for the data mining community to actively engage in the exciting field.

REFERENCES

Ananiadou, S., Kell, D. B., & Tsujii, J. (2006). Text mining and its potential applications in systems biology. *Trends in Biotechnology, 24*(12), 571–579. doi:10.1016/j.tibtech.2006.10.002

Blaschke, C., Leon, E., Krallinger, M., & Valencia, A. (2005). Evaluation of BioCreAtIvE assessment of task 2. *BMC Bioinformatics, 6*(Suppl 1), S16. doi:10.1186/1471-2105-6-S1-S16

Camon, E., Barrell, D., Dimmer, E., Lee, V., Magrane, M., & Maslen, J. (2005). An evaluation of GO annotation retrieval for BioCreAtIvE and GOA. *BMC Bioinformatics, 6*(Suppl 1), S17. doi:10.1186/1471-2105-6-S1-S17

Cohen, A., & Hersh, W. (2006). The TREC 2004 genomics track categorization task: classifying full text biomedical documents. *Journal of Biomedical Discovery and Collaboration, 1*(1), 4. doi:10.1186/1747-5333-1-4

Cohen, A. M. (2005). Unsupervised gene/protein named entity normalization using automatically extracted dictionaries. In *Proceedings of the ACL-ISMB Workshop on Linking Biological Literature, Ontologies and Databases: Mining Biological Semantics*, (pp. 17–24).

Cohen, A. M., & Hersh, W. R. (2005). A survey of current work in biomedical text mining. *Briefings in Bioinformatics*, 6(1), 57–71. doi:10.1093/bib/6.1.57

Cohen, K. B., Acquaah-Mensah, G. K., Dolbey, A. E., & Hunter, L. (2002). Contrast and variability in gene names. In *Proceedings of the ACL-02 workshop on natural language processing in the biomedical domain*, Morristown, NJ, (pp. 14–20).

Debole, F., & Sebastiani, F. (2003). Supervised term weighting for automated text categorization. In *Proceedings of 18th ACM Symposium on Applied Computing*, (pp. 784–788).

Fang, H. R., Murphy, K., Jin, Y., Kim, J., & White, P. (2006). Human gene name normalization using text matching with automatically extracted synonym dictionaries. In *Proceedings of the HLT-NAACL BioNLP Workshop on Linking Natural Language Processing and Biology*, (pp. 41–48).

Fukuda, K., Tsunoda, T., Tamura, A., & Takagi, T. (1998). Toward information extraction: Identifying protein names from biological papers. In . *Proceedings of the Pacific Symposium on Biocomputing*, 3, 705–716.

Hearst, M. A. (1999). Untangling text data mining. In *Proceedings of the 37th Annual Meeting of the Association for Computational Linguistics*, (pp. 3–10).

Hersh, W. (2004). Report on TREC 2003 genomics track first-year results and future plans. *SIGIR Forum*, 38(1), 69–72. doi:10.1145/986278.986292

Hersh, W., & Bhuptiraju, R. T. (2003). TREC 2003 genomics track overview. In *Proceedings of the 12th Text REtrieval Conference* (TREC).

Hersh, W., Bhuptiraju, R. T., Ross, L., Cohen, A. M., & Kraemer, D. F. (2004). TREC 2004 genomics track overview. In *Proceedings of the 13th Text REtrieval Conference* (TREC).

Hersh, W., Cohen, A. M., Roberts, P., & Rekapalli, H. K. (2006). TREC 2006 genomics track overview. In *Proceedings of the 15th Text REtrieval Conference* (TREC).

Hersh, W., Cohen, A. M., Ruslen, L., & Roberts, P. (2007). TREC 2007 genomics track overview. In *Proceedings of the 16th Text REtrieval Conference* (TREC).

Hersh, W., Cohen, A. M., Yang, J., Bhuptiraju, R. T., Roberts, P., & Hearst, M. (2005). TREC 2005 genomics track overview. In *Proceedings of the 14th Text REtrieval Conference* (TREC).

Hobbs, J. R. (2002). Information extraction from biomedical text. *Journal of Biomedical Informatics*, 35(4), 260–264. doi:10.1016/S1532-0464(03)00015-7

Hsu, C.-N., Chang, Y.-M., Kuo, C.-J., Lin, Y.-S., Huang, H.-S., & Chung, I.-F. (2008). Integrating high dimensional bi-directional parsing models for gene mention tagging. *Bioinformatics (Oxford, England)*, 24(13), i286–i294. doi:10.1093/bioinformatics/btn183

Lindsay, R. K., & Gordon, M. D. (1999). Literature-based discovery by lexical statistics. *Journal of the American Society for Information Science American Society for Information Science*, 50(7), 574–587. doi:10.1002/(SICI)1097-4571(1999)50:7<574::AID-ASI3>3.0.CO;2-Q

Maglott, D., Ostell, J., Pruitt, K. D., & Tatusova, T. (2005). Entrez Gene: gene-centered information at NCBI. *Nucleic Acids Research*, 33, D54–D58. doi:10.1093/nar/gki031

Manning, C. D., & Schütze, H. (1999). Foundations of statistical natural language processing. Cambridge, MA: MIT Press.

Metzler, D., & Croft, W. (2004). Combining the language model and inference network approaches to retrieval. *Information Processing & Management. Special Issue on Bayesian Networks and Information Retrieval, 40*(5), 735–750.

Morgan, A. A., Wellner, B., Colombe, J. B., Arens, R., Colosimo, M. E., & Hirschman, L. (2007). Evaluating the automatic mapping of human gene and protein mentions to unique identifiers. In . *Proceedings of the Pacific Symposium on Biocomputing, 12*, 281–291. doi:10.1142/9789812772435_0027

O'Donovan, C., Martin, M. J., Gattiker, A., Gasteiger, E., Bairoch, A., & Apweiler, R. (2002). High-quality protein knowledge resource: SWISS-PROT and TrEMBL. *Briefings in Bioinformatics, 3*(3), 275–284. doi:10.1093/bib/3.3.275

Ozgur, A., Vu, T., Erkan, G., & Radev, D. R. (2008). Identifying gene-disease associations using centrality on a literature mined gene-interaction network. *Bioinformatics (Oxford, England), 24*(13), i277–i285. doi:10.1093/bioinformatics/btn182

Perez-Iratxeta, C., Bork, P., & Andrade, M. A. (2002). Association of genes to genetically inherited diseases using data mining. *Nature Genetics, 31*(3), 316–319.

Perez-Iratxeta, C., Wjst, M., Bork, P., & Andrade, M. (2005). G2D: a tool for mining genes associated with disease. *BMC Genetics, 6*(1), 45. doi:10.1186/1471-2156-6-45

Pruitt, K. D., & Maglott, D. R. (2001). RefSeq and LocusLink: NCBI gene-centered resources. *Nucleic Acids Research, 29*(1), 137–140. doi:10.1093/nar/29.1.137

Reeve, L. H., Han, H., & Brooks, A. D. (2007). The use of domain-specific concepts in biomedical text summarization. *Information Processing & Management, 43*(6), 1765–1776. doi:10.1016/j.ipm.2007.01.026

Schuemie, M. J., Weeber, M., Schijvenaars, B. J. A., van Mulligen, E. M., van der Eijk, C. C., & Jelier, R. (2004). Distribution of information in biomedical abstracts and full-text publications. *Bioinformatics (Oxford, England), 20*(16), 2597–2604. doi:10.1093/bioinformatics/bth291

Schwartz, A. S., & Hearst, M. A. (2003). A simple algorithm for identifying abbreviation definitions in biomedical text. In . *Proceedings of the Pacific Symposium on Biocomputing, 8*, 451–462.

Sehgal, A., & Srinivasan, P. (2006). Retrieval with gene queries. *BMC Bioinformatics, 7*(1), 220. doi:10.1186/1471-2105-7-220

Seki, K., & Mostafa, J. (2005a). An application of text categorization methods to gene ontology annotation. In *Proceedings of the 28th annual international ACM SIGIR conference on research and development in information retrieval*, (pp. 138–145).

Seki, K., & Mostafa, J. (2005b). A hybrid approach to protein name identification in biomedical texts. *Information Processing & Management, 41*(4), 723–743. doi:10.1016/j.ipm.2004.02.006

Shatkay, H. (2005). Hairpins in bookstacks: Information retrieval from biomedical text. *Briefings in Bioinformatics, 6*(3), 222–238. doi:10.1093/bib/6.3.222

Sparck Jones, K. (1972). Statistical interpretation of term specificity and its application in retrieval. *The Journal of Documentation, 28*(1), 11–20. doi:10.1108/eb026526

Srinivasan, P. (2004). Text mining: generating hypotheses from Medline. *Journal of the American Society for Information Science and Technology*, *55*(5), 396–413. doi:10.1002/asi.10389

Stoica, E., & Hearst, M. (2006). Predicting gene functions from text using a cross-species approach. In . *Proceedings of the Pacific Symposium on Biocomputing*, *11*, 88–99.

Swanson, D. R. (1986a). Fish oil, Raynaud's syndrome, and undiscovered public knowledge. *Perspectives in Biology and Medicine*, *30*(1), 7–18.

Swanson, D. R. (1986b). Undiscovered public knowledge. *The Library Quarterly*, *56*(2), 103–118. doi:10.1086/601720

Swanson, D. R., & Smalheiser, N. R. (1997). An interactive system for finding complementary literatures: a stimulus to scientific discovery. *Artificial Intelligence*, *91*(2), 183–203. doi:10.1016/S0004-3702(97)00008-8

Swanson, D. R., Smalheiser, N. R., & Torvik, V. I. (2006). Ranking indirect connections in literature-based discovery: the role of medical subject headings. *Journal of the American Society for Information Science and Technology*, *57*(11), 1427–1439. doi:10.1002/asi.20438

Turtle, H., & Croft, W. B. (1991). Evaluation of an inference network-based retrieval model. *ACM Transactions on Information Systems*, *9*(3), 187–222. doi:10.1145/125187.125188

Weeber, M., Vos, R., Klein, H., de Jong-van den Berg, L. T., Aronson, A. R., & Molema, G. (2003). Generating Hypotheses by Discovering Implicit Associations in the Literature: A Case Report of a Search for New Potential Therapeutic Uses for Thalidomide. *Journal of the American Medical Informatics Association*, *10*(3), 252–259. doi:10.1197/jamia.M1158

Yang, Y., & Liu, X. (1999). A re-examination of text categorization methods. In *Proceedings of the 22nd annual international ACM SIGIR conference on Research and development in information retrieval*, (pp. 42–49).

Yang, Y., & Pedersen, J. O. (1997). A comparative study on feature selection in text categorization. In *Proceedings of the 14th International Conference on Machine Learning*, (pp. 412–420).

ENDNOTES

[1] http://umlsinfo.nlm.nih.gov/

[2] http://www.nlm.nih.gov/mesh/

[3] LocusLink has been superseded by Entrez Gene.

[4] http://geneticassociationdb.nih.gov/

[5] http://www..pubmedcentral.nih.gov/

[6] http://biocreative.sourceforge.net/resources.html

Chapter 18
Rainstorm Forecasting By Mining Heterogeneous Remote Sensed Datasets

Yu-Bin Yang
State Key Laboratory for Novel Software Technology, China

Hui Lin
The Chinese University of Hong Kong, Hong Kong

ABSTRACT

This chapter presents an automatic meteorological data mining system based on analyzing and mining heterogeneous remote sensed image datasets, with which it is possible to forecast potential rainstorms in advance. A two-phase data mining method employing machine learning techniques, including the C4.5 decision tree algorithm and dependency network analysis, is proposed, by which a group of derivation rules and a conceptual model for metrological environment factors are generated to assist the automatic weather forecasting task. Experimental results have shown that the system reduces the heavy workload of manual weather forecasting and provides meaningful interpretations to the forecasted results.

INTRODUCTION

Meteorological satellite data and images have been operationally utilized in weather services for more than 30 years. Since the inception of weather forecasting based on satellite remote sensed data, meteorologists have faced the challenge of using this tool to minimize the potential damage caused during adverse weather conditions by collecting and analyzing these images. Based on this analysis, responsible officers are able to take necessary action to minimize the potential damage caused

by weather-related disasters. This is particularly significant and urgent for China, particularly for the Yangtze River Basin, which suffers from frequent flooding that endangers life, disrupts transportation and commerce and results in serious economic losses. For example, the unprecedented, severe flood in the Yangtze River Basin in 1998 resulted in the deaths of 4,150 people and damage to property of approximately 32 billion US dollars. Since almost all floods are caused by heavy rainfall, advance forecasting of these adverse weather conditions has been a key factor in attempts to mitigate casualties and damages caused by floods.

DOI: 10.4018/978-1-61520-757-2.ch018

Meanwhile, the study of "Mesoscale Convective Systems" (MCS) clouds, including the study of their life cycles, trajectories and evolvement trends, remains an important and challenging issue in meteorology, by which severe weather situations, or, "mesoscale weather events" are often caused, such as strong winds, heavy rain falls, thunderstorms and hurricanes (Houze & Smull, 1990; Li & Plale, 2008).

In China, the MCS clouds over the Tibetan Plateau have recently been revealed to be the major factor in some disastrous weather phenomena occurring in the Yangtze River Basin. Meteorological observations have already shown that the eastward evolvement trends of MCS clouds over the Tibetan Plateau is the crucial factor leading to heavy rain falls in the Yangtze River Basin, which may be the direct cause of severe floods in Southern China (Jiang & Fan, 2002). Therefore, it is vital that we discover the evolvement trends of MCS over the Tibetan Plateau from the available meteorological satellite data (such as the meteorological environment parameters including temperature, wind divergence and water vapor flux divergence) and image collections, in order to effectively and efficiently predict and evaluate the potential occurrences of heavy rainstorms. The hidden correlations between the satellite data and the eastward evolvement trends of MCS clouds may then be discovered and revealed from similar historical remote sensed scenarios, if accurate data analysis and mining can be made. Most importantly, the meteorological environment factors causing eastward evolvement trends of MCS clouds can also be effectively modeled and explained, through which we may be able to forecast the future eastward evolvement trends of MCS clouds and subsequently locate and forecast potential heavy rainstorms.

Unfortunately, meteorologists still performed tracking, characterization and analysis tasks of MCS manually on most occasions. This so-called "expert-eye-scanning" tracking technique is both time and labour intensive, as expert meteorolo-

gists work to identify the movement trajectories and evolvement trends of MCS from the satellite remote sensed images (Arnaud & Desbios, 1992). Further, the quantity of satellite image data is so huge that this method is inadequate for the task of tracking MCSs in wide ranges and over long periods, despite its relatively high accuracy. It is too time-consuming, too ineffective, and the observation results are often unstable and vary between experts, which decreases the reliability and practicability of heavy rainfall forecasting. On the other hand, satellite remote sensed data used for this purpose have heterogeneous characteristics due to different data types, sensor properties and satellite specifications. Some data are infrared remote sensed images and the others are numeric observed or predicted data, describing different environmental properties of the activities of MCS clouds. Not only are the currently available data of different data types, but they also differ considerably in data quality, spatial resolution and temporal granularity. Since they have different spatial and temporal resolutions, it is necessary to model seamless integration of heterogeneous satellite data before MCS cloud analysis and mining is carried out.

To address the above issues, this chapter aims at presenting an automatic meteorological data mining approach based on analyzing and mining heterogeneous remote sensed image datasets, with which it is possible to forecast potential rainstorms in advance. Firstly, automatic MCS cloud detection and tracking methods are proposed to identify the geo-referenced cloud objects in satellite remote sensed images. Next, a data integration modeling mechanism is designed to extract meaningful properties of those detected clouds, by integrating the heterogeneous image data and observed data into a unified view. Finally, based on the integrated global data schema, a two-phase data mining method employing machine learning techniques, the C4.5 decision tree algorithm and dependency network analysis, is proposed to analyze and forecast the meteorological activities of all clouds in order to discover the hidden correlations between the satellite observed data and the eastward evolvement trends of MCS clouds. Moreover, the meteorological environment factors that may cause the eastward evolvement trends of MCS clouds are also analyzed and conceptually modeled. An MCS Cloud Analysis System (MCAS) is also successfully designed and implemented by applying the above approaches, through which it is possible for meteorologists to forecast potential heavy rainstorms more easily.

The remainder of this chapter is organized as follows. In Section II, the research background is briefly described, including related work on rainstorm forecasting by data mining techniques, and data sources used in this study. Section III discusses MCS cloud detection, tracking and characterization from remote sensed image sequences. In Section IV, an MCS data preparation model is proposed based on a heterogeneous data integration schema. Section V presents MCS data mining methods based on the C4.5 decision tree algorithm. MCS conceptual modeling based on dependency network analysis is described in Section VI to reveal relationships between MCS evolvement trends and meteorological environment factors. Experimental results are illustrated and analyzed in Section VII. Finally, concluding remarks with future work directions are provided in Section VIII.

BACKGROUND

Related Work

Meteorology has a long history of statistical approaches to weather and climate prediction based on different types of satellite data, by using empirical numerical modeling based on physics and dynamics. For instance, Plonski et al. (Plonski & Gustafson, 2000) performed high resolution cloud analysis based on statistical thresholding of satellite imaging. The results were fed into a cloud-

analysis numerical model to produce a global cloud analysis. Souto et al. (Souto & Balseirom, 2003) proposed a cloud analysis method aimed at rainfall forecasting in Spain, using a high-resolution non-hydrostatic numerical model applied to satellite observations. Both methods treated and handled the satellite images as ordinary data, rather than using image processing techniques to handle them. On the other hand, Arnaud et al. (Arnaud & Desbios, 1992) presented an automatic cloud tracking method based on area-overlapping analysis by treating satellite data as images and applying image processing techniques to them. Although building an empirical model works in many cases, it does not present issues of imprecision and uncertainty in the meteorology domain. Further, the complexity and difficulty of comprehension also raises considerable problems in many real-life applications such as weather forecasting, in which experts may need to reveal understandable correlations or associations. Moreover, the empirical model is usually very complicated and requires sophisticated computer modeling and simulation for accurate predictive results.

Emerging as a new paradigm in the computer science community, data mining has been successfully applied to many problems with a wide range of models and techniques, resulting in a growing recognition of data mining and knowledge discovery tools and techniques that develop newer approaches to weather and climate prediction based on satellite remote sensed data (Lance, 2000). Particularly in the meteorological community, in which satellite data prevail and play a very important role, the possibility of applying various data mining methods has attracted considerable research, since long-term climatic trends are generally meaningful. The study of these data mining methods can provide significant information about climate changes. Examples are as follows. Li et al. (Li & Harms, 2003) discovered representative association rules by using two association rule mining algorithms and two interpolation methods implemented in a Geospatial Decision Support System (GDSS) to predict drought risk based on various types of crop and environmental data obtained from the National Oceanic and Atmospheric Administration (NOAA) Advanced Very High Resolution Radiometer (AVHRR) satellite. Philip et al. (Philip & Joseph, 2003) adopted Neural Networks on rainfall studies based on 87 years of rainfall data. Basak et al. (Basak & Sudarshan, 2004) applied the independent component analysis technique for mining weather patterns, by using the time-series of monthly mean sea level pressure (SLP) data obtained from the NOAA Cooperative Institute for Research in Environmental Sciences (CIRES) satellite data center. Their results have been validated by matching the independent component activities with the spatio-temporal North Atlantic Oscillation (NAO) index. Basak et al. viewed the weather phenomena as a mixture of a certain number of signals with independent stable activity, but this assumption doesn't always hold true in meteorology since all factors are often correlated. Liu et al. (Liu & George, 2005) employed fuzzy logic techniques to mine the climate trends in the weather domain by discovering the Southern Ocean Index (SOI) from a global sea level pressure dataset taken between 1982 and 1993. Estevam et al. (Estevam & Eduardo, 2005) presented a meteorological data mining application using Bayesian Networks to classify "wet fog" weather and other weather conditions in an international airport, with a reported correct classification rate of approximately 80%. The attributes involved in the data mining process include records on pressure, temperature, humidity and precipitation. Lai et al. (Lai & Li, 2006) implemented a data mining method based on association rule to predict short duration rainfalls by using satellite cloud images. However, they converted the numeric satellite image values into categorical values in order to allow the use of the Apriori algorithm to generate associate rules, which made it impossible to handle continuous values and achieved only an average 2% improvement in accuracy. António

et al. (Tomé & Almeida, 2007) also investigated the time-series NAO index for rainfall forecast purpose. A number of derivative variables were firstly composed by using domain knowledge. Then machine learning algorithms, such as k-nearest neighbor (KNN) and Naïve Bayes, were used to perform pattern detection and prediction in 3 classes of weather conditions. These were reported to achieve prediction accuracies above 80% in the winter months and slightly less than that in other months. Li et al. (Li & Plale, 2008) proposed a prototype cyberinfrastructure to carry out storm detection and weather forecasting on a continuous basis in real time over large volumes of observational data obtained from the Weather Surveillance Radar –1988 Doppler (WSR-88D), using a data mining toolkit called ADaM to perform image processing and data mining tasks. The emphasis is laid on designing a work flow system to complete the task, rather than on the data mining algorithm itself.

In spite of the above progress in meteorological modeling and data mining, there are still many research issues and challenges to be met, which cannot be solved easily and generally by current data mining techniques, particularly in weather forecasting applications. Firstly, since heterogeneous satellites, weather stations and sensors collect large volumes of geospatial data on a wide range of parameters, the lack of a global schema of those heterogeneous satellite data sources, which can provide a unified view and access to the different types of data, will be a major problem for accurate analysis. Secondly, it is important to view the weather variables as sources of spatio-temporal signals characterized by high volumes of data. Severe weather events such as storms and rainfall all have a geo-spatial and a temporal component, in which the temporal component has been neglected in much research currently available. Thirdly, to achieve a solution with more generalization, hidden associations need to be discovered in the form of general knowledge from the data collections, and a domain specific conceptual model should also be constructed in order to generalize the properties. After that, the meteorological and geographical data can then ultimately be transformed into information, inference, and even a decision making process that can be easily understand and used by human experts.

Data Sources

Because of the multidisciplinary nature of the problem, different types of satellite data are used in this study.

Satellite Images

In order to track and analyze MCS clouds over the Tibetan Plateau, with the aim of discovering useful knowledge crucial to heavy rainfall forecasting, a large amount of satellite imaging is indispensable. For this purpose, the Temperature of Black Body (TBB) satellite infrared remote sensed images over the Tibetan Plateau from June 1998 to August 1998, collected by the Geostationary Meteorological Satellite (GMS-5) was provided by the China National Satellite Meteorological Center as one of the data sources in this study.

TBB is the radiant temperature at the top of a cloud in a cloud intensive area, which can be used to analyze and forecast the activities of specific weather systems. The meteorological satellite GMS-5 transmits TBB infrared remote sensed images every hour of every day. From June 1998 to August 1998, there are in total (30+31+31) × 24=2,208 images, with each picture having a resolution of 140×100 pixels. The range of a TBB image covers latitude 0°N~50°N and longitude 80°E~150°E, and the spatial resolution is 0.5° (longitude) × 0.5° (latitude). Since only the MCS clouds over the Tibetan Plateau are of interest to this research, the specific, useful data coverage is latitude 27°N~40°N and longitude 80°E~105°E, which is the geo-referenced range of the Tibetan Plateau. Figure 1 illustrates a snapshot sequence of GMS-5 TBB satellite imaging of MCS clouds.

Satellite Observed Data

Satellite observed data are also collected from the China National Satellite Meteorological Center for MCS cloud analysis. High resolution Limited area Analysis and Forecasting System (HLAFS) is a series of observed data utilized to accurately forecast weather systems, particularly heavy rainfalls, in China. HLAFS covers latitude 15°N~64°N and longitude 70°E~145°E with 1° (longitude) × 1° (latitude) spatial resolution; it gives a 48-hour forecast with values at five time slots, i.e., UTC hour 00, UTC hour 12, UTC hour 24, UTC hour 36 and UTC hour 48. The functional spatial coverage of HLAFS data is from latitude 27°N~40°N and longitude 80° E~105°E.

The HLAFS data include 16 meteorological environment variables, of which 9 variables related to our research interests, including geo-potential Height (H: 10^{-1}dagpm), Temperature (T: ^{0}C), Relative Humidity (RH: %), Vorticity (VOR: $10^{-6} \cdot s^{-1}$), Wind Divergence (DIV: $10^{-6} \cdot s^{-1}$), Vertical Wind Speed (W: $10^{-5} \cdot h \cdot Pa \cdot s^{-1}$), Water Vapor Flux Divergence (IFVQ: $10^{-10} \cdot g/cm^2 \cdot h \cdot Pa \cdot s$), Pseudo-

Figure 1. A snapshot sequence of GMS-5 satellite imaging of MCS clouds

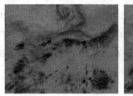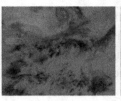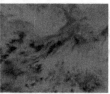

equivalent Potential Temperature (θSE: ^{0}C), and K index (K). These nine types of HLAFS variables in different UTC times were employed in order to model the relationships between the evolvement trends of MCS clouds and their meteorological environment conditions, i.e., to find out the patterns that may cause MCS clouds to move out of the Tibetan Plateau. This can be very helpful in forecasting heavy rainfalls.

It is clear that the above datasets pose heterogeneity problems. Firstly, TBB images and HLAFS observations provide different views of the factors related to the MCS cloud analysis task. After the MCS clouds have been detected and tracked from TBB images, they should be further analyzed according to their HLAFS variables. TBB images only contain the temperatures of the clouds, whereas HLAFS variables include more observation variables, such as humidity and wind speed, which are important for establishing the meteorological environment models around an MCS cloud. Secondly, they have different spatial resolutions, which make a geo-location binding operation necessary before the precise observation values around an MCS cloud can be retrieved. Moreover, they also appear with different temporal resolutions: TBB images were updated every hour and HLAFS were recorded three times a day. Knowing this, the data preparation model should be implemented before the data mining process, serving as a data integration solution including spatial calibration and temporal adjustment, mapping the heterogeneous data into a unified data schema.

MCS CLOUD DETECTION, TRACKING AND CHARACTERIZATION

The processing flow of our meteorological data mining system takes place in two stages: MCS tracking and MCS data mining. We firstly identify the presence of MCS clouds, where splitting, merging, vanishing and new-emergence of MCS clouds may be occurring, in order to track the same MCS from the satellite images and data. This is fundamental to exploring the MCS evolvement trends over the Tibetan Plateau, and all data used for knowledge discovery carry the characteristics of MCS clouds. Since the satellite TBB images and HLAFS data are both spatio-temporal, all MCS clouds need to be detected and tracked correctly and efficiently from complete image sequences. Subsequently, it is necessary to extract some representative attributes of the tracked MCS from the corresponding data collections in order to characterize them.

To address the above problems, we propose a fast tracking and characterization method of multiple moving clouds from meteorological satellite images based on feature correspondences (Yang & Lin, 2006). The method is based on the fact that in a relatively small time-span, the deformation of an MCS is progressive and detectable, which means that at two consecutive satellite images the same MCS will maintain a relatively similar moving speed, shape, area and texture.

From a meteorological stand-point, only the MCS of which TBB value is lower than a fixed threshold p (p=-32^{0}C) and cloud size large enough is needed for our study. Therefore, an image filter is applied to identify the qualified pixels in the satellite images, whose cloud-top temperatures (i.e. TBB values) are lower than the threshold p. An image thresholding process is then applied to segment the remaining qualified image pixels into several different clusters, followed by the application of 8-connectivity chain code representation (Freeman, 1974) on TBB images to produce MCS segmentation, through which all MCS clouds are identified and labeled.

The boundary of each MCS cloud is thus represented as a chain code. Figure 2 illustrates 8-connectivity directions and a detected MCS cloud whose boundary is represented as a chain code sequence.

Figure 2. 8-connectivity directions and an example of 8-connectivity chain code representation, where the middle section shows an original cloud structure and the right section gives its chain code sequence

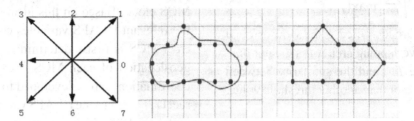

As shown in Figure 2, the eight neighboring directions are coded from 0 to 7, enabling the complete boundary of an MCS cloud to be represented as the following code sequence:

$$A_n = a_1 a_2 \ldots a_n, \ a_i \in \{0,1,2,\ldots,7\}, \ i=1,2,\ldots,n$$

Starting from the image segmentation results, a group of discriminative features of each MCS are extracted as its representation, including MCS size, MCS roundness, MCS protraction ratio, a Fourier descriptor of MCS shape and a texture descriptor of MCS. In addition, spatial self-correlation function is calculated for each cloud as its texture features (Yang & Lin, 2006). The final candidates qualified for tracking and characterization stage are those clouds whose sizes are larger than a threshold q. This step provides us with the initial positions of MCS. Next, we make use of feature correspondences to identify and track the original clouds in the time-consecutive satellite image sequences. Fig. 3 provides an instance of the result image after the MCS identification process, in which each region represents an identified MCS cloud represented as chain codes.

Two different kinds of feature correspondence are adopted in our study (Yang & Lin, 2004). Firstly, the overlapping area of the two detected regions belonging to the same MCS cloud, in two time-consecutive images, is used as the first feature correspondence and is computed as follows:

$$\Delta A = 1 - \frac{|M_j(t+1) - M_i(t)|}{\min[M_j(t+1), M_i(t)]} \quad (1)$$

where $M_i(t)$, $M_j(t+1)$ represent the size of MCS C_i in hour t, and MCS C_j in hour $t+1$, respectively.

The other feature correspondence is applied on the normalized feature vector of each MCS. The similarity between two MCSs is calculated as the normalized Euclidean distance between their feature vectors. Assume that feature vector of MCS C_i in hour t is $F_A = (f_{a1}, f_{a2}, \ldots, f_{aN})$, and feature vector of MCS C_j in hour $t+1$ is $F_B = (f_{b1}, f_{b2}, \ldots, f_{bN})$, then the similarity is computed as follows:

Figure 3. Identified MCS clouds

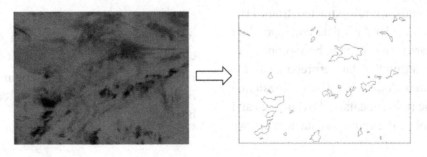

$$S(A,B) = 1 - \sqrt{\sum_{i=1}^{N} \left[\frac{(f_{ai} - f_{bi})}{\max(f_{ai}, f_{bi})} \right]^2} \qquad (2)$$

Two MCSs are identified as the same original MCS if their overlapping area ΔA is greater than threshold value $T_{\Delta A}$, and the similarity between them is also greater than another threshold value, $T_{S(A,B)}$.

Finally, in the characterization stage, the qualified MCSs are categorized into four types according to their evolvement trends indicated on the satellite images: (1) MCS moving East (E) out of the Tibetan Plateau; (2) MCS moving Northeast (NE) out of the Tibetan Plateau; (3) MCS moving Southeast (SE) out of the Tibetan Plateau; and (4) MCS staying in the Tibetan Plateau (STAY-IN). The categorization is implemented by computing the direction angle values from the movement trajectory of each MCS, and is crucial to meteorologists for predicting and evaluating the potential occurrences of heavy rain falls.

DATA PREPARATION

Based on the result of the MCS tracking and characterization stage, we can now begin the MCS data mining stage. However, due to the heterogeneity of our data sources, appropriate attributes of each MCS, including TBB value, HLAFS values and feature values, should be firstly integrated to constitute a consistent input dataset serving for data mining purposes.

In the MCS tracking and characterization stage, MCS data including MCS features, geo-locations, life cycle, average TBB value, trajectories and evolvement trends are all extracted from TBB images. Therefore, HLAFS data corresponding to each MCS are then needed to be appropriately integrated into the unified dataset prepared for the data mining step. A data integrator is designed to integrate the relevant data of TBB images and HLAFS variables. The common data item that we

can use to join TBB image and HLAFS datasets is geo-location and observational hour of each MCS cloud. Based on this idea, geo-location of the relevant HLAFS variables corresponding to each MCS is firstly determined in terms of the geo-location of each MCS. Next, a UTC time coordination step is developed to obtain the correct UTC hour of the HLAFS variables in order to match the UTC time of each MCS cloud. Finally, a spatial association is applied to a pre-defined geo-referenced neighborhood of each MCS to generate an integrated data schema, with which a unified dataset is generated based on all the useful information from multiple heterogeneous data sources, and provided to the data mining module as an input.

Data preparation includes the following steps.

Spatial Calibration

The geo-locations of HLAFS variables are the same as those of their corresponding MCS clouds. Since TBB images and HLAFS data have different spatial resolutions (TBB: 0.5^0 longitude $\times 0.5^0$ latitude, HLAFS: 1^0 longitude $\times 1^0$ latitude) the HLAFS data corresponding to each MCS cloud are extracted according to the geo-location binding operation in Eq. (3) (Yang & Lin, 2006):

$$\bar{H} = \begin{cases} H(x,y), & if\ (x\,/\,0.5)\bmod 2 = 0,\ (y\,/\,0.5)\bmod 2 = 0 \\ \dfrac{H(x-0.5,y) + H(x+0.5,y)}{2}, & if\ (x\,/\,0.5)\bmod 2 \neq 0, (y\,/\,0.5)\bmod 2 = 0 \\ \dfrac{H(x,y-0.5) + H(x,y+0.5)}{2}, & if\ (x\,/\,0.5)\bmod 2 = 0, (y\,/\,0.5)\bmod 2 \neq 0 \\ \dfrac{H(x-0.5,y) + H(x+0.5,y) + H(x,y-0.5) + H(x,y+0.5)}{4}, \\ \qquad\qquad if\ (x\,/\,0.5)\bmod 2 \neq 0, (y\,/\,0.5)\bmod 2 \neq 0 \end{cases}$$

$$(3)$$

where (x,y) is the geo-location of each MCS cloud (x is longitude, y is latitude), $H(x,y)$ is the HLAFS data in geo-location point (x,y), and $\bar{H}$ is the extracted HLAFS data after geo-location binding.

Temporal adjustment

A UTC time coordination operation is then performed according to Eq. (4) (Yang & Lin, 2006):

$$UTC = \begin{cases} 00, & if \quad 0 \leq t < 6 \\ 12, & if \quad 6 \leq t < 18 \\ 24, & if \quad 18 \leq t < 24 \end{cases} \quad (4)$$

where t is the observing hour of each MCS cloud in TBB images and UTC is the corresponding time slot of HLAFS data of the MCS.

Spatial Association

An MCS cloud moves out of the Tibetan Plateau only if its longitude value is greater than 105°E (the eastern longitude boundary of the Tibetan Plateau). Therefore, in order to increase the robustness to the noise of latitude values in our dataset, we apply a spatial association operation to each MCS with its geo-referenced neighborhoods to generate the final value of each HLAFS variable. The neighborhood size of the spatial association is decided according to prior information obtained by meteorologists. Not only is the geo-location of an MCS cloud considered, but also its adjacent geographical neighborhoods in latitude axis are taken into account from a spatial perspective, which is shown in Figure 4 (Yang & Lin, 2007).

As we can see from Figure 4, the geographical neighborhood regions considered in our study are labeled as A, B and C, respectively. The central cell of region B indicates the MCS cloud itself. The size of each neighboring region is 1° (longitude) × 3° (latitude). For each MCS located in region B the average values of HLAFS variables for geographical regions A, B and C are all computed. The differences of every HLAFS averages in regions B and A and for regions C and B are calculated as feature vectors D_{ba} and D_{cb}, respectively. Both the feature vectors include the corresponding values of all 9 HLAFS variables as their elements.

Integrated Data Schema

A new dataset consisting of all the features extracted from TBB images and HLAFS variables is then integrated for each MCS cloud as a unified schema prepared for data mining. The feature elements included in this unified dataset are listed as follows:

Figure 4. Spatial association

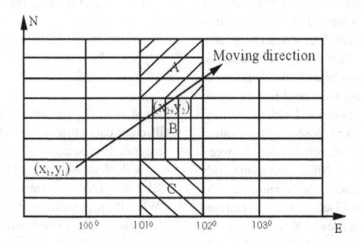

(1) All the elements of feature vector D_{ba}, including H_{ba}, T_{ba}, RH_{ba}, VOR_{ba}, DIV_{ba}, W_{ba}, $IFVQ_{ba}$, θSE_{ba}, and K_{ba};

(2) All the elements of feature vector D_{cb}, including H_{cb}, T_{cb}, RH_{cb}, VOR_{cb}, DIV_{cb}, W_{cb}, $IFVQ_{cb}$, θSE_{cb}, and K_{cb};

(3) All the HLAFS features of each MCS, indicated as H_{bb}, T_{bb}, RH_{bb}, VOR_{bb}, DIV_{bb}, W_{bb}, $IFVQ_{bb}$, θSE_{bb}, and K_{bb};

(4) The area of each MCS cloud;

(5) The shape of each MCS, which is categorized into "*Elliptical*", "*Circle*" or "*Other shapes*" according to its morphological features;

(6) The geo-location of each MCS cloud represented as latitude and longitude coordinate values;

(7) The lowest average TBB value of each MCS cloud;

(8) MCS types, i.e., "E", "NE","SE", and "STAY-IN".

Finally, all the above features of every tracked MCS cloud makes up the integrated dataset used for MCS data mining stage.

DECISION TREE BASED DATA MINING

To forecast the future eastward evolvement trends of MCS clouds is the crucial step to further forecast potential heavy rainstorms in the Yangtze River Basin. Although meteorology researchers have employed a variety of data analysis techniques, the methodologies have failed to clearly illustrate the correlations among the causal factors and to provide probabilities associated with the factors. Therefore, in order to propose a better method to highlight or expose any relationships between possible factors related to MCS movement trends and rainstorm occurrences, the data mining techniques were used to discover the correlations between MCS properties, MCS movements, meteorological environment factors (HLAFS

data) and rainstorm occurrences. A spatial data mining approach was then designed directly from the integrated dataset to yield the meteorological knowledge.

In the rainstorm forecasting task studied in this chapter, comprehensibility of the result, i.e., the transparency of discovered knowledge and the ability to explain the reasoning process is important for data mining techniques. The decision tree algorithm is one of the main techniques used to classify large amounts of data. Generally speaking, decision trees have good comprehensibility because the learned knowledge is explicitly represented in trees and every path from the root to a leaf forms a clear decision rule. The data classification procedure in a decision tree algorithm is generally separated into two steps, i.e., growing and pruning (Breiman & Friedman, 1984). In order to complete the data mining task involved in our relatively large integrated dataset, a data mining process is designed and implemented by adopting the C4.5 decision tree algorithm (Quinlan, 1993; Zhou & Jiang, 2003), outputting a set of knowledge primitives represented as decision rules. The aim of the data mining step is to analyze the meteorological activities of MCS clouds and further discover the hidden correlations between the satellite data and the eastward evolvement trends of MCS clouds, which is crucial for subsequent rainstorm forecasting.

The general form of the C4.5 decision rules is

'$P_1 \wedge \ldots \wedge P_m \rightarrow Q$'

where $P_1, \ldots, P_m$ are the rule antecedents, i.e., different data attributes of MCS existing in our integrated dataset; and Q is the rule consequence, one of the four categories of MCS, i.e. "E", "NE", "SE" or "STAY-IN". The rules are interpreted as: "When the precondition '$P_1 \wedge \ldots \wedge P_m$' is satisfied, the pattern 'Q' is to be determined as the evolvement trend of the MCS cloud with a definite probability". The C4.5 rules are generated as follows (Quinlan, 1993; Zhou & Jiang, 2003).

First, a C4.5 decision tree is trained. Then, every path from the root to a leaf is converted to an initial rule. The antecedent of the rule includes all the test conditions appearing in that path, while the consequence of the rule is assigned as the class label held by the leaf. Each initial rule then follows a generalization. Antecedents not helpful for distinguishing a specific class from other classes are removed. When an antecedent is removed, a new variant of the initial rule is generated. If the accuracy of the initial rule is less than that of the variant, the initial rule will be replaced by the variant. It is possible to remove several rule antecedents. If so, the removal of the antecedent that produces the lowest error rate compared to the generalized rule is kept and the removal process is repeatedly performed until the rule is generalized. After all the initial rules are generalized, rule sets corresponding to every class are generated. All rule sets are polished by using the minimum description length (MDL) principle so that rules that have no influence on the accuracy of a rule set are removed (Quinlan & Rivest, 1989). The rule sets are then sorted in ascending order according to their false positive error rates. Finally, a default rule with no antecedent is created for dealing with instances that are not covered by any of the generated rules. Its consequence is assigned as the class that contains the most training instances not covered by any rule.

One of the advantages of C4.5 algorithm is that useful information can be efficiently mined from large-scale databases, with high accuracy and relatively low computation burden. Moreover, both the categorical and the continuous attributes present in the integrated dataset can be handled properly and the rules generated by C4.5 decision tree algorithm are quite easy to understand.

Based on the mined C4.5 decision rules, the evolvement trend of an MCS cloud can be inferred provided that TBB data and HLAFS variables are both extracted.

MCS CONCEPTUAL MODELING

The resulting derivation rules define the pattern used to derive the evolvement trends of MCS clouds. However, revealing the possible relationships between MCS attributes and MCS evolvement trends is just one side of the coin and insufficient for predicting possible heavy rainfall occurrences. For meteorologists, it is also very important to extract and model meteorological environment patterns that indicate the meteorological conditions incurring heavy rain falls. It generally helps meteorologists achieve their heavy rainfall predictions. To achieve this goal, the relevant HLAFS variables, powerfully influencing the evolvement trends and moving trajectories of MCS clouds, should be selected and then a set of environmental model graphs can be established and plotted to illustrate how the selected attributes interact with each other and finally influence the evolvement trends of MCS. This is the MCS conceptual modeling part in the spatial data mining process. A group of environmental model graphs on the related attributes are generated as final knowledge used for heavy rainfall forecasting. By using those model graphs, the influence of each relevant attribute on the evolvement trends of MCS can be appropriately evaluated, and used to predict the actual evolvement of a new MCS. To address this issue, we proposed an MCS conceptual modeling method based on dependency network technique.

Graphical models represent a joint distribution over a set of variables represented as a group of nodes. The edges indicate the dependence between a pair of nodes. It is simply a set of conditional probability distributions for all of the variables. A dependency network is a graphical model of probabilistic relationships between a set of relevant attributes or events, which is an alternative to the Bayesian network (Heckerman & Chickering, 2000). Like a Bayesian network, a dependency network has both a graph and a probability component, in which the graph component is a directed graph and the probability component consists of the probability of a node given its parents.

Therefore, conditional independence can be interpreted using graph separation. Unlike Bayesian network, the dependency network cannot represent causal relationships. All the relationships indicated in a dependency network should only be considered predictive or correlational, which cannot be interpreted as causal (Heckerman & Chickering, 2000). This is also the reason why the dependency network is employed to depict the MCS conceptual model ---- the satellite observed data and the eastward evolvement trends of MCS clouds have hidden correlations but they do not necessarily imply causations. Also, since the Bayesian network is more appropriate for categorical variables while HLAFS variables are all continuous values, the dependency network is employed in this study to depict dependence and independence among all variables in our integrated data schema. With the discovered dependency, the relevant variables can be selected and then a set of environmental model graphs can be established and plotted.

By using dependency network techniques, each feature element in the integrated dataset is viewed as a node in the graph and the link between each pair of nodes indicates their mutual relationship, with a probability value depicting their relevance. All the data selected in the integrated dataset serve as the training data to establish the dependency network, which is implemented by the WinMine Toolkit (Chickering, 2000; Chickering, 2002), an analytic tool developed for identifying higher-order relationships in research data.

The WinMine Toolkit is a "set of tools for Windows 2000/NT/XP that allows the creation of statistical models from data and graphical representation of the results." (Chickering, 2002). WinMine graphically represents probabilistic dependencies found within a dataset in a dependency network, represented as a graph and with a probability component. In our study, each feature element is modeled to have the fol-

lowing local distribution types: for a continuous variable, such as HLAFS variables, Gaussian or Log-Gaussian distribution is chosen, depending on which local distribution best fits the marginal data. For categorical variables, such as MCS type, a multinomial distribution is used. Prior to performing a dependency analysis, we need firstly to specify whether a variable is to be modeled as an "input" or "output" variable, or "input-output" in WinMine's Plan Phase (Chickering, 2002). In that phase, defining the role of a variable serves as a way of specifying which dependency model to test. An "input" variable can only predict other variables. An "output only" variable is one that can only be predicted by other variables. An "input and output" variable is one that may be an internal link in a chain of events. That assignation decides how variables will be modeled, the role they will play in the analysis and how they will be displayed in WinMine's graphic output, called a decision tree. In the MCS conceptual modeling process, "MCS type" is actually an outcome or presumably the last event in a chain so that it is modeled in WinMine's Plan Phase as an "output only" variable with the goal of determining whether WinMine could show how the other factors might be related to this output variable. On the other hand, data elements related to the MCS cloud itself, including area, shape, geo-location values and the lowest average TBB value of each MCS cloud are modeled as "input" variables. Since we are unsure about the role that each HLAFS variable may play with regard to the output variable, i.e. "MCS type", and we aim at revealing their interactions among each other, each HLAFS variable is therefore best defined as "input and output" variable, which is one that is both predicted by other variables and can also serve as a predictor.

Once the structure is specified, a stochastic analysis can be executed to reveal the relationships between variables and identify probabilistic dependencies. WinMine learns the structure and the parameters of dependency networks from data and builds dependency networks with decision trees at each node to represent the conditional distributions. The generated dependency network is a summary of the set of all decision trees constructed for each variable in the integrated dataset, which can be used to model the relationship between different variables. A path on the decision tree is formed from conditional probabilities and is a graphical method of displaying dependencies found within the data. The decision tree for each node indicates the likelihood of an "output" if some other correlated variables were coded in a specific way, which means that certain other conditions co-exist.

Figure 5 shows an illustration of the generated dependency network for the integrated dataset for MCS conceptual modeling.

The dependency network shown in Fig. 5 is user-interactive, which helps users to visually check the relationships of any feature elements to any other elements present.

The output is generated using WinMine's visualizing tool, DNet Viewer, which is a graph containing nodes and arrows indicating relational links between the variables (Chickering, 2002).

DNet Viewer graphically displays the structure of the data and represents the variables with different colors. By clicking on each node in the graph, it will be indicated with green color, with all the correlated nodes highlighted in different colors. Take the "DIV_bb" node in Fig. 5 as an example. As can be seen from Fig. 5, there are three attributes: "IFVQ_bb", "DIV_ba", and "H_bc" linked to the "DIV_bb", which means they are all related to the "DIV_bb" attribute. Therefore, we may assume that the meteorological environment fields consisting of "DIV_bb" and one of the three linked attributes would be meaningful to model the environment pattern, under which MCS would have eastward evolvement and a high probability of causing heavy rainfall.. Each link represents a strength of dependency associated with probability distribution (Heckerman & Chickering, 2000), and only the strongest link (dependency) among the three nodes is chosen to combine with "DIV_bb" to model a concept interpretation and the corresponding meteorological environment model graph is plotted. From the entire group of generated model graphs, meteorologists can easily discover which HLAFS variables are crucial

Figure 5. Dependency network generated for MCS dataset

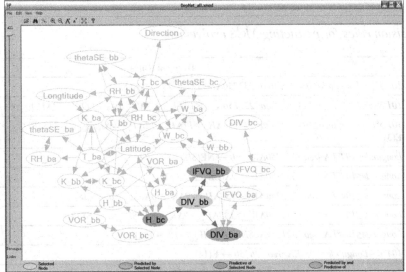

in influencing the evolvement trends of MCS clouds that will possibly incur heavy rainfall in the Yangtze River Basin.

It should be noted that the C4.5 rule is based on an individual MCS cloud. We can predict the evolvement trend of each newly identified MCS cloud from the mined decision rules. This conceptual model is different from those rules. It targets the attributes in the integrated dataset where all the correlated attributes of the same type of MCS clouds are selected from the generated dependency network. Their values are then spatially averaged to provide a meteorological relevance analysis for the MCS evolvement trends. Both of them are integrated and complementary components for analyzing the evolvement trends of MCS and evaluating their influence on heavy rain falls.

EXPERIMENTAL RESULTS AND ANALYSIS

Experiments are designed and implemented to test the proposed data mining method and generated conceptual model, based on the data sources described in subsection 2.2. After the MCS tracking and characterization stage, there are totally 320 MCSs that qualify for data mining

step, among which 50 clouds have moved out of the Tibetan Plateau (105^0E): 37 clouds for "E", 9 clouds for "NE" and 4 clouds for "SE". 70% of all the identified MCSs, i.e. 224 clouds, are used as train samples and the remaining 30% are kept for testing. A set of decision rules for predicting MCS evolvements are generated by using the C4.5 decision tree algorithm and a set of meteorological environment models corresponding to the relevant HLAFS attributes are also automatically constructed and plotted according to dependency network techniques.

Table 1 shows the generated decision rules, which have already been pruned, for predicting the evolvement trends of MCS clouds moving out of the Tibetan Plateau. After the tree pruning process, the number of misclassifications on test cases is 5 out of 96 clouds, achieving overall classification accuracy 94.8%.

From the above rules, we may garner important information about MCS evolvement and the satellite remote sensed data, which is presented as follows:

(1) HLAFS Variables Vorticity (VOR), Relative Humidity (RH), Temperature (T) and MCS shape are less important in influencing the evolvement trends of MCS clouds;

Table 1. The decision rules for predicting MCS evolvement

Rule No.	Decision Rules
1	$101.5°E < Longitude \leq 104°E \wedge Area \leq 233750 \wedge IFVQ_{c-b} \leq -74 \rightarrow$ **NE(2)**
2	$101.5°E < Longitude \leq 104°E \wedge Area \leq 233750 \wedge H_{b-a} \leq 17 \wedge K_{b-a} \leq 12 \wedge T_{b-a} > 9 \wedge IFVQ_{c-b} > -74 \wedge DIV_{c-b} \leq 6 \rightarrow$ **E(10)**
3	$101.5°E < Longitude \leq 104°E \wedge Area \leq 233750 \wedge H_{b-a} > 17 \wedge K_{b-a} \leq 12 \wedge T_{b-a} > 9 \wedge IFVQ_{c-b} > -74 \wedge IFVQ_{b-a} > 2 \wedge DIV_{c-b} \leq 6 \rightarrow$ **E(3)**
4	$Longitude \leq 104°E \wedge Area > 233750 \wedge K_{c-b} \leq 0 \rightarrow$ **NE(3/1)**
5	$Longitude \leq 104°E \wedge Area > 233750 \wedge H_{b-a} \leq 9 \wedge \theta SE_{c-b} \leq 0 \rightarrow$ **SE**
6	$Longitude \leq 104°E \wedge Area > 233750 \wedge W_{b-a} \leq 138 \wedge H_{b-a} > 9 \wedge K_{c-b} > 0 \wedge \theta SE_{c-b} \leq 0 \rightarrow$ **E(8)**
7	$Longitude \leq 104°E \wedge Area > 233750 \wedge W_{b-a} > 138 \wedge H_{b-a} > 9 \wedge K_{c-b} > 0 \wedge \theta SE_{c-b} \leq 0 \rightarrow$ **SE(3/1)**
8	$Longitude \leq 104°E \wedge Area > 521250 \wedge \theta SE_{c-b} > 0 \wedge DIV_{b-a} > -10 \rightarrow$ **E(2)**
9	$104°E < Longitude < 105°E \wedge Area > 26250 \rightarrow$ **E(14)**
10	$104°E < Longitude < 105°E \wedge Latitude > 30.5 \wedge Area \leq 26250 \rightarrow$ **E(2)**

(2) If the longitude of an MCS cloud's centroid is less than 104°E, the evolvement trend of that cloud is mainly determined by variables including MCS area, K index (K), geo-potential Height (H), Wind Divergence (DIV) and Water Vapor Flux Divergence (IFVQ).

(3) If the longitude of an MCS cloud's centroid is between 104°E and 105°E, and the MCS area is greater than 26,250 km², that cloud has much more chance of moving out of the Tibetan Plateau.

The experimental results in Table I also indicate that the meteorological environment features, i.e. HLAFS variables K, H, DIV and IFVQ are important in influencing the evolvement trends of MCS clouds. Jointly considering the dependency network generated by using dependency network techniques, it is then possible to construct and plot a set of environment model graphs corresponding to those variables, rendering a geographical relevance analysis tool for predicting the possibility of heavy rainfalls incurred by evolvements of MCS clouds. Figure 6 gives several instances

of the meteorological, environment model graph revealing the relationship between the "H-DIV" variable pair and eastward evolvement trends of MCS clouds.

The environment model graphs, together with the C4.5 decision rules, jointly constitute the forecasting model of MCS clouds as the final output of our MCS data mining system. These results have been validated by meteorologists from the National Satellite Meteorological Center of the China Meteorological Administration and by the Hong Kong Observatory, which not only provides a satisfactory prediction accuracy of MCS movement trends but also renders a novel tool for rainstorm forecasting.

The experimental results indicate that it is feasible to model and predict evolvement trends of MCSs on the Tibetan Plateau based on their meteorological environment attribute (i.e. HLAFS data) values and TBB images from the satellite databases. Moreover, it is also proven that our data mining approach provides an automatic and robust means for meteorologists to observe and analyze MCSs more effectively and efficiently. This may help meteorologists reveal the hidden connections

Figure 6. Instances of "H-DIV" environment model graphs incurring the eastward evolvement trend of MCS clouds

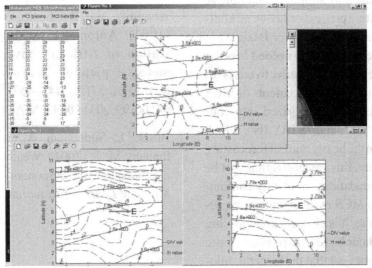

of MCS evolvements to heavy rainfalls occurring in China's Yangtze River Basin.

CONCLUSION

This chapter proposes an automatic meteorological data mining system based on analyzing and mining heterogeneous remote sensed image datasets, with which it is possible to forecast potential rainstorms in advance. An efficient MCS tracking, characterization and analysis tool based on meteorological satellite remote sensed images has been implemented and a two-phase data mining method employing machine learning techniques, including the C4.5 decision tree algorithm and dependency network technique, is proposed, by which decision rules and a conceptual model are generated to discover the correlations between MCS trends and the possible heavy rainfall in China's Yangtze River Basin.

Since the process is entirely automated, the output of the above method will largely help meteorologists produce their weather forecasting results quickly and efficiently, relieving them from the heavy workload of visually scanning a large amount of satellite images. Moreover, experimental results have shown that the proposed method is able to provide meaningful interpretations to the forecasted results and may simplify and improve the weather forecasting process on heavy rainfalls and floods in China's Yangtze River Basin.

However, further work is still needed in order to improve the accuracy and effectiveness of this process. Currently, the evolvements of MCS clouds are only roughly categorized into four types: "E", "NE", "SE", and "STAY-IN", which depends strongly on the heavy rainfall forecasting context. In the future, this categorization will be refined with finer gradations, or ideally continuously, to model the MCS evolvements more accurately. Furthermore, it is also worth improving the proposed methodologies to produce more generalization abilities, so that these methodolo-

gies can be used in many other similar MCS cloud analysis applications, in which TBB and HLAFS data sources from different geographical regions may be used.

Moreover, how to construct and output a more intuitive and straightforward model based on the integrated data schema remains an important issue for future research considerations. A novel solution to this problem will help reveal the unknown patterns of intensive occurrences of heavy rainfall and enable us to better understand them.

ACKNOWLEDGMENT

This work is supported by the "973" Program of China (Grant No. 2010CB327903), the National Natural Science Foundation of China (Grant Nos. 60875011, 60723003, 60721002), and the Natural Science Foundation of Jiangsu Province, China (Grant No. BK2007520). The authors also thank their collaborators in the National Satellite Meteorological Center of China Meteorological Administration and at the Hong Kong Observatory, for their stimulating discussion on domain-specific knowledge and provision of data sources.

REFERENCES

Arnaud, Y., Desbios, M., & Maizi, J. (1992). Automatic tracking and characterization of African convective systems on meteosat pictures. *Journal of Applied Meteorology, 31*(5), 443–453. doi:10.1175/1520-0450(1992)031<0443:ATACOA>2.0.CO;2

Basak, J., Sudarshan, A., Trivedi, D., & Santhanam, M. S. (2004). Weather Data Mining Using Independent Component Analysis. *Journal of Machine Learning Research, 5*(3), 239–253.

Breiman, L., Friedman, J. H., Olshen, R. A., & Stone, C. J. (1984). *Classification and Regression Trees*. Monterey, CA: Wadsworth International Group.

Chickering, D. M. (2002). *The WinMine Toolkit* (Tech. Rep. No. MSR-TR-2002-103). Redmond, WA: Microsoft Research.

Chickering, D. M., Heckerman, D., Meek, C., Platt, J. C., & Thiesson, B. (2000). *Goal-oriented clustering*. Tech. Rep. No. MSR-TR-2000-82. Redmond, WA: Microsoft Research.

Estevam, R. H., Eduardo, R. H., & Nelson, F. F. (2005, December). *Applying Bayesian Networks for Meteorological Data Mining*. Paper presented at the Twenty-fifth SGAI International Conference on Innovative Techniques and Applications of Artificial Intelligence, Cambridge, UK.

Freeman, H. (1974). Computer processing of line-drawing image. *Computing Surveys*, *6*(1), 57–97. doi:10.1145/356625.356627

Heckerman, D., Chickering, D. M., Meek, C., Rounthwaite, R., & Kadie, C. (2000). Dependency Networks for Inference, Collaborative Filtering, and Data Visualization. *Journal of Machine Learning Research*, *1*(9), 49–75.

Houze, R., Smull, B., & Dodge, P. (1990). Mesoscale organization of springtime rainstorms in Oklahoma. *Monthly Weather Review*, *18*(3), 613–654. doi:10.1175/1520-0493(1990)118<0613:MOOSRI>2.0.CO;2

Jiang, J., & Fan, M. (2002). Convective clouds and mesoscale convective systems over the Tibetan Plateau in summer. *Atmosphere Science*, *26*(1), 262–269.

Lai, X., Li, G., Gan, Y., & Ye, Z. (2006). An Association Rule Mining Approach for Satellite Cloud Images and Rainfall. In Y. Zhuang (Ed.), *Lecture Notes on Computer Sciences* (Vol. 4261, pp. 658–666), Heidlberg, Germany: Springer-Verlag.

Lance, S. (2000). *Use of Data Mining on Satellite Data Bases for Knowledge Extraction*. Paper presented at the 13th International Florida Artificial Intelligence Research Society Conference, Orlando, Florida.

Li, D., Harms, S., Goddard, S., Waltman, W., & Deogun, J. (2003). *Time-series data mining in a geospatial decision support system*. Paper presented at the 7th annual national conference on Digital government research, Boston.

Li, X., Plale, B., Vijayakumar, N., Ramachandran, R., Graves, S., & Conover, H. (2008). Real-time storm detection and weather forecast activation through data mining and events processing. *Earth Science Informatics*, *1*(2), 49–57. doi:10.1007/s12145-008-0010-7

Liu, Z., & George, R. (2005). Mining Weather Data Using Fuzzy Cluster Analysis. In E. P. Frederick, B. R. Vincent, & A. C. Maria (Eds.), *Fuzzy Modeling with Spatial Information for Geographic Problems*, (pp. 105-119). Heidelberg, Germany: Springer-Verlag.

Philip, N. S., & Joseph, K. B. (2003). A Neural Network Tool for Analyzing Trends in Rainfall. *Computers & Geosciences*, *29*(2), 215–223. doi:10.1016/S0098-3004(02)00117-6

Plonski, M. P., Gustafson, G., Shaw, B., Thomas, B., & Wonsick, M. (2000). *High resolution cloud analysis and forecast system*. Paper presented at the 10th Conference on Satellite Meteorology and Oceanography, Long Beach, CA.

Quinlan, J. R. (1993). *C4.5: Programs for Machine Learning.* San Francisco, CA: Morgan Kaufman.

Quinlan, J. R., & Rivest, R. L. (1989). Inferring decision trees using the minimum description length principle. *Information and Computation, 80*(3), 227–248. doi:10.1016/0890-5401(89)90010-2

Souto, M. J., Balseiro, C. F., Pérez-Muñuzuri, V., Xue, M., & Brewster, K. (2003). Impact of cloud analysis on numerical weather prediction in the galician region of spain. *Journal of Applied Meteorology, 42*(3), 129–140. doi:10.1175/1520-0450(2003)042<0129:IOCAON>2.0.CO;2

Tomé, A. R., & Almeida, P. D. (2007, April). *Usefull(ness) of NAO index for forecast of Monthly rainfall in Lisbon.* Paper presented at European Geosciences Union General Assembly 2007, Vienna, Austria.

Yang, Y., Lin, H., Guo, Z., & Jiang, J. (2004). Automatic Tracking and Characterization of Multiple Moving Clouds in Satellite Images. In W. Thissen, P. Wieringa, & M. Pantic (Eds.), *Proceedings of IEEE International Conference on Systems, Man and Cybernetics* (pp. 3088-3093). New York: IEEE press.

Yang, Y., Lin, H., Guo, Z., & Jiang, J. (2007). A data mining approach for heavy rainfall forecasting based on satellite image sequence analysis. *International Journal of Computers and Geosciences, 33*(1), 20–30. doi:10.1016/j.cageo.2006.05.010

Yang, Y., Lin, H., & Jiang, J. (2006). Cloud analysis by modeling the integration of heterogeneous satellite data and imaging. *IEEE Transactions on Systems, Man, and Cybernetics. Part A, Systems and Humans, 36*(1), 162–172. doi:10.1109/TSMCA.2005.859182

Zhou, Z. H., & Jiang, Y. (2003). Medical Diagnosis With C4.5 Rule Preceded by Artificial Neural Network Ensemble. *IEEE Transactions on Information Technology in Biomedicine, 7*(1), 37–42. doi:10.1109/TITB.2003.808498

Chapter 19
Learning Verifiable Ensembles for Classification Problems with High Safety Requirements

Sebastian Nusser
Otto-von-Guericke-University, Germany

Clemens Otte
Siemens AG, Germany

Werner Hauptmann
Siemens AG, Germany

Rudolf Kruse
Otto-von-Guericke-University, Germany

ABSTRACT

This chapter describes a machine learning approach for classification problems in safety-related domains. The proposed method is based on ensembles of low-dimensional submodels. The usage of low-dimensional submodels enables the domain experts to understand the mechanisms of the learned solution. Due to the limited dimensionality of the submodels each individual model can be visualized and can thus be interpreted and validated according to the domain knowledge. The ensemble of all submodels overcomes the limited predictive performance of each single submodel while the overall solution remains interpretable and verifiable. By different examples from real-world applications the authors will show that their classification approach is applicable to a wide range of classification problems in the field of safety-related applications - ranging from decision support systems over plant monitoring and diagnosis systems to control tasks with very high safety requirements.

INTRODUCTION

Machine learning methods are successfully applied in a wide range of applications – for instance – object recognition in computer vision, search engines, or stock market analysis. But in the field of safety-related applications such methods are regarded with suspicion by the domain experts because the learned models are often hard to verify, may tend to overfitting, and the exact inter- and extrapolation behavior is often unclear. In this chapter, a machine learning method is proposed that (1) is capable of

DOI: 10.4018/978-1-61520-757-2.ch019

tackling classification problems in application domains with high safety requirements and (2) satisfies the domain experts' demand for verification of the correctness of the learned solution for the given application problem.

A safety-related system is a system whose malfunction or failure can lead to serious consequences – for instance environmental harm, loss or severe damage of equipment, harm or serious injury of people, or even death. Examples of safety-related application domains are: aerospace engineering, automotive industry, medical systems, and process automation. The increasing complexity of such safety-related systems and the growth of the number of requirements and customer requests raise the interest in applying machine learning methods within this domain. For instance, the domain knowledge is often imperfect and, thus, purely analytical solutions cannot be provided by the domain experts. In addition, the data-driven generation of classification models offers a reduction of development time and costs. The classification performance can be improved by advanced classification models. Unfortunately, in the field of safety-related application domains, it is often not possible to rectify a wrong decision. For effectively applying data-driven classification methods within this domain, it is crucial to provide strong evidence that the learned solution is valid within the complete input space and correctly satisfies all given functional specifications. It must be guaranteed that the interpolation and extrapolation behavior of the solution is always correct. Therefore, it is imperative to provide an interpretable solution that can be validated according to the given domain knowledge. Figure 1 illustrates the issue of an unexpected change of a classifier's decision within a region of the input space where no data is available. Such unintended behavior can be regularly discovered by visualization for the two-dimensional case – but for a high-dimensional model this is infeasible. Often, statistical risk estimation methods are not

satisfactorily in real-world applications because the observed data is scarce and, therefore, vast regions of the high-dimensional input space do not contain any data.

This contribution is motivated by a real-world application within the field of automotive safety electronics. It concerns the deployment of restraint systems (for instance belt pretensioners and airbags) and serves as an example for control systems with high safety requirements. The malfunction might be fatal and it is impossible to rectify a wrong deployment decision since an airbag system can only be triggered once. Depending on the severity of a crash different restraint systems must be triggered: for instance, the belt pretensioners, the front airbag stage 1 (airbag is inflated to 70%) or stage 2 (airbag is inflated to 100%), the knee airbags, the side airbags (front or rear), or the curtain airbags. Furthermore, the airbag must be triggered within a certain time interval in order to ensure the best passenger protection – a front crash, for instance, must be triggered within 15 ms to 30 ms. The postponed deployment of an airbag can lead to severe injuries of the car occupants.

For each new car platform the control logic of the restraint systems has to be developed nearly from scratch since altered mechanical components, different sensor placements, or new functional requirements of the car platform can dramatically influence the signal characteristics and, for this reason, a solution of a previous platform will not be applicable anymore. Until now, most of the calibration work is done manually by domain experts. For each crash type many different sensor combinations are evaluated and a control logic based on those combinations is developed. This manual calibration is time and cost intensive. Due to cost pressure in the market, the increasing complexity of today's restraint systems must be handled with limited resources. Thus, there is a growing interest in automatically learning the control logic from crash test data in order to reduce

Figure 1. Unintended extrapolation behavior of a support vector machine classifier with a Gaussian kernel in a region of the input space where no training data is available

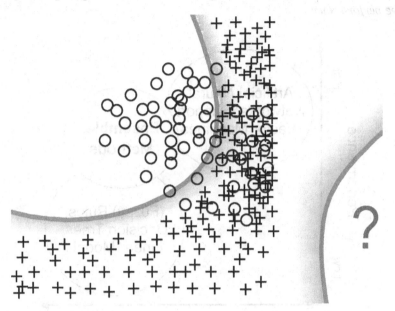

development time and costs. A solution of this challenging classification problem is discussed as an application example in Section 3.2.

The main focus of interest within this chapter can be summarized by the following objectives:

1. Data-driven generation of interpretable classification models that
2. achieve a good predictive accuracy and
3. allow the verification according to the given domain knowledge.

Here, the crucial aspect is to realize a suitable trade-off between (1) and (2). It is obvious that a complex model can achieve a higher predictive performance on the available data. However, a higher model complexity will lead to an increased effort for model verification. This trade-off and the corresponding characterization of common machine learning methods are illustrated in Figure 2. Methods that are known to achieve a high predictive performance – for instance sup-

port vector machines (SVMs) or artificial neural networks (ANNs) – are usually hard to interpret. On the other hand, methods that are known to be well-interpretable – for instance (fuzzy) rule systems, decision trees, or linear models – are usually limited with respect to their predictive performance. The use of ensemble methods provides an appealing solution of this conflict.

The remaining part of this chapter is organized as follows: Section 2 gives a short introduction into the field of safety-related systems and existing machine learning approaches for use in safety-related domains. In Section 3, an ensemble learning method is presented to solve binary classification problems in the field of safety-related applications. Section 4 extends the binary classification ensemble to deal with multi-class problems. Different data preprocessing methods that can be used to enhance the performance of the classification ensembles are discussed in Section 5. Section 6 concludes this chapter.

Figure 2. Interpretability versus predictive performance. Methods that can achieve a high predictive performance are typically hard to interpret and methods that show a good interpretability usually achieve a lower predictive performance

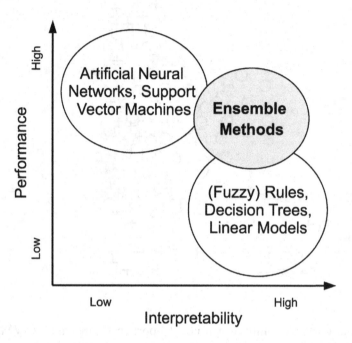

SAFETY-RELATED SYSTEMS

Safety is "a measure of the continuous delivery of a service free from occurrences of catastrophic failures" (Bowen & Hinchey, 1999). That is, safety is the property of a system that it will not endanger human life or the environment. Therefore, a safety-critical system is a system where a failure may result in injury or loss of life – an often quoted example of the malfunctioning of such a safety-critical system is the Therac-25 radiotherapy machine which killed several people (Leveson & Turner, 1993). Systems that involve safety aspects but are not necessarily safety-critical are so-called safety-related systems. Safety-critical systems can be seen as a subset of safety-related systems. Within this chapter, we will not distinguish between safety-critical and safety-related systems.

Safety-related systems can be grouped into three application classes where the safety requirements of each class are increasing:

Decision Support. This application class includes forecasts, planning supports, recommendations of control variables and decision support systems in medical engineering or system control. These systems take on a purely advisory role for the domain experts or the plant operators.

Monitoring and Diagnosis. Monitoring systems for engines, equipment, production or process facilities, and systems for fault diagnosis and early fault detection can be assigned to this application class. Typically, an alarm is activated in such systems leading to a subsequent user intervention. A wrong decision of such a monitoring system (for instance a false alarm) can be rectified by the domain expert or system operator.

Automation and Control. This class of applications is most challenging since the systems perform autonomously – without any user interaction – and directly affect the control or automation task. This application class has particularly high requirements on the functional safety and it is especially important to satisfy the domain experts' demand for the correctness of the learned solution. It must be guaranteed that the learned solution is valid within the complete input space.

The machine learning approaches discussed in Section 3 and Section 4 are developed for autonomous control tasks – but they are also applicable for the application classes with lower safety-requirements.

Assessing Solutions for Safety-Related Problems

The correctness and reliability of a safety-related system is usually assessed by formal verification and validation methods. Thereby, verification concerns the question whether the system is being built right. It is evaluated whether or not the system complies with the imposed specifications and conditions. Validation concerns the question whether the right system for the user needs is being built. This issue is related to statements on system reliability and failure rates. For successfully applying a safety-related system it is important to prove the trustworthiness and acceptability of the solution for the safety-related application problem. Therefore, it must be ensured that the system is stable and meets all given requirements.

In practical application tasks, the available training data is often scarce and the number of input dimensions is too large in order to sufficiently apply purely statistical risk estimation methods – for instance K-fold cross-validation (Kohavi, 1995). Assessing the quality of a learned solution only based on the error rate estimated on a testing set becomes intractable especially for high-dimensional problems for the reason that the required error rates cannot be achieved (for instance, the required error rate within the field of aviation is $\leq 10^{-9}$). In many applications, high-dimensional models are required to solve the given problem. Unfortunately, high-dimensional models are hard to verify (*curse of dimensionality* – a good illustration of this problem is given in (Hastie et al., 2001, Chapter 2.5)), may tend to overfitting,

and the interpolation and extrapolation behavior is often intransparent. An illustrative example of a counterintuitive behavior of a classifier is shown in Figure 1. While this classifier achieves a good performance on the training and testing data – there is an unexpected change of the prediction of the model within a region not covered by the given data set. Such undesired behavior becomes even more likely and much more difficult to discover in the high-dimensional case. Thus, a model building method is required which guarantees a well-defined interpolation and extrapolation behavior, that is, the decision bounds of the learned models can exactly be determined and evaluated for every point of the input space.

For the assessment of a data-driven generated solution for use in safety-related domains, it is important to take the following issues into account (Taylor, 2005, Chapter 3):

- The limited size of the testing data set may not allow a proper system evaluation.
- The limited size of the training data set may lead to an inappropriate approximation of the desired function.
- How will the solution deal with previously unseen data?
- The training and testing data might be insufficient – especially for rigorous testing and reliability estimation.
- The training and testing data must represent the entire input domain (completeness and correctness).

Reliability assessment and robustness analysis require a huge number of test cases which may not be available. Insufficient testing data make it impossible to prove the correctness of the learned solution. Furthermore, it must be ensured that proper model assumptions and parameters are chosen.

For successfully applying machine learning methods within the field of safety-related applications and providing solutions that are accepted by the domain experts, the following requirements arise:

Reliability. The learned solution must show a low probability of failure. It must be ensured that the learned solution is always within the specified conditions.

Correct Interpolation and Extrapolation. Overfitting of the learned solution must be avoided and a good generalization behavior must be guaranteed. On the other hand, the solution must be sensitive enough to capture the specific problem.

Data Efficiency. The learning algorithm must be capable to deal with small training sets, that is, a small number of independent training samples.

Expert Knowledge. It must be possible to include expert knowledge within the model building process.

Interpretability and Verification. Interpretability is essential to facilitate the domain experts to evaluate the decisions of the learned solution. Furthermore, the model should be understandable for people that are not experts in the field of machine learning theory.

It is a challenging task to prove that the learned solution is a correct solution of the application problem within the complete input space. The incorporation of a-priori knowledge into the model selection and model learning process can be helpful – for instance one can exploit monotonicity constraints, allow user interactions, or use active learning in order to achieve an improved generalization behavior (Cohn et al., 1994). Nevertheless, the quality of a data-driven generated solution depends on the quality and on the amount of data that is available for training. Often, the amount of data is insufficient for statistical risk estimation methods. Furthermore, the observed data might not be representative for the complete input space. Therefore, in order to ensure that the learned model is a correct solution of the problem and it is valid within the complete input space it is imperative to allow the domain experts to judge the learned model according to their domain knowledge.

Overview of the Usage of Machine Learning in Safety-Related Domains

Lisboa (2001) investigates the current usage of machine learning methods – especially artificial neural networks – in the field of safety-related applications. Recent approaches to adopt machine learning methods for use in safety-related applications can be found, for instance, in Zakrzewski (2001); Kurd et al. (2006); Kurd & Kelly (2007). Furthermore, there are different approaches of providing a verification and validation framework for machine learning methods, for instance Pullum et al. (2007) consider the verification and validation of artificial neural networks.

The important issue of the successful application of machine learning methods in a safety-related domain is to guarantee that the learned solution does not show any unintended inter- or extrapolation behavior – as already mentioned in Section 2.1 and illustrated in Figure 1. Using visualization techniques developed to map high-dimensional data to a low-dimensional space – for instance multidimensional scaling (Hastie et al., 2001; Rehm et al., 2006), principal curves (Hastie & Stuetzle, 1989), or self-organizing maps (Kohonen, 1990) – might give a good insight into the problem, but there is a loss of information and there is no guarantee that the mapping does not induce or hide inconsistencies of the originally learned solution.

One possibility of providing an interpretable solution is to use rule systems or tree-like models, or to extract such representations from non-symbolic models. There are numerous machine learning approaches that can be utilized for doing this – see, for instance, Breiman et al. (1984); Cohen (1995); Andrews et al. (1995); Boz (2002); Chen & Wang (2003); Tzeng & Ma (2005). Taylor (2005) recommends using rule extraction for generating rule bases from artificial neural networks in order to perform a formal safety analysis of the learned solution. The safety life cycle proposed by Kurd et al. (2006) combines rule extraction and knowledge insertion to an iterative process. It deals with three levels: a symbolic level, a translation level and a neural learning level. The symbolic level is associated with the domain knowledge, the translation level performs the rule insertion and rule extraction to the neural learning level, and the neural learning level is used to modify and refine the symbolic knowledge based on the given data. Fuzzy-rule systems (Nauck et al., 1997; Nauck, 2003) might be also a good option. They are often applied to controlling tasks. Unfortunately, data-driven methods of building such rule systems often result in huge rule bases which are hard to interpret.

Schlang et al. (1999) combine an RBF-network with an analytical model of the controlled process. The RBF-network multiplicatively corrects the output of the analytical model. For unknown inputs it is designed to produce a correction factor close to one so that the output in that case is determined by the analytical model. The advantage of their approach is that the analytical model guarantees a baseline performance which the RBF-network can optimize in its trusted input regions. The disadvantage of this approach is that it is only applicable on problems where an analytical model can be provided.

Another possibility to determine a data-driven model is proposed by Zakrzewski (2001). In this approach, an already validated reference implementation (for instance a look-up table) is used as deterministic data generator for an exhaustive evaluation of the machine learning solution. This approach compensates the limited number of data by generating data according to the reference implementation. Thus, it becomes possible to prove that the machine learning solution conforms to the reference implementation. This might be useful to reduce the memory usage by replacing large look-up tables by smaller artificial neural networks, but it is questionable why a second model should be built if there is an already validated reference solution of an application problem.

Confidence measures – for instance error bars provided by Gaussian Processes (GPs) (MacKay, 1998; Rasmussen & Williams, 2006) or multi-layer perceptrons (MLPs) with evidence propagation (MacKay, 1992) – can be used to estimate the uncertainty of the model's output. But for high-dimensional problems where the data might be sparse such confidence measures suffer from the limited number of data that is available. For instance, in the field of aviation and controlling nuclear power plants an error rate of at least 10^{-9} failures per hour is required – achieving such an error rate by purely assessing the solution based on the error rate estimated on a testing data set and computing some confidence measures becomes intractable for high-dimensional problems.

Another approach of providing an interpretable solution is to use ensemble methods, that is, the original high-dimensional problem is partitioned into smaller subproblems. Then it becomes possible to visualize and, thus, to interpret the solutions of the smaller subproblems. The methods described in Section 3 and Section 4 are based on this ensemble modeling idea.

LEARNING VERIFIABLE ENSEMBLES

The basic idea of this machine learning approach is to solve a high-dimensional classification problem by an ensemble of submodels. Each submodel utilizes only a low-dimensional subspace of the complete input space which facilitates the visual interpretation. The submodels are trained on the original input dimensions allowing the domain experts to directly evaluate the trained models within their domain. Thus, an unintended extrapolation and interpolation behavior of the learned solution can be avoided and the correctness of the solution can be guaranteed. The ensemble of the submodels compensates for the limited predictive performance of each single submodel and the possibility to visualize each submodel greatly assures the domain experts' acceptance of the data-driven generated models. This classification approach was introduced by Nusser et al. (2007, 2008b) and it is motivated by Generalized Additive Models (Hastie & Tibshirani, 1990) and Separate-&-Conquer approaches (Fürnkranz, 1999). It can be seen as variant of the Projection Pursuit (Friedman & Tukey, 1974; Huber, 1985).

The original ensemble classification framework is designed to solve binary classification problems, that is, the learning task is to determine an estimate of the unknown function $f: V^n \rightarrow Y$, where $V^n = X_1 \times X_2 \times \ldots \times X_n$ with $X_i \subseteq R$ and $Y = \{0,1\}$, given the observed data set $D = \{(\mathbf{v}_1, y_1), (\mathbf{v}_2, y_2), \ldots, (\mathbf{v}_m, y_m)\} \subset V^n \times Y$. The extension of our binary classification ensemble to deal with multi-class problems is discussed in Section 4.

The Binary Classification Ensemble

We are interested in determining an estimate of the unknown function $f: V^n \rightarrow Y$. Instead of considering the original high-dimensional input space V^n, we consider only two- or three-dimensional subspaces of V^n. Submodels are trained on these small subspaces. This facilitates the visual interpretation of the solution and, thus, unintended inter- and extrapolation behavior can be avoided. The submodels are combined to an ensemble of models to overcome the limited predictive performance of each single model. That is, the approach assumes that the original classification problem is separable into low-dimensional subproblems.

Projections of High-dimensional Data

The projection π maps the high-dimensional input space V^n to an arbitrary subspace V_β. This mapping is determined by a given index set $\beta \subset \{1, \ldots, n\}$. This index set defines the dimensions of V^n that will be included in the subspace V_β. Thus, the projection π can be defined as:

$$\pi_\beta(V^n) = V_\beta = \prod_{i \in \beta} X_i. \tag{1}$$

Submodels

The j-th submodel is defined as:

$$g_j: \pi_{\beta[j]}(V^n) \rightarrow Y, \tag{2}$$

where β_j denotes the index set of the subspace where the classification error of the submodel g_j is minimal. In order to determine the best projections, a wrapper method for feature selection (Kohavi & John, 1997) that performs an exhaustive search through all possible low-dimensional input combinations is used. For very high-dimensional data sets we advise to use a preceding feature selection (see for instance Guyon & Elisseeff (2006)) for reducing the computational costs. The final function estimate $f^*(\mathbf{v})$ of the global model is determined by the aggregation of the results of all submodels $g_j(\pi_{\beta[j]}(\mathbf{v}))$.

Learning the Verifiable Ensemble

The ensemble requires that the *default class* (c_{pref}), that is, the default state of the safety-related system, must not be misclassified by any of the trained submodels: $\forall y = c_{pref}: |y - g_j(\pi_{\beta[j]}(\mathbf{v}))| = 0$. This requirement typically leads to imbalanced misclassification costs. The submodels are trained on low-dimensional projections of the high-dimensional input space with the objective to avoid the misclassification of the default class. The submodels try to greedily separate the samples of the other class from all default class samples. Missed samples of the other class are used to build further sub-experts. Algorithm 1 shows the learning algorithm of the ensemble method. For the sake of simplicity it is defined that the default class is always encoded as zero by all submodels.

Figure 3. Algorithm 1. Learning a Verifiable Ensemble

Algorithm 1 Learning a Verifiable Ensemble

---

input: data set D, c_{pref} - label of default class, d_{limit} – limit of dimensions (fixed)

output: models – set of submodels

function models := buildModel(D, c_{pref})

1: solve $\forall (\mathbf{v}, y) \in D : \min \{ |y - g(\pi_\beta(\mathbf{v}))| \}$, $\beta \subset \{1, ..., n\}$ s.t.
   $|\beta| = d_{\text{limit}}$ and $\forall y = c_{\text{pref}} : |y - g(\pi_\beta(\mathbf{v}))| = 0$

2: $D_{new} := \{ (\mathbf{v}, y) | g(\pi_\beta(\mathbf{v})) = c_{\text{pref}} \}$

3: **if** $(D \setminus D_{new} \neq \emptyset)$ **then**

4:      models := $\{ g(\pi_\beta(\cdot)) \} \cup$ buildModel(D_{new}, c_{pref})

5: **else**

6:      models := $\emptyset$

7: **end if**

Applying the Verifiable Ensemble

The application of the ensemble framework is very simple. Due to the restriction that every submodel must not misclassify any sample of the default class, it is sufficient to determine the maximum of the output of all submodels, that is

$$f^*(\mathbf{v}) = \max_{(g[j], \beta[j]) \in models} g_j(\pi_{\beta[j]}(\mathbf{v})), \qquad (3)$$

where *models* is the set of submodels that is returned by Algorithm 1.

Discussion of the Learning Algorithm

In a high-dimensional space the observed data is sparse and the uncertainty about the correctness of the solution is large because vast regions of the high-dimensional input space do not contain any data. Using low-dimensional projections (as defined in Eq. 1) of the high-dimensional input space reduces this uncertainty because the regions without any data become smaller or might even vanish within these subspaces. Furthermore, for projections of size two or three it is feasible to visualize the relevant input space and to detect an unintended and possibly undesired behavior of the learned model. Because the submodels are built on the original input dimensions, the visual representations of the learned submodels can be easily evaluated according to the given domain knowledge – even for non-experts in the field of machine learning. Although the submodels are learned on small subspaces of the high-dimensional input space, each submodel can be extended to the high-dimensional space (via a cylindrical extension as used for instance in fuzzy logic) and therefore each submodel is valid within the complete input space. The maximum operator provides a simple but powerful aggregation function: for detecting a critical event (that is, the system leaves the default state) it is sufficient that one submodel is activated – there are no (hidden) dependencies among the submodels. Thus, all submodels can be evaluated independently. The ensemble compensates for the limited predictive performance of each submodels. As pointed out in the introduction, there is always a trade-off between the interpretability and the achievement of a high predictive performance. Since interpretability is imperative in the domain of safety-related applications in order to guarantee that the learned solution is valid within the complete input space, one must accept a reduced predictive accuracy on the observed data. In Section 5 we propose different methods to enhance the predictive performance on problems requiring a higher dimensionality than allowed by the submodels.

Safe Learning for Airbag Control

This application serves as an example for control systems with very high safety requirements. In this learning problem, based on a high-dimensional data set, a decision has to be derived whether to trigger the restraint system of a car (Fire) or not (NoFire). An example for such a restraint application is the deployment of an airbag system. This classification task is challenging because (1) the restraint system can be triggered only once – that is, a wrong decision cannot be rectified – and (2) a malfunction of the system might be fatal. Thus, it must be ensured that the obtained model is sensitive enough to trigger the restraint system and robust enough in order to avoid an unintended extrapolation or interpolation behavior – as illustrated in Figure 1. The control logic of a restraint system has to be developed almost from scratch for each new car platform since the signal characteristics of the sensors can considerably differ from a previous car platform and, thus, the previous solution will not be applicable anymore. Until now, most of this calibration work is done manually by the domain experts. Automatically learning the control logic from crash test data can significantly reduce the development time and costs.

The data set in this application example, which was first used in Nusser et al. (2007), is sparse and consists of approximately 40 000 data points, where each data point is 30-dimensional. These data points belong to 40 distinct time series. Each time series represents a certain standardized crash situation. Due to the limited number of crash tests, the guaranteed extrapolation (and interpolation) behavior of the models becomes essential. As the data set consists of a number of time series, it is sufficient to trigger the restraint system once in a defined time interval. The incorporation of domain knowledge facilitates the reduction of the model complexity by dividing the Fire class into subgroups (Fire.1 and Fire.2). These subgroups represent different types of crash situations which implicate input signals with different signal characteristics. Thus, in order to reduce the complexity of the learning problem, we can separate the original problem into two distinct subproblems (Fire.1 versus NoFire and Fire.2 versus NoFire) and solve these problems independently. NoFire is chosen as the default class. That is, all NoFire samples have to be correctly classified by all submodels. NoFire is encoded as 0 and Fire is encoded as 1.

This binary classification problem can be solved by an ensemble of four two-dimensional submodels – two submodels for the Fire.1 subgroup and two submodels for the Fire.2 subgroup. The prediction of the global model can simply be determined by the maximum of the prediction of each learned submodel:

$$f^*(\mathbf{v}) = \max\{g_1^{\text{F.1}}(\pi_{\beta[1,\text{F.1}]}(\mathbf{v})), g_2^{\text{F.1}}(\pi_{\beta[2,\text{F.1}]}(\mathbf{v})), g_1^{\text{F.2}}(\pi_{\beta[1,\text{F.2}]}(\mathbf{v})), g_2^{\text{F.2}}(\pi_{\beta[2,\text{F.2}]}(\mathbf{v}))\} \ .$$

The learned submodels per subgroup are illustrated in Figure 4. All submodels have smooth decision boundaries that are adequate according to domain knowledge. No NoFire sample is triggered. Due to the capability to divide the data set into two different subgroups and to combine the learned submodels disjunctively, all Fire samples can be triggered by at least one expert.

The binary classification ensemble solves this challenging classification problem and conforms to all given requirements. The visualization of each submodel facilitates the domain experts to perform a direct evaluation of the learned solution. The simple aggregation of the submodels by the maximum operator ensures the interpretation of the global model as well. Despite the sophisti-

Figure 4. Verifiable Ensemble and the autonomous control example. NoFire samples are marked with circles and Fire samples are marked with crosses. The trajectories of the Fire samples are shown as broken lines. The decision boundaries of the submodels are drawn as solid lines

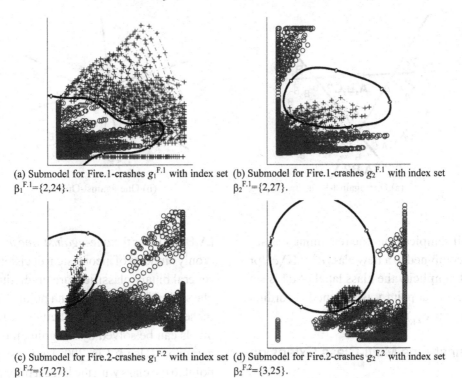

(a) Submodel for Fire.1-crashes $g_1^{F.1}$ with index set $\beta_1^{F.1}=\{2,24\}$.

(b) Submodel for Fire.1-crashes $g_2^{F.1}$ with index set $\beta_2^{F.1}=\{2,27\}$.

(c) Submodel for Fire.2-crashes $g_1^{F.2}$ with index set $\beta_1^{F.2}=\{7,27\}$.

(d) Submodel for Fire.2-crashes $g_2^{F.2}$ with index set $\beta_2^{F.2}=\{3,25\}$.

cated demands in the sensitive area of passenger safety, a verifiably correct solution is provided by our algorithm.

EXTENSION TO MULTI-CLASS ENSEMBLES

In this section, we will first briefly discuss common approaches to extend binary classifiers to deal with multi-class problems. We will point out the arising difficulties of these approaches that must be taken into account for use in safety-related applications. Later in this section, we discuss different strategies of extending the ensemble learning method of Section 3 to solve multi-class problems.

Common Multi-Class Extensions

There are two commonly used approaches to extend binary classifiers to solve multi-class problems: (1) a one-against-one extension and (2) a one-against-rest extension. A comparison of these methods and an experimental evaluation for support vector machines is given in Hsu & Lin (2002). Figure 5 illustrates both approaches.

One-Against-Rest Multi-Class Extension

This method constructs $k = |\mathbf{K}|$ classifiers, where $\mathbf{K} = \{1,\ldots,k\}$ is the set of classes. The model f_c for class $c \in \mathbf{K}$ is trained on all samples of class

Figure 5. Illustration of commonly used multi-class extensions of binary classifiers: There are three classes: A, B, C. The discriminant functions are given as solid lines. Regions with possible inconsistent decisions are labeled with question marks

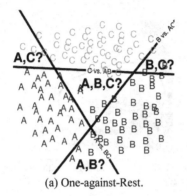

(a) One-against-Rest.

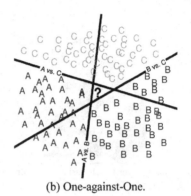

(b) One-against-One.

c against all samples from the remaining classes which are combined to a new class $c^* = \mathbf{K} \setminus c$, for the sake of simplicity the class label of c^* is set to -1. A new data point $\mathbf{v}$ is assigned according to $f(\mathbf{v}) = \arg \max_{c \in \mathbf{K}} f_c(\mathbf{v})$.

One-Against-One Multi-Class Extension

This method builds $k(k-1)/2$ classifiers, each for the pair-wise combination of the classes $c_k, c_l \in \mathbf{K}$, $k \neq l$. The final classification is performed by majority voting – that is, the most frequent predicted class label is returned as prediction of the multi-class model.

Risk of Inconsistent Decisions

The issue of inconsistent decisions of combining binary classifiers to multi-class classifiers is addressed for instance by Tax & Duin (2002). As illustrated in Figure 5, there can be regions of the input space where the decision of the multi-class models might be inconsistent. Those regions are marked with question marks in each figure. For the *one-against-rest method*, there are two possibilities of an inconsistent decision: (1) there are several binary classifiers predicting different class labels for one given data point. Such regions are (A,B ?), (A,C ?), (B,C ?). (2) there are regions, where all classifiers are predicting the "rest" class,

(A,B,C ?). For the *one-against-one method*, there is only one kind of inconsistent decisions possible: several binary classifiers are predicting different class label for one given data point. The problem of several classifiers predicting different class labels can be solved by assigning the class label at random (Hsu & Lin, 2002) or to assign the data point to the class with the largest prior probability (Tax & Duin, 2002). The second kind of inconsistent decisions of the one-against-rest method can be acceptable for some problems, where "no decision" might be better than a "wrong decision". Otherwise, one can use the same strategy as for the other kind of inconsistent decisions.

The Multi-Class Ensemble

There are two different approaches conceivable in order to extend the binary ensemble framework from Section 3.1. The first variant uses multi-class models as submodels. The second variant still uses binary submodels and performs the multi-class classification by the overall ensemble. Note: For safety-related problems it is crucial to take into account that the commonly used strategies of extending binary classifiers to multi-class classifiers, which are illustrated in Figure 5, may lead to regions with inconsistent decisions, cf. Section 4.1.

Hierarchy of Misclassification Costs.

In order to avoid inconsistent and undesired solutions, all extensions of the binary classification ensemble require a hierarchy of misclassification costs, that is, it is assumed that there exists an *ordering* of the class labels, which allows statements like: *"class c_1 samples should never be misclassified, class c_2 samples might be misclassified only as class c_1 samples, class c_3 might be classified as class c_1 or c_2 samples, ..."*

$$penalty(c_1) > penalty(c_2) > penalty(c_3) > ... .$$

Such a hierarchy of misclassification costs leads to a confusion matrix as depicted in Table 1. A new data point **v** is assigned to the class label of all predicted class labels which has the largest misclassification costs. For safety-related problems, such a hierarchy can be assumed because different states of a system might result in different perilous consequences. This issue is closely related to ordinal classification problems. An SVM-based approach for ordinal classification can be found in Cardoso et al. (2005).

Ensemble of Multi-Class Submodels

Combining several multi-class submodels becomes difficult because one can only rely on the prediction of the class c, which has the minimal misclassification cost – all other class label predic-

tions might be false positives, cf. Table 1. Thus, it is necessary to include all samples that are not predicted as class c in the training for the next submodel. Obviously, the problem becomes a binary classification task (separating class c from $\mathbf{K} \backslash c$) and using multi-class submodels becomes obsolete. Instead, we recommend to use the Hierarchical Separate-and-Conquer Ensemble.

Hierarchical Separate-and-Conquer Ensemble

This approach is related to the commonly used one-against-rest approach and is illustrated in Figure 6. It directly follows the hierarchy of the misclassification costs. Instead of building all one-against-rest combinations of models, the class with the minimal misclassification costs is separated from all samples of the other classes with (several) binary submodels. The learning procedure is the same as for the binary classification ensemble, which is described in Section 3.1. If the problem is solved for the class with minimal misclassification costs or further improvements are not possible, all samples of this class are removed from the training data set and the procedure is repeated for the class which has now the least misclassification costs. The learning procedure is repeated until the data set of the next iteration has only a single class label. The resulting binary classifiers are evaluated according to the hierarchy of misclassification costs, that is, in the first step

Table 1. Confusion Matrix for multi-class submodels in a Verifiable Ensemble. The following hierarchy of misclassification costs is assumed: penalty(c_1) > penalty(c_2) > penalty(c_3) > penalty(c_4) > penalty(...)

true class	predicted class				
	c_1	c_2	c_3	c_4	...
c_1	$n_{1,1}$	0	0	0	...
c_2	$n_{2,1}$	$n_{2,2}$	0	0	...
c_3	$n_{3,1}$	$n_{3,2}$	$n_{3,3}$	0	...
c_4	$n_{4,1}$	$n_{4,2}$	$n_{4,3}$	$n_{4,4}$	...
...	...	...	...	...	...

all submodels of the class with minimal misclassification costs are evaluated. If the novel sample cannot be assigned to this class, the procedure is repeated for the next class within the hierarchy of misclassification costs. If no submodel assigns the novel sample to a certain class the sample is assigned to the class with the maximal misclassification costs.

One-Versus-Rest Ensemble

This approach follows the commonly used one-against-rest multi-class classification approach. It is illustrated in Figure 7. For every class $c \in \mathbf{K}$ versus $c^* = \mathbf{K} \backslash c$ a complete binary Verifiable Ensemble $f_c(\mathbf{v})$ is trained, cf. Section 3.1. The class c^* is chosen as the default class c_{pref} in order to avoid the misclassification of any sample belonging to $\mathbf{K} \backslash c$. For the sake of simplicity c^* is encoded as -1. The resulting binary models can be combined by determining the maximum:

$$f^*(\mathbf{v}) = \arg \max_{c \in \mathbf{K}} f_c(\mathbf{v}) . \qquad (4)$$

This is the easiest way of extending the binary ensemble method in order to obtain a multi-class model, but it shows a lack of performance for overlapping data sets: it is possible that certain data points will be assigned to the class c^* by every submodel and that some classes cannot be

Figure 6. Hierarchical Separate-and-Conquer Ensemble trained on the data from Figure 5. The following hierarchy of misclassification costs is assumed: penalty(A) > penalty(B) > penalty(C)

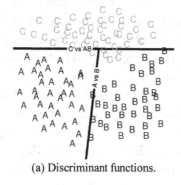

(a) Discriminant functions.

	predicted class		
true class	A	B	C
A	36	0	0
B	1	37	0
C	1	5	41

(b) Confusion matrix.

Figure 7. One-versus-Rest Ensemble trained on the data from Figure 5. Each submodel for class c is trained with the objective to avoid the misclassification of all samples belonging to $c^* = \mathbf{K} \backslash c$. Missed samples are denoted by '?' in the confusion matrix

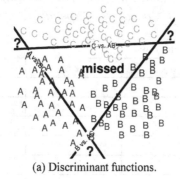

(a) Discriminant functions.

	predicted class			
true class	A	B	C	?
A	22	0	0	14
B	0	30	0	8
C	0	0	40	7

(b) Confusion matrix.

separated from the other classes due to overlapping of the classes in all projections. This approach still yields ambiguous decisions within the input space, as shown in Figure 7. Such ambiguities can be resolved by the hierarchy of misclassification costs.

Related Work

Szepannek & Weihs (2006) propose a pairwise variable subset selection method in order to extend binary classifiers to solve multi-class problems with an one-against-one classifier combination. In contrast to our ensemble methods this approach does not limit the number of dimensions included for learning the submodels – all input dimensions that provide statistically sufficient information are included for learning a single submodel to separate a pair of classes. Our ensemble method may use several submodels with limited dimensionality to solve the same subproblem, while each sub-model remains visually interpretable. Although the pairwise variable subset selection method can give a good insight into the importance of the different dimensions and might achieve a better predictive performance, this approach does not allow the validation of each submodel. Thus, this will not satisfy the requirements of safety-related application problems.

A Medical Diagnosis Example

The NewThyroid data set can be obtained from the UCI Machine Learning Repository (Asuncion & Newman, 2007). This problem concerns a typical medical data screening application. The classification task is to predict whether a patient's thyroid belongs to the class euthyroidism (normal = Class 1), hyperthyroidism (hyper = Class 2) or hypothyroidism (hypo = Class 3). The data set consists of 215 instances and each instance is described by five attributes. The attributes are:

T3-resin: T3-resin uptake test (a percentage). The T3 resin uptake test measures the level of thyroid hormone-binding proteins in the blood.

Thyroxin: Total serum thyroxin (T4) as measured by the isotopic displacement method.

Triiodothyronine: Total serum triiodothyronine (T3) as measured by radioimmuno assay.

Basal TSH: Basal thyroid-stimulating hormone (TSH) as measured by radioimmuno assay.

Diff TSH: Maximal absolute difference of TSH value after injection of 200 micro grams of thyrotropin-releasing hormone as compared to the basal value.

The data set is illustrated in Figure 8. The following hierarchy of misclassification costs is assumed: *penalty*(hypo) > *penalty*(hyper) > *penalty*(normal). That is, Class 3 samples must not be misclassified by any submodel, Class 2 samples might be misclassified as Class 3 samples only, and Class 1 samples might be misclassified as Class 3 or Class 2 samples. The idea behind this hierarchy is to avoid any misclassification of sick patients. Changing the hierarchy of misclassification costs between Class 3 and Class 2 does not influence the results because both classes are well-separated.

Hierarchical Separate-and-Conquer Ensemble

This approach results is three binary classification submodels which are illustrated in Figure 9. Following the given hierarchy of misclassification costs, the learning algorithm tries to separate the samples of Class 1 from all other samples without misclassifying any of the other samples. The first submodel, which is depicted in Figure 9(a), separates most of the Class 1 from the other samples using the input dimensions "Thyroxin" and "Diff TSH". Further Class 1 samples can be captured by the second submodel, which uses the input dimensions "T3-resin" and "Thyroxin" and is shown in Figure 9(b). The remaining Class 1 samples cannot be separated by further two-dimensional submodels. Thus, according to the hierarchy of misclassification costs in the next iteration the Class 2 samples are separated from

Figure 8. Scatter plot matrix of the five-dimensional NewThyroid data set

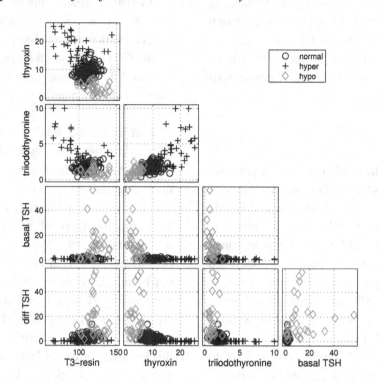

the remaining classes (i.e. the Class 3 samples). The Class 2 samples can be easily discriminated from the Class 3 samples by setting a threshold for the input dimension "Thyroxin" as in the third submodel. As one can see in Table 2, the Hierarchical Separate-and-Conquer Ensemble misclassifies only four instances, which belong all to Class 1. No sick patient is predicted as healthy. The three learned submodels are adequate to the given domain knowledge (a high level of thyroxin indicates hyperthyroidism and elevated TSH levels suggests hypothyroidism) and can be easily evaluated.

One-vs-Rest Ensemble

This classification approach ends up with four submodels. These submodels are shown in Figure 10. The One-versus-Rest Ensemble follows the one-against-rest strategy, that is, submodels are built for each class in order to separate this class from the samples of all other classes – with the important restriction of never misclassifying the samples that belong to the "other" class. The first and the second submodel of this solution are identical to the first and second model of the Hierarchical Separate-and-Conquer Ensemble. The third model

Table 2. Confusion matrix: Hierarchical Separate-and-Conquer Ensemble and the NewThyroid data

true class	predicted class		
	Class 3	Class 2	Class 1
Class 3	30	0	0
Class 2	0	35	0
Class 1	**2**	**2**	146

Figure 9. Two-dimensional submodels: Hierarchical Separate-and-Conquer Ensemble and the NewThyroid data

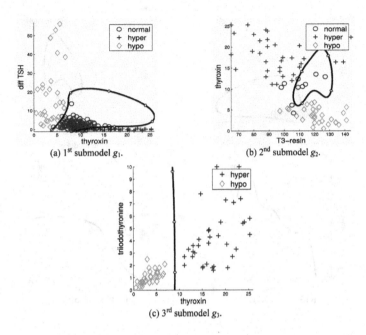

(a) 1st submodel g_1.

(b) 2nd submodel g_2.

(c) 3rd submodel g_3.

of the One-versus-Rest Ensemble separates the Class 2 samples from all other samples and the fourth submodel separates the Class 3 samples from all samples that do not belong to Class 3. As one can see in Table 3, the One-versus-Rest Ensemble misses 10 instances. All other samples are correctly assigned. This property of the One-versus-Rest Ensemble is advantageous especially for medical application problems, where further examinations can be carried out in order to judge the patient's status.

Discussion of the Results

Table 4 summarizes 10-fold-crossvalidation runs that are performed to estimate the error rate of the ensemble methods on previously unseen data. Both ensemble methods are compared with a high-dimensional SVM solution (we used the libSVM implementation of Chang & Lin (2001) with a Gausssian kernel) and a classification tree (treefit in Matlab). Both standard classification models are trained with imbalanced misclassification costs in order reproduce the hierarchy of

Table 3. Confusion matrix: One-versus-Rest Ensemble and the NewThyroid data. The last column shows the samples that are missed by all submodels

true class	predicted class			
	Class 3	**Class 2**	**Class 1**	**?**
Class 3	26	0	0	4
Class 2	0	33	0	2
Class 1	0	0	146	4

Figure 10. Two-dimensional submodels: One-versus-Rest Ensemble and the NewThyroid data

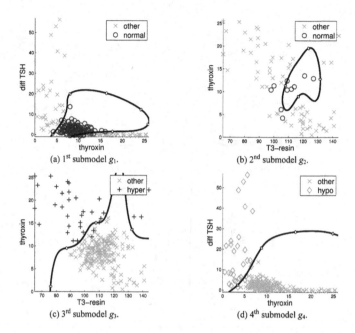

(a) 1st submodel g_1.

(b) 2nd submodel g_2.

(c) 3rd submodel g_3.

(d) 4th submodel g_4.

misclassification costs. The Hierarchical Separate-and-Conquer Ensemble (HSCE) achieves the best predictive performance on the NewThyroid data set. The best critical error rate is achieved by the One-versus-Rest Ensemble (OvRE). The high error rate of the One-versus-Rest Ensemble is due to the fact that missed samples (in average, 4.7% of the data points are missed by the One-versus-Rest Ensemble) are considered as misclassified within the crossvalidation experiments. Nevertheless, for screening medical data the information that an automated classification system cannot assign a sample to a certain class is a benefit as long as the method has a small critical error rate, because in such a situation further examinations can be carried out to ensure the patient's condition. Compared to the five-dimensional support vector machine, the ensemble models are superior with respect to the interpretability of the models, because each two-dimensional model can be visualized and, hence, easily interpreted. The model complexity of the treefit model with six decision nodes is comparable to the ensemble models. The disadvantage of the treefit model is that the decision nodes depend on their antecessors – while each submodel of the ensemble models can be interpreted independently.

DATA PREPROCESSING

The quality of the input dimensions is essential for the effective application of our ensemble modeling framework (cf. Section 3 and Section 4) to a given classification problem. In the following we will address two problems that can arise while applying the classification ensembles: (1) due to a large overlap of the classes within all low-dimensional subspaces the submodels might not be capable to find a good separation of the different classes and (2) the classification problem might not be solved with the restriction to two- or three-dimensional submodels because the underlying function requires a higher dimensionality. The first problem can be tackled by a preceding data filtering. Two examples of such filtering methods are given in Section 5.1. The second problem can be solved by a stacking-like approach (Wolpert, 1992; Gama

Table 4. NewThyroid data set: 10-fold crossvalidation evaluation. #M denotes the number of submodels or decision nodes within the decision tree and #D denotes the dimensionality of each model or decision node, respectively. The Error column denotes the overall classification error (including the missed samples of the One-versus-Rest Ensemble). The Critical Error column denotes the rate of samples that violate the hierarchy of misclassification costs

Method	#M	#D	Error		Critical Error
			mean (std)		mean (std)
HSCE	3	2	4.19% (5.03)	1.10% (2.86)	
OvRE	4	2	6.38% (5.63)		0.90% (2.41)
libSVM	1	5	4.62% (4.56)	1.90% (3.71)	
treefit	6	1	4.29% (4.36)		1.29% (2.12)

Further experiments showing similar results can be found in Nusser et al. (2008b).

& Brazdil, 2000), which is discussed in Section 5.2: additional input dimensions are generated by a MLP-architecture. These additional input dimensions can be interpreted as preceding soft classifiers.

Data Filtering

Insular regions as depicted in Figure 11(a) might be counterintuitive according to domain knowledge. Therefore, it becomes necessary to provide methods in order to avoid such undesired results during the model building process. Such unintended results can be avoided by removing conflicting data points from the data set. In the following we will show two heuristics, namely: (1) the convex hull filtering and (2) the upper envelope filtering. The basic idea behind both approaches is to remove data points which may conflict with monotony requirements in the resulting classification models. Furthermore, removing conflicting data points leads to a runtime reduction of the submodel learning process.

Convex Hull Filtering

This approach determines the convex hull of the samples of the default class c_{pref}. All samples which do not belong to the default class and which are within the convex hull are removed from training data set. The classifier is then trained on the reduced data set.

The advantages of this method are that the axes orientation does not influence the result of the algorithm and this approach can be extended to an arbitrary dimensionality. As one can see in Figure 11(c), the convex hull of the set of data points belonging to Class 1 includes regions of Class 2 which are separable from Class 1. Thus, a more sensitive filtering method is needed.

Upper Envelope Filtering

In this approach, the upper envelope of all default class samples is determined and all samples which do not belong to the default class and which are below the upper envelope are removed from training data set. Then, the classifier is then trained on the reduced data set.

For this approach the axes orientation influences the filter result. But this can be compensated by filtering both variants of a feature combination and presenting them both to the function that determines the best submodel. This variant of filtering is much more sensitive than the convex hull filter, see Figure 11(d), but this method works only on two-dimensional data where one dimension has a (local) monotony constraint.

Figure 11. Convex hull filtering and upper envelope filtering. The are two classes: Class 1 samples are depicted as circles and Class 2 samples are shown as crosses. The filter is applied for Class 1. The decision border of the resulting filter functions are plotted as dashed line

(a) Unintended insular region of a submodel.

(b) Submodel after applying the upper envelope filter.

(c) Convex hull filter.

(d) Upper envelope filter.

Feature Construction

As demonstrated in Section 3.2 and Section 4.3, the Verifiable Ensemble and its multi-class extensions show a good performance on real-world applications, but there are classification problems that cannot be solved with the restriction to two-dimensional submodels. To overcome this limitation, a feature construction method based on a multi-layer perceptron (MLP) architecture has been developed by Nusser et al. (2008a) that generates low-dimensional linear combinations of the original input dimensions. The additionally generated input dimensions can be interpreted as preceding soft classifiers – a similar approach is proposed by Liu & Setiono (1998), where the hidden units of a fully connected MLP architecture were used to build multivariate decision trees.

The original input dimensions $V^n = X_1 \times X_2 \times \ldots \times X_n$ are used in the input layer and the target variable Y is used in the output layer of the MLP. The hidden layer of this network consists of $n(n-1)/2$ nodes $hidden_{(i,j)}$, where $i,j \in \{1,\ldots,n\}$ and $i < j$.

Each hidden node is only connected to two of the original input dimensions. The connections from the hidden to the output layer are set to 1 and are fixed during the network training procedure. This MLP architecture is depicted in Figure 12.

Due to the chosen network design, the MLP is forced in the hidden layer to find local classifiers on the given input dimension. These classifiers are simple linear models where each uses only two input dimensions. The resulting weights of the hidden neurons are used to build additional input dimensions. An additional input dimension is generated by: $X_{(i,j)}^{new} = \tanh(X_i \cdot w_{(i,j)}^{hidden} + X_j \cdot w_{(j,i)}^{hidden} + b_{(i,j)}^{hidden})$, where X_i, X_j are the original input dimensions, $w_{(i,j)}^{hidden}$ is the connecting weight of the input dimension X_i to the hidden neuron $hidden_{(i,j)}$, and $b_{(i,j)}^{hidden}$ is the bias of the hidden neuron $hidden_{(i,j)}$. The additional input dimension $X_{(i,j)}^{new}$ can be seen as a preceding soft classifier. Finally, the additional input dimensions are appended to the original data set.

Using all $n(n-1)/2$ additional input dimensions drastically increases the effort to determine the best

Figure 12. Example of an MLP for feature construction used on a four-dimensional input space

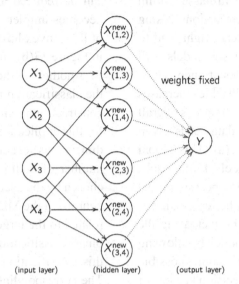

projections of the data set. Thus, it is necessary to reduce the number of additional input dimensions by adding only the "best" hidden neurons as additional input dimensions to the original data set. For instance, such selection can be performed by choosing the hidden neurons which are most correlated with the target variable.

The advantage of the MLP-based feature construction method is that the restricted dimensionality of the linear combinations facilitates the understanding of the additionally generated dimensions. In contrast to the original stacking method (Wolpert, 1992), the additionally generated input dimensions (meta-attributes) are only determined as linear combinations of the original input dimensions. It is not allowed to use the output of a meta-attribute to build an additional meta-attribute. We do not allow a higher complexity of the additionally generated dimensions because an increasing complexity prevents the acceptance of the solution by the domain experts in the field of safety-related problems.

A Naval Risk Detection Example

This data set serves as an example of the advantages to use data filtering or feature construction methods, to facilitate the low-dimensional submodels to solve a classification problem. The Sonar data set consists of 208 instances. Each instance is described by 60 attributes. The task is to discriminate between sonar signals bounced off a metal cylinder, that is possibly a mine, (Class 1) and those bounced off a roughly cylindrical rock (Class 0). This data set can be obtained from UCI Machine Learning Repository (Asuncion & Newman, 2007). The submodels are trained as support vector machines with a Gaussian kernel. The default class is set to Class 1, $c_{pref} = 1$, that is, a metal cylinder must not be classified as a rock by any model. In order to reduce the risk of misclassifying any novel Class 1 sample, the misclassification costs for Class 1 are 20 times higher than for Class 0.

This problem cannot be sufficiently solved by a binary classification ensemble with respect to the restriction to two-dimensional projections, since there is a large overlap of both classes within all possible two-dimensional projections. Using more sensitive model parameters might lead to a better performance, but the submodels will capture only one or two samples at once. Thus, numerous submodels will be built which increases the risk of overfitting. The global model's overall performance on the complete data set is given as confusion matrix in Table 5(a). This global model consists of three submodels. Further submodels cannot be determined. The best submodel is depicted in Figure 13(a). A better predictive performance can be achieved by increasing the number of dimensions per submodel: by allowing three-dimensional projections it becomes possible to solve this problem, but the decision borders of the submodels will become more complex.

Another possibility to tackle this problem is to apply one of the data filtering methods which are discussed in Section 5.1. By applying such a data filtering method, for instance the convex hull filtering, the submodels must only handle those data points that actually can be separated within the low-dimensional subspaces. Thus, the disadvantageous effect of the conflicting data points

can be reduced and the classification problem becomes simpler. The outcome of the application of the convex hull filtering method is illustrated in Figure 13(b) and Table 5(b).

Another method that can be used to solve the classification problem is to apply the feature construction method of Section 5.2. Hereby and for this application example, 20 additional input dimensions are added to the original data set. The number of additional input dimensions can be chosen by the user. In this example, those hidden neurons of the MLP are chosen that are most correlated to the target variable. This facilitates the binary classification ensemble to completely solve this classification problem with 18 submodels. The corresponding confusion matrix is given in Table 5(c). If one regards the first three submodels, which capture 61 of 97 Class 0 samples, one achieves already a higher predictive accuracy compared to the binary classification ensemble without additional input dimensions and without a preceding data filtering. The best submodel of the Verifiable Ensemble with additional input dimensions is depicted in Figure 13(c). This submodel uses one original input dimension and one

Table 5. Confusion matrices of the 60-dimensional Sonar data set

(a) Verifiable Ensemble trained without additional features and without filtering.		
	predicted class	
true class	Class 1	Class 0
Class 1	111	0
Class 0	63	34
(b) Verifiable Ensemble trained with preceding convex hull data filtering.		
	predicted class	
true class	Class 1	Class 0
Class 1	111	0
Class 0	5	92
(c) Verifiable Ensemble trained with additional features.		
	predicted class	
true class	Class 1	Class 0
Class 1	111	0
Class 0	0	97

Figure 13. Verifiable Ensemble and the Sonar data set: Class 1 samples are marked with circles and Class 0 samples are marked with crosses. The decision boundaries are drawn as solid lines

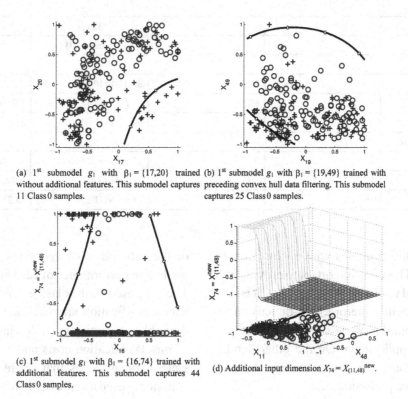

(a) 1st submodel g_1 with $\beta_1 = \{17,20\}$ trained without additional features. This submodel captures 11 Class 0 samples.

(b) 1st submodel g_1 with $\beta_1 = \{19,49\}$ trained with preceding convex hull data filtering. This submodel captures 25 Class 0 samples.

(c) 1st submodel g_1 with $\beta_1 = \{16,74\}$ trained with additional features. This submodel captures 44 Class 0 samples.

(d) Additional input dimension $X_{74} = X_{(11,48)}^{new}$.

additionally generated feature. By applying the feature construction method, which is described in Section 5.2, the following additional input dimension $X_{74} = X_{(11,48)}^{new}$ has been generated:

$$X_{74} = \tanh(X_{11} \cdot w_{(11,48)}^{hidden} + X_{48} \cdot w_{(48,11)}^{hidden} + b_{(11,48)}^{hidden}),$$

where $w_{(11,48)}^{hidden} = -36.829$, $w_{(48,11)}^{hidden} = -9.004$ and $b_{(11,48)}^{hidden} = -28.936$. This additional feature can be seen as preceding linear soft classifier that facilitates the (two-dimensional) submodels of the binary classification ensemble to solve the classification problem, while the model keeps interpretable. In Figure 13(d) the surface plot of the additional input dimension X_{74} and the resulting partitioning of the input space is depicted.

Table 6 illustrates the gain of predictive performance by applying our feature construction method. We compare the original Sonar data set with the Sonar (MLP) data set where 20 additionally generated input dimensions are appended to the original input dimensions. Therefore, it becomes possible to reduce the predictive error of the Verifiable Ensemble model by approx. 50% by using additionally generated input dimensions as preceding soft classifiers.

CONCLUSION

In order to successfully apply machine learning methods in the field of safety-related problems it is essential to satisfy the domain experts' demands for proving that the learned solution solves the

Table 6. Sonar data set: classification accuracy estimated by 10-fold cross-validation with 10 random set initializations

Method	#M	#D	Error	Critical Error
			mean (std)	mean (std)
Sonar data set				
Ensemble	6	2	36.35% (10.61)	*1.20% (2.57)*
libSVM	1	60	*11.10% (7.64)*	3.75% (4.46)
treefit	17	1	34.20% (11.09)	11.60% (7.78)
Sonar (MLP) data set				
Ensemble	16	2	17.05% (8.82)	4.80% (4.82)
libSVM	1	80	*14.90% (8.41)*	*4.70% (5.26)*
treefit	15	1	36.65% (11.35)	11.25% (6.83)

right problem and complies with all functional specifications. Thus, it is important to provide an interpretable and verifiable solution. Since it is infeasible to sufficiently interpret high-dimensional models, such complex models are not applied to safety-related applications. On the other hand, simple models that are easier to interpret show a lack of predictive performance.

The classification framework proposed in this chapter provides a good trade-off between the interpretability of the learned submodels and a high predictive accuracy. Our ensemble framework greatly facilitates the use of machine learning methods in the field of safety-related applications. It requires that the given input dimensions allow an (at least partial) separation of the classes within the low-dimensional subspaces. The learned submodels can be visually interpreted and evaluated by the domain experts in order to ensure a correct extrapolation and interpolation behavior. This is particularly facilitated by the fact that the submodels are trained on the original input dimensions, allowing the experts to directly evaluate the trained models within their known input domain. The correctness of the learned overall solution can be guaranteed although the submodels are trained on small subspaces of the input space and the training data might be sparse in the high-dimensional space. The ensemble of the submodels compensates for the limited predictive performance of each single submodel. The proposed multi-class extensions of the binary classification approach maintain the same desirable properties by following the hierarchy of misclassification costs and by avoiding possible inconsistencies that might be induced by commonly used multi-class extensions. The One-versus-Rest Ensemble is appropriate for problems where unassigned samples are acceptable but a very low false-negative rate is required – the Hierarchical Separate-and-Conquer Ensemble also achieves a low false-negative rate and can capture more samples by its sequential covering algorithm. Furthermore, we have shown that the proposed data filtering and feature construction methods can be utilized to overcome the limitations of the low-dimensional submodels for application problems that require a higher dimensionality.

The proposed classification approach is applicable to a wide range of classification problems in the field of safety-related applications - ranging from decision support systems (e.g. screening of medical data) over plant monitoring and diagnosis systems (e.g. fault prevention) to control tasks with very high safety-requirements (e.g. control of airbag systems in automotive safety electronics).

REFERENCES

Andrews, R., Diederich, J., & Tickle, A. B. (1995). Survey and critique of techniques for extracting rules from trained artificial neural networks. *Knowledge-Based Systems*, *8*(6), 373–389. doi:10.1016/0950-7051(96)81920-4

Asuncion, A., & Newman, D. J. (2007). *UCI Machine Learning Repository*. Available at http://www.ics.uci.edu/~mlearn/MLRepository.html

Bowen, J. P., & Hinchey, M. G. (1999). High-Integrity System Specification and Design. Secaucus, NJ: Springer-Verlag New York, Inc.

Boz, O. (2002). Extracting decision trees from trained neural networks. In *Proceedings of the 8th ACM SIGKDD international conference on Knowledge discovery and data mining* (pp. 456–461). Edmonton, Alberta, Canada.

Breiman, L., Friedman, J. H., Olshen, R. A., & Stone, C. J. (1984). Classification and Regression Trees. Boca Raton, FL: CRC Press.

Cardoso, J. S., da Costa, J. F. P., & Cardoso, M. J. (2005). Modelling ordinal relations with SVMs: An application to objective aesthetic evaluation of breast cancer conservative treatment. *Neural Networks*, *18*(5-6), 808–817. doi:10.1016/j.neunet.2005.06.023

Chang, C.-C., & Lin, C.-J. (2001). *LIBSVM: A library for support vector machines*. Software available at http://www.csie.ntu.edu.tw/~cjlin/libsvm

Chen, Y., & Wang, J. Z. (2003). Support vector learning for fuzzy rule-based classification systems. *IEEE Transactions on Neural Networks*, *11*(6), 716–728.

Cohen, W. W. (1995). Fast effective rule induction. In A. Prieditis & S. J. Russell (Eds.), *Proceedings of 12th International Conference on Machine Learning* (pp. 115–123), Tahoe City, CA.

Cohn, D., Atlas, L., & Ladner, R. (1994). Improving generalization with active learning. *Machine Learning*, *15*(2), 201–221.

Friedman, J. H., & Tukey, J. W. (1974). A projection pursuit algorithm for exploratory data analysis. *IEEE Transactions on Computers*, *23*(9), 881–890. doi:10.1109/T-C.1974.224051

Fürnkranz, J. (1999). Separate-and-conquer rule learning. *Artificial Intelligence Review*, *13*(1), 3–54. doi:10.1023/A:1006524209794

Gama, J., & Brazdil, P. (2000). Cascade generalization. *Machine Learning*, *41*(3), 315–343. doi:10.1023/A:1007652114878

Guyon, I., & Elisseeff, A. (2006). An introduction to feature extraction. In I. Guyon, S. Gunn, M. Nikravesh, & L. Zadeh (Eds.), Feature Extraction: Foundations and Applications (pp. 1–25). Berlin: Springer.

Hastie, T., & Stuetzle, W. (1989). Principal curves. *Journal of the American Statistical Association*, *84*(406), 502–516. doi:10.2307/2289936

Hastie, T., & Tibshirani, R. (1990). Generalized Additive Models. Boca Raton, FL: Chapman & Hall.

Hastie, T., Tibshirani, R., & Friedman, J. (2001). The Elements of Statistical Learning. Berlin: Springer.

Hsu, C.-W., & Lin, C.-J. (2002). A comparison of methods for multiclass support vector machines. *IEEE Transactions on Neural Networks*, *13*(2), 415–425. doi:10.1109/72.991427

Huber, P. J. (1985). Projection pursuit. *Annals of Statistics*, *13*(2), 435–475. doi:10.1214/aos/1176349519

Kohavi, R. (1995). A study of cross-validation and bootstrap for accuracy estimation and model selection. In *Proceedings of 14th International Joint Conference on Artificial Intelligence*, (Vol. 2, pp. 1137–1143). Montreal, Canada: Morgan Kaufmann.

Kohavi, R., & John, G. H. (1997). Wrappers for feature subset selection. *Artificial Intelligence, 97*(1-2), 273–324. doi:10.1016/S0004-3702(97)00043-X

Kohonen, T. (1990). The self-organizing map. *Proceedings of the IEEE, 78*(9), 1464–1480. doi:10.1109/5.58325

Kurd, Z., & Kelly, T. (2007). Using fuzzy self-organising maps for safety critical systems. *Reliability Engineering & System Safety, 92*(11), 1563–1583. doi:10.1016/j.ress.2006.10.005

Kurd, Z., Kelly, T., & Austin, J. (2006). Developing artificial neural networks for safety critical systems. *Neural Computing & Applications, 16*(1), 11–19. doi:10.1007/s00521-006-0039-9

Leveson, N. G., & Turner, C. S. (1993). An investigation of the Therac-25 accidents. *Computer, 26*(7), 18–41. doi:10.1109/MC.1993.274940

Lisboa, P. J. G. (2001). Industrial use of safety-related artificial neural networks. Contract research report 327/2001, Liverpool John Moores University.

Liu, H., & Setiono, R. (1998). Feature transformation and multivariate decision tree induction. In *Proceedings of the 1st International Conference on Discovery Science* (pp. 279 – 290), Fukuoka, Japan.

MacKay, D. J. C. (1992). *Bayesian methods for adaptive models*. PhD thesis, California Institute of Technology, Pasadena, CA.

MacKay, D. J. C. (1998). Introduction to Gaussian processes. In C. M. Bishop (Ed.), Neural Networks and Machine Learning (pp. 133–166). Amsterdam: Kluwer Academic Press.

Nauck, D. (2003). Fuzzy data analysis with NEFCLASS. *International Journal of Approximate Reasoning, 32*(2-3), 103–130. doi:10.1016/S0888-613X(02)00079-8

Nauck, D., Klawonn, F., & Kruse, R. (1997). Foundations of Neuro-Fuzzy Systems. Chichester, UK: Wiley.

Nusser, S., Otte, C., & Hauptmann, W. (2007). Learning binary classifiers for applications in safety-related domains. In R. Mikut & M. Reischl (Eds.), *Proceedings of 17th Workshop Computational Intelligence* (pp. 139–151). Dortmund, Germany: Universitätsverlag Karlsruhe.

Nusser, S., Otte, C., & Hauptmann, W. (2008a). Interpretable ensembles of local models for safety-related applications. In M. Verleysen (Ed.), *Proceedings of 16th European Symposium on Artificial Neural Networks* (pp. 301–306). Brugge, Belgium: D-facto publications.

Nusser, S., Otte, C., & Hauptmann, W. (2008b). Multi-class modeling with ensembles of local models for imbalanced misclassification costs. In O. Okun & G. Valentini (Eds.), *Proceedings of 2nd Workshop on Supervised and Unsupervised Ensemble Methods and Their Applications (at ECAI 2008)* (pp. 36–40). Patras, Greece.

Pullum, L. L., Taylor, B. J., & Darrah, M. A. (2007). Guidance for the Verification and Validation of Neural Networks. New York: Wiley.

Rasmussen, C. E., & Williams, C. K. I. (2006). Gaussian Processes for Machine Learning. Cambridge, MA: MIT Press.

Rehm, F., Klawonn, F., & Kruse, R. (2006). PO-LARMAP - a new approach to visualisation of high dimensional data. In *Proceedings of the 10th International Conference on Information Visualisation (IV'06)* (pp. 731–740), London, UK.

Schlang, M., Feldkeller, B., Lang, B., Poppe, T., & Runkler, T. (1999). Neural computation in steel industry. In Proceedings European Control Conf. ECC 99. Berlin: VDI-Verlag.

Szepannek, G., & Weihs, C. (2006). Local modelling in classification on different feature subspaces. In *Industrial Conference on Data Mining* (pp. 226–238), Leipzig, Germany.

Tax, D. M. J., & Duin, R. P. W. (2002). Using two-class classifiers for multiclass classification. In *Proceedings of the 16th International Conference on Pattern Recognition*, (Vol. 2, pp. 124–127), Quebec, Canada.

Taylor, B. J. (Ed.). (2005). Methods and Procedures for the Verification and Validation of Artificial Neural Networks. Berlin: Springer.

Tzeng, F.-Y., & Ma, K.-L. (2005). Opening the black box - data driven visualization of neural networks. In *Proceedings of IEEE Visualization '05 Conf.* (pp. 383–390). Washington, DC: IEEE.

Wolpert, D. H. (1992). Stacked generalization. *Neural Networks*, 5(2), 241–259. doi:10.1016/S0893-6080(05)80023-1

Zakrzewski, R. R. (2001). Verification of a trained neural network accuracy. In *Proceedings of International Joint Conference on Neural Networks (IJCNN'01)*, (Vol. 3, pp. 1657–1662). Washington, DC: IEEE Press.

Compilation of References

Abdel-Magid, Y. L., & Dawoud, M. M. (1997). Optimal AGC tuning with genetic algorithms. *Electric Power Systems Research*, *38*, 231–238. doi:10.1016/S0378-7796(96)01091-7

Abe, H., & Yamaguchi, T. (2005). Implementing an integrated time-series data mining environment – a case study of medical KDD on chronic hepatitis. In *Proceedings of the 1st International Conference on Complex Medical Engineering (CME2005)*.

Abido, M. A. (2002). Optimal design of power-system stabilizers using particle swarm optimization. *IEEE Transactions on Energy Conversion*, *17*(3), 406–413. doi:10.1109/TEC.2002.801992

Abramson, D., & Abela, J. (1991). *A parallel genetic algorithm for solving the school timetabling problem*. Technical Report, Division of Information Technology, CSIRO.

Abusina, Z. U. M., Zabir, S. M. S., Asir, A., Chakraborty, D., Suganuma, T., & Shiratori, N. (2005). An engineering approach to dynamic prediction of network performance from application logs. *Int. Network Mgmt*, *15*(3), 151–162. doi:10.1002/nem.554

Aditya, S. K., & Das, D. (2003). Design of load frequency controllers using genetic algorithms for two area interconnected hydro power system. *Electric Power Components and Systems*, *31*(1), 81–94. doi:10.1080/15325000390112071

Agrawal, R., Mannila, H., Srikant, R., Toivonen, H., & Verkamo, A. (1996). Fast discovery of association rules. In U.M. Fayyad, G. Piatetsky-Shapiro, P. Smyth, & R. Uthurusamy, (Eds.), *Advances in Knowledge Discovery and Data Mining* (pp. 307–328). Cambridge, MA: AAAI/MIT Press.

Aguilar-Ruiz, J., Giraldez, R., & Riquelme, J. (2007). Natural encoding for evolutionary supervised learning. *IEEE Transactions on Evolutionary Computation*, *11*(4), 466–479. doi:10.1109/TEVC.2006.883466

Aguilar-Ruiz, J., Riquelme, J., & Toro, M. (2003). Evolutionary learning of hierarchical decision rules. *IEEE Transactions on Systems, Man, and Cybernetics . Part B*, *33*(2), 324–331.

Aickelin, U., Bentley, P., Cayzer, S., Kim, J., & Mcleod, J. (2003) Danger theory: The link between AIS and IDS. In *Proceedings ICARIS-2003, 2nd International Conference on Artificial Immune Systems*, (pp.147-155).

Akkiraju, R., et al. (2005). *Web Service Semantics: WSDL-S*. W3C member submission. Retrieved from www.w3.org/SubmissionWSDL-S/

Alcalá, R., Alcalá-Fdez, J., Casillas, J., Cordón, O., & Herrera, F. (2006). Hybrid learning models to get the interpretability-accuracy trade-off in fuzzy modeling. *Soft Computing*, *10*(9), 717–734. doi:10.1007/s00500-005-0002-1

Alcalá, R., Alcalá-Fdez, J., Casillas, J., Cordón, O., & Herrera, F. (2007). Local identification of prototypes for genetic learning of accurate tsk fuzzy rule-based systems. *International Journal of Intelligent Systems*, *22*(9), 909–941. doi:10.1002/int.20232

Alcalá, R., Cordón, O., & Herrera, F. (2003). Combining rule weight learning and rule selection to obtain simpler and more accurate linguistic fuzzy models. In J. Lawry, J. Shanahan, & A. Ralescu (Eds.), Modelling with words (Vol. 2873, pp. 44–63). Berlin: Springer.

Al-Hamouz, Z. M., & Abdel-Magid, Y. L. (1993). Variable Structure Load Frequency Controllers for Multiarea Power Systems. *Electrical Power & Energy Systems*, *15*(5), 293–300. doi:10.1016/0142-0615(93)90050-W

Aliev, R. A., Fazlollahi, B., & Vahidov, R. M. (2001). Genetic algorithm- based learning of fuzzy neural networks. Part 1: Feed-forward fFuzzy neural networks. *Fuzzy Sets and Systems*, *118*, 351–358. doi:10.1016/S0165-0114(98)00461-8

Allman, M., & Paxson, V. (2008). A Reactive Measurement Framework, In *Proceedings 9th International Conference, PAM 2008, Passive and Active Measurement Conference,* (LNCS vol. 4979, pp. 92-101). Berlin: Springer.

Allman, M., Martin, L., Rabinovich, M., & Atchinson, K. (2008). On community-oriented Internet measurement. In *Proceedings 9th International Conference, PAM 2008, Passive and Active Measurement Conference,* (LNCS vol. 4979, pp. 112-121). Berlin: Springer.

Alpaydin, G., Dundar, G., & Balkir, S. (2002). Evolution-based design of fuzzy networks using self-adapting genetic parameters. *IEEE transactions on Fuzzy Systems*, *10*(2), 211–221. doi:10.1109/91.995122

Ananiadou, S., Kell, D. B., & Tsujii, J. (2006). Text mining and its potential applications in systems biology. *Trends in Biotechnology*, *24*(12), 571–579. doi:10.1016/j.tibtech.2006.10.002

Andrews, R., Diederich, J., & Tickle, A. B. (1995). Survey and critique of techniques for extracting rules from trained artificial neural networks. *Knowledge-Based Systems*, *8*(6), 373–389. doi:10.1016/0950-7051(96)81920-4

Angelov, P. P., & Filev, D. P. (2004). An approach to online identification of Takagi-Sugeno fuzzy models. *IEEE Transactions on Systems, Man, and Cybernetics*, *34*(1), 484–498. doi:10.1109/TSMCB.2003.817053

Ankolekar, A., Burstein, M., Hobbs, J., Lassila, O., Martin, D., McIlraith, S., et al. (2001). DAML-S: Semantic Markup for Web Services. In *Proceedings of the International Semantic Web Working Symposium* (SWWS) (pp. 39–54). Stanford University, California.

Arlit, M., & Jin, T. (2000). A Workload Characterization Study of the 1998 Word Cup Web Site. *IEEE Network*, (May/June): 30–373. doi:10.1109/65.844498

Arlit, M., Krishnamurthy, B., & Mogul, J. C. (2005). Predicting short-transfer latency from TCP arcane: A trace-based validation. In *Proceedings of International Measurement Conference* (pp. 119-124). USENIX Association.

Arnaud, Y., Desbios, M., & Maizi, J. (1992). Automatic tracking and characterization of African convective systems on meteosat pictures. *Journal of Applied Meteorology*, *31*(5), 443–453. doi:10.1175/1520-0450(1992)031<0443:ATACOA>2.0.CO;2

Arthur, D., & Vassilvi, S. (2006). How Slow is the K-means Method? In *Proceedings of the 22th Annual Symposium on Computational Geometry* (pp. 144-153).

Asuncion, A., & Newman, D. J. (2007). *UCI Machine Learning Repository.* Available at http://www.ics.uci.edu/~mlearn/MLRepository.html

Atkinson-Abutridy, J., Mellish, C., & Aitken, S. (2004). Combining information extraction with genetic algorithms for text mining. *IEEE Intelligent Systems*, 22–30. doi:10.1109/MIS.2004.4

Azeem, M. F., Hanmandlu, M., & Ahmad, N. (2003). Structure identification of generalized adaptive neuro-fuzzy inference systems. *IEEE transactions on Fuzzy Systems*, *11*(15), 666–681. doi:10.1109/TFUZZ.2003.817857

Bacardit, J., & Garrell, J. (2003). Evolving multiple discretizations with adaptive intervals for a pittsburgh rule-based learning classifier system. In Genetic and evolutionary computation conference (gecco'03) (p. 1818-1831). Berlin: Springer-Verlag.

Bacardit, J., & Garrell, J. (2004). Analysis and improvements of the adaptive discretization intervals knowledge representation. In Genetic and evolutionary computation conference (gecco'04) (p. 726-738). Berlin: Springer-Verlag.

Bacardit, J., & Garrell, J. (2007). Bloat control and generalization pressure using the minimum description length principle for a pittsburgh approach learning classifier system. In Learning classifier systems (Vol. 4399, pp. 59–79). London: Springer Berlin-Heidelberg.

Baek, J., & Yeom, H. (2003). d-Agent: an approach to mobile agent planning for distributed information retrieval. *IEEE Transactions on Consumer Electronics, 49*(1), 115–122. doi:10.1109/TCE.2003.1205463

Baek, J., Kim, G., & Yeom, H. (2002). Cost effective planning of timed mobile agent. In *Proceedings of the international conference on information technology: Coding and computing* (pp. 536–541).

Baek, J., Yeo, J., & Yeom, H. (2002). Agent chaining: An approach to dynamic mobile agent planning. In *Proceedings of the 22nd international conference on distributed computing systems* (pp. 579–586).

Baek, J., Yeo, J., Kim, G., & Yeom, H. (2001). Cost effective mobile agent planning for distributed information retrieval. In *Proceedings of the 21st international conference on distributed computing systems* (pp. 65–72).

Baker, J. E. (1985). Adaptive selection methods for genetic algorithms. In *Proceedings of an International Conference on Genetic Algorithms and their Application (pp.* 101–111). Hillsdale, NJ: Lawrence Erlbaum Associates.

Baker, M., Buyya, R., & Laforenza, D. (2002). Grids and grid technologies for wide-area distributed computing. *Software, Practice & Experience, 32*(15), 1437–146. doi:10.1002/spe.488

Banerjee, S., & Pedersen, T. (2002). An Adapted Lesk Algorithm for Word Sense Disambiguation Using WordNet. In *Proceedings of the Third International Conference on Computational Linguistics and Intelligent Text Processing* (LNCS Vol. 2276, pp. 136–145). Retrieved from http://www.d.umn.edu/~tpederse/Pubs/cicling2002-b.ps

Banerjee, S., & Pedersen, T. (2003). Extended gloss overlap as a measure of semantic relatedness. In *Proceedings of the 18th International Joint Conference on Artificial Intelligence,* (pp. 805–810), Acapulco, Mexico, 9–15 August, 2003. Retrieved from http://www.d.umn.edu/~tpederse/Pubs/ijcai03.pdf

Barford, P., Mirza, M., & Zhu, X. (2007). A machine learning approach to TCP throughput prediction . *ACM SIGMETRICS Performance Evaluation Review, 35*(1), 97–108. doi:10.1145/1269899.1254894

Barry, D. K. (2003). *Web Services and Service-Oriented Architectures: The Savvy Manager's Guide.* San Francisco, CA: Morgan Kaufmann Publishers.

Basak, J., Sudarshan, A., Trivedi, D., & Santhanam, M. S. (2004). Weather Data Mining Using Independent Component Analysis. *Journal of Machine Learning Research, 5*(3), 239–253.

Batista, G. E., & Monard, M. C. (2003). An analysis of four missing data treatment methods for supervised learning. *Applied Artificial Intelligence, 17*(5-6), 519–533. doi:10.1080/713827181

Battiti, R. (1992). First- and Second-order methods for learning: between steepest descent and Newton's method. *Neural Computation, 4,* 141–166. doi:10.1162/neco.1992.4.2.141

Bawa, V. S., & Lindenberg, E. B. (1977). Capital market equilibrium in a mean-lower partial moment framework. *Journal of Financial Economics, 5,* 189–200. doi:10.1016/0304-405X(77)90017-4

Beaufays, F., Abdel-Magid, Y., & Widrow, B. (1999). Application of neural network to load frequency control in power systems. *Neural Networks, 7*(1), 183–194. doi:10.1016/0893-6080(94)90067-1

Bell, S., & Brockhausen, P. (1995). *Discovery of data dependencies in relational databases.* Tech. Rep. LS-8. No. 14. Dortmund, Germany: University of Dortmund.

Belohlavek, R., & V. (2006). Relational Model of Data over Domains with Similarities: An Extension for Similarity Queries and Knowledge Extraction. In *Proceedings of IEEE IRI* (pp. 207-213).

Bernadó-Mansilla, E., & Garrell, J. (2003). Accuracy-based learning classifier systems: models, analysis and applications to classification tasks. *Evolutionary Computation, 1*(3), 209–238. doi:10.1162/106365603322365289

Bernadó-Mansilla, E., & Ho, T. K. (2005). Domain of competence of xcs classifier system in complexity measurement space. *IEEE Transactions on Evolutionary Computation, 9*(1), 82–104. doi:10.1109/TEVC.2004.840153

Bernasconi, J. (1990). Learning in neural networks. In R. Lima, R. Streit & R. Vilela Mendes (Eds.), *Dynamics and Stochastic Processes: Theory and Applications*, (LNCS Vol. 355, pp. 42-54). Berlin: Springer.

Berry, M. W. (1990). *Multiprocessor Sparse SVD Algorithms and Applications*. Doctoral dissertation, The University of Illinois at Urbana-Champaign, Urbana, IL.

Berry, M., & Sameh, A. (1989). An overview of parallel algorithms for the singular value and dense symmetric eigenvalue problems. *Journal of Computational and Applied Mathematics, 1*(27), 191–213. doi:10.1016/0377-0427(89)90366-X

Berthold, M. R., Cebron, N., Dill, F., Fatta, G. D., Gabriel, T. R., Georg, F., et al. (2006). Knime: the konstanz information miner. In Proceedings international workshop on multi-agent systems and simulation (mas & s), 4th annual industrial simulation conference (isc 2006) (p. 58-61), Palermo, Italy.

Bevrani, H., Mitani, Y., & Tsuji, K. (2004). Robust decentralized AGC in a restructured power system. *Energy Conversion and Management, 45*, 2297–2312. doi:10.1016/j.enconman.2003.11.018

Bezdek, J. C. (1973). *Fuzzy mathematics in pattern classification*. Master's thesis, Cornell University, Ithaca, NY.

Bezdek, J. C. (1981). *Pattern Recognition with Fuzzy Objective Function Algorithms*. New York: Plenum Press.

Bezdek, J. C. (1992). On the Relationship between Neural Networks, Pattern Recognition and Intelligence. *International Journal of Approximate Reasoning, 6*, 85–107. doi:10.1016/0888-613X(92)90013-P

Bezdek, J. C. (1994). What is Computational Intelligence? *Computational Intelligence: Imitating Life,* (pp. 1-11). Piscataway, NJ: IEEE Press.

Bhatia, M., Singh, H., & Kumar, N. (2007). A proposal for the management of mobile network's quality of service (QoS) using data mining methods. In *Proceedings of Wireless Communications, Networking and Mobile Computing Conference* (pp. 1-5).

Bhattacharya, A., Abraham, A., Vasant, P., & Grosan, C. (2007). Evolutionary artificial neural network for selecting flexible manufacturing systems under disparate level-of-satisfaction on decision maker. *International Journal of Innovative computing . Information and Control, 3*(1), 131–140.

Bhattacharya, S., Chattopadhyay, T., & Pal, A. (2006). A survey on different video watermarking techniques and comparative analysis with reference to H.264/AVC. In *Proceedings of IEEE Tenth International Symposium on Consumer Electronics* (pp. 1-6).

Bhatti, T. S., Al-Ademi, A. A. F., & Bansal, N. K. (1997). Load frequency control of isolated wind diesel hybrid power systems. *Energy Conversion and Management, 38*(9), 829. doi:10.1016/S0196-8904(96)00108-2

Bilbao-Terol, A., Perez-Gladish, B., Arenas-Parra, M., & Rodriguez-Uria, M. V. (2006). Fuzzy compromise programming for portfolio selection. *Applied Mathematics and Computation, 173*, 251–264. doi:10.1016/j.amc.2005.04.003

Bin, W., Yi, Z., Shaohui, L., & Zhongzhi, S. (2002). CSIM: A document clustering algorithm based on swarm intelligence. In *Proceedings of the 2002 Congress on Evolutionary Computation, Vol. 1,* (pp. 477-482).

Bingqian, L. (1990). The grey modelling for central symmetry sequence. *The Journal of Grey System, 2*(2), 95–103.

Birbil, S. I., & Fang, S. C. (2003). Electromagnetism-like mechanism for global optimization. *Journal of Global Optimization, 25*, 263–282. doi:10.1023/A:1022452626305

Birbil, S. I., Fang, S., & Sheu, R. (2005). On the convergence of a population-based global optimization algorithm. *Journal of Global Optimization, 30,* 301–318. doi:10.1007/s10898-004-8270-3

Biswas, S., Das, S. R., & Petriu, E. M. (2005). An adaptive compressed MPEG-2 video watermarking scheme. *IEEE Transactions on Instrumentation and Measurement, 54*(5), 1853–1861. doi:10.1109/TIM.2005.855084

Blaschke, C., Leon, E., Krallinger, M., & Valencia, A. (2005). Evaluation of BioCreAtIvE assessment of task 2. *BMC Bioinformatics, 6*(Suppl 1), S16. doi:10.1186/1471-2105-6-S1-S16

Bonarini, A. (2001). Evolutionary Learning, Reinforcement Learning, and Fuzzy Rules for Knowledge Acquisition in Agent-Based Systems. *Proceedings of the IEEE, 89*(9), 1334–1346. doi:10.1109/5.949488

Borgi, A., Corfini, S., & Popescu, R. (2008). Semantics-Based Composition-Oriented Discovery of Web Services. *ACM Trans. on Internet Technol., 8*(4), Article 19. DOI = 10.1145/1391949.1391953 http://doi.acm.org/10.1145/1391949.1391953

Borzemski, L. (2004). Data mining in evaluation of Internet path performance. In *Proceedings of the 17th International Conference on Industrial and Engineering Applications of Artificial Intelligence and Expert Systems,* (LNCS vol. 3029, pp. 643-652). Berlin: Springer.

Borzemski, L. (2006a). Testing, measuring and diagnosing Web sites from the user's perspective. *International Journal of Enterprise Information Systems, 2*(1), 54–66.

Borzemski, L. (2006b). The use of data mining to predict Web performance. *Cybernetics and Systems, 37*(6), 587–608. doi:10.1080/01969720600734586

Borzemski, L. (2007). Internet path behavior prediction via data mining: Conceptual framework and case study. *J. UCS, 13*(2), 287–316.

Borzemski, L. (2008). Measuring of Web performance as perceived by end-users. In A. Gunasekaran (Ed.), *Techniques and tools for the design and implementation of enterprise information systems* (pp. 293-325). Hershey, PA: IGI Publishing.

Borzemski, L., & Druszcz, A. (2006). Lessons from the application of domain-independent data mining system for discovering Web user access patterns. In *Proceedings of the 10th International Conference on Knowledge-Based & Intelligent Information & Engineering Systems,* (LNCS Vol. 4253, pp. 789-796). Berlin: Springer.

Borzemski, L., & Nowak, Z. (2004a). An empirical study of Web quality: Measuring the Web from the Wroclaw University of Technology campus. In *Engineering Advanced Web Applications* (pp. 307-320). Princeton, NJ: Rinton Publishers.

Borzemski, L., & Nowak, Z. (2004b). WING: A Web probing, visualization and performance analysis service. In *Proceedings of the 4th International Conference on Web Engineering,* (LNCS Vol. 3140, pp. 601-602). Berlin: Springer.

Borzemski, L., & Nowak, Z. (2008). Using Autonomous System topological information in Web server performance prediction. *Cybernetics and Systems, 39*(7), 751–767. doi:10.1080/01969720802257980

Borzemski, L., & Starczewski, G. (2009). Application of transform regression to TCP throughput prediction. In *Proceedings of the 1th Asian Conference on Intelligent Information and Database Systems ACIIDS 2009,* (pp. 28-33). Los Alamos, CA: IEEE Press.

Borzemski, L., Cichocki, Ł., Fraś, M., Kliber, M., & Nowak, Z. (2007). MWING: A multiagent system for Web site measurements. In *Proceedings of the First AMSTA KES International Symposium,* (LNCS Vol. 4496, pp. 278-287). Berlin: Springer.

Borzemski, L., Kliber, M., & Nowak, Z. (2008). Application of data mining algorithms to TCP throughput prediction in HTTP transactions. In *Proceedings of the 21st International Conference on Industrial, Engineering and Other Applications of Applied Intelligent Systems,* (LNCS Vol. 5027, pp. 159-168). Berlin: Springer.

Bosc, P., Lietard, L., & Pivert, O. (1997). Functional dependencies revisited under graduality and imprecision. In *Proceedings of NAFIPS* (pp. 57-62).

Bose, I., & Mahapatra, R. K. (2001). Business data mining - a machine learning perspective. *Information & Management, 39,* 211–225. doi:10.1016/S0378-7206(01)00091-X

Bowen, J. P., & Hinchey, M. G. (1999). High-Integrity System Specification and Design. Secaucus, NJ: Springer-Verlag New York, Inc.

Box, J. E., & Jenkins, G. M. (1970). *Time Series Analysis, Forecasting and Control.* Holden Day.

Boz, O. (2002). Extracting decision trees from trained neural networks. In *Proceedings of the 8th ACM SIG-KDD international conference on Knowledge discovery and data mining* (pp. 456–461). Edmonton, Alberta, Canada.

Branco, P. J. C., Dente, J. A., & Mendes, R. V. (2003). Using immunology principles for fault detection. *IEEE Transactions on Industrial Electronics, 50*(2), 362–374. doi:10.1109/TIE.2003.809418

Breiman, L., Friedman, J. H., Olshen, R. A., & Stone, C. J. (1984). *Classification and Regression Trees.* Monterey, CA: Wadsworth International Group.

Brownlee, N., & Claffy, K. C. (2004). Internet measurement. *IEEE Internet Computing, 8*(5), 30–33. doi:10.1109/MIC.2004.41

Brownlee, N., Claffy, K. C., Murray, M., & Nemeth, E. (2001). Methodology for passive analysis of a university Internet link. *Passive and Active Measurement Workshop*, Amsterdam, April 22-24. Retrieved October 10, 2008, from http://www.ripe.net/pam2001/program.html

Buckles, B. P., & Petry, F. E. (1982). A fuzzy representation of data for relational databases. *Fuzzy Sets and Systems, 7*, 213–226. doi:10.1016/0165-0114(82)90052-5

Buckley, J. J., & Hayashi, Y. (1992). Fuzzy neural nets and applications. *Fuzzy Systems and AI, 3*, 11–41.

Buckley, J. J., & Hayashi, Y. (1994). Fuzzy neural networks. In R. Yager, L. Zadeh (Eds.), Fuzzy Sets, Neural Networks, and Soft Computing. New York: Van Nostrand Reinhold.

Buckley, J. J., Reilly, K. D., & Penmetcha, K. V. (1996). "Backpropagation and genetic algorithms for training fuzzy neural nets", *IEEE International Conference on Fuzzy Systems, 1*, 2–6.

Cabrera, J. B. D., & Narendra, K. S. (1999). Issues in the application of neural networks for tracking based on inverse control. *IEEE Transactions on Automatic Control, 44*(11), 2007–2027. doi:10.1109/9.802910

Cai, X., Zhang, N., Venayagamoorthy, G. K., & Wunsch, D. C. (2007). Time series prediction with recurrent neural networks trained by a hybrid PSO-EA algorithm. *Neurocomputing, 70*(13-15), 2342–2353. doi:10.1016/j.neucom.2005.12.138

CAIDA. (2008). *The Cooperative Association for Internet Data Analysis.* Retrieved 10 October 2008, from http://www.caida.org

Calyam, P., Sridharan, M., Mandrawa, W., & Schopis, P. (2004). Performance measurement and analysis of H.323 Traffic. In *Proceedings of the Passive and Active Network Measurement Workshop*, (LNCS vol. 3015, pp. 137-146). Berlin: Springer.

Camon, E., Barrell, D., Dimmer, E., Lee, V., Magrane, M., & Maslen, J. (2005). An evaluation of GO annotation retrieval for BioCreAtIvE and GOA. *BMC Bioinformatics, 6*(Suppl 1), S17. doi:10.1186/1471-2105-6-S1-S17

Campbell, J. Y., Lo, A. W., & MacKinlay, A. C. (1997). *The Econometrics of Finance Markets.* Princeton, NJ: Princeton University Press.

Canham, R. O., & Tyrrell, A. M. (2003). A hardware artificial immune system and embryonic array for fault tolerant systems. *Genetic Programming and Evolvable Machines, 4*, 359–382. doi:10.1023/A:1026143128448

Cano, J. R., Herrera, F., & Lozano, M. (2003). Using evolutionary algorithms as instance selection for data reduction in kdd: an experimental study. *IEEE Transactions on Evolutionary Computation, 7*(6), 561–575. doi:10.1109/TEVC.2003.819265

Cao, L., & Zhang, C. (2007). The evolution of KDD: Towards domain-driven data mining. *International Journal of Pattern Recognition and Artificial Intelligence, 21*(4), 677–692. doi:10.1142/S0218001407005612

Cardellini, V., Casalicchio, E., Colajanni, M., & Yu, P. S. (2002). The state of the art in locally distributed Web-server systems. *ACM Computing Surveys, 34*(2), 263–311. doi:10.1145/508352.508355

Cardoso, J. S., da Costa, J. F. P., & Cardoso, M. J. (2005). Modelling ordinal relations with SVMs: An application to objective aesthetic evaluation of breast cancer conservative treatment. *Neural Networks, 18*(5-6), 808–817. doi:10.1016/j.neunet.2005.06.023

Cardoso, J., & Sheth, A. (2003). Semantic e-Workflow Composition. *Journal of Intelligent Information Systems, 21*(3), 191–225. doi:10.1023/A:1025542915514

Carey, M., & Johnson, D. (1979). *Computers and Intractability: A guide to the theory of NP-completeness.* San Francisco, CA: Freeman.

Carlsson, C., Fullér, R., & Majlender, P. (2002). A possibilistic approach to selecting portfolios with highest utility score. *Fuzzy Sets and Systems, 131*, 13–21. doi:10.1016/S0165-0114(01)00251-2

Carrasco, R. A., Vila, M. A., Galindo, J., & Cubero, J. C. (2000). FSQL: a Tool for obtaining fuzzy dependencies. In *8th International Conference on Information Processing and Management of Uncertainty in Knowledge-Based Systems*, (pp. 1916-1919).

Carse, B., Fogarty, T., & Munro, A. (1996). Evolving fuzzy rule based controllers using genetic algorithms. *Fuzzy Sets and Systems, 80*(3), 273–293. doi:10.1016/0165-0114(95)00196-4

Casillas, J., Cordón, O., & Herrera, F. (2002). Cor: a methodology to improve ad hoc data-driven linguistic rule learning methods by inducing cooperation among rules. *IEEE Transactions on Systems, Man, and Cybernetics . Part B, 32*(4), 526–537.

Casillas, J., Cordón, O., del Jesus, M. J., & Herrera, F. (2001). Genetic feature selection in a fuzzy rule-based classification system learning process for high-dimensional problems. *Information Sciences, 136*(1-4), 135–157. doi:10.1016/S0020-0255(01)00147-5

Casillas, J., Cordón, O., Herrera, F., & Villar, P. (2004). A hybrid learning process for the knowledge base of a fuzzy rule-based system. In X international conference on information processing and management of uncertainty in knowledge-based systems (ipmu´04) (pp. 2189-2196), Perugia, Italy.

Castillo, P. A., Carpio, J., Merelo, J. J., Prieto, A., Rivas, V., & Romero, G. (2000). Evolving multilayer perceptions. *Neural Processing Letters, 12*(2), 115–128. doi:10.1023/A:1009684907680

Castillo, P. A., Merelo, J. J., González, J., Prieto, A., Rivas, V., & Romero, G. (1996). G-Prop-III: Global optimization of multilayer perceptions using an evolutionary algorithm. *Proc. Of the Congress on Evolutionary Computation, 1*, 942-947.

Chakrabarti, K., Keogh, E. J., Pazzani, M., & Mehrotra, S. (2002). Locally adaptive dimensionality reduction for indexing large time series databases. *ACM Transactions on Database Systems, 27*(2), 188–228. doi:10.1145/568518.568520

Chakrabarti, S. (2003). *Mining the Web: Analysis of Hypertext and Semi Structured Data.* San Francisco, CA: Morgan Kaufmann.

Chan, C.-C., & Santhosh, S. (2003). Blem2: Learning Bayes' Rules From Examples Using Rough Sets. *NAFIPS 2003, 22nd Int. conf. of the North American Fuzzy Information Processing Society* (pp. 187–190), July 24 – 26, Chicago.

Chan, P. W., Lyu, M. R., & Chin, R. T. (2005). A novel scheme for hybrid digital video watermarking: approach, evaluation and experimentation. *IEEE Trans. on Circuits and Systems for Video Technology, 15*(12), 1638–1649. doi:10.1109/TCSVT.2005.856932

Chang, C. S., Fu, W., & Wen, F. (1998). Load frequency controller using genetic algorithm based fuzzy gain scheduling of PI controller. *Electric Machines and Power Systems, 26*, 39–52. doi:10.1080/07313569808955806

Chang, C.-C., & Lin, C.-J. (2001). *LIBSVM: A library for support vector machines.* Software available at http://www.csie.ntu.edu.tw/~cjlin/libsvm

Chang, J. F., Chu, S. C., Roddick, J. F., & Pan, J. S. (2005). A Parallel Particle Swarm Optimization Algorithm with Communication Strategies. *Journal of Information Science and Engineering, 21*(4), 809–818.

Chapple, M. (n.d.). *Regression (data mining) definition.* About.com: Databases. Retrieved from http://databases.about.com/od/datamining/g/regression.htm

Chatterjee, A., Pulasinghe, K., Watanabe, K., & Izumi, K. (2005). A particle-swarm-optimized fuzzy-neural network for voice-controlled robot systems. *IEEE Transactions on Industrial Electronics, 52*(6), 1478–1489. doi:10.1109/TIE.2005.858737

Chaturvedi, D. K., Satsangi, P. S., & Kalra, P. K. (1999). Load frequency control: a generalised neural network approach. *Electrical Power & Energy Systems, 21*, 405–415. doi:10.1016/S0142-0615(99)00010-1

Chen, C. H., Lin, C. T., & Lin, C. J. (2007). A functional-link-based fuzzy neural network for temperature control. In *2007 IEEE Symposium on Foundations of Computational Intelligence,* Honolulu, HI, (pp. 53-58).

Chen, C. K., & Tien, T. L. (1997). The indirect measurement of tensile strength by the deterministic grey dynamic model DGDM (1,1,1). *International Journal of Systems Science, 28*(7), 683–690. doi:10.1080/00207729708929428

Chen, D. S., & Jain, R. C. (1994). A robust backpropagation learning algorithm for function approximation. *IEEE Transactions on Neural Networks, 5*(3), 467–479. doi:10.1109/72.286917

Chen, G. Q. (1998). *Fuzzy Logic in Data Modeling: Semantics, Constraints, and Database Design.* Amsterdam: Kluwer Academic Publishers.

Chen, K. Y. (1998). *On the Study of the Learning Performance for Neural Networks and Neural Fuzzy Networks.* Master Thesis, Dept. of Electrical Eng., NTUST, Taiwan, R.O.C.

Chen, M. Han, S., J., & Yu, P. S. (1996). Data mining: An overview from a database perspective. *IEEE Transactions on Knowledge and Data Engineering, 8*(6), 866–883. doi:10.1109/69.553155

Chen, Y., & Wang, J. Z. (2003). Support vector learning for fuzzy rule-based classification systems. *IEEE Transactions on Neural Networks, 11*(6), 716–728.

Chen, Y., Wang, R., & Lin, H. (2002). The application and compare of training algorithms in MATLAB 6.0's neural network toolbox. *Computer and Information Technology, 3*, 1-6/18.

Chess, D., Harrison, C., & Kershenbaum, A. (1995). *Mobile agents: Are they a good idea?* IBM Research Report.

Chickering, D. M. (2002). *The WinMine Toolkit* (Tech. Rep. No. MSR-TR-2002-103). Redmond, WA: Microsoft Research.

Chickering, D. M., Heckerman, D., Meek, C., Platt, J. C., & Thiesson, B. (2000). *Goal-oriented clustering.* Tech. Rep. No. MSR-TR-2000-82. Redmond, WA: Microsoft Research.

Cho, Y. H., Kim, J. K., & Kim, S. H. (2002). A personalized recommender system based on Web usage mining and decision tree induction. *Expert Systems with Applications, 23*, 329–342. doi:10.1016/S0957-4174(02)00052-0

Christensen, E., Curbera, F., Meredith, G., & Weerawarana, S. (2001). *Web Services Description Language (WSDL) 1.1.* W3C Recommendation. Retrieved from http://www.w3.org/TR/2001/NOTE-wsdl-20010315

Christie, R. D., Wollenberg, B. F., & Wangensteen, I. (2000). Transmission management in the deregulated environment. *Proc. IEEE Special Issue on The Technology of Power System Competition, 88*(2), 170–195.

Christie, R., & Bose, A. (1996). Load-frequency control issues in power systems operation after deregulation. *IEEE Transactions on Power Systems, 11*, 1191–1200. doi:10.1109/59.535590

Chu, B.-H., Lee, Ch.-E., & Ho, Ch.-S. (2008). An ontology-supported database refurbishing technique and its application in mining actionable troubleshooting rules from real-life databases. *Engineering Applications of Artificial Intelligence, 21*, 1430–1442. doi:10.1016/j.engappai.2008.04.015

Chu, S. C., & Tsai, P. W. (2007). Computational Intelligence Based on the Behaviors of Cats. *International Journal on Innovative Computing . Information & Control, 3*(1), 163–173.

Chu, S. C., & Tsai, P. W. (2007). Computational intelligence based on the behavior of cats. *International Journal of Innovative computing . Information and Control, 3*(1), 163–173.

Chu, S. C., Roddick, J. F., & Pan, J. S. (2004). Ant Colony System with Communication Strategies. *Information Sciences, 167,* 63–76. doi:10.1016/j.ins.2003.10.013

Chu, S. C., Roddick, J. F., Su, C. J., & Pan, J. S. (2004). Constrained ant colony optimization for data clustering. In *8th Pacific Rim International Conference on Artificial Intelligence,* (LNAI Vol. 3157, pp. 534-543).

Chu, S. C., Tsai, P. W., & Pan, J. S. (2006). Cat swarm optimization. *9th Pacific Rim International Conference on Artificial Intelligence* (LNCS Vol. 4099, pp. 854-858). Berlin: Springer.

Chuang, A. (2000). An extendible genetic algorithm framework for problem solving in a common environment. *IEEE Transactions on Power Systems, 15*(1), 269–275. doi:10.1109/59.852132

Chuang, C. C., Su, S. F., & Chen, S. S. (2001). Robust TSK fuzzy modeling for function approximation with outliers. *IEEE transactions on Fuzzy Systems, 9*(6), 810–821. doi:10.1109/91.971730

Chuang, C. C., Su, S. F., & Hsiao, C. C. (2000). The annealing robust backpropagation (ARBP) learning algorithm. *IEEE Transactions on Neural Networks, 11*(5), 1067–1077. doi:10.1109/72.870040

Chuang, C. C., Su, S. F., Jeng, J. T., & Hsiao, C. C. (2002). Robust support vector regression networks for function approximation with outliers. *IEEE Transactions on Neural Networks, 13*(6), 1322–1330. doi:10.1109/TNN.2002.804227

Cichocki, A., & Unbehauen, R. (1993). *Neural Networks for Optimization and Signal Processing.* New York: John Wiley & Sons.

Claffy, K., Dovrolis, C., & Murray, M. (2003). Bandwidth estimation: metrics, measurement techniques, and tools. *IEEE Network, 17*(6), 27–35. doi:10.1109/MNET.2003.1248658

Clement, L., et al. (Eds.). (2004). *UDDI Version 3.0.2.* http://uddi.org/pubs/uddiv3.0.2-20041019.htm

Cohen, A. M. (2005). Unsupervised gene/protein named entity normalization using automatically extracted dictionaries. In *Proceedings of the ACL-ISMB Workshop on Linking Biological Literature, Ontologies and Databases: Mining Biological Semantics,* (pp. 17–24).

Cohen, A. M., & Hersh, W. R. (2005). A survey of current work in biomedical text mining. *Briefings in Bioinformatics, 6*(1), 57–71. doi:10.1093/bib/6.1.57

Cohen, A., & Hersh, W. (2006). The TREC 2004 genomics track categorization task: classifying full text biomedical documents. *Journal of Biomedical Discovery and Collaboration, 1*(1), 4. doi:10.1186/1747-5333-1-4

Cohen, K. B., Acquaah-Mensah, G. K., Dolbey, A. E., & Hunter, L. (2002). Contrast and variability in gene names. In *Proceedings of the ACL-02 workshop on natural language processing in the biomedical domain,* Morristown, NJ, (pp. 14–20).

Cohen, W. W. (1995). Fast effective rule induction. In A. Prieditis & S. J. Russell (Eds.), *Proceedings of 12th International Conference on Machine Learning* (pp. 115–123), Tahoe City, CA.

Cohn, D., Atlas, L., & Ladner, R. (1994). Improving generalization with active learning. *Machine Learning, 15*(2), 201–221.

Cohn, N. (1986). *Control of generation and power flow on interconnected systems.* New York: Wiley.

Comer, D. (2008). *Computer Networks and Internets,* (5th Ed.). Upper Saddle River, NJ: Prentice Hall.

Cooley, R., Mobasher, B., & Srivastava, J. (1999). Data preparation for mining World Wide Web browsing patterns. *Journal of Knowledge and Information System, 1*(1), 5–32.

Corcoran, A., & Sen, S. (1994). Using real-valued genetic algorithms to evolve rule sets for classification. In *Proceedings of the first ieee conference on evolutionary computation,* (Vol. 1, p. 120-124), Orlando, FL.

Cordón, O., & Herrera, F. (1997). A three-stage evolutionary process for learning descriptive and approximate fuzzy logic controller knowledge bases from examples. *International Journal of Approximate Reasoning, 17*(4), 369–407. doi:10.1016/S0888-613X(96)00133-8

Cordón, O., & Herrera, F. (1999). A two-stage evolutionary process for designing tsk fuzzy rule-based systems. *IEEE Transactions on Systems, Man, and Cybernetics . Part B, 29*(6), 703–715.

Cordón, O., & Herrera, F. (2001). Hybridizing genetic algorithms with sharing scheme and evolution strategies for designing approximate fuzzy rule-based systems. *Fuzzy Sets and Systems, 118*(2), 235–255. doi:10.1016/S0165-0114(98)00349-2

Cordón, O., del Jesus, M. J., & Herrera, F. (1998). Genetic learning of fuzzy rule-based classification systems cooperating with fuzzy reasoning methods. *International Journal of Intelligent Systems, 13*(10-11), 1025–1053. doi:10.1002/(SICI)1098-111X(199810/11)13:10/11<1025::AID-INT9>3.0.CO;2-N

Cordón, O., del Jesus, M. J., Herrera, F., & Lozano, M. (1999). Mogul: A methodology to obtain genetic fuzzy rule-based systems under the iterative rule learning approach. *International Journal of Intelligent Systems, 14*(9), 1123–1153. doi:10.1002/(SICI)1098-111X(199911)14:11<1123::AID-INT4>3.0.CO;2-6

Cordón, O., Herrera, F., Hoffmann, F., & Magdalena, L. (2001). Genetic fuzzy systems: Evolutionary tuning and learning of fuzzy knowledge bases. Singapore: World Scientific.

Corwin, E. M., Logar, A. M., & Oldham, W. J. B. (1994). An iterative method for training multilayer networks with threshold function . *IEEE Transactions on Neural Networks, 5,* 507–508. doi:10.1109/72.286926

Cowder, R. S. (1990). Predicting the Mackey-glass time series with cascade-correlation learning. In *Proc. of the 1990 Connectionist Models Summer School*, (pp. 117-123).

Cox, I., Miller, M., & Bloom, J. (2001). *Digital Watermarking.* San Francisco: Morgan Kaufmann.

Craenen, B. C., & Eiben, A. E. (2003). Computational Intelligence. *Encyclopedia of Life Support Sciences.* Oxford, UK: EOLSS Publishers Co. Ltd.

Crovella, M., & Krishnamurthy, B. (2006). *Internet Measurement: Infrastructure, Traffic, and Applications.* New York: John Wiley & Sons.

Czyzowicz, J., Kranakis, E., Krizanc, D., Pelc, A., & Martin, M. V. (2003). Enhancing hyperlink structure for improving Web performance. *Journal of Web Engineering, 1*(2), 93–127.

Danzig, D. B. (1955). Linear programming under uncertainty. *Management Science, 1,* 197–206. doi:10.1287/mnsc.1.3-4.197

Das, G., Lin, K., Mannila, H., Renganathan, G., & Smyth, P. (1998). Rule discovery from time series. In *Proceedings of the 4th International Conference on Knowledge Discovery and Data Mining,* (pp. 16–22).

Dasgupta, D. (1999). *Artificial Immune System and Their Applications.* Berlin: Springer-Verlag.

Davis, L. (1991). Handbook of Genetic Algorithms. New York: Van Nostrand Reinhold.

de Castro, L. N., & Von Zuben, F. J. (2002). Learning and optimization using clonal selection principle. *IEEE Transactions on Evolutionary Computation, 6*(3), 239–251. doi:10.1109/TEVC.2002.1011539

De Jong, K. (1980). Adaptive system design: a genetic approach . *IEEE Transactions on Systems, Man, and Cybernetics, SMC-10*(9), 1566–1574.

Debels, D., Reyck, B. D., Leus, R., & Vanhoucke, M. (2006). A hybrid scatter search/electromagnetism meta-heuristic for project scheduling. *European Journal of Operational Research, 169,* 638–653. doi:10.1016/j.ejor.2004.08.020

Debole, F., & Sebastiani, F. (2003). Supervised term weighting for automated text categorization. In *Proceedings of 18th ACM Symposium on Applied Computing,* (pp. 784–788).

del Jesus, M. J., Hoffmann, F., Navascués, L. J., & Sánchez, L. (2004). Induction of fuzzy-rule-based classiffers with evolutionary boosting algorithms. *IEEE transactions on Fuzzy Systems*, *12*(3), 296–308. doi:10.1109/TFUZZ.2004.825972

Delfino, B., Fornari, F., & Massucco, S. (2002). Load-frequency control and inadvertent interchange evaluation in restructured power systems. *Proc. IEE in Generation, Transmition & Distribution, 149*(5), 607–614.

Dempster, A. P., Laird, N. M., & Rubin, D. B. (1977). Maximum likelihood from incomplete data via the EM algorithm. *Journal of the Royal Statistical Society. Series A (General), 39*(1), 1–38.

Demsar, J. (2006). Statistical comparisons of classifiers over multiple data sets. *Journal of Machine Learning Research, 7*, 1–30.

Demsar, J., Zupan, B., Leban, G., & Curk, T. (2004). Orange: From experimental machine learning to interactive data mining. In Knowledge discovery in databases: Pkdd 2004 (p. 537-539). Berlin: Springer.

Demuth, H., Beale, M., & Hagan, M. (2007). Neural network toolbox 5 user's guide. Natick, MA: MathWorks Inc.

Denai, M. A., Palis, F., & Zeghbib, A. (2007). Modeling and Control of Non-Linear Systems Using Soft Computing Techniques. *Applied Soft Computing, 7*(3), 728–738. doi:10.1016/j.asoc.2005.12.005

Deneubourg, J. L., Goss, S., Franks, N., Sendova-Franks, A., Detrain, C., & Chrétien, L. (1991). The dynamics of collective sorting robot-like ants and ant-like robots. In *Proceedings of the first international conference on simulation of adaptive behavior on From animals to animates table of contents,* (pp. 356-363).

Deng, J. L. (1982). Control problem of grey system. *Systems & Control Letters, 5*, 288–294.

Deng, J. L. (1987). *The Essential Methods of Grey Systems.* Wuhan, China: Huazhong University of Science & Technology Press.

Devert, W., Mateen, M. R., & Louis, A. T. (2002). E-Net: Evolutionary neural network synthesis. *Neurocomputing, 42*, 171–196. doi:10.1016/S0925-2312(01)00599-9

Dietterich, T. G. (1998). Approximate statistical tests for comparing supervised classification learning algorithms. *Neural Computation, 10*(7), 1895–1923. doi:10.1162/089976698300017197

Djukanovic, M. B., Dobrijevic, D. M., Calovic, M. S., Novicevic, M., & Sobajic, D. J. (1997). Coordinated stabilizing control for the exciter and governor loops using fuzzy set theory and neural nets. *Electrical Power & Energy Systems, 19*(8), 489–499. doi:10.1016/S0142-0615(97)00020-3

Djukanovic, M., Novicevic, M., Sobajic, D. J., & Pao, Y. P. (1995). Conceptual development of optimal load frequency control using artificial neural networks and fuzzy set theory. *Int. J. of Eng. Intelligent Systems for Electrical Engineering and Communication, 3*(2), 95–108.

Donde, V., Pai, M. A., & Hiskens, I. A. (2001). Simulation and optimization in an AGC system after deregulation. *IEEE Transactions on Power Systems, 16*(3), 481–489. doi:10.1109/59.932285

Dong, X., et al. (2004). Similarity Search for Web Services. In *Proceedings of 2004 VLDB Conference* (pp. 372–383). Toronto, Canada. Retrieved from www.vldb.org/conf/2004/RS10P1.PDF

Dorigo, M., & Gambardella, L. M. (1997). Ant Colony System: A Cooperative Learning Approach to the Traveling Salesman Problem. *IEEE Transactions on Evolutionary Computation, 26*(1), 53–66. doi:10.1109/4235.585892

Dorigo, M., & Stutzle, T. (2004). *Ant Colony Optimization.* Cambridge, MA: MIT Press.

Dovrolis, C. (2005). End-to-end available bandwidth estimation. In *Proceedings of the ACM SIGMETRICS International Conference on Measurement and Modeling of Computer Systems,* (pp. 265–276).

Downey, A. B. (1999). Using pathchar to estimate Internet link characteristics. *SIGCOMM Comput. Commun. Rev., 29*(4), 241–250. doi:10.1145/316194.316228

Dubois, D., & Prade, H. (1980). Systems of linear fuzzy constraints. *Fuzzy Sets and Systems, 3*, 37–48. doi:10.1016/0165-0114(80)90004-4

Dubois, D., & Prade, H. (1988). *Possibility Theory: An Approach to Computerized Processing of Uncertainty.* New York: Plenum.

Duch, W. (2007). *What is Computational Intelligence and What Could It Become?* Tech. Rep., Department of Informatics, Nicolaus Copernicus University and School of Computer Engineering, Nanyang Technological University.

Duffield, N. (2004). Sampling for passive Internet measurement: A review. *Statistical Science, 19*(3), 472–498. doi:10.1214/088342304000000206

Eberhart, R. C. (1995). Computational Intelligence: A Snapshot. *Computational Intelligence - A Dynamic System Perspective Piscataway* (pp. 9-15). Piscataway, NJ: IEEE Press.

Eberhart, R. C. (1998). Overview of Computational Intelligence. *Proceedings of the 20th Annual International Conference of the IEEE Engineering in Medicine and Biology Society, 3*, 1125-1129.

Eberhart, R., & Kennedy, J. (1995). A new optimizer using particle swarm theory. In *Proc. of the Sixth International Symposium on Micro Machine and Human Science,* (pp. 39-43).

Eberhart, R., Simpson, P., & Dobbins, R. (1996). *Computational Intelligence PC Tools.* Boston: Academic Press.

Eiben, A. E., & Smith, J. E. (2003). Introduction to Evolutionary Computing. Berlin: SpringerVerlag.

Elgerd, O. I. (1982). *Electric Energy Systems Theory, an Introduction.* New Delhi, India: Tata McGraw-Hill.

Elgerd, O. I., & Fosha, C. E. (1970). Optimum megawatt frequency control of multi-area electric energy systems. *IEEE Trans. on PAS, PAS-89*, 556–563.

El-Ramly, M., & Stroulia, E. (2004). Analysis of Web-usage behavior for focused Web sites: a case study. *Journal of Software Maintenance and Evolution: Research and Practice, 16*(1-2), 129–150. doi:10.1002/smr.286

Elton, E. J., & Gruber, M. J. (1995). *Modern Portfolio Theory and Investment Analysis.* New York: Wiley.

Emmeche, C. (1994). Garden in the Machine: The Emerging Science of Artificial Life. Princeton, NJ: Princeton University Press.

Engin, O., & Doyen, A. (2004). A new approach to solve hybrid flow shop scheduling problems by artificial immune system. *Future Generation Computer Systems, 20*, 1083–1095. doi:10.1016/j.future.2004.03.014

Estevam, R. H., Eduardo, R. H., & Nelson, F. F. (2005, December). *Applying Bayesian Networks for Meteorological Data Mining.* Paper presented at the Twenty-fifth SGAI International Conference on Innovative Techniques and Applications of Artificial Intelligence, Cambridge, UK.

Facca, F., & Lanzi, P. (2005). Mining interesting knowledge from weblogs: A survey. *Data & Knowledge Engineering, 53*, 225–241. doi:10.1016/j.datak.2004.08.001

Fahlman, S. E., & Lebiere, C. (1991). *The cascade-correlation learning architecture* (Tech. Rep. CMU-CS-90-100). Pittsburgh, PA: Carnegie Mellon University, Dept. of CS.

Faloutsos, M., & Faloutsos, Ch. (2002). *Data-Mining the Internet: What We Know, What We Don't, and How We Can Learn More.* Full day Tutorial ACM SIGCOMM 2002 Conference, Pittsburgh.

Faloutsos, M., Faloutsos, P., & Faloutsos, C. (1999). On power-law relationships of the Internet topology. In *Proceedings of SIGCOMM* (pp. 251-262).

Fang, D. Y. (2004). *Information hiding in digital video with phase angle of motion vector.* Master's thesis, Dept. of Computer and Information Science, National Tsing Hua University, Hsinchu, Taiwan.

Fang, H. R., Murphy, K., Jin, Y., Kim, J., & White, P. (2006). Human gene name normalization using text matching with automatically extracted synonym dictionaries. In *Proceedings of the HLT-NAACL BioNLP Workshop on Linking Natural Language Processing and Biology,* (pp. 41–48).

Fang, T., Leng, X., Ma, X., & Guang, M. (2004). λ-*PDF* and Gegenbauer polynomial approximation for dynamic response problems of random structures. *Acta Mechanica Sinica, 20*(3), 292–298. doi:10.1007/BF02486721

Fellbaum, C. (1998). *WordNet: An Electronic Lexical Database*. Cambridge, MA: MIT Press.

Fellbaum, C. (2007). *WordNet: Connecting words and concepts*. Retrieved from http://colab.cim3.net/file/work/SICoP/2007-02-06/WordNet02062007.ppt

Feng, H. M. (2006). Self-generation RBFNs using evolutional PSO learning. *Neurocomputing, 70*(1-3), 241–251. doi:10.1016/j.neucom.2006.03.007

Flach, P. A. (1990). *Inductive characterization of database relations*. ITK Research Report.

Flach, P. A., & Savnik, I. (1999). Database dependency discovery: a machine learning approach. *AI Communications, 12*(3), 139–160.

Fleming, P. J., & Fonseca, C. M. (1993). *Genetic algorithms in control systems engineering*. Research Report No. 470. Sheffield, UK: University of Sheffield, Dept. of Automatic Control and Systems Engineering.

Fogel, D. B. (1994). Applying evolutionary programming to selected control problems. *Computers & Mathematics with Applications (Oxford, England), 11*(27), 89–104. doi:10.1016/0898-1221(94)90100-7

Fogel, D. B. (1995). Review of Computational Intelligence: Imitating Life. *IEEE Transactions on Neural Networks, 6*(6), 1562–1565.

Forrest, S., Javornik, B., Smith, R. E., & Perelson, A. S. (1993). Using genetic algorithm to explore pattern recognition in the immune system. *Evolutionary Computation, 1*(3), 191–211. doi:10.1162/evco.1993.1.3.191

Forrest, S., Perelson, A., Allen, L., & Cherukuri, R. (1994). Self-nonself discrimination in a computer. In *IEEE Symposium on Research in Security and Privacy*, (pp. 202-212).

Freeman, H. (1974). Computer processing of line-drawing image. *Computing Surveys, 6*(1), 57–97. doi:10.1145/356625.356627

Freitas, A. A. (2002). Data mining and knowledge discovery with evolutionary algorithms. Secaucus, NJ: Springer-Verlag New York, Inc.

Friedman, J. H., & Tukey, J. W. (1974). A projection pursuit algorithm for exploratory data analysis. *IEEE Transactions on Computers, 23*(9), 881–890. doi:10.1109/T-C.1974.224051

Fuggetta, A., Picco, G. P., & Vigna, G. (1998). Understanding Code Mobility. *IEEE Transactions on Software Engineering, 24*(5). doi:10.1109/32.685258

Fukuda, K., Tsunoda, T., Tamura, A., & Takagi, T. (1998). Toward information extraction: Identifying protein names from biological papers. In . *Proceedings of the Pacific Symposium on Biocomputing, 3*, 705–716.

Fukuda, T., & Shibata, T. (1992). Hierarchical intelligent control for robotic motion by using fuzzy. artificial intelligence, and neural network. In . *Proceedings of IJCNN, 92*, I-269–I-274.

Fürnkranz, J. (1999). Separate-and-conquer rule learning. *Artificial Intelligence Review, 13*(1), 3–54. doi:10.1023/A:1006524209794

Fürnkranz, J. (2005). Web mining. In *Data Mining and Knowledge Discovery Handbook*, (pp. 899-920). Berlin: Springer.

Furuhashi, T. (2001). Fusion of Fuzzy/Neuro/Evolutionary Computing for Knowledge Acquisition. *Proceedings of the IEEE, 89*(9), 1266–1274. doi:10.1109/5.949484

Gagné, C., & Parizeau, M. (2006). Genericity in evolutionary computation software tools: Principles and case-study. *International Journal of Artificial Intelligence Tools, 15*(2), 173–194. doi:10.1142/S021821300600262X

Gaing, Z. L. (2004). A particle swarm optimization approach for optimum design of PID controller in AVR system. *IEEE Transactions on Energy Conversion, 19*(2), 384–391. doi:10.1109/TEC.2003.821821

Galiano, F. B., Cubero, J. C., Cuenca, F., & Medina, J. M. (2002). Relational decomposition through partial functional dependencies. *Data & Knowledge Engineering, 43*(2), 207–234. doi:10.1016/S0169-023X(02)00056-3

Galindo, J., Urrutia, A., & Piattini, M. (2006). *Fuzzy databases: modeling, design and implementation*. Hershey, PA: Idea Group Publishing.

Gama, J., & Brazdil, P. (2000). Cascade generalization. *Machine Learning, 41*(3), 315–343. doi:10.1023/A:1007652114878

Ganjisaffar, Y., Abolhassani, H., Neshati, M., & Jamali, M. (2006). A Similarity Measure for OWL-S Annotated Web Services. In *2006 IEEE/WIC/ACM International Conference on Web Intelligence* (pp. 621–624).

Gao, X., & Cong, S. (2001). Comparative study on fast learning algorithms of BP networks. *Control and Decision, 16*(2), 167–171.

García, S., Cano, J., & Herrera, F. (2008). A memetic algorithm for evolutionary prototype selection: A scaling up approach. *Pattern Recognition, 41*(8), 2693–2709. doi:10.1016/j.patcog.2008.02.006

Garofalakis, M., & Rastogi, R. (2002). *Network data mining and analysis: The NEMES project*, (LNCS vol. 2336, pp. 1-12). Berlin: Springer.

Ghosh, A. (2005). *Evolutionary algorithms for data mining and knowledge discovery. Evolutionary computation in data mining*. In A. Gohsh & L. C. Jain (Eds.), *Studies in Fuzziness and Soft Computing*, (Vol. 163, pp. 1-19).

Ghosh, A., & Jain, L. C. (2005). *Evolutionary computation in data mining*. In A. Gohsh & L. C. Jain, (Eds.), *Studies in Fuzziness and Soft Computing*, (Vol. 163).

Gil-Pita, R., & Yao, X. (2007). Using a genetic algorithm for editing k-nearest neighbor classifiers. In *Proceedings of the 8th international conference on intelligent data engineering and automated learning (ideal)* (pp. 1141-1150), Birmingham, UK.

Glover, F. (1986). Future paths for integer programming and links to artificial intelligence. *Computers & Operations Research, 13*, 533–549. doi:10.1016/0305-0548(86)90048-1

Glover, F., & Laguna, M. (1997). Tabu Search. Dordrecht, The Netherlands: Kluwer Academic Publishers.

Goldberg, D. E. (1989). *Genetic algorithm in search. Optimization and machine learning*. Reading. MA: Addison-Wesley Publishing Company.

Golub, G. H., & Reinsch, C. (1970). Singular value decomposition and least squares solutions. *Numerische Mathematik, 14*, 403–420. doi:10.1007/BF02163027

Golub, G. H., & Van Loan, C. F. (1996). *Matrix Computations*. Baltimore: The Johns Hopkins University Press.

Gomm, J. B., & Yu, D. L. (2000). Selecting radial basis function network centers with recursive orthogonal least squares training. *IEEE Transactions on Neural Networks, 11*(2), 306–314. doi:10.1109/72.839002

González, A., & Pérez, R. (1999). Slave: a genetic learning system based on an iterative approach. *IEEE transactions on Fuzzy Systems, 7*(2), 176–191. doi:10.1109/91.755399

González, A., & Pérez, R. (2001). Selection of relevant features in a fuzzy genetic learning algorithm. *IEEE Transactions on Systems, Man, and Cybernetics . Part B, 31*(3), 417–425.

Gonzalez, J., Rojas, I., Pomares, H., Ortega, J., & Prieto, A. (2002). A new clustering technique for function approximation. *IEEE Transactions on Neural Networks, 13*(1), 132–142. doi:10.1109/72.977289

Goodman, R. M., & Zeng, Z. (1994) A learning algorithm for multi-layer perceptrons with hard-limiting threshold units. In IEEE Workshop of Neural Networks for Signal Processing, (pp. 219-228), Ermioni.

Green, R. K. (1996). Transformed Automatic Generation Control. *IEEE Transactions on Power Systems, 11*(4), 1799–1804. doi:10.1109/59.544645

Grefenstette, J. J. (1986). Optimization of control parameters for genetic algorithms. *IEEE Transactions on Systems, Man, and Cybernetics, SMC-16*, 122–128. doi:10.1109/TSMC.1986.289288

Grefenstette, J. J. (1994). Genetic algorithms for machine learning. Norwell, MA: Kluwer Academic Publishers.

Grossman, R. L., Gu, Y., Sabala, M., & Zhang, W. (2009). Compute and storage clouds using wide area high performance networks. *Future Generation Computer Systems, 25*, 179–183. doi:10.1016/j.future.2008.07.009

Grossman, R. L., Kamath, Ch., Kegelmeyer, P., Kumar, V., & Namburu, R. R. (Eds.). (2001). *Data Mining for Scientific and Engineering Applications*. Boston: Kluwer Academic Publishers.

Guo, P., & Tanaka, H. (1998). Possibility data analysis and its application to portfolio selection problems. *Fuzzy Economic Rev., 3*, 3–23.

Gupta, M. M. (1996). Fuzzy Logic and Fuzzy Systems: Recent Developments and Future Directions. In *The Biennial Conference of the North American Fuzzy Information Processing Society*, (pp. 155-159).

Gupta, M. M., & Knopf, G. K. (1990). Fuzzy neural network approach to control systems. In *Proceedings of the First International Symposium on Uncertainty Modeling and Analysis*, (pp. 483–488).

Gupta, M. M., & Qi, J. (1991). On fuzzy neuron models. In . *Proceedings of International Joint Conference on Neural Networks, II*, 4312–4436.

Gupta, M. M., Ragade, R. K., & Yager, R. R. (1979). *Advances in Fuzzy Set Theroy and Applications*. New York: North-Holland.

Guyon, I., & Elisseeff, A. (2006). An introduction to feature extraction. In I. Guyon, S. Gunn, M. Nikravesh, & L. Zadeh (Eds.), Feature Extraction: Foundations and Applications (pp. 1–25). Berlin: Springer.

Hagan, M. T., Demuth, H. B., & Beale, M. (1996). *Neural Network Design*. Boston: PWS.

Hale, J., & Shenoi, S. (1996). Analyzing FD inference in relational databases. *Data and Knowledge Engineering Journal, 18*, 167–183. doi:10.1016/0169-023X(95)00033-O

Han, J., & Chang, K. Ch.-Ch. (2002). Data mining for Web intelligence. *Computer*, (Nov): 54–60.

Han, J., & Kamber, M. (2007). *Data mining: Concepts and techniques*, (2nd Ed.). San Francisco: Morgan Kaufmann.

Hartung, F., & Girod, B. (1998). Watermarking of uncompressed and compressed video. *Signal Processing, 66*(6), 283–301. doi:10.1016/S0165-1684(98)00011-5

Hasegawa, G., Murata, M., & Miyahara, H. (1999). Performance evaluation of HTTP/TCP on asymmetric networks. *International Journal of Communication Systems, 12*(4), 281–296. doi:10.1002/(SICI)1099-1131(199907/08)12:4<281::AID-DAC402>3.0.CO;2-W

Hassan, M. A., Malik, O. P., & Hope, G. S. (1991). A fuzzy logic based stabilizer for a synchronous machine. *IEEE Transactions on Energy Conversion, 6*(3), 407–413. doi:10.1109/60.84314

Hastie, T., & Stuetzle, W. (1989). Principal curves. *Journal of the American Statistical Association, 84*(406), 502–516. doi:10.2307/2289936

Hastie, T., & Tibshirani, R. (1990). Generalized Additive Models. Boca Raton, FL: Chapman & Hall.

Hastie, T., Tibshirani, R., & Friedman, J. (2001). The Elements of Statistical Learning. Berlin: Springer.

Hasuike, T., & Ishii, H. (2005). Portfolio selection problem with two possibilities of the expected return. In *Proceedings of Nonlinear Analysis and Convex Analysis Okinawa*, (pp.115-25). Yokohama: Yokohama Publishers.

Hasuike, T., & Ishii, H. (2008). Portfolio selection problems considering fuzzy returns of future scenarios. *International Journal of Innovative Computing . Information and Control, 4*(10), 2493–2506.

Haux, R., & Eckert, U. (1985). Nondeterministic dependencies in relations: an extension of the concept of functional dependency. *Information Systems, 10*(2), 139–148. doi:10.1016/0306-4379(85)90032-8

Hayashi, Y., Buckley, J. J., & Czogula, E. (1993). Fuzzy neural network. *International Journal of Intelligent Systems, 8*, 527–537. doi:10.1002/int.4550080405

Haykin, S. (1999). *Neural Networks – A Comprehensive Foundation*. Upper Saddle River, NJ: Prentice-Hall.

He, Q., Dovrolis, C., & Ammar, M. (2007). On the predictability of large transfer TCP throughput. *Computer Networks, 51*(14), 3959–3977. doi:10.1016/j.comnet.2007.04.013

Hearst, M. A. (1999). Untangling text data mining. In *Proceedings of the 37th Annual Meeting of the Association for Computational Linguistics*, (pp. 3–10).

Heckerman, D., Chickering, D. M., Meek, C., Rounthwaite, R., & Kadie, C. (2000). Dependency Networks for Inference, Collaborative Filtering, and Data Visualization. *Journal of Machine Learning Research*, *1*(9), 49–75.

Hellerstein, J., Zhang, F., & Shahabuddin, P. (2001). A statistical approach to predictive detection. *Computer Networks*, *35*(1), 77–95. doi:10.1016/S1389-1286(00)00151-1

Herrera, F., Lozano, M., & Verdegay, J. (1995). Tuning fuzzy logic controllers by genetic algorithms. *International Journal of Approximate Reasoning*, *12*(3-4), 299–315. doi:10.1016/0888-613X(94)00033-Y

Hersh, W. (2004). Report on TREC 2003 genomics track first-year results and future plans. *SIGIR Forum*, *38*(1), 69–72. doi:10.1145/986278.986292

Hersh, W., & Bhuptiraju, R. T. (2003). TREC 2003 genomics track overview. In *Proceedings of the 12th Text REtrieval Conference* (TREC).

Hersh, W., Bhuptiraju, R. T., Ross, L., Cohen, A. M., & Kraemer, D. F. (2004). TREC 2004 genomics track overview. In *Proceedings of the 13th Text REtrieval Conference* (TREC).

Hersh, W., Cohen, A. M., Roberts, P., & Rekapalli, H. K. (2006). TREC 2006 genomics track overview. In *Proceedings of the 15th Text REtrieval Conference* (TREC).

Hersh, W., Cohen, A. M., Ruslen, L., & Roberts, P. (2007). TREC 2007 genomics track overview. In *Proceedings of the 16th Text REtrieval Conference* (TREC).

Hersh, W., Cohen, A. M., Yang, J., Bhuptiraju, R. T., Roberts, P., & Hearst, M. (2005). TREC 2005 genomics track overview. In *Proceedings of the 14th Text REtrieval Conference* (TREC).

Hicks, G. V., Jeyasurya, B., & Snow, W. F. (1997). *An investigation of automatic generation control for an isolated power system, IEEE PES Winter Meeting*, (pp. 31-34).

Hirose, Y., Yamashita, K., & Hijiya, S. (1991). Back-propagation algorithm which varies the number of hidden units. *Neural Networks*, *4*, 61–66. doi:10.1016/0893-6080(91)90032-Z

Hiyama, T. (1989). Application of rule based stabilizer controller to electric power system. *IEEE Proceedings . Part C*, *136*(3), 175–181.

Ho, S.-Y., Liu, C.-C., & Liu, S. (2002). Design of an optimal nearest neighbor classifier using an intelligent genetic algorithm. *Pattern Recognition Letters*, *23*(13), 1495–1503. doi:10.1016/S0167-8655(02)00109-5

Hobbs, J. R. (2002). Information extraction from biomedical text. *Journal of Biomedical Informatics*, *35*(4), 260–264. doi:10.1016/S1532-0464(03)00015-7

Holland, J. H. (1975). *Adaptation in Nature and Artificial Systems*. Ann Arbor, MI: University of Michigan Press.

Homaifar, A., & McCormick, E. (1995). Simultaneous design of membership functions and rule sets for fuzzy controllers using genetic algorithms. *IEEE transactions on Fuzzy Systems*, *3*(2), 129–139. doi:10.1109/91.388168

Hong, T. P., & Tseng, S. S. (1991). Trade-off between time complexity and accuracy of perceptron learning. In *IEEE Region 10 International Conference on EC3 - Energy, Computer, Communication and Control Systems: Vol. 2* (pp. 157-161), New Delhi.

Hong, T. P., Chen, C. H., Lee, Y. C., & Wu, Y. L. (2008). Genetic-Fuzzy Data Mining with Divide-and-Conquer Strategy. *IEEE Transactions on Evolutionary Computation*, *12*(2), 252–265. doi:10.1109/TEVC.2007.900992

Hopfield, J. J. (1982). Neural networks and physical systems with emergent collective computational abilities. *Proceedings of the National Academy of Sciences of the United States of America*, *79*, 2554–2558. doi:10.1073/pnas.79.8.2554

Hopfield, J. J., & Tank, D. W. (1985). 'Neural' computation of decisions in optimization problems. *Biological Cybernetics*, *52*, 141–152.

Hornik, K., Stinchcommbe, M., & White, H. (1989). Multilayer feedforward networks are universal approximators. *Neural Networks, 2,* 359–366. doi:10.1016/0893-6080(89)90020-8

Houze, R., Smull, B., & Dodge, P. (1990). Mesoscale organization of springtime rainstorms in Oklahoma. *Monthly Weather Review, 18*(3), 613–654. doi:10.1175/1520-0493(1990)118<0613:MOOSRI>2.0.CO;2

Hsia, T. C. (1979). *System Identification: Least Square Method.* Davis, CA: University of California, at Davis.

Hsu, C.-N., Chang, Y.-M., Kuo, C.-J., Lin, Y.-S., Huang, H.-S., & Chung, I.-F. (2008). Integrating high dimensional bi-directional parsing models for gene mention tagging. *Bioinformatics (Oxford, England), 24*(13), i286–i294. doi:10.1093/bioinformatics/btn183

Hsu, C.-W., & Lin, C.-J. (2002). A comparison of methods for multiclass support vector machines. *IEEE Transactions on Neural Networks, 13*(2), 415–425. doi:10.1109/72.991427

Hsu, Y. T., Cheng, C. S., & Wu, C. C. (1997). Reliability Evaluations based on Grey Models. *The Journal of Grey System, 9*(1), 25–39.

Hsu, Y. T., Lin, C. B., Mar, S. C., & Su, S. F. (1998). High noise vehicle plate recognition using grey system. *The Journal of Grey System, 10*(3), 193–208.

Huang, F. Y. (2008). A particle swarm optimized fuzzy neural network for credit risk evaluation. In *Proc. of the Second International Conference on Genetic and Evolutionary Computing,* (pp. 153-157).

Huang, M. J., Tsou, Y. L., & Lee, S. C. (2006). Integrating fuzzy data mining and fuzzy artificial neural networks for discovering implicit knowledge. *Knowledge-Based Systems, 19*(6), 396–403. doi:10.1016/j.knosys.2006.04.003

Huang, T., & Subhlok, J. (2005). Fast pattern-based throughput prediction for TCP bulk transfers. In *Proceedings of the Fifth IEEE International Symposium on Cluster Computing and the Grid* (pp. 410-417).

Huang, X. (2007). Two new models for portfolio selection with stochastic returns taking fuzzy information. *European Journal of Operational Research, 180,* 396–405. doi:10.1016/j.ejor.2006.04.010

Huber, P. J. (1981). *Robust Statistics.* New York: John Wiley.

Huber, P. J. (1985). Projection pursuit. *Annals of Statistics, 13*(2), 435–475. doi:10.1214/aos/1176349519

Huffman, D. A. (1952). A method for the construction of minimum redundancy codes. *Proc. IRE, 40*(10), 1098-1101.

Huhtala, Y., Karkkainen, J., Porkka, P., & Toivonen, H. (1998). Efficient discovery of functional and approximate dependencies using partitions. In *Proceedings of IEEE International Conference on Data Engineering* (pp. 392-410).

Hunt, J. E., & Cooke, D. E. (1996). Learning using an artificial immune system. *Journal of Network and Computer Applications, 19,* 189–212. doi:10.1006/jnca.1996.0014

Hunter, R., & Elliot, G. (1994). *Wind-Diesel Systems: A Guide to the Technology and Its Implementation.* Cambridge, UK: Cambridge University Press.

Hwang, C. L. (1999). Neural-network-based variable structure control of electrohydraulic servosystems subject to huge uncertainties without persistent excitation. *IEEE/ASME Transactions on Mechatronics, 4*(1), 50–59. doi:10.1109/3516.752084

IBM. (2008). *DB2 Intelligent Miner.* Retrieved October 10, 2008, from http://www.ibm.com

Ichimura, T., Oeda, S., Suka, M., & Yoshida, K. (2005). A learning method of immune multi-agent neural networks. *Neural Computing & Applications, 14,* 132–148. doi:10.1007/s00521-004-0448-6

Ilic, M., Galiana, F., & Fink, L. (Eds.). (1998). *Power Systems Restructuring: Engineering & Economics.* Boston: Kluwer Academic Publishers.

Indyk, P., Koudas, N., & Muthukrishnan, S. (2000). Identifying representative trends in massive time series data sets using sketches. In *Proceedings of the 26th International Conference on Very Large Data Bases*, (pp. 363–372).

Inuiguchi, M., & Ramik, J. (2000). Possibilisitc linear programming: A brief review of fuzzy mathematical programming and a comparison with stochastic programming in portfolio selection problem. *Fuzzy Sets and Systems, 111*, 3–28. doi:10.1016/S0165-0114(98)00449-7

Inuiguchi, M., & Tanino, T. (2000). Portfolio selection under independent possibilistic information. *Fuzzy Sets and Systems, 115*, 83–92. doi:10.1016/S0165-0114(99)00026-3

Inuiguchi, M., Ichihasi, H., & Tanaka, H. (1990). Fuzzy programming: A survey of recent development. In R. Slowinski & J. Teghem (Ed.), *Stochastic versus Fuzzy Approaches to Multiobjective Mathematical Programming under Uncertainty*, (pp. 45-68).

Ishibuchi, H., & Tanaka, H. (1991). Regression analysis with interval model by neural networks. In Proc. Int. Joint Conf. Neural Networks (IJCNN'91-Singapore), (pp. 1594–1599).

Ishibuchi, H., Fujioka, R., & Tanaka, H. (1992). An architecture of neural networks for input vectors of fuzzy numbers. In *Proc. IEEE Int. Conf. Fuzzy Syst. (FUZZ-IEEE'92)*, (pp. 1293–1300).

Ishibuchi, H., Kwon, K., & Tanaka, H. (1995). A learning algorithm of fuzzy neural networks with triangular fuzzy weights. *Fuzzy Sets and Systems, 71*, 277–293. doi:10.1016/0165-0114(94)00281-B

Ishibuchi, H., Nakashima, T., & Murata, T. (1999). Performance evaluation of fuzzy classifier systems for multidimensional pattern classification problems. *IEEE Transactions on Systems, Man, and Cybernetics . Part B, 29*(5), 601–618.

Ishibuchi, H., Nozaki, K., Yamamoto, N., & Tanaka, H. (1995). Selecting fuzzy if-then rules for classification problems using genetic algorithms. *IEEE transactions on Fuzzy Systems, 3*(3), 260–270. doi:10.1109/91.413232

Ishibuchi, H., Okada, H., Fujioka, R., & Tanaka, H. (1993). Neural networks that learn from fuzzy If-Then rules. *IEEE transactions on Fuzzy Systems, FS-1*(2), 85–89. doi:10.1109/91.227388

Ishibuchi, H., Yamamoto, T., & Nakashima, T. (2005). Hybridization of fuzzy gbml approaches for pattern classification problems. *IEEE Transactions on Systems, Man, and Cybernetics . Part B, 35*(2), 359–365.

Jacobs, R. A. (1988). Increased rates of convergence through learning rate adaptation. *Neural Networks, 1*, 295–307. doi:10.1016/0893-6080(88)90003-2

Jain, M., & Dovrolis, C. (2002). Pathload: A measurement tool for end-to-end available bandwidth. In *Proceedings of Passive and Active Measurements (PAM) Workshop* (pp. 14-25).

Jaleeli, N., VanSlyck, L. S., Ewart, D. N., Fink, L. H., & Hoffmann, A. G. (1992). Understanding Automatic Generation Control. *IEEE Transactions on Power Systems, 7*(3), 1106–1122. doi:10.1109/59.207324

Janeway, C. A., Jr., & Travers, P. (1997). *Immunobiology: The Immune System in Health and Disease*. São Paulo, Brazil: Artes Medicas.

Jang, J. S. R. (1993). Adaptive-network-based fuzzy inference systems. *IEEE Transactions on Systems, Man, and Cybernetics, 23*(3), 665–685. doi:10.1109/21.256541

Jang, J. S. R., Sun, C. T., & Mizutani, E. (1997). *Neuro-Fuzzy and Soft Computing: A Computational Approach to Learning and Machine Intelligence*. Upper Saddle River, NJ: Prentice-Hall.

Jang, J.-S. R. (1991). Fuzzy modeling using generalized neural networks and Kalman Filter algorithm. In *Proceedings of Ninth National Conference on Artificial Intelligence*, (pp. 762–767).

Jang, J.-S. R. (1992). Fuzzy controller design without domain expert. *IEEE International Conference on Fuzzy Systems*, (pp. 289–296).

Jang, J.-S. R., & Sun, C.-T. (1993). Functional equivalence between radial basic function networks and fuzzy inference systems. *IEEE Transactions on Neural Networks, 4*(1), 156–159. doi:10.1109/72.182710

Jang, J.-S. R., & Sun, C.-T. (1995). Neuro-fuzzy modeling and control. *Proceedings of the IEEE, 83*(3), 378–406. doi:10.1109/5.364486

Jang, J.-S. R., Sun, C.-T., & Mizutani, E. (1997). *Neuro-Fuzzy and Soft Computing.* Upper Saddle River, NJ: Prentice Hall.

Jenkins, W. M. (2006). Neural network weight training by mutation. *Computers & Structures, 84,* 2107–2112. doi:10.1016/j.compstruc.2006.08.066

Jerne, N. K. (1974). Towards a network theory of the immune system. *Annals of Immunology, 125C,* 373–389.

Jia, J. C., & Chong, C. C. (1995). Distributed normalisation input coding to speed up training process of BP-neural network classifier. *Electronics Letters, 31*(15), 1267–1269. doi:10.1049/el:19950854

Jiang, J., & Fan, M. (2002). Convective clouds and mesoscale convective systems over the Tibetan Plateau in summer. *Atmosphere Science, 26*(1), 262–269.

Jin, X., & Reynolds, R. G. (1999). Using knowledge-based evolutionary computation to solve nonlinear constraint optimization problems: a cultural algorithm approach. In *Proc. of IEEE Congress on Evolutionary Computation,* Washington, DC, (pp. 1672-1678).

Jin, Y. (2000). Fuzzy modeling of high-dimensional systems: complexity reduction and interpretability improvement. *IEEE transactions on Fuzzy Systems, 8*(2), 212–221. doi:10.1109/91.842154

Jones, K. S. (1971). *Automatic Keyword Classification for Information Retrieval.* North Haven, CT: Archon Books.

Jordan, F., Kutter, M., & Ebrahimi, T. (1997). Proposal of a watermarking technique for hiding/retrieving data in compressed and decompressed video. *ISO/IEC Doc. JTC1/SC29/WG11 MPEG97/ M2281.*

Jorion, P. (1992). Portfolio optimization in practice, *Financial Analysis Journal,* (Jan.-Feb.), 68-74.

Juang, C. F. (2004). A hybrid of genetic algorithm and particle swarm optimization for recurrent network design. *IEEE Trans. on Sys., Man and Cybern. Part B, 34*(2), 997–1006.

Juang, C. F., & Lin, C. T. (1998). An on-line self-constructing neural fuzzy inference network and its applications. *IEEE transactions on Fuzzy Systems, 6*(1), 12–32. doi:10.1109/91.660805

Juang, C., Lin, J., & Lin, C.-T. (2000). Genetic reinforcement learning through symbiotic evolution for fuzzy controller design. *IEEE Transactions on Systems, Man, and Cybernetics. Part B, Cybernetics, 30*(2), 290–302. doi:10.1109/3477.836377

Juang, C.-F. (2002). A TSK-type recurrent fuzzy network for dynamic systems processing by neural network and genetic algorithms. *IEEE transactions on Fuzzy Systems, 10*(2), 155–170. doi:10.1109/91.995118

Kanade, P. M., & Hall, L. O. (2003). Fuzzy ants as a clustering concept. In *Proceedings of the 22nd International Conference of the North American Fuzzy Information Processing Society,* (pp. 227-232).

Karaboga, D., & Basturk, B. (2008). On the performance of artificial bee colony (ABC) algorithm. *Applied Soft Computing, 8*(1), 687–697. doi:10.1016/j.asoc.2007.05.007

Karnavas, Y. L. (2005). AGC tuning of an interconnected power system after deregulation using genetic algorithms. In *Proc. of the 5th WSEAS International Conference on Power Systems and Electromagnetic Compatibility (PSE '05),* Corfu Island, Greece, (pp. 218-223).

Karnavas, Y. L. (2005). On the optimal control of interconnected electric power systems in a re-structured environment using genetic algorithms. *WSEAS Transactions on Systems Journal, 4*(8), 1248–1258.

Karnavas, Y. L. (2006). On the optimal load frequency control of an interconnected hydro electric power system using genetic algorithms. In *Proceedings of the 6th IASTED International Conference on European Power and Energy Systems (EuroPES'06),* Rhodes, Hellas, Cd Ref. No 521-099.

Karnavas, Y. L., & Pantos, S. (2008). Performance Evaluation of Neural Networks for μC Based Excitation Control of a Synchronous Generator. In *Proc. of the 18th International Conference on Electrical Machines (ICEM'08),* Vilamura, Portugal, CD Paper ID 885.

Karnavas, Y. L., & Papadopoulos, D. P. (2000). Excitation control of a power generating system based on fuzzy logic and neural networks. *European Transactions on Electrical Power, 10*(4), 233–241.

Karnavas, Y. L., & Papadopoulos, D. P. (2002). A genetic-fuzzy system for the excitation control of a synchronous machine. In *Proc. of the 15th International Conference in Electrical Machines (ICEM'02)*, Bruges, Belgium, CD paper Ref. No. 204.

Karnavas, Y. L., & Papadopoulos, D. P. (2002). AGC for autonomous power station using combined intelligent techniques. *Int. J. Electric Power Systems Research, 62*, 225–239. doi:10.1016/S0378-7796(02)00082-2

Karnavas, Y. L., & Papadopoulos, D. P. (2003). Power generation control of a wind-diesel system using fuzzy logic and pi-sigma networks. In *Proc. of the 12th International. Conference on Intelligent Systems Application to Power Systems (ISAP '03)*, Lemnos Island, Greece, Cd ref. no. 078.

Karnavas, Y. L., Polyzos, N. P., & Papadopoulos, D. P. (2006). On the design of a remote intelligent excitation controller for a synchronous generator. In *Proc. of the 17th International Conference in Electrical Machines (ICEM'06)*, Chania, Crete, Hellas, CD paper Ref. No. 063.

Karr, C. L. (1991). Design of an adaptive fuzzy logic controller using a genetic algorithm. In *Proc. of 4th Conf. Genetic Algorithms*, (pp. 450-457).

Kasabov, N. K., & Song, Q. (2002). DENFIS: dynamic evolving neural-fuzzy inference system and its application for time-series prediction. *IEEE transactions on Fuzzy Systems, 10*(2), 144–154. doi:10.1109/91.995117

Kassabalidis, I.N., El-Sharkawi, M.A., Marks, R.J. II, Moulin, L.S., & Alves, A.P. da Silva. (2002). Dynamic Security Border Identification Using Enhanced Particle Swarm Optimization. *IEEE Transactions on Power Systems, 17*(3). doi:10.1109/TPWRS.2002.800942

Katagiri, H., Ishii, H., & Sakawa, M. (2004). On fuzzy random linear knapsack problems. *Central European Journal of Operations Research, 12*(1), 59–70.

Katagiri, H., Sakawa, H., Kato, K., & Nishizaki, H. (2008). Interactive multiobjective fuzzy random linear programming: Maximization of possibility and probability. *European Journal of Operational Research, 188*, 530–539. doi:10.1016/j.ejor.2007.02.050

Katagiri, H., Sakawa, M., & Ishii, H. (2005). A study on fuzzy random portfolio selection problems using possibility and necessity measures. *Scientiae Mathematicae Japonocae, 65*(2), 361–369.

Katagiri, H., Sakawa, M., Kato, K., & Nishizaki, I. (2004). A fuzzy random multiobjective 0-1 programming based on the expectation optimization model using possibility and necessity measure. *Mathematical and Computer Modelling, 40*, 411–421. doi:10.1016/j.mcm.2003.08.007

Kaufmann, A. (1975). *Introduction to the Theory of Fuzzy Subsets*, (Vol.I). New York: Academic Press.

Keijzer, M., Guervós, J. J. M., Romero, G., & Schoenauer, M. (2002). Evolving objects: A general purpose evolutionary computation library. In Selected papers from the 5th european conference on artificial evolution (pp. 231-244). London, UK: Springer-Verlag.

Kennedy, J., & Eberhart, R. (1995). Particle swarm optimization. In *Proc. of IEEE Int. Conf. on Neural Networks*, (pp. 1942-1948).

Keogh, E. J. (2008). Indexing and mining time series data, *Encyclopedia of GIS 2008*, (pp. 493-497).

Keogh, E. J., & Pazzani, M. (1998). An enhanced representation of time series which allows fast and accurate classification, clustering and relevance feedback. In *Proceedings of the 4th International Conference on Knowledge Discovery and Data Mining*, (pp. 239–241).

Keogh, E. J., Lonardi, S., & Chiu, W. (2002). Finding surprising patterns in a time series database in linear time and space. In *The 8th ACM SIGKDD International Conference on Knowledge Discovery and Data Mining*, (pp. 550–556).

Keynote. (2008). *Web benchmarking service*. Retrieved October 10, 2008, from http://www.keynote.com

Khilwani, N., Prakash, A., Shankar, R., & Tiwari, M. (2008). Fast clonal algorithm. *Engineering Applications of Artificial Intelligence*, *21*, 106–128. doi:10.1016/j.engappai.2007.01.004

Kil, H., Oh, S.-C., & Lee, D. (2006). On the Topological Landscape of Web Services Matchmaking. In *VLDB Int'l Workshop on Semantic Matchmaking and Resource Retrieval (SMR06)*, Seoul, Korea.

Kim, H., Tan, J. K., Ishikawa, S., Khalid, M., Otsuka, Y., Shimizu, H., & Shinomiya, T. (2006). Automatic judgment of spinal deformity based on back propagation on neural network. *International Journal of Innovative computing . Information and Control*, *2*(6), 1271–1279.

Kincaid, D., & Cheney, W. (2003). Numerical analysis: mathematics of scientific computing. Beijing: China Machine Press.

King, A. J. (1993). Asymmetric risk measure and trcking models for portfolio optimization under uncertainty. *Annals of Operations Research*, *45*, 205–220. doi:10.1007/BF02282047

Kirkpatrick, A., Gelatt, A. K. C. J., & Vechi, M. P. (1983). Optimization by simulated annealing. *Science*, *220*, 671–680. doi:10.1126/science.220.4598.671

Klir, G. J., & Yuan, B. (1995). *Fuzzy Sets and Fuzzy Logic: Theory and Applications*. Upper Saddle River, NJ: Prentice Hall.

Kohavi, R. (1995). A study of cross-validation and bootstrap for accuracy estimation and model selection. In *Proceedings of 14th International Joint Conference on Artificial Intelligence*, (Vol. 2, pp. 1137–1143). Montreal, Canada: Morgan Kaufmann.

Kohavi, R., & John, G. H. (1997). Wrappers for feature subset selection. *Artificial Intelligence*, *97*(1-2), 273–324. doi:10.1016/S0004-3702(97)00043-X

Kohonen, T. (1990). The self-organizing map. *Proceedings of the IEEE*, *78*(9), 1464–1480. doi:10.1109/5.58325

Kokash, N. (2006). A comparison of web service interface similarity measures. *STAIRS 2006 - Proceedings of the Third Starting AI Researchers' Symposium: Frontiers in Artificial Intelligence and Applications* (pp.220–231), Riva del Garda, Trentino, Italy. Amsterdam: IOS Press.

Kong, X., Lui, Y., Lui, H., & Yang, D. (2004). Object watermarks for digital images and video. *Image and Vision Computing*, *22*(8), 583–594. doi:10.1016/j.imavis.2003.09.016

Konno, H. (1990). Piecewise linear risk functions and portfolio optimization. *Journal of the Operations Research Society of Japan*, *33*, 139–159.

Konno, H., Shirakawa, H., & Yamazaki, H. (1993). A mean-absolute deviation-skewness portfolio optimization model. *Annals of Operations Research*, *45*, 205–220. doi:10.1007/BF02282050

Kosko, B. (1992). *Fuzzy systems as universal approximators*. Paper presented at Proc. IEEE Int'l Conf. On Fuzzy Systems.

Kosko, B. (1992). *Neural Networks and Fuzzy Systems, A Dynamical Systems Approach to Machine Intelligence*. Upper Saddle River, NJ: Prentice-Hall.

Kosko, B. (1992). *Neural Networks and Fuzzy Systems*. Upper Saddle River, NJ: Prentice Hall.

Krasnogor, N., & Smith, J. (2000, July 8-12). Mafra: A java memetic algorithms framework. In *Proceedings of the 2000 international genetic and evolutionary computation conference (GECCO 2000)* (pp. 125–131), Las Vegas, NV.

Krishnamurthy, B., & Willinger, W. (2008). What are our standards for validation of measurement-based networking research? *ACM SIGMETRICS Performance Evaluation Review*, *36*(2), 64–69. doi:10.1145/1453175.1453186

Kukolj, D., & Levi, E. (2004). Identification of complex systems based on neural and Takagi-Sugeno fuzzy model. *IEEE Transactions on Systems, Man, and Cybernetics. Part B, Cybernetics*, *34*(1), 272–282. doi:10.1109/TSMCB.2003.811119

Kumar, A., Malik, O. P., & Hope, G. S. (1985). Variable-structure-system control applied to AGC of an interconnected power system. *IEE Proceedings Part C, 132*(1), 23–29.

Kumar, J., Ng, K. H., & Sheble, G. (1997). AGC simulator for price-based operation-part I: A model. *IEEE Transactions on Power Systems, 12*(2), 527–532. doi:10.1109/59.589593

Kung, C. H., Jeng, J. H., Lee, Y. C., Hsiao, H. H., & Cheng, W. S. (2003). Video watermarking using motion vector. In *Proceedings of the 16th IPPR Conference on Computer Vision Graphics and Image,* (pp. 547-551).

Kuo, R. J. (2001). A sales forecasting system based on fuzzy neural network with initial weights generated by genetic algorithm. *European Journal of Operational Research, 129,* 496–517. doi:10.1016/S0377-2217(99)00463-4

Kuo, R. J., & Cohen, P. H. (1998). Manufacturing process control through integration of neural networks and fuzzy model. *Fuzzy Sets and Systems, 98*(1), 15–31. doi:10.1016/S0165-0114(96)00382-X

Kuo, R. J., & Xue, K. C. (1999). Fuzzy neural networks with application to sales forecasting. *Fuzzy Sets and Systems, 108,* 123–143. doi:10.1016/S0165-0114(97)00326-6

Kuo, R. J., Chen, C. H., & Hwang, Y. C. (2001). An intelligent stock trading decision support system through integration of genetic algorithm based fuzzy neural network and artificial neural network. *Fuzzy Sets and Systems, 118,* 21–45. doi:10.1016/S0165-0114(98)00399-6

Kuo, R. J., Wu, P., & Wang, C. P. (2000). Fuzzy neural networks for learning fuzzy If-Then rules. *Applied Artificial Intelligence, 14,* 539–563. doi:10.1080/08839510050076963

Kuo, R. J., Wu, P., & Wang, C. P. (2002). An intelligent sales forecasting system through integration of artificial neural networks and fuzzy neural networks with fuzzy weight elimination. *Neural Networks, 15,* 909–925. doi:10.1016/S0893-6080(02)00064-3

Kurd, Z., & Kelly, T. (2007). Using fuzzy self-organising maps for safety critical systems. *Reliability Engineering & System Safety, 92*(11), 1563–1583. doi:10.1016/j.ress.2006.10.005

Kurd, Z., Kelly, T., & Austin, J. (2006). Developing artificial neural networks for safety critical systems. *Neural Computing & Applications, 16*(1), 11–19. doi:10.1007/s00521-006-0039-9

Laarhoven, P. J. M. V., & Aarts, E. H. L. (1987). Simulated Annealing: Theory and Applications. Dordrecht, The Netherlands: Kluwer Academic Publishers.

Lai, X., Li, G., Gan, Y., & Ye, Z. (2006). An Association Rule Mining Approach for Satellite Cloud Images and Rainfall. In Y. Zhuang (Ed.), *Lecture Notes on Computer Sciences* (Vol. 4261, pp. 658–666), Heidlberg, Germany: Springer-Verlag.

Lance, S. (2000). *Use of Data Mining on Satellite Data Bases for Knowledge Extraction.* Paper presented at the 13th International Florida Artificial Intelligence Research Society Conference, Orlando, Florida.

Lange, D. B., & Oshima, M. (1998). *Programming mobile agents in java—with the java aglet API.* Reading, MA: Addison-Wesley.

Lange, D. B., & Oshima, M. (1999). Seven good reasons for mobile agents: Dispatch your agents, shut off your machine. *Communications of the ACM, 42*(3), 88–89. doi:10.1145/295685.298136

Lanzi, P. (1997). Fast feature selection with genetic algorithms: A filter approach. In *Conference on ieee international evolutionary computation,* (pp. 537-540), Indianapolis, IN.

Lee, C. C. (1990). Fuzzy logic in control systems – Parts I and II. *IEEE Transactions on Systems, Man, and Cybernetics, 20*(2), 404–435. doi:10.1109/21.52551

Lee, C. H., & Teng, C. C. (2000). Identification and control of dynamic systems using recurrent fuzzy neural network. *IEEE transactions on Fuzzy Systems, 8*(4), 349–366. doi:10.1109/91.868943

Lee, C., & Maxwell, T. (1987). Learning, invariance, and generalization in high-order neural network. *Applied Optics, 26*(23).

Lee, J. D., & Huang, Z. X. (1999). Automatic color image segmentation with fuzzy C-means algorithm. In *Proceedings of the National Computation Symposium,* (pp. 99-106).

Lee, J.-S. (2004). Hybrid genetic algorithms for feature selection. *IEEE Transactions on Pattern Analysis and Machine Intelligence, 26*(11), 1424–1437. doi:10.1109/TPAMI.2004.105

Lee, S.-J., & Ouyang, C.-S. (2003). A neuro-fuzzy system modeling with self-constructing rule generation and hybrid SVD-based learning. *IEEE transactions on Fuzzy Systems, 11*(3), 341–353. doi:10.1109/TFUZZ.2003.812693

Lee, Y.-S., & Yen, S.-J. (2008). Incremental and interactive mining of web traversal patterns. *Information Sciences, 178*, 287–306. doi:10.1016/j.ins.2007.08.020

Leithead, W. E., & Zhang, Y. (2007). O(N^2)-operation approximation of covariance matrix inverse in Gaussian process regression based on quasi-Newton BFGS methods. *Communications in Statistics Simulation and Computation, 36*(2), 367–380. doi:10.1080/03610910601161298

Lesk, M. (1986). Automatic sense disambifuation using machine readable dictionaries: how to tell a pine cone from an ice cream cone. In *Proceedings of the 1986 SIGDOC Conference* (pp. 24–26).

Leung, S. H., Luk, A., & Ng, S. C. (1994). Fast convergent genetic-type search for multi-layered network. *IEICE Trans. Fundamentals . E (Norwalk, Conn.), 77-A*(9), 1484–1492.

Leveson, N. G., & Turner, C. S. (1993). An investigation of the Therac-25 accidents. *Computer, 26*(7), 18–41. doi:10.1109/MC.1993.274940

Li, C., & Lee, C. Y. (2003). Self-organizing neuro-fuzzy system for control of unknown plants. *IEEE transactions on Fuzzy Systems, 11*(1), 135–150. doi:10.1109/TFUZZ.2002.805898

Li, D., Harms, S., Goddard, S., Waltman, W., & Deogun, J. (2003). *Time-series data mining in a geospatial decision support system*. Paper presented at the 7th annual national conference on Digital government research, Boston.

Li, M., Mehrotra, K., Mohan, C., & Ranka, S. (1990). Sunspot numbers forecasting using neural networks. *Proc. of IEEE Int. Conf. Intelligent Control, 1*, 524-529.

Li, S. H. (2002). *Neural Network Based Fusion of Global and Local Information in Predicting Time Series*. Master Thesis, Dept. of Electrical Eng., NTUST, Taiwan, R.O.C.

Li, S. T., Chen, C. C., & Li, J. W. (2007). A multi-objective particle swarm optimization algorithm for rule discovery. *3rd International Conference on Intelligent Information Hiding and Multimedia Signal Processing,* (pp. 597-600).

Li, X., Plale, B., Vijayakumar, N., Ramachandran, R., Graves, S., & Conover, H. (2008). Real-time storm detection and weather forecast activation through data mining and events processing. *Earth Science Informatics, 1*(2), 49–57. doi:10.1007/s12145-008-0010-7

Li, X., Song, L., & Garcia-Diaz, A. (2008). Adaptive web presence and evolution through web log analysis. *International Journal of Electronic Customer Relationship Management, 2*(3), 195–214. doi:10.1504/IJECRM.2008.020408

Liang, X., & Tso, S. K. (2002). An improved upper bound on step-size parameters of discrete-time recurrent neural networks for linear inequality and equation system. *IEEE Transactions on Circuits and Systems I, 49*(5), 695–698. doi:10.1109/TCSI.2002.1001961

Liano, K. (1996). Robust error measure for supervised neural network learning with outliers. *IEEE Transactions on Neural Networks, 7*(1), 246–250. doi:10.1109/72.478411

Lin, C. (2007). Numerical analysis. Beijing: Science Press.

Lin, C. B. (2000). *Grey System Applications and Its Utilization in Prediction*. Ph.D Dissertation, Department of Electrical Engineering, National Taiwan University of Science and Technology, Taiwan, R.O.C.

Lin, C. B., Su, S. F., & Hsu, Y. T. (2001). High precision forecast using grey models. *International Journal of Systems Science, 32*(5), 609–619. doi:10.1080/002077201300155791

Lin, C. H., & Wang, J. F. (2006). Solving the Mobile Agent Planning Problem with a Hopfield-Tank Neural Network. In *Proceedings of the 2006 IAENG International Workshop on Artificial Intelligence and Applications,* (pp. 104–114).

Lin, C. H., & Wang, J. F. (2007). The Hopfield-Tank Neural Network Applied to the Mobile Agent Planning Problem. *Applied Intelligence, 27*(2), 167–187. doi:10.1007/s10489-006-0021-3

Lin, C. J. & Chin, C. C. (2004). Prediction and identification using wavelet-based recurrent fuzzy neural networks. *IEEE Trans. Systems, Man, and Cybernetics (Part:B), 34*(5), 2144-2154.

Lin, C. J. (2008). An efficient immune-based symbiotic particle swarm optimization learning algorithm for TSK-type neuro-fuzzy networks design. *Fuzzy Sets and Systems, 159*(21), 2890–2909. doi:10.1016/j.fss.2008.01.020

Lin, C. T. (1995). A neural fuzzy control system with structure and parameter learning. *Fuzzy Sets and Systems, 70*, 183–212. doi:10.1016/0165-0114(94)00216-T

Lin, C. T., & Lee, C. S. G. (1991). Neural network-based fuzzy logic control and decision system. *IEEE Transactions on Computers, C-40*(12), 1320–1336. doi:10.1109/12.106218

Lin, C. T., & Lee, C. S. G. (1996). *Neural Fuzzy Systems: A Neural Fuzzy Synergism to Intelligent Systems.* Upper Saddle River, NJ: Prentice Hall.

Lin, C. T., & Lu, Y. C. (1995). A neural fuzzy system with linguistic teaching signals. *IEEE transactions on Fuzzy Systems, 3*(2), 169–189. doi:10.1109/91.388172

Lin, C. Y., & Hajela, P. (1992). Genetic algorithms in optimization problems with discrete and integer design variables. *Engineering Optimization, 19*(4), 309–327. doi:10.1080/03052159208941234

Lin, D.-T., & Liao, G.-J. (2008a). Embedding watermarks in compressed video using fuzzy c-means clustering. In *Proceedings of the IEEE International Conference of System Man and Cybernetics,* (pp. 1053-1058).

Lin, D.-T., & Liao, G.-J. (2008b). Swarm Intelligence Based Fuzzy C-Means Clustering for Motion Vector Selection in Video Watermarking. *International Journal of Fuzzy Systems, 10*(3), 185–194.

Lin, F. J., Hwang, W. J., & Wai, R. J. (1999). Supervisory fuzzy neural network control system for tracking periodic inputs. *IEEE transactions on Fuzzy Systems, 7*(1), 41–52. doi:10.1109/91.746304

Lin, Y., Cunningham, G. A. III, & Coggeshall, S. V. (1997). Using fuzzy partitions to create fuzzy systems from input-output data and set the initial weights in a fuzzy neural network. *IEEE transactions on Fuzzy Systems, 5*(4), 614–621. doi:10.1109/91.649913

Lindsay, R. K., & Gordon, M. D. (1999). Literature-based discovery by lexical statistics. *Journal of the American Society for Information Science American Society for Information Science, 50*(7), 574–587. doi:10.1002/(SICI)1097-4571(1999)50:7<574::AID-ASI3>3.0.CO;2-Q

Ling, S. H., Leung, F. H. F., Lam, H. K., Lee, Y. S., & Tam, P. K. S. (2003). A novel genetic-algorithm-based neural network for short-term load forecasting. *IEEE Trans. Industrial electornic., 50*(4), 793-799.

Lintner, B. J. (1965). Valuation of risky assets and the selection of risky investments in stock portfolios and capital budgets. *The Review of Economics and Statistics, 47*, 13–37. doi:10.2307/1924119

Lippmann, R. P. (1987). An introduction to computing with neural nets. *IEEE ASSP Magazine*, 4–22. doi:10.1109/MASSP.1987.1165576

Lippmann, R. P. (1989). Pattern classification using neural networks. *IEEE Communications Magazine*, 47–64. doi:10.1109/35.41401

Lisboa, P. J. G. (2001). Industrial use of safety-related artificial neural networks. Contract research report 327/2001, Liverpool John Moores University.

Liu, B. (2002). *Theory and Practice of Uncertain Programming*. Heidelberg, Germany: Physica Verlag.

Liu, B. (2004). *Uncertainty Theory*. Heidelberg, Germany: Physica Verlag.

Liu, H., & Setiono, R. (1998). Feature transformation and multivariate decision tree induction. In *Proceedings of the 1st International Conference on Discovery Science* (pp. 279 – 290), Fukuoka, Japan.

Liu, H., Hussain, F., Tan, C., & Dash, M. (2002). Discretization: An enabling technique. *Data Mining and Knowledge Discovery*, 6(4), 393–423. doi:10.1023/A:1016304305535

Liu, Z., & George, R. (2005). Mining Weather Data Using Fuzzy Cluster Analysis. In E. P. Frederick, B. R. Vincent, & A. C. Maria (Eds.), *Fuzzy Modeling with Spatial Information for Geographic Problems*, (pp. 105-119). Heidelberg, Germany: Springer-Verlag.

Llorà, X. (2006). E2k: evolution to knowledge. *SIGEVOlution*, 1(3), 10–17. doi:10.1145/1181964.1181966

Llorà, X., & Garrell, J. M. (2003). Prototype induction and attribute selection via evolutionary algorithms. *Intelligent Data Analysis*, 7(3), 193–208.

Looney, C. G. (1996). Advances in feedforward neural networks: demystifying knowledge acquiring black boxes. *IEEE Transactions on Knowledge and Data Engineering*, 8(2), 211–226. doi:10.1109/69.494162

Lu, C.-S., & Liao, H.-Y. M. (2001). Multipurpose watermarking for image authentication and protection. *IEEE Transactions on Image Processing*, 10(10), 1579–1592. doi:10.1109/83.951542

Lu, Z. M., Li, Y. N., Wang, H. X., & Sun, S. H. (2006). Multipurpose video watermarking algorithm in the hybrid compressed domain. *IEEE Proceedings of Information Security*, 153(4), 173–182. doi:10.1049/ip-ifs:20060034

Luenberger, D. G. (1997). *Investment Science*. Oxford, UK: Oxford Univ. Press.

Luhandjura, M. K. (1987). Linear programming with a possibilistic objective function. *European Journal of Operational Research*, 13, 137–145.

Luke, S., Panait, L., Balan, G., Paus, S., Skolicki, Z., Bassett, J., et al. (2007). *Ecj: A java based evolutionary computation research system*. Retrieved from http://cs.gmu.edu/ eclab/projects/ecj

MacKay, D. J. C. (1992). *Bayesian methods for adaptive models*. PhD thesis, California Institute of Technology, Pasadena, CA.

MacKay, D. J. C. (1998). Introduction to Gaussian processes. In C. M. Bishop (Ed.), Neural Networks and Machine Learning (pp. 133–166). Amsterdam: Kluwer Academic Press.

MacQueen, J. B. (1967). Some methods for classification and analysis of multivariate observations. In *Proceedings of the Fifth Symposium on Math, Statistics, and Probability* (pp. 281-297).

Maeda, T. (2001). Fuzzy linear programming problems as bi-criteria optimization problems. *Applied Mathematics and Computation*, 120, 109–121. doi:10.1016/S0096-3003(99)00237-4

Maglott, D., Ostell, J., Pruitt, K. D., & Tatusova, T. (2005). Entrez Gene: gene-centered information at NCBI. *Nucleic Acids Research*, 33, D54–D58. doi:10.1093/nar/gki031

Mahanta, A. K., Mazarbhuiya, A. F., & Baruah, H. K. (2008). Finding calendar-based periodic patterns. *Pattern Recognition Letters*, 29, 1274–1284. doi:10.1016/j.patrec.2008.01.020

MAL. *The Mobile Agent List* (n.d.). Retrieved from http://reinsburgstrasse.dyndns.org/mal/preview/preview.html

Mamdani, E. H., & Assilian, S. (1975). An experiment in linguistic synthesis with a fuzzy logic controller. *International Journal of Man-Machine Studies*, 7(1), 1–13. doi:10.1016/S0020-7373(75)80002-2

Mandischer, M. (2002). A comparison of evolution strategies and backpropagation for neural network training. *Neurocomputing, 42,* 87–117. doi:10.1016/S0925-2312(01)00596-3

Mañdziuk, J. (1996). Solving the Traveling Salesperson Problem with Hopfield—type neural network. *Demonstration Math, 29*(1), 219–231.

Manganaris, S., Christensen, M., Zerkle, D., & Hermiz, K. (2000). A data mining analysis of RTID alarms. *Computer Networks, 34,* 571–577. doi:10.1016/S1389-1286(00)00138-9

Mannila, H., & Toivonen, H. (1997). Levelwise search and borders of theories in knowledge discovery. *Data Mining and Knowledge Discovery, 1*(3), 241–258. doi:10.1023/A:1009796218281

Manning, C. D., & Schütze, H. (1999). *Foundations of statistical natural language processing.* Cambridge, MA: MIT Press.

Mansour, M., Mekhamer, S. F., & El-Sherif El-Kharbawe, N. (2007). A modified particle swarm optimizer for the coordination of directional overcurrent relays. *IEEE Transactions on Power Delivery, 22*(3), 1400–1410. doi:10.1109/TPWRD.2007.899259

Markowitz, H. (1959). *Portfolio Selection.* New York: Wiley.

Marks, R. (1993). Computational versus Artificial. *IEEE Transactions on Neural Networks, 4*(5), 737–739.

Martin., et al. (2004). *OWL-S: Semantic Markup for Web Services.* Retrieved from http://www.w3.org/Submission/OWL-S/

Martínez, A., Martínez, F., Hervás, C., & García, N. (2006). Evolutionary product unit based neural networks for regression. *Neural Networks, 19*(4), 477–486. doi:10.1016/j.neunet.2005.11.001

Martínez, F., Hervás, C., Gutiérrez, P., & Martínez, A. (in press). Evolutionary product-unit neural networks classifiers. *Neurocomputing.*

Mathews, J. H., & Fink, K. D. (2004). Numerical methods using MATLAB. Beijing: Pearson Education Inc.

McClelland, J., & Rumelhart, D. (1987). *Parallel Distributed Processing* (Vol.1). Cambridge, MA: The MIT Press.

Mellia, M., Stoica, I., & Zhang, H. (2002). TCP model for short lived flows. *IEEE Communications Letters, 6*(2), 85–87. doi:10.1109/4234.984705

Mendel, J. M. (2007). Type-2 fuzzy sets and systems: an overview. *IEEE Computational Intelligence Magazine, 2*(1), 20–29. doi:10.1109/MCI.2007.380672

Mendes, R., Cortez, P., Rocha, M., & Neves, J. (2002). Particle swarms for feedforward neural network training. In *The 2002 International Joint Conference on Neural Networks,* (pp. 1895-1899).

Metzler, D., & Croft, W. (2004). Combining the language model and inference network approaches to retrieval. *Information Processing & Management. Special Issue on Bayesian Networks and Information Retrieval, 40*(5), 735–750.

Meyer, M., & Hufschlag, K. (2006). A generic approach to an object-oriented learning classifier system library. *Journal of Artificial Societies and Social Simulation, 9*(3). Available from http://jasss.soc.surrey.ac.uk/9/3/9.html

Meyer, S. C. (2005). Analysis of base flow trends in urban streams, northeastern Illinois, USA. *Hydrogeology Journal, 13,* 871–885. doi:10.1007/s10040-004-0383-8

Michalewicz, Z. (1994). Genetic Algorithms +Data Structures=Evolution Programs, New York: Springer-Verlag.

Microsoft. (2008). *Microsoft SQL Server.* Retrieved October 10, 2008, from http://www.microsoft.com

Mierswa, I., Wurst, M., Klinkenberg, R., Scholz, M., & Euler, T. (2006). Yale: rapid prototyping for complex data mining tasks. In *Kdd '06: Proceedings of the 12th acm sigkdd international conference on knowledge discovery and data mining,* (pp. 935–940). New York: ACM.

Miller, D. A., Arguello, R., & Greenwood, G. W. (2004). Evolving artificial neural network structures: experimental results for biologically-inspired adaptive mutations. In *Congress on Evolutionary Computation: Vol. 2* (pp. 2114-2119), Portland, OR.

Miller, G., Todd, P., & Hedge, S. (1989). Designing neural networks using genetic algorithms. In *Proceedings of the 3rd international conference on genetic algorithm and their applications* (p. 379-384). Arlington, VA: George Mason University.

Minsky, M., & Papert, S. (1969). *Perceptrons.* Cambridge, MA: The MIT Press.

Mitra, N. (Ed.). (2003). *SOAP Version 1.2 Part 0: Primer.* W3C Recommendation, 2003. Retrieved from http://www.w3.org/TR/2003/REC-soap12-part0-20030624/

Mitra, S., Pal, S. K., & Mitra, P. (2002). Data mining in soft computing framework: a survey. *IEEE Transactions on Neural Networks, 13*(1), 3–14. doi:10.1109/72.977258

Mizutani, E., & Jang, J.-S. R. (1995). Coactive neural fuzzy modeling. In *Proc. of Int. Conf. Neural Networks*, (pp. 760-765).

Mo, G., & Liu, K. (2003). Function approximation methods. Beijing: Science Press.

Moizumi, K. (1998). *Mobile agent planning problems.* PhD thesis, Thayer School of Engineering, Dartmouth College.

MOME. (2008). *MOnitoring and MEsurement project.* Retrieved October 10, 2008, from http://www.ist-mome.org

Monmarche, N., Slimane, M., & Venturini, G. (1999). AntClass: discovery of clusters in numeric data by an hybridization of an ant colony with the K-means algorithm. *Internal Report*, 1-21.

Morgan, A. A., Wellner, B., Colombe, J. B., Arens, R., Colosimo, M. E., & Hirschman, L. (2007). Evaluating the automatic mapping of human gene and protein mentions to unique identifiers. In . *Proceedings of the Pacific Symposium on Biocomputing, 12*, 281–291. doi:10.1142/9789812772435_0027

Morik, K., & Scholz, M. (2004). The miningmart approach to knowledge discovery in databases. In N. Zhong & J. Liu (Eds.), Intelligent technologies for information analysis (pp. 47-65). Berlin: Springer-Verlag.

Mossin, J. (1966). Equilibrium in capital asset markets. *Econometrica, 34*(4), 768–783. doi:10.2307/1910098

Mucientes, M., Moreno, L., Bugarín, A., & Barro, S. (2006). Evolutionary learning of a fuzzy controller for wall-following behavior in mobile robotics. *Soft Computing, 10*(10), 881–889. doi:10.1007/s00500-005-0014-x

Murtagh, F. (1985). *Multidimensional Clustering Algorithms.* Heidelberg, Germany: Physica-Verlag.

Murtagh, F. (2002). *Multivariate data analysis software and resources.* Retrieved from http://astro.u-strasbg.fr/~fmurtagh/mda-sw

Nahmias, S. (1978). Fuzzy variables. *Fuzzy Sets and Systems, 1*, 97–110. doi:10.1016/0165-0114(78)90011-8

Nakayama, S., Horikawa, S., Furuhashi, T., & Uchikawa, Y. (1992). Knowledge acquisition of strategy and tactics using fuzzy neural networks. In *Proc. IJCNN'92*, (pp. II-751–756).

Nambiar, U., & Kambhampati, S. (2004). Mining approximate functional dependencies and concept similarities to answer imprecise queries. In *Seventh International Workshop on the Web and Databases,* (pp. 73-78).

Nanda, J., & Kaul, B. (1978). Automatic generation control of an interconnected power system . *IEE Proceedings, 125*(5), 385–390.

Nanni, L. (2006). Mechine learning algorithms for T-cell epitopes prediction. *Neurocomputing, 69*, 866–868. doi:10.1016/j.neucom.2005.08.005

Narendra, K. S., & Parthasarathy, K. (1990). Identification and control of dynamical systems using neural networks. *IEEE Transactions on Neural Networks, 1*(1), 4–27. doi:10.1109/72.80202

Nasrouri, O., Rojas, C., & Cardona, C. (2006). A framework for mining evolving trends in Web data streams using dynamic learning and retrospective validation. *Computer Networks, 50*, 1488–1512. doi:10.1016/j.comnet.2005.10.021

Nauch, D., Klawonn, F., & Kruse, R. (1997). *Foundations of Neuro-Fuzzy Systems*. New York: John Wiley & Sons.

Nauck, D. (2003). Fuzzy data analysis with NEFCLASS. *International Journal of Approximate Reasoning, 32*(2-3), 103–130. doi:10.1016/S0888-613X(02)00079-8

Ng, S. C., Leung, S. H., & Luk, A. (1996). Evolution of connection weights combined with local search for multi-layered neural networks. *IEEE,* 726-731.

NGG. (2008). *Future for European Grids: Grids and Service Oriented Knowledge Utilities - Vision and Research Directions 2010 and Beyond.* The 3rd report of the NGG Expert Group. Retrieved October 10, 2008, from ftp://ftp.cordis.europa.eu

Nobile, E., Bose, A., & Tomsovic, K. (2000). Bilateral market for load following ancillary services. In *Proc. Power Energy Systems Summer Power Meeting*, Seattle, WA.

Nomura, H., Hayashi, I., & Wakami, N. (1992). A learning method of fuzzy inference rules by descent method. In *Proceedings of IEEE International Conference on Fuzzy Systems*, San Diego, CA, (pp. 203–210).

Nusser, S., Otte, C., & Hauptmann, W. (2007). Learning binary classifiers for applications in safety-related domains. In R. Mikut & M. Reischl (Eds.), *Proceedings of 17th Workshop Computational Intelligence* (pp. 139–151). Dortmund, Germany: Universitätsverlag Karlsruhe.

Nusser, S., Otte, C., & Hauptmann, W. (2008a). Interpretable ensembles of local models for safety-related applications. In M. Verleysen (Ed.), *Proceedings of 16th European Symposium on Artificial Neural Networks* (pp. 301–306). Brugge, Belgium: D-facto publications.

Nusser, S., Otte, C., & Hauptmann, W. (2008b). Multi-class modeling with ensembles of local models for imbalanced misclassification costs. In O. Okun & G. Valentini (Eds.), *Proceedings of 2nd Workshop on Supervised and Unsupervised Ensemble Methods and Their Applications (at ECAI 2008)* (pp. 36–40). Patras, Greece.

O'Donovan, C., Martin, M. J., Gattiker, A., Gasteiger, E., Bairoch, A., & Apweiler, R. (2002). High-quality protein knowledge resource: SWISS-PROT and TrEMBL. *Briefings in Bioinformatics, 3*(3), 275–284. doi:10.1093/bib/3.3.275

Ogata, K. (1970). *Modern control engineering*. Upper Saddle River, NJ: Prentice Hall.

Otero, J., & Sánchez, L. (2006). Induction of descriptive fuzzy classifiers with the logitboost algorithm. *Soft Computing, 10*(9), 825–835. doi:10.1007/s00500-005-0011-0

Ouyang, C.-S., Lee, W.-J., & Lee, S.-J. (2005). A TSK-type neurofuzzy network approach to system modeling problems. *IEEE Transactions on Systems, Man, and Cybernetics. Part B, Cybernetics, 35*(4), 751–767. doi:10.1109/TSMCB.2005.846000

Ozgur, A., Vu, T., Erkan, G., & Radev, D. R. (2008). Identifying gene-disease associations using centrality on a literature mined gene-interaction network. *Bioinformatics (Oxford, England), 24*(13), i277–i285. doi:10.1093/bioinformatics/btn182

Pabarskaite, Z., & Raudys, A. (2007). A process of knowledge discovery from Web log data: Systematization and critical review. *Journal of Intelligent Information Systems, 28*, 79–104. doi:10.1007/s10844-006-0004-1

Pai, G. A. V. (2004). A fast converging evolutionary neural network for the prediction of uplift capacity of suction caissons. In *IEEE Conference on Cybernetics and Intelligent Systems* (pp. 654-659), Singapore.

Pal, S. K., & Wang, P. P. (1996). Genetic algorithms for pattern recognition. Boca Raton, FL: CRC Press, Inc.

Pan, C. T., & Lian, C. M. (2005). An adaptive controller for power system load frequency control. *IEEE Transactions on Power Systems, 4*(1), 122–128. doi:10.1109/59.32469

Pan, J. S., Huang, H. C., Jain, L. C., & Fang, W. C. (2007). *Intelligent Multimedia Data Hiding: New Directions*. Berlin: Springer.

Pan, J. S., McInnes, F. R., & Jack, M. A. (1996). Application of parallel genetic algorithm and property of multiple global optima to VQ codevector Index assignment. *Electronics Letters*, *32*(4), 296–297. doi:10.1049/el:19960194

Pandey, S. K., & Mishra, R. B. (2006). Intelligent Web mining model to enhance knowledge discovery on the Web. In *Proceedings of the 7th Parallel and Distributed Computing, Applications and Technologies International Conference*, (pp. 339-343).

Panella, M., & Gallo, A. S. (2005). An input-output clustering approach to the synthesis of ANFIS networks. *IEEE transactions on Fuzzy Systems*, *13*(1), 69–81. doi:10.1109/TFUZZ.2004.839659

Pao, Y. H. (1989). *Adaptive Pattern Recognition and Neural Networks*. Reading, MA: Addison-Wesley.

Papadopoulos, D.P., & Amanatidis. (1984). Frequency deviations of steam turbogenerator in isolated operation with representative governor and turbine models. In *Proc. of the International Conference on Electrical Machines (ICEM'84)*, Lausanne, Switzerland, Part 3, (pp. 979-982).

Park, D., Kandel, A., & Langholz, G. (1994). Genetic-based new fuzzy reasoning models with application to fuzzy control. *IEEE Transactions on Systems, Man, and Cybernetics*, *24*(1), 39–47. doi:10.1109/21.259684

Parpinelli, R., Lopes, H., & Freitas, A. (2002a). An ant colony algorithm for classification rule discovery. In H. Abbass, R. Sarker, & C. Newton (Eds.), Data mining: a heuristic approach (pp. 191-208). Hershey, PA: Idea Group Publishing.

Parpinelli, R., Lopes, H., & Freitas, A. (2002b). Data mining with an ant colony optimization algorithm. *IEEE Transactions on Evolutionary Computation*, *6*(4), 321–332. doi:10.1109/TEVC.2002.802452

Passino, K. M. (2002). Biomimicry of Bacterial Foraging for Distributed Optimization and Control. *Control Systems Magazine, IEEE*, 52-67.

Patra, J. C., Pal, R. N., Chatterji, B. N., & Panda, G. (1999). Identification of nonlinear dynamic systems using functional link artificial neural networks. *IEEE Trans. on Syst., Man, and Cybern. - . Part B*, *29*, 254–262.

Paxson, V. (2004). Strategies for sound Internet measurement. In *Proceedings of ACM SIGCOMM Internet Measurement Conference*, (pp. 263 – 271).

Pechenizkiy, M., Tsymbal, A., & Puuronen, S. (2005). Knowledge management challenges in knowledge discovery systems. In *Proceedings of the 16th International Workshop on Database and Expert Systems Applications*, (pp. 433-437).

Pedersen, T. (2005). Word sense disambiguation. *The AAAI 2005 Tutorial Advances in Word Sense Disambiguation*, Pittsburgh, PA., July 9, 2005. Retrieved from http://www.d.umn.edu/~tpederse/WSDTutorial.html

Pedersen, T., Patwardhan, S., & Michelizzi, J. (2004). WordNet:Similarity -- Measuring the relatedness of concepts. *Demonstrations of the Human Language Technology Conference of the North American Chapter of the Association for Computational Linguistics* (pp. 267–270), Boston, Mass., 2–7 May 2004. Available online at http://www.cs.utah.edu/~sidd/papers/PedersenPM04b.pdf

Pednault, E. (2006). Transform regression and the Kolmogorov superposition theorem, In *Proceedings of the Sixth SIAM International Conference on Data Mining*, (pp. 35-46).

Pedrycz, W. (1986). Structured fuzzy models. *Cybernetics and Systems*, *16*, 103–117. doi:10.1080/01969728508927757

Pedrycz, W., & Card, H. C. (1992). Linguistic interpretation of self-organizing maps. In *Proceedings of IEEE International Conference on Fuzzy Systems*, San Diego, CA, (pp. 371–378).

Pelanda, R., & Torres, R. M. (2006). Receptor editing for better or for worse. *Current Opinion in Immunology*, *18*, 184–190. doi:10.1016/j.coi.2006.01.005

Perelson, A. S. (1993). Immune network theory. *Immunological Reviews*, *110*, 5–36. doi:10.1111/j.1600-065X.1989.tb00025.x

Perez-Iratxeta, C., Bork, P., & Andrade, M. A. (2002). Association of genes to genetically inherited diseases using data mining. *Nature Genetics, 31*(3), 316–319.

Perez-Iratxeta, C., Wjst, M., Bork, P., & Andrade, M. (2005). G2D: a tool for mining genes associated with disease. *BMC Genetics, 6*(1), 45. doi:10.1186/1471-2156-6-45

Philip, N. S., & Joseph, K. B. (2003). A Neural Network Tool for Analyzing Trends in Rainfall. *Computers & Geosciences, 29*(2), 215–223. doi:10.1016/S0098-3004(02)00117-6

Plonski, M. P., Gustafson, G., Shaw, B., Thomas, B., & Wonsick, M. (2000). *High resolution cloud analysis and forecast system.* Paper presented at the 10th Conference on Satellite Meteorology and Oceanography, Long Beach, CA.

Poole, D. I., Goebel, R. G., & Mackworth, A. (1998). Computational Intelligence: A Logical Approach. *Computational Intelligence and Knowledge,* (pp. 1-22). New York: Oxford University Press.

Porter, M. F. (1980). An algorithm for suffix stripping. *Program, 14*(3), 130–137.

Prasad, R. S., Murray, M., Dovrolis, C., & Claffy, K. C. (2003). Bandwidth estimation: Metrics, measurement techniques, and tools. *IEEE Network, 17*(6), 27–35. doi:10.1109/MNET.2003.1248658

Pruitt, K. D., & Maglott, D. R. (2001). RefSeq and LocusLink: NCBI gene-centered resources. *Nucleic Acids Research, 29*(1), 137–140. doi:10.1093/nar/29.1.137

Pu, C., Sun, Z., & Zhao, S. (2006). Comparison of BP algorithms in MATLAB NN toolbox. *Computer Simulation, 23*(5), 142–144.

Pullum, L. L., Taylor, B. J., & Darrah, M. A. (2007). Guidance for the Verification and Validation of Neural Networks. New York: Wiley.

Punch, B., & Zongker, D. (1998). *Lib-gp 1.1 beta.* Retrieved from http://garage.cse.msu.edu/software/lil-gp

Puuronen, S., Pechenizkiy, M., & Tsymbal, A. (2006). Data mining researcher, who is your customer? Some issues inspired by the information systems field. In *Proceedings of the 17th International Conference on Databases and Expert Systems Applications,* (pp. 579-583).

Pyle, D. (1999). *Data Preparation for Data Mining.* San Francisco, CA: Morgan Kaufmann Publishers, Inc.

Python. (2009). *Python Programming Language - Official Website.* Retrieved February 10, 2009, from http://www.python.org/

Quinlan, J. R. (1993). *C4.5: Programs for Machine Learning.* San Francisco, CA: Morgan Kaufman Publishers Inc.

Quinlan, J. R., & Rivest, R. L. (1989). Inferring decision trees using the minimum description length principle. *Information and Computation, 80*(3), 227–248. doi:10.1016/0890-5401(89)90010-2

Rahman, R. M., Alhajj, R., & Barker, K. (2008). Replica selection strategies in data grid. *Journal of Parallel and Distributed Computing.* doi:.doi:10.1016/j.jpdc.2008.07.013

Raju, K. V. S. V. N., & Majumdar, A. K. (1988). Fuzzy functional dependencies and losses join decomposition of fuzzy relational database systems. *ACM Transactions on Database Systems, 13*(2), 129–166. doi:10.1145/42338.42344

Rakotomalala, R. (2005). Tanagra: un logiciel gratuit pour l'enseignement et la recherche. In proccedings of the 5th journées d'extraction et gestion des connaissances (Vol. 2, p. 697-702), Paris, France.

Rasmussen, C. E., & Williams, C. K. I. (2006). Gaussian Processes for Machine Learning. Cambridge, MA: MIT Press.

Rasmussen, D., & Yager, R. R. (1999). Finding fuzzy and gradual functional dependencies with SummarySQL. *Fuzzy Sets and Systems, 106,* 131–142. doi:10.1016/S0165-0114(97)00268-6

Reeve, L. H., Han, H., & Brooks, A. D. (2007). The use of domain-specific concepts in biomedical text summarization. *Information Processing & Management, 43*(6), 1765–1776. doi:10.1016/j.ipm.2007.01.026

Rehm, F., Klawonn, F., & Kruse, R. (2006). POLARMAP - a new approach to visualisation of high dimensional data. In *Proceedings of the 10th International Conference on Information Visualisation (IV'06)* (pp. 731–740), London, UK.

Reid, M. B. (1989). Rapid Training of Higher-order Neural Networks for Invariant Pattern Recognition. In [], Washington D.C.]. *Proceedings of IJCNN, 1*, 689–692.

Ren, Y., & Zhou, L. (2008). PMSM control research based on particle swarm optimization BP neural network. In *International Conference on Cyberworlds* (pp. 832-836), Hangzhou.

Resnik, P. (1999). Semantic similarity in a taxonomy: an information based measure and its application to problems of ambiguity in natural language. *Journal of Artificial Intelligence Research, 11*, 95–130.

Reynolds, R. G. (1994). An introduction to cultural algorithms. In A.V. Sebald & L.J. Fogel (eds.), *Proc. of the 3rd Annual Conference on Evolutionary Programming,* (pp. 131- 139). River Edge, NJ: World Scientific.

RFC1945. (2008). Hypertext Transfer Protocol - HTTP/1.0. *Request for Comments: 1945.* Retrieved October 10, 2008, from http://www.ietf.org/rfc/rfc1945.txt

RFC4656. (2008). A One-way Active Measurement Protocol (OWAMP). *Request for Comments: 1945.* Retrieved October 10, 2008, from http://www.ietf.org/rfc/rfc4656.txt

Rivera, A. J., Rojas, I., Ortega, J., & del Jesús, M. J. (2007). A new hybrid methodology for cooperative-coevolutionary optimization of radial basis function networks. *Soft Computing, 11*(7), 655–668. doi:10.1007/s00500-006-0128-9

Rockafellar, R. T., & Uryasev, S. (2000). Optimization of conditional value-at-risk. *Journal of Risk, 2*(3), 1–21.

Rodríguez, J. J., Kuncheva, L. I., & Alonso, C. J. (2006). Rotation forest: A new classifier ensemble method. *IEEE Transactions on Pattern Analysis and Machine Intelligence, 28*(10), 1619–1630. doi:10.1109/TPAMI.2006.211

Romero, C., Ventura, S., & de Bra, P. (2004). Knowledge discovery with genetic programming for providing feedback to courseware author. user modeling and user-adapted interaction. *The Journal of Personalization Research, 14*(5), 425–465.

Rooij, A. V., Lakhmi, J., & Ray, J. (1998). Neural Networks Training Using Genetic Algorithms. Singapore: World Scientific.

Roubos, H., & Setnes, M. (2001). Compact and transparent fuzzy models and classifiers through iterative complexity reduction . *IEEE transactions on Fuzzy Systems, 9*(4), 516–524. doi:10.1109/91.940965

Roughan, M. (2006). A comparison of Poisson and uniform sampling for active measurements. *IEEE Journal on Selected Areas in Communications, 24*(12), 2299–2312. doi:10.1109/JSAC.2006.884028

Rovithakis, G. A., Gaganis, V. I., Perrakis, S. E., & Christodoulou, M. A. (1999). Real-time control of manufacturing cells using dynamic neural networks. *Automatica, 35*(1), 139–149. doi:10.1016/S0005-1098(98)00139-3

Rumehart, D. E., & McClelland, J. L. & the PDP Research Group (1986). *Parallel Distributed Processing (Two Volumes).* Cambridge, MA: MIT Press Brandford Books.

Rumelhart, D. E. (1994). The Basic Ideas in Neural Networks. *Communications of the ACM, 37*(3), 87–92. doi:10.1145/175247.175256

Rumelhart, D. E., Hinton, G. E., & Williams, R. J. (1986). *Learning internal* representations by error propagation. *Parallel Distribution Processing, 1*, 318–362.

Rummler, A. (2007). *Evolvica: a java framework for evolutionary algorithms.* Retrieved from http://www.evolvica.org.

Rushing, J., Ramachandran, R., Nair, U., Graves, S., Welch, R., & Lin, H. (2005). Adam: a data mining toolkit for scientists and engineers. *Computers & Geosciences, 31*(5), 607–618. doi:10.1016/j.cageo.2004.11.009

Sachar, H. (1986). *Theoretical aspects of design of and retrieval from similarity-based relational database systems.* Ph.D. Dissertation, University of Texas at Arlington, TX.

Sadeghi, B. H. M. (2000). A BP-neural network predictor model for plastic injection molding process. *Journal of Materials Processing Technology, 103,* 411–416. doi:10.1016/S0924-0136(00)00498-2

Saha, S., Murthy, C. A., & Pal, S. K. (2008). Classification of web services using tensor space model and rough ensemble classifier. *ISMIS 2008,* ([). Berlin: Springer-Verlag.]. *LNAI, 4994,* 508–513.

Saharia, A. N., & Barron, T. M. (1995). Approximate dependencies in database systems. *Decision Support Systems, 13,* 335–347. doi:10.1016/0167-9236(93)E0049-J

Sakawa, M. (1993). *Fuzzy sets and Interactive Multiobjective Optimization.* New York: Plenum.

Saleem, S. M. (2001). *Knowledge-based solution to dynamic optimization problems using cultural algorithms.* PhD thesis, Wayne State University, Detroit, Michigan.

Salton, G., Wong, A., & Yang, C. S. (1975). A vector space model for automatic indexing. *Communications of the ACM, 18*(11), 613–620. doi:10.1145/361219.361220

Sánchez, L., & Couso, I. (2000). Fuzzy random variables-based modeling with ga-p algorithms. In B. Bouchon, R. Yager, & L. Zadeh (Eds.), Information, uncertainty and fusion (pp. 245-256). Norwell, MA: Kluwer Academic Publishers.

Sanchez, L., & Couso, I. (2007). Advocating the use of imprecisely observed data in genetic fuzzy systems. *IEEE transactions on Fuzzy Systems, 15*(4), 551–562. doi:10.1109/TFUZZ.2007.895942

Sánchez, L., & Otero, J. (2007). Boosting fuzzy rules in classification problems under single-winner inference. *International Journal of Intelligent Systems, 22*(9), 1021–1034. doi:10.1002/int.20236

Sánchez, L., Couso, I., & Corrales, J. A. (2001). Combining gp operators with sa search to evolve fuzzy rule based classifiers. *Information Sciences, 136*(1-4), 175–191. doi:10.1016/S0020-0255(01)00146-3

Schlang, M., Feldkeller, B., Lang, B., Poppe, T., & Runkler, T. (1999). Neural computation in steel industry. In Proceedings European Control Conf. ECC 99. Berlin: VDI-Verlag.

Schroder, C. (2008). *Measure Network Performance: iperf and ntop.* Retrieved October 10, 2008, from http://www.enterprisenetworkingplanet.com/netos/article.php/3658331

Schuemie, M. J., Weeber, M., Schijvenaars, B. J. A., van Mulligen, E. M., van der Eijk, C. C., & Jelier, R. (2004). Distribution of information in biomedical abstracts and full-text publications. *Bioinformatics (Oxford, England), 20*(16), 2597–2604. doi:10.1093/bioinformatics/bth291

Schultz, W. C., & Rideout, V. C. (1961). Control system performance measures: past, present and future. *I.R.E. Transactions on Automatic Control, AC-6*(22), 22–35.

Schwartz, A. S., & Hearst, M. A. (2003). A simple algorithm for identifying abbreviation definitions in biomedical text. In . *Proceedings of the Pacific Symposium on Biocomputing, 8,* 451–462.

Scoot, G. W., Wilreker, V. F., & Shaltens, R. K. (1984). Wind turbine generator interaction with diesel generators on an isolated power system. *IEEE Trans. on PAS, 103*(5), 933.

Sehgal, A., & Srinivasan, P. (2006). Retrieval with gene queries. *BMC Bioinformatics, 7*(1), 220. doi:10.1186/1471-2105-7-220

Seki, K., & Mostafa, J. (2005a). An application of text categorization methods to gene ontology annotation. In *Proceedings of the 28th annual international ACM SIGIR conference on research and development in information retrieval,* (pp. 138–145).

Seki, K., & Mostafa, J. (2005b). A hybrid approach to protein name identification in biomedical texts. *Information Processing & Management, 41*(4), 723–743. doi:10.1016/j.ipm.2004.02.006

Shapiro, A. F. (2002). The merging of neural networks, fuzzy logic, and genetic algorithms. *Insurance, Mathematics & Economics, 31*, 115–131. doi:10.1016/S0167-6687(02)00124-5

Sharpe, W. F. (1964). Capital asset prices: A theory of market equivalent under conditions of risk. *The Journal of Finance, 19*(3), 425–442. doi:10.2307/2977928

Shatkay, H. (2005). Hairpins in bookstacks: Information retrieval from biomedical text. *Briefings in Bioinformatics, 6*(3), 222–238. doi:10.1093/bib/6.3.222

Sheble, G. B. (1999). *Computational Auction Mechanisms for Restructured Power Industry Operation.* Boston: Kluwer Academic Publishers.

Shenoi, S., Melton, A., & Fan, L. T. (1990). An equivalence class model of fuzzy relational databases. *Fuzzy Sets and Systems, 38*, 153–170. doi:10.1016/0165-0114(90)90147-X

Shi, Y., & Eberhart, R. (1999). Empirical study of particle swarm optimization. *Congress on Evolutionary Computation*, 1945-1950.

Shi, Y., Eberhart, R., & Chen, Y. (1999). Implementation of evolutionary fuzzy systems. *IEEE transactions on Fuzzy Systems, 7*(2), 109–119. doi:10.1109/91.755393

Shin, Y., & Ghosh, J. (1991). The pi-sigma network: An efficient higher-order neural network for pattern classification and function approximation. In [), Seattle.]. *Proceedings of IJCNN, 1*, 13–18.

Sikdar, B., Kalyanaraman, S., & Vastola, K. S. (2001). An integrated model for the latency and steady-state throughput of TCP connections. *Performance Evaluation, 46*(2-3), 139–154. doi:10.1016/S0166-5316(01)00048-7

Silva, A., Neves, A., & Costa, E. (2002). An empirical comparison of particle swarm and predator prey optimization. *Lecture Notes in Computer Science, 2464*, 103–110. doi:10.1007/3-540-45750-X_13

Simon, H. D. (1984). Analysis of the symmetric Lanczos algorithm with reorthogonalization methods. *Linear Algebra and Its Applications, 61*, 101–131. doi:10.1016/0024-3795(84)90025-9

Simpson, T., & Dao, T. (2005). *WordNet-based semantic similarity measurement.* Retrieved from http://www.codeproject.com/cs/library/semanticsimilaritywordnet.asp van Rijsbergen, C.J., Robertson, S.E., & Porter, M.F. (1980). *New Models in Probabilistic Information Retrieval.* British Library Research and Development Report, no. 5587. London: British Library.

Sinha, A. P., & Zhao, H. (2008). Incorporating domain knowledge into data mining classifiers: An application in indirect lending. *Decision Support Systems.* Available online 16 July 2008, doi:10.1016/j.dss.2008.06.013

SLAC. (2008). *Stanford Linear Accelerator Center. Network Monitoring Tools.* Retrieved October 10, 2008, from http://www.slac.stanford.edu/xorg/nmtf/nmtf-tools.html

Smalz, R., & Conrad, M. (1994). Combining evolution with credit apportionment: A new learning algorithm for neural nets. *Neural Networks, 7*(2), 341–351. doi:10.1016/0893-6080(94)90028-0

Song, Y., Chen, Z., & Yuan, Z. (2007). New chaotic PSO-based neural network predictive control for nonlinear process. *IEEE Transactions on Neural Networks, 18*(2), 595–601. doi:10.1109/TNN.2006.890809

Sonnenburg, S., Braun, M. L., Ong, C. S., Bengio, S., Bottou, L., & Holmes, G. (2007). The need for open source software in machine learning. *Journal of Machine Learning Research, 8*, 2443–2466.

Sousa, T., Silva, A., & Neves, A. (2004). Particle swarm based data mining algorithms for classification tasks. *Parallel Computing, 30*(5-6), 767–783. doi:10.1016/j.parco.2003.12.015

Souto, M.J., Balseiro, C.F., Pérez-Muñuzuri, V., Xue, M., & Brewster, K. (2003). Impact of cloud analysis on numerical weather prediction in the galician region of spain. *Journal of Applied Meteorology, 42*(3), 129–140. doi:10.1175/1520-0450(2003)042<0129:IOCAON>2.0.CO;2

Sparck Jones, K. (1972). Statistical interpretation of term specificity and its application in retrieval. *The Journal of Documentation, 28*(1), 11–20. doi:10.1108/eb026526

Spiliopoulou, M. (2000). Web usage mining for Web site evaluation. *Communications of the ACM, 43*(8), 127–134. doi:10.1145/345124.345167

Spiliopoulou, M., & Pohle, C. (2001). Data mining for measuring and improving the success of Web sites. *Data Mining and Knowledge Discovery, 5*, 85–114. doi:10.1023/A:1009800113571

Srinivasan, P. (2004). Text mining: generating hypotheses from Medline. *Journal of the American Society for Information Science and Technology, 55*(5), 396–413. doi:10.1002/asi.10389

Srivastava, J., Cooley, R., Deshpande M. & Tan, P. N. (2000). Web usage mining: Discovery and applications of usage patterns from Web data. *2000 SIGKDD Explorations, 1*(2), 12-23.

Stankovic, A. M., Tadmor, G., & Sakharak, J. A. (1998). On robust control analysis and design for load frequency regulation. *IEEE Transactions on Power Systems, 13*(2), 449–455. doi:10.1109/59.667367

Stejic, Z., Takama, Y., & Hirota, K. (2007). Variants of evolutionary learning for interactive image retrieval. *Soft Computing, 11*(7), 669–678. doi:10.1007/s00500-006-0129-8

Steriti, R. J., & Fiddy, M. A. (1993). Regularized image reconstruction using SVD and a neural network method for matrix inversion. *IEEE Transactions on Signal Processing, 41*(10), 3074–3077. doi:10.1109/78.277813

Sterne, J. (2002). *Web Metrics: Proven Methods for Measuring Web Site Success.* Toronto: John Wiley &Son, Inc. Canada.

Stoica, E., & Hearst, M. (2006). Predicting gene functions from text using a cross-species approach. In . *Proceedings of the Pacific Symposium on Biocomputing, 11*, 88–99.

Storn, R. (1999). System design by constraint adaptation and differential evolution. *IEEE Transactions on Evolutionary Computation, 3*(1), 22–34. doi:10.1109/4235.752918

Su, G., & Deng, F. (2003). On the improving backpropagation algorithms of the neural networks based on MATLAB language: a review. *Bulletin of Science and Technology, 19*(2), 130–135.

Su, S. F., & Chen, K. Y. (2004). Fuzzy hierarchical data fusion networks for terrain location identification problems. *IEEE Transactions on Systems, Man, and Cybernetics. Part B, Cybernetics, 34*(1), 731–739. doi:10.1109/TSMCB.2003.811292

Su, S. F., & Chen, K. Y. (2005). Conceptual discussions and benchmark comparison for neural networks and fuzzy systems. *Differential Equations and Dynamical Systems., 13*(1), 35–61.

Su, S. F., & Huang, S. R. (2003). Applications of model-free estimators to the stock market with the use of technical indicators and non-deterministic features. *Journal of the Chinese Institute of Engineers, 26*(1), 21–36.

Su, S. F., & Lee, C. S. G. (1992). Uncertainty manipulation and propagation and verification of applicability of actions in assembly tasks. *IEEE Transactions on Systems, Man, and Cybernetics, 22*(6), 1376–1389. doi:10.1109/21.199463

Su, S. F., & Yang, F. P. (2002). On the dynamical modeling with neural fuzzy networks. *IEEE Transactions on Neural Networks, 13*(6), 1548–1553. doi:10.1109/TNN.2002.804313

Su, S. F., Lin, C. B., & Hsu, Y. T. (2002). A high precision global prediction approach based on local prediction approaches. *IEEE Trans. on Systems, Man, and Cybernetics . Part C: Applications and Reviews, 32*(4), 416–425.

Su, S. F., Tao, T., & Hung, T. H. (2003). Credit assigned CMAC and its application to online learning robust controllers. *IEEE Trans. on Systems, Man, and Cybernetics . Part B: Cybernetics, 33*(2), 202–213.

Sudkamp, T., Knapp, A., & Knapp, J. (2003). Model generation by domain refinement and rule reduction. *IEEE Transactions on Systems, Man, and Cybernetics . Part B, 33*(1), 45–55.

Sugeno, M., & Kang, G. T. (1988). Structure identification of fuzzy model. *Fuzzy Sets and Systems, 28*(1), 15–33. doi:10.1016/0165-0114(88)90113-3

Sun, F., Sun, Z., Li, L., & Li, H. X. (2003). Neuro-fuzzy adaptive control based on dynamic inversion for robotic manipulators. *Fuzzy Sets and Systems, 134*, 117–133. doi:10.1016/S0165-0114(02)00233-6

Sun, Z.-L., Au, K.-F., & Choi, T.-M. (2007). A neuro-fuzzy inference system through Integration of fuzzy logic and extreme learning machines. *IEEE Transactions on Systems, Man, and Cybernetics. Part B, Cybernetics*, *37*(5), 1321–1331. doi:10.1109/TSMCB.2007.901375

Swanson, D. R. (1986a). Fish oil, Raynaud's syndrome, and undiscovered public knowledge. *Perspectives in Biology and Medicine*, *30*(1), 7–18.

Swanson, D. R. (1986b). Undiscovered public knowledge. *The Library Quarterly*, *56*(2), 103–118. doi:10.1086/601720

Swanson, D. R., & Smalheiser, N. R. (1997). An interactive system for finding complementary literatures: a stimulus to scientific discovery. *Artificial Intelligence*, *91*(2), 183–203. doi:10.1016/S0004-3702(97)00008-8

Swanson, D. R., Smalheiser, N. R., & Torvik, V. I. (2006). Ranking indirect connections in literature-based discovery: the role of medical subject headings. *Journal of the American Society for Information Science and Technology*, *57*(11), 1427–1439. doi:10.1002/asi.20438

Swany, M., & Wolski, R. (2002). Multivariate resource performance forecasting in the network weather service. In *Proceedings of the IEEE/ACM SC2002 Conference*, (pp. 1-10).

Szepannek, G., & Weihs, C. (2006). Local modelling in classification on different feature subspaces. In *Industrial Conference on Data Mining* (pp. 226–238), Leipzig, Germany.

Takagi, H., Suzuki, N., Koda, T., & Kojima, Y. (1992). Neural networks designed on approximate reasoning architecture and their application. *IEEE Transactions on Neural Networks*, *3*, 752–759. doi:10.1109/72.159063

Takagi, T., & Hayashi, I. (1991). NN-driven fuzzy reasoning. *International Journal of Approximate Reasoning*, *5*, 191–212. doi:10.1016/0888-613X(91)90008-A

Takagi, T., & Sugeno, M. (1985). Fuzzy identification of systems and its application to modeling and control. *IEEE Transactions on Systems, Man, and Cybernetics*, *15*(1), 116–132.

Takashima, S. (1989). *100 Examples of Fuzzy Theory Application mostly in Japan*. Trigger.

Takeda, M., & Goodman, J. W. (1986). Neural networks for computation: number representations and programming complexity. *Applied Optics*, *25*(18), 15. doi:10.1364/AO.25.003033

Talavan, P., & Yanez, J. (2002). Parameter setting of the Hopfield network applied to TSP. *Neural Networks*, *15*, 363–373. doi:10.1016/S0893-6080(02)00021-7

Tan, C. L., & Chang, S. P. (1996). Residual correction method of Fourier series to GM(1,1) model. *1996 First National Conference on Grey Theory and Applications*, (pp. 93-101).

Tan, C. L., & Lu, B. F. (1996). Grey Markov chain forecasting model. *1996 First National Conference on Grey Theory and Applications*, (pp. 157-162).

Tan, G., & Jarvis, S. A. (2006). Prediction of short-lived TCP transfer latency on bandwidth asymmetric links. *Journal of Computer and System Sciences*, *72*(7), 1201–1210. doi:10.1016/j.jcss.2006.01.006

Tan, K., Lee, T., Khoo, D., & Khor, E. (2001). A multiobjective evolutionary algorithm toolbox for computer-aided multiobjective optimization. *IEEE Transactions on Systems, Man, and Cybernetics . Part B*, *31*(4), 537–556.

Tan, K., Tay, A., & Cai, J. (2003). Design and implementation of a distributed evolutionary computing software. *IEEE Transactions on Systems, Man, and Cybernetics . Part C*, *33*(3), 325–338.

Tan, P. N., & Kumar, V. (2002). Discovery of the Web robot sessions based on their navigational patterns. *Data Mining and Knowledge Discovery*, *6*, 9–35. doi:10.1023/A:1013228602957

Tan, P.-N., Steinbach, M., & Kumar, V. (2005). Introduction to data mining, (first edition). Boston: Addison-Wesley Longman Publishing Co., Inc.

Tanaka, H., & Guo, P. (1999). Portfolio selection based on upper and lower exponential possibility distributions. *European Journal of Operational Research*, *114*, 115–126. doi:10.1016/S0377-2217(98)00033-2

Tanaka, H., Guo, P., & Turksen, I. B. (2000). Portfolio selection based on fuzzy probabilities and possibility distributions. *Fuzzy Sets and Systems, 111*, 387–397. doi:10.1016/S0165-0114(98)00041-4

Tanaka, H., Ichihashi, H., & Asai, K. (1984). A formulation of fuzzy linear programming problem based on comparison of fuzzy numbers. *Control Cybernet, 13*(3), 185–194.

Tanaka, K., & Sano, M. (1994). A Robust Stabilization Problem of Fuzzy Control Systems and Its Application to Backing up Control of a Truck-Tailer. *IEEE transactions on Fuzzy Systems, 2*(2), 1–14. doi:10.1109/91.277961

Tax, D. M. J., & Duin, R. P. W. (2002). Using two-class classifiers for multiclass classification. In *Proceedings of the 16th International Conference on Pattern Recognition*, (Vol. 2, pp. 124–127), Quebec, Canada.

Taylor, B. J. (Ed.). (2005). Methods and Procedures for the Verification and Validation of Artificial Neural Networks. Berlin: Springer.

Thrift, P. (1991). Fuzzy logic synthesis with genetic algorithms. In *Proceedings of the fourth international conference on genetic algorithms (icga)* (pp. 509-513), San Diego, USA.

Timmis, J., & Neal, M. (2001). A resource limited artificial immune system. *Knowledge-Based Systems, 14*(3), 121–130. doi:10.1016/S0950-7051(01)00088-0

Tomé, A. R., & Almeida, P. D. (2007, April). *Usefull(ness) of NAO index for forecast of Monthly rainfall in Lisbon*. Paper presented at European Geosciences Union General Assembly 2007, Vienna, Austria.

Tong, H. (1990). *Non-linear Time Series: A Dynamical System Approach*. Oxford, UK: Oxford University Press.

Tripathy, S. C., Chandramohanan, P. S., & Balasubramanium, R. (1998). Self tuning regulator for adaptive load frequency control of power system. *The Journal of Institution of Engineers (India), EL79*, 103–108.

Tripathy, S. C., Kalantor, M., & Balasubramanian, R. (1992). Stability Simulation and Parameter Optimization of a Hybrid Wind-Diesel Power Generation System. *International Journal of Energy Research, 16*, 31. doi:10.1002/er.4440160105

Tsai, P. W., Pan, J. S., Chen, S. M., Liao, B. Y., & Hao, S. P. (2008). Parallel cat swarm optimization. *7th International Conference on Machine Learning and Cybernetics*, 3328-3333.

Turtle, H., & Croft, W. B. (1991). Evaluation of an inference network-based retrieval model. *ACM Transactions on Information Systems, 9*(3), 187–222. doi:10.1145/125187.125188

Tzeng, F.-Y., & Ma, K.-L. (2005). Opening the black box - data driven visualization of neural networks. In *Proceedings of IEEE Visualization '05 Conf.* (pp. 383–390). Washington, DC: IEEE.

Vajda, S. (1982). *Probabilistic Programming*. New York: Academic Press.

Van den Bergh, F., & Engelbrecht, A. P. (2004). A cooperative approach to particle swarm optimization. *IEEE Transactions on Evolutionary Computation, 8*(3), 225–239. doi:10.1109/TEVC.2004.826069

Vazhkudai, S., & Schopf, J. M. (2002). Predicting sporadic grid data transfers. In *Proceedings of 11th International Symposium on High Performance Distributed Computing HPDC-11*, (pp. 188-196).

Vazhkudai, S., & Schopf, J. M. (2003). Using regression techniques to predict large data transfers. *International Journal of High Performance Computing Applications, 17*(3), 249–268. doi:10.1177/1094342003173004

Velásquez, J. D., & Palade, V. (2007). A Knowledge Base for the maintenance of knowledge extracted from web data. *Knowledge-Based Systems, 20*(3), 238–248. doi:10.1016/j.knosys.2006.05.015

Ventura, S., Romero, C., Zafra, A., Delgado, J. A., & Hervás, C. (2007). JCLEC: a java framework for evolutionary computation. *Soft Computing, 12*(4), 381–392. doi:10.1007/s00500-007-0172-0

Venturini, G. (1993). Sia: A supervised inductive algorithm with genetic search for learning attributes based concepts. In Machine learning: Ecml-93 (Vol. 667, pp. 280–296). London: Springer Berlin-Heidelberg.

Vercher, E., Bermúdez, J. D., & Segura, J. V. (2007). Fuzzy portfolio optimization under downside risk measures. *Fuzzy Sets and Systems, 158*, 769–782. doi:10.1016/j.fss.2006.10.026

W3C. (2008). *Extended Log File Format*. Retrieved October 10, 2008, from http://www.w3.org/TR/WD-logfile

Wang, C. P. (1999). *A shipping forecasting model of distribution center through integration of genetic algorithm and fuzzy neural network*. Unpublished Master thesis, I-Shou University, Kaohsiung County, Taiwan.

Wang, H., & Wang, S. (2007). Making data mining relevant to business. In *Proceedings of Wireless Communications, Networking and Mobile Computing Conference*, (pp. 5516-5518).

Wang, J. S., & Lee, C. S. G. (2000). Structure and learning in self-adaptive neural fuzzy inference systems. *International Journal on Fuzzy Systems, 2*(1), 12–22.

Wang, J. S., & Lee, C. S. G. (2002). Self-adaptive neuro-fuzzy inference systems for classification applications. *IEEE transactions on Fuzzy Systems, 10*(6), 790–802. doi:10.1109/TFUZZ.2002.805880

Wang, L. X. (1992). *Fuzzy systems are universal approximators*. Paper presented at Proc. IEEE Int'l Conf. On Fuzzy Systems.

Wang, L. X., & Mendel, J. M. (1992). Generating fuzzy rules by learning from examples. *IEEE Transactions on Systems, Man, and Cybernetics, 22*(6), 1414–1427. doi:10.1109/21.199466

Wang, R., Cheng, Q., & Huang, T. (2001). Identify regions of interest (ROI) for video watermark embedment with principle component analysis. In *Proceedings of the eighth ACM international conference on Multimedia* (pp. 459-461).

Wang, S. L., & Li, P. Y. (1991). Neural networks for medicine: two cases. In *Electro International Conference* (pp. 586-590), New York.

Wang, S. L., Shen, J. W., & Hong, T. P. (2000). Discovering Functional Dependencies Incrementally from Fuzzy Relational Databases. In *Proceedings of the Eighth National Conference on Fuzzy Theory and Its Applications*, (17).

Wang, S. L., Tsai, J. S., & Hong, T. P. (2001). Discovering Functional Dependencies from Similarity-based Fuzzy Relational Databases. *Journal of Intelligent Data Analysis, 5*(1), 131–149.

Wang, X., & Mendel, J. M. (1992). Generating fuzzy rules by learning from examples. *IEEE Transactions on Systems, Man, and Cybernetics, 22*(6), 1414–1427. doi:10.1109/21.199466

Wang, X., Abraham, A., & Smith, K. A. (2005). Intelligent web traffic mining and analysis. *Journal of Network and Computer Applications, 28*, 147–165. doi:10.1016/j.jnca.2004.01.006

Wang, X., Nauck, D., Spott, M., & Kruse, R. (2006). Intelligent data analysis with fuzzy decision trees. *Soft Computing, 11*(5), 439–457. doi:10.1007/s00500-006-0108-0

Wang, Y., & Stroulia, E. (2003a). Flexible interface matching for web-service discovery. In *Proceedings of the 4th Int. Conf. on Web Information Systems Engineering (WISE) 2003* (pp. 147–156), December 10–12, 2003.

Wang, Y., & Stroulia, E. (2003b). Similarity structure matching for assessing web-service similarity. In *ICSOC 2003*, (LNCS Vol. 2910, pp. 194–207). Berlin: Springer-Verlag.

Watada, J. (1997). Fuzzy portfolio selection and its applications to decision making. *Tatra Mountains Math. Pub., 13*, 219–248.

Watson, D., Malan, G. R., & Jahanian, F. (2004). An extensible probe architecture for network protocol performance measurement. *Software, Practice & Experience, 34*, 47–67. doi:10.1002/spe.557

Weeber, M., Vos, R., Klein, H., de Jong-van den Berg, L. T., Aronson, A. R., & Molema, G. (2003). Generating Hypotheses by Discovering Implicit Associations in the Literature: A Case Report of a Search for New Potential Therapeutic Uses for Thalidomide. *Journal of the American Medical Informatics Association, 10*(3), 252–259. doi:10.1197/jamia.M1158

Weigle, M. C., Jeffay, K., & Smith, F. D. (2005). Delay-based early congestion detection and adaptation in TCP: impact on web performance. *Computer Communications, 28*(8), 837–850. doi:10.1016/j.comcom.2004.11.011

Wen, J. W., Zhao, J. L., Luo, S. W., & Han, Z. (2000). The improvements of BP neural network learning algorithm, In *International Conference on Signal Processing: Vol. 3* (pp. 1647-1649), Beijing.

Wenwei, L., Dafang, Z., Jinmin, Y., & Gaogang, X. (2007). On evaluating the differences of TCP and ICMP in network measurement. *Computer Communications, 30*, 428–439. doi:10.1016/j.comcom.2006.09.015

Wilson, D. R., & Martinez, T. R. (2000). Reduction techniques for instance-based learning algorithms. *Machine Learning, 38*(3), 257–286. doi:10.1023/A:1007626913721

Wilson, D. R., & Martinez, T. R. (2001). The need for small learning rates on large problems. In *International Joint Conference on Neural Networks: Vol. 1* (pp. 115-119), New York.

Wilson, S. W. (1995). Classifier fitness based on accuracy. *Evolutionary Computation, 3*(2), 149–175. doi:10.1162/evco.1995.3.2.149

Witten, I., & Frank, E. (2005). Data mining: Practical machine learning tools and techniques, (2nd ed.). San Francisco: Morgan Kaufmann Publishers.

Wolpert, D. H. (1992). Stacked generalization. *Neural Networks, 5*(2), 241–259. doi:10.1016/S0893-6080(05)80023-1

Wolski, R. (1998). Dynamically forecasting network performance using the network weather service. *Cluster Computing, 1*(1), 119–132. doi:10.1023/A:1019025230054

Wong, C.-C., & Chen, C.-C. (1999). A hybrid clustering and gradient descent approach for fuzzy modeling. *IEEE Transactions on Systems, Man, and Cybernetics. Part B, Cybernetics, 29*(6), 686–693. doi:10.1109/3477.809024

Wong, J. T., Chen, K. H., & Su, C. T. (2008). Designing a system for a process parameter determined through modified PSO and fuzzy neural network. In *Proc. of the 12th Pacific-Asia Conference on Knowledge Discovery and Data Mining*, (pp. 785-794).

Wong, M. L., & Leung, K. S. (2000). Data mining using grammar-based genetic programming and applications. Norwell, MA: Kluwer Academic Publishers.

WordNet Similarity lib. (n.d.). Retrieved from http://search.cpan.org/src/SID/WordNet-Similarity-1.04/lib/WordNet/Similarity/wup.pm

Wu, C. J., & Huang, C. H. (1997). A hybrid method for parameter tuning of PID Controllers. *Journal of the Franklin Institute, JFI, 334B*, 547–562. doi:10.1016/S0016-0032(96)00094-4

Wu, C., Zhang, H., & Fang, T. (2007). Flutter analysis of an airfoil with bounded random parameters in incompressible flow via Gegenbauer polynomial approximation. *Aerospace Science and Technology, 11*, 518–526. doi:10.1016/j.ast.2007.03.003

Wu, E. H. C., Ng, M. K., & Huang, J. Z. (2004). On improving Website connectivity by using Web-log data streams. In *Proceedings of DASFAA 2004 Conference*, (pp. 352-364).

Wu, J., & Wu, Z. (2005). Similarity-based Web service matchmaking. In *Proceedings of 2005 IEEE International Conference on Services Computing* (Vol. 1, pp. 287–294).

Wu, P., & Chiang, H. C. (2005). An EM+K-opt methods for the TSPs. In *Proceeding of the Operations Research Society of Taiwan Annual Meeting*, Taipei, Taiwan, R.O.C.

Wu, P., & Chiang, H. C. (2005). The application of electromagnetism-like mechanism for solving the traveling salesman problems. In *Proceeding of the Chinese Institute of Industrial Engineering Annual Meeting*, HsinChu, Taiwan, R.O.C.

Wu, P., & Fang, H. C. (2006). A revised electromagnetism-like mechanism for the traveling salesman problem. In *Proceeding of the 36th International Conference on Computers & Industrial*, Taipei, Taiwan, R.O.C.

Wu, P., Yang, K. J., & Hung, Y. Y. (2005). *The study of electromagnetism-like mechanism based fuzzy neural network for learning fuzzy if–then rules.* (. *LNCS, 3684*, 382–388.

Wu, P., Yang, W. H., & Wei, N. C. (2004). An electromagnetism algorithm of neural network analysis -an application to textile retail operation . *Journal of the Chinese Institute of Industrial Engineers, 21*(1), 59–67.

Wu, S., Er, M. J., & Gao, Y. (2001). A fast approach for automatic generation of fuzzy rules by generalized dynamic fuzzy neural networks. *IEEE transactions on Fuzzy Systems, 9*(4), 578–594. doi:10.1109/91.940970

Wu, S.-Y., & Yen, E. (2008). Data mining-based intrusion detectors. *Expert Systems with Applications.* doi:. doi:10.1016/j.eswa.2008.06.138

Wu, Z., & Palmer, M. (1994). Verb semantics and lexical selection. In *Proceedings of the 32nd Annual Meeting of the Associations for Computational Linguistics* (pp. 133–138).

Xi, X., Keogh, E. J., Shelton, C. R., Li, W., & Ratanamahatana, C. A. (2006). Fast time series classification using numerosity reduction. In *Proceedings of the 23rd International Conference on Machine Learning, (ICML 2006)*, (pp. 1033–1040).

Xia, F., Tian, Y.C., Sun, Y., & Dong, J. (2008). Neural Feedback Scheduling of Real-time Control Tasks. *International Journal on Innovative Computing, Information & Control, 4*(11).

Xing, D., & Shen, J. (2004). Efficient data mining for Web navigation patterns. *Information and Software Technology, 46*(1), 55–63. doi:10.1016/S0950-5849(03)00109-5

Xu, X., Mathur, R. M., Jiang, J., Roger, G. J., & Kundur, P. (1996). Modeling of generators and their controls in power system simulations using singular perturbations. *IEEE Transactions on Power Systems, 1*(1), 109–114.

Yager, R. R. (1980). On choosing between fuzzy subsets. *Kybernetes, 9*, 151–154. doi:10.1108/eb005552

Yager, R. R. (1993). On a Hierarchical Structure for Fuzzy Modeling and Control. *IEEE Transactions on Systems, Man, and Cybernetics, 23*(4), 1189–1197. doi:10.1109/21.247901

Yager, R. R., & Filev, D. P. (1994). Approximate clustering via the mountain method. *IEEE Transactions on Systems, Man, and Cybernetics. Part B, Cybernetics, 24*(8), 1279–1284.

Yager, R. R., & Filev, D. P. (1994). *Essentials of Fuzzy Modeling and Control.* Hoboken, NJ: John Wiley & Sons.

Yang, B., Liu, D.-Y., Yang, K., & Wang, S.-S. (2003). Strategically migrating agents in itinerary graph. In *Proceedings of the second international conference machine learning and cybernetics,* (pp. 1871–1876).

Yang, T. C., Cimen, H., & Zhu, Q. M. (1998). Decentralized load-frequency controller design based on structured singular values. *IEEE Proc. in Generation . Transmission & Distribution, 145*(1), 7–14. doi:10.1049/ip-gtd:19981716

Yang, W. H. (2002). *A study on the intelligent neural network training using the electromagnetism algorithm.* Unpublished Master Thesis, I-Shou University, Kaohsiung County, Taiwan.

Yang, Y., & Liu, X. (1999). A re-examination of text categorization methods. In *Proceedings of the 22nd annual international ACM SIGIR conference on Research and development in information retrieval,* (pp. 42–49).

Yang, Y., & Pedersen, J. O. (1997). A comparative study on feature selection in text categorization. In *Proceedings of the 14th International Conference on Machine Learning,* (pp. 412–420).

Yang, Y., Lin, H., & Jiang, J. (2006). Cloud analysis by modeling the integration of heterogeneous satellite data and imaging. *IEEE Transactions on Systems, Man, and Cybernetics. Part A, Systems and Humans, 36*(1), 162–172. doi:10.1109/TSMCA.2005.859182

Yang, Y., Lin, H., Guo, Z., & Jiang, J. (2004). Automatic Tracking and Characterization of Multiple Moving Clouds in Satellite Images. In W. Thissen, P. Wieringa, & M. Pantic (Eds.), *Proceedings of IEEE International Conference on Systems, Man and Cybernetics* (pp. 3088-3093). New York: IEEE press.

Yang, Y., Lin, H., Guo, Z., & Jiang, J. (2007). A data mining approach for heavy rainfall forecasting based on satellite image sequence analysis. *International Journal of Computers and Geosciences*, *33*(1), 20–30. doi:10.1016/j.cageo.2006.05.010

Yao, H., Hamilton, H., & Butz, C. (2002). *FD_Mine: discovering functional dependencies in a database using equivalences*. Technical Report TR 2002-04. Regina, Canada: University of Regina.

Yao, X. (1999). Evolving artificial neural networks. *Proceedings of the IEEE*, *87*(9), 1423–1447. doi:10.1109/5.784219

Yazici, A., & George, R. (1999). *Fuzzy Database Modeling*. Heidelberg: Physica-Verlag.

Yen, J., Wang, L., & Gillepie, C. W. (1998). Improving the interpretability of TSK fuzzy models by combining global learning and local learning. *IEEE transactions on Fuzzy Systems*, *6*(4), 530–537. doi:10.1109/91.728447

Yeung, D. S., & Zeng, X. (2002). Hidden neuron pruning for multilayer perceptrons using a sensitivity measure. In *International Conference on Machine Learning and Cybernetics* (pp. 1751-1757), New York.

Yoshida, H., Kawata, K., Fukuyama, Y., Takayama, S., & Nakanishi, Y. (2000). A particle swarm optimization for reactive power and voltage control considering voltage security assessment. *IEEE Transactions on Power Systems*, *15*(4), 1232–1239. doi:10.1109/59.898095

Yousaf, M., & Welzl, M. (2005). *A reliable network measurement and prediction architecture for grid scheduling*. Paper presented at the 1st IEEE/IFIP International Workshop on Autonomic Grid Networking and Management AGNM'05, Barcelona 28th October, 2005.

Yu, J., Guo, S., Su, H., Zhang, H., & Xu, K. (2007, May 8-12). A kernel based structure matching for web services search. [Banff, Alberta, Canada.]. *WWW, 2007*, 1249–1250.

Yu, O., Tan, K. C., & Lee, T. H. (2005). Knowledge discovery in data mining via an evolutionary algorithm. In A. Gohsh & L. C. Jain, (Eds.), *Evolutionary computation in data mining: Studies in Fuzziness and Soft Computing*, (Vol. 163, pp. 101-121).

Yu, W. D. (2007). Hybrid soft computing approach for mining of complex construction databases. *Journal of Computing in Civil Engineering*, *21*(5), 343–352. doi:10.1061/(ASCE)0887-3801(2007)21:5(343)

Yu, X. H., & Chen, G. A. (1995). On the local minima free condition of backpropagation learning. *IEEE Transactions on Neural Networks*, *6*(5), 1300–1303. doi:10.1109/72.410380

Yu, X. H., Chen, G. A., & Cheng, S. X. (1993). Acceleration of backpropagation learning using optimised learning rate and momentum. *Electronics Letters*, *29*(14), 1288–1290. doi:10.1049/el:19930860

Zadeh, L. (1973). Outline of a new approach to the analysis of complex systems and decision process. *IEEE Transactions on Systems, Man, and Cybernetics*, *14*(1), 28–44.

Zadeh, L. A. (1965). Fuzzy Set. *Information and Control*, *8*, 338–353. doi:10.1016/S0019-9958(65)90241-X

Zadeh, L. A. (1971). Similarity relations and fuzzy orderings. *Information Sciences*, *3*(1), 177–200. doi:10.1016/S0020-0255(71)80005-1

Zadeh, L. A. (1973). Outline of a New Approach to the Analysis of Complex Systems and Decision Processes. *IEEE Transactions on Systems, Man, and Cybernetics*, *3*(1), 28–44.

Zadeh, L. A. (1975). The concept of a linguistic variable and its application to approximate reasoning. *Information Sciences*, *8*, 199–251. doi:10.1016/0020-0255(75)90036-5

Zadeh, L. A. (1978). Fuzzy sets as a basis for a theory of possibility. *Fuzzy Sets and Systems*, *1*, 3–28. doi:10.1016/0165-0114(78)90029-5

Zadeh, L. A. (1988). Fuzzy Logic. *IEEE Computer*, *21*(4), 83–93.

Zadeh, L. A. (1993). *Fuzzy Logic, Neural Networks and Soft Computing*. Tech. Rep. University of California at Berkeley, November.

Zadeh, L. A. (1994). Soft Computing and Fuzzy Logic. *IEEE Software*, *11*(6), 48–56. doi:10.1109/52.329401

Zakrzewski, R. R. (2001). Verification of a trained neural network accuracy. In *Proceedings of International Joint Conference on Neural Networks (IJCNN'01)*, (Vol. 3, pp. 1657–1662). Washington, DC: IEEE Press.

Zha, H., Ding, C., Gu, M., He, X., & Simon, H. D. (2001). Spectral relaxation for K-means clustering. In *Neural Information Processing Systems vol.14* (pp. 1057–1064).

Zhang, C., Lin, M., & Tang, M. (2008). BP neural network optimized with PSO algorithm for daily load forecasting. In *International Conference on Information Management, Innovation Management and Industrial Engineering: Vol. 3*, (pp. 82–85). Taipei.

Zhang, D., & Dong, Y. (2002). A novel Web usage mining approach for search engines. *Computer Networks*, *39*, 303–310. doi:10.1016/S1389-1286(02)00211-6

Zhang, J., Ho, A. T. S., Qui, G., & Marziliano, P. (2007). Robust video watermarking of H.264/AVC. *IEEE Transactions on Circuits and Systems*, *54*(2), 205–209. doi:10.1109/TCSII.2006.886247

Zhang, J., Li, J., & Zhang, L. (2001). Video watermark technique in motion vector. In *Proceedings Xiv Brazilian Symposium Computer Graphics and Image Processing* (pp. 179-182).

Zhang, S., Zhang, C., & Yang, Q. (2003). Data preparation for data mining. *Applied Artificial Intelligence*, *17*, 375–381. doi:10.1080/713827180

Zhang, X., & Yin, X. (2008). Design of an information intelligent system based on Web data mining. In *Proceedings of International Conference on Computer Science and Information Technology*, (pp. 88-91). Los Alamos, CA: IEEE Press.

Zhang, X., Edwards, J., & Harding, J. (2007). Personalised online sales using web usage data mining. *Computers in Industry*, *58*(8-9), 772–782. doi:10.1016/j.compind.2007.02.004

Zhang, Y. (1999). *Software implementation of artificial neural networks using JAVA and object oriented programming (OOP) technique*. Unpublished master's thesis, South China University of Technology, Guangzhou.

Zhang, Y. (2002). *Analysis and design of recurrent neural networks and their applications to control and robotic systems*. Unpublished doctoral dissertation, Chinese University of Hong Kong, Hong Kong.

Zhang, Y. Q., Fraser, M. D., Gagliano, R. A., & Kandel, A. (2000). Granular neural networks for numerical-linguistic data fusion and knowledge discovery. *IEEE Transactions on Neural Networks*, *11*(3), 658–667. doi:10.1109/72.846737

Zhang, Y., & Chen, K. (2008). Global exponential convergence and stability of Wang neural network for solving online linear equations. *Electronics Letters*, *44*(2), 145–146. doi:10.1049/el:20081928

Zhang, Y., & Ge, S. S. (2005). Design and analysis of a general recurrent neural network model for time-varying matrix inversion. *IEEE Transactions on Neural Networks*, *16*(6), 1477–1490. doi:10.1109/TNN.2005.857946

Zhang, Y., & Wang, J. (2001). Recurrent neural networks for nonlinear output regulation. *Automatica*, *37*, 1161–1173. doi:10.1016/S0005-1098(01)00092-9

Zhang, Y., & Wang, J. (2002). Global exponential stability of recurrent neural networks for synthesizing linear feedback control systems via pole assignment. *IEEE Transactions on Neural Networks*, *13*(3), 633–644. doi:10.1109/TNN.2002.1000129

Zhang, Y., Duffield, N., Paxson, V., & Shenker, S. (2001). On the constancy of Internet path properties. In *Proceedings of the 1st ACM SIGCOMM Workshop on Internet Measurement* (pp. 197-211).

Zhang, Y., Ge, S. S., & Lee, T. H. (2004). A unified qua-dratic-programming based dynamical system approach to joint torque optimization of physically constrained redundant manipulators. *IEEE Transactions on Systems, Man, and Cybernetics . Part B, 34*(5), 2126–2132.

Zhang, Y., Jiang, D., & Wang, J. (2002). A recurrent neural network for solving Sylvester equation with time-varying coefficients. *IEEE Transactions on Neural Networks, 13*(5), 1053–1063. doi:10.1109/TNN.2002.1031938

Zhang, Y., Leithead, W. E., & Leith, D. J. (2005). Time-series Gaussian process regression based on Toeplitz computation of O(N^2) operations and O(N)-level stor-age. In *IEEE Conference on Decision and Control* (pp. 3711-3716), Seville.

Zhang, Y., Li, W., Liu, W., Tan, M., & Chen, K. (2007). Power-activation feed-forward neural network with its weights immediately determined. In *Chinese Conference on Pattern Recognition* (pp. 72-77). Beijing: Science Press.

Zhang, Y., Li, W., Yi, C., & Chen, K. (2008). A weights-directly-determined simple neural network for nonlinear system identification. In *IEEE International Conference on Fuzzy Systems* (pp. 455-460), Hong Kong.

Zhang, Y., Zhong, T., Li, W., Xiao, X., & Yi, C. (2008). Growing algorithm of Laguerre orthogonal basis neural network with weights directly determined. In D.-S. Huang *et al* (Eds.), *International Conference on Intelligent Computing: Vol. 5227. Lecture Notes in Artificial Intelligence* (pp. 60-67), Shanghai. Berlin: Springer-Verlag.

Zhao, X. Z., Zeng, J. F., Gao, Y. B., & Yang, Y. P. (2006). A particle swarm algorithm for classification rules gen-eration. In *6th International Conference on Intelligent Systems Design and Applications,* (pp. 957-962).

Zhou, K., & Kang, Y. (2005). Neural network models and their MATLAB simulation program design. Beijing: Tsinghua University Press.

Zhou, Z. H., & Jiang, Y. (2003). Medical Diagnosis With C4.5 Rule Preceded by Artificial Neural Net-work Ensemble. *IEEE Transactions on Information Technology in Biomedicine, 7*(1), 37–42. doi:10.1109/TITB.2003.808498

Zimmermann, H. J. (1978). Fuzzy programming and linear programming with several objective functions. *Fuzzy Sets and Systems, 1,* 45–55. doi:10.1016/0165-0114(78)90031-3

Ziv, J., & Lempel, A. (1978). Compression of individual sequences via variable-rate coding. *IEEE Transactions on Information Theory, 24*(5), 530–536. doi:10.1109/TIT.1978.1055934

About the Contributors

Leon Shyue-Liang Wang received his Ph.D. from State University of New York at Stony Brook in 1984. From 1984 to 1987, he joined the University of New Haven as assistant professor. From 1987 to 1994, he joined New York Institute of Technology as assistant/associate professor. From 1994 to 2002, he joined I-Shou University in Taiwan and served as Director of Computing Center, Director of Library, and Chairman of Information Management Department. In 2002, he joined National University of Kaohsiung, Taiwan. In 2003, he rejoined NYIT. He is now professor and chairman in National University of Kaohsiung, Taiwan. He has published over 150 papers in the areas of data mining and soft computing, and served as a PC member of several national and international conferences. He is a member of the board of Chinese American Academic and Professional Society, USA.

Tzung-Pei Hong received his B.S. degree in chemical engineering from National Taiwan University in 1985, and his Ph.D. degree in computer science and information engineering from National Chiao-Tung University in 1992. He was a faculty at the Department of Computer Science in Chung-Hua Polytechnic Institute from 1992 to 1994, and at the Department of Information Management in I-Shou University from 1994 to 2001. Since 2001, he has served as Director of Library and Computing Center, Dean of Academic Affair, and Vice President of National University of Kaohsiung. He is currently a distinguish professor at the Department of Electrical Engineering and the department of Computer Science and Information Engineering in National University of Kaohsiung. His current research interests include machine learning, data mining, soft computing, management information systems, WWW applications and has published more than 300 technical papers.

****

Jesus Alcalá-Fdez received the M.Sc. degree in Computer Science in 2002 and Ph.D. degree in Computer Science in 2006, both from the University of Granada, Spain. He is an Assistant Professor in the Department of Computer Science and Artificial Intelligence at the University of Granada. He has over 31 international publications, 13 of them published in international journals. As edited activities, he co-edited the IEEE Transactions on Fuzzy Systems Special Issue on "Genetic Fuzzy Systems: What's next". He currently is member of the IEEE Task force on **Fuzzy Systems Software**. His research interests include fuzzy association rules, genetic fuzzy systems and Data Mining software.

Ester Bernadó-Mansilla received the B.Sc. degree in telecommunications engineering, the M.Sc. degree in electronic engineering, and the Ph.D. degree in computer science from the Enginyeria i Ar-

474

quitectura La Salle, Universitat Ramon Llull, Barcelona, Spain, in 1992, 1995, and 2002, respectively. During 2002, she was a visiting researcher at the Computing Sciences Research Center, Bell Laboratories, Lucent Technologies, Murray Hill, NJ, USA. She is currently associate professor at the Computer Engineering Department of Enginyeria i Arquitectura La Salle, Ramon Llull University, and director of the Research Group in Intelligent Systems. Dr. Bernadó-Mansilla's research interests are focused on the study of genetic-based machine learning and related areas: machine learning, data mining, pattern recognition, etc. Bernadó-Mansilla has co-edited two books on Learning Classifier Systems and Data Mining, and serves on the editorial board of *Pattern Recognition Letters*.

Leszek Borzemski received his M.Sc., Ph.D. and D.Sc. (post-PhD habilitation) degrees in computer science from Wroclaw University of Technology, in 1976, 1980 and 1992, respectively. He is a professor in computer science at the Institute of Informatics (I), Wroclaw University of Technology, Wroclaw, Poland. He is also the vice-director of II and the Chair of Distributed Computer Systems. He is the vice-chairman of the Council of the Wroclaw Academic Computer Network. In 1993-2007 he was elected to the Committee on Informatics of the Polish Academy of Sciences. His research interests include Internet and Web performance, data mining, systems engineering, quality analysis and modeling. He has published about 200 publications including book chapters, journal articles and refereed conference papers. He is the member of the editorial board of the *Theoretical and Applied Informatics*. He has served as a PC member of several national and international conferences. He is the member of KES International.

Yuanyuan Chai, who was born in Zhejiang province on March 1st, 1980, is a candidate for Ph.D. in Traffic and Transportation School, Beijing Jiaotong University. She obtained her master's degree at Beijing Institute of Technology in 2006. She is majoring in System Engineering in her doctoral study. Her research interests include issues related to computational intelligence, CI hybrid algorithms, fuzzy neural networks and complex system modeling. She is author of a great deal of research studies published at national and international journals, conference proceedings as well as book chapters, all of which have been indexed by EI and/or ISTP, SCI. Now she is engaged full time in research.

Chien-Chung Chan is a professor of Computer Science at the University of Akron, Akron, Ohio, USA. He received his Ph.D. in computer science from the University of Kansas in 1989. His areas of research include data mining, expert systems, machine learning algorithms, web-based systems, and rough set theory and its applications to data mining and bioinformatics.

Cheng-Hung Chen was born in Kaohsiung, Taiwan, R.O.C. in 1979. He received the B.S. and M.S. degrees in computer science and information engineering from the Chaoyang University of Technology, Taiwan, R.O.C., in 2002 and 2004, respectively, and the Ph.D. degree in electrical and control engineering from the National Chiao-Tung University, Taiwan, R.O.C., in 2008. His current research interests are fuzzy systems, neural networks, evolutionary algorithms, image processing, intelligent control, and pattern recognition.

Shu-Chuan Chu received the B.S. in Department of Industrial Management from the National Taiwan of Science and Technology, Taiwan, in 1988 and the Ph.D. degree in School of Informatics and Engineering, Flinders University of South Australia, Australia, in 2004. Dr. Chu joints the editorial board for ICIC Express Letters. Currently, she is an assistant professor in the Department of Information Management, Cheng Shiu University, Taiwan. Her current research interests include Data Mining Computational Intelligence Information Hiding and Signal Processing.

Shangce Gao received a B.S. degree from Southeast University, Nanjing, China in 2005 and an M.S. degree from University of Toyama, Toyama, Japan in 2008. From 2005 to 2006, he was a technical support engineer in Wicrosoft Co. Ltd., Shanghai, China. Now, he is working toward the D.E. degree at University of Toyama, Toyama, Japan. His main research interests are multiple-valued logic, artificial immune system and artificial neural networks. He is a member of IEICE and IEEJ.

Salvador García received the M.Sc. and Ph.D. degrees in computer science from the University of Granada, Granada, Spain, in 2004 and 2008, respectively. He is currently an Assistant Professor in the Department of Computer Science, University of Jaén, Jaén, Spain. He has published more than 10 papers in international journals. As edited activities, he currently serves as managing editor of the International Journal of Computational Intelligence Research. His research interests include data mining, data reduction, imbalanced problems, statistical inference, data complexity and evolutionary algorithms.

Takashi Hasuike received his BS degree from School of Engineering at Osaka University, Japan, in 2005, MS degree from Graduate School of Information Science and Technology at Osaka University, Japan, in 2006, and PhD degree of "Information Science" from Graduate School of Information Science and Technology at Osaka University, Japan. He is a member of The Institute of Electrical and Electronics Engineers (IEEE), Japan Society for Fuzzy Theory and Intelligent Informatics (SOFT) and The Operations Research Society of Japan (ORSJ). His research papers are published in Fuzzy Sets and Systems, Omega, Central European Journal of Operations Research, International Journal of Innovative Computing, Information and Control, etc.. His research interests include portfolio selection problem, product planning problem and mathematical programming such as stochastic programming and fuzzy programming.

Werner Hauptmann received the Diploma in electrical engineering from the Technical University of Braunschweig, Germany, in 1989 and the M.S. degree in digital signal processing from the Georgia Institute of Technology, Georgia, USA in 1990. Since 1995 he has been with the Learning Systems group at Siemens Corporate Technology in Munich, where he currently holds the position of a program manager in the area of information fusion. His research interests include machine learning for system modelling and control, knowledge integration and decision support.

Francisco Herrera received the M.Sc. degree in Mathematics in 1988 and the Ph.D. degree in Mathematics in 1991, both from the University of Granada, Spain. He is currently a Professor in the Department of Computer Science and Artificial Intelligence at the University of Granada. He has published more than 140 papers in international journals. He is coauthor of the book *Genetic Fuzzy Systems: Evolutionary Tuning and Learning of Fuzzy Knowledge Bases*. As edited activities, he has co-edited four international books and co-edited 17 special issues in international journals on different Soft Computing topics. He acts as associated editor of the journals: IEEE Transactions on Fuzzy Systesms, Mathware and Soft Computing, Advances in Fuzzy Systems, **Advances in Computational Sciences and Technology**, and International Journal of Applied Metaheuristic Computing. He currently serves as area editor of the Journal Soft Computing (area of genetic algorithms and genetic fuzzy systems), and he serves as member of the editorial board of the journals: Fuzzy Sets and Systems, Applied Intelligence, Knowledge and Information Systems, Information Fusion, Evolutionary Intelligence, International Journal of Hybrid Intelligent Systems, Memetic Computation, International Journal of Computational Intelligence Research, The Open Cybernetics and Systemics Journal, Recent Patents on Computer Science, Journal of Advanced Research in Fuzzy and Uncertain Systems, and International Journal of Information Technology and Intelligent and Computing. His current research interests include computing with words and decision making, data mining, data preparation, instance selection, fuzzy rule based systems, genetic fuzzy systems, knowledge extraction based on evolutionary algorithms, memetic algorithms and genetic algorithms.

Tzung-Pei Hong received his B.S. degree in chemical engineering from National Taiwan University in 1985, and his Ph.D. degree in computer science and information engineering from National Chiao-Tung University in 1992. He was a faculty at the Department of Computer Science in Chung-Hua Polytechnic Institute from 1992 to 1994, and at the Department of Information Management in I-Shou University from 1994 to 2001. He is currently a professor at the Department of Electrical Engineering in National University of Kaohsiung. His current research interests include machine learning, data mining, soft computing, management information systems, and www applications.

Yung-Yao Hung received his B.S. and M.S. degrees in industrial engineering and management from the I-Shou University, Kaohsiung, Taiwan, R.O.C., in 2002 and 2004, respectively. He is currently working toward the Ph.D. degree in industrial engineering and management at the I-Shou University, Kaohsiung, Taiwan, R.O.C.. His research interests include fuzzy neural network, electromagnetism-like mechanism algorithm, meta-heuristic algorithm, and intelligent systems.

María José del Jesus received the M.Sc. and Ph.D. degrees in computer science from the University of Granada, Spain, in 1994 and 1999, respectively. She is currently an associate professor with the Department of Computer Science, University of Jaén. She has authored or coauthored several publications in international journals indexed at the JCR Science Citation Index. She has also coedited 2 special issues in international journals on topics such as genetic fuzzy systems and the interpretability-accuracy trade-off and on metaheurisctic based data mining. She has worked on 10 research projects (as coordinator of four of them) supported by the Spain's and Andalusian Governments and the University of Jaén concerning several aspects of genetic fuzzy systems, data mining and applications. Her research interests include data mining, data preparation, fuzzy rule-based systems, genetic fuzzy systems, soft computing, knowledge extraction based on evolutionary algorithms and evolutionary radial basis neural networks.

Yannis L. Karnavas was born in Volos, Hellas in 1969. He received the Diploma and the Ph.D. in Electrical & Computer Engineering, both from the Dept. of Electrical & Computer Engineering of Democritus University of Thrace, Xanthi, Hellas, in 1994 and 2002 respectively. Currently, he is with the Lab. of Electrical Machines and Installations, Dept. of Electrical Engineering, School of Technological Applications, Technological Educational Institution of Crete, where he is a full time Assistant Professor. He is also a Chartered Electrical Engineer and he carries out technical studies. His research interests mainly include operation and control of electrical machines and power systems as well as applications of artificial intelligence techniques to them. He serves as an Associate Editor in 2 International Journals, as an Editorial Board Member in 3 International Journals, as an International Program Committee Member of 15 International Conferences, and also as a Member of 6 IASTED Technical Committees. He has served as a Conference Reviewer in more than 60 International Conferences. He is a member of IEEE, PES (Power Engineering Society), NNC (Neural Network Council), RAS (Robotics and Automation Society), TEE (Technical Chamber of Hellas), ΠΣΔΜΗΕ (National Board of Electrical and Mechanical Engineers), EETN (Greek Artificial Intelligence Society) and ΕΠΥ (Greek Computer Society).

Aparna Konduri has been involved in the research and development of intelligent software applications. She is currently a Senior Software Engineer at Farmers Insurance Inc. She has a Masters Degree in Computer Science from University of Akron, USA and a Masters Degree in Chemical Engineering from Birla Institute of Technology and Science, India. She enjoys mentoring and playing with her four-year-old son Praket in her free time!

Rudolf Kruse is professor for computer science at the Otto-von-Guericke University of Magdeburg, Germany. He received a master degree in mathematics (1979), a Ph.D. degree in mathematics (1980), and the venia legendi in mathematics (1984) from University of Braunschweig, Germany. The working group of Prof. Kruse conducts research on methods of Artificial Intelligence. Currently, the main focus is on new methods of *Intelligent Data Analysis*. Prof. Kruse is a Fellow of IFSA, ECCAI, and IEEE.

Mei-Chiao Lai received her B.S. in 1976 in Pharmaceutical Department from China Medical University, Taiwan, the M.S. in 1994 in Department of Quality Management from University of Paisley, U.K., and the Ph.D. degree in School of Business & Informatics in 2004 from Australian Catholic University, Australia. Currently, she is an Assistant Professor in the department of Health Care Administration, Diwan University, Taiwan. Her research interests include quality management, marketing management, case management, and medical tour.

Sou-Horng Li received the diploma degree in electronic engineering, in 1995, from Chien-Hsing Industrial College, Jung-Li, Taiwan, R.O.C., and the M.S. degree in electrical engineering, in 2002, from National Taiwan University of Science and Technology, Taiwan, R.O.C.

Bin-Yih Liao received his B.S. in 1972, M.S. in 1974 from National Cheng Kung University, Taiwan, and Ph.D. in Electronic Engineering in 1994 from National Cheng Kung University, Taiwan. Currently, he is a Professor in the department of Electronic Engineering and serves concurrently as the dean of Electronic Engineering and Computer Science, National Kaohsiung University of Applied Sciences, Taiwan. He joints the editorial board for International Journal of Innovative Computing, Information and Control. His research interests include computational intelligence, embedding system, pattern recognition and intelligent video processing.

Guan-Jhih Liao received the B.Sc. degree in computer science and information engineering from Tamkang University, Taiwan. In 2008, he received the M. Sc. Degree in computer science from Chung-Hua University, Hsin-Chu, Taiwan. His research interests include video watermarking and steganography, video coding and image processing.

Cha-Hwa Lin is director of the Knowledge Engineering Laboratory in the Department of Computer Science and Engineering at National Sun Yat-sen University in Taiwan. She is assistant professor of the Center for General Education at National Sun Yat-sen University. She received her Ph.D. degree in Computer Science from the University of Southern California in 2002. Her research interests include artificial intelligence, knowledge discovery, database systems and information management, structured domain ontologies, user-customized information access, and personalized information management environments. She is conducting research in intelligent adaptive systems, multiagent systems, e-Learning systems, semantic web services, and information management environments for scientific and engineering data.

Cheng-Jian Lin received the B.S. degree in electrical engineering from Ta-Tung University, Taiwan, R.O.C., in 1986 and the M.S. and Ph.D. degrees in electrical and control engineering from the National Chiao-Tung University, Taiwan, R.O.C., in 1991 and 1996. Currently, he is a full Professor of Computer Science and Information Engineering Department, National Chin-Yi University of Technology, Taichung County, Taiwan, R.O.C. His current research interests are soft computing, pattern recognition, intelligent control, image processing, bioinformatics, and FPGA design.

Daw-Tung Lin received the B.S. degree in control engineering from National Chiao Tung University, Hsin Chu, Taiwan, in 1985, and the M.S. and Ph.D. degrees in electrical engineering from the University of Maryland at College Park, MD, U.S.A., in 1990 and 1994, respectively. He was an Associate Professor (1995-2005) of the Department of Computer Science and Information Engineering at the Chung Hua University, Hsin Chu, Taiwan. During his service at the Chung Hua University, he was the Director (2001-2003) of the Computer Center. In 2003, he was the Dean of the Admission and Development Office at the Chung Hua University. From 2003 to 2005, he was the Dean of the Engineering School at the university. Since 2005, he has been an Associate Professor of the Department of Computer Science and Information Engineering at the National Taipei University, Taipei County, Taiwan. Currently, he is the Chairperson of the department. He is a member of IEEE. His current research interests are pattern recognition, image processing, neural networks, fuzzy systems, and intelligent surveillance.

Hui Lin received the Graduate degree in aerophotogrammetric engineering from Wuhan Technical University of Surveying and Mapping, Wuhan, China, in 1980, the M.Sc. degree in remote sensing and cartography from the Graduate School of Chinese Academy of Sciences, Beijing, China, in 1983, and the Ph.D. degree in geographical information systems from the State University of New York at Buffalo, Buffalo, in 1992. He is currently a Professor and the Director of the Space and Geoinformation Science Institute, Chinese University of Hong Kong, Shatin, N.T., Hong Kong. His current research interests include virtual geographic environments, cloud-prone and rainy area remote sensing, spatially integrated humanities, and social science. Prof. Lin was elected as an Academician of the International Eurasian Academy of Sciences in 1995.

Javed Mostafa is the Francis Carroll McColl Term Professor at the University of North Carolina at Chapel Hill, USA, with a joint appointment in information science and in the Biomedical Research and Imaging Center (a medical school entity). He is the Assistant Director of Clinical Data Management at the Translational Clinical Sciences Institute and he is the Director of the Laboratory of Applied Informatics Research – both are based in UNC. His main area of research is information retrieval, with a particular focus on developing effective computational functions for analysis, visualization, and personalization of biomedical information. He is also involved in developing educational programs in health informatics and digital libraries. He is an associate editor of the ACM Transactions on Information Systems.

Sebastian Nusser is a Ph.D. student at the Otto-von-Guericke-University of Magdeburg, Germany. He received a master degree in computer science (Diplom-Informatiker) in 2005 from the Otto-von-Guericke-University of Magdeburg. His research focus is on machine learning algorithms for use in safety-related domains. His research was supported by Siemens AG, Corporate Technology, Information & Communications, Learning Systems in Munich.

Clemens Otte received a Diploma degree in computer science in 1993 from the Technical University of Braunschweig, Germany and a Ph.D. degree in computer science in 1998 from the University of Oldenburg, Germany. He currently works as a Senior Engineer for the Siemens AG - Corporate Technology in Munich. His research interests include machine learning, statistical data analysis, pattern recognition and the application of these methods in safety-related systems.

Chen-Sen Ouyang was born in Kin-Men, Taiwan, R.O.C., on December 21, 1976. He received the B.S. and Ph.D. degrees from the Department of Applied Mathematics and Department of Electrical Engineering, National Sun Yat-Sen University, Kaohsiung, Taiwan, in 1998 and 2004, respectively. He joined the faculty of the Department of Information Engineering, I-Shou University, Kaohsiung, Taiwan, in 2005. His research interests include soft computing, computer vision, data mining, and biometrics. Dr. Ouyang is a member of the Institute of Electrical and Electronics Engineers (IEEE) and the Taiwanese Association of Artificial Intelligence (TAAI).

Jeng-Shyang Pan received the B.S. degree in Electronic Engineering from the National Taiwan University of Sciences and Technology, Taiwan in 1986, the M.S. degree in Communication Engineering from the National Chiao Tung University, Taiwan in 1988, and the Ph.D. degree in An Adaptive Online Recursive Learning Algorithm for Least Squares SVM Classifiers Electrical Engineering from the University of Edinburgh, U.K. in 1996. Currently, he is a Professor in the Department of Electronic Engineering, National Kaohsiung University of Applied Sciences, Taiwan. He joints the editorial board for LNCS Transactions on Data Hiding and Multimedia Security, Springer, International Journal of Knowledge-Based Intelligent Engineering Systems, and International Journal of Hybrid Intelligent System, Advanced Knowledge International. He currently is the Chair of IEEE Tainan Chapter. He is the Co-Editors-in-Chief for Journal of Information Hiding and Multimedia Signal Processing and International Journal of Innovative Computing, Information and Control. His current research interests include data mining, information security and pattern recognition.

Antonio Peregrín received the M.Sc. and Ph.D. degrees in computer science, both from the University of Granada, Granada, Spain, in 1995 and 2000, respectively. Currently, he is an Associate Professor with the Department of Information Technologies, University of Huelva, Huelva, Spain. His research interests include genetic fuzzy systems, fuzzy rule-based systems, evolutionary algorithms, linguistic modeling and distributed data mining.

Ignacio Robles was born in Granada, Spain, in 1983. He received the Technical Engineering degree and the M.Sc. degree in Computer Science from the University of Granada, Spain. Also he was given the Extraordinary Award from the University of Granada, an award given to the most outstanding graduate in 2007. He is a member of the Soft Computing and Intelligent Information Systems (SCI2S) group and he is currently working on his PhD under the program Soft Computing and Intelligent Systems in the University of Granada. His main areas of interest are parallel and distributed computational intelligence, real coding genetic algorithms and metaheuristics.

Luciano Sanchez received the electrical engineering degree and the Ph.D. degree from Oviedo University, Spain, in 1991 and 1994, respectively. He is currently an Associate Professor of Computer Science at Oviedo University. In the summers of 1995 and 1996, he was a Visiting Professor at the University of California at Berkeley and at General Electric CRD, Schenectady, NY. His research interests include genetic fuzzy systems and the processing of imprecise data in machine learning problems. Responsible of the Metrology and Models research group (University of Oviedo). Professor Sánchez has been Director or responsible of research in 5 of national projects and 13 contracts with Spanish industries. Member of the international program committees of many relevant congresses in his area. Frequent reviewer of leading scientific journals.

Kazuhiro Seki received his Ph.D. in information science from Indiana University, Bloomington. His research interests are in the areas of natural language processing, information retrieval, machine learning, and their applications to intelligent information processing and management systems. He is currently an assistant professor in the Organization of Advanced Science and Technology at Kobe University, Japan.

Ju-Wen Shen received her B.S. and M.S. degree from the I-Shou University, Taiwan, R.O.C., in 1999 and 2001, respectively, in the department of Information Management and Institute of Information Engineering. She is currently a service manager at the South Office of Chungwa Telecom Enterprise Business Group, Taiwan.

Shun-Feng Su received the B.S. degree in electrical engineering, in 1983, from National Taiwan University, Taiwan, R.O.C., and the M.S. and Ph.D. degrees in electrical engineering, in 1989 and 1991, respectively, from Purdue University, West Lafayette, IN. He is a Professor of the Department of Electrical Engineering, National Taiwan University of Science and Technology, Taiwan, R.O.C. He is an IET Fellow. He has published more than 140 refereed journal and conference papers in the areas of robotics, intelligent control, fuzzy systems, neural networks, and non-derivative optimization. His current research interests include computational intelligence, machine learning, virtual reality simulation, intelligent transportation systems, smart home, robotics, and intelligent control.

Hiroki Tamura received the B.E and M.E degree from Miyazaki University in 1998 and 2000, respectively. From 2000 to 2001, he was an Engineer in Asahi Kasei Corporation, Japan. In 2001, he joined University of Toyama, Toyama, Japan, where he was currently a Technical Official in Department of Intellectual Information Systems. In 2006, he joined Miyazaki University, Miyazaki, Japan, where he is currently an Assistant Professor in the Department of Electrical & Electronic Engineering. His main research interests are neural networks and optimization problems.

Ning Tan was born in Xinxing, Guangdong, China, in 1984. He received the B.S. degree in Information Engineering in June 2007 from Guangdong University of Technology (GDUT), Guangzhou, China. Since September 2007, he has been a postgraduate student, completing his Master degree in Software Engineering at School of Software, Sun Yat-Sen University (SYSU), Guangzhou, China. His current research interests include artificial neural networks and intelligent information processing.

Zheng Tang received the B.S. degree from Zhejiang University, Zhejiang, China in 1982 and an M.S. degree and a D.E. degree from Tshinghua University, Beijing, China in 1984 and 1988, respectively. From 1988 to 1989, he was an Instructor in the Institute of Microelectronics at Tshinhua University. From 1990 to 1999, he was an associate professor in the Department of Electrical and Electronic Engineering, Miyazaki University, Miyazaki, Japan. In 2000, he joined University of Toyama, Toyama, Japan, where he is currently a professor in the Department of Intellectual Information Systems. His current research interests include intellectual information technology, neural networks, and optimizations.

Pei-Wei Tsai received his B.S. and M.S. in Electronic Engineering in 2005 and 2007 respectively from National Kaohsiung University of Applied Sciences, Taiwan. He is currently working toward his Ph.D. degree in Electronic Engineering in National Kaohsiung University, Taiwan. He was invited to give a speech at the 1st Student-Organizing International Mini-Conference on Information Electronics Systems for the Global COE (Center of Excellence) Program in the field of Electrical Communication, Electronic Engineering, and Information Science of Tohoku University, Japan, in October, 2008. His research interests include computational intelligence, information hiding, image processing, intelligent video processing and signal processing.

Kuniaki Uehara received his B.E., M.E. and D.E. degrees in information and computer sciences from Osaka University, Japan. He was an assistant professor in the Institute of Scientific and Industrial Research at Osaka University and was a visiting assistant professor at Oregon State University. Currently, he is a professor in the Graduate School of Engineering at Kobe University, Japan. His is widely conducting research in the areas of machine learning, data mining, and multimedia processing. He is a member of the Information Processing Society of Japan, Japan Society for Software Science and Technology, and AAAI.

Sebastian Ventura was born in Cordoba, Spain, in 1966. He received the B.S. degree in Chemistry from the University of Cordoba, Spain, in 1989 and the Ph.D. degree in sciences from the University of Cordoba, Spain, in 1996. He is an Associate Professor with the University of Cordoba in the Department of Computer Science and Numerical Analysis in the area of computer science and artificial intelligence. His current research interests include machine learning and data mining with evolutionary algorithms, and their applications to real world problems.

Jin-Fu Wang is a software engineer of a Taiwan based computer manufacturer and is a member of the Knowledge Engineering Laboratory in the Department of Computer Science and Engineering at National Sun Yat-sen University in Taiwan. He received his M.S. degree in Computer Science from the National Sun Yat-sen University in 2006. His research interests include intelligent adaptive systems, multiagent systems, Computer Networks and Internets, and information management environments for scientific and engineering data. His work include researching, designing, and writing new software programs; testing new programs and fault finding; developing existing programs by analyzing and identifying areas for modification, and investigating new technologies.

Shyue-Liang Wang received his Ph.D. from State University of New York at Stony Brook in 1984. From 1984 to 1987, he joined the University of New Haven as assistant professor. From 1987 to 1994, he joined New York Institute of Technology as assistant/associate professor. From 1994 to 2002, he joined I-Shou University in Taiwan and served as Directors of Computing Center and Library, Chairman of Information Management Department. In 2002, he joined National University of Kaohsiung, Taiwan. In 2003, he rejoined NYIT. He is now professor in National University of Kaohsiung, Taiwan. He has published over 150 papers in the areas of data mining and soft computing, and served as a PC member of several national and international conferences. He is a member of the board of Chinese American Academic and Professional Society, USA

Peitsang Wu received his M.S. degrees in industrial manufacturing and system engineering from the Iowa State University, Ames, IA, U.S.A., in 1992 and his Ph.D. degree in Operations Research from North Carolina State University, Raleigh, NC, U.S.A., in 1997, respectively. He is currently an associate professor of Industrial Engineering and Management at I-Shou University, Kaohsiung, Taiwan, R.O.C.. His research interests are heuristic algorithm, soft computing, decision support system and operations research.

Yu-Bin Yang received the B.Sc. degree in computer science from Wuhan Technical University of Surveying and Mapping, Wuhan, China, in 1997, and the M.Sc. and Ph.D. degrees in computer science from Nanjing University, Nanjing, China, in 2000 and 2003, respectively. He is currently an Associate Professor of the State Key Laboratory for Novel Software Technology, Nanjing University. He is also a Research Fellow of the Space and Geoinformation Science Institute, Chinese University of Hong Kong, Shatin, N.T., Hong Kong. His current research interests include spatial data mining and knowledge discovery, image processing and analysis, machine learning, and intelligent virtual geographical environment.

Yunong Zhang was born in Xinyang, Henan, China, in 1973. He received the B.S., M.S., and Ph.D. degrees from Huazhong University of Science and Technology (HUST), South China University of Technology (SCUT), and Chinese University of Hong Kong (CUHK), respectively, in 1996, 1999, and 2003. He is currently a professor at School of Information Science and Technology, Sun Yat-Sen University (SYSU), Guangzhou, China. Before joining SYSU in 2006, he had been with National University of Ireland (NUI), University of Strathclyde, and National University of Singapore (NUS) since 2003. His main research interests include neural networks, robotics and Gaussian processes. His webpage is now available at http://www.ee.sysu.edu.cn/teacher/detail.asp?sn=129.

Index